KJV

STANDARD LESSON COMMENTARY®

2003-2004

International Sunday School Lessons

Edited by

Ronald G. Davis, Ronald L. Nickelson,
and Jonathan Underwood

Published by
STANDARD PUBLISHING

Mark A. Taylor, Publisher
Paul D. Learned, Executive Director, Church Resources
Carla J. Crane, Production Manager
Jonathan Underwood, Senior Editor, Adult Curriculum
Cheryl Frey, Associate Editor

Fifty-first Annual Volume

©2003
STANDARD PUBLISHING
A division of STANDEX INTERNATIONAL Corporation
8121 Hamilton Avenue, Cincinnati, Ohio 45231
Printed in U. S. A.

In This Volume

Artists

TITLE PAGES: James E. Seward

Cover design by DesignTeam

Lessons based on International Sunday School Lessons © 2001 by the Lesson Committee.

CD-ROM AVAILABLE

The *Standard Lesson Commentary*® is available in an electronic format in special editions of the *Standard Lesson Commentary*® (King James edition) and *The NIV*® *Standard Lesson Commentary*®. These editions (order #20004 for KJV and 30004 for NIV®) contain a compact disk for use with Windows®-based computers.

System Requirements: Windows XP/2000/ME/98/95; Pentium 133 MHz processor (300MHz recommended), 64 Meg RAM (128 recommended); 60 Meg Available Hard Drive Space; 2x or better CD-ROM drive.

If you have any questions regarding the use of this CD-ROM, please contact Logos Customer Service, at (800) 875-6467, or Technical Support by telephone at (360) 685-2337, by e-mail at tech@logos.com, or online at www.logos.com/support.

Index of Printed Texts, 2003-2004

The printed texts for 2003-2004 are arranged here in the order in which they appear in the Bible. Opposite each reference is the number of the page on which it appears in this volume.

Cumulative Index

A cumulative index for the Scripture passages used in the STANDARD LESSON COMMENTARY®
for the years September, 1998—August, 2004, is provided below.

VI

Fall Quarter, 2003

Faith Faces the World

Special Features

Lessons

Unit 1: Live in Faith

Unit 2: Live in Hope

Unit 3: Live as God's Children

Unit 4: Live With Purpose

About These Lessons

The lessons of the present quarter are about putting faith into practice. Faith is easy to talk about, especially in Sunday school. The next thirteen lessons will encourage and challenge each participant to do more than talk, to take faith beyond the walls of the Sunday school classroom.

Sep 7
Sep 14
Sep 21
Sep 28
Oct 5
Oct 12
Oct 19
Oct 26
Nov 2
Nov 9
Nov 16
Nov 23
Nov 30

Fifty Years and Beyond

"THOU ART NOT YET FIFTY YEARS OLD," the Jews challenged Jesus, "and hast thou seen Abraham?" (John 8:57). With the year 2004, the STANDARD LESSON COMMENTARY® *is* fifty years old. Through the past half-century we have seen Abraham in its pages, along with Moses, Joshua, David, Solomon, Isaiah, Jeremiah, Jesus and the apostles, and many others.

Of course, we have not seen their actual likeness. We have seen them in their works and in their teachings. We have come to know a little more of the way of life because of their examples.

With this fiftieth-anniversary edition of the STANDARD LESSON COMMENTARY® we continue in that tradition. This year's studies conclude another six-year study of the Scriptures, following the International Sunday School Lesson plan (see the chart below). It is not the plan that is important, however, but the purpose. For fifty years we have striven to achieve the same purpose as expressed by the apostle Paul: "that ye might be filled with the knowledge of his will in all wisdom and spiritual understanding; that ye might walk worthy of the Lord unto all pleasing, being fruitful in every good work, and increasing in the knowledge of God" (Colossians 1:9, 10).

We pray that this volume, and every volume published in the future, will help you to see that goal realized in your life and in the lives of your learners.

International Sunday School Lesson Cycle
September, 1998—August, 2004

YEAR	FALL QUARTER (Sept., Oct., Nov.)	WINTER QUARTER (Dec., Jan., Feb.)	SPRING QUARTER (Mar., Apr., May)	SUMMER QUARTER (June, July, Aug.)
1998-1999	God Calls a People to Faithful Living (Old Testament Survey)	God Calls Anew in Jesus Christ (New Testament Survey)	That You May Believe (John)	Genesis: Beginnings (Genesis)
1999-2000	From Slavery to Conquest (Exodus, Leviticus, Numbers, Deuteronomy, Joshua)	Immanuel: God With Us (Matthew)	Helping a Church Confront Crisis (1 and 2 Corinthians)	New Life in Christ (Ephesians, Philippians, Colossians, Philemon)
2000-2001	Rulers of Israel (Judges, 1 and 2 Samuel, 1 Kings 1-11)	Good News of Jesus (Luke)	Continuing Jesus' Work (Acts)	Division and Decline (1 Kings 12-22, 2 Kings 1-17, Isaiah 1-39, Hosea, Amos, Micah)
2001-2002	Jesus' Ministry (Miracles, Parables, Sermon on the Mount)	Light for All People (Isaiah 9:1-7; 11:1-9; 40-66; Ruth, Jonah)	The Power of the Gospel (Romans, Galatians)	Worship and Wisdom for Living (Psalms, Proverbs)
2002-2003	Judgment and Exile (2 Kings 18-25, Jeremiah, Lamentations, Ezekiel, Habakkuk, Zephaniah)	Portraits of Faith (Personalities in the New Testament)	Jesus: God's Power in Action (Mark)	God Restores a Remnant (Ezra, Nehemiah, Daniel, Joel, Obadiah, Haggai, Zechariah, Malachi)
2003-2004	Faith Faces the World (James, 1 and 2 Peter, 1, 2, 3 John, Jude)	A Child Is Given (Samuel, John the Baptist, Jesus) Lessons From Life (Esther, Job, Ecclesiastes, Song of Solomon)	Jesus Fulfills His Mission (Death, Burial, and Resurrection Texts) Living Expectantly (1, 2 Thessalonians, Revelation)	Hold Fast to the Faith (Hebrews) Guidelines for the Church's Ministry (1, 2 Timothy, Titus)

Faith With Substance

by Orrin Root

Now FAITH IS THE SUBSTANCE of things hoped for, the evidence of things not seen" (Hebrews 11:1). Therefore, faith may seem to be at a disadvantage in a world of things seen and touched and enjoyed. But faith is more durable. It will emerge triumphant when the visible world is no more (2 Corinthians 4:18). So in the hearts and minds where faith is strong, faith is triumphant even now (1 John 5:4).

In the next three months our Sunday school lessons will trace some of the adventures of faith, an unseen power in a visible world. If we are confident of the "substance" of what we hope for and accept the "evidence" of what we do not see, we shall find ourselves growing more confident week by week.

These lessons also will make us more familiar with the seven short books we find in our Bibles between Hebrews and Revelation. Five of the seven were written by Peter and John, apostles of Jesus. The other two were written by James and Jude, half-brothers of Jesus. All of these men were involved in the church from its beginning, and all were well aware of its condition and its problems in the second half of the first century.

For our study the thirteen lessons of the quarter are presented in four units. These are listed below with short previews of the lessons in each unit.

Unit 1. September
Live in Faith

Lesson 1: Faith and Temptation. Some versions of the Bible have *trials* where the *King James Version* has *temptations*. The many troubles that try our strength and our patience and our faith are distressing, but James challenges us to face them with joy because we know they will make better persons of us. Shall we rise to his challenge? Shall we face each distressing problem with delight instead of grim determination?

Lesson 2: Faith and Action. Faith is believing and more than believing. So James challenges us again: "Be ye doers of the word, and not hearers only" (James 1:22). And he warns us that faith without works is dead (James 2:17). So if our faith is feeble we need to revive it and put it to work. Quick, before it dies!

Lesson 3: Faith and Wisdom. Without faith one may think wisdom is skill in promoting himself and putting others down. This kind of wisdom is "earthly, sensual, devilish" (James 3:15). With faith in God we seek wisdom from Him, wisdom that "is first pure, then peaceable, gentle, and easy to be entreated, full of mercy and good fruits, without partiality, and without hypocrisy" (James 3:17). May we all emerge with more wisdom of that kind!

Lesson 4: Faith and Attitudes. A selfish attitude leads to conflict. Be unselfish (James 4:1). Too much affection for the godless world makes one an enemy of God. Put God first (James 4:4). A proud attitude forfeits God's grace. Be humble before Him (James 4:10). Save your hostility for the devil. Resist him and defeat him (James 4:7). A judgmental attitude usurps God's place. Leave judging to Him. An arrogant attitude in planning is unwise. Make your plans subject to God's will (James 4:15). Remember that you are just a human being, and God is God.

Unit 2. October
Live in Hope

Lesson 5: Live as God's People. The text of this lesson begins with a burst of praise to God because He in His mercy has brought us to rebirth, by which we are His children. As His children we have the hope of eternity, not an eternity of poverty and trouble, but an eternity blessed by the inheritance that falls to the children of the Almighty. If we believe as God's children ought, His power will keep us safe through earth's perils and bring us to that glorious eternity. Responsibility goes with such privilege, of course. We are to be holy, dedicated to God's service, obedient to His will. If we do that, the family of God is pictured as a spiritual house, a royal priesthood, and a holy nation. Then let us all exert ourselves to be holy, as our Father in Heaven is holy (1 Peter 1:15, 16).

Lesson 6: Set a Good Example. Of course, every child of God ought to set a good example for other Christians and everyone else. This not only assures for him a glorious inheritance in eternity; it brings glory to God even now. If our lives are as good as they ought to be, even some of the heathen will give honor and praise to our Father because He teaches us to do right. Since God gives us glory eternal, don't we owe it to Him to bring Him all the glory we can while we live on earth? Shall we then persist in doing right, even when everything seems to go wrong? Shall we then seek to help our fellow Christians rather than seek their help? This is good for us, and for those we help, and for the glory of God.

Lesson 7: Grow in Faith. In an earlier lesson we heard James say faith is dead unless it makes a difference in what we do. Now we hear Peter name some things that should accompany our faith: virtue, knowledge, temperance, patience, godliness, brotherly kindness, charity. All of these help faith make a difference in what we do. They make us fruitful in our Christian service, and ensure our entrance into the everlasting kingdom of our Lord. Peter said he was repeating what the readers had heard before, and meant to keep repeating it as long as he lived on earth. As long as we live on earth, shall we keep on rereading the advice of Peter and other New Testament writers to help us grow in Christian faith and character and action?

Lesson 8: Trust God's Promise. When Jesus was preparing to leave this world, He promised to come again, bringing changes in sky and earth. Thirty years later, scoffers were laughing at that promise. They said the earth had been going along in the same way ever since creation and would continue in the same way. Peter said those scoffers were misinterpreting history. The world had not always gone along in the same way. Once a great flood had drowned most of earth's people. There will be changes greater than that when Jesus comes again. Earth and sky will disappear. But there will be a new creation where righteousness will live. Do we trust the promise? Are we looking for Jesus to come back and getting ready to live with righteousness in the new creation?

Unit 3. November
Live as God's Children
Lesson 9: Enjoy Fellowship With God. Darkness is a symbol of ignorance and evil, but God is light. If we have fellowship with Him, we are free from darkness. But the call of the godless world is strong, and sometimes we stumble into darkness. Then our advocate is Jesus, who died to atone for our sin. Forgiveness is ready when we turn back to the light. Shall we not guide our lives daily by the Word of God and live in the light?

Lesson 10: Love One Another. The world about us provides abundant examples of hatred, but we know that one who hates his brother is a murderer at heart. We do not take our example from the world, but from Heaven. God so loves us that He sent His Son to die for us; Jesus so loves us that He accepted death. We cannot give our lives as He gave His to atone for others' sins; but shall we not give large parts of our lives in helping the brothers we love?

Lesson 11: Live With Confidence. We believe that Jesus is God's Son and our Savior. Because of that faith we become children of God, and by that same faith we overcome the godless world

that would turn us away from God. Because we are obedient children of God, we know that we have eternal life. While we live on this earth we know God will give us what we ask if we ask according to His will. Shall we not then obey God with all confidence, knowing that faith is the victory that overcomes the world?

Unit 4. November
Live With Purpose
Lesson 12: Remain Loyal. Writing to a Christian lady, John expressed his joy at seeing some of her children walking in truth. But he warned that many deceivers would like to turn them from that way, and he urged the lady to be loyal to Christ and the truth. In another letter John approved the Christian life of Gaius, especially the help he gave to traveling evangelists. But again he warned that false teachers were opposing the good. Taking these two letters to heart, shall we not examine ourselves to be sure we are loyal to Christ and we are helpers of the good?

Lesson 13: Maintain Steadfast Faith. Writing to Christians like us, Jude warned that many false teachers were trying to turn Christians away from their faith. He urged his readers not only to cling to their faith, but also to contend earnestly for it, not with railing accusations, but with calm reasoning and truth. He urged the long-ago readers and the present readers not only to maintain their own faith, but to help their fellow Christians do the same.

Answers to Quarterly Quiz
on page 8
Lesson 1—1. ask God for it. 2. the crown of life. 3. false (God does not tempt any man). **Lesson 2**—1. doers, hearers. 2. "Love thy neighbor as thyself." 3. confess faults to one another and pray for each other. **Lesson 3**—1. the tongue. 2. self-assurance. **Lesson 4**—1. proud, humble. 2. a vapor. **Lesson 5**—1. the precious blood of Christ. 2. Jesus. 3. false (all Christians are part of the "royal priesthood"). **Lesson 6**—1. hope. 2. a roaring lion. **Lesson 7**—1. faith, virtue, knowledge, temperance, patience, godliness, brotherly kindness, charity. 2. He knew that shortly he would die. **Lesson 8**—1. water, fire. 2. true. 3. Paul. **Lesson 9**—1. true. 2. keep his commandments. 3. walk. **Lesson 10**—1. death, life. 2. Spirit. **Lesson 11**—1. our faith. 2. blood. 3. true. **Lesson 12**—1. Jesus Christ did not come in the flesh. 2. walked in truth. **Lesson 13**—1. the faith. 2. Michael the archangel.

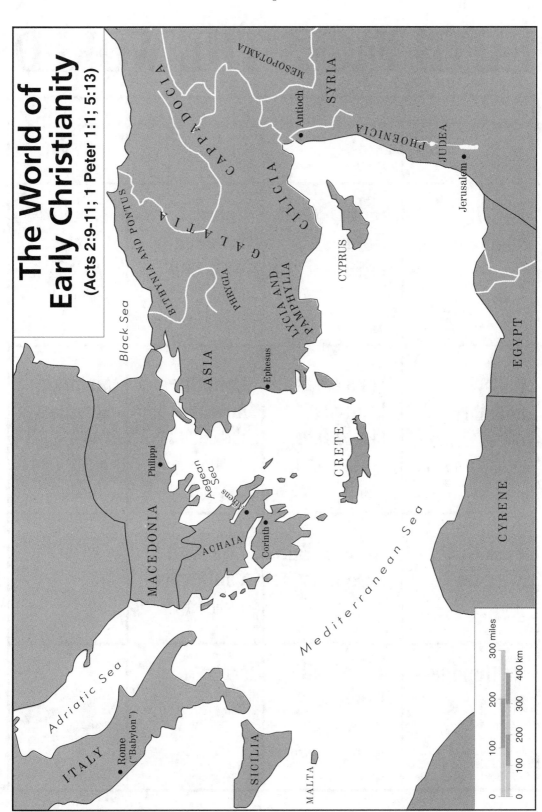

The World of Early Christianity
(Acts 2:9-11; 1 Peter 1:1; 5:13)

FAITH FACES THE WORLD

Live in Faith	Live in Hope	Live in Love	Live with Purpose
Resist Temptation James 1:1-8, 12-18	**Imitate God's Holiness** 1 Peter 1:3-5, 13-21; 2:4-10	**Enjoy Fellowship With God** 1 John 1:5–2:6, 15-17, 29–3:1	**Remain Loyal** 2 John 4-9; 3 John 3-12
Believe and Act James 1:22-27; 2:8, 9, 14-17; 5:13-16	**Set a Good Example** 1 Peter 2:11, 12; 3:13-17; 4:7-11; 5:6-10	**Love One Another** 1 John 3:11-16; 4:7-16	**Maintain Steadfast Faith** Jude 3, 4, 8-13, 16-23
Seek God's Wisdom James 3	**Grow in Faith** 2 Peter 1:3-15	**Live With Confidence** 1 John 5:1-15	
Be Humble James 4	**Trust God's Promise** 2 Peter 3:3-18		

Drawing From the Well of Truth

by Mark B. Reed

WHY IS IT THAT WHEN OUR WORLD talks about religious truth, the meaning of the word *truth* suddenly changes?

We examine a historical record and credit it as right or wrong. No one says that a historical fact like the assassination of John F. Kennedy is both true and false. The details of the case might be disputed, but everyone agrees that a chain of historical events led to his death—events that actually happened.

In the courtroom judges and juries do not hand down ambiguous verdicts saying, "We feel that the defendant is guilty in the eyes of his accusers, but innocent in the eyes of his friends. So we suggest that each person make up his own mind, as his heart leads. And the defendant will be guilty to him or her, or innocent to him or her, as each chooses to believe." How absurd! The defendant is guilty or not guilty, based on the evidence—the truth.

However, when it comes to moral and religious truth, our society takes the relativity route: whatever seems good to you—no hard facts—no absolutes. The word *truth* suddenly changes into some mystical abstraction that cannot be defined or relied upon.

The Bible rejects the notion that religious truth is relative. It declares that truth is by definition absolute and available through the one true God.

A Thirsty World

Never has the world been so desperate for truth and yet so blind to its presence—except perhaps on the day Christ died. People are thirsty; yet they walk past the well of truth and head for the saloon, looking for something that will kill the pain, something that will make them happy. Instead they come away drunk, their mouths bitter, their spirits still dissatisfied.

In his two letters Peter warns against false teachers who exploit students, doctoring up the truth until it tastes more palatable—the "new and improved" truth with more zest and better taste! They offer synthetic truth, and people throng around them for a sip. Our culture's fascination with the spirit world, eastern mysticism, the "health and wealth" gospel, and the teaching of many cults attests to this thirst for truth. People want a code by which to live, a standard in which to trust. Without a core of absolute truth, they are left with no foundation.

Daily Nourishment

Truth is more than a courtroom verdict or a historical statistic. It is a life-giving force. It sustains mental and spiritual life. The ability to think on truth is in itself a refreshing truth.

Peter reminds us to cling tightly to the truth Christ has given. If we fail to review it and remind one another of it, we will drift from truth into near truths and from near truths to half-truths and from half-truths to outright lies. And the whole process will seem logical.

Peter says that through God's promises, which are truth, we commune with God and participate in His nature (2 Peter 1:4). Those who build on the truth of God's promises grow in the qualities listed in 2 Peter 1:5-7—faith, virtue, knowledge, temperance, patience, godliness, brotherly kindness, and charity (love). Those who doubt God's truth (Peter calls them scoffers) rely on their own judgment, experience, and natural instincts. They forget that God's truth is unchanging, while their version of truth changes as their experience, feelings, and instincts change.

Drawing Others to the Well of Truth

The best way to confront a lie is to teach the truth. Every time we state a truth of God, we nourish ourselves and those who hear it. No matter how simple the truth, we must keep on speaking it to ourselves, to our children, to the woman at the coffee shop, to the other fathers at the soccer game, to every available ear.

We can also help others by demonstrating the truth of truth—not with arrogance, but with humble and consistent obedience to the principles of God's Word, especially when it would be much easier to doubt or deny the Word. For example, one of my coworkers, a Christian, told me about his financial problems, but affirmed his faith in God's provision. He said that his family had agreed that even during their financial crisis they would continue giving 15 percent of their income to Christ's kingdom work. What a testimony to the truth!

Both Peter and Jude predicted that an age of falsehood and scoffing would come. It has, but the situation is not hopeless. The Bible declares that God's truth will continue and that lies will fade away. And in the end, His truth will be known and vindicated before every eye and ear.

Quarterly Quiz

The questions on this page may be used in several ways: as a pretest at the beginning of the quarter; as a review at the end of the quarter; or as a review after each lesson. The questions are based on the Scripture text of each lesson (King James Version). **The answers are on page 4.**

Lesson 1

1. What does James tell us to do if we lack wisdom? (seek Christian advice, ask God for it, meditate on Scripture?) *James 1:5*

2. What reward is promised to those who are tried and show their love for the Lord? *James 1:12*

3. God tempts us with evil to enable us to learn how to endure temptation. T/F *James 1:13*

Lesson 2

1. James tells us to be _____ of the word, and not _____ only. *James 1:22*

2. What is the "royal law"? *James 2:8*

3. What two activities should be done by believers so that they "may be healed"? *James 5:16*

Lesson 3

1. What does James say cannot be tamed? (the love of money, lust, the tongue?) *James 3:8*

2. Which of the following is *not* a quality of wisdom that comes from above: purity, mercy, self-assurance, impartiality? *James 3:17*

Lesson 4

1. God resists the _____ but gives grace to the _____. *James 4:6*

2. James compares life to what? (a tree, a vapor, a river?) *James 4:14*

Lesson 5

1. We have been redeemed, not by silver and gold, but by what? *1 Peter 1:18, 19*

2. Who is referred to as "a stone of stumbling, and a rock of offense"? (Satan, Peter, Jesus?) *1 Peter 2:6-8*

3. In the church, there is no longer any "priesthood." T/F *1 Peter 2:9*

Lesson 6

1. We should always be ready to give an answer to anyone who asks us the reason for the _____ that is in us. *1 Peter 3:15*

2. Peter warns us about the devil and compares him with which creature? (a slinking snake, a roaring lion, a ravenous wolf?) *1 Peter 5:8*

Lesson 7

1. List the eight qualities that should be in all Christians so that they will live fruitful lives. *2 Peter 1:5-8*

2. Why did Peter feel a sense of urgency about helping the early Christians remember the truth about the everlasting kingdom of Jesus Christ? *2 Peter 1:12-15*

Lesson 8

1. The first time the world was destroyed by _____; for the final judgment, destruction will come by _____. *2 Peter 3:6, 7*

2. The Lord is longsuffering because He wants everyone to come to repentance. T/F *2 Peter 3:9*

3. What other apostle does Peter mention? (Paul, John, Matthew?) *2 Peter 3:15, 16*

Lesson 9

1. If we say that we have not sinned, we make God a liar. T/F *1 John 1:10*

2. What must we do to show that we know Jesus? *1 John 2:3*

3. We abide in Jesus when we (pray, walk, obey) as He did. *1 John 2:6*

Lesson 10

1. By loving the brethren, we pass from _____ to _____. *1 John 3:14*

2. We know that we dwell in Him and He dwells in us because He has given us His (love, Spirit, life). *1 John 4:13*

Lesson 11

1. What gives us the victory that overcomes the world? *1 John 5:4*

2. The three that bear witness in earth are the spirit, the water, and the _____. *1 John 5:8*.

3. Anyone who does not have the Son of God does not have life. T/F *1 John 5:12*

Lesson 12

1. What lie were the deceivers telling about Jesus Christ? *2 John 7*

2. John's greatest joy was to hear that his children (did good deeds, were successful, walked in truth). *3 John 4*

Lesson 13

1. What is it for which we should earnestly contend? (the faith, our salvation, authority over evil?) *Jude 3*

2. Who disputed with the devil about Moses' body? *Jude 9*

Faith and Temptation

September 7
Lesson 1

DEVOTIONAL READING: 2 Corinthians 4:5-11.

BACKGROUND SCRIPTURE: James 1:1-18.

PRINTED TEXT: James 1:1-8, 12-18.

James 1:1-8, 12-18

1 James, a servant of God and of the Lord Jesus Christ, To the twelve tribes which are scattered abroad, Greeting.

2 My brethren, count it all joy when ye fall into divers temptations;

3 Knowing this, that the trying of your faith worketh patience.

4 But let patience have her perfect work, that ye may be perfect and entire, wanting nothing.

5 If any of you lack wisdom, let him ask of God, that giveth to all men liberally, and upbraideth not; and it shall be given him.

6 But let him ask in faith, nothing wavering: for he that wavereth is like a wave of the sea driven with the wind and tossed.

7 For let not that man think that he shall receive any thing of the Lord.

8 A double-minded man is unstable in all his ways.

. . . .

12 Blessed is the man that endureth temptation: for when he is tried, he shall receive the crown of life, which the Lord hath promised to them that love him.

13 Let no man say when he is tempted, I am tempted of God: for God cannot be tempted with evil, neither tempteth he any man:

14 But every man is tempted, when he is drawn away of his own lust, and enticed.

15 Then when lust hath conceived, it bringeth forth sin; and sin, when it is finished, bringeth forth death.

16 Do not err, my beloved brethren.

17 Every good gift and every perfect gift is from above, and cometh down from the Father of lights, with whom is no variableness, neither shadow of turning.

18 Of his own will begat he us with the word of truth, that we should be a kind of firstfruits of his creatures.

GOLDEN TEXT: My brethren, count it all joy when ye fall into divers temptations; knowing this, that the trying of your faith worketh patience.—James 1:2, 3.

Faith Faces the World
Unit 1: Live in Faith
(Lessons 1-4)

Lesson Aims

After participating in this lesson, each student should be able to:

1. Tell what James says about trials and temptations—and how to achieve victory through them.

2. Explain how to use wisdom from God to overcome temptation.

3. Identify a specific temptation that he or she is experiencing and pray for help to do what is right.

Lesson Outline

INTRODUCTION
    A. Letters in the New Testament
    B. Lesson Background
  I. AUTHOR AND AUDIENCE (James 1:1)
    A. The Writer (v. 1a)
    B. The Readers (v. 1b)
 II. TEMPTATION AND TRIUMPH (James 1:2-8, 12)
    A. Joy in Temptation (v. 2)
    B. Happy Results (vv. 3, 4)
       When Circumstances Stress Us
    C. Wisdom to Win (vv. 5-8)
    D. Reward of Victory (v. 12)
III. EVIL AND GOOD (James 1:13-18)
    A. Sources of Evil (vv. 13-15)
       Costly Desires
    B. Source of Good (vv. 16-18)
CONCLUSION
    A. Advice From James
    B. Prayer
    C. Thought to Remember

Introduction

Being a hermit by nature, I was fortunate to have a wife as social as I am unsocial. Thanks to her, both of us had a multitude of friends living near and far away. When we composed our annual "Christmas letter" for them, we had to make five hundred copies.

But to members of our family we wrote a different kind of letter, and we wrote more often. Instead of giving a summary of our lives for a year, each letter spoke of matters of special interest to the person or couple to whom that letter was sent. One copy was enough.

A. Letters in the New Testament

About one-third of the New Testament consists of letters. Some of those letters are like our letters to family members. Some in that group are addressed to special individuals such as Timothy, Titus, or Philemon. Some are addressed to all the Christians in certain cities such as Rome or Corinth. One is addressed to the Christians in Galatia, a district including a number of cities. These are called "special letters" because each one was specially written for a certain individual or a certain group.

New Testament letters of another group are called "general letters" because the identity of specific recipients is hard to determine; this brings up the possibility that they were written for Christians in general, not for specific individuals or groups. Each of these letters is named for its writer: James, Peter, John, or Jude. Peter wrote two of the general letters, and John wrote three. Second John and 3 John actually are special letters, since one is addressed to a certain lady and her children, and the other to a man named Gaius. But those two very short works are grouped with 1 John among the general letters for convenience. These seven letters appear in the Bible after the book of Hebrews (which itself often is considered to be one of the general letters), and before the final book, Revelation. Our lessons for the fall will be drawn from these books that are called "general letters" or "general epistles."

B. Lesson Background

The book of James is not heavy on doctrine as are many other letters in the New Testament. The focus, instead, is on how Christians are to conduct themselves. Of course, the author cannot teach his readers lessons about proper conduct without solid doctrine as a foundation. But here that doctrinal foundation is assumed to be already in place; this allows the author to focus on his main concern: right behavior. As we shall see, much of this letter bears a strong resemblance to things Jesus had to say in His Sermon on the Mount.

I. Author and Audience
(James 1:1)

If we pick up a new book dealing with space travel, we look for the name of the author. If he is a well-known writer of fiction, we expect this story to be fiction as well. If the writer is one of those who walked on the moon years ago, perhaps the book will have interesting reminiscences of what it felt like to be literally out of this world. If the new book comes from an official of NASA, we expect to learn something about the latest developments in travel in outer space. So when we know who wrote the book of James perhaps we will know what to expect in the book.

A. The Writer (v. 1a)

1a. James, a servant of God and of the Lord Jesus Christ.

Ancient letters customarily begin with the name of the writer. The New Testament notes several men by the name of *James*. Two of Jesus' twelve disciples bore the name: the son of Zebedee and brother of John (Matthew 10:2) and the son of Alpheus (Matthew 10:3). "James the Less" (Mark 15:40) is generally assumed to be the apostle James, son of Alpheus. One of Jesus' brothers was also named James (Matthew 13:55; Mark 6:3). Another James is mentioned in Luke 6:16 and Acts 1:13, but nothing more than his relationship to Judas is known.

So who was this James who wrote the letter we are beginning to read? Modestly he calls himself *a servant of God and of the Lord Jesus Christ.* That is also a description of you or me or any active Christian. Most likely this is "James, the Lord's brother" (Galatians 1:19). James is named first among Jesus' brothers in both Matthew and Mark, perhaps indicating that he was the oldest of those siblings.

When Jesus began His ministry, all His siblings must have learned that He was doing miracles (Matthew 4:23-25) and teaching amazing things (7:28, 29). They must have known their brother was the most popular teacher in Israel, for when they went with their mother to talk with Him, they found the crowd so big and so tightly packed that they could not reach Him. The people of God had replaced them as His family (Luke 8:19-21).

After more than two years of miracles and teaching, Jesus' brothers still did not believe Jesus was Israel's Messiah and the world's Savior (John 7:5). They did not become convinced until He rose from the dead. After that, His brothers were among His disciples in Jerusalem (Acts 1:13, 14). Peter thought highly enough of James to mention him by name (Acts 12:17). Later, Paul named James along with two of the other apostles as pillars of the church (Galatians 2:9). During an important doctrinal debate, it was James who stated the conclusion reached by the apostles, the elders, and the church at Jerusalem (Acts 15:13-29). When we look at the book of James, then, we are seeing a letter from one of the strongest, wisest, and most trusted leaders of the first church in Jerusalem. From such a writer we can expect good counsel, and the inspiration of the Holy Spirit assures us that we shall find no mistakes.

B. The Readers (v. 1b)

1b. To the twelve tribes which are scattered abroad, Greeting.

Taken literally this would refer to all the Jews living outside their homeland of Palestine. Jews lived in various parts of the sprawling Roman Empire. Acts 2:9-11 lists some of the places from which they came for the feast of Passover in Jerusalem.

However, since those who are expected to read this letter have faith in "our Lord Jesus Christ, the Lord of glory" (James 2:1), we conclude that James writes it for Jewish Christians in many places outside of Palestine. Certainly it contains good advice for all Christians everywhere, even to us who live two thousand years later.

II. Temptation and Triumph (James 1:2-8, 12)

After the very short greeting of verse 1, James dives right into the subjects he wants to discuss.

A. Joy in Temptation (v. 2)

2. My brethren, count it all joy when ye fall into divers temptations.

Scarcely has the sound of James's greeting died away when he introduces a word that we may prefer not to hear: *temptations.* (Some versions read "trials" instead.) This refers to things, events, or circumstances that test our strength of character. Sometimes the trials and temptations of life entice us to relieve our distress by doing wrong. But James recommends an unusual way of responding to trouble or distress: meet it with *joy!* (See Matthew 5:12.) [See question #1, page 16.]

We probably have a hard time imagining ourselves clapping our hands in joy when we break a leg, lose a job, or wreck the car! Such trials test our faith, our patience, and our godly disposition. Trials like this tempt us to do something wrong, such as trying to defraud the insurance company or blaming God for our careless driving. In any

---

How to Say It

ABRAHAM. *Ay*-bruh-ham.
ALPHEUS. Al-*fee*-us.
CORINTH. *Kor*-inth.
GAIUS. *Gay*-us.
GALATIA. Guh-*lay*-shuh.
HEBREWS. *Hee*-brews.
JERUSALEM. Juh-*roo*-suh-lem.
MESSIAH. Meh-*sigh*-uh.
PHILEMON. Fih-*lee*-mun or Fye-*lee*-mun.
TITUS. *Ty*-tus.

case, the disaster is not likely to be greeted with delight. But James is not insane. He is taking the long view, as the next verse shows.

B. Happy Results (vv. 3, 4)

3, 4. Knowing this, that the trying of your faith worketh patience. But let patience have her perfect work, that ye may be perfect and entire, wanting nothing.

Catastrophe may indeed test our *faith*. It may tempt us to turn away from God. But if our faith is strong and healthy, it passes the test. Strong faith does not ask, "Where was God when that wild driver rammed me?" Instead, with gratitude this faith says, "Thank God I'm alive." So the test of your faith produces *patience*. This word *patience* does not suggest that we simply wait out our troubles passively. Instead, it includes the idea of active persistence. We persevere. We keep on thinking straight, speaking truthfully, and doing right. When patience is allowed to *have her perfect work*, we become mature and complete, lacking nothing that belongs in Christian character and life. As a result, we emerge from our troubles better people. We are firmer, stronger, more secure in our faith. Isn't that reason enough for the joy recommended in verse 2? (See also v. 12, below.) [See question #2, page 16.]

WHEN CIRCUMSTANCES STRESS US

Somewhere over Africa on December 29, 2000, British Airways flight 2069 suddenly went out of control. Dr. Mark Jasmine, his wife Mary, and their two daughters were on that flight, heading for a vacation safari.

As the plane fell into a steep dive, it vibrated horribly and parts of the ceiling and luggage from the overhead bins cascaded onto the passengers. The Jasmines embraced the children, sure that all would die soon. Mary started singing a gospel song by Twila Paris that spoke of God's being in control.

Unbeknownst to most of the passengers, a deranged man had burst into the cockpit and disengaged the autopilot, causing the plane to plunge nineteen thousand feet before the crew could subdue him and bring the plane under control.

VISUALS FOR THESE LESSONS

The visual pictured in each lesson (e.g., page 13) is a small reproduction of a large, full-color poster included in the *Adult Visuals* packet for the Fall Quarter. The packet is available from your supplier. Order No. 192.

Mary Jasmine said later, "I had this island of calm right in the middle of all this chaos . . . the holy presence inside me. . . . Hang onto that place. Call on it regularly, not just when the chips are down. [God's] grace is more than sufficient."

The Jasmine family learned the lesson of today's text: when life's circumstances threaten to destroy us, God will provide not only momentary peace, but lasting, patient trust and confidence in His loving care.   —C. R. B.

C. Wisdom to Win (vv. 5-8)

5. If any of you lack wisdom, let him ask of God, that giveth to all men liberally, and upbraideth not; and it shall be given him.

Easily we fall into the foolish habit of blaming someone else for our problems. If we cannot put the blame on the other driver, we put it on God. Why didn't He rescue me from that awful situation? It takes more than human wisdom to see clearly a situation that involves ourselves. So *ask of God*. (See also Matthew 7:7.)

When you ask God, you allow Him to teach you something through your trials. But you should not expect God to give you a clear understanding against your will. Do your best to see your situation and yourself fairly, impartially. Imagine yourself in someone else's place. How would your conduct look to him? Or imagine someone else in your place. Would you find excuses for her as easily as you find them for yourself? [See question #3, page 16.]

6. But let him ask in faith, nothing wavering: for he that wavereth is like a wave of the sea driven with the wind and tossed.

Ask wisdom from God, fully expect to receive it, and be willing and eager to accept God's view of the situation even if it makes you look bad. If you waver between your wish for clear understanding and your wish to make yourself look good, you can't be satisfied either with God's clear understanding or your own biased view. You're like a wind-tossed *wave of the sea*.

7, 8. For let not that man think that he shall receive any thing of the Lord. A double-minded man is unstable in all his ways.

So we must make up our minds: Do we want God's clear wisdom or our own self-justifying opinions? God knows what we really want, and that is what we will get. (See also James 4:8.)

D. Reward of Victory (v. 12)

12. Blessed is the man that endureth temptation: for when he is tried, he shall receive the crown of life, which the Lord hath promised to them that love him.

In verse 2 James urged us to be joyful in the midst of our trials and temptations. Now he looks forward to the end of all those trials and temptations. When their end comes, we shall stand before God as mature Christians, strengthened by every battle with *temptation*. By His grace we at long last shall be as Christlike as we have been trying to be throughout our lives. Then we shall be crowned with *life*, endless life, life without trials and temptations, life in the presence of God. Isn't that worth all the struggles you have had and will ever have in this life on earth? (See also Matthew 24:13; James 5:11.) [See question #4, page 16.]

III. Evil and Good
(James 1:13-18)

Sometimes it is hard to trace a matter to its source or to find the cause of a result that is plain before us. When rainfall makes a river overflow its banks, can we say that God caused the resulting destruction? Did the devil cause it? (Compare Job 1:6-19.) Or was the owner of the house at fault by foolishly building on a flood plain? In the last part of our text, James gives us some guidelines for our thinking about sources.

A. Sources of Evil (vv. 13-15)

13. Let no man say when he is tempted, I am tempted of God: for God cannot be tempted with evil, neither tempteth he any man.

The word *tempt* has different meanings. "God did tempt Abraham" (Genesis 22:1) in that *God* tested Abraham to show to him and to us the depth and power of Abraham's faith (Genesis 22:1-13). But in verse 13 of our text, *tempted* has the meaning that it most often has today. James is saying God does not entice anyone to commit sin. If you are wondering who or what is trying to make you do wrong, here is a starting point for your thinking: God is not doing it.

14. But every man is tempted, when he is drawn away of his own lust, and enticed.

Does this shock you? The source of temptation is inside you. It is your *own lust,* your own desire, your own wish. This does not deny the devil's part in temptation (see 1 Peter 5:8). But the devil cannot make you do anything wrong unless some wish of yours cooperates with him. Alert for every opportunity, the devil uses your own wish to entice you into wrongdoing in order to get what you desire. The devil may be stronger than you are, but God is even stronger (1 John 4:4). He will strengthen us in our time of temptation, if we let Him. [See question #5, page 16.]

15. Then when lust hath conceived, it bringeth forth sin; and sin, when it is finished, bringeth forth death.

FAITH FACES THE WORLD

Live in Faith	Live in Hope	Live in Love	Live with Purpose
Resist Temptation James 1:1-8, 12-18	Imitate God's Holiness 1 Peter 1:3-5, 13-21; 2:4-10	Enjoy Fellowship With God 1 John 1:5-2:6, 15-17, 29-3:1	Remain Loyal 2 John 4-9; 3 John 3-12
Believe and Act James 1:22-27; 2:8-9, 14-17; 3:13-16	Set a Good Example 1 Peter 2:11, 12; 3:15-17; 4:7-11; 5:6-10	Love One Another 1 John 3:11-16; 4:7-16	Maintain Steadfast Faith Jude 3, 4, 8-13, 16-25
Seek God's Wisdom James 3	Grow in Faith 2 Peter 1:3-15	Live With Confidence 1 John 5:1-15	
Be Humble James 4	Trust God's Promise 2 Peter 3:3-18		

Visual for lesson 1

Use this poster from the Adult Visuals *packet to provide an overview of the lessons this quarter.*

"Every man" in verse 13 is generic, meaning every person. But having said "man," James is able to draw a vivid picture. Lust, your desire, your wish, is pictured as a woman. Beautiful but evil, she tries to entice the "man" to do wrong. If he gives in to her pleading, she leads him to her bed; the child *conceived* of their union with her is *sin*—your sin. And when that sin *is finished*, that is, when it is grown up, it is worse than the wish. The sin results in *death*—your death. Now aren't you glad you stood firm against your wish when first it tried to entice you to do wrong? Aren't you glad you resisted its pleading, put it in its place, and refused to do anything wrong? In so doing, you allowed God to save you for eternity.

COSTLY DESIRES

Would you like to travel the world over, but not have to eat any "strange" food or sleep in a stranger's bed every night? You say you want the comforts of home but still want to see exotic sights? When we want our desires to be fulfilled without the normal cost that comes with that fulfillment, usually there's not much help.

But some of us keep trying. How about the possibility of visiting cities around the world, sleeping in our own bed every night, eating our customary diet while doing so, and never having to pay the penalty of discomfort in our travels? Now it can be done! *The World* of ResidenSea, a new cruise ship launched in 2002, is an ocean-going condominium with 110 units ranging from 1,100 to 3,200 square feet each. You may cook in your own kitchen and eat on your own terrace, or you can patronize one of the four restaurants on board. All this for only $2 million to $6.8 million! (But don't forget the 5 percent annual fee that includes all but food and drink.)

Most of us don't have desires as grandiose as that, but what we do want gives us trouble when we don't want to pay the price. When what we want is wrong and the price is too high, James says, "Don't blame God; it's your own fault!" When we allow evil desires to be incubated in our hearts, we should not be surprised that the price is more than we want to pay!   —C. R. B.

B. Source of Good (vv. 16-18)

16. Do not err, my beloved brethren.

"Make no mistake about this," says James. James already has assured us that God does not tempt anyone (v. 13). Now he tells us what God does instead. He is the provider of good. James wants us to be fully convinced of this truth.

17. Every good gift and every perfect gift is from above, and cometh down from the Father of lights, with whom is no variableness, neither shadow of turning.

Notice that the word *gift* appears twice. The first refers to an "act of giving" that is *good* in motive, method, and result. The *gift* that results is *perfect*, complete, all that it ought to be, all the recipients need. Such wonderful generosity is beyond the reach of us ordinary human beings; they are *from above*, from Heaven. In fact, they come *down from the Father* who made the heavenly *lights* (Genesis 1; Psalm 136:7-9). This imagery naturally makes us think of the blazing sun by day and the mellow moon and the sparkling stars by night. The lights we see above are variable. They are dimmed by clouds and eclipses; they brighten in a clear sky. But the Father of them all is forever changeless, forever dependable, forever in the good act of giving perfect gifts.

18. Of his own will begat he us with the word of truth, that we should be a kind of firstfruits of his creatures.

Through *the word of truth,* it is God who grants the power and the right to be born again, born of water and of the Spirit (John 3:3-5). Thus He makes us to be new creatures (2 Corinthians 5:17) and the *firstfruits of his creatures.* When our salvation is completed in Heaven, the "bondage of corruption" shall be no more (Romans 8:21).

Conclusion

Nearly every scholar who comments on the book of James tells us it is a very practical book. So, what practical advice for daily living have we seen in this lesson?

A. Advice From James

First, James counsels us to live with joy, especially to find joy in things that trouble and distress us. Those troubles can be beneficial. If we meet them with courage and keep on doing right, they make us better people. Isn't that what we want? And, after all, most of us are not greatly troubled or distressed most of the time. Still, we know God's tomorrow will be better than today if we meet life with courage and keep on doing right. How can we not be filled with joy?

Second, James tells us to live for victory. One of the things that troubles us is the constant presence of temptation, the urge to do wrong in order to gain some short-term advantage. Don't let it scare you. With wisdom from God, you can beat the devil. "Resist the devil, and he will flee from you" (James 4:7). More dangerous may be the enemy within you, your own wish to do something wrong (4:1). You can beat that wish with a better one. More than anything else, wish for God's kingdom (Matthew 6:33). That is, wish to be ruled by God, to do His will. And wish for God's righteousness. You can never get that for yourself, but God can give it to you by His gracious forgiveness (1 John 1:9).

Third, James tells us to live for the future. As Paul puts it, "the sufferings of this present time are not worthy to be compared with the glory which shall be revealed in us" (Romans 8:18). Go for the glory!

B. Prayer

Our Father in Heaven, it is good to be assured that all things work together for good to them that love You, as Romans 8:28 promises. We do love You, Lord, and we do want to serve You. "Lead us not into temptation." Give us, instead, the wisdom to know what is right and the courage to do it. In Jesus' name, amen.

C. Thought to Remember

Trust God and do right.

Home Daily Bible Readings

Learning by Doing

This page contains an alternative lesson plan emphasizing learning activities.
Classes desiring such student involvement will find these suggestions helpful.

Learning Goals

After this lesson each student will be able to:

1. Tell what James says about trials and temptations—and how to achieve victory through them.

2. Explain how to use wisdom from God to overcome temptation.

3. Identify a specific temptation that he or she is experiencing and pray for help to do what is right.

Into the Lesson

Begin by stating, "People respond differently to the same event. For example, some rejoice over the outcome of a football game; others are quite disappointed." To help illustrate different reactions to the same event, ask for volunteers to serve in two skit groups of at least two people. Each skit group will illustrate both a positive and a negative response to a particular situation.

Group 1 prepares two skits describing the reaction of parents to their teenage son's car accident. Group 2 describes the reaction of an employee who should have received a job promotion to another employee who actually did. Ask the groups to give the negative reaction first, then the positive reaction. After both groups have finished, say: "As we have seen, people react differently to the same situation. Today we will think about how people react differently to temptation or trials. Our text today describes how we should respond if we want to receive eternal life. Turn to the book of James, and let's read our text, James 1:1-8, 12-18."

Into the Word

Ask two class members to read the two sections of the text aloud. Prior to this class session, ask a member of the class to prepare a three-minute monologue on the author of this epistle. Give the class member the following Scriptures to look up in preparation: Matthew 4:23-25; 7:28, 29; Mark 6:3; Luke 8:19-21; John 7:5; Acts 1:13, 14; 15:13-29; Galatians 1:19; 2:9. State: "To begin our study, I've asked _____ to tell us a little about the identity of this James."

Following the monologue, state: "Now let's see what James the Lord's brother has to say about trials and temptations." Ask the following questions.

1. How does James say we should respond to trials and temptations? *("Count it all joy," v. 2.)*

2. What are the benefits of responding to trials in that way? *(It develops patience, v. 3, and that*

leads to becoming *"perfect and entire, wanting nothing," v. 4.)*

3. What does James promise will be the reward for enduring? *("The crown of life," v. 12.)*

Say: "Have you ever considered why some people 'break' under trials while others get stronger? A different response is often due to different focus. People who 'break' under trials see only the immediate difficulty. But what do people who grow stronger see? They see the future, the end result, not the present difficulty."

4. What does James say a person should do to know how to endure personal trials and temptations? *("Let him ask of God," v. 5.)*

5. What determines whether a person's prayer is granted? *("Ask in faith, nothing wavering," v. 6.)*

Assign half of the class to each of the following two questions. Allow about three minutes for the students to work together; then ask for the answers. Discuss as needed to clarify the answers.

1. What qualities or characteristics does James say a person who endures temptation has? *(Wisdom, v. 5; faith, v. 6; love for the Lord, v. 12.)*

2. Why should we not say that God tempts us? *(He does not tempt any man, v. 13; God gives only good and perfect gifts, and God does not change, v. 17.)*

State: "Notice that the source of temptation is inside us. Our own lust leads to our own sin, resulting in our own death" (vv. 14, 15).

Into Life

No one is exempt from temptation. But how we respond to temptation determines whether we sin. Ask, "What are the most common temptations that come to Christians in our community?" and "Why do Christians fall into those temptations?" As the students suggest answers, write these answers for all to see.

Assign a group of students to each temptation listed. Ask: "In light of what James says to Christians who face temptation, what practical steps do you recommend to a struggling Christian to overcome falling?"

Allow time for the groups to work. While they do, write all of the temptations across the chalkboard as headings for separate columns. After several minutes, call for recommended solutions from each group. Write the suggestions in the appropriate columns. Lead the class in prayer for help in applying these solutions.

Let's Talk It Over

The questions on this page are designed to promote discussion of the lesson by the class and to encourage application of the lesson Scriptures. The answers provided are only discussion starters. Let your class talk it over from there.

1. "Are we having fun yet?" That question exposes the shallow ambitions of worldly people. What can the church do to help the average Christian seek lasting joy instead of pursuing that which brings only temporary happiness?

Happiness is the temporary result of what is currently happening—perhaps whatever is currently "fun." As soon as the excitement wears off, the internal emptiness quickly returns. In contrast, James says the real blessing comes from having joy that lasts even through the toughest times. The church must continue to point out to modern pleasure-seekers the superiority of this lasting contentment. Our calm assurance—our joy!—comes from knowing that God is faithful in all circumstances. He provides daily care and ensures that an eternal reward is waiting for those faithful to Him through Christ.

2. Many Christians feel that they are failures if they repeatedly have to deal with the same trial or temptation. In what ways can the church effectively teach that these experiences, while potentially dangerous, are not sin in and of themselves, and are also opportunities for growth?

Being tempted does not mean a person has sinned. We sin only when we yield to temptation. If a Christian successfully resists the same temptation five hundred times in the same day, sin has not entered the picture. However, it is important that Christians develop effective ways to distance themselves from repeated temptations. Training the mind to think on positives is one help (Philippians 4:8). Following through on the commitment to stay away from sources of temptation can also help ensure success. An "accountability partner" can provide a valuable service; this is someone who agrees to be available at any time to help a person navigate past a powerful temptation (see James 5:19, 20).

3. It's easy to say we need to ask God for wisdom. It's much harder to remember to do it. Perhaps hardest yet is discerning His answer. How do you do what James is telling us to do in this passage?

How often we hear someone say, "God told me. . . ." Seldom, if ever, does that person claim to have heard an audible voice. Rather, the expression means that one has determined what he or she ought to do and is crediting God with the answer. But is the answer truly from God? Brainstorm some specific ways class members can incorporate asking for God's wisdom in their private devotional times, in public prayers, and in spiritually-oriented conversations. Talk also about how to check the "answer." Is it consistent with God's revealed Word, the Bible? Do mature and godly people concur? Is it the easy way out, or does it require the kind of patience and perseverance James writes of in the text?

4. James seems to describe both the short- and long-term results of dealing successfully with trials and temptations. How can Christians effectively communicate both perspectives?

The church has done an excellent job of describing how wonderful Heaven will be. However, we have not always held high the expectation that *every* Christian can and should use their struggles as stepping stones to spiritual maturity in the here and now. One teaching tool we can use in this regard is to encourage Christians to share their testimonies. Have the congregation review the lives of those they know who have grown as a result of adversity. (A reminder: if any class member has confidential information about the person being discussed, that information must remain confidential.)

5. One part of the Alcoholics Anonymous experience includes conducting a "fearless moral inventory" in which struggling individuals look at what they have done, whom they have hurt, and what continues to be the source of the problem in their lives. How can Christians use such an "inventory" to help them grow?

Sometimes Christians are so happy to be forgiven for their sins that they do not take the time to learn from their experiences. As a result, they do not gain wisdom for dealing with the next temptation. A "fearless inventory" is not designed to destroy a person's self-concept. Done correctly, it will give the Christian a tool to look deeply into oneself to discover "what's really going on." As a result, it will reveal ways to overcome temptations. Have the class list questions that Christians can ask themselves to complete such an in-depth search process successfully.

Faith and Action

DEVOTIONAL READING: Matthew 7:21-27.

BACKGROUND SCRIPTURE: James 1:19–2:26; 5:7-20.

PRINTED TEXT: James 1:22-27; 2:8, 9, 14-17; 5:13-16.

James 1:22-27

22 But be ye doers of the word, and not hearers only, deceiving your own selves.

23 For if any be a hearer of the word, and not a doer, he is like unto a man beholding his natural face in a glass:

24 For he beholdeth himself, and goeth his way, and straightway forgetteth what manner of man he was.

25 But whoso looketh into the perfect law of liberty, and continueth therein, he being not a forgetful hearer, but a doer of the work, this man shall be blessed in his deed.

26 If any man among you seem to be religious, and bridleth not his tongue, but deceiveth his own heart, this man's religion is vain.

27 Pure religion and undefiled before God and the Father is this, To visit the fatherless and widows in their affliction, and to keep himself unspotted from the world.

James 2:8, 9, 14-17

8 If ye fulfil the royal law according to the Scripture, Thou shalt love thy neighbor as thyself, ye do well:

9 But if ye have respect to persons, ye commit sin, and are convinced of the law as transgressors.

. . . .

14 What doth it profit, my brethren, though a man say he hath faith, and have not works? can faith save him?

15 If a brother or sister be naked, and destitute of daily food,

16 And one of you say unto them, Depart in peace, be ye warmed and filled; notwithstanding ye give them not those things which are needful to the body; what doth it profit?

17 Even so faith, if it hath not works, is dead, being alone.

James 5:13-16

13 Is any among you afflicted? let him pray. Is any merry? let him sing psalms.

14 Is any sick among you? let him call for the elders of the church; and let them pray over him, anointing him with oil in the name of the Lord:

15 And the prayer of faith shall save the sick, and the Lord shall raise him up; and if he have committed sins, they shall be forgiven him.

16 Confess your faults one to another, and pray one for another, that ye may be healed. The effectual fervent prayer of a righteous man availeth much.

GOLDEN TEXT: Be ye doers of the word, and not hearers only, deceiving your own selves.—James 1:22.

Faith Faces the World
Unit 1: Live in Faith
(Lessons 1-4)

Lesson Aims

After participating in this lesson, each student should be able to:

1. List several features of a living and active faith.

2. Explain why faith must be active to be real.

3. Work with others in the class to develop a project that would enable members to help the needy.

Lesson Outline

INTRODUCTION
  A. Forgetting and Neglecting
  B. Lesson Background
 I. ACCEPTABLE RELIGION (James 1:22-27)
  A. The Call to Action (v. 22)
  B. The Forgetful Non-doer (vv. 23, 24)
  C. The Blessed Doer (v. 25)
    Needed: An External Reference Point
  D. An Active Self-discipline (v. 26)
  E. A Pure Religion (v. 27)
 II. ACTIVE LOVE AND FAITH (James 2:8, 9, 14-17)
  A. The Kingly Law (v. 8)
    Living (and Dying) by the Royal Law
  B. Transgression Against the King (v. 9)
  C. Dead Faith (vv. 14-17)
III. ADVICE FOR SPECIAL CASES (James 5:13-16)
  A. The Afflicted (v. 13a)
  B. The Merry (v. 13b)
  C. The Sick (vv. 14, 15)
  D. The Faulty (v. 16)
CONCLUSION
  A. Not "Living It Up," but "Living It Out"
  B. Prayer
  C. Thought to Remember

Introduction

"Wash your hands, boys," Mom called. "We'll have supper in a minute." That was so long ago that our farm home had no running water and no bathroom. My brother beat me to the wash bench just inside the kitchen door. Savoring his victory, he took his time about dipping water from the bucket to the basin and washing his hands. Meanwhile I looked through the screen door at a robin gathering his supper bug by bug from the tiny lawn behind the house. Then the plot thick-ened. I saw a cat crouching behind a clump of mums, obviously hoping the bird would come close enough to become his supper. Breathless, I watched the little drama of life and death while minutes ticked away. Finally the robin did come within range, and the cat pounced. But the bird was too quick for him. He took flight a scant inch ahead of the slashing claws, and I started breathing again.

At that moment Mom called again: "Come on, boys. Supper's on." We took our places at the table and bowed our heads while Dad spoke a short prayer. Then Mom turned to me with a gentle rebuke: "Go back and wash your hands."

A. Forgetting and Neglecting

I wish I could say I quickly outgrew the habit of forgetting my duty, but I didn't. Only yesterday, engrossed in lesson 1 of this series, I forgot it was my turn to help distribute the mail in the retirement home where I live. I did not remember until the telephone rang and a good friend gave me the gentle rebuke.

Do we Christians become so engrossed in earning our living and enjoying our lives that we forget our duties to God? I mean the duty of reading His Word and applying it in our daily living, the duty of helping one another at every opportunity, the duty of keeping up an attractive and helpful program of worship in the church and teaching in the Sunday school, the duty of maintaining happy fellowship and mutual encouragement among the saints, the duty of doing "good unto all men, especially unto them who are of the household of faith" (Galatians 6:10), the duty of sharing the gospel with people who need it, the duty of supporting those who give their full time to various Christian ministries, the duty of being the salt of the earth and the light of the world (Matthew 5:13-16).

Is it also possible that some of us do not *forget* all these duties but *neglect* them anyway? That is even worse than forgetting, for "to him that knoweth to do good, and doeth it not, to him it is sin" (James 4:17).

B. Lesson Background

As noted in last week's lesson, practical James is interested in what we do. Today he reminds us of our duties and rebukes our neglect of them. The immediate background of our text lies in the verse just before it: "Lay apart all filthiness and superfluity of naughtiness, and receive with meekness the engrafted word, which is able to save your souls" (James 1:21). But James says it is not enough to receive the Word and cherish it in our hearts. We need it to direct the work of our hands.

I. Acceptable Religion
(James 1:22-27)

Many people have used or heard the phrase, "That's a dead church." Dead churches are all about us, unfortunately. But James has the solution for bringing dead churches and lifeless Christians back to life.

A. The Call to Action (v. 22)

22. But be ye doers of the word, and not hearers only, deceiving your own selves.

Christian teaching is designed to graft God's Word into our minds and hearts (v. 21), to make it a vital part of our thinking and our emotions. But you are fooling yourself if you think you are a good Christian when you have *the word* in your mind and heart but not in your hands and feet. [See question #1, page 24.]

B. The Forgetful Non-doer (vv. 23, 24)

23, 24. For if any be a hearer of the word, and not a doer, he is like unto a man beholding his natural face in a glass: for he beholdeth himself, and goeth his way, and straightway forgetteth what manner of man he was.

You don't look in a mirror just for the privilege of admiring yourself for a few seconds. You look to see if you need to comb your hair, adjust your tie, or renew your makeup. If any of these is needed, you provide it without delay. That is what makes the look in the mirror worthwhile. But some people, even some Christians, hear the Word of God point out some error or sin in their behavior and then go on their *way* and forget what they just heard! In that case the hearing is worthless. A change to better conduct is what gives value to the hearing.

C. The Blessed Doer (v. 25)

25. But whoso looketh into the perfect law of liberty, and continueth therein, he being not a forgetful hearer, but a doer of the work, this man shall be blessed in his deed.

God's Word is called *the perfect law of liberty* (see also James 2:12) because those who hear it and obey it are made free (John 8:31, 32). They are made free from the bondage of sin (John 8:34) and free from the punishment of sin (Romans 6:23). If anyone looks into God's Word and changes his conduct to match God's teaching and continues to live by that teaching, *this man shall be blessed* in what he does. Our godly actions and deeds don't "earn" this blessing, of course, but they do demonstrate the sincerity of our faith (see James 2:17, 18). In His Sermon on the Mount, Jesus also stressed the importance of being a "doer" (see Matthew 5:19; 7:21, 26, 27).

Visual for lesson 2

Use this poster from the Adult Visuals *packet to illustrate James 1:22.*

NEEDED: AN EXTERNAL REFERENCE POINT

Jerry Dragoo is a biology professor at the University of New Mexico. He dresses in traditional "western" style—cowboy boots, jeans, and a belt with a big, fancy buckle. But instead of the usual silver and turquoise inlays, the buckle features a spotted skunk standing on its front legs, ready to defend itself as only a skunk can do!

Skunks are Dragoo's academic specialty. They are in his lab, his backyard, and there are even three in his home—none of which has been "fixed." He says, "My wife has a problem with that." On his first assignment as a student studying skunks, Dragoo got "sprayed." When he couldn't smell anything, he wondered why people spoke so disparagingly of skunks. But back at school, he was kicked out of the building. Since then he has often been a *persona non grata* and has been ejected from meetings, evicted from his residence, and generally avoided in public, all because he has almost no sense of smell. His work is significant, but it hasn't made people like to be around him!

We all need an external reference point—someone or something that can give us an unbiased evaluation of how we look and act (and smell!). For our actions and thoughts, the Word of God provides that point of reference. However, it is of practical value only if we pay attention to what it says about our lives.   —C. R. B.

D. An Active Self-discipline (v. 26)

26. If any man among you seem to be religious, and bridleth not his tongue, but deceiveth his own heart, this man's religion is vain.

Picture a man who goes to church every Sunday, who perhaps leads in prayer when he is asked, and who may even be a deacon. But he fails to control *his tongue*. Perhaps he repeats unfounded gossip. Perhaps he is cruel and loud in judging others. Perhaps he loses his temper and curses. Such a person may fool himself, thinking himself to be a good Christian. He may make some others think he is a genuine and ardent follower of Christ. But when he lets his tongue run wild, he shows that his *religion is vain*, empty, worthless. James will have much more to say about the tongue in 3:1-12.

E. A Pure Religion (v. 27)

27. Pure religion and undefiled before God and the Father is this, To visit the fatherless and widows in their affliction, and to keep himself unspotted from the world.

We have just seen one mark of a phony Christian: an unruly tongue. Now we see two marks of a real Christian. First is generosity in taking care of orphans and *widows*, people unable to earn their own living. The Old Testament frequently connects these two groups of people as being some of the most helpless and vulnerable in the ancient world (see Exodus 22:22-24; Deuteronomy 10:18; 14:28, 29; and many others). [See question #2, page 24.]

Second is keeping oneself morally pure, or *unspotted from the world*. In the Christian's thinking, there is to be none of the world's selfishness or lust. Moral purity is an important theme in the New Testament (see 1 Timothy 5:22; 6:14; Titus 2:12; James 1:21; 2 Peter 1:4; 2:20; 3:14). [See question #3, page 24.]

II. Active Love and Faith (James 2:8, 9, 14-17)

Surely every Christian is aware of the high place love holds in Christianity (see Matthew 22:37-40; 1 John 3:11; 4:7-10). But faith is no less important. "Without faith it is impossible to please [God]: for he that cometh to God must believe that he is, and that he is a rewarder of them that diligently seek him" (Hebrews 11:6). Practical James would have us know that love and faith in our hearts and minds are powerless until they find expression in what we do.

A. The Kingly Law (v. 8)

8. If ye fulfil the royal law according to the Scripture, Thou shalt love thy neighbor as thyself, ye do well.

The *Scripture* James refers to is Leviticus 19:18. See also Jesus' use of this Scripture in Matthew 5:43; 19:19; and Mark 12:31, 33. Loving *thy neighbor as thyself* is *the royal law*, the kingly law. That may mean this law is established by

the King of Heaven and earth, the Lord God Almighty. Or it may mean the law itself is the king of laws, ruling over all the other laws that regulate our relationships with others (see Romans 13:8-10). Whichever meaning James intends, we *do well* when we obey this royal law, when we really do love our neighbors as we love ourselves. How well are we doing that?

LIVING (AND DYING) BY THE ROYAL LAW

Adam Mayblum was on the eighty-seventh floor of the north tower of the World Trade Center when a terrorist-commanded plane slammed into the building on September 11, 2001. He made it to safety, and then wrote an E-mail to twenty-five friends, describing his escape from the burning tower. His friends were so moved that they passed the story on to many others. Within twenty-four hours one hundred people whom Mayblum did not know had written to thank him for the story's impact on their lives; within four months one thousand strangers from around the world had written to him.

In his E-mail Mayblum described the smoke and fire at the top, his conversations with people who did not escape. He also told of meeting the firefighters at the forty-fourth floor as they struggled to the top, sacrificing their lives (as we would learn later) for people they did not know, regardless of their race, nationality, or social station in life.

We don't know how many of those rescue workers were Christians. Some may merely have been doing their duty; others perhaps were simply expressing their humanitarian spirit. Regardless of what motivated them and regardless of what their faith may have been, they were living—and soon to be dying—examples of the royal law of which James speaks. Whether in crisis or in daily life, do we do as well as they in living up to the royal law of our King? —C. R. B.

B. Transgression Against the King (v. 9)

9. But if ye have respect to persons, ye commit sin, and are convinced of the law as transgressors.

To *have respect to persons* is to discriminate, to show more love to one neighbor than to another—perhaps because of who he or she "is" or has. See the example in verses 1-4 of this chapter in which a church welcomes a rich man more cordially than it welcomes a poor man. If we show such partiality instead of loving rich and poor alike, we *commit sin*. The royal law itself convicts us of transgression against that king of laws and against the great King who made that law. God Himself "is no respecter of persons" (Acts 10:34), so why should we be?

C. Dead Faith (vv. 14-17)

14. What doth it profit, my brethren, though a man say he hath faith, and have not works? can faith save him?

Emphatically the apostle Paul teaches that we are saved by God's grace through our *faith*, not by the good works we do (Romans 3:21-31; Galatians 2:16; Ephesians 2:8, 9). James does not contradict Paul, but adds that genuine *faith* makes a difference in what we do. If we really believe in God and love Him, we try to do what He tells us to do (John 14:15). If a person says he or she believes in the God of the Bible, but still goes on in a life of wickedness, we know that that person's faith is fraudulent. Both Paul and James use Abraham as an example of a man with the right kind of faith (Romans 4; James 2:20-24).

15, 16. If a brother or sister be naked, and destitute of daily food, and one of you say unto them, Depart in peace, be ye warmed and filled; notwithstanding ye give them not those things which are needful to the body; what doth it profit?

Suppose a fellow Christian is out of a job and out of money. He is hungry; he is cold. Suppose you greet him with a cordial handshake and give him your good wishes, but nothing more. He is still hungry and cold. Your good wishes are worthless without food for the stomach and fuel for the furnace. Likewise, worthless is faith that does nothing but "believe" (cf. James 2:19). Certainly James isn't saying that we should reward lazy people by feeding them (see 2 Thessalonians 3:10). We put faith to work by meeting genuine needs, especially those of fellow Christians (Galatians 6:10; 1 John 3:17, 18).

17. Even so faith, if it hath not works, is dead, being alone.

We have been saying that inactive *faith* is phony. Practical James is even more blunt. He says inactive faith *is dead*. What mourning there would be if we would have a mass funeral for all the dead faith in the church!

III. Advice for Special Cases (James 5:13-16)

Again we note that James is a practical writer. He knows the specific things that concern his readers, and he has suggestions—actually, requirements from God!—about what to do.

A. The Afflicted (v. 13a)

13a. Is any among you afflicted? let him pray.

So many things afflict us! There is poverty. There are people who don't like us. There is loss of a loved one. There is loneliness. Whatever your affliction, James says to tell your Heavenly

---

How to Say It

EPHESIANS. Ee-*fee*-zhunz.
GALATIANS. Guh-*lay*-shunz.
HEBREWS. *Hee*-brews.

Father about your misery. That in itself may help more than you think it can. In his 1904 book *Quiet Talks on Prayer*, S. D. Gordon observes that, "You can do more than pray, *after* you have prayed. But you can *not* do more than pray *until* you have prayed." Perhaps God will help you make a plan to bring cheer to someone whose affliction is worse than yours. You are sure to feel better as you carry out that plan. Or perhaps you will think of a way to do something good for that person who dislikes you. You'll be surprised to see how much that will help you.

The New Testament stresses the importance of prayer in many places (e.g., Romans 15:30-32). Acts 16:25 demonstrates that we can both pray and sing in the midst of affliction.

B. The Merry (v. 13b)

13b. Is any merry? let him sing psalms.

Many of the *merry* folk today choose to celebrate with bawdy songs and booze. The next day they think they will never be merry again. James has a better idea. And see what a collection of songs for the merry is found in Psalms 103–107! Some of the *psalms* have been set to music in our modern praise choruses. Or, if you prefer, perhaps you will call family and friends to the piano to sing grand old Christian hymns. If you don't have other songs in mind, look at the index of your hymnbook. And the next day you will be merry still.

C. The Sick (vv. 14, 15)

14. Is any sick among you? let him call for the elders of the church; and let them pray over him, anointing him with oil in the name of the Lord.

Today's *elders* agree about praying for the *sick*, but many are puzzled about *anointing him with oil*. Some obey literally without question: "James says to do it, so we do it." Some note that oil had medicinal value in the ancient world. Since our medical technology has improved, they say, using oil isn't much needed any longer. Still others point out that anointing with oil in the Bible is symbolic for setting things and people apart for God in a special way (cf. Exodus 40:9, 15). They say it should be taken that way here as well.

Some students like to debate this question; others like to avoid debate and let each elder do as he thinks best about anointing the sick. The most important thing is to recognize our need to place ultimate trust in *the Lord* since healing comes from no other.

15. And the prayer of faith shall save the sick, and the Lord shall raise him up; and if he have committed sins, they shall be forgiven him.

Whatever we think about anointing the sick with oil, it is notable that James attributes the outcome to *the prayer of faith,* not to the anointing. But a skeptic thinks this promise is far too confident. "Sometimes," says the skeptic, "a sick person dies instead of getting well." But the Greek word translated *save* often refers to salvation in the New Testament. If you pause to think about it, you know death is the best possible recovery for a Christian who is sick. The one who dies is safe from illness forever, safe also from pain and grief and fear. Note the reference to the forgiveness of *sins.* That is the best part of the promise. This Christian is safe in Heaven for eternity. He or she is raised up far higher than mere restoration to health on earth.

D. The Faulty (v. 16)

16. Confess your faults one to another, and pray one for another, that ye may be healed. The effectual fervent prayer of a righteous man availeth much.

This seems to broaden the instruction given in verse 15. All of us have *faults* or sins, don't we? We can confess them *one to another* instead of only to the elders or other church leaders. [See question #4, page 24.] All of us, elders or not, can *pray one for another, that ye may be healed* either from physical sickness or from moral weakness. If I am troubled by some fault or sin of mine, I can be greatly helped by telling a good Christian friend about it. He can help me keep from continuing or repeating my wrongdoing. If I have to go where I will be tempted, perhaps he

---

Home Daily Bible Readings

Monday, Sept. 8—A Good Heart Produces Good (Luke 6:43-49)

Tuesday, Sept. 9—Act on the Word (James 1:19-25)

Wednesday, Sept. 10—Live Out Pure Religion (James 1:26–2:4)

Thursday, Sept. 11—Do Not Show Favoritism (James 2:5-13)

Friday, Sept. 12—Faith and Works Go Together (James 2:14-18)

Saturday, Sept. 13—Live With Patience (James 5:7-12)

Sunday, Sept. 14—Pray for One Another (James 5:13-20)

---

can go with me and give me strength. He can pray with me and for me. We do well to keep in mind that the *effectual fervent prayer of a righteous man availeth much,* whether he is an elder or not. [See question #5, page 24.]

Conclusion

James has had some very important things to say to every church in every century. In light of that, are you satisfied with how you're "living out" your Christianity? Do your love and faith just make you feel comfortable in church on Sunday, or do they make you feel uncomfortable until you make some improvements in your Christian living, or until you do something to help someone else?

A. Not "Living it Up," but "Living it Out"

A year ago, Juan was a ten-year-old immigrant from Mexico. He was in third grade because he was too big for a first-grade seat. He couldn't even do first-grade work because he spoke only Spanish. Joe was working a night shift, so he could tutor Juan. He bought third-grade books, and the two worked together every day after school. They kept on working through the summer, and now Juan is ready for fourth grade.

As a landscape artist, Jason thought a bare parking lot was an unfit setting for a beautiful church building. After consulting the elders, he drew a plan for some planting. The plan was displayed; a special offering was taken for plants; church members were invited to work on a "Transformation Saturday." The result was amazing and better still when the flowers bloomed and the little lawn was green.

Jeremy was haunted by the thought that he was not doing enough for the Lord. He planned to be a missionary, but when he talked with advisors at a Bible college, another plan emerged. He kept his well-paying job; he increased his contributions for missions; he sent his two sons to Bible college. Now they are ministers, and Jeremy believes that they are doing twice as much for the Lord as he would be doing if he had become a missionary.

How do these examples affect you?

B. Prayer

Heavenly Father, we believe in You, we believe in Jesus, and we love You both. Give us wisdom to see what our faith and love ought to be doing, and give us energy and enthusiasm to do it joyfully. In Jesus' name, amen.

C. Thought to Remember

What you do today is your gift to God.

Learning by Doing

This page contains an alternative lesson plan emphasizing learning activities.
Classes desiring such student involvement will find these suggestions helpful.

Learning Goals

After this lesson each student will be able to:

1. List several features of a living and active faith.

2. Explain why faith must be active to be real.

3. Work with others in the class to develop a project that would enable members to help the needy.

Into the Lesson

Prior to this week's lesson, purchase several packs of different kinds of chewing gum. Open all the packs and slide the foil-wrapped gum sticks out of the paper sleeves. Mix up the various sticks of gum, and re-insert each foil-wrapped gum stick into a different paper sleeve, one that does not match the actual gum in the foil. Next, place the gum sticks back into the same kind of gum pack so that the label on the sticks of gum match the label on the packs.

Hold up the various packs of gum and say, "To begin the lesson this week, I'd like each of you to select a stick of chewing gum from one of the various packs I have to pass around. Pull it out of the pack and put it down on your Bible." After the gum has made it around the room and everyone has taken a stick of gum, say, "Now that each of you has a stick of gum, move your chairs into small groups with those who selected the same kind of gum you did."

After the class moves into groups, say, "Now, unwrap the gum and begin chewing it." Wait briefly to see if anyone in the class recognizes that the whole class has been deceived. Then say, "All of you have been deceived. The gum you selected was not the kind you thought it was. I changed the wrappers! Some recognized it; others did not. That happens in life, too. How do people deceive others today?" After a brief discussion, say, "Our text talks about another kind of deception, self-deception. Turn to the book of James and let's see how Christians sometimes deceive themselves."

Into the Word

Assign James 1:22-27 to one group, James 2:8, 9, 14-17 to a second, and James 5:13-16 to a third. Appoint a member of each group to read the text aloud to the whole class. Have the following questions for each group on a separate sheet of paper. Hand the question sheet to each group and ask groups to discuss these issues.

Questions for Group One

1. What is the characteristic of those whose faith is living and active? *(They are "doers of the word," 1:22.)*

2. How does James indicate a person could be self-deceived? *(If one is a hearer only, 1:22, or "bridleth not his tongue," 1:26.)*

3. What two qualities describe pure, undefiled religion? *(See 1:27.)*

4. What kind of person does James say is blessed by God? *("A doer of the work," 1:25.)*

Questions for Group Two

1. Meeting what physical needs demonstrates genuine faith? *(Clothing and food, 2:15.)*

2. What happens when Christians show preference to some people? *(They "commit sin" and become "transgressors," 2:9.)*

3. What are the characteristics of a faith that is living and active? *(Love for one's neighbor, 2:8.)*

4. Why must faith be active to be real? *(Otherwise it is "dead, being alone," 2:17.)*

Questions for Group Three

1. What does James recommend that the elders do for a sick member? *(Pray and anoint with oil, 5:14.)*

2. What should Christians do when they recognize personal failures and faults? *(Confess faults to one another and pray, 5:16.)*

3. What characterizes faith that is living and active? *(Prayer, singing psalms, worship regardless of circumstances, 5:13, 14.)*

4. Why must faith be active to be real? *("The effectual fervent prayer of a righteous man availeth much," 5:16.)*

After six to eight minutes, have a member of each group give the group's answers.

Into Life

Say, "James makes it clear that faith means action. Let's develop a class project to demonstrate our faith to the needy." Ask the class to brainstorm projects. Write them on the board. Next, ask each small group to decide the one they will do. Prior to this week's lesson design a Project Planning Sheet that contains the following questions: What? Why? When? Where? Who? Give one to each small group and ask them to plan a specific project to demonstrate faith. Conclude the class period by letting each group explain its project. Close the session with a prayer circle asking God's blessing on the projects that have been planned.

Let's Talk It Over

The questions on this page are designed to promote discussion of the lesson by the class and to encourage application of the lesson Scriptures. The answers provided are only discussion starters. Let your class talk it over from there.

1. James says deception and real Christianity do not mix. What can each Christian do to avoid spiritual self-deception?

Three times in chapter 1 James states that it is very easy to deceive ourselves. It is easy to blame God for our problems and fail to give Him credit for each blessing. It is easy to listen to God's Word and then claim we are being faithful even when we are obviously faltering. It is easy to claim great spiritual depth while also "running off at the mouth." The problem comes when a Christian cannot accurately assess his or her attitudes, behavior, and status of faith. Self-deceit may be preventing needed correction. Have the class discuss how the following techniques can be helpful: pray for wisdom and discernment in self-assessment; look for everyday applications of principles from Scripture, sermons, and lessons; ask mature Christians for constructive spiritual feedback.

2. What is our church doing to help those who are powerless to help themselves? What more ought to be done?

If your students can identify some active ministries in this area, celebrate the fact that the church is helping people as James directs. If not, try to see why not. (Use Proverbs 14:31 and James 2:9; 4:17 in your discussion.)

As creatures of habit, it is easy to continue with what we have done in the past without asking what is being missed. Hospitals, colleges, and school systems are evaluated regularly by accrediting institutions that identify strengths and weaknesses and make suggestions for improvement. What if each congregation willingly and regularly invited a select group to give a constructive evaluation? Perhaps once a year the congregation should search for potential blind spots that keep it from fully honoring Christ in sacrificial ministry.

3. A complete Christian, according to James, is one who deals well with temptation (avoids sin) and is known for taking positive action to reach out to others (performs good deeds). How can Christians do both?

In many sports, the complete athlete is the one who can play well on both offense and defense. James paints the same picture. Avoiding tempta-

tions and the trickery of Satan means playing good defense. Doing positive, godly things with and for other people is playing good offense. Using two scales from 1-10, challenge students to identify which is their stronger emphasis: (1) self-examination to avoid sinning, or (2) going outside one's comfort zone to help others. Then brainstorm specific ways Christians can maintain the emphasis in their stronger dimension while at the same time finding ways to improve in the weaker area.

4. James makes no provision for passing on confessional information to anyone but God. Does this *forbid* sharing with another? When would such sharing become gossip, and what steps can the church take both to discourage gossiping and discipline the gossips?

Confessing one's sins to another can be dangerous if the other person cannot keep confidences. Paul condemns gossiping in 2 Corinthians 12:20. The church can teach all age groups that negative information about anyone should not be shared unless the hearer can play a specific role in the solution. The church takes important spiritual action when it teaches this principle and confronts those who violate it. Leaders must model what they teach and must never act out of the spirit of judgmentalism. Their task is to call all Christians to live their lives to honor Christ. Sadly, most congregations have no intention or means to confront those who spread information.

5. Notice that James does not say, "fervent prayer availeth much." James's requirement is that of persistent prayer coming from a righteous person. How can the church teach both the discipline of prayer as well as the attitudes and actions expected of the one who prays?

First Peter 3:7 also affirms that a person's actions may interfere with the effectiveness of his or her prayer life. The entire book of James proclaims, "You have to live out what you say you believe." While it is valuable to encourage Christians to deepen their prayer lives (in quantity and in quality), it is equally important to stress that God wants to see that our "walk-life" matches our "talk-life." Remembering Jesus' instructions about prayer in Matthew 6:5-8 is also important.

Faith and Wisdom

DEVOTIONAL READING: Colossians 1:3-14.

BACKGROUND SCRIPTURE: James 3.

PRINTED TEXT: James 3.

James 3:1-18

1 My brethren, be not many masters, knowing that we shall receive the greater condemnation.

2 For in many things we offend all. If any man offend not in word, the same is a perfect man, and able also to bridle the whole body.

3 Behold, we put bits in the horses' mouths, that they may obey us; and we turn about their whole body.

4 Behold also the ships, which though they be so great, and are driven of fierce winds, yet are they turned about with a very small helm, whithersoever the governor listeth.

5 Even so the tongue is a little member, and boasteth great things. Behold, how great a matter a little fire kindleth!

6 And the tongue is a fire, a world of iniquity: so is the tongue among our members, that it defileth the whole body, and setteth on fire the course of nature; and it is set on fire of hell.

7 For every kind of beasts, and of birds, and of serpents, and of things in the sea, is tamed, and hath been tamed of mankind:

8 But the tongue can no man tame; it is an unruly evil, full of deadly poison.

9 Therewith bless we God, even the Father; and therewith curse we men, which are made after the similitude of God.

10 Out of the same mouth proceedeth blessing and cursing. My brethren, these things ought not so to be.

11 Doth a fountain send forth at the same place sweet water and bitter?

12 Can the fig tree, my brethren, bear olive berries? either a vine, figs? so can no fountain both yield salt water and fresh.

13 Who is a wise man and endued with knowledge among you? let him show out of a good conversation his works with meekness of wisdom.

14 But if ye have bitter envying and strife in your hearts, glory not, and lie not against the truth.

15 This wisdom descendeth not from above, but is earthly, sensual, devilish.

16 For where envying and strife is, there is confusion and every evil work.

17 But the wisdom that is from above is first pure, then peaceable, gentle, and easy to be entreated, full of mercy and good fruits, without partiality, and without hypocrisy.

18 And the fruit of righteousness is sown in peace of them that make peace.

GOLDEN TEXT: Who is a wise man and endued with knowledge among you? let him show out of a good conversation his works with meekness of wisdom.
—James 3:13.

Faith Faces the World
Unit 1: Live in Faith
(Lessons 1-4)

Lesson Aims

After participating in this lesson, each student should be able to:

1. Recall the various sins that are caused by an unwise use of the tongue.

2. Compare the way the tongue is used by one who has "wisdom from below" with that of one with godly wisdom.

3. Create a personal reminder to use wisdom in his or her speech during the coming week.

Lesson Outline

INTRODUCTION
    A. Words That Wound
    B. Lesson Background
I. TEACHERS AND TONGUES (James 3:1-12)
    A. Warning! (v. 1)
    B. Stumbling (v. 2)
    C. Illustrations and Applications (vv. 3-6)
    D. Our Dominion (v. 7)
    E. The Tongue's Freedom (v. 8)
    F. The Inconsistent Tongue (vv. 9-12)
      Conflicting Identities
II. WORDS AND WISDOM (James 3:13-18)
    A. The Proof (v. 13)
    B. The Lower Wisdom (vv. 14-16)
    C. The Higher Wisdom (vv. 17, 18)
      Living With Integrity
CONCLUSION
    A. Decisions, Decisions
    B. Prayer
    C. Thought to Remember

Introduction

Mary was delighted when husband John not only remembered her birthday but also took her out for a fabulous dinner at their favorite restaurant. The evening was pure joy till Mary was taken by a fit of coughing. She smothered the coughs with a napkin, and they were not loud. In fact, they were so quiet that Mary distinctly heard a low-voiced but angry comment from another table: "That coughing! She makes me sick!"

Mary almost strangled in trying to stop coughing, but she failed. She struggled to her feet and staggered from the room, blinded by her streaming tears, tears of mingled grief and rage. John

had no choice but to follow, leaving the fabulous dinner unfinished and the pretty little birthday cake untouched.

Mary and John have never seen their favorite restaurant again. Dining out has lost all its charm for Mary. Even on their wedding anniversary, she wants to eat at home. Tears flood her eyes anew when she thinks how she made another diner sick, and how cruelly that diner responded.

And the woman who was sickened? Probably she never gave it a second thought, was not really sick, finished her dinner complacently, and never suspected that she had hurt anyone.

A. Words That Wound

There are many words that wound. Some of them are spoken maliciously, with the intention of wounding. More are spoken thoughtlessly or jokingly. But they hurt. Don't you remember a time when you wept over a careless or malicious remark? Worse than that, do you remember when you carelessly or maliciously wounded someone else's spirit with your words? This is not new in the twenty-first century. James took note of it back in century one.

B. Lesson Background

Although brought up under the strict standards of Jewish law, James knew that the accepted teachers did not always live by their own teaching (Matthew 23:1-3). Writing to Jewish Christians living abroad among the Gentiles, he also knew about the so-called "wisdom" that continually circulated in the ancient world. In this lesson we shall see how he urged those readers to be careful with their talk: to be always truthful, always sincere, always helpful. We shall see also how he urged them to see the difference between God's wisdom and human wisdom, and to make God's wisdom their own.

I. Teachers and Tongues
(James 3:1-12)

In everyday conversation we answer one another promptly, not taking time to think before we speak. With the best of intentions sometimes we say things that are untrue, unkind, or are unhelpful. There will be no conversation if we must stop and think for an hour, or even ten minutes, before we respond. So we need to be armed in advance with Christian truth, principles, and motives—so well armed that we shall rarely lose our way in conversation or teaching.

A. Warning! (v. 1)

1. My brethren, be not many masters, knowing that we shall receive the greater condemnation.

Here the word *masters* means "teachers," as it usually did in 1611, when the *King James Version* of the Bible was issued. If your Sunday school is constantly trying to enlist more teachers, you may be disappointed to see James's advice that *not many* Christians undertake that work. Paul urged Timothy to be training teachers (2 Timothy 2:2). Then why does James advise as he does?

James certainly does not want Christians to be untaught. But he *does* want them to be taught truly, correctly, properly. So he warns would-be teachers: if they do not teach properly, they will be condemned not only for their own wrongdoing but also for leading others to do wrong. Teachers in the first-century church had a high status (Acts 13:1; Ephesians 4:11). This status is a dangerous temptation for those thinking that their own wisdom makes them natural teachers. But more is expected of a teacher than of a new Christian, who needs to be taught. The teacher is held to a higher standard, has a greater responsibility, and is subject to receiving *the greater condemnation* for failure. [See question #1, page 32.]

If our churches need more teachers we certainly must be looking for them; and we must search for people who not only understand Christian teaching and live by it, but also have the ability to teach it clearly and convincingly.

B. Stumbling (v. 2)

2. For in many things we offend all. If any man offend not in word, the same is a perfect man, and able also to bridle the whole body.

The opening *for* connects the next thought with what we have just learned in verse 1. The fact that *in many things we offend all* means that all teachers (including James himself) go astray at some time or other in a variety of ways.

None of us intends to go astray *in word*. But sins of the tongue are especially hard to control. Frequently we need to say something quickly, and we fail to take time to think about it. So it's easy to slip up, to say the wrong thing, just as a person walking may accidentally stumble over a rough place in the path. As a result, we say something that we later wish we had not said, or we fail to say what we should have said.

The wrong word seems to slip out so easily, so quickly, so uncontrollably—to be able to *offend not in word* is so difficult! But when we become mature in this area, we are *able also to bridle the whole body*. What a worthwhile goal for teachers and non-teachers alike!

C. Illustrations and Applications (vv. 3-6)

3. Behold, we put bits in the horses' mouths, that they may obey us; and we turn about their whole body.

A "bit" is a small part of a bridle, and a bridle is only as big as the horse's head, and the horse is many times as big as the head. But think about how that tiny bit controls the whole horse!

4. Behold also the ships, which though they be so great, and are driven of fierce winds, yet are they turned about with a very small helm, whithersoever the governor listeth.

If you have ever seen a ship in dry dock, you may have been surprised to see how small the rudder was. Yet that little rudder turns a huge ocean liner to the right or the left, wherever the helmsman *(governor)* wants it to go. [See question #2, page 32.]

5a. Even so the tongue is a little member, and boasteth great things.

The tongue is not a large body part, and usually it is hidden from sight. Yet the tongue can tell a tremendous truth or a monstrous lie, make or break a friendship, start or stop a war. People such as Hitler, Hussein, and bin Laden led entire nations astray with their tongues.

5b, 6. Behold, how great a matter a little fire kindleth!

And the tongue is a fire, a world of iniquity: so is the tongue among our members, that it defileth the whole body, and setteth on fire the course of nature; and it is set on fire of hell.

In bold figures of speech James sets forth the damage done by evil talk. *The tongue is a fire:* that is, a small thing with tremendous destructive power (cf. Proverbs 16:27; 26:21). Some forest fires are started when campers go home without extinguishing their campfires completely. The small smoldering embers that remain ignite a great conflagration that destroys thousands of acres of woodland.

The tongue is like that. Every kind of *iniquity* in the *world* can be generated by evil talk

Home Daily Bible Readings

Monday, Sept. 15—Search for Wisdom (Proverbs 2:1-5)

Tuesday, Sept. 16—God Gives Wisdom (Proverbs 2:6-11)

Wednesday, Sept. 17—Be Careful to Live Wisely (Ephesians 5:11-17)

Thursday, Sept. 18—A Prayer for Wisdom (Colossians 1:9-14)

Friday, Sept. 19—Keep the Tongue in Check (James 3:1-6)

Saturday, Sept. 20—Bless and Do Not Curse (James 3:7-12)

Sunday, Sept. 21—Godly Wisdom Is Pure (James 3:13-18)

(Proverbs 7:21-23; Romans 16:18). [See question #3, page 32.]

The relation of the tongue to the other *members* of the body is such that a foul tongue *defileth the whole body:* dirty talk makes the whole person dirty, corrupt, despicable (cf. Mark 7:15). A fiery tongue sets *on fire the course of nature:* it so inflames a person's very being that the effect of his or her life is destructive. We can guess easily the source of the foul talk that defiles and destroys—it comes from *hell.*

D. Our Dominion (v. 7)

7. For every kind of beasts, and of birds, and of serpents, and of things in the sea, is tamed, and hath been tamed of mankind.

A circus is a fascinating illustration of what is written here, and of God's original decree of humanity's dominion (Genesis 1:26). Massive elephants and savage tigers move in smooth harmony at the ringmaster's command, as if they could understand his language. Perhaps your own dog will "sit," "stay," or "come" when you speak the word.

E. The Tongue's Freedom (v. 8)

8. But the tongue can no man tame; it is an unruly evil, full of deadly poison.

A man may control elephants and tigers, and still let his *tongue* escape his control and strike with *deadly poison.* Someone who loses his or her temper is likely to lose control of the tongue at the same time. Even within a loving family circle a tongue liberated by anger may utter ugly sarcasm, cruel criticism, or unjust accusations. Thus the tongue may deeply wound someone dearly loved by the owner of the tongue. [See question #4, page 32.]

However, let us concede that James uses a bit of hyperbole when he says *the tongue can no man tame.* Some people can and do control their tongues. My own parents were such people. In more than twenty years of living with them, I never heard either of their tongues break free and rant against the other, or against anyone else. Even when they were provoked, their speech was rational, temperate, controlled. We must remember, however, that a hyperbole is not a falsehood. What James says is true even though there are exceptions to it. People do lose control of their tongues. Uncontrolled tongues do rant irrationally, intemperately, even falsely. So what do you do? You keep your own tongue under control. You know you can do it if God helps you. So you pray, as David did (Psalm 39:1-3).

F. The Inconsistent Tongue (vv. 9-12)

9, 10. Therewith bless we God, even the Father; and therewith curse we men, which are made after the similitude of God. Out of the same mouth proceedeth blessing and cursing. My brethren, these things ought not so to be.

What an amazing thing—we use our tongues to *bless . . . God* and then turn right around and *curse* people who *are made* in His image (Genesis 1:26, 27)! Of course, some people have horribly defaced the image of God by their sin. We have to take a stand against evil and rebuke it (Luke 17:3). Sometimes we ought to do that privately (Matthew 18:15); sometimes we have to do it publicly (1 Timothy 5:20). But we do that by using God's Word to point out the right way and show the wrong that has been done, not by cursing the one who has done wrong. Of course, some people really are eternally accursed, but that judgment is not for us to make; it is for the Lord (Matthew 25:41-46).

11, 12. Doth a fountain send forth at the same place sweet water and bitter? Can the fig tree, my brethren, bear olive berries? either a vine, figs? so can no fountain both yield salt water and fresh.

Ancient villages depended on nearby springs to produce usable water. So it is with a Christian's talk. *The fig tree* produces figs every year, never olives, never grapes, never thorns or thistles. That is how you know what kind of a tree it is (Matthew 7:16-20). Likewise a Christian can be identified by his or her talk. It is always good, clean, wholesome, uplifting Christian talk (cf. Ephesians 4:29; 5:4).

CONFLICTING IDENTITIES

In September 2001, San Francisco police arrested a man for robbing eight banks and attempting to rob another. When taken into custody, the man admitted his crimes. He was an unlikely suspect, since in daily life he had a $98,000 job as an air traffic controller. He was known to be very cool under the pressure of his job, a trait he exhibited during his short career as a bank robber. Described by friends as a nice, friendly person, he took his teenage sons and their friends camping and to ball games.

Investigation showed he was unable to make his salary stretch far enough to cover his expenses, which included large bills for alimony,

---

How to Say It

CORINTHIANS. Kor-*in*-thee-unz (*th* as in *thin*).

EPHESIANS. Ee-*fee*-zhunz.

GALATIANS. Guh-*lay*-shunz.

PHILIPPIANS. Fih-*lip*-ee-unz.

child support, and school tuition. So he apparently allowed another side of himself to grow alongside his law-abiding, family-man persona. The court ordered that he undergo psychiatric evaluation to determine his sanity.

It could be argued that there must be something "insane" about a man who risked a good job and his reputation in everyday life to take up a second, risky and unlawful, identity. But James says we demonstrate a similar type of split in our persona when we let our tongues get out of control. When Christians bless God in worship and curse others elsewhere, it may not be a mark of insanity, but it certainly doesn't make sense.

—C. R. B.

Visual for lesson 3

II. Words and Wisdom (James 3:13-18)

This poster from the Adult Visuals *packet illustrates the Golden Text, James 3:13.*

After thinking so much about the tongue with its follies and failures, it is fitting to turn our thoughts to wisdom. Wisdom is what every tongue needs to restrain and guide it. But sometimes wisdom is not easily recognized, for human folly likes to masquerade as wisdom, and capable but unwary people may be deceived. With a few well-chosen words, James describes the true wisdom and the phony.

A. The Proof (v. 13)

13. Who is a wise man and endued with knowledge among you? let him show out of a good conversation his works with meekness of wisdom.

If asked, each one of us would like to state with confidence, "I am a *wise* person who is *endued with knowledge.*" But James wants an answer in the form of our *works* (deeds). A person who does foolish things is not wise. In the antique English of the *King James Version* the word *conversation* does not mean "talk." It means, rather, one's entire manner of living (Galatians 1:13; Ephesians 4:22). If a person is wise, that lifestyle is *good,* unselfish, helpful. That good lifestyle is the stage on which each individual work is done. Further, it is done with wise *meekness* or humility (cf. Matthew 5:5). Now, how wise are you?

B. The Lower Wisdom (vv. 14-16)

14. But if ye have bitter envying and strife in your hearts, glory not, and lie not against the truth.

Imagine a popular leader in a certain church. Perhaps he is a handsome man with a ready smile and charming manners. With his pleasant ways and flattering words he wins followers easily, but this fellow is winning them for himself

rather than for Christ. His *heart* is full of *bitter envying* of other leaders. Instead of cooperating with them, he belittles them, their opinions, and their plans. In so doing, he generates *strife* (factionalism) instead of unified fellowship. James warns such a one to *glory not*—don't brag, don't be proud of yourself and your accomplishments and opinions. Speak well of other leaders rather than praising yourself. (This is part of the meekness of v. 13.) Don't exaggerate your own goodness, your own wisdom, your own accomplishment because when you do you *lie . . . against the truth.*

15. This wisdom descendeth not from above, but is earthly, sensual, devilish.

The *wisdom* that glorifies self is not God-given. It arises out of *earthly* ambition, selfishness, and the prompting of the devil (cf. 1 Corinthians 1:20; 2:5, 6). One who asks God for wisdom (Proverbs 2:6; James 1:5) is rewarded with the kind described in verse 17 (below).

16. For where envying and strife is, there is confusion and every evil work.

If *envying and strife* are prompted by *evil* (v. 15), we can be sure they are not good for us. This kind of disorder infected the church at Corinth (2 Corinthians 12:20). But *confusion and every evil work* please no one but Satan and some victims of his deceit.

C. The Higher Wisdom (vv. 17, 18)

17. But the wisdom that is from above is first pure, then peaceable, gentle, and easy to be entreated, full of mercy and good fruits, without partiality, and without hypocrisy.

Paul lists the "fruit of the Spirit" in Galatians 5:22, 23. Here, James lists what may be called the "fruit of *wisdom.*" Wisdom that is *pure* has no trace of the phoniness that is earthly, sensual, and devilish. *Peaceable* wisdom will not produce strife, as selfishness and pride often do. A person of *gentle* (considerate) wisdom does not try to overpower others and force opinions on them.

A wise person stands firm for truth and righteousness. In matters of opinion, however, this kind of person is *easy to be entreated*. This means such a person listens to reason and compromises when appropriate. A wise person shows *mercy* by being kind, helpful, and quick to forgive. Wisdom is evident in a person's *good fruits* or deeds to others, especially to fellow Christians (Galatians 6:10). *Partiality* and *hypocrisy* are two of the baser things that have no place in wisdom that is pure.

LIVING WITH INTEGRITY

It seemed like a good idea at the time. A professor at Columbia University Business School decided to do some research on how businesses handle customer complaints. So he wrote—on official university stationery—identical letters of complaint to two hundred and forty restaurants. In the letter he falsely complained that he had contracted food poisoning on an evening when he and his wife had eaten there. The poisoning ruined a "romantic wedding anniversary," and also resulted in his curling up—violently ill—in the fetal position on the floor of their home bathroom all night.

Several of the restaurants checked their reservation lists for the evening in question and found the professor's claims to be spurious. Although his research was well-intentioned, he was forced to send out letters of apology to each of the firms, admitting his lack of integrity. Then he had to face an academic review board to determine the fate of his career.

James tells us that our manner of life should demonstrate the integrity that comes from living in accordance with the wisdom that comes from above. The Bible is a ready source of instruction as to the kind of attitudes, speech, and actions that are to characterize the life of the Christian. True wisdom will demonstrate itself in relationships that are honest, pure, and straightforward. Do our lives show it?   —C. R. B.

18. And the fruit of righteousness is sown in peace of them that make peace.

Envying and strife provide the soil where confusion grows along with "every evil work" (v. 16). But wise people *that make peace* find in that peace the soil where they can plant the seeds that grow into *the fruit of righteousness*, their own and that of others. (See also 2 Corinthians 9:10; Philippians 1:11.) [See question #5, page 32.]

Conclusion

As Christians we are called to "put on the whole armor of God" (Ephesians 6:10-18) and "fight the good fight of faith" (1 Timothy 6:12). So we sing "Onward, Christians Soldiers" with our feet tapping in martial tempo. But through the drumbeat we hear Paul urging, "If it be possible, as much as lieth in you, live peaceably with all men" (Romans 12:18). Jesus Himself pronounced a blessing on "the peacemakers" in the Sermon on the Mount (Matthew 5:9). Wise indeed is the Christian who knows when to fight and when to make peace.

A. Decisions, Decisions

Of course, we are to resist the devil and drive him back in defeat (James 4:7). Naturally, we are to live in peace with our brothers and sisters in the family of God. But the devil is a master of disguise (2 Corinthians 11:14); and—let's face it—some of God's people stumble into ungodliness. So what do we do?

When there is a clear-cut decision between right and wrong, we choose the right. Example: May a Christian continue to live openly in an adulterous relationship? No, he may not. He must either give up that relationship or give up his membership in the church. That is the teaching of Scripture (1 Corinthians 5).

But some questions are not so readily answered. Example: May our teenagers conduct a series of car washes to pay their way to a Christian camp? The Bible does not say yes or no. Some of us think it is a great idea; some of us think Christian activities should be supported solely by the gifts of Christians (cf. 3 John 7). Each of us may express an opinion, but we do not quarrel to the point of splitting the church. One congregation may take a vote of its members. Another may accept the decision of its elders. In either case, the matter (which is not a doctrinal issue) is settled and peace is unbroken.

To revert to our lesson title, this is the way of faith and wisdom.

B. Prayer

Our gracious Father in Heaven, we thank You for the clear guidance of Your Word, and we thank You for the privilege of using the minds and wisdom You have given us to make decisions in the light of Your Word. Give us wisdom day by day according to our need. We pray in Jesus' name, amen.

C. Thought to Remember

"Wisdom is the principal thing; therefore get wisdom" (Proverbs 4:7).

Learning by Doing

This page contains an alternative lesson plan emphasizing learning activities.
Classes desiring such student involvement will find these suggestions helpful.

Learning Goals

After this lesson each student will be able to:

1. Recall the various sins that are caused by an unwise use of the tongue.

2. Compare the way the tongue is used by one who has "wisdom from below" with that of one with godly wisdom.

3. Create a personal reminder to use wisdom in his or her speech during the coming week.

Into the Lesson

In preparation for this week's lesson, prepare the following chart on either a transparency to project or on the chalkboard. The title of the chart is, "The Tongue." Below the title there are two columns: the left, "Godly Use"; the right, "Sinful Use." Begin class this week by saying: "Today's lesson focuses on the tongue. I'd like us to brainstorm uses of the tongue. Note the two columns on this chart. The tongue can be used in a godly way, but it can also be used in a sinful way. As you think of a use of the tongue, call it out and I'll write it in the appropriate column." *(Godly uses include praying, thanking someone, asking forgiveness, encouraging. Sinful uses include lying, gossiping, taking God's name in vain, using profanity.)* After a few minutes, say, "As you can see, the tongue can be an instrument of evil, or it can be an instrument of good. Our lesson text today explains the difficulty we have in controlling the tongue, and it suggests what we need to do. Let's read James 3, our lesson text."

Into the Word

Ask each of six adults to read three verses of the lesson text aloud to the class. After the reading, say, "To help us understand this text, move into small groups of three students each. In your group, I want you to answer the following questions."

1. List the ten analogies to the tongue that James makes in this passage. *(Bits in horses' mouths, v. 3; helm of a ship, v. 4; a fire, v. 6; beasts, birds, serpents, things in the sea, v. 7; fountain, v. 11; fig tree, vine, v. 12.)*

2. List the five descriptions of the tongue that James gives. *("A little member," v. 5; "a fire," "a world of iniquity," v. 6; "an unruly evil," "full of deadly poison," v. 8.)* Allow several minutes for the groups to look up the answers. Then ask the groups to report their answers. Write them on the chalkboard or overhead transparency.

For the next activity, give a poster board and two color markers to each small group. Say, "James makes it perfectly clear that the tongue can be used either as an explosive instrument in a sinful way or as an instrument of good in a godly way. Prepare two lists from James 3:13-18. First, list all the characteristics of the way the tongue is used by one who has 'wisdom from below.' Second, list all the characteristics of the way the tongue is used by one who has 'wisdom from above.' Then arrange your lists into a crossword puzzle format on the poster board provided. List the 'wisdom from below' characteristics vertically in one color and those of the 'wisdom from above' horizontally in the other color. When you are finished, post your work on the wall and we'll compare the two lists." *(Wisdom from below: "bitter envying," "strife," v. 14; "earthly," "sensual," "devilish," v. 15; "confusion," "evil work," v. 16. Wisdom from above: "good conversation," "meekness," v. 13; "pure," "peaceable," "gentle," "easy to be entreated," "full of mercy," "good fruits," "without partiality," "without hypocrisy," v. 17.)*

Say, "James tell us that a perfect man is one who does not offend people by what he says (v. 2). To live that way requires wisdom from above. Perhaps we have seen sins we need to overcome. We need to be reminded daily to speak with godly wisdom. Let's create a personal reminder to use wisdom in our speech."

Into Life

People use all sorts of reminders to make certain they do not forget to perform specific actions. Create a "Personal Reminder Card" prior to this week's lesson. Below the title of the card write out James 3:17, 18. Underline the characteristics of godly wisdom. Then provide several blank lines for the students to write personal goals for the week that practically apply the use of godly wisdom in their speech and relationships with others.

Make a copy of the card for each class member. Give these cards to the class. Say, "For several minutes, think about how you can apply this concept of godly wisdom in your life this week. Write a personal goal on the lines provided on the card, stating what you will either do or not do this week. Then, put the card where you will see it every day." Close with a prayer for God's wisdom.

Let's Talk It Over

The questions on this page are designed to promote discussion of the lesson by the class and to encourage application of the lesson Scriptures. The answers provided are only discussion starters. Let your class talk it over from there.

1. James says that teachers will be held to a higher standard. What does that mean for people other than teachers? To what degree are they accountable?

It is true that people want to look up to their leaders. Therefore, they tend to expect them to live by a higher standard. And James confirms that leaders will be judged more rigorously by God on their speech. (See also Hebrews 13:17.)

But James also makes it clear that all Christians are responsible to God on the use of the tongue. Because of the great damage the tongue can create, the church must stress holiness in regard to the tongue just as strongly as it stresses holiness in other areas. Jesus says we all will give an account for "every idle word" (Matthew 12:36).

2. James says that keeping the tongue in check is the first step to keeping all other parts of the body under control. What are some steps to take in controlling the tongue?

The secret to controlling the tongue is to filter all thoughts through God's wisdom before speaking. But this can be extremely difficult to do in a rapid, back-and-forth conversation in which it's impossible to pause before every sentence and ask oneself, "What does God think?" The solution is to be so familiar with the Word of God *in advance* that holiness of speech is natural (Psalm 119:11, 105). This familiarity starts with the weekly Bible study that you are in right now, but that's only a beginning point. There is no substitute for daily, personal Bible study when it comes to putting the Word of God into our hearts—and, ultimately, on our tongues.

3. Hurtful words spoken by those with differences of opinion often are the root cause of many church fights or splits. How can the church develop ways to help resolve disputes and at the same time help bring to maturity those who would use their tongues in destructive ways?

Read Proverbs 6:16-19. Three of the things God hates specifically in this passage involve the improper use of the tongue. Ideally, when one Christian has said something to hurt another, either one of them should be mature enough to approach the other to seek a resolution of the differences (Matthew 5:23, 24; 18:15-17).

But often these folks need assistance. Those who intervene must use the principles of Galatians 6:1 and 2 Timothy 4:2 as well as the qualities of James 3:17, 18. The goal is threefold: find a resolution to the dispute between the individuals at odds, protect the integrity of the church as a whole, and help those in the conflict learn a better way to settle differences in the future.

4. There is an old saying, "You can't unscramble an egg." If a Christian does misspeak, what steps can be taken to reduce the possibility of creating the terrible results listed in verses 5, 6, and 8?

Many hurt feelings can be healed if individuals are willing to admit their error and ask the injured parties to work with them toward a solution. An apology is the first step. An invitation to find some way for the two to stand side by side is even better. The best place to start is for the two to kneel before Christ, asking that the mind of Christ (Philippians 2:1-8) guide both their words and actions.

Church leaders also should consider the motives of the person who misspeaks. Corrective action for those who speak out of wrong motives can be very different from corrective action for those who have good motives but need help with their interpersonal skills. Compare with 2 Timothy 4:2 with Titus 3:10.

5. Using the principles in today's lesson, what ingredients do Christians need to make use of in order to be good peacemakers?

Some people picture the Christian life as having to live like a doormat, allowing everyone to walk all over them in order to keep the peace (cf. Matthew 5:9.) A peacemaker is a person who willingly steps into a difficult situation, seeks God's wisdom, listens carefully without partiality, and behaves gently while insisting on a workable, God-honoring resolution. Remember that not only are we to have peace with one another, we are also to have peace with God. If we simply "sweep things under the rug" to keep people on friendly terms with one another, we may very well end up angering God (e.g., Revelation 2:20). Paul had to be rather stern at times in putting a stop to sinful activities (e.g., 1 Corinthians 4:21; 5).

Faith and Attitudes

DEVOTIONAL READING: 1 Peter 5:1-6.

BACKGROUND SCRIPTURE: James 4:1–5:6.

PRINTED TEXT: James 4.

James 4:1-17

1 From whence come wars and fightings among you? come they not hence, even of your lusts that war in your members?

2 Ye lust, and have not: ye kill, and desire to have, and cannot obtain: ye fight and war, yet ye have not, because ye ask not.

3 Ye ask, and receive not, because ye ask amiss, that ye may consume it upon your lusts.

4 Ye adulterers and adulteresses, know ye not that the friendship of the world is enmity with God? whosoever therefore will be a friend of the world is the enemy of God.

5 Do ye think that the Scripture saith in vain, The spirit that dwelleth in us lusteth to envy?

6 But he giveth more grace. Wherefore he saith, God resisteth the proud, but giveth grace unto the humble.

7 Submit yourselves therefore to God. Resist the devil, and he will flee from you.

8 Draw nigh to God, and he will draw nigh to you. Cleanse your hands, ye sinners; and purify your hearts, ye double-minded.

9 Be afflicted, and mourn, and weep: let your laughter be turned to mourning, and your joy to heaviness.

10 Humble yourselves in the sight of the Lord, and he shall lift you up.

11 Speak not evil one of another, brethren. He that speaketh evil of his brother, and judgeth his brother, speaketh evil of the law, and judgeth the law: but if thou judge the law, thou art not a doer of the law, but a judge.

12 There is one lawgiver, who is able to save and to destroy: who art thou that judgest another?

13 Go to now, ye that say, Today or tomorrow we will go into such a city, and continue there a year, and buy and sell, and get gain:

14 Whereas ye know not what shall be on the morrow. For what is your life? It is even a vapor, that appeareth for a little time, and then vanisheth away.

15 For that ye ought to say, If the Lord will, we shall live, and do this, or that.

16 But now ye rejoice in your boastings: all such rejoicing is evil.

17 Therefore to him that knoweth to do good, and doeth it not, to him it is sin.

GOLDEN TEXT: Humble yourselves in the sight of the Lord, and he shall lift you up.
—James 4:10.

Faith Faces the World
Unit 1: Live in Faith
(Lessons 1-4)

Lesson Aims

After participating in this lesson, each student should be able to:

1. Recall key points from James's warning against evil passions and his call to submission to God.

2. Tell how wrong attitudes can lead to conflicts between Christians.

3. Identify and confess a sinful attitude that has led to a disagreement with another believer.

Lesson Outline

INTRODUCTION
    A. No Winner
    B. Lesson Background
  I. CHURCH PROBLEMS (James 4:1-5)
    A. Wrong Desires (v. 1)
    B. Bad Results (vv. 2, 3)
      "Holy Wars"
    C. Conflicting Friendships (vv. 4, 5)
  II. GOD'S SOLUTIONS (James 4:6-10)
    A. Accept God's Grace (v. 6)
      The Smartest Kid in the World
    B. Choose Your Master (vv. 7-10)
 III. DON'T TRY TO BE GOD (James 4:11-17)
    A. Let God Be the Judge (vv. 11, 12)
    B. Consider God's Will (vv. 13-17)
CONCLUSION
    A. Key Thoughts
    B. Prayer
    C. Thought to Remember

Introduction

Brenda and Linda are cousins, but they were born in the same week and they look like identical twins. Although both are girls, their mothers soon learned to dress one in pink and the other in blue when they were to be together at Grandma's. Thus each mom was sure of going home with her own baby.

When the two were old enough to ramble on all fours, it was fascinating to watch their antics as they got acquainted with each other and explored their environment. On Christmas Day Grandma's floor was littered, and the babies went from toy to toy too swiftly to give attention to any. Not surprisingly, both of them chanced to pick up one item at the same time. It was a bright paper Santa Claus designed to be hung in the window, but now on the floor Brenda clung to its head and Linda clung to its feet. There was a brief tug-of-war with wordless sounds of protest. Then Santa was in two pieces, and two little girls were in tears.

A. No Winner

How often we see an adult tug-of-war with like results! Neither contestant gets what he or she wants, and both are disappointed. And when the result is decisive and the winner takes all, that may be no better. The loser feels defeated, defrauded, and resentful; the winner learns the victory was not worth the struggle. When will grown-ups learn that cooperation is better than conflict?

B. Lesson Background

In last week's lesson James drew a contrast between two kinds of wisdom. The lower kind produces "confusion and every evil work"; the higher kind is "first pure, then peaceable." Our text concluded with this declaration: "The fruit of righteousness is sown in peace of them that make peace" (James 3:13-18). But that conclusion is not the end of what James has to say on that subject. This week we shall read more about war and peace, and the attitudes that produce them. As with our previous studies in James, we shall see several parallels to Jesus' "Sermon on the Mount."

I. Church Problems
(James 4:1-5)

Conflict in the church is as old as the church itself. (See Acts 5:1-11; 9:26-28; and 15:1-31.) As we consider the word of James, we discover some typical sources of church conflict.

A. Wrong Desires (v. 1)

1. From whence come wars and fightings among you? come they not hence, even of your lusts that war in your members?

Wars and fightings—these are strong terms. We cannot think that James's readers were having among them literal *wars* with swords and spears, however. The first century was the time of the famed "Roman peace." The Romans did not allow such wars among the people they ruled. We must suppose James was writing of church fights such as are all too common among Christians now. Perhaps he used those strong terms to help his readers understand that church fights were really serious matters, matters to be avoided. [See question #1, page 40.]

Where do *fightings* come from, *fightings* between individuals and between factions in the church? They often come from our self-centered *lusts*, our desires, our cravings. Craving for power can lead to competition between two leaders and the groups that follow them. It is bad enough when one person fights with selfish desires and is led to do wrong for personal gain. But the damage can be more than doubled when two talented people both use "no holds barred" tactics to gain popularity and leadership. In 1 Corinthians 1:10-13 Paul pleads with Christians to put an end to such unseemly competition in the church (cf. 3 John 9, 10).

B. Bad Results (vv. 2, 3)

2. Ye lust, and have not: ye kill, and desire to have, and cannot obtain: ye fight and war, yet ye have not, because ye ask not.

Again we see those strong words, *fight, lust,* and *war.* Now another is added: *kill.* Again we must doubt that it is to be taken literally. It hardly seems possible that Jewish Christians were accustomed to killing one another to gain some advantage in a church fight. Perhaps James was thinking, as John did, that anyone who hates a brother is a murderer at heart, even though never actually killing anyone (1 John 3:15).

But even without bloodshed, a church fight can be tragic. One Christian belittles or denounces another, or two groups defame each other's integrity, and the conflict is almost as disgraceful as a bloody battle would be. Nobody wins. Each fierce fighter or group gains shame instead of honor and prestige. Why don't all the Christians unite in harmonious work for the progress of the church and then *ask* God for success? Instead of that, the battling groups end up taking glory from Christ and giving it to themselves. Surely we do not need to be told that it is futile for such groups to ask the Lord for success!

"HOLY WARS"

We've heard a lot about "holy wars" in recent years, but church fights are not in that category! A few years ago, a minister's stubbornness conspired with the power needs of some of the members to bring the congregation's temperature to "fever level." Some members had unreasonable expectations of the minister; he resisted accommodating their desires in *any* way.

The board chair called a church meeting to allow each side to express its concerns. The rules were as follows: there would be no personal attacks, no one could speak twice until everyone had spoken once, and no action would be taken during that meeting (it was not a business meeting; the purpose was to restore some long-lost communication). Some on each side found those rules *very* hard to live by, since their anger had been seething for a long time.

Opinions were split 45 percent to 45 percent, with 10 percent in the middle wishing the rest would act more like Christians. The minister would have stayed had he been able to count on the support of half of the congregation. Lacking that support, he soon resigned. As a result, several who had sided with the minister also left the church, and many of his opponents dug in to consolidate their gain in power. Many of the rest found themselves helpless to heal the broken spirit of a now declining congregation. Obviously, *no one won the battle.* James is telling us that is what always happens!   —C. R. B.

3. Ye ask, and receive not, because ye ask amiss, that ye may consume it upon your lusts.

The fighters do not get what they want from God because their attitudes, aims, and wants are wrong. They are not concerned about God's kingdom and His righteousness (Matthew 6:33); rather, they are concerned about satisfying their own *lusts*, their own desires. They want money for their own pleasures; they want influence and power for their own pride. The Bible speaks to the importance of our motives in other places as well (see 1 Chronicles 28:9; Proverbs 16:2; 1 Corinthians 4:5). [See question #2, page 40.]

C. Conflicting Friendships (vv. 4, 5)

4. Ye adulterers and adulteresses, know ye not that the friendship of the world is enmity with God? whosoever therefore will be a friend of the world is the enemy of God.

Now James digs deeper. The cause of those selfish and worldly desires lies in a damaged relationship with God. In the Old Testament Scriptures, so well known to James and the other Jewish Christians, the relationship of God to His people sometimes is pictured as that of husband and wife (e.g., Isaiah 54:5). Israel's worship of idols is described as adultery, and God punished her with divorce (Jeremiah 3:6-9). He no longer took care of Israel, and as a result she was destroyed by pagans.

In a similar figure of speech we now see James accusing his readers of giving more devotion to worldly interests than to God, and that is a type of adultery. Perhaps there are cases of "physical" adultery among James's readers, but James is saying those readers are guilty of "spiritual" adultery when they gave their devotion to the godless *world* and its attractions rather than to *God* Himself (cf. Revelation 17:1, 2). God wants to be supreme in our hearts and lives. If we give the greater part of it to anyone or anything else, we

---

How to Say It

COLOSSIANS. Kuh-*losh*-unz.

CORINTHIANS. Kor-*in*-thee-unz (*th* as in *thin*).

ISAIAH. Eye-*zay*-uh.

JEREMIAH. Jair-uh-*my*-uh.

LEVITICUS. Leh-*vit*-ih-kus.

NEHEMIAH. *Nee*-huh-*my*-uh (strong accent on *my*).

---

become God's enemies (Colossians 1:21). So choose which *friend* you want.

5. Do ye think that the Scripture saith in vain, The spirit that dwelleth in us lusteth to envy?

This verse puzzles us because the part that seems to be a quotation from *Scripture* is not found in the Scriptures we know. Was James quoting a Scripture that God has chosen not to preserve except in this very passage? Or are we reading a mistranslation that has crept in along the way? (This verse is not the same in all the ancient manuscripts, so some scholars think the original wording has been lost.)

In any case, we do know the Holy Spirit lives in us if we are Christians (1 Corinthians 3:16). The verse seems to be saying that the Holy Spirit in us longs for our full devotion. (We think of lust as an inappropriate desire, but the New Testament uses the word for any strong longing. In Romans 1:11 the same word, translated "long," is used of Paul's desire to visit the Christians in Rome.) God longs so ardently for us that He actually is jealous over (or envies) us. Exodus 20:5 says God is jealous over us, so maybe that is the Scripture James had in mind as he wrote this.

II. God's Solutions
(James 4:6-10)

An old saying goes, "It's not enough to smell a rotten egg, you have to lay a better one!" James doesn't leave his readers condemned with problems—he provides solutions.

A. Accept God's Grace (v. 6)

6. But he giveth more grace. Wherefore he sayeth, God resisteth the proud, but giveth grace unto the humble.

God's Spirit living in us does not desert us if we fall short of the full devotion He longs for. In fact, *he giveth more grace*—more favor than we deserve. This is verified by Proverbs 3:34. James quotes that verse from the Greek translation used by Greek-speaking Jews. That is the reason it does not read quite like our own version of Proverbs 3:34 (see also 1 Peter 5:5). No doubt all of us

sometimes fail to follow the leading of the Holy Spirit, who lives in us. With His grace He gives us forgiveness if we are *humble* and willing to receive it (cf. Matthew 5:3). If we are *proud* and defiant in rejecting His leading, we find ourselves in opposition to God Almighty. Nothing could be worse than that!

THE SMARTEST KID IN THE WORLD

For a while, Justin Chapman was the smartest kid in the world. At age three his IQ tested off the charts. At six he scored a record 298-plus. On the SAT math test he scored a perfect 800. He was taking on-line high school classes at age five and enrolled at New York's University of Rochester when he was six. Justin was a celebrity, being interviewed by the governor of New York, appearing in a BBC documentary that focused on young geniuses, and speaking at numerous conferences on the unique needs of gifted children.

Mom, of course, was justly proud of her boy genius and specialized in bragging about him, adding fuel to the fire of his fame. But everything changed when, at age eight, he began to exhibit bizarre behavior and was hospitalized for severe mental problems. As evidence of psychological pressure on Justin came to light, the court took the boy away from his mother. In hopes of regaining custody, she admitted that she had falsified the IQ scores and stolen a neighbor's SAT scores. She said, "It just happened, and I let things get out of control."

There is no doubt that Justin is very bright. But his mother's exaggerated and misguided pride brought pathetic results in terms of her son's health and well-being. Eventually, God will judge our pride and bring us down. Worse, we often take others with us!   —C. R. B.

B. Choose Your Master (vv. 7-10)

7. Submit yourselves therefore to God. Resist the devil, and he will flee from you.

When we *submit* ourselves *to God*, we follow the leading of His written Word in our hands and His gracious Spirit in our hearts. In verse 1 of our text, James attributes some of our wrongdoing to our own wrong desires. But now James leads us to consider the cause of our wrong wishes. *The devil* is always trying to implant them and encourage them. The devil is like a roaring lion eager to devour us (1 Peter 5:8), but he pretends to be an angel of light (2 Corinthians 11:14). If we are fooled by his pretense, he will lead us into all kinds of wrong thinking, wishing, and doing. But if we recognize his evil influence and *resist* it, he can only take to his heels. We are safe from the devil's wiles if we know the Bible and apply it in our lives.

8. Draw nigh to God, and he will draw nigh to you. Cleanse your hands, ye sinners; and purify your hearts, ye double-minded.

So you choose God to be your master. You renounce the devil, and you renounce your own devilish desires (cf. Matthew 6:24). But when you decide to serve the Lord, do not try to serve Him from afar. Instead, *draw nigh* to Him—seek His presence. He is not hard to find, for He is looking for you, too (Acts 17:27). But you will not be comfortable in His presence with those sin-stained hands. So *cleanse your hands* in His loving forgiveness (cf. 1 John 1:9).

Remember, God wants no half-hearted service. So *purify your heart* if you have been wavering between the call of God and the call of the godless world. A *double-minded* person can expect no blessing from the Lord (James 1:7, 8).

9, 10. Be afflicted, and mourn, and weep: let your laughter be turned to mourning, and your joy to heaviness. Humble yourselves in the sight of the Lord, and he shall lift you up.

In Nehemiah 8:9-12, the people are told to stop *mourning* and start rejoicing. Now circumstances call for the opposite to be done. This weeping is for the sinners and the double-minded who are addressed in verse 8. They (and we) are not to come proudly to the Lord; they are not to hold their heads high and demand His cleansing. Instead, they (and we) are to come with a broken spirit and a contrite heart (Psalm 51:17). Then the Lord will purify hearts and *lift* up those ready to serve Him.

III. Don't Try to Be God
(James 4:11-17)

We have been warned against destructive conflicts with Christian brothers and sisters. We have been warned against our own desires that cause conflicts. We have been warned against the godless world that constantly tries to make us as godless as itself. We have been warned against the devil, who is out to destroy us. But God gives us power to overcome all these problems. We are exalted by the thought that we are God's friends and have His Spirit living in us.

Now in the last part of our text we are warned against thinking we are more than we can be. God's friends are not God. Let us not be foolish enough to take on ourselves the judging that only God can do. Let us not be arrogant enough to think we can plan and direct our lives with no thought of God's will.

A. Let God Be the Judge (vv. 11, 12)

11. Speak not evil one of another, brethren. He that speaketh evil of his brother, and judgeth his brother, speaketh evil of the law, and judgeth the law: but if thou judge the law, thou art not a doer of the law, but a judge.

Jesus warns us against judging our fellow Christians (Matthew 5:22; 7:1-5). So does Paul (Romans 14:3, 10, 13). Now we see a like warning from James. Sometimes such warnings are misunderstood. They are taken to mean that we should shut our eyes to a fellow Christian's wrongdoing and let it go on without rebuke. That is a mistake. If a fellow Christian is doing something that is plainly contrary to Bible teaching, we ought to call his or her attention to God's judgment of what he or she is doing (Luke 17:3). We ought to help the person stop the wrongdoing when we can.

First, we take up the issue privately with the wrongdoer (Matthew 18:15). Too often we do just the opposite: we tell the wrongdoer's fault to everyone but the wrongdoer. It becomes common gossip in the church and community, but no one mentions it to the one who could make the needed change! Surely Jesus, Paul, and James do warn us against such irresponsible gossip.

Passing judgment on fellow Christians is tantamount to speaking *evil of the law* and sitting in judgment on *the law.* Some careful students conclude that James is alluding to what he calls "the royal law": "Thou shalt love thy neighbor as thyself" (Leviticus 19:18; Matthew 5:43; 19:19; James 2:8). Jesus said that this commandment was one of two upon which hang "all the law and the prophets" (Matthew 22:37-40). This one law is the whole law of human relations condensed into one statement (Romans 13:8-10). Anyone who speaks evil of his brother is breaking that royal law, and thereby judging it unworthy of obedience—thus speaking evil of it.

Visual for
lesson 4

Humble yourselves in the sight of the Lord, and he shall lift you up. James 4:10

Display this poster as you discuss James 4:10. It is in the Adult Visuals *packet.*

12. There is one lawgiver, who is able to save and to destroy: who art thou that judgest another?

The Lord God Almighty is the *one lawgiver.* Remember that *to save* and *to destroy* is His prerogative, not ours (Isaiah 33:22). [See question #3, page 40.]

B. Consider God's Will (vv. 13-17)

13. Go to now, ye that say, Today or tomorrow we will go into such a city, and continue there a year, and buy and sell, and get gain.

In the antique English of the *King James Version, Go to now* is a call to thought or action. It seems to carry a bit of rebuke for not having thought or acted already. In today's English we sometimes say, "Come on, now!" with the same meaning. Here James calls his readers to rethink the attitude with which they make their plans. In the Roman Empire as today, many in the church are astute businessmen. It is not unusual for one of them to see a business opportunity in another city and to plan to go there immediately.

14. Whereas ye know not what shall be on the morrow. For what is your life? It is even a vapor, that appeareth for a little time, and then vanisheth away.

In our hearts we know the plans we make are breakable. You may be disabled in a traffic accident. I may drop dead with a heart attack (cf. Luke 12:20). That city to which we plan to go may be so damaged by earthquake, fire, flood, or terrorism that no wise person would conduct business there.

15. For that ye ought to say, If the Lord will, we shall live, and do this, or that.

Keeping *the Lord* in our thinking and planning allows us to maintain a proper perspective. When we do that, we make plans that He can approve of; we ensure that we can make a profit without defrauding anyone. Perhaps you have heard people say, "Lord willing" when they tell of their plans. It is a healthy reminder. [See question #4, page 40.]

16. But now ye rejoice in your boastings: all such rejoicing is evil.

The fault of James's readers is not in making business plans by itself. Rather, their problem is in leaving God out of the planning. J. B. Adamson calls this "practical atheism." The arrogant *rejoicing* in human wisdom, power, and success *is evil.* God's people ought to have Him always on their minds, ought to depend on Him, ought to serve Him, ought to seek His kingdom and His righteousness above their own profit (Matthew 6:33).

17. Therefore to him that knoweth to do good, and doeth it not, to him it is sin.

All of James's readers, including us, ought to know that:

1. It is good to control our desires, and not be controlled by them.

2. It is good to seek to be friends of God rather than to be friends of the world.

3. It is good to serve God humbly, not to try to take His place.

So watch your step. If you do not do what you know is *good,* that is *sin.* Failing *to do good* can also be called a "sin of omission." [See question #5, page 40.]

Conclusion

Perhaps we can best conclude this lesson by listing key thoughts from its three main sections, those sections numbered with Roman numerals in the outline and in the body of the lesson.

A. Key Thoughts

I. Problems arise in the church when people fail to control their desires. Beware!

II. God, through His Word, provides solutions to those problems. Practice those solutions!

III. God's people are not God; they are His humble servants. Serve Him well!

B. Prayer

Our Father in Heaven, we thank You for the wisdom You have given to James and that he has passed on to us. Please give us increasing wisdom to grasp more of Your truth. Give us the strength to control our desires and attitudes, and grant us the courage to do what is right. In Jesus' name, amen.

C. Thought to Remember

"Surely he scorneth the scorners: but he giveth grace unto the lowly" (Proverbs 3:34).

Learning by Doing

This page contains an alternative lesson plan emphasizing learning activities.
Classes desiring such student involvement will find these suggestions helpful.

Learning Goals

After this lesson each student will be able to:

1. Recall key points from James's warning against evil passions and his call to submission to God.

2. Tell how wrong attitudes can lead to conflicts between Christians.

3. Identify and confess a sinful attitude that has led to a disagreement with another believer.

Into the Lesson

Prepare a scrambled word and sentence activity. The sentence is James 4:7, "Submit yourselves therefore to God." Estimate how many small groups of three students you will have in class. For each group, prepare a set of four three-by-five index cards and place them in an envelope. On one card you will write "BIMSTU" *(submit)*; on another, "EELORSSUVY" *(yourselves)*; on a third, "EEEFHORRT" *(therefore)*; and on the final card you will write two words "OT DGO" *(to God)*.

Shuffle the cards before placing them into the envelopes. After moving the class into groups of three, begin class by saying, "Each of these envelopes contains index cards that have one or more scrambled words written on them. When I tell you to begin, take the cards out of the envelope, unscramble the words, and then arrange the words to form a verse from our lesson text today."

Say, "Our lesson text today describes what happens when people have a broken relationship with God and what is necessary to restore that relationship. Open your Bible to James 4."

Into the Word

Prepare three question sheets using the questions given below. Ask someone to read aloud James 4. Then move the class into three groups, giving each group one of the question sheets to answer. Allow about eight minutes for the groups to work. When they have finished, ask each group to tell the answers to their questions.

Group A

1. What are the characteristics of one who has a broken relationship with God (vv. 1-6)? *(Wars, fightings, lusts, murder, adultery, pride, selfishness.)*

2. What does James say explains why believers did not have the things they wanted (vv. 2, 3)? *(They did not ask God; when they did ask, they did not ask correctly.)*

3. What is a proper attitude for Christians (v. 6)? *(Humility.)*

Group B

1. What should you do to restore a broken relationship with God (vv. 7-10)? *(Submit to God; resist the devil; draw nigh to God; cleanse your hands; purify your hearts; be afflicted, mourn, weep; humble yourselves.)*

2. What does James say is the source of the wars and fightings among believers (v. 1)? *(Individual lusts that lead to sinful deeds.)*

3. What metaphor does James use to describe a person's life (v. 14)? *(A vapor.)*

Group C

1. What does James call those believers who engage in wars and fightings among themselves (vv. 4, 8, 11)? *(Adulterers, adulteresses; sinners, double-minded; judges of the law rather than doers.)*

2. How should Christians make plans for the future (vv. 13-15)? *(Plans should be made with the contingency, "If the Lord will.")*

3. What does James say indicates sin in a person's life (v. 17)? *(Not doing the good that one knows should be done.)*

After discussing the answers, say, "James isn't the only one who dealt with conflicts between Christians. Unfortunately, we all face it too often. This lesson is called, 'Faith and Attitudes'; conflicts often begin with wrong attitudes that lead to sinful behaviors. Let's explore this concept."

Into Life

Project a chart entitled, "Disagreements Between Believers," using an overhead projector or chalkboard. Have two columns with the headings, "Sinful Attitudes" and "Broken Relationships." Ask the class to identify wrong attitudes that cause conflicts between Christians. As the ideas are suggested, write them down the left column. Draw a horizontal arrow from each attitude to the right column and note the direct relationship between sinful attitudes and broken relationships with people. Ask each student to pick one sinful attitude that has led to a disagreement with another believer. Distribute three-by-five cards and ask each student to write a prayer confessing an attitude that has broken a relationship. Remind learners of James 4:10: "Humble yourselves in the sight of the Lord, and he shall lift you up."

Let's Talk It Over

The questions on this page are designed to promote discussion of the lesson by the class and to encourage application of the lesson Scriptures. The answers provided are only discussion starters. Let your class talk it over from there.

1. Bickering among church members often undermines the spirit and effectiveness of the local church. What must the local congregation teach its members in order to reduce the risk of strife within the church?

Most church quarrels start because of a lack of personal humility or a failure to see issues from God's perspective. Church leaders must teach Christians to pray for wisdom and to compare their behavior constantly with God's standards. Passages such as 1 Corinthians 13; Galatians 6:1-5; Ephesians 4:2, 3; and Philippians 2:3, 4 are very helpful in this regard.

The following story provides a blueprint for solving such conflicts when people are committed to resolution rather than insisting on being right. In one area of Scotland when two people disagree, they are required to go to a small island named the "Isle of Discussion." They are given an ample supply of cheese and are required to stay there until the issue is settled. Afterward they go over to another island, called the "Isle of Reconciliation," to celebrate their agreement. The area has had only one murder in over a century!

2. Many people have become good at shifting blame. The old saying, "The devil made me do it" is an example. How can we teach individuals that the source of their ungodly attitudes lies within themselves?

Some would have us defeat evil and wrong attitudes by focusing all our effort on closing down sinful establishments as opposed to dealing with the internal problem. It is helpful to remember that during Prohibition in the 1920s the demand for alcoholic beverages was still high because the source of desire had not been changed or controlled. While it is helpful to remove as many temptation sources as possible, it is more important to give individuals the resources to overcome their own evil desires. Christians need to learn how to recognize the real source of temptation, to ask for help from God and others, to find or be an accountability partner, and to satisfy their longings in a constructive way (Philippians 4:8).

3. How can Christians come to understand just how serious is the sin of being judgmental?

Christians continually need to be reminded that God is the only eternal lawgiver and there-fore the only judge of eternal destinies. We need to be warned repeatedly that a judgmental person is usurping God's position and role and that God will not tolerate such arrogance.

Positive alternatives are always helpful. Believers need to know that, instead of becoming judges, their work is to tell about and demonstrate the mercy they have received from God. Even so, God has given Christians a judging, or discerning, role (Matthew 7:15-20). We can describe and analyze. We do that for the purposes of responding to needs, proposing solutions, and avoiding sin.

4. The Bible teaches the virtue of being an industrious self-starter (e.g., Proverbs 10:4). On the other hand, James seems to be saying that a person's planning for tomorrow may be fruitless, since God is in control of what happens in the future. What should the church teach in order to clarify this seeming contradiction?

The Lord spoke approvingly of advance planning in Luke 14:28-31. Paul planned his journeys (Romans 15:23-29). In the passage at hand, James is not attacking the idea of planning ahead. Rather, he is highlighting the problem of pride and arrogance. Our sense of invincibility leads to a boastful spirit as we assume we are in control, rather than God.

5. Over time, most church members unconsciously fall into the habit of emphasizing some types of sin and not others. What can we do to explore this "blind side" in reference to sin?

Sometimes there is more talk about sins of action (adultery, theft, murder) while there is little mention of the sins of attitude (envy, jealously, pride, hatred). In some circles, Christians have developed a list of reasons explaining why little effort should be placed on helping the poor, visiting prisoners, correcting injustices, etc. These inactions become sins of omission (which often result from the sins of attitude).

Help your learners discover the collective blind sides of churches and Sunday school classes as well as the personal blind sides of individual Christians. Discuss ways to correct imbalances. James's summary statement covers all of these areas: "Therefore to him that knoweth to do good, and doeth it not, to him it is sin."

Live as God's People

DEVOTIONAL READING: Leviticus 19:1-10.

BACKGROUND SCRIPTURE: 1 Peter 1:1–2:10.

PRINTED TEXT: 1 Peter 1:3-5, 13-21; 2:4-10.

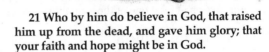

1 Peter 1:3-5, 13-21

3 Blessed be the God and Father of our Lord Jesus Christ, which according to his abundant mercy hath begotten us again unto a lively hope by the resurrection of Jesus Christ from the dead,

4 To an inheritance incorruptible, and undefiled, and that fadeth not away, reserved in heaven for you,

5 Who are kept by the power of God through faith unto salvation ready to be revealed in the last time.

. . . .

13 Wherefore gird up the loins of your mind, be sober, and hope to the end for the grace that is to be brought unto you at the revelation of Jesus Christ;

14 As obedient children, not fashioning yourselves according to the former lusts in your ignorance:

15 But as he which hath called you is holy, so be ye holy in all manner of conversation;

16 Because it is written, Be ye holy; for I am holy.

17 And if ye call on the Father, who without respect of persons judgeth according to every man's work, pass the time of your sojourning here in fear:

18 Forasmuch as ye know that ye were not redeemed with corruptible things, as silver and gold, from your vain conversation received by tradition from your fathers;

19 But with the precious blood of Christ, as of a lamb without blemish and without spot:

20 Who verily was foreordained before the foundation of the world, but was manifest in these last times for you,

21 Who by him do believe in God, that raised him up from the dead, and gave him glory; that your faith and hope might be in God.

1 Peter 2:4-10

4 To whom coming, as unto a living stone, disallowed indeed of men, but chosen of God, and precious,

5 Ye also, as lively stones, are built up a spiritual house, a holy priesthood, to offer up spiritual sacrifices, acceptable to God by Jesus Christ.

6 Wherefore also it is contained in the Scripture, Behold, I lay in Zion a chief corner stone, elect, precious: and he that believeth on him shall not be confounded.

7 Unto you therefore which believe he is precious: but unto them which be disobedient, the stone which the builders disallowed, the same is made the head of the corner,

8 And a stone of stumbling, and a rock of offense, even to them which stumble at the word, being disobedient: whereunto also they were appointed.

9 But ye are a chosen generation, a royal priesthood, a holy nation, a peculiar people; that ye should show forth the praises of him who hath called you out of darkness into his marvelous light:

10 Which in time past were not a people, but are now the people of God: which had not obtained mercy, but now have obtained mercy.

GOLDEN TEXT: As he which hath called you is holy, so be ye holy
in all manner of conversation.—1 Peter 1:15.

Lesson Aims

After participating in this lesson, each student should be able to:

1. List several qualities that characterize Christians who respond to the challenge of our text.

2. Explain how these qualities help draw others to the Lord.

3. Suggest a course of action that will help him or her to improve on at least one of these qualities.

Lesson Outline

INTRODUCTION
  A. Our Job
  B. Lesson Background
 I. PRAISE GOD (1 Peter 1:3-5)
  A. Praise God for Our Hope (v. 3)
  B. Praise God for Our Inheritance (v. 4)
  C. Praise God for Our Safekeeping (v. 5)
 II. PREPARE YOURSELF (1 Peter 1:13-21)
  A. Call to Holiness (vv. 13-16)
   Applying the Right Principles
  B. Call to Reverence (vv. 17-21)
III. YOUR SPIRITUAL HOUSE (1 Peter 2:4-10)
  A. The Materials (vv. 4, 5)
  B. The Cornerstone (vv. 6-8)
   The Only Stone That Lasts for Ages
  C. The Building (vv. 9, 10)
CONCLUSION
  A. Practical Ideas
  B. Prayer
  C. Thought to Remember

Introduction

"It's not fair," Rob grumbled. "Everybody expects a preacher's kid to be good for nothing."

Rob's father, the preacher, answered with a laugh. "Then your work is cut out for you, Robbie," he said. "Your job is to disappoint everybody by being good for something."

This preacher's kid indeed has proven to be good for many things, and he has won increased respect for his father as well as for himself.

A. Our Job

This week's lesson title challenges us to "Live as God's People." If anyone expects Christians to be hypocrites, our job is to disappoint that one!

When we are sincere, honest, and devoted to the Lord we win respect not only for ourselves but also for our Father in Heaven. Isn't that what Jesus asks? "Let your light so shine before men, that they may see your good works, and glorify your Father which is in heaven" (Matthew 5:16).

B. Lesson Background

After our four lessons from the epistle of James, we now turn to the first of two letters by Simon Peter. Not many heroes of the infant church are better known than this man! He was one of the first of Jesus' disciples (John 1:35-42), and was taught intensively through the years of Jesus' earthly ministry. After Jesus died and rose again, Peter was the one who preached on that memorable Day of Pentecost when the church began its tremendous growth (Acts 2:1-41). Later, God chose Peter as the first to carry the gospel to the Gentiles (Acts 10). We know little about Peter's movements after that, but certainly he remained a tower of strength in the growing church (Galatians 2:9).

I. Praise God
(1 Peter 1:3-5)

Peter probably wrote his first letter in about A.D. 64. That means he had been a Christian for more than thirty years. He wrote from a place he called "Babylon" (1 Peter 5:13), probably a code word for pagan Rome. He wrote to Christians in Asia Minor (1:1), that large landmass south of the Black Sea and north of the east part of the Mediterranean Sea, where modern Turkey is today.

A. Praise God for Our Hope (v. 3)

3. Blessed be the God and Father of our Lord Jesus Christ, which according to his abundant mercy hath begotten us again unto a lively hope by the resurrection of Jesus Christ from the dead.

The word *blessed* should be understood as *praise*, as in "Bless the Lord, O my soul" (Psalm 103:1). Thus we understand the first clause to say, "May God be praised." Naturally we take that as a suggestion that we ourselves praise Him. What a privilege!

Next, God is described as *Father of our Lord Jesus Christ*. Since the Father *hath begotten us again*, He is our Father as well. Of course God did not beget us in the same way He begot Jesus (Luke 1:26-35). No one else is God's Son in the same way Jesus is. But in another way all Christians are children of God since He has caused us to be born again as His children (cf. Galatians 3:26, 27). This statement is true not because we have a right to rebirth or deserve it, but it is *according to his abundant mercy* that He gave that rebirth to us when we did not deserve it.

By His mercy we are born again, born into *a lively hope,* a living and active hope that will not be disappointed (see the next verse). God brought us to that hope *by the resurrection of Jesus Christ from the dead.* Because we know Jesus had the power to live again and is living still, we know that He has the power to cause us to live again—and to live forever—after our own deaths. [See question #1, page 48.]

B. Praise God for Our Inheritance (v. 4)

4. To an inheritance incorruptible, and undefiled, and that fadeth not away, reserved in heaven for you.

Born again as God's children, we are "heirs of God, and joint-heirs with Christ" (Romans 8:17). Our *inheritance* is secure forever, *reserved in heaven for* us. Inheritance is an important theme in the Bible (e.g., Psalm 37:9; Matthew 5:5; 19:29; 25:34; 1 Peter 3:9).

C. Praise God for Our Safekeeping (v. 5)

5. Who are kept by the power of God through faith unto salvation ready to be revealed in the last time.

Can we be sure of receiving that matchless inheritance that is reserved for us? Yes—and no. *The power of God* guarantees it, if we are faithful. It is God who keeps us safe against every attack of the world, the flesh, and the devil. But God does it *through* our *faith,* and the maintenance of our faith is our own responsibility (cf. Hebrews 2:1).

II. Prepare Yourself
(1 Peter 1:13-21)

The word *wherefore* that begins our next section means that what Peter has to say next is the logical conclusion of what he has said just before. In 1:6-12 (not in our text), he recognizes the trials his readers are suffering. He also reminds them of the reality of their salvation. This leads him to exhort his readers to do certain things and think certain ways.

A. Call to Holiness (vv. 13-16)

13. Wherefore gird up the loins of your mind, be sober, and hope to the end for the grace that is to be brought unto you at the revelation of Jesus Christ.

Gird up the loins means "get ready for action." In Peter's day a man's daily garb was rather like a modern bathrobe. In preparing to run or to work vigorously, a man would lift the hem of his robe above his knees and tuck it into the belt around his waist. Peter is not asking us to free our legs

for a footrace, but to free our minds for proper thinking.

In Greek, as in English, *be sober* can mean either "don't be drunken" or "be serious and thoughtful, not careless or facetious." *Hope to the end* does not mean until the end of time; it means to hope fully, completely, confidently. Peter is telling us to expect the *grace,* the favor of God, that forgives our sins and welcomes us to Heaven when *Jesus Christ* returns.

14. As obedient children, not fashioning yourselves according to the former lusts in your ignorance.

Most of the Christians receiving this letter had been pagans before they had heard the gospel. In their *ignorance* of Christian teaching they had fashioned themselves according to their natural *lusts* and desires. But now as Christians they must shape themselves in a different fashion, the fashion of *obedient children* of God. The apostle Paul also wrote to some of these same people to remind them of the life they should have left behind (see Galatians 4:8-11). [See question #2, page 48.]

15. But as he which hath called you is holy, so be ye holy in all manner of conversation.

Holy things and holy people are dedicated to the service of God. Christians must pattern themselves to be like Jesus, to be holy and dedicated to God's service. Holiness will affect their whole *manner of conversation.* Here "conversation" does not merely mean "talk"; it means an entire lifestyle. [See question #3, page 48.]

16. Because it is written, Be ye holy; for I am holy.

The call to holiness is *written* more than once in the Old Testament (Leviticus 11:44, 45; 19:2; 20:7). That Testament was given to the people of Israel (the Jews); now Peter repeats the same call to Christians, whether Jewish or Gentile in background.

APPLYING THE RIGHT PRINCIPLES

Rudolph Giuliani, former mayor of New York City, is most famous for his commanding and comforting presence at the horrendous scene of the terrorist attacks on the World Trade Center on September 11, 2001. However, he had become famous (or infamous, depending on one's politics) for changes he brought about earlier in his tenure as mayor.

Giuliani came to office at a time when the city was crime-ridden and the streets overrun by cast-off derelicts of society. *A New York Times* poll indicated that more than 50 percent of the adults in the city were planning to leave. A decade later, the murder rate was one-third of what it had been, the homeless had been moved into facilities where they could be helped, and street prostitution, drug-dealing, and graffiti had all declined due to aggressive law enforcement. The mayor's promotion of "middle-class values" (in other words, the advocacy of principles of human decency) had made New York City livable again.

Regardless of sociological and political fads that try to make humanity's sinful condition excusable—or even laudable—the Biblical values of sobriety, morality, and holiness that Peter advocates are the only principles that will make society work. With anything else, we are merely fooling ourselves.   —C. R. B.

B. Call to Reverence (vv. 17-21)

17. And if ye call on the Father, who without respect of persons judgeth according to every man's work, pass the time of your sojourning here in fear.

"Reverence" is in the subtitle above to suggest that that word would be an acceptable translation where our text has *fear.* Wise Solomon concluded a long discussion by saying, "Fear God, and keep his commandments: for this is the whole duty of man" (Ecclesiastes 12:13). That does not mean we ought to try to hide from God, as guilty Adam did (Genesis 3:8). We are not tormented by fear as Adam was. When we *call on the Father* in prayer, our fear of God is an attitude of reverence and awe.

As we learned in lesson 2, God shows no *respect of persons,* meaning He does not discriminate or show favoritism (Acts 10:34). He evaluates us on the basis of our *work* for His kingdom, not on the basis of race or ethnic group.

18, 19. Forasmuch as ye know that ye were not redeemed with corruptible things, as silver

Visual for lesson 5

Drawing from 1 Peter 2:5, this visual illustrates that the church is people, not a building.

and gold, from your vain conversation received by tradition from your fathers; but with the precious blood of Christ, as of a lamb without blemish and without spot.

Before they became Christians, most of Peter's audience had been pagan. Their *conversation* (i.e., their way of life) that they had *received by tradition* was *vain*—concerned with worldly values and false religion, with no hope for eternity. But their Christian redemption has not come about on the basis of *silver and gold. The precious blood of Christ* was required for that. *A lamb* offered in sacrifice had to be perfect, *without blemish and without spot* (Leviticus 22:21). "The Lamb of God, which taketh away the sin of the world!" (John 1:29) had to be God's faultless Son.

20, 21. Who verily was foreordained before the foundation of the world, but was manifest in these last times for you, who by him do believe in God, that raised him up from the dead, and gave him glory; that your faith and hope might be in God.

Before God began to make *the world,* He had a plan for the redemption of people whose own actions would make them slaves of sin and doomed to death. God planned to send His own Son to live a sinless life among sinful people, to take upon himself the punishment that all those sinners deserved, and thus to ransom the sinners from sin and death (Mark 10:45). In Peter's time the Redeemer *was manifest*—was seen and known. According to God's ancient plan Jesus gave His life to redeem lost sinners today just as much as He did it for those people in Asia Minor who received this letter originally.

Peter's audience had forsaken their old, imaginary gods for Jesus. The real God was the one who *raised him up from the dead, and gave him glory.* Those people of Asia Minor had learned about that, and that was the reason they put their *faith and hope* in God. And don't we put our faith and hope in the same God for the same reasons?

III. Your Spiritual House
(1 Peter 2:4-10)

In language mostly literal, the first two parts of our text tell something about what we "do" as God's people. Now Peter switches to figurative language to tell us more about our relationship to Jesus. In his metaphor we appear as things rather than people, but in a way that enhances our human dignity.

A. The Materials (vv. 4, 5)

4, 5. To whom coming, as unto a living stone, disallowed indeed of men, but chosen of God, and precious, ye also, as lively stones, are built

up a spiritual house, a holy priesthood, to offer up spiritual sacrifices, acceptable to God by Jesus Christ.

A glance at verse 3 (not in our text) shows that *to whom* means to the Lord, to Jesus. In Peter's metaphor, Jesus is *a living stone* to whom we Christians, as *lively* (living) *stones,* come. As the Christians in Asia Minor came to Jesus and were built into *a spiritual house* (the church), so are we.

Adding to the imagery, Peter notes that we "lively stones" are also priests *to offer up spiritual sacrifices.* Now that the Old Testament era is past, there is no longer any need for a separate category of priests. We are all priests (Revelation 1:6; 5:10), and Jesus is our Great High Priest (Hebrews 6:20). [See question #4, page 48.]

Romans 12:1 helps us understand the nature of our spiritual sacrifices. That passage urges us to offer up to God our very bodies—not killed at the altar like ancient sacrifices, but living and serving.

B. The Cornerstone (vv. 6-8)

6. Wherefore also it is contained in the Scripture, Behold, I lay in Zion a chief corner stone, elect, precious: and he that believeth on him shall not be confounded.

The *Scripture* Peter quotes is Isaiah 28:16, a seven-hundred-year-old prophecy of Jesus as *chief corner stone. Zion* is another name for Jerusalem and the hill on which it stands. Jerusalem had been one of the important places of Jesus' ministry, and the church of which He is the cornerstone began its amazing growth there (Acts 2). Jesus the cornerstone is forever secure, forever dependable. Those who believe *on him shall not be confounded,* shall never be discredited or put to shame. [See question #5, page 48.]

7. Unto you therefore which believe he is precious: but unto them which be disobedient, the stone which the builders disallowed, the same is made the head of the corner.

This verse alludes to Psalm 118:22, 23. That passage sings of a building *stone* rejected by builders whom God overrules. That rejected stone becomes the chief cornerstone, the most important stone in the building. Long before Peter wrote this letter we are reading, he presented that bit of Psalm 118 as a fulfilled prophecy of Jesus (Acts 4:8-12). Jesus was rejected by the official builders of Israel—the priests and scholars and teachers. But God overruled them (cf. Mark 12:10, 11).

We who believe in Jesus understand how *precious* He is: the secure cornerstone of the eternal church to which we commit ourselves. No other foundation is necessary or possible (cf.

How to Say It

CEPHAS. *See*-fus.
CORINTHIANS. Kor-*in*-thee-unz (*th* as in *thin*).
DEUTERONOMY. Due-ter-*ahn*-uh-me.
ECCLESIASTES. Ik-*leez*-ee-*as*-teez (strong accent on *as*).
EPHESIANS. Ee-*fee*-zhunz.
GALATIANS. Guh-*lay*-shunz.
LEVITICUS. Leh-*vit*-ih-kus.
MEDITERRANEAN. *Med*-uh-tuh-*ray*-nee-un (strong accent on *ray*).
PISA. *Pee*-zuh.
ZION. *Zi*-un.

---

1 Corinthians 3:10; Ephesians 2:20). Those who are *disobedient,* the non-Christians, take their stand with the mistaken builders who rejected Him at His first appearance on earth. Unbelievers may be loud in their denial now, but in the end they will be confounded, discredited, and put to shame. This very cornerstone ultimately will crush them (Luke 20:17, 18).

8. And a stone of stumbling, and a rock of offense, even to them which stumble at the word, being disobedient: whereunto also they were appointed.

Peter now cites Isaiah 8:14. The *word,* the good news of Jesus and salvation, was told in Peter's time and is told now in our century. Each person who hears it has the same opportunity to submit to Jesus as Lord. Those who do are built into a spiritual house with Him, saved for eternity. Those who refuse stumble and fall for eternity. God has not *appointed* anyone to reject Christ. But those who do reject Christ of their own free will are indeed appointed to stumble over Him, *a rock of offense.*

THE ONLY STONE THAT LASTS FOR AGES

The pyramids and Sphinx of Egypt, the Tower of London, the Cathedral of Notre Dame in Paris, the Washington Monument in Washington, D.C.—throughout history, when people have wanted to build an edifice that would last for ages, they have built with stone. Yet these monuments show the effects of time: the pyramids and Sphinx have eroded and the other structures have had to undergo periodic restoration to preserve them.

One of the most striking examples of this need to expend great amounts of effort and money to preserve our monuments is the "Leaning Tower" of Pisa. The 190-foot-tall bell tower was begun in 1173. Before the third of its eight levels was completed, however, its foundation had begun to sink, and the tilt began. Through the centuries numerous attempts were made to stop the tilting, all without success. It was not until 1990, after a ten-year, twenty-seven million dollar effort, that engineers finally succeeded in keeping the tower from falling down.

Nothing we build in this life, even when made of the hardest stone, will last forever. It will gradually wear away and ultimately crumble or have to be demolished. But Peter tells us that Christ is a precious, living stone and the only sure foundation for our lives. Some may reject this stone or stumble over it, but those who build their lives on it will never be disappointed. They are incorporated into a spiritual building that will last forever. —C. R. B.

C. The Building (vv. 9, 10)

9. But ye are a chosen generation, a royal priesthood, a holy nation, a peculiar people; that ye should show forth the praises of him who hath called you out of darkness into his marvelous light.

We are not only a spiritual house (v. 5), but also *a chosen generation,* a group of people related by being born again (1 Peter 1:3). We are *a royal priesthood,* a group of priests (2:5) associated with Jesus the King. As *a holy nation* we are dedicated to God's service. Being *a peculiar people* does not mean we are odd or strange in our ways. Rather, the idea is that of being a distinctive possession (cf. Exodus 19:5, 6; Deuteronomy 7:6). All these mean that we ought to *show forth the praises of him who hath called you out of darkness into his marvelous light* (cf. Isaiah 43:20, 21).

10. Which in time past were not a people, but are now the people of God: which had not obtained mercy, but now have obtained mercy.

Peter now draws on Hosea 1:6, 9, 10; 2:23. Before becoming Christians, Peter's audience in Asia Minor had been scattered among several nations, with little in common (1 Peter 1:1). As Christians they are all bound together as *the people of God.* Likewise today's Christians are all members of one body (Ephesians 4:4-6). Before we were Christians we *had not obtained mercy.* We were loaded with the guilt of our sins, doomed to die. But now we *have obtained mercy* and forgiveness and eternal life (Romans 6:23). Praise God!

Conclusion

Through the month of September we read parts of a letter from James. Often we noted that James was a practical man, interested in what we do. Now we are starting to read a letter from Peter. Can we glean from him some practical ideas for our "doing"?

A. Practical Ideas

Part 1 of our lesson is about praising God. When you praise a store or a physician, your praise may bring a new customer to the store or a new patient to the doctor. How many non-Christians have been brought to God by your praise of Him?

Part 2 of our lessons is about being holy and reverent. We have to do some thinking about that. If we make a big show of being holy as the Pharisees did (Matthew 6:1-6; 23:5-12) we may turn people away from us and from God. But Jesus asks us to let people see our good works so they will glorify our Father in Heaven (5:16). Has anyone become more holy and reverent by following your example?

Part 3 of our lesson is about being built into a spiritual house, the church. What are you in that house? Are you a pillar of strength, like James, Cephas (Peter), and John (Galatians 2:9)? Or are you an area of weakness, leaning on the strength of others? Can you be stronger?

B. Prayer

Our Father, we never can praise You enough. How matchless are Your power, love, mercy, and grace! Thank You for calling us out of darkness and into Your marvelous light. Grant us wisdom—not the wisdom of the world, but Your wisdom. May we have strength and courage to walk in that wisdom, that light, to behave as Your children in the spiritual house where we live with Your people. In Jesus' name, amen.

C. Thought to Remember

Live as children of light!

Home Daily Bible Readings

Monday, Sept. 29—God's Treasured Possession (Deuteronomy 7:6-11)

Tuesday, Sept. 30—People Led by a Holy God (Leviticus 19:1-5)

Wednesday, Oct. 1—New Birth Into a Living Hope (1 Peter 1:1-7)

Thursday, Oct. 2—People of a Glorious Joy (1 Peter 1:8-12)

Friday, Oct. 3—Disciplined and Holy People (1 Peter 1:13-21)

Saturday, Oct. 4—People Longing for Spiritual Milk (1 Peter 1:22–2:3)

Sunday, Oct. 5—God's Own People (1 Peter 2:4-10)

Learning by Doing

This page contains an alternative lesson plan emphasizing learning activities.
Classes desiring such student involvement will find these suggestions helpful.

Learning Goals

After participating in this lesson, each student will be able to:

1. List several qualities that characterize Christians who respond to the challenge of our text.

2. Explain how these qualities help draw others to the Lord.

3. Suggest a course of action that will help him or her to improve on at least one of these qualities.

Into the Lesson

To begin this lesson write, "Change is . . ." in big letters on a poster board or butcher paper. Have space on the paper for written comments from the class. Place this on the classroom wall and have available several markers in different colors. After the learners have arrived, say, "Notice the graffiti poster on the wall. The word *change* produces a number of emotions and thoughts. Think about change for a moment; then come to the poster and use one of these markers to write on the poster an emotion or thought about change." *(Some possible responses include scary, uncomfortable, disliked, resisted, exciting.)*

After everyone has added a word or phrase, say, "Let's talk about the responses you have written." Read the responses and ask for an example or further explanation for each. Once these responses have been reviewed, make the transition to Bible study by saying, "The idea of change certainly carries much emotion. Yet, our text makes it clear that change is an expected result of coming to Christ. Open your Bibles to 1 Peter 1, and let's see what changes occurred in these Christians."

Into the Word

To begin, move the class into three or more small groups of five students. Ask each group to select a reader to read the lesson Scripture aloud to their own groups. Prior to class, prepare a work sheet for each group with three columns labeled: PAST (What were they?), PRESENT (What are they?), and FUTURE (Where will they be or have?). Give a work sheet to each group and ask them to find text descriptions to help answer those questions, and to write those under the appropriate column heading. Allow about fifteen minutes for this activity. *(Possible answers include the following: PAST—lustful, ignorant, 1:14; vain conversation, 1:18; disobedient, 2:8; in darkness, 2:9;*

PRESENT—hope, 1:3, 13; faith, power of God, 1:5; gird the mind, sober, 1:13; holy, 1:15, 16; redeemed, 1:18; chosen, precious, 2:4; priesthood, holy nation, peculiar people, 2:9; FUTURE—inheritance in Heaven, 1:4; salvation, 1:5; revelation of Jesus, 1:13; built into a spiritual house, 2:5.) When time is up, ask for answers. Point out the radical change that has taken place.

Ask each group to prepare a mock TV show interview with some of these Christians to cover the transition from past, through the present, and to the future. Have one-third of the groups focus on the past, one-third on the present, and one-third on the future. Ask the groups to write questions and to gather insights into what each of these time periods may have been like to the believers. Allow ten minutes for this activity, and then ask for volunteer groups to demonstrate their interviews before the whole class.

After the "TV news shows" have been completed, move the class back into one large group. Say, "Now that we have a better understanding of these early believers, what qualities from the text characterize Christians?" *(Possible answers are self-disciplined, sober, 1:13; obedient, 1:14; holy, 1:15; demonstrate faith and hope, 1:21; proclaim His praises, 2:9.)* Write answers on the chalkboard or on an overhead transparency for all to see. Say, "These qualities that characterize Christians are like a magnet to iron shavings. They attract people to Jesus. Turn to a neighbor and decide how these qualities draw others to the Lord." Ask volunteers to report their answers.

Into Life

Make certain the learners understand that these qualities represent the changes Christians develop throughout their lives. Ask them to evaluate their own level of attracting others to Jesus through these qualities. Then say, "How could a Christian improve some of these qualities? What specific steps can we take to improve one that appears to be weak?" Discuss with the class various suggestions to improve these qualities. Prior to class, prepare another work sheet, this time for each student. Name it "Action Plan," and provide a space for identifying a quality to improve and several lines for specific steps to be taken toward improvement. Ask each learner to select a quality and identify ways he or she can improve that quality in daily life.

Let's Talk It Over

The questions on this page are designed to promote discussion of the lesson by the class and to encourage application of the lesson Scriptures. The answers provided are only discussion starters. Let your class talk it over from there.

1. What steps can Christians take to ensure their praise is a fitting response to being born into "a lively hope," celebrating the Giver of the greatest gift ever received?

We have been born again from the dead, born into a living hope, and promised a sure inheritance. God promises to keep us in Him by His power as we exercise our faith. Wow! That is worth celebrating and celebrating and celebrating some more. Joy, thanksgiving, praise, and awe are just a few words that describe these responses. Worship services need to celebrate life in Christ! Worship services also can reflect our sorrow over our sinful pasts and our resolve not to return to that lifestyle. In personal devotions, Christians have the freedom to express their praise in many ways (singing jubilantly, dancing enthusiastically as David before the Lord, walking and talking with God in joyful conversation). There are many ways to honor the giver of every good and perfect gift!

2. When children are obedient, it is a testimony to the parents' skill in child-rearing. What needs to be done to teach Christians that God is to receive the glory when a person becomes obedient to His commands?

Peter's message here matches Paul's message that we are God's workmanship (Ephesians 1:3-14; 2:8-10). In your discussion, observe that Christians can feel good about and appreciate their growth, but they should realize that it is God who ultimately deserves all our praise. That lesson can be taught by example—testimonies of the faithful ought to include praise. They should never be a rehearsal of how good a person is on his or her own. The lesson can be taught in the classroom—as it is being done now. How about displaying posters praising God for His continued grace?

3. Chapter 1 uses many verbs to describe what Christians are to do as a result of being born into God's family. What are some actions a Christian can take to live out each of these?

Peter's list covers every aspect of a Christian's being—body, mind, and spirit. Channel your discussion along those three lines. For example, we can prepare our bodies for holy living through proper diet and exercise; we can prepare our minds for action by keeping the amount of our TV-watching under control; we maintain holiness of spirit by remembering at all times where our true home is. These are just a very few ideas! You can also discuss how each of the three aspects has an effect on the other two.

4. Peter describes God's people as being very special, based on what has been accomplished through the sacrifice of Jesus. What can the church do to awaken all its members to practice the unity—character, purpose, and direction—that Peter describes with the figures of speech in 1 Peter 2:5?

The lively stones (the church) are to be united (one building and one holy nation), serving together (royal priesthood), and unique in character (peculiar people). This is consistent with Christ's prayer before His betrayal in which He prayed for oneness among His followers (John 17:20, 21).

Instead of fighting each other, God's will is that believers be united in faith under the authority of Christ. They can do this by loving and caring for the needs of each other, by joining in one mission to proclaim Jesus as Savior, and by being an example (living lives worthy of the high calling of Christ) to those who are still controlled by the world.

5. Our faith is not a blind leap in the dark. Our faith is based on the solidness of Jesus Christ and the historical evidence about Him. How can Christians demonstrate in daily life their confidence in this sure foundation (Jesus)?

We begin by recognizing the nature of a cornerstone. For a large building, the cornerstone has to be strong enough to bear the considerable weight of the structure, and placed accurately enough to give direction to the layout. In the church Jesus is that cornerstone, strong and straight enough to support and give direction to His redeemed people.

Christians can live out this fact by singing and worshiping boldly, sharing the message of Christ with confidence, taking risks to help others (some of whom will never appreciate the effort), and sending forth missionaries with the message that can transform both individuals and nations. The old hymn, "The Church's One Foundation" is a great reminder of Who helps us.

Set a Good Example

DEVOTIONAL READING: Galatians 5:16-26.

BACKGROUND SCRIPTURE: 1 Peter 2:11–5:14.

PRINTED TEXT: 1 Peter 2:11, 12; 3:13-17; 4:7-11; 5:6-10.

1 Peter 2:11, 12

11 Dearly beloved, I beseech you as strangers and pilgrims, abstain from fleshly lusts, which war against the soul;

12 Having your conversation honest among the Gentiles: that, whereas they speak against you as evildoers, they may by your good works, which they shall behold, glorify God in the day of visitation.

1 Peter 3:13-17

13 And who is he that will harm you, if ye be followers of that which is good?

14 But and if ye suffer for righteousness' sake, happy are ye: and be not afraid of their terror, neither be troubled;

15 But sanctify the Lord God in your hearts: and be ready always to give an answer to every man that asketh you a reason of the hope that is in you, with meekness and fear:

16 Having a good conscience; that, whereas they speak evil of you, as of evildoers, they may be ashamed that falsely accuse your good conversation in Christ.

17 For it is better, if the will of God be so, that ye suffer for well doing, than for evildoing.

1 Peter 4:7-11

7 But the end of all things is at hand: be ye therefore sober, and watch unto prayer.

8 And above all things have fervent charity among yourselves: for charity shall cover the multitude of sins.

9 Use hospitality one to another without grudging.

10 As every man hath received the gift, even so minister the same one to another, as good stewards of the manifold grace of God.

11 If any man speak, let him speak as the oracles of God; if any man minister, let him do it as of the ability which God giveth; that God in all things may be glorified through Jesus Christ: to whom be praise and dominion for ever and ever. Amen.

1 Peter 5:6-10

6 Humble yourselves therefore under the mighty hand of God, that he may exalt you in due time:

7 Casting all your care upon him; for he careth for you.

8 Be sober, be vigilant; because your adversary the devil, as a roaring lion, walketh about, seeking whom he may devour:

9 Whom resist steadfast in the faith, knowing that the same afflictions are accomplished in your brethren that are in the world.

10 But the God of all grace, who hath called us unto his eternal glory by Christ Jesus, after that ye have suffered a while, make you perfect, stablish, strengthen, settle you.

GOLDEN TEXT: Having your conversation honest among the Gentiles: that, whereas they speak against you as evildoers, they may by your good works, which they shall behold, glorify God in the day of visitation.—1 Peter 2:12.

Faith Faces the World
Unit 2: Live in Hope
(Lessons 5-8)

Lesson Aims

After participating in this lesson, each student should be able to:

1. Tell some ways Peter says a Christian can set a good example.

2. Explain why setting a good example is important for the sake of other believers and also unbelievers.

3. Spend time with a new Christian and give him or her guidance and encouragement.

Be an example ## Lesson Outline

INTRODUCTION
  A. Bad Examples
  B. Lesson Background
I. DO RIGHT FOR GOD'S GLORY (1 Peter 2:11, 12)
  A. What to Do (v. 11)
  B. Why to Do It (v. 12)
II. DO RIGHT IN ALL CIRCUMSTANCES (1 Peter 3:13-17; 4:7-11)
  A. Blessing, Fear, Heart, and Hope (3:13-15)
  B. Conscience, Shame, God's Will, and Suffering (vv. 16, 17)
     Living Above Criticism
  C. Self-Control, Prayer, Love, and Sin (4:7-9)
     How Brothers Should Treat Each Other
  D. Gifts, Grace, Speaking, and Serving (vv. 10, 11)
III. DO RIGHT WITH AWARENESS (1 Peter 5:6-10)
  A. Trust God to Exalt You (v. 6)
  B. Trust God to Care for You (v. 7)
  C. Trust God and Resist the Devil (vv. 8, 9)
  D. Trust God to Perfect You (v. 10)
CONCLUSION
  A. Washing Our Feet
  B. Prayer
  C. Thought to Remember

Introduction

A. Bad Examples

"Follow the Leader" was the game on our country schoolyard, and Jake was the leader. Some of us fell in line reluctantly, for we knew we soon would be shamed by failure to follow. Jake was the tallest boy in school. Easily he jumped high enough to catch the lowest limb of the ash tree and pull himself up among the branches—but only two of the boys could follow him. Beaming with pride, Jake came down and hopped on one foot till half the boys dropped out with weariness. Next, our leader put his hands on the top rail of the fence and vaulted over into the area beside the road. It was against the rules to leave the schoolyard, but all of us vaulted or clambered over the fence. Then Jake tried what was meant to be his greatest stunt. Running at top speed across the road, he leaped over the irrigation ditch beyond it. His feet landed on the other bank, but his body had not quite kept up with his feet. With arms flailing, he fell back into the waist-deep water.

Every boy in the line was happy to see our leader fail. We surrounded him with jests and ridicule as he climbed from the ditch, dripping from head to toe. Then the bell sounded to end our afternoon recess a few minutes early, and we went to form orderly lines in front of the schoolhouse door.

From the top of the steps the teacher faced us with a heavy frown. No questioning was needed; she had been watching from a window. "Jake," she said, "go home and get into some dry clothes. Tell your parents you will be staying after school tomorrow."

So Jake got his bicycle and rode away, while the teacher led us into the schoolroom and gave us a lecture on the peril of following a bad example. I have forgotten the lecture, but I remember the clincher of it. The teacher said, "Next time anyone leaves the schoolyard before four o'clock, he will learn what *that* is for." She jerked a thumb over her shoulder at the big switch on the wall behind her.

Children often begin to smoke, or drink, or use illegal drugs because other children are doing it. A child usually knows better, but he or she dares not refuse to follow the leader. Sometimes "children" twenty or forty or sixty years old do the same thing. They want to be congenial, so they embrace the customs of the people around them. In other surroundings, they may fall (or jump!) into customs of double-dealing, fraud, or simple stealing. In yet another environment they may adopt the prevailing customs of infidelity, adultery, and divorce. Too late such folks may discover that evil examples corrupt good character (cf. Proverbs 24:1, 2; 1 Corinthians 15:33).

B. Lesson Background

Paul was a wise old Christian made wiser still by the Holy Spirit, who inspired him. He wanted his trainee to be an example to the Christians whom he taught. So Paul told Timothy to be an example "in word, in conversation, in charity, in spirit, in faith, in purity" (1 Timothy 4:12). What a list! These are the kinds of examples each Christian should set, and that is the background against which we look at the thoughts about example in our text.

I. Do Right for God's Glory (1 Peter 2:11, 12)

First Peter 2:9, 10, the verses just before our text, remind us that as Christians we are a separate people, the people of God, and a holy nation apart from the nations of the world. We are good citizens of the earthly countries where we live (vv. 13, 14 of our text), but our primary citizenship is in Heaven (Philippians 3:20). Our first allegiance is to God, the Heavenly King. His standards are our standards, His will is our will.

A. What to Do (v. 11)

11. Dearly beloved, I beseech you as strangers and pilgrims, abstain from fleshly lusts, which war against the soul.

Repeating from 1:1, Peter reminds his readers that they are *strangers* in this world. This is the mind-set that all Christians must have in order to be able to resist the *fleshly lusts* that are all around us. No province in ancient Asia Minor had laws against gluttony, drunkenness, or fornication resulting from such lusts. In fact, many pagans looked forward to the festival of "Bacchanalia," a Roman feast that was little more than a drunken orgy. But Christians do right according to the standards of the Heavenly King, not those of the prevailing culture.

B. Why to Do It (v. 12)

12. Having your conversation honest among the Gentiles: that, whereas they speak against you as evildoers, they may by your good works, which they shall behold, glorify God in the day of visitation.

Pagans of Peter's day often spoke in a variety of ways *against* Christians *as evildoers*. Christians will not worship the imaginary gods of their neighbors, so they are called atheists. In some places the emperor is worshiped as a god, so the Christians are accused of rebellion against Rome's government and religion. And Christians are called cannibals because they eat the body of Jesus and drink His blood.

How could Christians defend themselves? It is true that they will worship no god but One. It is true that they, in a symbolic way, eat Jesus' body and drink His blood at Communion. So the Christians' defense is simply to do good so constantly that no one will believe the evil that is spoken against them. As noted in previous lessons, the word *conversation* means an entire

way of life (not just "talk"), as it usually does in the *King James Version*. And the Greek word translated *honest* is more often translated "good" or "beautiful." A Christian's way of life must be so plainly above reproach that every accusation of wrongdoing falls flat. But beware: if we advertise our goodness, we spoil it. No one admires the Pharisees who did good to be seen by others (Matthew 23:5-11). We do good in such a way that those who see it will give credit to God rather than to us (Matthew 5:16).

Finally, when is the *day of visitation?* God is said to "visit" people for punishment (Isaiah 10:3; Jeremiah 51:18) or for rescue (Genesis 50:24, 25; Ruth 1:6; Psalm 106:4). If Christians perform *good works* in such a way as to lead their neighbors to Christ, those neighbors will *glorify God*. So the day any of them becomes a Christian may rightly be called a day of visitation. Or the day of visitation may be the day Christ returns, giving punishment to those who have not accepted Him and salvation to those who have. [See question #1, page 56.]

II. Do Right in All Circumstances (1 Peter 3:13-17; 4:7-11)

Some of the pagans are calling Christians evildoers (2:12), but the persecution goes beyond name-calling. Peter calls it a "fiery trial" (4:12) and indicates that it is being inflicted on Christians elsewhere (5:9). This seems to speak of violent opposition, which the Christians must endure even as Christ endured the suffering inflicted on Him (2:21-23). They must not meet violence with violence, but simply go on doing right (3:9-12).

A. Blessing, Fear, Heart, and Hope (3:13-15)

13, 14. And who is he that will harm you, if ye be followers of that which is good? But and if ye suffer for righteousness' sake, happy are ye: and be not afraid of their terror, neither be troubled.

The best way to prevent *harm*, either to body or to reputation, is simply to do right. No one can justly attack you for that.

But sometimes doing right is not enough to keep you from being mistreated. People may

---

How to Say It

BACCHANALIA. Bah-keh-*nail*-yuh.
FORNICATION. for-neh-*kay*-shun.
GETHSEMANE. Geth-*sem*-uh-nee (G as in *get*).
JEREMIAH. Jair-uh-*my*-uh.
PHILIPPIANS. Fih-*lip*-ee-unz.

abuse you just because your conduct highlights their own evil. In that case their attack is a compliment. Rather than being upset or troubled, rejoice that your right conduct brings forth opposition (Acts 5:41).

15. But sanctify the Lord God in your hearts: and be ready always to give an answer to every man that asketh you a reason of the hope that is in you, with meekness and fear.

Your opponents have hurt you in some way— physically, emotionally, or financially. They can't understand why you still smile. So you explain, if you have their attention. In your heart you have sanctified *the Lord God.* You have given Him first place. In His own time He will reward you. You can wait for His time because He is Lord forever and you will live forever, too. *The hope that is in you* will surely be realized, for God is unconquerable.

You explain all this to the questioner *with meekness* (gentleness) and *fear.* Again we must note that there are two kinds of fear. You are not afraid of your opponents (v. 14), but you answer the questioner with reverence before God, who is far above all of us on earth. [See question #2, page 56.]

B. Conscience, Shame, God's Will, and Suffering (3:16, 17)

16. Having a good conscience; that, whereas they speak evil of you, as of evildoers, they may be ashamed that falsely accuse your good conversation in Christ.

Keep your *conscience* clear by doing right— doing it so continuously and so obviously that those who falsely *speak evil* of your good way of life will be *ashamed* of their falsehood. [See question #3, page 56.] This repeats and emphasizes what we read in 1 Peter 2:12. Again, *conversation* refers to one's lifestyle.

LIVING ABOVE CRITICISM

During the Cold War thousands of East Germans escaped Communist repression by crossing the border into West Berlin. In response to calls for sealing the border, Walter Ulbricht, Communist Party leader, promised in 1961 that it would not happen. Less than two months later the infamous Berlin Wall arose, complete with minefields and watchtowers, to make sure no one escaped from the "worker's paradise."

Democratic Socialists are today's successors to the old Communist Party. They are still condemned for the broken promise regarding the Wall. People are calling on the Party to admit its past inhumanity and apologize for its actions. The past will be hard to live down: evidence of Communism's sins is found in pieces of the Wall

in various places around the world and at the Berlin memorial, where a section of the Wall still stands amidst a re-created section of the "death strip" where hundreds were murdered as they tried to escape.

Those sins should long be remembered lest they be committed again. But the evil claims spoken against the church in Peter's day were unfounded. How should Christians respond? Peter says to live so that the charges are obviously groundless, accept the world's attack as proof the church is doing what is right, and share your hope in Christ. Two thousand years later God's plan remains the same for us.   —C. R. B.

17. For it is better, if the will of God be so, that ye suffer for well doing, than for evildoing.

Most would agree that suffering for evildoing is a good thing; perhaps the one suffering will learn to stop doing evil! But suffering for doing good is more difficult to accept. The constant question in such cases is "why?" The suffering of Job is one example. (See also Judges 6:13.) Peter deals with this issue in more depth in 4:12-19 (not in today's text). Christ suffered and so shall we (but not in all the same ways). [See question #4, page 56.]

C. Self-Control, Prayer, Love, and Sin (4:7-9)

7. But the end of all things is at hand: be ye therefore sober, and watch unto prayer.

The end of all things speaks of the end of the present creation as associated with the Lord's return (cf. 2 Peter 3:10). We sometimes think that if something is *at hand,* then we can expect it right away. But *at hand* can easily indicate that the event can happen at any time. Thus, the Lord's return has been *at hand* ever since Peter's day— and still it can happen at any time. By encouraging his readers to *watch unto prayer,* perhaps Peter is thinking back to his own failure in this regard in the Garden of Gethsemane (Matthew 26:40, 41).

8. And above all things have fervent charity among yourselves: for charity shall cover the multitude of sins.

Charity is a word that has changed in meaning over the centuries. Today, charity means "giving to the needy." But when the *King James Version* was made it referred to the emotion that prompts such giving. Thus today we might say "love" instead of "charity."

Love among Christians ought to be *fervent*—enthusiastic, deep, and constant (see 1 Peter 1:22). Such love *shall cover the multitude of sins* in several ways. Such a love "thinketh no evil" (1 Corinthians 13:5); it is able to forgive (Matthew

18:21, 22); it persuades others to stop sinning (James 5:19, 20).

HOW BROTHERS SHOULD TREAT EACH OTHER

Gary Klahr met Steven Barbin when Steven was twenty-one and Gary was twenty-four. They struck up one of those special friendships that seems to "click" automatically. Gary was best man at Steven's wedding. Once he even gave Steven a photograph inscribed, "You are truly my brother."

Twenty-five years later, they discovered from an adoption caseworker that they *really are* brothers! It turns out that they were two of nine children (out of thirteen) whose parents had given them up for adoption. For twenty-five years they had not known the truth but had acted in the spirit of true brotherhood anyway.

We don't always "click" in our relationships with other Christians. In fact, sometimes we have real trouble with them! Peter tells us how to be resolve such conflicts: prayerfully, seriously develop good intentions toward others; offer loving forgiveness when it is needed; and demonstrate generous hospitality toward fellow Christians. This is the attitude we show to "best friends," and it *should* characterize our relationships with other Christians. The fact that Peter had to admonish his readers (and us) in this regard indicates how important these Christian graces are for the well-being of the family of God.   —C. R. B.

9. Use hospitality one to another without grudging.

What Peter stresses here is nothing new (see Romans 12:13; Hebrews 13:2; 3 John 5, 6; contrast 2 John 10, 11), but it does bear repeating. *Hospitality* to fellow Christians is especially important in a time of persecution, and persecution in Asia Minor is severe enough to be called a "fiery trial" (1 Peter 4:12). Christians may be afraid to go home because hostile neighbors are waiting to meet them with physical violence. A Christian's home might even be destroyed by a mob of persecutors. The need to offer hope to fellow Christians *without grudging* is part of our Christian witness as well (see Philippians 2:14).

D. Gifts, Grace, Speaking, and Serving (4:10, 11)

10. As every man hath received the gift, even so minister the same one to another, as good stewards of the manifold grace of God.

Whatever spiritual gifts, talents, or abilities you have are gifts from God. God does not give them to us to be used selfishly, however, but for the benefit of others. You can find lists of spiritual gifts in Romans 12; 1 Corinthians 12; and Ephesians 4.

Visual for lessons 6 and 12. *This visual suggests an application of the message of 1 Peter 4:7-11. Have the class suggest other specific acts of love.*

11. If any man speak, let him speak as the oracles of God; if any man minister, let him do it as of the ability which God giveth; that God in all things may be glorified through Jesus Christ: to whom be praise and dominion for ever and ever. Amen.

The context of the opening command is that of speech a preacher or teacher uses when we assemble for worship. What sobering challenge it is to ensure that they *speak as the oracles of God!* This includes knowing, understanding, and following what God says in the Bible. Many who are not called to speak in this way are able to *minister*, to help others in various ways (v. 10, above). Each helpful Christian should let it be known that it is God who makes him or her able to help. Thus through the Christians and through Christ the credit will be given to God, for *praise and dominion* properly belong to God *for ever and ever.*

III. Do Right With Awareness (1 Peter 5:6-10)

The title of our lesson is, "Set a Good Example." Naturally this puts strong emphasis on doing right, for that is the way to set a good example. But people who do right face a strong temptation to become proud of their goodness, like the Pharisee whose prayer consisted of telling God how good that Pharisee thought himself to be (Luke 18:11, 12). So the last section of our text reminds us to be humble and trust in God rather than in ourselves.

A. Trust God to Exalt You (v. 6)

6. Humble yourselves therefore under the mighty hand of God, that he may exalt you in due time.

The word *therefore* looks back to the verse before this, which ends by saying, "God resisteth the proud, and giveth grace to the humble." *Therefore* we had better be among the humble, for God's grace is better than anything we can gain for ourselves. As Peter reflects on humility and our coming exaltation, perhaps he is recalling the Master's teaching in this regard of some thirty years previous (see Matthew 23:12).

B. Trust God to Care for You (v. 7)

7. Casting all your care upon him; for he careth for you.

Remember that Peter is writing to people who are enduring a "fiery trial" of persecution (1 Peter 4:12). They may be overwhelmed with care, but God is not. It is good to remember this when our own cares seem overwhelming (Psalm 55:22; Luke 12:22).

C. Trust God and Resist the Devil (vv. 8, 9)

8. Be sober, be vigilant; because your adversary the devil, as a roaring lion, walketh about, seeking whom he may devour.

Casting all our care on God does not mean we become careless. If you give *the devil* a chance, he, like a *roaring lion,* will *devour* you (cf. Psalm 22:13; Jeremiah 51:34). This calls for vigilance, alertness. Trust God, yes; but don't expect Him to keep you safe when you recklessly deliver yourself right into the enemy's camp. [See question #5, page 56.]

9. Whom resist steadfast in the faith, knowing that the same afflictions are accomplished in your brethren that are in the world.

The devil is not so terrible as some people think. He gains great power by enslaving weaklings who surrender to him. If you strongly *resist* him, he runs away (James 4:7). It is encouraging

Home Daily Bible Readings

Monday, Oct. 6—Be Zealous in Serving God (Romans 12:9-18)

Tuesday, Oct. 7—Conduct Yourselves Honorably (1 Peter 2:11-17)

Wednesday, Oct. 8—Don't Repay Evil for Evil (1 Peter 3:8-12)

Thursday, Oct. 9—Be Ready With a Gentle Defense (1 Peter 3:13-22)

Friday, Oct. 10—Live by the Will of God (1 Peter 4:1-6)

Saturday, Oct. 11—Maintain Love for One Another (1 Peter 4:7-11)

Sunday, Oct. 12—Keep Alert, Resist the Devil (1 Peter 5:7-14)

to know that *your brethren* all over *the world* are fighting and winning the same spiritual battle that you are.

D. Trust God to Perfect You (v. 10)

10. But the God of all grace, who hath called us into his eternal glory by Christ Jesus, after that ye have suffered a while, make you perfect, stablish, strengthen, settle you.

Verses 6 and 7 call us to trust in *God,* but verses 8 and 9 emphasize our own responsibility. Then we come to verse 10, the verse of blessed assurance. His *grace* is His favor that we do not deserve, favor purchased by the death of Christ. If in our hearts we remain truly devoted to Him, He graciously forgives our faults and failures. The *eternal glory by Christ Jesus* into which He has *called us* surely shall come after we *have suffered a while.* But we are not there yet. When those sufferings come we greet them with joy because we know they can make us better (Romans 5:3-5). In the meantime we fix our eyes on *the God of all grace* who prepares us for eternal glory. [See question #6, page 56.]

Conclusion

A. Washing Our Feet

We do set a good example most of the time, don't we? But did you, today or yesterday or last week, stumble into some small wrong? Even Jesus' dearest disciples did that. On the eve of the day of His death they lapsed into selfish wrangling (Luke 22:24). Jesus rebuked them with an object lesson for the ages. He, the Lord and Master, took a basin of water and took the place of a lowly slave as He washed their dirty feet (John 13:1-17).

When we came to the Lord, God washed away our sins and made us clean (Acts 22:16). Yet we walk in an unclean world and dirty ourselves with small wrongs. Even so, God is still ready to wash us: "If we confess our sins, he is faithful and just to forgive us our sins, and to cleanse us from all unrighteousness" (1 John 1:9). As God set an example of service to us, let us set an example as well.

B. Prayer

Forgive us, Father. How we do dirty ourselves! How we thank You for Your cleansing day by day. And for today and tomorrow we pray for faith, wisdom, and courage to walk without fouling ourselves again. In Jesus' name, amen.

C. Thought to Remember

Be a "pattern to them . . . to life everlasting" (1 Timothy 1:16).

Learning by Doing

This page contains an alternative lesson plan emphasizing learning activities.
Classes desiring such student involvement will find these suggestions helpful.

Learning Goals

After this lesson each student will be able to:

1. Tell some ways Peter says a Christian can set a good example.

2. Explain why setting a good example is important for the sake of other believers and also unbelievers.

3. Spend time with a new Christian and give him or her guidance and encouragement.

Into the Lesson

In preparation for the application section of this week's lesson, secure a list of the church's new Christians in the past year. To begin, move the class into groups of four or five. Say, "This week's lesson is called, 'Set a Good Example.' To help us get started, I would like each small group to prepare a twenty-second radio commercial. We all have heard radio commercials trying to encourage us to eat at a certain restaurant or to buy a certain product. What we don't hear are commercials that encourage us to be good examples for others or simply to do something that is good. Discuss in your group what it is you want to encourage. Then prepare your commercial to present to the class."

Allow six to eight minutes for each group to prepare the commercial. Then ask the groups to present their commercials. Say, "We've heard some very creative commercials encouraging us to set a good example. Our text today describes ways Christians can be an example for others. Turn to 1 Peter 2, and let's see how God encourages us to set a good example."

Into the Word

Keep the same small groups for this section of the lesson. Ask a class member to stand and read the lesson text aloud. Then give each group a copy of the questions below. Say, "As we look carefully at what the lesson text says, answer each of the questions on this sheet. I will give you about ten minutes." Prepare the following questions on the handout.

1. What are some ways Peter says a Christian can set a good example? *(Abstain from fleshly lusts, 2:11; have an honest conversation [i.e., way of life], 2:12; be sober, 4:7.)*

2. What attitudes should Christians have when they suffer for "well doing" (3:17)? *(Happy, not afraid or troubled, 3:14.)*

3. In what sense does Peter want us to be prepared? *("Be ready always to give an answer," 3:15.)*

4. How does a "good conversation" influence evildoers who speak evil of you? *("They may be ashamed that falsely accuse your good conversation," 3:16.)*

5. In light of the coming "end of all things," what does Peter urge Christians to do? *("Be . . . sober, and watch unto prayer," 4:7.)*

6. How are Christians to use the gifts they receive from God? *("Minister the same one to another, as good stewards," 4:10.)*

7. What is the ultimate purpose of the gift received by Christians? *("God . . . may be glorified through Jesus Christ," 4:11.)*

8. How are the two words for *care* in 1 Peter 5:7 used differently? *("Your care" refers to their trials and persecution; "He careth" refers to God's compassion for His own.)*

9. What warning does Peter give these Christians in light of the plea to "be vigilant," 5:8? *(The devil is "seeking whom he may devour.")*

10. What positive benefits come to those who "suffered a while," 5:10? *(God will "make you perfect, stablish, strengthen, settle you.")*

Into Life

Answer the questions with the class. Then bring the whole class together. Write on the chalkboard, "Why Be Good?" Below that label two columns: "Believers" and "Unbelievers." Ask, "Why should Christians set a good example for believers, and why should they set a good example for unbelievers?" Write in the proper column each suggested answer.

Prior to class, prepare a "Compassion Covenant" sheet for each student. Include spaces for name, date, person to be encouraged, opportunity to spend time, specific guidance to share, and specific encouragement to give. Ask the following two questions and write suggested answers on the board: "What are some ways to encourage a new Christian?" "What are some ways to guide a new Christian?" Distribute the "covenant" sheet and the list of new Christians. Say, "Select one new Christian to spend time with this week, providing both guidance and encouragement. Fill in the information on your 'covenant' and sign your name." After giving a few minutes to complete the form, make a prayer circle and ask for God's blessing on the covenants made today.

Let's Talk It Over

The questions on this page are designed to promote discussion of the lesson by the class and to encourage application of the lesson Scriptures. The answers provided are only discussion starters. Let your class talk it over from there.

1. What can the church do to prepare believers to stand strong when being teased or persecuted?

Christians need to understand that godly behavior is likely to cause a response. Some will respectfully inquire about why a person wants to be a Christian. Others will react with disdain.

Young Christians need to be encouraged to take a stand. They must be taught that opposition is to be expected. They need sound instruction in what they believe and in how to present that. They need good models of how to turn an attack into an opportunity to share Christ. Ask the class to list the ways Christians can turn trying circumstances into opportunities to introduce others to the Savior. (See 1 Peter 2:13-25; 4:4, 12-16, 19 and John 15:18-25.) You could also ask the class to name individuals in the church who are especially good models from whom other Christians can learn.

2. What is a response Christians can prepare in advance to give whenever he or she is being ridiculed or persecuted?

When a Christian is being accused or attacked, it is important to realize that one of the questions in the persecutor's mind is, "Why do you continue to live this way?" But in the emotion of the moment, the believer may find it difficult to explain the reason for his or her faith. For that reason, Christians ought to prepare in advance a short testimony to answer this question, explaining what Christ has done in their lives. This can open a door to sharing what He can do for the persecutor. Ask volunteers in your class to suggest what they might say in their own testimonies. Others in the class can learn from their examples.

3. Why is "having a good conscience" important to ensure that a Christian's witness sounds and looks credible to unbelievers, particularly those who are hostile?

Peter implies that having a good conscience is important in showing the accuser the error of his or her criticisms. The person who is living a godly life doesn't have a conscience that is always worrying about being found out and having the message compromised. When the accused cannot back up the accusations, the accuser will be ashamed for falsely accusing the Christian of any wrongdoing.

4. Suppose a Christian friend is being discriminated against at work because of his faith. After one more episode, he comes to you for advice. "It's just not fair!" he says. How do you answer?

Persecution is, of course, unfair. No one should ever suffer for doing right. Focusing on the way Jesus' own teaching and handling of persecution and unfairness will help us follow His example (see Mark 10:29-31; 1 Peter 3:8-16). Remember that a thief (Luke 23:40-43) and a centurion (Luke 23:47) were affected positively by the way Jesus graciously dealt with His most difficult hour.

5. What can Christians do collectively and individually to protect themselves from the devil's tactics?

Satan stalks all Christians like a lion, looking for the weakest individual. Peter says the secret in resisting the attacks of Satan is to be strong, self-controlled, and alert; this requires constant attention to one's worship, devotional, and prayer life.

In the animal world, some species "circle up" to protect the weaker members from an attacking lion. Likewise, Christians can come to the aid of those being attacked. When one finds himself or herself "all alone" in a specific circumstance, a Christian can remember all the other Christians who have remained strong all around the world. Jesus set examples for us during His own time of testing (see question #4), as did the early disciples (e.g., Stephen in Acts 7).

6. What other promises can we commit to memory that will keep us from losing heart even in the face of the toughest situations? Why are these promises important?

Peter reminds us that God is full of grace and always supplies what we need. Just when we begin to doubt our ability to hold on any longer, God provides strength and sufficient blessings (Romans 8:26-28; Philippians 4:19). If the Christian felt strong in every situation, he or she would sense no need for God and would soon start praising self and relying on personal strength. When the Christian acknowledges weakness, then he or she is very excited about praising the God who supplies all strength for both the good times and the bad. (See 2 Corinthians 12:7-10.)

Grow in Faith

DEVOTIONAL READING: Ephesians 3:14-21.

BACKGROUND SCRIPTURE: 2 Peter 1.

PRINTED TEXT: 2 Peter 1:3-15.

2 Peter 1:3-15

3 According as his divine power hath given unto us all things that pertain unto life and godliness, through the knowledge of him that hath called us to glory and virtue:

4 Whereby are given unto us exceeding great and precious promises; that by these ye might be partakers of the divine nature, having escaped the corruption that is in the world through lust.

5 And besides this, giving all diligence, add to your faith virtue; and to virtue, knowledge;

6 And to knowledge, temperance; and to temperance, patience; and to patience, godliness;

7 And to godliness, brotherly kindness; and to brotherly kindness, charity.

8 For if these things be in you, and abound, they make you that ye shall neither be barren nor unfruitful in the knowledge of our Lord Jesus Christ.

9 But he that lacketh these things is blind, and cannot see afar off, and hath forgotten that he was purged from his old sins.

10 Wherefore the rather, brethren, give diligence to make your calling and election sure: for if ye do these things, ye shall never fall:

11 For so an entrance shall be ministered unto you abundantly into the everlasting kingdom of our Lord and Saviour Jesus Christ.

12 Wherefore I will not be negligent to put you always in remembrance of these things, though ye know them, and be established in the present truth.

13 Yea, I think it meet, as long as I am in this tabernacle, to stir you up by putting you in remembrance;

14 Knowing that shortly I must put off this my tabernacle, even as our Lord Jesus Christ hath showed me.

15 Moreover I will endeavor that ye may be able after my decease to have these things always in remembrance.

Oct 19

GOLDEN TEXT: According as his divine power hath given unto us all things that pertain unto life and godliness, through the knowledge of him that hath called us to glory and virtue.—2 Peter 1:3.

Faith Faces the World
Unit 2: Live in Hope
(Lessons 5-8)

Lesson Aims

After this lesson each student should be able to:

1. Cite the characteristics of a mature Christian as described in today's text.

2. Identify aspects in his or her life that help encourage Christian growth.

3. Make arrangements with another student to hold each other accountable for working on a specific area of growth.

Lesson Outline

INTRODUCTION
    A. No-Learners in the Church
    B. Lesson Background
  I. GOD'S GIFTS (2 Peter 1:3, 4)
    A. His Power (v. 3)
      Ingredients of "The Good Life"
    B. His Promises (v. 4)
 II. GOD'S EXPECTATIONS (2 Peter 1:5-9)
    A. The Means (vv. 5-7)
    B. The Ends (vv. 8, 9)
III. OUR REWARD (2 Peter 1:10, 11)
    A. Calling and Election (v. 10)
    B. Welcome and Kingdom (v. 11)
IV. PETER'S PLEA (2 Peter 1:12-15)
    A. Repeated Reminder (v. 12)
    B. Limited Time (vv. 13, 14)
      Remember . . . and Remember
    C. Never Forget (v. 15)
CONCLUSION
    A. Learners, Doers, and Repeaters
    B. Summary
    C. Prayer
    D. Thought to Remember

Introduction

Watching the children pour out of a third-grade classroom, I was surprised to see one student taller than I was, though I was a full-grown man. Later I asked the teacher, "Why is that big boy in third grade?"

She answered with a half-smile. "Because he's too big to sit in a first-grade seat where he belongs. He can't even read at first-grade level."

"What kind of a handicap does he have?"

"Who knows? His eyesight and hearing are normal. We've had them checked."

"What about his IQ?"

"He doesn't have one. With a psychiatrist as with a teacher, he has one answer to every question: 'I don't know.'"

"So he's just mentally incompetent?"

"I don't think so. He seems normal on the playground. He plays sports with the big boys—soccer, basketball, or softball, you name it."

"So it's only in the classroom that you'd call him a slow learner?"

"I don't call him a slow learner," the teacher snapped. "He's a no-learner!"

A. No-Learners in the Church

Are there any no-learners in your church? The first-century church had some. A wise leader wrote, "When for the time ye ought to be teachers, ye have need that one teach you again which be the first principles of the oracles of God; and are become such as have need of milk, and not of strong meat. For every one that useth milk is unskilful in the word of righteousness: for he is a babe" (Hebrews 5:12, 13).

We all know some people like that in our twenty-first-century churches. They are not nitwits. They are well-informed and capable farmers, mechanics, and professional people. Such folks are eager to learn ever more about their trades and professions, but have no similar desire to grow in Christianity. They are saved! What more can anyone want? So they sit through sermons without listening and through Bible lessons without learning.

The apostle Peter will not have such complacency. As we shall see in our text, he exhorts every Christian to become a better Christian. Paul likewise calls us to keep on improving "till we all come . . . unto a perfect man, unto the measure of the stature of the fulness of Christ" (Ephesians 4:13). Until we all become like Jesus Himself! What boundless room we all have for Christian growth!

B. Lesson Background

The text we consider this week is from "Simon Peter, a servant and an apostle of Jesus Christ" (2 Peter 1:1). It was originally sent "to them that have obtained like precious faith with us" (1:1). That is, it was addressed to Christians like us. Exactly who they were and to which churches they belonged, we cannot say. They were aware of some of the apostle Paul's writings (3:15). Either they had received letters from Paul or Paul's letters to some other churches had been shared with them. Apparently, however, they had not taken Paul's instructions to heart; some of Peter's readers were complacent, self-satisfied, and not eager to improve themselves and the church.

But was there ever a time when the church did not have self-satisfied members? Perhaps we can profit most from our text by considering today's lesson against the background of the church and Christians as we see them today. Then we can make today some of the improvements that Peter recommended two thousand years ago.

I. God's Gifts
(2 Peter 1:3, 4)

Before speaking of what we need to do to grow in faith, Peter reminds us of what God already has done for us. Let us, then, first look at God's gifts that underlie and encourage the growth that He expects.

A. His Power (v. 3)

3. According as his divine power hath given unto us all things that pertain unto life and godliness, through the knowledge of him that hath called us to glory and virtue.

We are not alone in caring for ourselves and building the kind of character that Peter recommends. God has given us all the essential materials we need for *life and godliness.* For physical *life* we need food, clothing, shelter, and the like. These are rightly seen as God's gifts (Matthew 6:25-33). We suspect, however, that Peter is talking about more than physical life. This is the "everlasting life," the "abundant life," that Jesus came to bring (John 3:16; 5:24; 10:10).

For *godliness* we need the guidance of God's own Word, and God has given us that, too. It is His Word that provides us *the knowledge of him that hath called us to glory and virtue.* This understanding doesn't come through personal visions, crystal balls, or horoscopes—it comes through the written Word. The more we study that Word, the more we come to realize how much He has given us in calling *us to glory and virtue.* When we think about this "glory and virtue," we must be careful to understand that this is referring to God's own "glory and virtue," and not ours! It is not until we come to recognize the glory and virtue (or goodness) of God do we hear and respond to His call. [See question #1, page 64.]

Virtue here translates a Greek word that can mean almost any kind of goodness. It is used of the goodness of God, the goodness of people on earth, the goodness of a cow or a sheep, even the goodness of a table or chair. It is fitting, then, that human beings made in the image of God are called, not only to virtue, but also to godliness (also v. 6, below). God Himself is the model for our goodness. We cannot hope or even wish to match His power and glory, but in our human relations we can aspire to God's own perfection (Matthew 5:48). Can we then be satisfied with anything less?

INGREDIENTS OF "THE GOOD LIFE"

Have you ever felt like all the "stuff" you have is more of a burden than a blessing? Actor Tim Robbins appeared on television some time ago, talking about "downsizing" his life. He said he was getting rid of stuff he didn't need, such as voice mail. When asked how people would contact him, he said, "They'll have to call me when I'm home." The audience cheered!

The late twentieth century brought us gadgets by the score that soon became "necessities" for many: computers, cell phones, and laptops, for example. We learned a new vocabulary: PDAs, CDs, DVDs, RAM, etc. High-powered executives—and even middle-school students!—found they couldn't function without a cell phone. But we also found that last year's computer wasn't fast enough and didn't have enough memory for all the new programs we wanted to use. Last year's cell phone was a bit bulky, so we "needed" a new, smaller one. Social philosophers have been warning us for decades that technology is not a savior; on the contrary, it can send life spinning out of control.

What a marvelous contrast is the text for today! The foundational provisions God makes for us, accompanied by His wonderful promises—that's what makes life good. Then, when we respond faithfully and begin to grow in the Christian graces mentioned in our text, that's when life *really* takes on meaning! —C. R. B.

B. His Promises (v. 4)

4. Whereby are given unto us exceeding great and precious promises; that by these ye might be partakers of the divine nature, having escaped the corruption that is in the world through lust.

God's greatest gifts to us are His *exceeding great and precious promises.* According to those promises we become *partakers of the divine nature,* meaning that we become children of God (Galatians 3:26), growing more and more like Jesus (Ephesians 4:13). Quarrels, fighting, and other kinds of *corruption* come from our lusts,

---

How to Say It

COLOSSIANS. Kuh-*losh*-unz.
CORINTHIANS. Kor-*in*-thee-unz (*th* as in *thin*).
EPHESIANS. Ee-*fee*-zhunz.
MASAAKI. Mah-sah-*ah*-key.
PHILIPPIANS. Fih-*lip*-ee-unz.

our selfish desires for money, pleasure, power, or popularity. We read about that in our lesson for September 28 (James 4:1-4). In becoming God's children, we escape from such corruption. Our thinking is turned way from evil; we think on things that are good (Philippians 4:8).

II. God's Expectations
(2 Peter 1:5-9)

God gives us all we need for life and godliness (v. 3); in so doing, He sets us free from worldly corruption and makes us His children (v. 4). We respond with gratitude, of course, and we show our gratitude by acting as God's children ought to act. That means we keep growing in all the good traits of Christian character.

A. The Means (vv. 5-7)

5. And besides this, giving all diligence, add to your faith virtue; and to virtue, knowledge.

Diligence is earnest and continuing effort. That is what we use in trying to be what God's children ought to be. We have *faith*, of course; we couldn't be Christians without it. To that we add *virtue*. As noted above in verse 3, that means goodness—every kind of goodness the children of God ought to have. But how can we add goodness to our character and our living unless we know what is good and what is bad? We get that kind of *knowledge* by reading the Bible. If we read several chapters of it every day, we shall not pass many days without seeing something that is good for us to do. [See question #2, page 64.]

6. And to knowledge, temperance; and to temperance, patience; and to patience, godliness.

Temperance is moderation. Some students translate it "self-control." With that added to our

personality, we keep a cool head in all situations and we control our behavior (cf. 2 Corinthians 12:20; Ephesians 4:25-32; Colossians 3:8; 1 Timothy 2:8). We keep our voice down as we reason with another, trying to win him or her to the same kind of goodness. *Patience* is not just waiting quietly and doing nothing. The same Greek word is sometimes translated "steadfastness" or "perseverance." This is the quality of Christian character that keeps us earnestly doing and promoting what is right, but doing it with temperance and self-control, not with violence (James 5:7-11). *Godliness* is a lifestyle consistent with reverence for our awesome God, a lifestyle designed to please Him (see 2 Peter 1:3, above). Indeed, knowledge of truth leads to godliness (cf. Titus 1:1).

7. And to godliness, brotherly kindness; and to brotherly kindness, charity.

Brotherly kindness is the affectionate mutual helpfulness seen in blood siblings at their best. Peter extends the idea to all Christianity (cf. 2 Corinthians 6:6; Galatians 5:22; Colossians 3:12). The crowning feature of this whole list is *charity*, which in modern English we would call "love" (see page 52). This is not romantic love—especially not the idealistic romance of novels and movies. This is love like that of God for the needy world (John 3:16). This is a heartfelt wish to do what is best for others, even at great cost to oneself. [See question #3, page 64.]

B. The Ends (vv. 8, 9)

8. For if these things be in you, and abound, they make you that ye shall neither be barren nor unfruitful in the knowledge of our Lord Jesus Christ.

If we keep on adding knowledge to our faith, we shall come to greater *knowledge of our Lord Jesus Christ* and His will. But such knowledge in and of itself is worthless—it needs to lead us to fruitful service. As we continue to add the things listed in verses 5-9 above, we shall find more and more opportunities to help people who need help.

9. But he that lacketh these things is blind, and cannot see afar off, and hath forgotten that he was purged from his old sins.

He that lacketh these things is blind and unproductive in the Lord's work. Jesus had a lot to say about the dangers of spiritual blindness (Matthew 23:16-19). A person so afflicted cannot look ahead and catch a vision of God's glory to which he or she is called (1 Peter 1:3, above). Therefore he or she is not motivated by the hope of glory (Colossians 1:27). Neither can such a person look back and recall *that he was purged from his old sins.* This person is therefore not motivated by gratitude for this cleansing, and sees no reason to work for the Lord. Such a person is idle.

Spiritual Addition

Faith
+ *Virtue*
+ *Knowledge*
+ *Temperance*
+ *Patience*
+ *Godliness*
+ *Brotherly Kindness*
+ *Charity*

Maturity

Visual for lesson 7

The visual for today's lesson provides a convenient summary of the qualities cited in verses 5-7.

III. Our Reward
(2 Peter 1:10, 11)

As we have just seen, the dangers of neglecting to grow in the Christian life are real and sobering. But Peter doesn't want merely to point out the negative. The positive aspects of Christian growth have magnificent eternal consequences!

A. Calling and Election (v. 10)

10. Wherefore the rather, brethren, give diligence to make your calling and election sure: for if ye do these things, ye shall never fall.

Rather than being blind and idle like the person described in verse 9, every Christian is to make his or her *calling and election sure*. We do this by allowing God to work through us (Philippians 2:12, 13). It is God who saves us; but He does not do it against our will. We are not saved by any good works we do, but neither are we saved without doing any good works. God saves us by His grace and through our faith (Ephesians 2:8, 9), but our faith is dead unless it causes us to do something (James 2:17). So Peter urges us to add to our faith all the good things listed in verses 5-7. That is the way to make our salvation sure, *for if ye do these things, ye shall never fall!* [See question #4, page 64.]

B. Welcome and Kingdom (v. 11)

11. For so an entrance shall be ministered unto you abundantly into the everlasting kingdom of our Lord and Saviour Jesus Christ.

How can we be sure of being in Christ's *everlasting kingdom?* In addition to having faith in King Jesus, we simply obey Him, do His will, and serve Him (John 14:15). Evidence of our allegiance is seen in all the things that Peter urges us to add to our faith in 2 Peter 1:5-7, above. When we have these in abundance, we are constant in our service to Christ (v. 8), and there can be no doubt about our citizenship in His kingdom.

IV. Peter's Plea
(2 Peter 1:12-15)

Simon Peter never went to teacher's college (Acts 4:13), but he understood the importance of repetition in Christian education. He wants us to know Christian principles so well that we apply them automatically and come up with the right answers.

A. Repeated Reminder (v. 12)

12. Wherefore I will not be negligent to put you always in remembrance of these things, though ye know them, and be established in the present truth.

These things that Peter is teaching (vv. 5-7) were not new to first-century Christians, and they are not new to us. But they are so important to good Christian living (vv. 8, 9) and so important to citizenship in Heaven (vv. 10, 11) that Peter repeats them to people who already *know* them.

B. Limited Time (vv. 13, 14)

13. Yea, I think it meet, as long as I am in this tabernacle, to stir you up by putting you in remembrance.

A *tabernacle* is a temporary structure (cf. Exodus 26). Peter's tabernacle as he writes is his physical body. (Paul uses the same metaphor in 2 Corinthians 5:1.) Peter thinks it is proper to continue reminding his readers of what they already know as long as he is living in that body and is able to write. His purpose is not just to repeat well-known words; it is *to stir* them *up*, and to stir us up—to motivate every Christian to do what is taught in this text.

REMEMBER . . . AND REMEMBER

The year was 1944. Two students at a Christian college in Texas were engaged to be married. They were deeply in love, but their peers and professors discouraged the interracial relationship. Anne was a white American. Her fiance, Masaaki, was also an American but of Japanese descent. In those times in America anyone of Japanese ancestry was looked upon with great suspicion. Eventually the force of this prejudice drove them apart.

In the years to come each married someone else, raised a family, and was eventually widowed. But "first loves" have a way of being remembered. Now single again, Masaaki tracked Anne down using the Internet. Fifty-six years after they had parted, Masaaki and Anne married, with their families celebrating the event at their sides. Anne said of the phone call when she first heard Masaaki's voice again, "I knew instantly that he wanted me back. During all those years he was always in the back of my mind."

Peter says of the Lord, who should be the first love of our hearts and spirits, that He should ever be in the back of our minds, always directing our thoughts and behavior. We are to remember (and remember . . . and remember . . .) that we are the bride of Christ, whose love for us never dims or fades. And neither should our love for Him.   —C. R. B.

14. Knowing that shortly I must put off this my tabernacle, even as our Lord Jesus Christ hath showed me.

Peter knows his time for teaching is short; he will not live much longer. *Jesus* Himself had told him that. John 21:18, 19 records a time when Jesus had warned that enemies of the cross would put Peter to death. Peter remembers the warning, and he means to make good use of the time he has on earth. (Tradition has it that Peter was crucified in Rome.)

C. Never Forget (v. 15)

15. Moreover I will endeavor that ye may be able after my decease to have these things always in remembrance.

Peter is writing about things that are vastly important to Christians living on earth (v. 8) for their eternal life in Heaven (vv. 10, 11). He intends to repeat *these things* so that his readers will not forget them after his death. Even today they are fresh in our memory. If we heed them well, they will guide us through our earthly life and ensure our entrance into the kingdom eternal (v. 11). [See question #5, page 64.]

Conclusion

We introduced this lesson by taking note of slow learners and no-learners in the church. Most churches have some of them. These people are Christians, they say, and that is enough. They seem to have no desire to be moving upward toward "the measure of the stature of the fulness of Christ" (Ephesians 4:13). But there is another side of the picture.

A. Learners, Doers, and Repeaters

Mary Ann thinks her class of third graders is the best in the Sunday school. "These little people are so eager," she says. "They soak up facts and Bible stories like so many sponges. This is

---

Home Daily Bible Readings

Monday, Oct. 13—Trust God, Send Out Roots (Jeremiah 17:5-10)

Tuesday, Oct. 14—The Righteous Grow, Produce Fruit (Psalm 92:5-15)

Wednesday, Oct. 15—Be Rooted and Grounded in Christ (Ephesians 3:14-21)

Thursday, Oct. 16—Live in the Spirit (Romans 8:9-17)

Friday, Oct. 17—Support Your Faith With Goodness (2 Peter 1:1-7)

Saturday, Oct. 18—Eagerly Confirm Your Call (2 Peter 1:8-15)

Sunday, Oct. 19—Be Attentive to the Prophetic Message (2 Peter 1:16-21)

---

the learning-est class!" And we remember that Jesus said, "Except ye be converted, and become as little children, ye shall not enter into the kingdom of heaven" (Matthew 18:3).

Brandon thinks his class is the best in the Sunday school. His students are middle-aged, prime-of-life people. On Saturday they may visit the church to pick up litter, weed the flower beds, or mow the lawn. This is the class that sends a welcoming committee to greet newcomers in the neighborhood. Brandon says they have been learning for a long time, and now they are the doing-est class. From an earlier lesson we remember that James exhorts all of us to be "doers of the word, and not hearers only" (James 1:22).

Nels teaches the old folks' class, and he thinks that is the best class of all. Seldom does he startle his students with anything they have not heard before, but they love to go over passages they learned long ago. When the teacher wants to call attention to a verse of Scripture, he quotes its opening words and pauses. Half a dozen voices in unison finish the verse. The old folks do take an interest in the few things they hear for the first time, but their greater delight is in recalling and repeating what they learned long ago. That does not mean the old folks are not doers. Those who are physically able are right there alongside the younger men and women whenever the church has ministries that need done.

B. Summary

The children may be the fastest learners, and they are learning what Christians do as well as what Christians know. The middle-agers may be the greatest doers, and they are learning from their doing as well as from the Bible. The old folks grow stronger spiritually as they review their learning. If their doing is limited by failing strength, it is refined by growing wisdom. So in your church and my church the slow learners and no-learners are outnumbered by the learners, doers, and repeaters—God's work is being done as they grow in faith.

C. Prayer

Father in Heaven, thank You for holding before us the ideal toward which we grow: "the measure of the stature of the fulness of Christ." Thank You for the unfailing guidance of Your Word; thank You for minds that can learn and plan; thank You for strength to do. In gratitude we promise our best efforts to learn Your will and do it. In Jesus' name, amen.

D. Thought to Remember

You're either growing in Christ or withering away—there is no standing still.

Learning by Doing

This page contains an alternative lesson plan emphasizing learning activities.
Classes desiring such student involvement will find these suggestions helpful.

Learning Goals

After this lesson each student will be able to:

1. Cite the characteristics of a mature Christian as described in today's text.

2. Identify aspects in his or her life that help encourage Christian growth.

3. Make arrangements with another student to hold each other accountable for working on a specific area of growth.

Into the Lesson

Create the following word-find activity on a large poster board or an overhead transparency. Display it and say, "There are seven words of at least four letters hidden in this puzzle, spelled forward or backward, up or down, or diagonally. When you find a word, call it out and I'll circle it for all to see." (These words are hidden: *child, appetite, seed, grass, weed, hair, love*.)

```
F D S A G V U C M F O Z
R E P R R I A H E N T Y
W E A P P E T I T E U E
O S E J O L S L P Q V M
S F A C W E E D X O I S
T I D H A G N P L E B Z
```

Allow a few minutes for all the words to be found. Then say, "Now discuss with your neighbor what these words all have in common." Allow a minute or two for ideas to be discussed. Then ask for suggestions from the class.

If the answer is not suggested by the class, tell them: "These are all things that grow." Say, "Today, we focus on something else that grows: our faith. Turn to 2 Peter 1:3-15, and let's see how God says our own faith can grow."

Into the Word

Ask a class member to read the lesson text aloud to the class. For this question-and-answer activity, move the class into groups of three students each. Prior to class time, prepare the following questions on a work sheet and make enough copies so that each group has one

1. What has God's divine power given us? *(All that pertains to life and godliness, 2 Peter 1:3.)*

2. What have God's precious promises to believers empowered them to be able to do? *(Be partakers of the divine nature; escape the corruption in the world, 2 Peter 1:4.)*

3. What did Peter say contributed to the world's corruption? *(Lust, 2 Peter 1:4.)*

4. What are the characteristics of a mature Christian that a believer who "gives all diligence" can add? *(Faith, virtue, knowledge, temperance, patience, godliness, brotherly kindness, charity, 2 Peter 1:5-7.)*

5. What result does Peter promise for believers who have those characteristics in their lives? *(Neither be barren nor unfruitful, 2 Peter 1:8.)*

6. How does Peter describe believers who do not have these characteristics? *(Blind, have forgotten about purging of personal sin, 2 Peter 1:9.)*

7. What promise does Peter give to those who "make your calling and election sure"? *(You will never fall, 2 Peter 1:10.)*

8. As long as Peter was alive, what did he say was necessary for him to do? *(Stir them up by helping them to remember these principles, 2 Peter 1:12, 13.)*

9. What did Peter mean by the word *tabernacle* in 2 Peter 1:13? *(His physical body.)*

Allow six to eight minutes for groups to work. As a whole class, review the answers.

Into Life

Prior to class, prepare a "Christian Maturity Indicator Scale—Self-Analysis Graph" and make enough copies so each student has one. This is a blank line chart with eight columns and ten rows. At the bottom of each column write one of the eight characteristics from question 4 above. Number the rows "1" to "10" from the bottom to the top. Say: "Peter teaches that faith grows. I'd like each of you to evaluate the strength of these eight characteristics in your own life. Then, place a dot on the line from each characteristic at the point indicating the strength of that characteristic in your own life. Draw a line from dot to dot."

Allow time for reflection and for completing this self-analysis line chart. Say: "Peter identifies several qualities that help encourage Christian growth: promises of God, v. 4; diligence, v. 5; remembrance of cleansing, vv. 9, 13, 15. What are some aspects in your life that help encourage Christian growth?" Write suggested answers on the board. Say, "Peter held these believers accountable by reminding them of God's promises. We all need to be held accountable. Select a classmate and make a commitment to contact each other several times during this week to encourage growth in one of the low-ranked characteristics. Close the class time by praying for each other."

Let's Talk It Over

The questions on this page are designed to promote discussion of the lesson by the class and to encourage application of the lesson Scriptures. The answers provided are only discussion starters. Let your class talk it over from there.

1. What can the church do to ensure its new members will receive knowledge "unto life and godliness"?

People must first hear the truth before they can accept it (Romans 10:14-17; Hebrews 4:2, 3). The church must not fail to provide quality teacher training to help this "hearing" take hold. This training can be done through on-site workshops, or by providing scholarships for members to travel to various seminars or Bible colleges. These trainees will need to learn a variety of teaching methods, since some of their students will learn best by hearing, others by seeing, and still others by doing. Preachers, for their part, must stay fresh—always reading, always learning.

2. What can the church do to convince believers that they must put consistent effort into becoming mature spiritual Christians?

The church has to become interested in making disciples, not just in getting people to "make decisions" for Christ. Evangelism is part of the discipleship effort. Getting people to accept Christ is the first step. But many churches stop there. The church must stress maturity. It must hold up maturity as the norm, not the exception. Perhaps senior saints can be given opportunities to tell of their struggles and their victories. Or the church can sponsor special in-depth classes, spiritual retreats, and other programs that challenge believers to grow to new levels of maturity.

3. Peter gives a recipe for spiritual success. What must Christians do to add these essential ingredients into their lives?

Christians won't be motivated to add these ingredients until they see why they're important. One way to communicate their importance is by asking, "What would a person's life be like without _____?" One by one, insert each of the spiritual qualities into the blank.

This discussion may lead to questions about how one or more of the qualities should be defined; use the commentary for help with definitions. Move the discussion to brainstorming about all the ways each quality can be added to a Christian's life. For example, brotherly kindness is added by doing good deeds, both for those who appreciate the effort and those who do not; patience or perseverance is added by learning to wait through prayer and serve faithfully through continued effort; etc. Enrich the discussion by using concrete examples of how each quality can be applied to your learners' lives.

4. How can the church warn new or long-time Christians that they have a responsibility to "make [their] calling and election sure"? How can the church accomplish this without falling into the trap of teaching "salvation by works"?

The church has a great responsibility to teach the Scriptures carefully and completely in this regard since eternity is at stake! If your church offers a basic "what we believe" class, it should include the teaching that believers need to persevere in the faith and not abandon their relationship with Christ by reverting to their sinful lifestyles (Hebrews 10:26-31; 2 Peter 2:20-22; 3:17; Revelation 3:14-16). Both new and long-time Christians can be included in such classes.

The church must also stress that others will be rejected by God in the judgment because they tried to reach salvation through their own effort (Romans 4:1-8; James 2:14-26). We are saved by the power and grace of God. This class could benefit from comparing Christianity with other world religions, all of which teach some form of salvation by works.

5. Peter was eager that the Christians be assured and convinced of the things he wrote about. He wanted to be sure they clung to them even after his death. How can churches or individual Christians develop a zeal and a faith that last beyond the influence of certain leaders?

Some churches grow and thrive under the leadership of a dynamic preacher. But when that preacher retires or passes away, the church seems to dwindle. Many of those who were active in ministry are no longer. Young people who were excited about the church are drawn away little by little to other interests.

Some mega-churches are now using multiple preachers, trying to ensure that one preacher is not the only focal point of the church. Have the students suggest other ways to downplay the significance of individual leaders and exalt the lordship of Christ in the thinking of the members. Sunday school classes, small groups, and ministry teams surely will play a part.

Trust God's Promise

DEVOTIONAL READING: Hebrews 10:19-25.

BACKGROUND SCRIPTURE: 2 Peter 3.

PRINTED TEXT: 2 Peter 3:3-18.

2 Peter 3:3-18

3 Knowing this first, that there shall come in the last days scoffers, walking after their own lusts,

4 And saying, Where is the promise of his coming? for since the fathers fell asleep, all things continue as they were from the beginning of the creation.

5 For this they willingly are ignorant of, that by the word of God the heavens were of old, and the earth standing out of the water and in the water:

6 Whereby the world that then was, being overflowed with water, perished:

7 But the heavens and the earth, which are now, by the same word are kept in store, reserved unto fire against the day of judgment and perdition of ungodly men.

8 But, beloved, be not ignorant of this one thing, that one day is with the Lord as a thousand years, and a thousand years as one day.

9 The Lord is not slack concerning his promise, as some men count slackness; but is long-suffering to us-ward, not willing that any should perish, but that all should come to repentance.

10 But the day of the Lord will come as a thief in the night; in the which the heavens shall pass away with a great noise, and the elements shall melt with fervent heat, the earth also and the works that are therein shall be burned up.

11 Seeing then that all these things shall be dissolved, what manner of persons ought ye to be in all holy conversation and godliness,

12 Looking for and hasting unto the coming of the day of God, wherein the heavens being on fire shall be dissolved, and the elements shall melt with fervent heat?

13 Nevertheless we, according to his promise, look for new heavens and a new earth, wherein dwelleth righteousness.

14 Wherefore, beloved, seeing that ye look for such things, be diligent that ye may be found of him in peace, without spot, and blameless.

15 And account that the long-suffering of our Lord is salvation; even as our beloved brother Paul also according to the wisdom given unto him hath written unto you;

16 As also in all his epistles, speaking in them of these things; in which are some things hard to be understood, which they that are unlearned and unstable wrest, as they do also the other Scriptures, unto their own destruction.

17 Ye therefore, beloved, seeing ye know these things before, beware lest ye also, being led away with the error of the wicked, fall from your own steadfastness.

18 But grow in grace, and in the knowledge of our Lord and Saviour Jesus Christ. To him be glory both now and for ever. Amen.

Oct 26

GOLDEN TEXT: Wherefore, beloved, seeing that ye look for such things, be diligent that ye may be found of him in peace, without spot, and blameless. And account that the long-suffering of our Lord is salvation.—2 Peter 3:14, 15.

Lesson Aims

After participating in this lesson, each student should be able to:

1. Summarize Peter's teaching about the Lord's return.

2. Compare the scoffing of the first-century mockers with that of modern disbelievers.

3. Suggest a specific way to obey the command of 2 Peter 3:14.

Lesson Outline

INTRODUCTION
  A. Trusting Jesus
  B. Lesson Background
 I. ANTICIPATING THE SCOFFERS (2 Peter 3:3-7)
  A. Their Attitude (vv. 3, 4)
  B. Their Error (vv. 5, 6)
  C. The Promise (v. 7)
    D. B. Cooper and Jesus
 II. REMEMBERING THE TRUTH (2 Peter 3:8-10)
  A. Explanation of Delay (vv. 8, 9)
  B. End of Delay (v. 10)
    "A-maze-ingly Complicated"
III. IMPLEMENTING THE TRUTH (2 Peter 3:11-18)
  A. What We Do and Expect (vv. 11-14)
  B. What Paul Says (vv. 15, 16)
  C. What We Avoid (v. 17)
  D. What We Do, Part 2 (v. 18a)
  E. Glory to Jesus (v. 18b)
CONCLUSION
  A. The Spot Remover
  B. Prayer
  C. Thought to Remember

Introduction

A. Trusting Jesus

The Ampro Writers' Club invited an editor of Christian publications to discuss the kinds of writing used in those publications. Part of the discussion is printed below, with a writer called W and the editor called E.

W: Do you teach that Jesus is going to come back?

E: Yes, we do. He promised.

W: I'm afraid I can't go along with you on that. He's not coming back.

E: May I ask where you got that information?

W: From history. From science. From observation. From common sense. After all, it's been two thousand years. How long do you wait for a promise to be kept?

E: That depends on who made the promise. For Jesus' promise, we wait as many thousands of years as it takes. He is dependable.

B. Lesson Background

Very plainly Jesus said He would come back. He said His coming would be announced by the failure of sun, moon, and stars. He said angels would gather Jesus' people from all over the world (Matthew 24:29-31). Jesus said also that He will judge the people of the world and separate those destined for a prepared kingdom from those destined for everlasting fire (25:31-46). If we believe Jesus, we had better give heed to His warning, "Watch therefore; for ye know neither the day nor the hour wherein the Son of man cometh" (25:13).

But as Peter writes his second and final letter in the mid-60s A.D., it's now been about thirty-five years since Jesus made His promise to return. Some fear that Jesus already has returned and that somehow they have missed it. (See 2 Thessalonians 2:1-3.) Others are becoming skeptical that Jesus will *ever* return.

But Peter has the solution to their skepticism. In last week's text he was emphatic in telling his readers that he was repeating things they already knew. He said that he was going to keep on repeating them as long as he lived on earth so his readers would remember those repeated teachings long after he was dead (2 Peter 1:12-15).

In the opening verses of chapter 3 he returns to that theme. He is stirring up his readers' minds "by way of remembrance": he is making sure that they will keep in mind the teaching of the inspired prophets and the apostles of Jesus (3:1, 2). In the beginning of this week's text he explains why it is so necessary to keep that true teaching in mind. Scoffers are coming to make fun of the truth—indeed, they already abound. Christians must be ready to respond to them with "pure minds" (3:1).

I. Anticipating the Scoffers
(2 Peter 3:3-7)

Like the first readers of this letter, we need to be prepared with the ancient truth taught by the prophets and apostles. Scoffers can cause a lot of damage if we're not alert to their activities and quick to respond. (See 1 Timothy 4:1-3; 2 Timothy 3:1-9; and Jude 17-19.) We begin by anticipating the scoffers and their arguments. As the old saying goes, "Forewarned is forearmed!"

A. Their Attitude (vv. 3, 4)

3. Knowing this first, that there shall come in the last days scoffers, walking after their own lusts.

The last days are all the days of the Christian era, all the time between Jesus' first coming to His second coming (Hebrews 1:2; 1 Peter 1:20; 1 John 2:18). This is the last era of the earth as we know it. *Scoffers* have been busy throughout most of this era, trying to turn God's people away from the truth. Their foundational problem is that they follow *their own lusts* instead of following Jesus. They are concerned about their own profit, pleasure, and pride, and not about the kingdom of God and His righteousness (Matthew 6:33). It is not in their selfish interest to accept that history might come to an end at any time.

4. And saying, Where is the promise of his coming? for since the fathers fell asleep, all things continue as they were from the beginning of the creation.

It's been about thirty-five years since Jesus made *the promise of his* return. *"Where* is it?" the scoffers ask. *The fathers* may mean the scoffers' own fathers—the first generation of Christians, the men who had come to Christ in the beginning days of the church. They had believed the promise that Jesus will come back; they had lived out their lives expecting to see Him. But now they are dead. The scoffers say that it is silly for the next generation to continue believing a promise that has not been kept. And since Jesus has not kept His promise, they say it is pointless to be bound by His teaching. Why not be crooked in business if it is profitable? Why not commit adultery if it is fun? Why do anything for the poor and sick who cannot do anything in return?

The Bible promises that spectacular events will accompany Jesus' return (Luke 21:25-28). But *all things continue as they were from the beginning of the creation.* It must be time to abandon Christianity, the scoffers say, because the passing of time has proven it to be a failure. [See question #1, page 72.]

B. Their Error (vv. 5, 6)

5, 6. For this they willingly are ignorant of, that by the word of God the heavens were of old, and the earth standing out of the water and in the water: whereby the world that then was, being overflowed with water, perished.

There is nothing wrong with ignorance when it cannot be helped. Everyone is *ignorant* of some things. But willful ignorance—ignorance of truth one ought to be aware of—is, in fact, a rejection of the truth. This is the sin of the scoffers: they *willingly* ignore the fact that it was *by the word of God* that the *heavens* and *earth* came into being

Visual for lesson 8

Display this visual from the Adult Visuals *packet as you discuss verses 5 and 6 of the text.*

in the first place! This same Word of God, as expanded by Jesus, is what promises an end to that old creation.

Further, it simply is not true that the ordinary course of nature has gone on since the beginning of creation. Long after the creation the normal course of nature was interrupted by another spectacular event: the great flood of Noah's day. *The world that then was* standing out of the water was *overflowed with water,* and most of humanity *perished* in a judgment scarcely less spectacular than the one promised in Matthew 25:31-46 (see Genesis 6–8).

C. The Promise (v. 7)

7. But the heavens and the earth, which are now, by the same word are kept in store, reserved unto fire against the day of judgment and perdition of ungodly men.

The heavens and the earth came into being by the word of God (v. 5). By the same word a flood destroyed most of the conscious living things of that world (Genesis 6:13). *By the same word* the creation we see is reserved unto fire. It will be burned up (v. 10), and the *ungodly* will perish.

D. B. COOPER AND JESUS

On November 24, 1971, D. B. Cooper boarded a plane in Portland, Oregon, showed a flight attendant what appeared to be a bomb in his carry-on luggage and demanded two hundred thousand dollars and four parachutes. When the plane landed at Seattle, Cooper was given the money and parachutes; he then directed the pilot to fly to Mexico. Shortly after takeoff he opened the rear door of the plane and jumped out, never to be seen again. No body was ever found. The only clue to his disappearance was found nine years later: a pack of twenty-dollar bills matching the serial numbers recorded by the FBI.

For nearly thirty years, a tavern in Ariel, Washington, has held a celebration on the anniversary of Cooper's escapade. Some people think of him as a folk hero; some probably consider the day simply an excuse for revelry.

It's been nearly two thousand years since Christ arose and promised to return. Every year we celebrate His resurrection and anticipate His second coming. Peter warned that skeptics would have fun at our expense, and it is so. What is the difference between Jesus and D. B. Cooper? At least two significant differences exist. First, Cooper risked the lives of others for his own profit; Christ gave His life so others could gain. Second, Cooper is almost certainly dead, but Jesus lives again. We can admire what Jesus did and trust the promise of what He is yet to do.
—C. R. B.

II. Remembering the Truth
(2 Peter 3:8-10)

Scoffers who ridiculed the idea of Christ's return also probably ridiculed the idea that the earth would be burned up. I knew a high-school teacher who mocked that prospect. "The earth was born in fire," he said. "It was burned to a cinder in its birth. It's fireproof." But nothing in this world is immune to God's fire.

A. Explanation of Delay (vv. 8, 9)

8. But, beloved, be not ignorant of this one thing, that one day is with the Lord as a thousand years, and a thousand years as one day.

Limited as we are by time, it is hard for us to grasp eternity. Eighty years is a long time to a person on earth, for it leaves him or her only a few more years to live. But when God lives *a thousand years,* He has as many years to live as He had when the thousand years began, for His life has neither beginning nor end (cf. Psalm 90:4). [See question #2, page 72.]

9. The Lord is not slack concerning his promise, as some men count slackness; but is long-suffering to us-ward, not willing that any should perish, but that all should come to repentance.

Distressed by the evil reported in halls of government, in places of business, in schools, on the street, and in homes, do you ever wonder why God hasn't destroyed this wicked world before now? Here is the answer: God is waiting for more people to repent. God's *long-suffering* (patience) is an important Biblical theme (Exodus 34:6; Romans 2:4; 9:22). And some are indeed repenting, but not nearly enough. Do you suppose God is

satisfied with what we are doing to bring more people *to repentance?* [See question #3, page 72.]

B. End of Delay (v. 10)

10. But the day of the Lord will come as a thief in the night; in the which the heavens shall pass away with a great noise, and the elements shall melt with fervent heat, the earth also and the works that are therein shall be burned up.

In this context *the day of the Lord* means the time of Jesus' second coming (v. 4). It is also the day of other tremendous events. *A thief in the night* comes when he is not expected, and so will *the day of the Lord.* The New Testament describes Jesus' return "as a thief" in several places (see Matthew 24:42-44; Luke 12:39; 1 Thessalonians 5:2; Revelation 3:3; 16:15), so we must be ready. [See question #4, page 72.]

The day of the Lord, however, will not also depart unseen and unheard as *a thief in the night* does. On that day the people of earth "shall see the Son of man coming in the clouds of heaven with power and great glory" (Matthew 24:30). God's people will see the angels bringing them together to meet their Savior (24:31). Every person in the world will hear himself or herself pronounced blessed or cursed (25:34, 41). It is a day on which *the Lord* will bring about the end of the world and the universe that we know (Joel 2:10; Mark 13:24-27; Revelation 20:11). *The heavens* that we admire on a clear night *shall pass away with a great noise.*

"A-MAZE-INGLY" COMPLICATED

Justin Taylor and Chris Taylor, recent college graduates, took out a small business loan, rented five acres of land just a few miles outside Memphis, Tennessee, bought some seed corn, and started Mid-South Maze. They became part of a franchise business that has built about one hundred mazes across America. The Taylors pay 6 percent of their profits to the parent company for the privilege of confusing patrons of their maze.

Their field was planted at about twice the density of a normal cornfield. When the plants were a foot tall, they cut the maze into it with a weed cutter. By the time the crop matured, one could not see through the closely planted rows of corn. The two miles of paths winding through the field were five feet wide, and had so many turns and dead ends that it typically took people an hour or so to find their way through it.

Complicated as these mazes can be, it is as nothing compared with what some Christians do with the prophecies surrounding the end of the world. It is "a-maze-ing" how complicated some preachers and teachers make the simple message of Scripture, trying to plot an intricate series of events leading up to the end and pinpoint the time at which it will come. Peter says the day will come unexpectedly, so our concern should not be when the day will come, but whether we will be prepared for it.   —C. R. B.

III. Implementing the Truth
(2 Peter 3:11-18)

In modern culture the question "So what?" usually is a flippant one. Often it is intended to imply that nothing important will come from what has been said or done. But in this case, "So what?" is a serious and important question since the answer points to eternal truth. This truth assures us that Jesus will come back according to His promise. The events He predicted in Matthew 24 and 25 will come to pass: the gathering of His people and the judgment of all humanity. This future reality should cause us to live our lives in certain ways.

A. What We Do and Expect (vv. 11-14)

11. Seeing then that all these things shall be dissolved, what manner of persons ought ye to be in all holy conversation and godliness?

We must remember that in the *King James Version* the word *conversation* does not mean "talk"; it means our whole way of life. Peter asks a rhetorical question, and the answer he expects is obvious. The way we live and act day by day should make it plain that we are God's people, *holy*, dedicated, set apart for His service. *Godliness* is reverence and awe before God, along with continual obedience to His teaching. "The world passeth away, and the lust thereof: but he that doeth the will of God abideth for ever" (1 John 2:17).

12. Looking for and hasting unto the coming of the day of God, wherein the heavens being on fire shall be dissolved, and the elements shall melt with fervent heat.

We know the ground where we stand is going to be burned up along with the rest of the earth and the universe, but that knowledge brings us no terror (cf. Revelation 6:12-17). Eagerly we are *looking for* that day; gladly we are *hasting unto* it. Some students understand that to mean that we actually speed that day's arrival. In either case, that great day is the climax of all history; it brings the realization of all our hopes. In this light we can pray, as John does in the next to the last verse of the Bible, "Even so, come, Lord Jesus."

13. Nevertheless we, according to his promise, look for new heavens and a new earth, wherein dwelleth righteousness.

God's *promise* of *new heavens and a new earth* is seen in Isaiah 65:17; 66:22. John saw the new

---

How to Say It

CORINTHIANS. Kor-*in*-thee-unz (*th* as in *thin*).
EPISTLES. ee-*pis*-uls.
GALATIANS. Guh-*lay*-shunz.
HEBREWS. *Hee*-brews.
JEREMIAH. Jair-uh-*my*-uh.
PHILIPPIANS. Fih-*lip*-ee-unz.
THESSALONIANS. *Thess*-uh-*lo*-nee-unz (strong accent on *lo*; *th* as in *thin*).

---

creation in a vision (Revelation 21:1), and he gives a marvelous description of the New Jerusalem that he saw "coming down from God out of heaven" (21:2). Peter says nothing about the size or shape of the new heavens and earth, but he states the most important difference between them and the earth we know: the new heavens and earth are the home of *righteousness* (cf. Jeremiah 23:5-7; 33:16; Revelation 21:27).

14. Wherefore, beloved, seeing that ye look for such things, be diligent that ye may be found of him in peace, without spot, and blameless.

Since we are to live in that new creation where righteousness lives, we are to take care to be righteous here and now. Just as Christ was *without spot* and *blameless* (see 1 Peter 1:19), so are we to be. It is His blood that makes us so. When we see that our daily lives are not quite spotless, we are disappointed but not dismayed. Our hope remains sure; we know that we are forgiven (1 John 1:9).

B. What Paul Says (vv. 15, 16)

15. And account that the long-suffering of our Lord is salvation; even as our beloved brother Paul also according to the wisdom given unto him hath written unto you.

The Lord's long wait before coming provides an opportunity for more and more people to repent and be saved. This repeats what has been said in verse 9. Paul's letters offer similar information—see especially Romans 2:4.

16. As also in all his epistles, speaking in them of these things; in which are some things hard to be understood, which they that are unlearned and unstable wrest, as they do also the other Scriptures, unto their own destruction.

When Peter speaks of *the other Scriptures,* he is recognizing that Paul's *epistles* have the authority of Scripture as well (cf. 1 Corinthians 14:37). Although Paul had to correct Peter on one occasion (Galatians 2:11-21), it was a correction of behavior and not of teaching. We never find any contradictions between these two apostles. Different as their writings are, there are no mistakes in either, for the Holy Spirit inspired both.

However, Peter says Paul's writings contain *some things hard to be understood,* and we would agree. Jesus spoke difficult things as well (John 6:60). That should not surprise us. It would be more surprising if we could easily understand all the deep things of God that are spoken and written by inspiration of His Spirit.

All of us need to be careful not to *wrest* those difficult passages—twisting them into some meaning not intended by the writers. Scripture-twisting is a never-ending problem (see Jeremiah 23:36; Acts 20:30; 2 Corinthians 4:2; and Jude 4). The way to avoid such error is to seek truth and truth teachers all our lives (2 Thessalonians 2:10-13; 2 Timothy 2:15; 1 Peter 1:22; 2 Peter 1:12). Then we shall not stand condemned as *unlearned and unstable* people who twist Paul's writing and *the other Scriptures* as well. [See question #5, page 72.]

C. What We Avoid (v. 17)

17. Ye therefore, beloved, seeing ye know these things before, beware lest ye also, being led away with the error of the wicked, fall from your own steadfastness.

Jesus warned of shallow believers in Matthew 13:5. As Peter writes this letter, only about thirty-five years after Jesus returned to Heaven, already some people are losing confidence in His promise to come back. Two thousand years later, relatively few people are seriously guiding their lives today by the thought that He may return tomorrow.

But when Jesus does indeed return, He will find that countless people, including some so-called Christians, have been *led away with the error of the wicked.* They will find themselves cursed rather than blessed in the judgment (Matthew 25:34, 41). That is what we want to avoid. So we hold ourselves in a dual readiness. We are ready to drop what we are doing and soar with joy to meet our Lord in the air (1 Thessalonians 4:17); and we are no less ready to go on with our customary life on earth, without spot, and blameless (2 Peter 3:14)—and quick to admit it when we find we are not quite spotless (1 John 1:9).

D. What We Do, Part 2 (v. 18a)

18a. But grow in grace, and in the knowledge of our Lord and Saviour Jesus Christ.

We grow *in the knowledge of* Jesus as we read about Him in the Bible, as we walk with Him day by day, and when we die to sin with Him. This was Paul's own earnest desire (Philippians 3:10, 11). We *grow in grace* when we increase our service in various ways (e.g., 2 Corinthians 8:7) and continually recognize how gracious God has been to us. This is true Christian growth! [See question #6, page 72.]

E. Glory to Jesus (v. 18b)

18b. To him be glory both now and for ever. Amen.

We grow in grace and the knowledge of Jesus also for the *glory* of Jesus. All we do can never earn life everlasting. Jesus redeemed us with His death; in paying sin's price, He saved us by His grace, His mercy, His forgiveness. All praise, honor, and glory properly belong to Him now and forever. *Amen!*

Conclusion

A. The Spot Remover

Let's conclude this lesson with a long look at ourselves in the light of the ideal set forth in verse 14 of our text. Is the life we are living really "without spot, and blameless"? If a long look reveals a few spots in our way of life, let's apply the spot remover recommended in 1 John 1:9 (see next week's lesson). And let us do so with full trust in the One who always has kept His promises, and always will.

B. Prayer

Forgive us, Father. We do confess the sins that spot our holiness and make us less than we want to be. And along with Your gracious forgiveness that makes us clean, please give us wisdom, strength, and courage to keep ourselves clean today and tomorrow and all through the week. In Jesus' name, amen.

C. Thought to Remember

All of God's promises are trustworthy.
Are we?

Home Daily Bible Readings

Monday, Oct. 20—Hold Fast to Our Hope (Hebrews 10:19-25)

Tuesday, Oct. 21—God Is Faithful (1 Corinthians 1:4-9)

Wednesday, Oct. 22—In Christ, It Is "Yes" (2 Corinthians 1:18-22)

Thursday, Oct. 23—God's Word Shall Not Return Empty (Isaiah 55:8-12)

Friday, Oct. 24—Where Is the Promise? (2 Peter 3:1-7)

Saturday, Oct. 25—God Is Not Slow (2 Peter 3:8-13)

Sunday, Oct. 26—Regard God's Patience as Salvation (2 Peter 3:14-18)

Learning by Doing

This page contains an alternative lesson plan emphasizing learning activities.
Classes desiring such student involvement will find these suggestions helpful.

Learning Goals

After participating in this lesson, each student will be able to:

1. Summarize Peter's teaching about the Lord's return.

2. Compare the scoffing of the first-century mockers with that of modern disbelievers.

3. Suggest a specific way to obey the command of 2 Peter 3:14.

Into the Lesson

In preparation for this week's lesson, prepare the following statement-completion activity and make a copy for each student. The statement to introduce the lesson and to be completed is this: "When people break promises they have made to me, it affects both my own attitude and my perception of them. My attitude becomes _____, and I begin to think of them as _____."

Say, "Each of us has had the experience of someone breaking a promise made to us. Today we begin by reflecting on how broken promises affect both our attitudes and our perceptions of those who failed to keep their promises. Complete the statement by writing your thoughts and feelings about how broken promises affect you." Distribute the statement-completion sheet, and give a minute or two for class members to write their answers. Then ask class members to reveal their answers; write these on the board. (Take all the answers to the first part before discussing the second part.) Say, "Broken promises tend to discredit the trustworthiness of those who made the promises. Our text from 2 Peter 3 identifies those who believe God has broken His promise to us."

Into the Word

Prior to class, prepare the following matching activity and make copies for all class members. Ask a class member to read aloud 2 Peter 3:3-18. Pass the activity sheet out to the class and say, "Read each phrase on the left side and select the best answer from those on the right. Write the letter of your selected answer in the space provided. An answer may be used more than once."

List the following phrases on the left side, each with a short blank line in front for writing the letter of the selected answer.

1. elements shall melt, v. 10
2. earth reserved unto fire, v. 7
3. come as a thief, v. 10

4. heavens on fire, v. 12
5. new heavens and earth, v. 13
6. world perished, v. 6
7. fall from steadfastness, v. 17
8. holy conversation and godliness, v. 11
9. walking after their own lusts, v. 3
10. in peace, without spot, and blameless, v. 14.

List the following answers to the right.

A. Ignorant scoffers
B. Promise of God
C. Beware
D. Be diligent
E. Day of God
F. Day of the Lord
G. All shall be dissolved
H. Day of judgment and perdition.

The answers are: 1-F; 2-H; 3-F; 4-E; 5-B; 6-A; 7-C; 8-G; 9-A; 10-D.

Move the students into groups of three and say, "As scoffers mocked the first-century believers, so the mockery continues. Compare the scoffing that Peter addressed with that of modern disbelievers." Prior to class, prepare a comparison chart with two columns: "First-Century Mockers," and "Present-Day Disbelievers." Working in small groups, students should list how scoffers mocked first-century believers in the first column and ways scoffers mock believers today in the other. Give about seven minutes for the groups to write answers. Then ask for volunteers to report their answers to the class.

Into Life

Say, "Mockers are a reality, but the the Lord's patience is an opportunity for mockers to come to repentance. What does a clear understanding of the coming day of the Lord lead us to do?" *(Be holy and godly, v. 11; look for that day, v. 12; be diligent, v. 14; beware that we don't fall, v. 17; grow in grace and knowledge, v. 18.)*

Prepare a work sheet titled "Be Diligent" prior to class. In the left column, write the words "in peace," "without spot," and "blameless" on separate rows. Title the right column, "To bring this about I need to . . . ." Give a copy of this action sheet to each student. Ask, "What do you need to do to bring these realities about in your own life?" Encourage students to give serious thought and reflection and to write what they intend to do. Close the class time with a prayer of dedication and commitment.

Let's Talk It Over

The questions on this page are designed to promote discussion of the lesson by the class and to encourage application of the lesson Scriptures. The answers provided are only discussion starters. Let your class talk it over from there.

1. What are some good techniques for Christians to use when witnessing to scoffers?

Until they develop the wisdom to distinguish truth from error, perhaps it would be best for new Christians to avoid getting into prolonged discussions with a scoffer. Christians who tend to be argumentative should be taught to use a gentler approach. James gives a brief summary of one good way to respond: "Let every man be swift to hear, slow to speak, slow to wrath" (James 1:19). The prepared Christian can listen with courtesy to the scoffer. Good listening techniques earn the right to speak, providing the opening to share the message of Christ.

2. God's perspective of time is much different from ours. How important do you think that is? Why?

God is a timeless being; for Him, time never "runs out." He is not limited by our twenty-four-hour clock. This means He always has "the bigger picture" of history in view. Humans always want to know "how long?" (cf. Revelation 6:10), but length of time is much less important to God. Before the creation, God had a plan that included the salvation of all true believers (Ephesians 3:4, 5; 2 Thessalonians 2:13). There was considerable time between the creation and the flood. And then in "the fulness of the time" He sent Jesus (Galatians 4:4). The timing of Jesus' second coming already has been determined by the Father (Matthew 24:36).

The fact that we do not know God's timetable does not give credibility to claims that Jesus will not return. Our job is to live each day with our lives in order, ready to be called to be with Christ. The church must stress both God's timetable and the eventual return of Christ.

3. What do we learn about God's nature from the fact that He has not yet brought about the Day of Judgment?

If God's nature included a short fuse, perhaps all of us would have already experienced the full magnitude of His wrath. Because He is righteous, He cannot allow evil to go unpunished. He could have decided to zap every person after every sin. If He had applied a speedy punishment, everyone would be dead (Romans 3:23) and lost in their sins. From this delay in final judgment we learn about His patience and His love. He wants all to come to Jesus.

4. What can every Christian do (or not do!) to be prepared for the second coming of Christ?

First, we should not waste time trying to pinpoint the date of the second coming. (See Matthew 24:36; 25:13; Revelation 3:3.) It would be much better to assume that Jesus could return at any minute. This doesn't mean quitting our jobs and waiting on the roof! (See 2 Thessalonians 3:12.) We prepare ourselves by living an evermore godly life (2 Peter 3:11-13). An important part of this is personal holiness (1 Peter 1:15, 16)—keeping guard on our thoughts and actions. We prepare others for Jesus' second coming by sharing Christ's love with as many as we can through our words and actions.

5. Which is the greater threat to the average Christian, a scoffer or a supposed believer who distorts the Word of God? Why?

Scoffers are often easier to identify and thus easier to guard against. They may exhibit a flippant or sarcastic tone. They usually don't bother to come to church, so they are not "in our midst."

On the other hand, those who twist the Scripture often are right among us. They can be very serious about what they teach (see 2 Thessalonians 2:1-5; 2 Timothy 4:4, 5; Titus 3:9-11). They really do seem to be on "our side" (Matthew 7:15). It takes a very wise Christian to recognize their counterfeit doctrine. This is the reason every Christian should study the Scriptures regularly (2 Timothy 3:14-17), ask mature Christians for help when something is unclear, be slow to jump to conclusions, and pray for wisdom (James 1:5-8).

6. Why is it important for Christians to grow in grace as well as in knowledge?

Knowledge by itself can lead to arrogance (see 1 Corinthians 8:1). An arrogant attitude won't win anyone to Christ. But when we grow in grace—which includes coming to grips with the depths of God's grace to us—we become more humble. This, in turn, results in our being more *gracious* to those around us. This demeanor, coupled with our Christian "knowledge," is what will allow us to win the most people to Christ.

Enjoy Fellowship With God

DEVOTIONAL READING: Ephesians 5:1-10.

BACKGROUND SCRIPTURE: 1 John 1:1–3:10.

PRINTED TEXT: 1 John 1:5–2:6, 15-17, 29–3:1.

1 John 1:5-10

5 This then is the message which we have heard of him, and declare unto you, that God is light, and in him is no darkness at all.

6 If we say that we have fellowship with him, and walk in darkness, we lie, and do not the truth:

7 But if we walk in the light, as he is in the light, we have fellowship one with another, and the blood of Jesus Christ his Son cleanseth us from all sin.

8 If we say that we have no sin, we deceive ourselves, and the truth is not in us.

9 If we confess our sins, he is faithful and just to forgive us our sins, and to cleanse us from all unrighteousness.

10 If we say that we have not sinned, we make him a liar, and his word is not in us.

1 John 2:1-6, 15-17, 29

1 My little children, these things write I unto you, that ye sin not. And if any man sin, we have an advocate with the Father, Jesus Christ the righteous:

2 And he is the propitiation for our sins: and not for ours only, but also for the sins of the whole world.

3 And hereby we do know that we know him, if we keep his commandments.

4 He that saith, I know him, and keepeth not his commandments, is a liar, and the truth is not in him.

5 But whoso keepeth his word, in him verily is the love of God perfected: hereby know we that we are in him.

6 He that saith he abideth in him ought himself also so to walk, even as he walked.

. . . .

15 Love not the world, neither the things that are in the world. If any man love the world, the love of the Father is not in him.

16 For all that is in the world, the lust of the flesh, and the lust of the eyes, and the pride of life, is not of the Father, but is of the world.

17 And the world passeth away, and the lust thereof: but he that doeth the will of God abideth for ever.

. . . .

29 If ye know that he is righteous, ye know that every one that doeth righteousness is born of him.

1 John 3:1

1 Behold, what manner of love the Father hath bestowed upon us, that we should be called the sons of God: therefore the world knoweth us not, because it knew him not.

GOLDEN TEXT: If we walk in the light, as he is in the light, we have fellowship one with another, and the blood of Jesus Christ his Son cleanseth us from all sin.—1 John 1:7.

Faith Faces the World
Unit 3: Live as God's Children
(Lessons 9-11)

Lesson Aims

After participating in this lesson, each student will be able to:

1. Tell the various ways John says that a Christian can develop a relationship with God.

2. Give examples of the things of the world that hinder our fellowship with the Lord.

3. Memorize 1 John 1:7 and ask God to help him or her to walk in the light.

Lesson Outline

INTRODUCTION
    A. Darkness
    B. Lesson Background
  I. AVAILABLE LIGHT (1 John 1:5-10)
    A. God Is Light (v. 5)
    B. Walking in the Light (vv. 6, 7)
       Brightening Up the Night
    C. Don't Fool Yourself (vv. 8-10)
 II. SIN AND CLEANSING (1 John 2:1-6)
    A. Our Advocate (v. 1)
    B. Our Propitiation (v. 2)
    C. Knowing Our Advocate (vv. 3, 4)
    D. Perfection of Love (vv. 5, 6)
III. MORE ABOUT LOVE (1 John 2:15-17, 29–3:1)
    A. Mistaken Love (vv. 15-17)
       Persistent Desires
    B. The Father's Love (2:29–3:1)
CONCLUSION
    A. Looking at Ourselves
    B. Prayer
    C. Thought to Remember

Introduction

Deep in New Mexico's Carlsbad Cavern, a guide halted our tourist group on the trail and asked, "Would you like to see what total darkness looks like? Perhaps some of you have never seen darkness as complete as it is in here when the lights are out." There was a murmur of assent, and the guide went on: "See if you can find something to hang on to, or lean against, or sit on. I don't mean you can't stand alone, but it will be good to feel something solid closer than the soles of your feet."

My wife and I put our backs against a wall of solid rock. Others lined up beside us. Perhaps half of the tourists simply sat down in the middle of the trail. A few found a chair-high ledge of rock to sit on. Then the lights went out.

What came to my mind was a line from Exodus 10:21: "Darkness which may be felt." I imagined the darkness was a living thing, pushing us back against the cold stone. I shivered and pressed closer to the warmth of my wife. The eerie silence was as oppressive as the darkness. It was as if we were alone, cut off from the world, lost, helpless, and hopeless.

Then the lights came on. There was a flutter of talk and relieved laughter.

A. Darkness

Darkness is a symbol of ignorance, the ignorance from which we Christians have escaped because God has called us "out of darkness into his marvelous light" (1 Peter 2:9). We are children of God (John 1:12), and therefore children of light (1 Thessalonians 5:4, 5).

Darkness is a symbol of evil, the evil that had its hour of power when Jesus was arrested (Luke 22:53). As Jesus was dying, the world was darkened as evil seemed to be victorious (Matthew 27:45). But our Father in Heaven "hath delivered us from the power of darkness, and hath translated us into the kingdom of his dear Son" (Colossians 1:13). Therefore we "have no fellowship with the unfruitful works of darkness, but rather reprove them" (Ephesians 5:11).

Darkness is also a symbol of punishment (see Matthew 25:29, 30; Jude 6, 13). What a privilege and joy it is for Christians who have been turned "from darkness to light, and from the power of Satan unto God" (Acts 26:18)!

B. Lesson Background

For more about light and darkness, we turn to the first letter of John. This letter was written by one of the fishermen who became apostles of Jesus. None of the Twelve was closer to Jesus than was John. After Jerusalem was destroyed in A.D. 70, John lived in Ephesus, a city on the western coast of Asia Minor (modern Turkey). It was probably there that John wrote his first letter (epistle) between A.D. 80 and 90. More than half a century had passed since Jesus rose from the dead and ascended to Heaven. The church was being invaded by false teachers who valued human opinion more than divine revelation, much as some false teachers do today.

In response to such false teaching John began his letter with a strong declaration of his own personal acquaintance with Jesus and his own accurate knowledge of the Master's teaching (1 John 1:1-4). Then our text begins by presenting some of what John had learned from Jesus.

I. Available Light
(1 John 1:5-10)

False teachers were telling lies instead of truth, and some people were accepting the falsehoods. In other words, darkness was being promoted instead of light, and deceived people were turning away from the light to wander in darkness. The false teaching sounded so scholarly! How could the hearers know it was not true?

A. God Is Light (v. 5)

5. This then is the message which we have heard of him, and declare unto you, that God is light, and in him is no darkness at all.

John brought *the message* that he and the other apostles *heard* from Jesus himself. Jesus said *that God is light.* In Him there is no trace of ignorance or evil. Since God's Son spoke God's word on earth, everyone ought to know that any contradiction of it was false.

B. Walking in the Light (vv. 6, 7)

6. If we say that we have fellowship with him, and walk in darkness, we lie, and do not the truth.

To *walk in darkness* is to do wrong, to behave in evil ways. Anyone who does that makes it plain that he or she is not in *fellowship* with God, for God is light. Fellowship with Him means walking in the light: that is, doing right. Some of the false teachers agree that God is altogether good; but they say everything material is evil, including the physical bodies of people. What those evil bodies do is not important, say the false teachers. They say their spirits are in fellowship with God, even while their bodies are doing wrong. John says that is a *lie.* [See question #1, page 80.]

7. But if we walk in the light, as he is in the light, we have fellowship one with another, and the blood of Jesus Christ his Son cleanseth us from all sin.

To *walk in the light, as he is in the light* is to do right according to the teaching we have from God. All of us who accept God's standards and live by them *have fellowship one with another* as well as with God. That does not mean we never do anything wrong, for we are not so wise or so strong as we would like to be. "In many things we offend" (James 3:2). But Jesus died to atone for our sins. If we believe in Him and accept His gift of grace, His blood *cleanseth us from all sin.* [See question #2, page 80.]

BRIGHTENING UP THE NIGHT

In less than a month, many people will be placing Christmas lights on their houses and in their yards. Lighting up the darkness of long winter evenings is a fitting symbol for our celebration of the coming of the One who is the "light of the world." But sometimes darkness tries to prevail in spite of us.

An eighty-five-year-old handicapped widow responded to a young man's plea for work by giving him forty-five dollars to buy some Christmas lights for her. She never saw him again. At her daughter's insistence, she reported the matter to the police. The young police officer who took the report couldn't get it out of his mind. A few days later, he and his wife and a fellow officer showed up at the widow's door with enough lights to light the eaves and bushes around her house and then proceeded to put the lights in place. When the widow offered to pay them for their efforts, they refused, because they wanted to do something to brighten what would have been a dreary season for her otherwise.

We don't know whether the officers were Christians, but they were acting as if they were! Their act of kindness was perfectly in keeping with John's instruction for us to walk in the light. When we demonstrate compassion for the unfortunate, we show that we are walking in the light of Christ, and in the process we help to brighten up a very dark world. —C. R. B.

C. Don't Fool Yourself (vv. 8-10)

8. If we say that we have no sin, we deceive ourselves, and the truth is not in us.

Some people think they can have fellowship with God even while their physical bodies are doing wrong (v. 6). They claim that they have *no sin* in their spirits even while their physical bodies are sinning. But they are only fooling themselves with that kind of thinking.

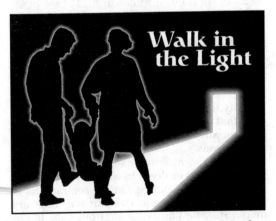

Visual for lesson 9. *This stark image is a dramatic illustration of verse 7. Discuss the significance of the parents' leading the child to the light.*

How to Say It

COLOSSIANS. Kuh-*losh*-unz.
DEMAS. *Dee*-mus.
ECCLESIASTES. Ik-*leez*-ee-*as*-teez (strong accent on *as*).
EPHESUS. *Ef*-uh-sus.
EPISTLE. ee-*pis*-ul.
ISAIAH. Eye-*zay*-uh.
PROPITIATION. pro-*pih*-she-*ay*-shun (strong accent on *ay*).
THESSALONIANS. *Thess*-uh-*lo*-nee-unz (strong accent on *lo*; *th* as in *thin*).

9. If we confess our sins, he is faithful and just to forgive us our sins, and to cleanse us from all unrighteousness.

It is better to be honest, to *confess our sins* instead of trying to deny them with the nonsensical theory that the sins of our bodies are not our sins. Then God is ready to *forgive us our sins, and to cleanse us from all unrighteousness.* [See question #3, page 80.]

10. If we say that we have not sinned, we make him a liar, and his word is not in us.

It is bad enough to fool ourselves and say we are sinless when we are not (v. 8). It is worse to accuse God of lying. We do that *if we say that we have not sinned,* for He says all of us have sinned. He says it emphatically and repeatedly in His written Word (1 Kings 8:46; Psalm 14:3; Ecclesiastes 7:20; Isaiah 53:6; 64:6; Romans 3:23).

II. Sin and Cleansing
(1 John 2:1-6)

All of us are sinners (Romans 3:23), and "the wages of sin is death" (Romans 6:23). [See question #4, page 80.] But not all sinners must accept what they have earned. Romans 6:23 adds, "The gift of God is eternal life through Jesus Christ our Lord." How can we escape the wages we have earned and receive the gift we have not earned?

A. Our Advocate (v. 1)

1. My little children, these things write I unto you, that ye sin not. And if any man sin, we have an advocate with the Father, Jesus Christ the righteous.

John has been writing that all human beings are sinners, but he does not want that to be taken as an excuse for sinning. On the contrary, he is writing to help his readers keep from sinning any more. Still, he points out that our case is not hopeless even if we do sin. *We have an advocate with the Father, Jesus Christ the righteous.* In any courtroom a criminal needs *an advocate,* a

lawyer who can argue his case better than he himself can. If guilt cannot be denied, perhaps the advocate can point to mitigating circumstances or some other reason to treat this criminal with mercy. Jesus is our *advocate* in God's court of justice. He is righteous; He will not resort to lying or anything wrong to save us from punishment. He knows we have sinned, and God knows it, and we know it. Then why should God have mercy on us? See the next verse.

B. Our Propitiation (v. 2)

2. And he is the propitiation for our sins: and not for ours only, but also for the sins of the whole world.

Jesus is *the propitiation,* the atoning sacrifice, the means of appeasing God's wrath and gaining His favor for us in spite of our sins. He died in our place. The punishment we deserve has been given to Him, and so we can receive God's mercy instead. Furthermore, the sacrifice Jesus made is enough to atone for *the sins of the whole world;* but that does not mean all the sinners will receive mercy instead of justice. There are proud sinners who declare they will gain Heaven by their own merits or not at all. Unless they repent, it will be not at all. There are other sinners who deny that there is a God or a Savior, a Heaven or a Hell. Unless they repent, they will learn the truth too late.

C. Knowing Our Advocate (vv. 3, 4)

3. And hereby we do know that we know him, if we keep his commandments.

Do we really know Jesus, our advocate, our propitiation, our Savior? There is an easy way to answer that question. If we ignore *His commandments* and do as we please, that is proof that we do not know Christ. On the other hand, if we consistently shape our lives by His commandments, that is convincing evidence that we know Him. This is true even if sometimes we are tricked into disobedience. [See question #5, page 80.]

4. He that saith, I know him, and keepeth not his commandments, is a liar, and the truth is not in him.

With this powerful blow the writer clinches the truth he drove home in verse 3. What one does is more convincing than what one says.

D. Perfection of Love (vv. 5, 6)

5. But whoso keepeth his word, in him verily is the love of God perfected: hereby know we that we are in him.

Keeping God's *word* is the same as keeping His commandments in verses 3 and 4. It is guiding one's life by God's directions. One who does that shows that his or her *love* for God is *perfected,* is mature, made complete, is what it ought to be. But the Greek word translated *perfected* can also mean "brought to its goal." With that in mind, some students take this verse to mean that God's love for us intends to bring us to obey God; and when we do obey God, His love for us is brought to its goal (cf. Psalm 119:11).

6. He that saith he abideth in him ought himself also so to walk, even as he walked.

The way we *walk* means the way we live, the way we conduct ourselves, the way we behave. Everyone who claims to be in Christ ought to live as Christ did. Of course that does not mean every Christian ought to walk on water and do other miracles as Jesus did. But every Christian ought to copy Jesus' attitudes and His actions that were not miraculous. Every Christian ought to be honest, kind, generous, helpful, considerate, courteous. If one does not act like Jesus, that shows that he really is not in Jesus; he is not a real Christian.

III. More About Love
(1 John 2:15-17, 29; 3:1)

Our lesson concludes with some important reflections on the objects of our love. One is very common, and one is not.

A. Mistaken Love (vv. 15-17)

15. Love not the world, neither the things that are in the world. If any man love the world, the love of the Father is not in him.

God loved *the world*—loved it so much that He gave His only begotten Son to die for it (John 3:16). We are God's people. How can John tell us not to *love* the world that God loves?

That is a legitimate question, but it's not hard to find an answer, is it? With about a minute's thought we see that the word *world* in our text does not mean what the same word means in John 3:16.

John 3:16 is saying God loved the people of the world, loved them so much that He sent His Son to redeem them. God still loves the people of the world, and so do God's people. Missionaries sacrifice much to take the message of God's love and salvation to people who need it. The rest of God's people sacrifice a little to support the missionaries. That is good.

When John says, *Love not the world,* he is not thinking of people, but *the things that are in the world,* such things as money and things money will buy: fine clothes, fine cars, fine homes. We ought to earn money enough to support ourselves (2 Thessalonians 3:11, 12) and our families (1 Timothy 5:8). But if anyone is so in love with money that he will lie or cheat or steal to get it, that is bad (1 Timothy 6:10). That greedy

kind of love for things of the world can so fill a person's heart that there is no room for the love of God, as we see in the last part of verse 15.

16. For all that is in the world, the lust of the flesh, and the lust of the eyes, and the pride of life, is not of the Father, but is of the world.

Lust is desire. *The flesh* is the physical body. Our bodies desire the food they need, but they do not stop there. They desire more than they need. If we do not take control and stop eating when we have enough, we become fat. Some people actually train their bodies to lust for nicotine or alcohol or some illegal drug. Such a lust of the flesh is likely to overpower a person and make him or her a slave.

The eyes desire what looks good. If a person does not control that lust, he may drive a more expensive car than he can afford, or she may fill her closet with more lovely clothes than she can use in a lifetime. [See question #6, page 80.]

The pride of life lusts for better things than the neighbors have. If we do not keep that lust under control, our happiness will always be marred by envy.

The Father in Heaven gives us the desires for all we need to be at our best. All our desire for what is bad, and all our desire for too much of what is good, *is not of the Father, but is of the world.* If we do not control those worldly desires, they will control us, and they will make us less than our best.

PERSISTENT DESIRES

"Models for Millionaires" was the heading of an advertisement in a slick-paper, upscale metropolitan magazine. Along with the picture of an attractive, thirty-five-ish woman were these teasers: "Now there is a way to find a relationship with model quality, commitment-minded women who want a lifetime partner. . . . If you are ready to settle down with a 9 or 10, we need to talk. . . . This is a no nonsense way of bringing you the type of woman you deserve." In just a quarter-page of copy and photo, the advertiser managed to appeal to every one of the persistent desires John mentions in our text. First, the ad was for an "escort service"—there you have the lust of the flesh; second, the photo appealed to the lust of the eyes; and third, the phrase "the type of woman *you deserve*" was a direct appeal to the pride of life of the "millionaire gentlemen" (as well as the women who would like to date a millionaire).

But you don't have to be a millionaire looking for a beautiful "trophy" to find temptations in our world today. Even the most common of us is daily bombarded with appeals to our base desires or attempts to raise our legitimate desires to a covetous level. But John puts life in its proper perspective: everything in this world and our desires for it will pass away. Only those who do God's will shall survive forever.   —C. R. B.

17. And the world passeth away, and the lust thereof: but he that doeth the will of God abideth for ever.

This *world* is not forever. No worldly lust will outlast the world. But God is forever, and Heaven is forever, and we are forever if we do God's will. So let's be in training for eternity.

B. The Father's Love (2:29–3:1)

29. If ye know that he is righteous, ye know that every one that doeth righteousness is born of him.

A person is not born again as a child of God by living right, but a life of *righteousness* is convincing evidence that one has been *born of* God. A man can go through the motions of becoming a Christian just to please his wife. He can profess repentance without really repenting. He can mouth a confession of faith with no real faith in his heart. He can be baptized without really being born again. But it is hardly possible to live a life of righteousness like that of God without really being a child of God. Such a life, day after day and year after year, is the proof that a person has been born of God.

3:1. Behold, what manner of love the Father hath bestowed upon us, that we should be called the sons of God: therefore the world knoweth us not, because it knew him not.

God called the Christians His children. What kind of love do you think that meant He had given them? It must have been a very great love. It must have been an everlasting love. Certainly it was a love that the Christians valued highly. And surely it was a love that made them very important. But

God's love gave them no importance in the eyes of the people around them. Most of those people were pagans. They worshiped many imaginary gods. They probably thought that the Christians' God was no better than one of theirs. Since they did not know God was important, they did not know His children were important. But the Christians knew. They knew God was the only real God, the Almighty. They knew His love set them apart from all the other people. They knew they were the most favored people on earth.

Conclusion

Some things never change. God is eternally the same; His righteousness is the same, and so is His love. In the course of centuries we have replaced the Christians to whom John wrote, but is that really a change?

A. Looking at Ourselves

Like the first-century Christians, we know God's righteousness is flawless, and we know ours is flawed. Like those Christians of long ago, we are trying to prove that we are God's children by matching our righteousness with His. But we have no referee to blow the whistle when we fall short. Each one of us must be his own referee.

So take a critical backward look. Examine what you have done in the week just past. Count the times when your righteousness has been less perfect than God's. If you find no such time, look again. But do not be dismayed if you find more flaws than you expected. "If we confess our sins, he is faithful and just to forgive us our sins, and to cleanse us from all unrighteousness" (1 John 1:9).

Then take a look at the week that lies ahead. Plan not to repeat any of the fouls of last week, and plan to commit no new fouls. Perhaps you will not be as perfect as you plan to be, but you can make some progress. Thus you will be growing toward "the measure of the stature of the fulness of Christ" (Ephesians 4:13).

B. Prayer

Father in Heaven, we can never say enough in praise of Your perfect righteousness and Your perfect love. Thank You for holding before us a faultless example, and thank You for sending Jesus to show us that faultless righteousness is possible even where we live. Again we must beg forgiveness for our recurrent unrighteousness, and again we must ask for wisdom and strength as we try daily to be more like You. In Jesus' name, amen.

C. Thought to Remember

"Truly our fellowship is with the Father"
(1 John 1:3).

Learning by Doing

This page contains an alternative lesson plan emphasizing learning activities.
Classes desiring such student involvement will find these suggestions helpful.

Learning Goals

After participating in this lesson, each student will be able to:

1. Tell the various ways John says that a Christian can develop a relationship with God.

2. Give examples of the things of the world that hinder our fellowship with the Lord.

3. Memorize 1 John 1:7 and ask God to help him or her to walk in the light.

Into the Lesson

Prepare an opening activity work sheet called "At One With God," a statement completion based on 1 John 1:7. The statement, including the missing words (blanks), is as follows: "But if we ___ in the ___, as ___ is in the ___, we have ___ one with ___, and the ___ of ___ his ___ us from all ___." (Make certain the spaces or lines are long enough for the words.) On the work sheet place the following missing words either above or below the statement: "*blood, fellowship, Christ, sin, walk, He, light, another, Jesus, cleanseth, light, son.*"

Give each student a copy of the work sheet and say, "This week's lesson focuses on the topic, 'Enjoy Fellowship With God.' To begin looking at this subject, fill in the missing words of the sentence by selecting the correct word for each blank space from those provided. Each word is to be used only once. When you complete the sentence, look up so I'll know you are finished."

When you have determined that nearly all have completed this activity, ask for someone to volunteer to read the completed sentence. Make corrections, if needed. Say, "The apostle John gives us a number of ways we can develop our relationships with God. Turn to our lesson text in 1 John, and let's discover those ways."

Into the Word

Ask a class member to read 1 John 1:5–2:6, 15–17, 29–3:1 aloud. After the reading, ask the following questions:

What are the various ways John says we can develop our relationships with God? *(Possible answers: walk as He walked, 1 John 2:6; confess our sins, 1 John 1:9; do the will of God, 1 John 2:17; do righteousness, 1 John 2:29.)*

What do you think John means when he uses the phrase, "walk in darkness" (1 John 1:6)? *(To do wrong, to behave in evil ways.)*

John says in 1 John 2:16 that the "lust of the flesh, and the lust of the eyes, and the pride of life" hinder our fellowship with God. What are some examples of things that hinder a Christian's relationship with God?"

Move the class members into at least three groups of no more than five. Label the groups A, B, and C. Say, "John gives us several verses that describe what we say (our talk), what we do (our walk), and even verses that combine what we say and do. Group A will look for those verses that describe what we say; Group B will look for those verses that describe what we do; and Group C will focus on those verses that describe both. You have ten minutes to do the following:

"1. Find those verses that apply to your group.

"2. Identify what we are to say and/or do, and the natural result of such responses.

"3. Identify those that are positive and those that are negative.

Group A: 1 John 1:9 (positive); 1 John 1:8, 10 (negative). *Group B:* 1 John 1:7, 9; 1 John 2:5, 17, 29 (positive); 1 John 2:1, 15 (negative). *Group C:* 1 John 2:6 (positive); 1 John 1:6; 2:4 (negative).

When the time is up, ask each group to report. After Group C's report, say, "John makes it clear that walking the talk is what is needed in each of our lives. We need to memorize 1 John 1:7." Divide the verse and the class into four groups and assign a phrase to each. Have the groups recite their phrases in order so that the total verse is rehearsed aloud. Shift the phrase to a different section and repeat the process until each has stated all four phrases: "But if we walk in the light, as he is in the light," "we have fellowship one with another," "and the blood of Jesus Christ his Son," "cleanseth us from all sin."

Into Life

Ask your class to list hymns and songs that share some of the ideas of 1 John 1:7. Some possible entries: "Stepping in the Light," "Heavenly Sunlight," "Blest Be the Tie That Binds," "Are You Washed in the Blood?" "Whiter Than Snow," "The Blood Will Never Lose Its Power," "Nothing But the Blood."

Direct the class to select seven, with one to be used each day this coming week in their personal (or family) devotional times. Suggest that each day they read 1 John 1:7 immediately before the singing of the selected song.

Let's Talk It Over

The questions on this page are designed to promote discussion of the lesson by the class and to encourage application of the lesson Scriptures. The answers provided are only discussion starters. Let your class talk it over from there.

1. Why is it important to have a healthy caution for the risk of having friendships with the children of spiritual darkness?

Paul tells us that "evil communications corrupt good manners" (1 Corinthians 15:33). Stated in modern English, "Bad company corrupts good character" *(New International Version).* That's why conscientious parents closely monitor their children's associations.

Peer pressure, however, can be very real to adults as well. While friendships with unbelievers can be the doorway to evangelism, the ungodly influences of worldly companions can at the same time jeopardize one's relationship with Christ and His church. We do well to remember Demas, who forsook the apostle Paul's ministry team, "having loved this present world" (2 Timothy 4:10).

2. How can Christians live in the midst of a sin-darkened world without becoming "of the darkness" themselves?

Jesus teaches in the Parable of the Sower that "the care of this world, and the deceitfulness of riches, choke the word," with the result that some become "unfruitful" (Matthew 13:22). What a challenge it is to live in this world without allowing our minds and souls to be corrupted! Spiritual victory is available in Christ, of course; Jesus prays for us and the Spirit strengthens us (John 17:9, 15-17). With proper caution and the power of the Holy Spirit we can keep our "boats in the water" without letting "the water into our boats."

3. Do we confess our sins only to God? Why, or why not?

The context of this lesson teaches us to confess our sins to God, as He is the only one who is able and willing "to forgive us" and "to cleanse us" for eternal life. Even so, the epistle of James exhorts, "Confess your faults one to another, and pray one for another" (James 5:16). Though we are not required to confide our shortcomings and wrongdoings to everyone in the church, a certain personal transparency is important if we are to be forgiven by anyone against whom we have sinned. Confession of wrongdoing to another person requires humility—we admit we were wrong!

We should remember, however, that in the New Testament era we do not confess sins to any particular person in the sense of thinking of him or her as a special mediator between us and God. That "priesthood" idea was abolished by Jesus, our great high priest (Hebrews 8:1-6). Today, we have a priesthood of all believers (1 Peter 2:5).

4. Is fear of death and Hell a legitimate motivation for deciding to follow Jesus? Why, or why not?

Some Christians who make life's most important decision only "to save their spiritual neck" later may wonder if the conversion was true and effective. However, in light of all the warnings in Scripture, including much in the teaching of Jesus regarding the eternal destinies of the righteous and the wicked, fear of punishment for sins surely is one acceptable motive for commitment to Christ. When Christians grow to greater spiritual maturity, they may come to realize that a higher motive for accepting Christ is a desire to please God.

5. How is it possible for us to presume upon God's grace when we willingly decide to sin?

Some professing Christians may disobey divine commandments intentionally while planning to seek and receive pardon later on. They know of God's love and mercy, and of His promise to forgive every sin that is confessed. But such presumption will not go unpunished. The writer of Hebrews warns that only eternal judgment awaits those who sin willfully after having received "the knowledge of the truth" (Hebrews 10:26, 27). We all slip back into sin from time to time, and God's continuing forgiveness is available when we stumble. But Paul warns against the utter folly of making sin a habit all over again (Romans 6).

6. What does our reaction to our culture's consumerism say about our sincerity in regard to the Biblical teaching about worldliness?

Overconsumption is a serious affliction of our times. Ultimately, where we spend our money reveals our priorities and our true allegiance (cf. Luke 12:34). When we indulge ourselves with luxuries while the needs of the church go unmet we rob God!

Love One Another

DEVOTIONAL READING: **1 Corinthians 13.**

BACKGROUND SCRIPTURE: **1 John 3:11–4:21.**

PRINTED TEXT: **1 John 3:11-16; 4:7-16.**

1 John 3:11-16

11 For this is the message that ye heard from the beginning, that we should love one another.

12 Not as Cain, who was of that wicked one, and slew his brother. And wherefore slew he him? Because his own works were evil, and his brother's righteous.

13 Marvel not, my brethren, if the world hate you.

14 We know that we have passed from death unto life, because we love the brethren. He that loveth not his brother abideth in death.

15 Whosoever hateth his brother is a murderer: and ye know that no murderer hath eternal life abiding in him.

16 Hereby perceive we the love of God, because he laid down his life for us: and we ought to lay down our lives for the brethren.

1 John 4:7-16

7 Beloved, let us love one another: for love is of God; and every one that loveth is born of God, and knoweth God.

8 He that loveth not, knoweth not God; for God is love.

9 In this was manifested the love of God toward us, because that God sent his only begotten Son into the world, that we might live through him.

10 Herein is love, not that we loved God, but that he loved us, and sent his Son to be the propitiation for our sins.

11 Beloved, if God so loved us, we ought also to love one another.

12 No man hath seen God at any time. If we love one another, God dwelleth in us, and his love is perfected in us.

13 Hereby know we that we dwell in him, and he in us, because he hath given us of his Spirit.

14 And we have seen and do testify that the Father sent the Son to be the Saviour of the world.

15 Whosoever shall confess that Jesus is the Son of God, God dwelleth in him, and he in God.

16 And we have known and believed the love that God hath to us. God is love; and he that dwelleth in love dwelleth in God, and God in him.

GOLDEN TEXT: Beloved, if God so loved us, we ought also to love one another.
—1 John 4:11.

Faith Faces the World
Unit 3: Live as God's Children
(Lessons 9-11)

Lesson Aims

After participating in this lesson, each student should be able to:

1. Tell the source, expression, and result of Christian love.

2. Compare God's love for us with our love for others.

3. Suggest one specific way to demonstrate godly love to someone this week.

Lesson Outline

Introduction

English-speaking people are fascinated with the word *love*, and we use it in a wide variety of contexts. We love our spouses and we love chocolate sundaes, but we love our spouses with all our hearts and love sundaes with our taste buds. We love our children and we love holidays, but those two loves are different things. We love our friends and, if we are Christians, we love our enemies; but even if both those loves are sincere, they do not feel exactly alike. So many shades of meaning for such a small word!

A. Love, Then and Now

The English language actually has over a dozen "specialized" words for *love* when we need them. Words such as *adore, cherish* (verbs), *endearment,* and *friendship* (nouns) are examples. The same is true of the word *love* in the Bible. In our English translations some form of this word occurs in the New Testament over three hundred times, and love is a major theme in the writings of the apostle John. In today's lesson we sift through a small part of what he has to say about love.

B. Lesson Background

In the background of last week's lesson we noted that the first century saw the rise of false teachers who valued human opinion more than divine revelation. These false teachers led many people away from God's truth. John wanted his readers to reject such mistaken leading and cling to the truth that he and the other apostles had heard from Jesus while He was teaching on earth.

Years before John wrote this letter, Paul warned Timothy against men whose teaching was perverted because their love was perverted. They loved themselves more than they loved their fellowman, and they loved pleasures more than they loved God. Therefore they became bad characters indeed (2 Timothy 3:1-5). In contrast with such perverted love and its evil results, we now hear John urging Christians toward proper love.

I. Love for Others
(1 John 3:11-16)

In the world around us we see evidence of mistaken love (1 John 2:15-17). John helps clarify our thinking about the proper objects of our love.

A. Message of God (v. 11)

11. For this is the message that ye heard from the beginning, that we should love one another.

To *love one another* is a theme John already has introduced in 1 John 2:9-11. This theme was important *from the beginning*, during Jesus' earthly ministry (John 13:34, 35). It still bears repeating as John becomes the church's elder statesman in the latter years of the first century. A lack of brotherly love is evidently a problem in some parts of the church as time moves on (Galatians 5:15; James 4:1-3, 11, 12). [See question #1, page 88.]

B. Example of Evil (vv. 12, 13)

12. Not as Cain, who was of that wicked one, and slew his brother. And wherefore slew he him? Because his own works were evil, and his brother's righteous.

Cain is an example of the extreme opposite of what a Christian ought to be (see Genesis 4:1-16). His problem was that he *was of that wicked one,* the devil. As a result, he did wrong instead of right. That was the reason the Lord refused to accept his offering (Genesis 4:7; Hebrews 11:4). But instead of repenting, Cain went wild with jealousy and murdered *his brother* Abel.

So I am warned. If I feel inclined to hate a fellow Christian, is it possibly because he or she is more *righteous* than I am? Should I be cleaning up my own way of living instead of envying someone whose godly living wins for him or her some honor that is denied to me?

13. Marvel not, my brethren, if the world hate you.

The world has a lot of people who are of the evil one, as Cain was. They are doing wrong, and they hate you because you are doing right. Don't be surprised at that (cf. John 15:18–16:4), and don't worry about it. It is far better to do right and be hated by the world (Mark 13:13) than to do wrong and hate those who are doing right.

C. Evidence of Life (vv. 14, 15)

14. We know that we have passed from death unto life, because we love the brethren. He that loveth not his brother abideth in death.

Before we became Christians we were "dead in trespasses and sins" (Ephesians 2:1). We were condemned to death because of those sins (Romans 6:23). But when we became Christians we *passed from death unto life*—eternal life! Our sins were forgiven; we were made alive (Ephesians 2:1-5). As children of God, we love God's other children, the other Christians. They have their faults as we have ours, but we love them because they are our brothers and sisters. This proves that *we have passed from death unto life,* that we really are Christians. Likewise anyone who does not love the brethren proves that he or she is still dead; such a person is not really a Christian even if his or her name is on the church roll.

15. Whosoever hateth his brother is a murderer: and ye know that no murderer hath eternal life abiding in him.

Anyone who hates a fellow Christian *is a murderer* at heart, even if he or she lacks the courage to kill. This verifies the last part of verse 14. Since the one who hates a fellow Christian does not have *eternal life abiding in him,* such a person is not really a Christian. See Matthew 5:21, 22. [See question #2, page 88.]

D. Example of Love (v. 16)

16. Hereby perceive we the love of God, because he laid down his life for us: and we ought to lay down our lives for the brethren.

You probably have noticed in your own Bible that some words in the *King James Version* are italicized. The translators did this to indicate words that are not in the Greek original but (in their opinion) are necessary for smooth English. In the verse at hand, however, this procedure confuses us rather than helps us. The words *of God* do not appear in the Greek text, and their insertion seems to say that God, rather than God's Son, *laid down his life for us.*

The Son's *love* is a model for us in that *we ought to lay down our lives for the brethren.* Of course we cannot (and need not) do this just as Jesus did: we cannot atone for others' sins by giving our lives. But the verse that follows (not in our text for today) makes it clear that God expects us to spend our time and resources in providing help for fellow Christians who need it. If we refuse to help, we demonstrate that we are lacking in love. [See question #3, page 88.]

TWISTED VALUES

Juanita Baird told police she thought she had been shot by someone she knew. Little did she know how right she was! Nothing had been taken from her modest home in Houston, so it was clear that robbery was not the motive. As detectives pieced together the story, it became ever stranger. For a least a year the plot had been hatching, and the principals in the story turned out to be Mrs. Baird's daughter and four teenage grandchildren.

Those five family members paid sixty dollars to a fourteen-year-old girl to shoot the grandmother and her husband. Another fifteen dollars was paid to a thirteen-year-old male accomplice. The reason for the attempted murder is just as surprising: the daughter and children were on

Visual for lesson 10

Display today's visual as you begin to discuss 1 John 3:16.

welfare and received room and board in the Baird home under what they felt were overly-strict rules. But the shooting was precipitated by the fact that the Bairds refused to build a swimming pool or basketball court for the younger family members!

The incident tends to confirm statistics that indicate a person is more likely to be murdered by an acquaintance than by a stranger. What twisted values our society sometimes exhibits! Unlike the Baird family, however, the family of God lives by a different standard—one established by our Lord, who laid down His life for us. In addition to paying sin's price, this sets an example of love as the standard for our treatment of others.

—C. R. B.

II. God's Love and Ours
(1 John 4:7-11)

Children are expected to be like their parents. Even Jesus became a carpenter like His step-father Joseph; and indeed, Jesus' Heavenly Father was the first and greatest of all carpenters, the maker of Heaven and earth (Genesis 1:1). As children of God, we shape ourselves to be like our Father in Heaven—not necessarily in the work of our hands, but certainly in the love of our hearts (Luke 6:35, 36).

A. Source of Love (vv. 7, 8)

7. Beloved, let us love one another: for love is of God; and every one that loveth is born of God, and knoweth God.

Although God's children are to love their enemies (Luke 6:27-29), this lesson is about loving *one another*—about loving our fellow Christians. *Love is of God* (indeed, "God is love," v. 8), and all of God's children ought to be loving as He is loving. Such love in us is powerful evidence that we really are God's children.

8. He that loveth not, knoweth not God; for God is love.

Sadly, the opposite is true as well. Unloving people do not even know God. He is a stranger to them.

B. Proof of Love (vv. 9, 10)

9. In this was manifested the love of God toward us, because that God sent his only begotten Son into the world, that we might live through him.

No Christian can doubt that God loves *His only begotten Son*, Jesus. Yet God sent Jesus from Heaven to earth not only to live as a man among men, but also to be despised, rejected, persecuted, tortured, and killed! A loving God subjected His beloved Son to all that in order *that we*

might live through him. Then how great is God's love for us! It is beyond measure, beyond understanding. But thank God it is not beyond belief. It cannot be doubted, for God proved it by sacrificing His Son to pay sin's penalty for us (John 3:16, 17). [See question #4, page 88.]

10. Herein is love, not that we loved God, but that he loved us, and sent his Son to be the propitiation for our sins.

We discussed the idea of *propitiation* in lesson 9 (see page 76). Love in all its fullness, love in all its power, love in all its splendor is not seen in our puny love for God. Rather, it is seen in God's tremendous love for us. God demonstrated it by sending His Son to give His life in propitiation (atonement) for our sins.

GIVING UP A CHILD

There always have been unwanted children. The "abortion on demand" movement in Western society is a sufficient—if grisly—indication that the trend is alive and thriving. But even among women who do not abort their babies, unwanted children are still a significant social problem. All too frequently we hear of a newborn baby left at the door of a hospital or a church—or worse yet, in a trash dumpster in a back alley.

A few years ago the city of Hamburg, Germany, resurrected and updated an old approach to this perennial problem. Project *Findelbaby*—for "foundling"—offers desperate mothers a delivery slot where they can place their babies in a warm bed and then leave anonymously. A sensor makes attendants aware that a baby has been delivered to their care. Impetus for the project came from testimony at a murder trial where a woman admitted hiding three pregnancies and snuffing out the tender lives shortly after birth. Her husband

Home Daily Bible Readings

Monday, Nov. 3—Love Believes, Hopes, Endures (1 Corinthians 13:1-7)

Tuesday, Nov. 4—Love Never Ends (1 Corinthians 13:8-13)

Wednesday, Nov. 5—Lay Down Life for Another (1 John 3:11-17)

Thursday, Nov. 6—Love in Truth and Action (1 John 3:18-24)

Friday, Nov. 7—Love Is From God (1 John 4:1-7)

Saturday, Nov. 8—God Is Love (1 John 4:8-12))

Sunday, Nov. 9—We Love Because God Loved Us (John 4:13-21)

How to Say It

AGAPE (Greek). uh-*gah*-pay.
EPHESIANS. Ee-*fee*-zhunz.
GALATIANS. Guh-*lay*-shunz.
HEBREWS. *Hee*-brews.
PROPITIATION. pro-*pih*-she-*ay*-shun (strong accent on *ay*).

---

had said he would kill her if she bore another child.

Such cases are tragedies for all concerned. How starkly they contrast to what God did in giving up His Son, not abandoning Him to a foundling home, but giving Him to a caring mother and father. They would raise Him to love us enough to give His own life to save us. As John says, this is what love is all about! —C. R. B.

C. Result of Love (v. 11)

11. Beloved, if God so loved us, we ought also to love one another.

To despise a fellow Christian for whom God's Son died is unthinkable! This week, how can we be more helpful and loving to fellow Christians, those here at home as well as those on the other side of the world? [See question #5, page 88.]

III. We in Him, He in Us (1 John 4:12-16)

We do love one another, don't we? We cannot take pride in that, however, because our love seems tiny in comparison with God's immeasurable love for us. As we read the final verses of our text, we see that we are in God and He is in us. We can rejoice because we are so close to Him; but we cannot boast, because the closeness is His doing, not ours. He redeemed us; He forgave us; He made us His children. Thank God!

A. Our Status (vv. 12, 13)

12. No man hath seen God at any time. If we love one another, God dwelleth in us, and his love is perfected in us.

In John 1:18 the apostle also stresses that *No man hath seen God at any time*. There, however, he adds that the "Son . . . hath declared him." We can know God very well by learning about His Son, who walked the earth in the visible form of a man and spoke God's truth (John 6:46; 14:9). In a much smaller way, people who do not know Jesus form their idea of God from the way we, God's other children, imitate His love, for *God dwelleth in us*. What a sobering thought!

God's *love is perfected* (meaning "completed") *in us* as *we love one another*. God's love com-

pletes its work when we copy His love and give help to one another in His name. In love God wants to give us help; He enables His loving people to give that help.

13. Hereby know we that we dwell in him, and he in us, because he hath given us of his Spirit.

John's observation that *we dwell in him, and he in us* is a way of saying our relationship with God is close and complete (cf. 1 John 2:24; 4:15). When we imitate God's love and help one of His needy people, God *in us* is doing it. But if we were not *in him*, we would not imitate His love and do His work. It is a mutual indwelling, but we do not live together as equals. He is God, the Creator, the all-wise, the all-powerful. He lives in us as director and controller. In old-fashioned terms, He is our Lord and Master and we are His willing slaves. We live in Him as devoted and obedient servants. Let us say, as Jesus said, "Not my will, but thine, be done" (Luke 22:42).

We know we dwell in God *because he hath given us of his Spirit*. God is the one "who hath also sealed us, and given the earnest of the Spirit in our hearts" (2 Corinthians 1:22). The Spirit indwells us as God's temple (1 Corinthians 3:16). We know also because we find ourselves abandoning our own wills to do God's will.

BECOMING ONE WITH THE STORY

The 1965 film *The Sound of Music* is one of the greatest movie hits of all time. One measure of its success is the fairly recent phenomenon known as the "Sing-along Sound of Music," which got its start in England and has been making the rounds of American cities on tour.

The fact that this is a "feel good" movie shows in the way people come to the sing-along version. They dress in costumes representing the various characters in the film. As the lyrics to the songs appear in subtitles on the screen, the audience sings heartily without self-consciousness. Voices range from good to bad, and everything in between. Caught up in the spirit of the film, the viewer-participants live out, for a few moments, the positive message portrayed on the screen. As one reviewer put it, "the teary-eyed woman to my right cradled her darling daughter in her lap as they earnestly sang along to 'Edelweiss.'" At the end of the film, "when love conquers all and hope waits on the horizon, my neighbor leaned over and kissed his wife."

Isn't this a picture of what John is calling us to? Today will we be so caught up in the spirit of what God has done for the world in Christ—the greatest "love story" of all time!—that we willingly and unself-consciously give ourselves over to living out God's story of selfless love, and letting that story live in us?

—C. R. B.

B. Our Testimony (v. 14)

14. And we have seen and do testify that the Father sent the Son to be the Saviour of the world.

John and the other apostles actually had *seen* Jesus (1 John 1:1-3). They had been with Him almost continually for three years. From His teaching and the teaching of the Holy Spirit they knew *the Father sent the Son to be the Saviour of the world.* Over and over they have given that testimony, have given it far and wide. We have not seen Jesus, and we are not inspired as the apostles were; but we can repeat the apostles' testimony as confidently as they gave it: God indeed did send His Son to be the Savior of the world.

C. Our Confession (vv. 15, 16)

15. Whosoever shall confess that Jesus is the Son of God, God dwelleth in him, and he in God.

In recent times the word *confess* has come to be used in admitting something wrong: a crime or sin, even a mistaken thought. For modern ears it may be better to say *agree* instead of "confess." One who says *that Jesus is the Son of God* agrees with the truth, and agrees also with countless Christians who have said the same thing before.

Of course, this agreement is more than merely saying so. If one really agrees that Jesus is the Son of God, then he or she lives a life in agreement with what the Son says. He or she loves, honors, and obeys Jesus even as Jesus loves, honors, and obeys His Father. Thus such a person makes it evident that *God dwelleth in him, and he in God.*

16. And we have known and believed the love that God hath to us. God is love; and he that dwelleth in love dwelleth in God, and God in him.

We might have expected to read "believed and known" rather than *known and believed.* Usually we think *known* is a stronger word than *believed.* We progress from believing to knowing as the evidence piles up till it cannot be denied. But in another way, *believed* is stronger than *known;* for believing is faith, and faith includes trust and commitment as well as conviction. If we have faith in our Savior, we trust His promise. We are sure we have everlasting life. To Jesus we turn over all we are and all we have, sure that in Him we shall be more than we could be without Him.

We know that *God is love.* But we know that that is not all that God is. He is also light (1 John 1:5), Spirit (John 4:24), a consuming fire (Hebrews 12:29), our refuge and strength (Psalm 46:1), King of all the earth (Psalm 47:7), my helper (Psalm 54:4), my defense (Psalm 59:9), and my salvation and glory (Psalm 62:7). But in our text John is writing about God as love. Evidence

of God's love is everywhere, from the sunshine and rain and bountiful harvest to the gift of His Son to rescue us from death and give us life everlasting. Every good thing that nourishes our life or brings us joy is evidence of God's love.

Love is intrinsic to God. Without His love, God would not be the God we know. Perhaps He would be a frightening monster like some of the imaginary gods of the pagans. And it is sobering to think what monsters we would be if we had no love either for God or for our fellow humans.

But God is love, and anyone *that dwelleth in love dwelleth in God.* We live in God, and He lives in us. There are comfort and security in these thoughts. Even our fear of God is not terror; it is reverence and awe that live alongside our love.

Conclusion

To write the conclusion of this lesson, we have only to copy the title printed above it: "Love One Another." This is the badge that identifies us as Christians, for Jesus said, "By this shall all men know that ye are my disciples, if ye have love one to another" (John 13:35). God's love for us is the model we follow in loving one another. The towering evidence of God's love was the sacrifice of His Son. So let us not turn thoughtlessly away when we see an opportunity for a great sacrifice for our brothers and sisters. Our Father's love is seen continually in daily bread, in the beauty of a sunset or a rose, in "every good gift and every perfect gift" that makes us glad (James 1:17). Our love for one another is seen most often in tiny bits of kindness, courtesy, and help.

A. One More Thought

We can hardly leave the subject of love without mentioning one thought that is not in this lesson, but is in the teaching of Jesus. He said, "Love your enemies" (Matthew 5:44). In this also we follow the example of our Father. It was a world of lost sinners that He "so loved . . . that he gave his only begotten Son" (John 3:16), and sinners share His gifts of sunshine and rain (Matthew 5:45). "As we have therefore opportunity, let us do good unto all men, especially unto them who are of the household of faith" (Galatians 6:10).

B. Prayer

Our Father in Heaven, how can we begin to thank You for Your example of unfailing love? Forgive our failure to model your love, and so stir our minds and hearts that we shall not fail again. In Jesus' name, amen.

C. Thought to Remember

God is love, and so are we.

Learning by Doing

This page contains an alternative lesson plan emphasizing learning activities. Classes desiring such student involvement will find these suggestions helpful.

Learning Goals

After participating in this lesson, each student will be able to:

1. Tell the source, expression, and result of Christian love.

2. Compare God's love for us with our love for others.

3. Suggest one specific way to demonstrate godly love to someone this week.

Into the Lesson

Prepare an agree/disagree work sheet activity entitled, "Love: Pinning It Down." Print the five statements below with a 1-7 scale next to each. Explain that the 7 indicates "strongly agree," and the 1 indicates "strongly disagree."

1. Love that is verbally expressed to others is genuine.

2. Love that is outwardly demonstrated toward others is genuine.

3. Only love that is both verbally expressed and outwardly demonstrated toward others is genuine.

4. Love that is expressed verbally to others can be insincere.

5. Love that is demonstrated outwardly to others can be insincere.

To begin class, distribute the work sheets and say, "Our topic today is 'Love One Another.' To help us begin thinking, I've prepared an agree/disagree work sheet. Read each statement and circle the number that best represents your opinion: strongly agree, 7, to strongly disagree, 1." Allow a few minutes for the class to complete the work sheet. Then, go over each statement to see whether there are different levels of agreement or disagreement. Ask class members to tell their numbers and their reason(s). Say, "We've discussed a number of interesting positions. It's not as easy as you may have thought to pin down a set formula or expression. However, in our text today, the apostle John describes this concept of love and adds an essential component of genuineness. Turn to 1 John 3, and let's see whether we can identify that component."

Into the Word

Ask a class member to read the whole lesson text aloud. Then ask each class member to review the text with a neighbor and try to identify the essential component of genuine love. After a few minutes, ask for suggested answers. *(The essential component is personal sacrifice for others.)*

Ask the following questions to review the text.

1. What is the source of Christian love? *(God, 4:7.)*

2. What is the ultimate expression of Christian love? *(God's sending His Son into the world, 4:9.)*

3. What is the result of Christian love? *(God's love is perfected in us, 4:12.)*

4. Why is the Old Testament example of Cain presented in the lesson text? *(He failed to love his brother, was influenced by the evil one, and sinned, 3:12.)*

5. What does a failure to love others reveal about the person? *(He abides in death, 1 John 3:14; he is a murderer, 3:15; he does not know God, 4:8.)*

6. What conclusions can be drawn from the text about a person who does love others? *(He has passed from death unto life, 3:14; he is born of God, he knows God, 4:7; God dwells in him and His love is perfected in him, 4:12.)*

7. From the lesson text, what is necessary for God to dwell in us? *(We need to love one another, 4:12; we have been given His Spirit, 4:13; we have confessed that Jesus is the Son of God, 4:15; we dwell in love, 4:16.)*

Into Life

Prepare a half-page work sheet called, "Measuring Our Love for Others." List the following terms down the left column: *family, friends, neighbors, work associates, homeless, prisoners.* In the right column place a 1-7 scale beside each term. Give each student a copy, and ask each to evaluate his or her intensity of love for others. Say, "We know that we all need to strengthen the way we love others. What practical ways can we demonstrate godly love to others?" As suggestions are given, write them on the board.

Give each class member a three-by-five index card. Say, "Think about someone to whom you would like to demonstrate God's love this week. Write his or her name on one side of the card. Next, think about some specific ways that you can demonstrate godly love to this person. Write those ways on the other side of the card." Encourage the students to carry the cards with them all week to remind them to demonstrate God's love. Close the class time with a prayer of commitment to show love to someone this week.

Let's Talk It Over

The questions on this page are designed to promote discussion of the lesson by the class and to encourage application of the lesson Scriptures. The answers provided are only discussion starters. Let your class talk it over from there.

1. How do people misuse the word *love*?

Probably the most serious misuse is to confuse the meanings of *love* and *lust*. For example, during premarital counseling couples often claim that they want to marry because they are "in love" when the truth may be that they are actually just "in lust." They want to marry for selfish reasons.

The love John talks about, however, is "something you do, not always something that you feel." This type of love is based on a decision, not on an emotion. It puts someone else's well-being above one's own. It is not passive, but active. This type of love "is not puffed up, doth not behave itself unseemly, seeketh not her own, is not easily provoked, thinketh no evil; rejoiceth not in iniquity" (1 Corinthians 13:4-6). None of this is true of lust, whether sexual lust or lust after material things.

2. If I find that I have hateful feelings toward someone, what should I do? Does 1 John 3:15 mean I am lost?

Jesus made it clear that hateful anger is equal to the sin of murder (Matthew 5:21, 22). Mental attitudes eventually find expression in words or actions (Matthew 12:33-37; 15:19, 20). Christ's standards are indeed high (Matthew 5:48), but the Holy Spirit gives us strength for greater holiness.

If I find I have hateful feelings toward a person, I need to pray—both for my own attitude and for the other person. I need to practice love, the active *agape* type of love that is more than merely a feeling. I need to seek the help of mature believers to overcome my hateful feelings.

The message of 1 John 3:15 applies to someone who gives over to such attitudes, who hates without remorse or repentance. The message of 1 John 1:9 is that repentant sinners can find grace.

3. In what ways is it possible to love others as much as Jesus loves us? In what ways is it impossible?

One thing we can do is to speak the truth in love, just as Christ did. We can show kindness by sharing material blessings, although we cannot perform miracles. There are documented cases where one person literally sacrificed his or her life so that another could live. But no one can (or needs to) die to pay the price for sin as Christ did.

Literal martyrdom is not an option for every Christian, but we can begin "laying down our lives" for needy neighbors as we sacrifice leisure time and personal resources for their benefit. As Jesus taught, our lives do not consist of material possessions (Luke 12:15); rather, it is in giving of ourselves and our resources to benefit others that we demonstrate the Christian love that He expects (Matthew 10:42).

4. The lesson writer says God's love "is beyond measure, beyond understanding." How, then, can he say, "Thank God it is not beyond belief"? How can we believe what we cannot really grasp?

Our limitations mean that we cannot understand *everything* about God and His love. But the fact that Jesus walked the earth and taught things about His Father means that we are expected to understand *some things* about God and His love.

We begin to get an inkling of that love when we look at some of the things God has done for us: creation itself, providential care through the forces of nature, and the death of Christ to pay sin's price. Those things we see (or others have seen) enable us to walk by faith concerning all that we have not yet seen or experienced (2 Corinthians 5:7). Until we see Jesus face to face, we rejoice and are content with the limited grasp of God's love that He has allowed us to have. It is enough.

5. What one characteristic, more than any other, identifies us as followers of Christ? Why?

Selfless love for one another marks us as disciples of Jesus. "By this shall all men know that ye are my disciples, if ye have love one to another" (John 13:35). This type of love shows itself in attitudes and actions, and is a consistent theme in the New Testament. The old saying, "People don't care how much you know until they know how much you care" is true!

Selfless love means we expect nothing in return. This is an effective witness for Christ because it shows the world what our true motives are. We aren't out to manipulate people. We don't love people because of what they can do for us in return (see James 2:1-13). The negative implication of this truth is that the grace of Christ is obscured when we are unloving in our words and deeds.

Live With Confidence

DEVOTIONAL READING: Romans 5:1-11.

BACKGROUND SCRIPTURE: 1 John 5.

PRINTED TEXT: 1 John 5:1-15.

1 John 5:1-15

1 Whosoever believeth that Jesus is the Christ is born of God: and every one that loveth him that begat loveth him also that is begotten of him.

2 By this we know that we love the children of God, when we love God, and keep his commandments.

3 For this is the love of God, that we keep his commandments: and his commandments are not grievous.

4 For whatsoever is born of God overcometh the world: and this is the victory that overcometh the world, even our faith.

5 Who is he that overcometh the world, but he that believeth that Jesus is the Son of God?

6 This is he that came by water and blood, even Jesus Christ; not by water only, but by water and blood. And it is the Spirit that beareth witness, because the Spirit is truth.

7 For there are three that bear record in heaven, the Father, the Word, and the Holy Ghost: and these three are one.

8 And there are three that bear witness in earth, the spirit, and the water, and the blood: and these three agree in one.

9 If we receive the witness of men, the witness of God is greater: for this is the witness of God which he hath testified of his Son.

10 He that believeth on the Son of God hath the witness in himself: he that believeth not God hath made him a liar; because he believeth not the record that God gave of his Son.

11 And this is the record, that God hath given to us eternal life, and this life is in his Son.

12 He that hath the Son hath life; and he that hath not the Son of God hath not life.

13 These things have I written unto you that believe on the name of the Son of God; that ye may know that ye have eternal life, and that ye may believe on the name of the Son of God.

14 And this is the confidence that we have in him, that, if we ask any thing according to his will, he heareth us:

15 And if we know that he hear us, whatsoever we ask, we know that we have the petitions that we desired of him.

Nov 16

GOLDEN TEXT: This is the record, that God hath given to us eternal life, and this life is in his Son.—1 John 5:11.

Lesson Aims

After participating in this lesson, each student should be able to:

1. Summarize the facts that we know about Jesus Christ from today's text.

2. Tell how faith in these facts helps us to live as confident Christians.

3. Write a statement of confident faith in Jesus as Lord and Savior.

Lesson Outline

INTRODUCTION
    A. Are We Bright Enough?
    B. Lesson Background
  I. CHILDREN OF GOD (1 John 5:1-5)
    A. Requirements (vv. 1-3)
    B. Results (vv. 4, 5)
    Faith That Overcomes
  II. WITNESSES TO TRUTH (1 John 5:6-8)
    A. Spirit, Water, and Blood, Part 1 (v. 6)
    B. Spirit, Water, and Blood, Part 2 (vv. 7, 8)
  III. DECLARATION OF LIFE (1 John 5:9-15)
    A. Testimony and Result (vv. 9-12)
    B. Knowledge and Confidence (vv. 13-15)
    The Promise of Immortality
CONCLUSION
    A. Living With Confidence
    B. Prayer
    C. Thought to Remember

Introduction

Some people think Pete is not very bright, but Pete thinks he is bright enough. He earns a living and lives alone in his own little house. He goes to church every Sunday and reads from the Bible every day. He likes best to read what Jesus did, and especially about the time Jesus walked on the water (John 6:16-21). Pete likes to imagine Jesus, tall and handsome, walking across the little lake outside the town where Pete lives.

One day Pete read that Jesus said, "He that believeth on me, the works that I do shall he do also" (John 14:12). Didn't that mean Pete could walk on water, too? He hurried out to the lake and straight into it. In a minute he knew he could not walk on water.

Pete had some disappointments worse than that. Seeing a man with terminal cancer, he prayed that the man would be well. But the man died. How could that be? Didn't Jesus say, "All things, whatsoever ye shall ask in prayer, believing, ye shall receive" (Matthew 21:22)?

Pete always had thought the Bible was true in every detail, but now he had to wonder. Is it possible that the Bible is wrong sometimes? Is it possible that not all of Jesus' promises are kept? Pete had to do some heavy thinking about that. In the midst of his thoughts he chanced to notice 1 John 5:14: "If we ask any thing according to his will, he heareth us."

So Jesus' will makes a difference, and Jesus' will is the same as God's will. Of course it makes a difference! God didn't want Pete to walk on water. Thinking about it again, Pete knew it would be a pretty silly thing for him to do. God allowed that cancer patient to die because that was the only way he could get to Heaven. Being well in Heaven is much better than being well on earth.

Now Pete has a new purpose in his Bible reading. Daily he is looking for what God wants him to do. When he finds that, he does it. Some people still think Pete is not very bright, but through the Word of God the Holy Spirit is teaching him something every day.

A. Are We Bright Enough?

Like Pete, most of us have made our peace with the fact that we don't always get what we pray for. We, too, have read Jesus' promise in Matthew 21:22 about receiving "whatsoever ye shall ask in prayer." But even as we read it, we know that the promise is not really as absolute as it seems.

First of all, we know God will not do anything wrong, even if dozens of us are begging for it every day. God knows what is right and what is wrong much better than we do.

Second, our own experience confirms the saying that is repeated often among Christians: "God has three ways of answering our prayers. Sometimes He says 'Yes,' sometimes He says 'No,' and sometimes He says 'Wait.'" Our confidence in God is unshaken even when He says "No" because we know His "No" is for our greater benefit.

Third, we are bright enough to see that it's logically impossible for God to say "Yes" to all our prayers. Perhaps I am asking a sunny day for my picnic while you, at the same time, are asking for a heavy rain for your cornfield. Neither of us is going to find fault with God because my picnic is rained out or your cornfield is dry for another day or two.

B. Lesson Background

Last week's lesson centered our attention on loving one another, but we gave a passing thought to the outreach of our love beyond the circle of our fellow Christians. Our love reaches out in two directions. First, it reaches upward to our Heavenly Father, who loves us with a love that is close and personal even while it is transcendent and supernatural. Second, our love reaches out horizontally to people. This includes enemies who do not love us (Matthew 5:43-45; 22:37-39) as well as friends and family who do.

This week's lesson overlaps that of last week. Beginning with thoughts on love, it leads us on to think of faith and confidence. Let us be not slow to follow where it leads, for faith and confidence can give a heavenly serenity even in the midst of worldly troubles.

I. Children of God
(1 John 5:1-5)

Our lesson title counsels us to "Live With Confidence," and that is excellent advice. Confidence frees us from anxiety and worry, makes us optimistic, and helps us do our best each day. But let us understand at the outset that John is not talking about self-confidence. He's actually talking about something much better than that: our confidence in the Son of God, Jesus (verses 13 and 14 of our text). We trust Jesus; we obey Him; we expect His help, and we get it.

The word *confidence* appears near the end of our printed text. Near the beginning of our lesson we see the words *believeth* and *faith.* Faith in Jesus includes believing in Jesus. This type of faith trusts Him, depends on Him, and does His will. It shapes our lives! So the words *confidence* and *faith* are related. In this lesson we do not want to get lost in word games, but we do want to understand the words we are reading.

A. Requirements (vv. 1-3)

1. Whosoever believeth that Jesus is the Christ is born of God: and every one that loveth him that begat loveth him also that is begotten of him.

When we believe *that Jesus is the Christ*, He gives us the "power to become the sons of God" (John 1:12). [See question #1, page 96.] Because of our belief, our faith, God brings us to rebirth (John 1:13; Galatians 3:26). Our bodies look as they did before, but our spirits are reborn (John 3:3-6). We are new creatures (2 Corinthians 5:17). Since God brings about our rebirth, the new creatures we become are God's children. As proper children do, we love our Father, God; and we love all His other children,

our fellow Christians. This repeats and reemphasizes the theme of last week's lesson, "Love One Another."

2, 3. By this we know that we love the children of God, when we love God, and keep his commandments. For this is the love of God, that we keep his commandments: and his commandments are not grievous.

John's thinking is easier to understand when we begin at the end of this two-verse section and work backward through it. God's *commandments are not grievous*—obedience to them does not place a heavy burden on us. Jesus said, "My yoke is easy, and my burden is light" (Matthew 11:30). It is our *love* for *God*, not a sense of obligation, that motivates us to *keep his commandments* in our daily living. *When we love God, and keep his commandments*, of course, *we love the children of God*. That is one of God's clear commandments. Jesus taught on this theme often (see John 14:21, 23; 15:14; cf. 1 John 3:23).

B. Results (vv. 4, 5)

4, 5. For whatsoever is born of God overcometh the world: and this is the victory that overcometh the world, even our faith. Who is he that overcometh the world, but he that believeth that Jesus is the Son of God?

Whatsoever is born of God is any one of the children of God whom we have been reading about, any faithful Christian. Here *the world* refers to the godless world, the selfish world, the world that is constantly tempting a Christian to turn away from God for the sake of worldly profit and pleasure. Any faithful Christian resists the world's temptations and so *overcometh the world*. (In his Gospel, John speaks more of "the world" than the three other Gospel writers combined!)

It is *our faith*, our belief in Jesus, the Son of God that enables us to overcome. [See question #2, page 96.] *The world* is insistent with offers of dishonest gain and wicked pleasure, but we have a better offer, an inheritance reserved in Heaven for us (1 Peter 1:4). That inheritance is better than anything the world can offer, and it is ours forever. This is not the first time that John has spoken of overcoming (see John 16:33; 1 John 2:13, 14; 4:4), and it will not be the last (see Revelation 2:7, 11, 17, 26; 3:5, 12, 21; 21:7).

How to Say It

CORINTHIANS. Kor-*in*-thee-unz (*th* as in *thin*).
CRYONICS. cry-*ahn*-iks.
GALATIANS. Guh-*lay*-shunz.
HEBREWS. *Hee*-brews.

FAITH THAT OVERCOMES

Floyd Goodman, Jr. was trapped! While working at his job in a peanut warehouse, he fell into a silo containing tons of unshelled peanuts. As he sank into the peanuts he did two things: he refused to panic, and he prayed. He later said his prayer was, "Lord, help me. This is not the way I would like to go. Lord, I know that's not the way you want me to go." It took an hour and a half to rescue him. Later, at the hospital, he was found to be in good condition.

So, did Floyd Goodman's faith save him? It can't be proved scientifically, of course. Did being rescued prove he was right about "knowing" that wasn't the way God wanted him to die? Again, there is no way to prove it. To say "yes" to either question is an assertion of *our* faith, which, of course, is just as legitimate an assertion as saying "no" to the questions.

But this much we can say: Floyd Goodman's faith in the power of God to help him overcome the avalanche of peanuts that engulfed him gave him the power to focus on what he needed to do. Floyd prayed for help, and God answered, giving him the calmness of spirit to slow down his breathing, which raised considerably the likelihood of his survival. Perhaps that is one of the most practical results of faith: it enables us to approach the troubles of this world with a calm spirit, knowing that God will see us through.

—C. R. B.

II. Witnesses to Truth
(1 John 5:6-8)

We who believe that Jesus is the Son of God (v. 5) have good reasons for that belief. No doubt the first-century believers were as sure as we are. But there were false teachers who boldly said many false things about Jesus—about how He came to this world and about His true nature. So John wrote briefly about why we believe that Jesus is the Son of God.

A. Spirit, Water, and Blood, Part 1 (v. 6)

6. This is he that came by water and blood, even Jesus Christ; not by water only, but by water and blood. And it is the Spirit that beareth witness, because the Spirit is truth.

When *Jesus Christ* was about thirty years old He was baptized in the Jordan River, and then began His great work of teaching. So *by water*, that is, by His baptism, He *came* as the teacher of Israel. More than three years later He was crucified and shed His *blood* on Calvary. So by *blood*, that is, by His death, He came to be the Redeemer of believers. Jesus was fully human and fully God.

The Holy *Spirit* is the One who *beareth witness* to these facts (John 1:32-34). John and the other apostles give the testimony in human language, but the Holy Spirit inspires them. Jesus Himself promised that the Holy Spirit would guide those apostles into all truth (John 16:13). The Spirit not only speaks truth, He *is* truth (cf. John 14:17). He cannot be mistaken.

B. Spirit, Water, and Blood, Part 2 (vv. 7, 8)

7, 8. For there are three that bear record in heaven, the Father, the Word, and the Holy Ghost: and these three are one. And there are three that bear witness in earth, the spirit, and the water, and the blood: and these three agree in one.

It is true that God *the Father*, Jesus *the Word* (cf. John 1:1), and the *Holy Ghost* are *one* even while they are *three*. And, of course, they all agree that Jesus is the Son of God. However, there is good reason to believe that the *King James Version* of these two verses gives us more than what John originally wrote. Newer versions of the Bible present these two verses in shorter form. The words *in heaven, the Father, the Word, and the Holy Ghost: and these three are one. And there are three that bear witness in earth*, are not included.

So, why is a part of these verses in the *King James Version* "left out" of the newer versions? It is simply because that part is not found in the older manuscripts of John's letter, those made closer to the time of the original writing. It's not so much that it was "left out" of the newer versions; it was "added to" the *King James Version*. But if it is not in the older manuscripts, then how did it get into the later ones? On that question we can only conjecture, but we know that Bible readers, ancient and modern, use the margins in their Bibles to jot down thoughts as they read. Perhaps some ancient reader did just that as he read about the witnesses who testified that Jesus was the Son of God.

Then years (or centuries) later, some scribe may have been making a new copy from that timeworn manuscript. When he saw the writing in the margin, he supposed the earlier scribe had accidentally left out a line or two and that, upon discovering his mistake, had written that bit in the margin instead of rewriting the whole page. So the later scribe wrote the bit from the margin into the text, and so any scribe that copied this new copy would include the added bit. Thus the addition found its way into the Greek Bible used by the translators of the *King James Version*.

It does seem strange to say water and blood are witnesses, but the strangeness disappears when we realize that the word *water* means

Jesus' baptism and the word *blood* means His death. At Jesus' baptism God Himself spoke from Heaven, saying, "Thou art my beloved Son, in whom I am well pleased" (Mark 1:11). You can't find better testimony than that. While Jesus was on the cross, His enemies derided Him by saying His death proved that He was not the Son of God (Matthew 27:39-43). How wrong they were! Jesus' manner and words on the cross, three hours of darkness before He died, an earthquake at His death—all these were so convincing that even pagan soldiers decided that Jesus really was the Son of God (Matthew 27:45-54). Any remaining doubts were dispelled by the resurrection (John 20:24-28). [See question #3, page 96.]

III. Declaration of Life
(1 John 5:9-15)

Our closing verses summarize our certainty about Jesus and the life He brings.

A. Testimony and Result (vv. 9-12)

9. If we receive the witness of men, the witness of God is greater: for this is the witness of God which he hath testified of his Son.

We do indeed accept the testimony *of men*. In every court of law it is the basis of decisions (cf. John 8:17; 19:35). More than that, almost every day of our lives we accept what people tell us, making their statements the basis of decision and action.

The testimony *of God*, however, *is greater* than the testimony of man, as much greater as God is greater than people on earth (cf. John 5:36). And it is God's own testimony that tells us Jesus is God's *Son*. The three witnesses of the Holy Spirit, the water (Jesus' baptism), and the blood

God hath given us eternal life, and this life is in his Son.
—1 John 5:11

Visual for lesson 11

Display this poster from the Adult Visuals *packet as you discuss verse 11.*

(Jesus' death) give us God's own testimony. The apostles put in human language the testimony of the Holy Spirit, and the Spirit is God. The voice from Heaven at Jesus' baptism was God's own voice. The darkness and the earthquake gave power to the testimony of Jesus' death, and the darkness and the earthquake were God's own work. Thus in different ways God is telling us that Jesus is His Son. How can anyone doubt it?

10. He that believeth on the Son of God hath the witness in himself: he that believeth not God hath made him a liar; because he believeth not the record that God gave of his Son.

If we accept God's testimony and believe that Jesus is God's Son, then we have God's testimony in ourselves. It is in our minds to guide us in everything we think or say or do; it is in our hearts to make us give glad obedience to every command of the Father or the Son. "He that hath received his testimony hath set to his seal that God is true. For he whom God hath sent speaketh the words of God" (John 3:33, 34; cf. 12:44-50).

There is no middle ground here: you either believe God's *record* of *his Son* or you don't. And if you don't, then you're calling God *a liar.*

11. And this is the record, that God hath given to us eternal life, and this life is in his Son.

The *record* doesn't stop with the fact that Jesus is God's *Son*. The record goes on to proclaim the *eternal life* He brings. This doesn't mean "life forever" with all the problems, trials, temptations, and distresses that beset us now. It is life forever in Heaven! (See Revelation 22.) [See question #4, page 96.]

12. He that hath the Son hath life; and he that hath not the Son of God hath not life.

The line is clearly drawn. Despite modern ideas of "many paths to God," there really is only Jesus. "I am the way, the truth, and the life: no man cometh unto the Father, but by me" (John 14:6). This path is very narrow (Matthew 7:13, 14). Eternal life is for those redeemed by Jesus, and for no one else.

B. Knowledge and Confidence (vv. 13-15)

13. These things have I written unto you that believe on the name of the Son of God; that ye may know that ye have eternal life, and that ye may believe on the name of the Son of God.

This verse is the "purpose statement" for John's letter (cf. John 20:30, 31). No doubt John's readers already *know* that God is giving them *eternal life* because they *believe* in Jesus. But John wants to reinforce that knowledge, wants to fix the truth so firmly in their minds that they will never forget it. As a result, John's readers

Home Daily Bible Readings

Monday, Nov. 10—We Walk by Faith (2 Corinthians 5:4-9)

Tuesday, Nov. 11—We Speak of What We Know (John 3:11-21)

Wednesday, Nov. 12—Hope Doesn't Disappoint (Romans 5:1-5)

Thursday, Nov. 13—God Proves His Love in Christ (Romans 5:6-11)

Friday, Nov. 14—Our Faith Conquers the World (1 John 5:1-5)

Saturday, Nov. 15—A Testimony in Our Hearts (1 John 5:6-12)

Sunday, Nov. 16—That You May Know (1 John 5:13-21)

will find encouragement in it when life on earth is troubled. We, no less than they, find encouragement in the same assurance. If this time is full of trouble, it is good to know that it is only the prelude to an untroubled eternity.

Since John is writing to people who already believe that Jesus is God's Son, the words *may believe* can be taken to mean "keep on believing." John wants his readers of that time and our time to cling to that belief, to keep it in mind even when false teachers are denying it. However, this is another place where we cannot be sure we know exactly what John wrote. Very many of the older and most highly valued manuscripts of John's letter do not contain the closing part of verse 13.

THE PROMISE OF IMMORTALITY

For a mere twenty-eight thousand dollars, you can be guaranteed immortality! Well, maybe "guaranteed" is putting it a bit strongly, but the *possibility* of immortality through having your body quick-frozen at death is at least suggested by the advertisements.

Robert C. W. Ettinger is credited with starting the cryonics movement in the mid-1960s with the publication of a book entitled *The Prospect of Immortality*. Soon after that book was published, the Immortalist Society was founded, and today it publishes *The Immortalist* magazine. The movement continues to play on humanity's fears of nonexistence. As one of the many cryonics organizations says on its web site, cryonics is "the only hope for the elderly or terminally ill, or for those who die suddenly. Cryonics—the only alternative to the despair of death and disease. A new technology of life potentially without limits."

The movement appeals to peoples' hopes—some would say their gullibility—by noting that

many things are possible today that were once thought impossible. This is true, of course, but the Bible presents a profoundly different view of life everlasting. True eternal life is found, not in the genius of modern science—or, more realistically, in the prospect of a scientific process that may *never* be developed—but in identification with the Son of God, who alone is the source of life. He offers us abundant life both here and now, and in God's eternal future.   —C. R. B.

14, 15. And this is the confidence that we have in him, that, if we ask any thing according to his will, he heareth us: and if we know that he hear us, whatsoever we ask, we know that we have the petitions that we desired of him.

We do have this same *confidence*, don't we? We expect that God will do what *we ask* Him to do. Without such confidence, we have no promise of a favorable answer. Jesus said, "What things soever ye desire, when ye pray, believe that ye receive them, and ye shall have them" (Mark 11:24). Speaking of one who prays for wisdom, James said, "Let him ask in faith, nothing wavering" (James 1:6). Even so, we try to be reasonable in our prayers and our expectations. We pray for daily bread (Matthew 6:11), but we do not expect God to cook our dinner and put it on the table while we watch TV in the living room! God does not promise to do what we ask unless it is *according to his will;* so if we do not get what we ask, perhaps we can amend our asking to match His will. And if we are not getting what we ask for, the fault is ours, not God's (James 4:2, 3). [See question #5, page 96.]

Conclusion

A. Living With Confidence

How blessed it is to live with confidence! We know God can do anything, and He will do what we ask,

    . . . if it is the right thing to do.

    . . . if we really believe He will do it.

    . . . if we do our part in accomplishing it.

So we trust God and concentrate on doing our part.

B. Prayer

Father in Heaven, we know Your power and goodness and love are complete and faultless forever. Thank You for being dependable. In Jesus' name, amen.

C. Thought to Remember

"Cast not away therefore your confidence, which hath great recompense of reward" (Hebrews 10:35).

Learning by Doing

This page contains an alternative lesson plan emphasizing learning activities. Classes desiring such student involvement will find these suggestions helpful.

Learning Goals

After this lesson each student will be able to:

1. Summarize the facts that we know about Jesus Christ from today's text.

2. Tell how faith in these facts helps us to live as confident Christians.

3. Write a statement of confident faith in Jesus as Lord and Savior.

Into the Lesson

Prepare an opening activity work sheet called, "Modest Metaphors." This work sheet should contain the following statements: "If confidence were a color, it would be _____ because. . . ." "If confidence were an animal, it would a _____ because. . . ." "If confidence were an object, it would be a _____ because. . . ."

Give a work sheet to each student, and say, "Today our lesson is on confidence. To help us begin to think about this subject, I've prepared a few metaphors for you to complete. If confidence were a color, an animal, or an object, what would it be, and why? I'll give you three minutes to complete these sentences and then we can share them with the class." After several minutes, ask for some volunteers to reveal their answers on the color. Then ask for suggested answers to the animal and object that would describe confidence. Once you hear several, say, "Confidence is something we desire when we sense that we don't have it. The apostle John, in our lesson text, encourages us to live in confidence. Turn to 1 John 5:1-15, and let's read why we can have such confidence."

Into the Word

Ask a class member to read the lesson text aloud. Move the class into groups of three and distribute a copy of a work sheet you have prepared: "Confident Christian Faith: How Belief Influences Our Lives." There are two columns and eight rows in this work sheet. The left column contains the following verse numbers: 1a, 1b, 2, 3, 4, 6-13, 14, 15. The right column is blank for each row. State: "Our confidence is tied directly to our faith. Read the verses in the left column. Then write in the space provided the impact belief has our lives." *Possible answers include: (1a) born of God; (1b) loves God; (2) loves God's children; (3) keeps His commandments; (4) overcomes the world; (6-13) eternal life; (14) confident*

prayer; *(15) answered prayer.* After about five minutes, ask for answers.

Move the class back together as one group and ask the following questions:

1. What does John mean by the terms *water* and *blood* in 1 John 5:6? *(Baptism by water and shed blood on the cross.)*

2. What facts do we learn from today's text about Jesus Christ? *(Son of God, v. 5; baptized, v. 6; shed His blood, v. 6.)*

3. How does John say we know that we love our brothers and sisters in Christ? *(Love God and keep His commandments, v. 2.)*

4. What does John mean by the phrase, "his commandments are not grievous"? *(Not a heavy burden, not very hard to obey.)*

5. What confidence can we have by John's use of the phrase "overcometh the world"? *(We can resist the temptations in the world.)*

6. What are the witnesses that bear record in Heaven and the witnesses that bear record in earth that Jesus is the Son of God? *(Heaven: Father, Word, Holy Ghost; Earth: Spirit, water, blood, vv. 7, 8.)*

Into Life

Prepare the following work sheet and give a copy to each of your learners. Ask the students to use the work sheet in their quiet times this week.

My Level of Confidence

In matters of my daily life this week, my level of confidence in each of the following is as follows (5=absolute confidence, 0=no confidence):

My Job Status	5	4	3	2	1	0
The Economy	5	4	3	2	1	0
World Peace	5	4	3	2	1	0
My Spouse	5	4	3	2	1	0
My Friends	5	4	3	2	1	0
Local Government	5	4	3	2	1	0
National Government	5	4	3	2	1	0
Church Leaders	5	4	3	2	1	0
Jesus as Lord	5	4	3	2	1	0

Include these questions on the work sheet:

1. What criteria am I using to determine my level of confidence for each?

2. What would need to happen to increase my level of confidence in each area?

Suggest a time of prayer of thanksgiving for the factors that give us confidence and a time of supplication for greater confidence when it is merited.

Let's Talk It Over

The questions on this page are designed to promote discussion of the lesson by the class and to encourage application of the lesson Scriptures. The answers provided are only discussion starters. Let your class talk it over from there.

1. Is it possible to love God without loving His Son, Jesus Christ? Why, or why not?

There seems to be an unwritten rule that says, "If you value my friendship, you will accept and love my children, too." Most of us insist that our children be treated in loving ways by those who claim to be our friends. It's a package deal: love me, love my kids! My surrogate grandfather would decline invitations to anyone's home if I (his "little buddy") were not welcome as well.

The same will be true in Heaven. Many today claim to "believe in God" or to "love God" in an abstract way, but they disregard the Son. Yet we can make our way to the Father only through the Son! (See John 14:6.)

2. Some people claim that belief in Christ requires a "leap in the dark." What conclusive evidence can you cite to refute that claim?

There is no serious doubt, even among atheists, that a Jewish teacher named "Jesus" actually existed in first-century Palestine. Both secular history and the Biblical record testify to this. Following that fact, His uniqueness is proven true by many miracles, hundreds of eyewitnesses, and His own resurrection as recorded in the reliable, "God-breathed" pages of Scripture. The Christian faith is founded on the objective facts of history (Luke 1:1-4).

We also trust the truth of Christ because we have experienced His presence in our lives. Faith is neither a risk nor a gamble, for we have everything to gain and nothing to lose by giving ourselves to Him. The Christian faith looks back to facts of history while it also looks forward to the certainty "of things not seen" (Hebrews 11:1).

3. If a fellow believer confessed that he felt guilty because he sometimes had doubts about Jesus, how would you counsel him?

Lynn Anderson shares some helpful insights about doubting in his book *If I Really Believe, Why Do I Have These Doubts?* There he suggests that "doubt is not the absence of faith. . . . Unbelievers have made a conscious or unconscious decision *not* to believe; doubters still *want* to believe."

"Honest doubt" can be valuable. Those who are prompted by doubt to investigate the evidence will find the truth. A case in point is Thomas, the doubting disciple. When confronted by Christ's presence, Thomas discovered that he had the conclusive proof he needed and his doubts were erased (John 20:24-28). That proof is still with us today through the testimony of the eyewitnesses. Doubt becomes sinful only when we reject evidence for truth that we should accept.

4. What assurance does John give you when he says, "God hath given to us eternal life"? (Note the verb tense suggests completed action— He *has given* it to us, not He *will give* it to us.)

Eternal life begins when we accept Christ (Acts 2:38; Romans 6:4). From then on death no longer has a permanent hold on us (Colossians 2:12).

The eternal life we now possess becomes all the richer when we realize that "quantity of existence"—unending years of life—also includes "quality of existence." Life in Christ is "life to the full" as God intended from the beginning. It is a life of hope, confidence, and holiness. The eternal life we have right now is characterized by the blessed assurance that we have been saved from the *penalty* of sin, that we are being saved from the *power* of sin, and that we will one day be saved from the very *presence* of sin. Eternal life includes enjoying the best of God's blessings right now as well as in the hereafter.

5. Why does prayer seem to work for some people some of the time, but not for *all* people *all* of the time?

Although often a mystery, God sometimes allows us insight in the pages of Scripture on how He responds to prayer. For example, prayer just didn't seem to "work" for Job; but we the readers are privileged to know why as we read the dialogue that goes on between God and Satan. As our lesson text notes, some people pray with wrong motives. God ignores other prayers because the people who would receive the benefits are just too evil (Jeremiah 7:16; 11:14; 14:11, 12).

God has other reasons for not answering prayer (see Lamentations 3:8, 44; 1 Peter 3:7). If we make the mistake of thinking God to be arbitrary or unjust, then we run the risk of having God correct us as He did Job. One key to understanding effectual prayer can be found in verse 14 of our text: our prayers must be submissive to God's will—not just to get what we want, but to become all that He wants us to be.

Remain Loyal

DEVOTIONAL READING: John 15:1-11.

BACKGROUND SCRIPTURE: 2 and 3 John.

PRINTED TEXT: 2 John 4-9; 3 John 3-12.

2 John 4-9

4 I rejoiced greatly that I found of thy children walking in truth, as we have received a commandment from the Father.

5 And now I beseech thee, lady, not as though I wrote a new commandment unto thee, but that which we had from the beginning, that we love one another.

6 And this is love, that we walk after his commandments. This is the commandment, That, as ye have heard from the beginning, ye should walk in it.

7 For many deceivers are entered into the world, who confess not that Jesus Christ is come in the flesh. This is a deceiver and an antichrist.

8 Look to yourselves, that we lose not those things which we have wrought, but that we receive a full reward.

9 Whosoever transgresseth, and abideth not in the doctrine of Christ, hath not God. He that abideth in the doctrine of Christ, he hath both the Father and the Son.

3 John 3-12

3 For I rejoiced greatly, when the brethren came and testified of the truth that is in thee, even as thou walkest in the truth.

4 I have no greater joy than to hear that my children walk in truth.

5 Beloved, thou doest faithfully whatsoever thou doest to the brethren, and to strangers;

6 Which have borne witness of thy charity before the church: whom if thou bring forward on their journey after a godly sort, thou shalt do well:

7 Because that for his name's sake they went forth, taking nothing of the Gentiles.

8 We therefore ought to receive such, that we might be fellow helpers to the truth.

9 I wrote unto the church: but Diotrephes, who loveth to have the preeminence among them, receiveth us not.

10 Wherefore, if I come, I will remember his deeds which he doeth, prating against us with malicious words: and not content therewith, neither doth he himself receive the brethren, and forbiddeth them that would, and casteth them out of the church.

11 Beloved, follow not that which is evil, but that which is good. He that doeth good is of God: but he that doeth evil hath not seen God.

12 Demetrius hath good report of all men, and of the truth itself: yea, and we also bear record; and ye know that our record is true.

GOLDEN TEXT: Beloved, follow not that which is evil, but that which is good.
He that doeth good is of God: but he that doeth evil hath not seen God.
—3 John 11.

Faith Faces the World
Unit 4: Live With Purpose
(Lessons 12, 13)

Lesson Aims

After participating in this lesson, each student should be able to:

1. Describe the course of faithfulness and love for the truth that John commends in 2 and 3 John.

2. Name some current false teachings that cause doubt and confusion about who Jesus is.

3. Select one person who is faithful in his or her discipleship and express gratitude to that person.

Lesson Outline

INTRODUCTION
    A. The Big Picture
    B. Lesson Background
 I. OUR WALK (2 John 4-6)
    A. Walk of Truth (v. 4)
       The Test of Loyalty
    B. Walk of Love (vv. 5, 6)
 II. OUR ENEMY (2 John 7-9)
    A. Avoiding Deceivers (vv. 7, 8)
       Lies—No Matter How They Are Told!
    B. Avoiding Deceit (v. 9)
III. OUR FAITHFULNESS (3 John 3-8)
    A. Faithful to Truth (vv. 3, 4)
    B. Faithful in Hospitality (vv. 5-8)
IV. OUR EXAMPLES (3 John 9-12)
    A. A Bad Example (vv. 9, 10)
    B. A Good Example (vv. 11, 12)
CONCLUSION
    A. Three Kinds of Loyalty
    B. Prayer
    C. Thought to Remember

Introduction

A. The Big Picture

One of the helpers of a noted evangelist gave up that kind of work because he "loved this present world" (2 Timothy 4:10). That was back in the first century, but in the twentieth century a young preacher's wife deserted her husband and took a job in her uncle's law firm because she thought the preacher "was never going to make any money." Also in the twentieth century a whole family dropped out of church because they moved to a town where the church full of strangers "just didn't seem like church." They didn't realize that they were leaving the Lord as well as His church. In the twenty-first century three families left a church because they wanted red carpet in the auditorium, and all the other members voted for green carpet.

At times we all fail to see the big picture. The church is Christ's body, and He is the head of it (Ephesians 1:22, 23; Colossians 1:18). In this picture only the head is perfect. The parts of the body all have their faults, but we put up with them because we have faults, too. There is no way to forsake Christ's body without forsaking its head as well. To be faithful and loyal to Christ (the head), and to the church (His body), and to the Bible (His Word) is our constant challenge.

B. Lesson Background

After three lessons from 1 John, we turn to 2 John and 3 John for more instruction from that inspired apostle.

Second John is addressed to a Christian lady and her children, who are well loved by other Christians (2 John 1). Nothing is said about her husband, so we may suppose that she was a widow. Some think that he was still living, but was a pagan with no interest in Christianity. On the other hand, some think "the lady" to be figurative language for a local church, or possibly for the church universal, consisting of all the churches in the world. If that is what John had in mind, the lady's children would be the members of the church, or of all the churches. In either case, John's thoughts are helpful for Christians everywhere.

Third John is addressed to a good Christian man named Gaius. Here again we find teaching that is beneficial for all Christians as we read this man's mail. Let us see how those two letters encourage all of us to remain loyal.

I. Our Walk
(2 John 4-6)

John frames our loyalty to Christ in terms of our Christian walk. He begins his thoughts with an example.

A. Walk of Truth (v. 4)

4. I rejoiced greatly that I found of thy children walking in truth, as we have received a commandment from the Father.

Walking in truth means living in accordance with the Christian teaching given by the apostles as passed on by those who learned from them. *We have received a commandment from the Father* to live in that way (cf. 1 John 3:23). John has encountered some of the lady's *children* who are doing that, and he is delighted.

To say that some things are true means that other things are not true. When we walk in *truth,* we reject those things that are not true. All truth ultimately comes from God, whether He reveals it to us in His Word or allows us to discover it by some natural means. But John is speaking of spiritual truth—the truth that *we have received . . . from the Father.* This is the truth that keeps us on the road to eternal life. We stray from that truth at our peril. [See question #1, page 104.]

THE TEST OF LOYALTY

What is loyalty? Sometimes we talk about loyalty to a sports team. Fans of the New York Mets stuck with their baseball team for years through losing seasons before they finally won the World Series in 1969. But more often loyalty in sports is like that of Los Angeles Dodgers' pitcher Don Sutton when he was discussing free agency several years ago: "I'm not disloyal. I'm the most loyal person money can buy."

Politics has its own standards of loyalty also. Political pundits generally agree that Hubert Humphrey lost the presidential election to Richard Nixon in 1968 because, as Vice President, Humphrey had acquiesced to Lyndon Johnson's Vietnam War policy. Humphrey later explained his actions by saying, "Where you stand often depends on where you sit."

However, the apostle John's standard of loyalty is expressed differently: walk in the truth and live out the Lord's commandments regardless of the consequences. Economic, social, or political outcomes are not to be a part of the equation. This is difficult for us to do, isn't it? But no more so than for first-century Christians who also faced the possibility of persecution because of their stand for the truth. The call to discipleship is still the same today: walk in the truth and keep God's commandments. —C. R. B.

B. Walk of Love (vv. 5, 6)

5. And now I beseech thee, lady, not as though I wrote a new commandment unto thee, but that which we had from the beginning, that we love one another.

In previous lessons we have noted more than once that both Peter and John vigorously repeated teaching that already was well known. Peter gave special emphasis to his repeating (2 Peter 1:12-15). Now we read John's urgent request to the lady, and it does not concern anything new. It is a plea for remembering and continuing in *that which we had from the beginning, that we love one another.*

6. And this is love, that we walk after his commandments. This is the commandment,

That, as ye have heard from the beginning, ye should walk in it.

Easily we understand that our love for God is shown by keeping *His commandments* (John 14:15, 24; 15:10). But now we are reading of our *love* for one another, and it is a bit surprising to read that loving people is composed of keeping God's commandments. See how this is confirmed by Romans 13:8-10, where Paul points out that all of God's commandments about human relations are summed up in one commandment, "Thou shalt love thy neighbor as thyself." The commandment to love one another is one that we *have heard from the beginning* of our acquaintance with Christian teaching. Now, as always, we *should walk in it.* That is, we should be obeying that commandment continually in our daily living.

II. Our Enemy (2 John 7-9)

From our lessons in 1 John we recall that John was writing fifty-some years after Jesus ended His life as a man on earth. Many people had come along to contradict the truths taught by Christian teachers (1 John 2:18). Men, proud of their intellect, thought their own opinions to be more dependable than God's own revelation (cf. 1 Corinthians 2:13; Colossians 2:8). Now we come to one more warning against false teachers and one more call for Christians to remain loyal to the truth.

A. Avoiding Deceivers (vv. 7, 8)

7. For many deceivers are entered into the world, who confess not that Jesus Christ is come in the flesh. This is a deceiver and an antichrist.

Christians take care to be loyal to the truth because *many deceivers are entered into the world* and are teaching falsehood. Some are even in the church itself (2 Peter 2:1), and some have come into the church and left—taking others with them as they go. The falsehood at issue in this

---

How to Say It

BEREANS. Buh-*ree*-unz.
CORINTH. *Kor*-inth.
CORINTHIANS. Kor-*in*-thee-unz (*th* as in *thin*).
DEMETRIUS. De-*mee*-tree-us.
DIOTREPHES. Die-*ot*-rih-feez.
EPHESIANS. Ee-*fee*-zhunz.
GAIUS. *Gay*-us.
GALATIANS. Guh-*lay*-shunz.
PHILIPPIANS. Fih-*lip*-ee-unz.

verse is that they *confess not that Jesus Christ is come in the flesh.* This could mean that the deceivers deny that Jesus had been a human being, born in a body of flesh. It could also mean that they deny that Jesus, the man in the flesh, was the *Christ* (the Messiah), the eternal Word described in John 1:1-5. Anyone who denies either *is a deceiver and an antichrist.* (Contrast Martha's godly confession in John 11:27.)

LIES—NO MATTER HOW THEY ARE TOLD!

Have you heard about the program that has been in your computer for months taking pictures of you unawares and sending them out over the Internet? Or the map put out by the Fuji company that deletes Israel from the Middle East? Or the poisoned envelopes at the automatic bank teller? Or the HIV-infected hypodermic needles attached to the underside of gas pump handles? Or the . . . well, you get the idea!

All of the above are hoaxes! They can be checked out at http://hoaxbusters.ciac.org or similar Web sites. Something about us humans makes us fall for lies, whether fraudulent moneymaking schemes or chain letters or almost-plausible stories that trigger our fears and fantasies.

Falling for falsehoods is an age-old human trait; only the technology seems to have changed! John warns us strictly against those who deny the testimony of the eyewitnesses that Jesus, the man, was God's Son. It doesn't matter how (or by how many) the message is spread. It is still a lie. —C. R. B.

8. Look to yourselves, that we lose not those things we have wrought, but that we receive a full reward.

John expresses a fear somewhat similar to that of Paul: "I am afraid of you, lest I have bestowed upon you labor in vain" (Galatians 4:11). A *full reward* in eternity is our goal (cf. Matthew 5:12; 1 Corinthians 3:8; Revelation 11:18; 22:12). That is the reason John charges his readers to *look to yourselves*—in other words, "Be careful!" [See question #2, page 104.]

All these *things*—meaning Christian faith, Christian action, and full reward in Heaven—will be lost by Christians who let themselves be deceived by false teachers who spread lies about Jesus. If you're not strong enough to resist what these deceivers have to say, then just stay away from them!

B. Avoiding Deceit (v. 9)

9. Whosoever transgresseth, and abideth not in the doctrine of Christ, hath not God. He that abideth in the doctrine of Christ, he hath both the Father and the Son.

Doctrine means "that which is taught." In this case, John refers specifically to *the doctrine of Christ.* The deceivers mentioned in verse 8 are spreading deceit—bad doctrine. Any person who does not stay with correct teaching, but leaves it for the false teaching of liars, abandons God as well. On the other hand, any person who remains loyal to the true teaching of Christ remains loyal both to God the Father and to Jesus His Son. Paul has a lot to say about the importance of sound doctrine in his pastoral letters (see 1 Timothy 1:3, 10; 4:16; 6:3; 2 Timothy 4:3; Titus 1:9; 2:1).

III. Our Faithfulness (3 John 3-8)

As we turn from 2 John to 3 John, we consider specific Christian action; and before we finish the lesson we shall be reading also of specific un-Christian action.

This short letter is addressed to a certain man named Gaius (v. 1). The New Testament mentions several men of that name, but there is no way to know whether this Gaius was the same as any of them. All we really know about him is learned from the letter now before us.

A. Faithful to Truth (vv. 3, 4)

3. For I rejoiced greatly, when the brethren came and testified of the truth that is in thee, even as thou walkest in the truth.

Without any wild flights of imagination we can be sure that some *brethren,* some fellow Christians, have seen Gaius and have told John that *the truth* is in him. As we saw in our brief study from 2 John, what the apostle calls *the truth* is the gospel and other Christian teaching that he and other teachers have been spreading for half a century. Gaius holds all that teaching in his mind and cherishes it in his heart. He is shaping his life by true Christian teaching. He is doing what that teaching indicates he ought to do.

4. I have no greater joy than to hear that my children walk in truth.

John is now an old man, perhaps the only apostle of Jesus still living on earth. He has devoted his life to teaching, and most of his pupils are younger than he. Undoubtedly John has seen many of his spiritual *children* fall away from the *truth* (cf. 2 Timothy 4:10). How sad this must be! Even so, John focuses on the *joy* he has over those who continue to *walk in truth.*

B. Faithful in Hospitality (vv. 5-8)

5. Beloved, thou doest faithfully whatsoever thou doest to the brethren, and to strangers.

Gaius has done something good for *the brethren,* and John commends him. Without further information it seems reasonable to suppose Gaius had extended them hospitality, giving them food and lodging while they were in his town. Most Bible students agree that the *strangers* are Christians who had been unknown to Gaius. Probably they carried a letter of introduction from John or some other trusted person so Gaius could know they really were fellow Christians. One way we "walk in truth" (v. 4) is by extending hospitality (see Romans 12:13; 1 Timothy 3:2; 5:10; Hebrews 13:2; and 1 Peter 4:9). We are not to give the same kind of help to false teachers. In fact, we are specifically prohibited from doing so (2 John 10, 11).

6. Which have borne witness of thy charity before the church: whom if thou bring forward on their journey after a godly sort, thou shalt do well.

When traveling Christians return to their own city and their home church, they tell the whole congregation how helpful Gaius has been. Gifts of food and lodging might be called *charity* on a modern income-tax return, but we do not often use that term otherwise today. Gaius is simply demonstrating love on a personal level. In contemporary English we would say "love" here.

The latter part of verse 6 recommends another way of helping our fellow Christians. After supplying food and lodging while they are in town, it is good to bring them *forward on their journey* with silver in their pockets for purchasing food and lodging in other towns where there will be no Christians to provide for them (cf. John 13:20; Galatians 4:14, 15). The next verse helps us understand why this is appropriate.

7. Because that for his name's sake they went forth, taking nothing of the Gentiles.

Traveling *for his name's sake* means that these Christians are traveling evangelists, teachers, and missionaries. They move about to spread the gospel and plant churches in places where there are none. They are traveling to strengthen and encourage existing churches by winning new converts for them and by repeating the Christian teaching that Peter was eager to reinforce (2 Peter 1:12-16). As these Christians travel about in their ministries, they are *taking nothing of the Gentiles*—they are not asking or receiving any pay from the pagans to whom they offer the gospel.

The apostle Paul followed that same policy. Traveling evangelists could accept contributions from Christians in established churches (2 Corinthians 9:12-14; Philippians 4:15-18), and Paul would earn much of his living by secular work (Acts 18:1-4). He would "make the gospel of Christ without charge" to the sinners who needed

Visual for lessons 6 and 12. *This poster illustrates a practical way to "Remain Loyal" to the Lord. Display it as you begin the lesson.*

it (1 Corinthians 9:18). The fact that these Christians are "taking nothing of the Gentiles" may have something to say about the various "fund raisers" that churches engage in today.

8. We therefore ought to receive such, that we might be fellow helpers to the truth.

Because the traveling Christians are taking nothing from the pagans, other Christians ought to welcome these fellow believers and help them by supplying room and board without charge. Thus Christians will be *fellow helpers* to travelers who are walking in *the truth,* helping to spread it far and wide. Many years previously, John himself was on "the receiving end" of such hospitality (Mark 6:7-10). [See question #3, page 104.]

IV. Our Examples
(3 John 9-12)

Past lessons reminded us of false teachers who constantly opposed those loyal to Christ and the truth. After giving us a thumbnail sketch of the good work of Gaius, our text brings us a glimpse of the evil work of one of the false teachers. That is followed by another good example.

A. A Bad Example (vv. 9, 10)

9. I wrote unto the church: but Diotrephes, who loveth to have the preeminence among them, receiveth us not.

No doubt *the church* to which John *wrote* is the one where Gaius is a member. And no doubt John wrote a letter of instruction and advice such as Paul wrote to churches in Rome, Corinth, and elsewhere. Then we read no more about John's letter to that church, and the adversative conjunction *but* indicates that what follows is somehow in opposition to that letter.

The problem seems to be centered on a certain *Diotrephes*. We recognize his attitude of loving *to have the preeminence* as existing yet today. He wants to be Number One among the church members. He wants to be in charge. He wants to run the show. Consequently, he resents any advice from John. [See question #4, page 104.]

As Diotrephes sees it, John is butting in. As a matter of fact, the Holy Spirit is guiding John into all truth (John 16:13). What John is saying or writing is God's Word, so this apostle properly has authority over churches and Christians everywhere. But Diotrephes wants to be the top authority in his church. We can imagine that Diotrephes intercepted John's letter, and most of the church members knew nothing about it. If the letter had been read in the congregation, Gaius would have known it; it would not be necessary for John to tell him he had written it.

10. Wherefore, if I come, I will remember his deeds which he doeth, prating against us with malicious words: and not content therewith, neither doth he himself receive the brethren, and forbiddeth them that would, and casteth them out of the church.

Here we have a list of four wrongs of which Diotrephes is guilty. First, *with malicious words* he is *prating against* John and others who speak God's truth. Gossip is condemned in Romans 1:29; 2 Corinthians 12:20; and 1 Timothy 5:13. Second, he is not welcoming loyal teachers such as those Gaius welcomed and helped. Third, he is forbidding other church members to welcome such loyal teachers. These two violate the Christian obligation to extend hospitality (Romans 12:13; 1 Peter 4:9). Fourth, he cast *out of the church* any church member who defies him.

Diotrephes is someone who thinks "of himself more highly than he ought to think" (Romans 12:3). If by himself he can expel members of the church—perhaps even Gaius himself—then this is indeed a church run by one man. If John could visit that church, he would *remember* (call attention to) Diotrephes's evil *deeds* to denounce them.

B. A Good Example (vv. 11, 12)

11, 12. Beloved, follow not that which is evil, but that which is good. He that doeth good is of God: but he that doeth evil hath not seen God. Demetrius hath good report of all men, and of the truth itself: yea, and we also bear record; and ye know that our record is true.

If Diotrephes (v. 10) personifies *that which is evil*, then *Demetrius* personifies *that which is good*. It's one thing to give general advice to embrace good and avoid evil. Some folks, however, can benefit from concrete examples. Perhaps Gaius is one of those, and that is the reason John seems to be saying to him, "Imitate *this* guy and not *that* guy!" As Gaius is urged to remain loyal to God and His truth, so are we—even if the whole congregation is led away to falsehood and wrongdoing. One who keeps on doing *good* is one of God's people; one who does wrong is not. [See question #5, page 104.]

Conclusion

A. Three Kinds of Loyalty

Our lesson title invites us to remain loyal, to be faithful, to be dependable, to take a firm stand. Gaius, John, and Demetrius were loyal to God, to Christ, and to the truth that the Holy Spirit spoke by the mouths of the apostles and prophets. This is the kind of loyalty for us!

Diotrephes, on the other hand, was loyal to himself and his selfish ambition. Undoubtedly he had made some kind of confession of Christ, but what good was it?

"The world" has made no confession of Christ at all. The world still offers us the deceivers of 2 John 7. Since they "confess not that Jesus Christ is come in the flesh," they are loyal to their lies. Make no mistake: our spiritual health depends on where our loyalties lie!

B. Prayer

Our Father in Heaven, how good it is to know that You have verified the great Christian truths by the miracles of Your Son, and by His resurrection and ascension. Today we pledge our loyalty to Your Son and the truth You have given us; and we look to You for wisdom, strength, and courage to remain loyal. In Jesus' name, amen.

C. Thought to Remember

Before we were loyal to God, He was loyal to us.

Home Daily Bible Readings

Monday, Nov. 17—I Press On (Philippians 3:10-15)

Tuesday, Nov. 18—Hold Fast (Philippians 3:16-21)

Wednesday, Nov. 19—Abide in Christ (John 15:1-7)

Thursday, Nov. 20—Walk in Truth (2 John 1-6)

Friday, Nov. 21—Be on Guard, Don't Lose Out (2 John 7-12)

Saturday, Nov. 22—Be Faithful to the Truth (3 John 1-8)

Sunday, Nov. 23—Imitate What Is Good (3 John 9-15)

Learning by Doing

This page contains an alternative lesson plan emphasizing learning activities.
Classes desiring such student involvement will find these suggestions helpful.

Learning Goals

After participating in this lesson, each student will be able to:

1. Describe the course of faithfulness and love for the truth that John commends in 2 and 3 John.

2. Name some current false teachings that cause doubt and confusion about who Jesus is.

3. Select one person who is faithful in his or her discipleship and express gratitude to that person.

Into the Lesson

Prior to this week's lesson, prepare a half-page work sheet titled "Acrostic Antonym Puzzle." Part A has seven words for clues. Beside each word there are blanks representing the total number of letters for the correct words, antonyms (opposites) of the clue words. A selected letter is underlined in each correct word. Combined with the other selected letters, they can be arranged to form the unscrambled word in Part B. The puzzle is to look like this:

PART A:

_ _ _ _ _ _	war
_ _ _	sorrow
_ _ _ _	hate
_ _ _ _	hot
_ _ _ _ _	energetic
_ _ _ _ _ _	sad
_ _ _ _ _ _ _ _ _	finish

PART B:__ _ _ _ _ _ _ _

Give a copy of the puzzle to each class member. Say, "Today, we begin with an 'acrostic antonym puzzle.' The missing words are antonyms of the clue words. After filling in the words, select the letters underlined and unscramble them into a word. You have five minutes."

Go over the correct answers *(peace, joy, love, cold, lazy, happy, initiate)* and the unscrambled word: *loyalty.* Say, "One can be loyal to a spouse, a job or company, and even to a product. Our text talks about loyalty to Christ. Let's turn to 2 and 3 John and see what John says about loyalty."

Into the Word

Ask one class member to read 2 John 4-9 and another to read 3 John 3-12 aloud. Move the class into groups of four and ask each group to answer the following question: "What does John

indicate are characteristics of faithfulness?" *(Answers: walking in truth, 2 John 4; love one another, 2 John 5; walk after His commandments, walk in love, 2 John 6; showing hospitality, 3 John 7, 8; follow what is good, 3 John 11.)* After several minutes, ask for answers.

Say, "Faithfulness is also demonstrated by not being deceived by false teachers, as 3 John 7, 8 says. To help remove some confusion about what three religious groups teach about Jesus, I've asked _____ (give names) to serve on a panel. Will you come to the front now and tell us what these groups teach about Jesus?"

In preparation for this, select three members from the class to serve as a panel on "Mormonism, Islam, and Jehovah's Witnesses: False Teaching About Jesus." Panelists will need more than a week to research the assigned religion's teaching on the identity and role of Jesus. Have each panelist make a three-minute presentation on what the religion teaches about Jesus; then allow a few minutes for questions.

Say, "These groups sometimes lead Christians astray. And sometimes they are led astray like Diotrephes in 3 John 10. What are his four errors?" *(Spoke maliciously against John, failed to receive the brethren, forbade those that did receive them, and cast them out of the church.)*

Into Life

State: "In 3 John 12 notice the example of Demetrius, a faithful believer with a good report. There are still loyal Christians. In our own congregation there are individuals who have demonstrated faithfulness to God. Who are some of these?" As individuals are suggested, write their names for all to see.

In preparation for the next activity, prepare a certificate called, "Giving Thanks for Faithfulness." Give each class a copy, and say, "Today, we want to honor those in our congregation who have remained loyal, who have demonstrated faithfulness. On this certificate write the name of a person you want to thank. For the next few minutes, express your gratitude to this person by describing the specific areas in which the person has demonstrated loyalty to Christ." Give the class about five minutes to complete this activity. Encourage them to hand deliver these certificates to the ones selected.

Close the session with a prayer of thanksgiving.

Let's Talk It Over

The questions on this page are designed to promote discussion of the lesson by the class and to encourage application of the lesson Scriptures. The answers provided are only discussion starters. Let your class talk it over from there.

1. Every teacher in the church wants his or her learners to be "walking in truth." What does a teacher need to do to ensure that this happens?

Teaching Bible content is crucial! (See Psalm 119:11; 2 Timothy 3:16, 17.) We should note with a word of caution that some "small group" ministries tend to de-emphasize Bible content in favor of creating either support groups or groups that concentrate on studying topics. While topical studies and support groups fill important needs, it is dangerous to allow the teaching of the Bible to get squeezed out in the process. Small-group leaders need to emphasize solid Bible study within their groups or make sure that group members are involved in significant Bible studies that complement the small-group efforts.

An emphasis on teaching Bible content won't be effective, however, if the teacher isn't "practicing what he preaches." Teachers must model personally what they teach (1 Timothy 4:12b). People can see through hypocrisy or inconsistent lifestyles. Teachers who cause their learners to stumble in their faith-walk will be held accountable (cf. Luke 17:1).

2. John warns believers to "Look to yourselves that we lose not those things we have wrought, but that we receive a full reward." What are some specific things believers can do to heed this warning?

In the context here, John is specifically warning about false teachers. To recognize a counterfeit, one must be so thoroughly acquainted with the genuine as to see the difference. So believers must spend time in the Word, becoming so familiar with it that any false teaching is immediately recognized. Like the noble Bereans (Acts 17:11), they need to search the Scriptures daily and compare what they find with what they hear from those who claim to teach the Word.

Ask class members to tell what they do, besides attending Sunday school, to be familiar with the Bible. Do some read through the Bible each year? What reading plan do they follow? What other ideas can they suggest?

3. Why does Christian hospitality seem to be a dying ministry today?

Frazzled by their "busy-ness," people today are increasingly protective of their personal time.

After a long day at work, running the kids to-and-fro, and just generally keeping up with modern life, it's easy and tempting to stay at home and relax with whatever time in the day remains.

The result is that Christians rarely share personal accommodations or "time off" with friends, let alone with strangers. Even when a host makes his or her time available, the visitors often are taken to a restaurant rather than treated to a home-cooked meal. Evangelists and other church guests frequently are put up in motels instead of being invited to sleep in members' homes. In fact, some travelers prefer the commercial type of "hospitality" because it allows them to avoid having to interact with people. But wiser Christians know that they—and we—are missing a blessing.

4. How can we develop new leaders in the church while at the same time helping keep those emerging leaders from the sin of loving "to have the preeminence"?

This is difficult! Each of us probably can tell a tragic story of someone we knew who let power go to his head in the church. Our most important safeguard undoubtedly is to make sure we use Paul's requirements listed in 1 Timothy 3:1-10 and Titus 1:6-9. Paul probably is talking about the same problem as John when warning against leaders "being lifted up with pride" (1 Timothy 3:6).

Part of Diotrephes's problem was that he thought himself to be accountable to no one but himself. The elders in the local church need to hold each other accountable for their actions. They also can encourage and support one another in their demanding role as shepherds.

5. What are some sources of evil that people imitate? How do we resist imitating what we see in those sources?

The actions and lifestyles of other people are a great temptation to many. Television allows us easy access to view (and envy) the lives of sinful leisure that many "high profile" people live—an access that did not exist in John's day.

We can resist imitating evil by committing some Scriptures to memory. Then when we need them in order to remain strong we can easily call them up! Some good Scriptures to memorize include Psalm 101:3; Proverbs 23:17; 24:1, 2; and, of course, 3 John 11.

Maintain Steadfast Faith

DEVOTIONAL READING: Galatians 6:1-10.

BACKGROUND SCRIPTURE: Jude.

PRINTED TEXT: Jude 3, 4, 8-13, 16-23.

Jude 3, 4, 8-13, 16-23

3 Beloved, when I gave all diligence to write unto you of the common salvation, it was needful for me to write unto you, and exhort you that ye should earnestly contend for the faith which was once delivered unto the saints.

4 For there are certain men crept in unawares, who were before of old ordained to this condemnation, ungodly men, turning the grace of our God into lasciviousness, and denying the only Lord God, and our Lord Jesus Christ.

. . . .

8 Likewise also these filthy dreamers defile the flesh, despise dominion, and speak evil of dignities.

9 Yet Michael the archangel, when contending with the devil he disputed about the body of Moses, durst not bring against him a railing accusation, but said, The Lord rebuke thee.

10 But these speak evil of those things which they know not: but what they know naturally, as brute beasts, in those things they corrupt themselves.

11 Woe unto them! for they have gone in the way of Cain, and ran greedily after the error of Balaam for reward, and perished in the gainsaying of Korah.

12 These are spots in your feasts of charity, when they feast with you, feeding themselves without fear: clouds they are without water, carried about of winds; trees whose fruit withereth, without fruit, twice dead, plucked up by the roots;

13 Raging waves of the sea, foaming out their own shame; wandering stars, to whom is reserved the blackness of darkness for ever.

. . . .

16 These are murmurers, complainers, walking after their own lusts; and their mouth speaketh great swelling words, having men's persons in admiration because of advantage.

17 But, beloved, remember ye the words which were spoken before of the apostles of our Lord Jesus Christ;

18 How that they told you there should be mockers in the last time, who should walk after their own ungodly lusts.

19 These be they who separate themselves, sensual, having not the Spirit.

20 But ye, beloved, building up yourselves on your most holy faith, praying in the Holy Ghost,

21 Keep yourselves in the love of God, looking for the mercy of our Lord Jesus Christ unto eternal life.

22 And of some have compassion, making a difference:

23 And others save with fear, pulling them out of the fire; hating even the garment spotted by the flesh.

GOLDEN TEXT: Keep yourselves in the love of God, looking for the mercy of our Lord Jesus Christ unto eternal life. And of some have compassion, making a difference.—Jude 21, 22.

Lesson Aims

After participating in this lesson, each student should be able to:

1. Tell what it is to contend for the faith and why it is so important to do so.

2. Cite some contemporary issue that is, or may become, the source of a challenge to one's faith, similar to the challenge described by Jude.

3. Suggest some specific manner of dealing with that challenge.

Lesson Outline

INTRODUCTION
    A. War and Peace
    B. Lesson Background
  I. ALARM (Jude 3, 4)
    A. Contend for the Faith (v. 3)
    B. Enemies of the Faith (v. 4)
 II. INFORMATION (Jude 8-13, 16)
    A. Character of the Enemies, Part 1 (vv. 8-10)
      Speaking Evil
    B. Similarities to the Past (v. 11)
    C. Character of the Enemies, Part 2 (vv. 12, 13, 16)
III. ADVICE (Jude 17-23)
    A. Remember the Warnings (vv. 17-19)
    B. Keep the Faith (vv. 20, 21)
    C. Save the Doubters (vv. 22, 23)
      The Power of Encouraging Words
CONCLUSION
    A. Caution
    B. Prayer
    C. Thought to Remember

Introduction

Jesus is the Prince of Peace (Isaiah 9:6). He blesses the peacemakers (Matthew 5:9). On the other hand, He Himself said that He "came not to send peace, but a sword" (Matthew 10:34). The text of this week's lesson urges Christians to "earnestly contend for the faith" (see also 1 Timothy 6:12). So, which way is it? Shall we fight, or shall we make peace?

A. War and Peace

An extended family moved to our town: an elderly couple with two grown sons, each of whom had a wife and family of his own. The three men came to town to work in a department store that had recently been purchased and added to a chain of such stores. The adults and older children quickly became members of the local church, and the six adults took their places in two adult Sunday school classes, where they happily joined in the discussions.

These newcomers liked Jesus' teaching and meant to follow it, they said. But they were impatient with what they called "Christian myths." They were full of questions. "What difference does it make whether Jesus was born of a virgin or not? If He was, does that make His teaching any truer?" "Who cares whether Jesus did miracles or not? If He did, does that add value to what He said?" "Did Jesus really rise from the dead and take His body to Heaven with Him, or did He just die and go to Heaven as we do? In either case, His teaching is good for us to follow." "Can't we follow Him without pretending He is a demigod?"

Long-time members of both adult classes were firmly convinced that what the Bible says is true, and they were quick to say so. So lively debates arose.

Two thousand years ago, Jude addressed a similar (but more dangerous) situation. His short letter is "to them that are sanctified by God the Father, and preserved in Jesus Christ, and called" (Jude 1). Our lesson is about what he had to say to "them"—and to us.

B. Lesson Background

Jude describes himself as "the servant of Jesus Christ, and brother of James" (Jude 1). This James wrote the book that bears his name, from which we took our lessons in September. Paul calls James "the Lord's brother" (Galatians 1:19). So we see that both James and Jude were sons of Joseph and Mary, and half-brothers of Jesus (see Matthew 13:55, where "Jude" is spelled "Judas"). Neither James nor Jude was a disciple of Jesus before His resurrection (John 7:5).

Jude's letter is addressed to faithful Christians without specifying any place. This is the reason it is included among the "general" epistles. It is not dated either, and many scholars say merely that it was written in the latter half of the first century. Its message, as we shall see, is timeless.

I. Alarm
(Jude 3, 4)

Jude wishes peace, mercy, and love for his readers (Jude 2). He does not pause to praise the beauty and glory of peace, however, nor to cite Jesus' blessing for peacemakers (Matthew 5:9).

Instead he issues an unabashed call for contenders and warriors—not fighters with swords and spears, but contenders with ideas, words, and character. Remember the armor of God that Paul recommends in Ephesians 6:10-18.

A. Contend for the Faith (v. 3)

3. Beloved, when I gave all diligence to write unto you of the common salvation, it was needful for me to write unto you, and exhort you that ye should earnestly contend for the faith which was once delivered unto the saints.

The common salvation is given to Jude and all faithful Christians. No doubt Jude could write lengthy books about that salvation; but as he thinks about it, he sees that one thing is more *needful:* his readers must *earnestly contend for the faith.* That applies to his readers in the first century and to those in the twenty-first.

In our New Testament, *faith* normally means belief and trust in Jesus. Here, however, *the faith* refers to the body of Christian doctrine to be believed—all that was taught by the apostles and passed on by faithful teachers. This includes both the "milk" and "meat" beliefs of Christianity (Hebrews 5:12-14). That body of doctrine was *once delivered unto the saints,* or all Christians (cf. Acts 2:42; Romans 6:17). Having received this faith, Christians must be on the alert, ready and able to defend it against all the attacks made by false teachers.

B. Enemies of the Faith (v. 4)

4. For there are certain men crept in unawares, who were before of old ordained to this condemnation, ungodly men, turning the grace of our God into lasciviousness, and denying the only Lord God, and our Lord Jesus Christ.

Jude speaks of *certain men* who are not real Christians since they do not hold to the faith once delivered to the saints. They *crept in* before the other members became aware that they were not real Christians. Jesus warned of wolves who "come to you in sheep's clothing" (Matthew 7:15). How difficult it can be to recognize such dangerous people! But rest assured that God has known about them from eternity past and has *of old ordained* their *condemnation.*

These phony Christians are *ungodly men;* they prove it by *turning the grace of our God into lasciviousness.* God's grace is His favor, the mercy by which He forgives our sins. The *ungodly men* think, or pretend to think, that grace gives us license to keep on sinning in whatever evil way our *lasciviousness* may suggest, and still count on God to forgive us. Even worse than misinterpreting the promise of forgiveness, the *ungodly men* put their own opinions above God's Word,

thus *denying the only Lord God, and our Lord Jesus Christ.* These men may fool themselves into thinking they're following Christ. But if their teaching doesn't match His then they have replaced Him with something false. That's idolatry! [See question #1, page 112.]

II. Information
(Jude 8-13, 16)

Verse 4 introduces some phony Christians and announces their condemnation. Jude has more to say about them, but first he pauses to give some examples of people and angels who were condemned and punished. This he does in verses 5-7, which are omitted from our printed text. With such examples on the record, everyone ought to know unbelief and disobedience will be punished. But these pretended Christians ignore the warning and continue in their wrong ways.

A. Character of the Enemies, Part 1 (vv. 8-10)

8. Likewise also these filthy dreamers defile the flesh, despise dominion, and speak evil of dignities.

The word *likewise* ties the sins of the ungodly men of verse 4 with the sexual perversion of Sodom and Gomorrah in verse 7 (cf. 2 Peter 2:6). The types of perverse activities such *filthy dreamers* involve themselves in to *defile* their *flesh* we try not to imagine! When they *despise dominion, and speak evil of dignities,* they prove they have no respect for leaders who ought to be respected. Some students believe the *dignities* here are angels. If so, then these ungodly men have no respect for God's servants in Heaven or on earth.

9. Yet Michael the archangel, when contending with the devil he disputed about the body of Moses, durst not bring against him a railing accusation, but said, The Lord rebuke thee.

Michael the archangel is probably the one who spoke with Daniel many centuries earlier (Daniel 10:13, 21; 12:1). Michael's struggles against *the devil* are ongoing (see Revelation 12:7). The dispute between the two *about the body of Moses* is not recorded in any other Scripture. But it is generally supposed that Michael was God's agent in the burial of *Moses* (Deuteronomy 34:5, 6), and that the devil claimed that Moses' body was his because of Moses' sin at the water of Meribah (Numbers 20:12, 13).

The point Jude is making is that a holy angel did not use insulting language even when he was disputing with the most evil of all beings, the devil himself (2 Peter 2:11). How much less should we use such language against our fellow human beings who are created in God's image! [See question #2, page 112.]

Home Daily Bible Readings

Monday, Nov. 24—The Steadfast Are Kept in Peace (Isaiah 26:1-6)

Tuesday, Nov. 25—O Lord, We Wait for You (Isaiah 26:7-13)

Wednesday, Nov. 26—The Righteous Have Steady Hearts (Psalm 112:1-8)

Thursday, Nov. 27—Keep My Word (Revelation 3:7-13)

Friday, Nov. 28—Don't Give Up in Doing Right (Galatians 6:1-10)

Saturday, Nov. 29—Contend for the Faith (Jude 1-13)

Sunday, Nov. 30—Build Up Your Faith (Jude 16-25)

10. But these speak evil of those things which they know not: but what they know naturally, as brute beasts, in those things they corrupt themselves.

Unlike the angel Michael, the phony Christians freely use insulting talk whether they know what they are talking about or *not*. There are some things they do indeed *know naturally, as brute beasts* do: hunger and thirst, sexual desire, and power (cf. Mark 10:42-45). By such things these phonies *corrupt themselves*. For the sake of selfish desires they give up truth and decency.

SPEAKING EVIL

Nearly everyone agrees that there has been a coarsening of Western culture in the last fifty years or so. Rudeness and disrespect, from "road rage" and abuse of elderly family members to simple lack of courtesy in everyday interactions, have all been documented. Television and movies now often use formerly forbidden profanities. In fact, such expressions are so common as to have lost their shock value.

A newspaper reporter recently questioned college students about why there is so much foul language at college athletic events. One said, "It's a lot of fun. . . . Foul language debases my self-image, but I use it anyway out of habit." Another does it because he wants to "encourage" his team. He added that it probably isn't appropriate because "there are little kids there. But I don't feel bad."

Jude tells us that disrespect for others—especially leaders—is just one of many attitudes that impugn our character and have a destructive effect on the life of the church and society. As Christians we ought to provide an example that is strongly contrary to the way the cultural winds are blowing.   —C. R. B.

B. Similarities to the Past (v. 11)

11. Woe unto them! for they have gone in the way of Cain, and ran greedily after the error of Balaam for reward, and perished in the gainsaying of Korah.

Out of envy, *Cain* killed his brother Abel (Genesis 4:3-8; 1 John 3:12). For a fee, *Balaam* tried to call down a curse on Israel (Numbers 22–24; 2 Peter 2:15, 16; Revelation 2:14). In a lust for power, *Korah* staged a rebellion against Moses (Numbers 16:1-33). The phony Christians will all come to *woe*, as did Cain, Balaam, and Korah.

C. Character of the Enemies, Part 2 (vv. 12, 13, 16)

12a. These are spots in your feasts of charity, when they feast with you, feeding themselves without fear.

In first-century churches the Sunday meetings featured meals that we might call fellowship dinners. After such a meal they would observe the Lord's Supper. These *feasts of charity* are called "love feasts" in other versions.

The phony Christians mar the beauty and joy of these occasions because their love is only for themselves and members of their clique. They sit together and share their food with no one else. They do this *without fear* of spoiling the fellowship this custom is meant to cultivate. This is why they are *spots*, or blemishes (cf. 2 Peter 2:13). Or perhaps *without fear* means not having any reverence for the sacredness of the occasion (cf. 1 Corinthians 11:20, 21).

12b, 13. Clouds they are without water, carried about of winds; trees whose fruit withereth, without fruit, twice dead, plucked up by the roots; raging waves of the sea, foaming out their own shame; wandering stars, to whom is reserved the blackness of darkness for ever.

Now Jude uses some metaphors to add to what he says in verse 12a. As *clouds* that bring no rain, and as *trees* that are both fruitless and *plucked up by the roots,* the phonies are unproductive and useless (cf. Luke 13:6-9). Further, as *raging waves of the sea* they make a lot of noise but do not get any useful work done (cf. 2 Peter 2:17). [See question #3, page 112.]

The Greek word for *wander* provides the root for our English word *planet.* People in ancient times had no concept of what planets were. But when they looked up into the night sky, they could see that almost all the heavenly points of light kept their place night after night. However, a few of those points of light—which today we know as the planets Venus, Mars, Jupiter, and Saturn—shifted positions nightly. As *wandering stars* they are unreliable reference points. Any mariner setting the course of his ship by them is in danger!

16. These are murmurers, complainers, walking after their own lusts; and their mouth speaketh great swelling words, having men's persons in admiration because of advantage.

Can't you hear these phonies complaining and whining when they don't get their way? This sounds quite different from the raging mentioned in verse 13, and we are reminded that "problem people" do not all sound alike. And perhaps all of them change their tune from time to time, now whining in frustration, now raging in anger, now bragging with *great swelling words*. Sometimes they flatter people in order to take *advantage* of them (cf. Romans 16:18; 1 Thessalonians 2:5; 2 Peter 2:18). [See question #4, page 112.]

III. Advice
(Jude 17-23)

Jude does not suggest that we spend time denouncing the enemies as he has been doing. There is certainly a time and place for that (see Titus 3:10), but Jude wants to stress something else.

A. Remember the Warnings (vv. 17-19)

17. But, beloved, remember ye the words which were spoken before of the apostles of our Lord Jesus Christ.

Our faith is based on the testimony of *the apostles* who saw what *Jesus* did and heard what He taught. Of the four gospel writers, Matthew and John were apostles; their books are the testimonies of eyewitnesses. We do not know how much Mark knew of Jesus personally, but there is ancient testimony that Mark recorded what the apostle Peter taught. Luke came to Jerusalem years after Jesus was gone. As a careful historian he interviewed many eyewitnesses and separated verified truth from fiction (Luke 1:1-4). He was also a companion of the apostle Paul.

We can depend on the writings of these men. They recorded the supernatural events that show that Jesus is the Son of God (John 20:30, 31).

18. How that they told you there should be mockers in the last time, who should walk after their own ungodly lusts.

The apostles plainly foretold the coming of unbelievers who would make fun of the miracles mentioned above (e.g., 2 Peter 3:3, 4). Such *mockers* are not so much interested in God's truth as in *their own ungodly lusts*.

19. These be they who separate themselves, sensual, having not the Spirit.

Scholars point out that the word *themselves* is not in the best original manuscripts. Making adjustment for this means that the mockers "create divisions" among the Christians by convincing some of them that the miracle stories cannot be

true. In their sensuality the mockers put the testimony of their own senses above the testimony of the apostles. The mockers never saw a miracle, so they suppose no one else ever saw one.

But the apostles did see miracles. In addition, they had the Holy Spirit to guide them so they would make no mistake in the record (John 16:13). *Having not the Spirit*, the mockers can and do make mistakes.

B. Keep the Faith (vv. 20, 21)

20. But ye, beloved, building up yourselves on your most holy faith, praying in the Holy Ghost.

As it was in verse 3, *faith* here is substantive. It means "the body of Christian doctrine to be believed." We become firmer, stronger, more assured in all that we believe by reviewing the evidence presented in Scripture and by recognizing the enemies of the faith for who they are. *Praying in the Holy Ghost* means shaping our prayers according to the wishes of the Holy Spirit, who lives in us (1 Corinthians 3:16).

21. Keep yourselves in the love of God, looking for the mercy of our Lord Jesus Christ unto eternal life.

Keeping ourselves *in the love of God* means honoring God's will as He reveals it to us in the Bible. We do that by *looking for* and expecting *the mercy of our Lord Jesus Christ* to bring us to *eternal life*. When we have a proper understanding of eternal life, our current, earthly life stays in perspective (2 Corinthians 4:18).

C. Save the Doubters (vv. 22, 23)

22. And of some have compassion, making a difference.

There are differences in translation here because of uncertainty in the original Greek text.

Visual for lesson 13

Display this poster from the Adult Visuals *packet as you discuss verse 22.*

Some versions have something like, "Have compassion on some who are in doubt." This points to weak Christians who have listened to enemies of the faith and are beginning to have doubts. We do not denounce them or regard those who are wavering as enemies. Rather, we *have compassion* on them. We reason with them gently, lovingly—reviewing the evidence for the truth and trying to build them up in the most holy faith. [See question #5, page 112.]

23. And others save with fear, pulling them out of the fire; hating even the garment spotted by the flesh.

The *others* are those who have gone further in their doubting, who have almost joined the enemy. With them we reason more vigorously, perhaps even pointing out the eternal *fire* that lies at the end of the road they are taking. We reason *with fear* of losing them—or does Jude mean we reason *with fear* that we ourselves may be contaminated by our contact with those far gone in doubt? If the *flesh* of anyone's body is filthy, the garment in contact with that flesh is likely to become *spotted* or soiled. So in our contact with one far advanced in doubt we must be sure not to become contaminated ourselves by that doubt. But if we succeed in bringing doubters back to the true faith, it is like *pulling them out of the fire.*

THE POWER OF ENCOURAGING WORDS

The early days of World War II were dark ones for Great Britain. Hitler's armies had swept across Europe with no more than short-lived resistance. Then came the blitz of London, when night after night the German *Luftwaffe* fire-bombed the city. But rather than waste his words with condemnation of the Nazis, Prime Minister Winston Churchill "mobilized the English

---

How to Say It

AQUILA. *Ack*-wih-luh.
APOLLOS. Uh-*pahl*-us.
BALAAM. *Bay*-lum.
CORINTHIANS. Kor-*in*-thee-unz (*th* as in *thin*).
DEUTERONOMY. Due-ter-*ahn*-uh-me.
EPISTLES. ee-*pis*-uls.
GOMORRAH. Guh-*more*-uh.
JUDE. Jood.
KORAH. *Ko*-rah.
LASCIVIOUSNESS. luh-*sih*-vee-us-nuss.
MERIBAH. *Mehr*-ih-buh.
SODOM. *Sod*-um.
THESSALONIANS. *Thess*-uh-*lo*-nee-unz (strong accent on *lo; th* as in *thin*).
PRISCILLA. Prih-*sil*-uh.

---

language and sent it into battle," as John F. Kennedy said.

With British and French forces reeling from the German conquest of France, Churchill said on June 4, 1940, "We shall defend our Island, whatever the cost may be. We shall fight on the beaches, we shall fight on the landing grounds, we shall fight in the fields and in the streets, we shall fight in the hills; we shall never surrender." Two weeks later he added, "Let us therefore brace ourselves to our duties, and so bear ourselves that, if the British Empire and its Commonwealth last for a thousand years, men will still say, 'This was their finest hour.'"

The words of Jude reflect this same spirit: although he had harsh words for those who were doing evil, he chose a different approach in advising Christians on what their course of action should be. To them he offered strong words of encouragement, strengthening their faith so that they could reach out to the lost and save them from their painful destiny. Never underestimate the power of encouraging words!   —C. R. B.

Conclusion

We need to remember that Jude advises us first to strengthen ourselves and our own faith, then to help others do the same for themselves and their faith. This calls for a word of caution.

A. Caution

No doubt enemies of the faith have infiltrated churches of our time as they did churches of the first century. If we set ourselves to find them and expose them, we face a triple danger to ourselves. First, we may make false accusations, for fellow believers who need to strengthen their faith may be at heart as loyal as we are. Second, we may become as divisive as the enemies are (v. 19). Third, we may become too critical, too judgmental, too disagreeable in lacking discernment between issues of doctrine and opinion. For those who need help in strengthening themselves in our most holy faith, Jude advises us to be helpers, not detectives and prosecutors.

B. Prayer

How good it is to have a clear record of the truth taught by Jesus and His apostles! Thank You, Father, for the security we find in our faith based on that truth. Keep us from unseemly pride, and make us humble helpers of fellow Christians in need of help. In Jesus' name, amen.

C. Thought to Remember

Maintain steadfast faith—your own and that of your Christian brothers and sisters.

Learning by Doing

This page contains an alternative lesson plan emphasizing learning activities.
Classes desiring such student involvement will find these suggestions helpful.

Learning Goals

After this lesson each student will be able to:

1. Tell what it is to contend for the faith and why it is so important to do so.

2. Cite some contemporary issue that is, or may become, the source of a challenge to one's faith, similar to the challenge described by Jude.

3. Suggest some specific manner of dealing with that challenge.

Into the Lesson

Prepare a handout with two parts; title it "Greatest Challenge." The first part lists three individuals—a parent, an athlete, and Jesus—and asks the students to describe the greatest challenge ever faced by each of these. Leave plenty of space between these identifications for class members to write. Part two asks the students for a two-word definition or description of *challenge*.

Give each student a work sheet, and say, "This morning I want us to think about the topic of *challenge*. On this work sheet, write what you think is the greatest challenge a parent, an athlete, and Jesus ever faced. Then, after describing those challenges, write a two-word definition or description of *challenge* in part two. I'll give you three minutes to complete this."

Encourage class members to reveal their answers. Possible answers to part two: *great opportunity, difficult situation, personal struggle,* or *serious threat.* Say, "The word *challenge* can be looked at either as a positive or a negative concept. Today, our lesson text focuses upon the serious threat that challenges Christians in their struggle to 'maintain steadfast faith.' Turn to the book of Jude, and let's read about the challenge of contending for the faith."

Into the Word

Ask a student to read the whole lesson text aloud. Say, "As you heard, there were some 'Fakes Among the Family' who had crept in unawares. In pronouncing woe upon them, Jude uses several Old Testament illustrations. To help us understand those illustrations, I've prepared another work sheet for you to complete in small groups."

Move the class into groups of four students each. Prior to class prepare the work sheet entitled, "Fakes Among the Family." This chart contains four rows and three columns. The first row contains the column headings: The Example; The Point; The Application. The left column (The Example) contains: Cain (Genesis 4:3-8; 1 John 3:12), Balaam (Numbers 22–24), and Korah (Numbers 16:1-33).

Give one work sheet to each group. Assign some groups to start with Cain, some with Balaam, and some with Korah. (That way you'll be sure all three rows will be completed.)

Allow ten minutes; then ask the groups to report their answers to The Point and The Application. Then move the groups back into one group for the following questions:

1. What does Jude mean when he exhorts Christians to "contend for the faith" (v. 3)? *(Be alert, ready, and able to defend the faith against all attacks of false teachers.)*

2. Why is it important for Christians to contend for the faith? *(To avoid being pulled away from Christ; to provide a stronger witness of the trustworthiness of the gospel.)*

3. How did ungodly men treat God and His grace (v. 4)? *(They denied God and Jesus and turned grace into lasciviousness.)*

4. What is meant by the phrase "despise dominion, and speak evil of dignities" (v. 8)? *(They don't respect leaders in the church and in the world.)*

5. What is the point of the illustration about Michael and the devil (v. 9)? *(Michael did not use abusive language when disputing with the devil; neither should we when talking with any person.)*

6. Describe the character of the intruders (v. 16) and the type of response Jude instructs Christians to make (vv. 20-23). *(They murmur, complain, follow their lusts, boast, and flatter others selfishly. We pray, build ourselves up in the faith, show compassion, try to save them.)*

Into Life

Ask, "What contemporary issues challenge a Christian's faith?" Write suggested issues on the board for all to see. Prior to class, prepare a four-by-six-inch card for each student. Put the heading "Challenging the Challenge!" on each card. Ask each student to identify an issue that creates a personal challenge to him or her. He or she will write that challenge on the card in a section titled "My Challenge." Another section is called "My Challenging Response." There the student will write a specific response to the issue. After two minutes, close the class time in prayer asking God to help each one maintain steadfast faith.

Let's Talk It Over

The questions on this page are designed to promote discussion of the lesson by the class and to encourage application of the lesson Scriptures. The answers provided are only discussion starters. Let your class talk it over from there.

1. How can Christians prepare themselves to recognize and refute false teaching?

One is able to recognize falsehood only after knowing what is true. Knowledge of spiritual truth comes through spending much time in God's Word—meditating, studying, listening, and discussing (2 Timothy 3:14-17). Jesus stressed the importance of truth in John 4:23, 24.

Watching what we "feed" our minds in other ways is also important; people have been known to believe lies after hearing those lies repeated often enough. Watching TV programs that depict ungodly morality can lead one to accept that morality after a while.

Prayer is crucial because that is the way we invite the Holy Spirit's help in our struggles. Worship reminds us continually of who the Author of all truth really is. These disciplines are difficult to maintain because of all the distractions and claims on our time. But failure in this area has eternal consequences!

2. How should we confront those calling themselves Christians who believe and teach doctrinal errors?

"Contending" (v. 3) does not mean being contentious. Those who err should be approached with the respect that is due anyone who has been created in the image of God. Common courtesy, nonbelligerent tones, and friendly body language should prevail. When Apollos preached in Corinth, he knew "only the baptism of John." Aquila and Priscilla took him aside privately and explained "the way of the Lord more perfectly" (Acts 18:24-26). Their example of "speaking the truth in love" (Ephesians 4:15) is helpful for us.

Even so, another aim is to protect the purity of the church. No matter how hard we try, no matter how gentle we are, there will be some who will not accept the truth. The leadership of the church will have to deal with them as appropriate, from not allowing them to teach to, in extreme cases, actually disfellowshiping them. (See, for example, 1 Corinthians 5; Titus 1:10, 11; 3:10, 11.)

3. True Christians can be recognized by their productive lives (Matthew 7:15-20). What "fruit" can rightly be expected in the lives of genuine followers of Christ?

A good place to start is the "fruit of the Spirit" in Galatians 5:22, 23: "love, joy, peace, long-suffering, gentleness, goodness, faith, meekness, temperance." To the nine listed there we might add other important tasks of the Christian life such as evangelism, prayer, hospitality, worship, stewardship, benevolence, and leadership. Christians show fruit by earning their own livelihood to avoid being a burden to others if possible (2 Thessalonians 3:6-14). Undoubtedly your class can think of others to add to this list.

4. What character flaws might betray a professing Christian as a person of shallow, superficial faith? How dangerous are these flaws?

Alongside "the fruit of the Spirit" in Galatians 5:22, 23 is what we might call "the fruit of the devil" in 5:19-21: "adultery, fornication, uncleanness, lasciviousness, idolatry, witchcraft, hatred, variance, emulations, wrath, strife, seditions, heresies, envyings, murders, drunkenness, revelings, and such like." Amazingly, we note that what we may think of as the "more harmful" sins such as *adultery* and *idolatry* are placed right alongside *strife* and *envyings*. Many who faithfully attend church also gripe, criticize, and speak negatively about individuals, programs, and trivial matters. What may seem to be rather harmless sins actually are the same things that Paul says are typical of those who "shall not inherit the kingdom of God" (5:21).

5. What are some ways we can have compassion on weak Christians who are listening to enemies of the faith?

Before trying to "straighten someone out," a good first step is to become a true friend. This is not the same as being merely a Sunday-morning friend! Being a true friend includes being a good listener. Good listeners know how to connect with the depths of someone else's feelings. People who are questioning the faith and wavering, but are sincerely seeking the truth, should not have to fear that you are going to "whack them upside the head with the Bible."

Developing good listening skills leads to having good questioning skills. Someone who is good at asking questions can let the wavering person's own answers to thoughtful, probing questions lead him or her back to the path of truth.

Winter Quarter, 2003–2004

Special Features

Lessons

A Child Is Given

Lessons From Life

Unit 1: Job: Integrity in Times of Testing

Unit 2: Wisdom for the Times of Our Lives

About These Lessons

Our two sets of lessons for the quarter could be called "Expecting and Reflecting." The first set tells of births that changed history. Let us expect them to change us as well! The second set challenges us to stop and reflect about life in various ways. May our service improve as we do!

Dec 7
Dec 14
Dec 21
Dec 28
Jan 4
Jan 11
Jan 18
Jan 25
Feb 1
Feb 8
Feb 15
Feb 22
Feb 29

Quarterly Quiz

The questions on this page may be used in several ways: as a pretest at the beginning of the quarter; as a review at the end of the quarter; or as a review after each lesson. The questions are based on the Scripture text of each lesson (King James Version). **The answers are on page 116.**

Lesson 1

1. Who received Samuel when Hannah presented him to the Lord? (Elkanah, Ehud, Eli?) *1 Samuel 1:25*

2. According to Hannah, how long would Samuel be "lent" to the Lord? *1 Samuel 1:28*

3. In Hannah's prayer of praise she said, "There is none _____ as the Lord: . . . neither is there any _____ like our God." *1 Samuel 2:2*

Lesson 2

1. Which Old Testament character was *not* mentioned in Zechariah's prophecy? (David, Abraham, Moses?) *Luke 1:69, 73*

2. What title would be given to Zechariah's son, John? *Luke 1:76*

3. John the Baptist lived in Jerusalem until he began preaching. T/F *Luke 1:80*

Lesson 3

1. Who told Joseph to take Mary as his wife? (Zechariah, Michael, the angel of the Lord?) *Matthew 1:20*

2. Which name did the prophet Isaiah say would be given to the son born of a virgin? *Matthew 1:22, 23*

Lesson 4

1. How old was Jesus when He questioned the doctors in the temple? *Luke 2:42, 46*

2. What was the reaction of those who heard Jesus' answers? (skepticism, mild interest, astonishment?) *Luke 2:47*

3. "Jesus increased in _____ and stature, and in favor with _____ and man." *Luke 2:52*

Lesson 5

1. Satan came to present himself before the Lord. T/F *Job 2:1*

2. With what did Satan smite Job? *Job 2:7*

3. Who told Job to "curse God, and die"? (Job's wife, his friend, Satan?) *Job 2:9*

Lesson 6

1. What did Job ask God to help him know? *Job 13:23*

2. Job believed that even after his body was destroyed, he would see God in his flesh. T/F *Job 19:26*

3. Job esteemed God's words more than which necessity of life? (water, food, air?) *Job 23:12*

Lesson 7

1. According to Job, who was vexing his soul? *Job 27:2*

2. Job admitted that he had a few sins, such as greed for gold and pride. T/F *Job 31:24-28*

Lesson 8

1. When God laid the foundations of the earth, what did the sons of God do? *Job 38:4, 7*

2. Job answered the Lord and said, "I know that thou canst do _____ _____." *Job 42:1, 2*

Lesson 9

1. To every thing there is a _____. *Ecclesiastes 3:1*

2. To eat and drink and enjoy the good of labor is the gift of God. T/F *Ecclesiastes 3:13*

Lesson 10

1. The young man is warned that God will (bring him into judgment, cause him to feel sorrow, not hear his prayers). *Ecclesiastes 11:9*

2. What poetic phrase expresses the idea of an older person waking up early? *Ecclesiastes 12:4*

3. What happens to the spirit of a person who dies? *Ecclesiastes 12:7*

Lesson 11

1. What two fruits are mentioned by "the beloved"? *Song of Solomon 2:13*

2. Many waters cannot quench _____, neither can the floods drown it. *Song of Solomon 8:7*

Lesson 12

1. Who refused to bow down before Haman? *Esther 3:2*

2. Haman's entire plan of revenge against Mordecai was to humiliate and destroy him. T/F *Esther 3:6*

3. What did Esther request that the Jews of Shushan do for her? *Esther 4:16*

Lesson 13

1. What happened to Haman? (beaten, banished, hanged?) *Esther 8:7*

2. The fourteenth and fifteenth of the month of Adar were days of fasting and sorrow for the Jews. T/F *Esther 9:19-21*

3. What acts of generosity were part of the Jews annual celebration? *Esther 9:22*

Variety, the Spice of Life

by John W. Wade

IF VARIETY IS INDEED THE SPICE OF LIFE, and if you enjoy spices, you will enjoy the lessons of this quarter. They include lessons from both the Old and New Testaments, involving familiar Scriptures and Scriptures that we rarely study in the Uniform Lesson Series. This great variety we find in the Bible is one reason for its universal appeal. If one is willing to search, he or she is certain to find something to meet every human need.

The theme for the first four lessons is "A Child Is Given." Since the lessons begin in December, one's first thought would be that they deal with the traditional Christmas story about the birth of Christ. But that supposition would be only half true, for the first two lessons deal with the births of Samuel and John the Baptist, while the last two deal with Jesus' birth and growth.

Lesson 1 provides us information about the events that surrounded the birth of Samuel. Elkanah had two wives, a not uncommon practice in that day. One wife, Peninnah, had borne him several children, while the other wife, Hannah, was barren. Since children were considered a precious blessing, Hannah became the object of scorn and ridicule. On one of her visits to the tabernacle, she prayed earnestly that God would grant her a son. So desperate was she for a son that she promised to dedicate him to God if her prayer were heard. God heard her prayer and granted her a son, whom she named Samuel. When Samuel was weaned, she was true to her promise and brought him to the tabernacle where she left him to be reared by the elderly priest, Eli.

Lesson 2 also tells of a barren woman, Elisabeth, whose husband, Zechariah, was a priest. On one occasion when he was serving in the temple, the angel Gabriel appeared to him, telling him that he would have a son. But he doubted the divine messenger and was left dumb, unable to speak until after the birth of his son, John. Much of the lesson text deals with the prophecy that the aged priest uttered concerning his son.

Lesson 3 relates a portion of the Christmas story that we never grow tired of hearing. At the heart of the lesson is the virginal conception of Jesus by the Holy Spirit. This created a delicate situation that Joseph sought to avoid by putting Mary aside quietly without making a public scandal of it. But before he could take this action, Joseph was confronted in a dream by an angel of the Lord, who assured him that he need not hesitate to take Mary as his wife. What was

happening was a fulfillment of a prophecy that a virgin would conceive and bear a child.

The closing verses of the second chapter of Luke is the basis for **Lesson 4:** "Jesus: Growing in God's Favor." We read about Jesus' visit to Jerusalem as He accompanied His parents there to observe the feast of Passover. This is the only account we have about the life of Jesus from the time His parents returned to Nazareth and the beginning of His ministry. Christians have often wondered what those growing-up years were like. To satisfy this curiosity, various apocryphal stories of those years have been circulated. Of course, many of them are quite fanciful and even silly. We have every reason to believe that Jesus was an obedient son, obeying His parents and not burdening them with the worries that most parents have to deal with—with the exception of the incident related in this lesson. Here He behaved like, well, a typical twelve-year-old, driven by curiosity about the inner activities of the temple. But even in this activity, which so upset Mary and Joseph, He was obeying His Heavenly Father.

The next unit of this quarter, beginning in January, is titled "Job: Integrity in Times of Testing." It consists of four lessons dealing with the life of this great man of faith.

Lesson 5 introduces us to Job and the problem of human suffering that he struggles to deal with for the remainder of the book. The traditional orthodox view was that suffering came as the result of sin, either the sin of the sufferer or the sin of someone else. But in Job's experience this theory did not square with the facts in the situation. Job was a good man—a very good man, by normal human standards—and yet he suffered. Of course, what he didn't realize at the time was that he was caught in a struggle between God and Satan. The first chapter of Job tells how he lost his possessions and his children. The second chapter, the basis for this lesson, relates the terrible physical suffering he underwent. Only his wife was left, and she certainly wasn't any help to him in this situation.

Lesson 6 uses four short texts scattered from chapter 9 to chapter 23 to give us glimpses of the struggle Job was going through. He pleads for God to give him a chance to prove his innocence. The fact that God had not answered his plea leaves him bewildered. Yet, in the midst of his pain and emotional struggle, he still does not lose his faith in God. "I know that my Redeemer liveth," he cries out, "and that he shall stand at the latter day upon the earth" (Job 19:25). This statement alone makes the study of the book of Job worthwhile.

In the midst of all his suffering, Job is visited by three of his friends, Eliphaz, Bildad, and Zophar. But with friends like these, he didn't need enemies! They only added to his burden. In **Lesson 7,** "Integrity in Everyday Life," Job responds to his friends' challenges. He maintains his integrity by refusing to admit that he was guilty of any of the sins his friends accused him of.

The final lesson in this unit, **Lesson 8,** gives us the conclusion of Job's agonizing struggle. In the depths of his trial, Job comes dangerously close to challenging God's wisdom. God answers him out of a whirlwind, asking Job a series of questions that demonstrate Job's ignorance and finiteness. Job is completely humbled, affirming "I have heard of thee by the hearing of the ear; but now mine eye seeth thee." This experience led him to abhor himself and repent in dust and ashes.

The book of Job is one of the great pieces of literature that comes to us from the ancient world. The fact that it is part of the Holy Bible makes it imperative to study.

The next unit, "Wisdom for the Times of Our Lives," allows us to explore some other precious gems from the Old Testament. **Lesson 9** is based on the book of Ecclesiastes, and the issues it deals with sound as contemporary as this morning's newspaper. Many believe the author was King Solomon, and he had it all. But in the end, "vanity of vanities, all is vanity" is his conclusion. Yet in this lesson he passes along some of the wisdom he had accumulated through his life. His theme is "timeliness." There is an appropriate time for all of our activities. If we could just get this one lesson from this study, it would be worth the effort we spend on it.

Lesson 10, "A Time to Remember," is an appropriate follow-up on the previous lesson from Ecclesiastes. Much of the content of this book is rather cynical. While it stresses the importance of doing everything at an appropriate time, its emphasis upon things in this world does not give the reader much of a glimpse of the more important things beyond. The message of this lesson is especially important for young people: "Remember now thy Creator in the days of thy youth." Young people often want to "sow their wild oats" while they are young, expecting to survive and later settle down to become responsible citizens. Unfortunately, it doesn't always work that way. We all have seen young people who have become caught up in sex and drugs with devastating results. They don't live long enough to reach maturity! Remembering God in one's youth not only protects a person from the ravages of these evils, but gives a person many more years to serve the Lord.

Lesson 11 is quite unusual. In the long history of the Uniform Lesson Series, only a couple of times has the Song of Solomon been used for a lesson. The reason is quite obvious: the book speaks quite frankly about the physical aspects of love. In past years sexual matters were rarely spoken about in public, much less studied in a Sunday school lesson. Yet this book is in the Bible, and that makes it worthy of study. But further, God made us physical beings, and He expects us to deal with sexual matters in an honest and wholesome manner.

The final two lessons of the quarter are based on the book of Esther. **Lesson 12** has all the drama of a Hollywood production. Esther, an orphan girl, brought up by her uncle or cousin, Mordecai, becomes the queen of Ahasuerus, king of the Persian Empire. The villain, Haman, hates Mordecai and plots to take him out by having all the Jews in the empire killed. The king, ignorant of what was behind the plot, goes along with it. Then Esther, encouraged by Mordecai, courageously puts her life on the line to save her people. Her courage certainly serves as a model for us today. In the end Haman is hanged because of his treacherous plot, and Mordecai takes his place as the king's counselor.

Lesson 13 closes the quarter by telling how the Jews were able to escape the trap set for them by Haman. Their victory becomes the occasion for their feasting and rejoicing. The feast of Purim, one of the minor festivals in the Jewish calendar, is based on this incident.

Answers to Quarterly Quiz on page 114

Lesson 1—1. Eli. 2. as long as he lived. 3. holy, rock. **Lesson 2**—1. Moses. 2. the prophet of the Highest. 3. false (lived in the deserts). **Lesson 3**—1. the angel of the Lord. 2. Immanuel. **Lesson 4**—1. twelve years old. 2. astonishment. 3. wisdom, God. **Lesson 5**—1. true. 2. sore boils. 3. Job's wife. **Lesson 6**—1. his sin. 2. true. 3. food. **Lesson 7**—1. the Almighty. 2. false. **Lesson 8**—1. shouted for joy. 2. every thing. **Lesson 9**—1. season. 2. true. **Lesson 10**—1. bring him into judgment. 2. "he shall rise up at the voice of the bird." 3. it returns unto God. **Lesson 11**—1. figs, grapes. 2. love. **Lesson 12**—1. Mordecai. 2. false (he wanted to destroy all the Jews). 3. fast. **Lesson 13**—1. hanged. 2. false (gladness and feasting). 3. sending portions to each other and giving gifts to the poor.

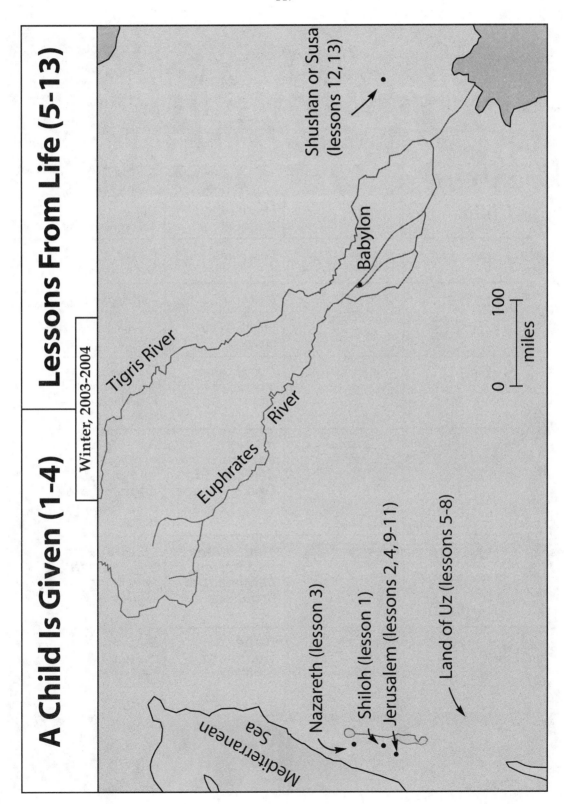

UNIQUE BIRTHS OF SPECIAL CHILDREN

Child	Text(s)	How the Child Is Special	Life Accomplishment
Cain	Genesis 4:1	First human child	Cursed as the first murderer
Isaac	Genesis 18:1-15; 21:1-7	Mother old and barren; prophesied by an angel	Fathered Jacob, the father of Israel
Samson	Judges 13:2-24	Mother barren; announced by an angel	Championed Israel against the Philistines; died in shame
Samuel (Lesson 1)	*1 Samuel 1:1-20*	*Mother barren; dedicated to God's service*	*As judge, prophet, and priest, anointed the first kings of Israel*
John the Baptist (Lesson 2)	*Luke 1:5-25, 57-66*	*Mother old and barren; fulfillment of prophecy*	*Forerunner of the Messiah; herald of God's kingdom*
Jesus (Lesson 3,4)	*Matthew 1:18-25; Luke 1:26-35; 2:1-7*	*Father is God; born of a virgin*	*Messiah and Savior of all believers*

A Context for Learning

A Good Start

by Ronald G. Davis

CLASSROOMS SHOULD CREATE "wide-eyed children" of learners, no matter the age. A "learning enriched environment," as educators use the term, has the potential to do so. Usually the proponents are referring to a space filled with content-related elements, both decorative and educational. From decorations to furnishings to a library of books, teachers want the room both to support and encourage learning. When learners walk in (or even approach), something reminds or tells them, "Oh, yes, this is what we're studying." Some visual, aural, or other sensory stimulus helps learners recall what has been studied or piques their curiosity and interest as to what will be. A leader of classroom Bible study with adults wants a "learning enriched environment."

Nursery and Nativity

The first four lessons in this quarter's study are all about births and babies. The unit title is "A Child Is Given," and three special baby stories are reviewed. A classroom furnished and arranged to resemble an infant nursery in some fashion has excellent learning enhancement possibilities. Consider some of the following ideas.

Set in prominent position selected nursery furnishings: a bassinet, an infant child seat, a hanging mobile. Add a container of baby talc and baby lotion. As learners arrive, have lullaby music playing. A study display collection of baby pictures—both of class members and of their children or grandchildren—can add "flavor" to the context.

As each of the new babies is introduced in the lesson series, prepare a list of "shower" gifts that will be appropriate for the parents or baby. Either as a preview activity handed out a week before or as a session introductory activity, ask the learners to decide how each "gift" on the list is relevant to the text revelation. Consider the following lists, here given with explanatory notes.

For Samuel and his parents: an athletic shirt with the number 11 (based on Elkanah's statement that he was better to Hannah than ten sons); a razor without a blade (based on Hannah's promise that her son would never have his hair cut; anything blue (Hannah prayed for a "man child"); a "golden ear" locket (for Samuel's name means, "heard of God"); an AA membership card (Eli thought Hannah was drunk in her

praying); a cow (for Hannah's sacrifice at the time she gives her son to the Lord); happy face stickers (see 1 Samuel 1:18b); musical staff sheets (for Hannah to record her song of chapter 2); a "Get out of worship free" card (for Hannah's skipping the annual pilgrimage to Shiloh until her son's weaning).

For John and his parents: two senior citizen discount cards (for both parents are "well stricken in years"); a book teaching sign language (for Zechariah to use for communication during his mute period of nine months); stick or cone incense (for Zechariah's duty in the temple); a book of "Names for Boys" (though the parents won't need this one); carton of soft drinks (for John will drink no "strong drink"); a five-month supply of knitting supplies (for Elisabeth's self-imposed five-month hiding); party supplies for an "It's a boy!" celebration (see Luke 1:58); a small chalkboard and chalk (for Zechariah's use in indicating the baby's name); a big jar of honey (for John's food in the wilderness); a baby camel (for John's later clothes of camel's hair, Matthew 3:4).

For Jesus and His parents: a book on dream interpretation (though neither will need it!); engagement ring (they were "espoused"); a fold-out map of Jerusalem (for Mary and Joseph's search for Jesus); a safe deposit box in the First Bank of Bethlehem (for safe storage of the wise men's gifts); round-trip tickets to Egypt (see Matthew 2:13-15); outdated Holiday Inn® coupon (for there was "no room in the inn"); bundle of cloth strips (for "swaddling cloths" for the newborn); wooden folding bassinet with a straw tick (for the manger bed); a journaling notebook (for Mary to "keep and ponder" all the events); a pair of turtledoves (for the temple sacrifice at Jesus' circumcision).

"It's Always One O'Clock"

Two key words are used in the titles of the last nine lessons in this quarter's study: *integrity* and *time*. Have an artistic member of your class prepare a large cut-out analog clock for the wall, a clock that at every hour position is the number 1.

Have this on display as lesson 5 is introduced. Be prepared to make an explanation when someone notes and questions the design of the clock. Use words something like these:

"The basic root of the word *integrity* is the word, *integer*, a whole number. Integrity has to do with wholeness, consistency, predictability. Integrity is a round-the-clock concept. No one has integrity when living a fractured, disjunctive life. The person with integrity can be counted on, counted on to speak truth and to be true." Note that the first four lessons in the coming units deal with integrity, and that the last five have to do with time. And that integrity reveals itself at all times, whatever the circumstance.

As an alternative introductory visual, bring in as many clocks as you can and display them randomly around the room. Set each one to one o'clock. Make an explanation similar to the previous paragraph.

For each lesson, then, consider ways to apply lesson themes and to review lesson truths.

For lesson five, consider some of the following "context" ideas: hand out an adhesive strip to each learner arriving (to represent Job's suffering); hand out a broken piece of clay pottery (inexpensive flowerpot) to each (see 2:8); give each a "praying for you" card (at the end you can recommend that it be sent to someone in physical and emotional distress).

For lesson six, set whatever clock(s) you are displaying to 12 o'clock, both hands pointing up. When members arrive, ask if they notice the difference on the clock(s). Ask, "Why would 12 o'clock be the best reminder to seek God in prayer?" Someone will probably note: "Both hands are 'lifted up' toward Heaven." Assign and have read the following Bible verses that include references to both time and to praying: Psalm 5:3; Psalm 55:17; Psalm 88:13; Psalm 119:164. As class continues, note that the title is "Integrity in Seeking God," and ask, "Is there a best time to seek God? Is there a best way?"

For lesson seven, collect enough newspapers (or newsmagazines) to have one on the chair for each class member as the class assembles. If possible, have items from a variety of dates, including some older items. Direct the class members to, "Find an article in your paper or magazine that clearly depicts someone living without integrity in everyday life." You may note, "These resources are records of people in everyday life— records of people choosing integrity or choosing dissimulation."

In lesson eight, one part of the text (Job 38:1-7) is God's "Final Exam" for Job, an examination for which Job has no answers. Secure a set of the traditional blue books used by schools and colleges for tests. Hand one to each person as he or she enters. Tell the class, "Number your test booklet one to twenty." Either prepare and hand out or simply present orally test questions learn-

ers will most likely be unable to answer: for example, "What is the standard deviation of the top ten batting averages of last year's American League baseball batters?"; "On Moh's hardness scale, what is the number of the earth's most common mineral?"; "How many kilometers is it from the earth to the nearest star?"; "Translate this clause, 'God is good,' into Urdu script"; "Draw a contour map of the Pacific Ocean floor"; "Write the steps necessary to program a computer to do a spell check in a language not using the English alphabet"; and other such "impossible" questions. After only four or five, the point will be obvious. Launch into the text.

For lesson nine, "A Time for All Things," if you did not collect and display a variety of clocks earlier, do so for today's study. Label each clock with a daily activity of necessity and/or importance. Such items as "brushing teeth," "putting shoes on," "praying," "Bible reading," "eating," "sleeping," "helping someone," and others can be included. Make the labels large enough to be legible across the room. Begin by saying, "Each day some things we just don't have time for." Select a clock, read the label aloud, and put the clock conspicuously in the wastebasket. Put some of the "necessary" items in first. At some point say, "What makes a daily activity 'necessary'?"

For lesson ten, "A Time to Remember," have someone tie a loose bow of ribbon or string around a finger of each arriving student. When all are in and seated, ask all to hold up their hands with the bows and ask, "Now what was that you were supposed to remember?"

For lesson eleven, the day after Valentine's Day, have the room decorated with valentines or simple cut-out hearts. Students should realize quickly that this lesson is "A Time for Love."

For lesson twelve you can use the hearts from the previous Sunday. Arrange a group of hearts into one large heart shape on display. Ask the class, "How does a heart relate to today's study, 'A Time for Courage'?" Note that the "core" of "courage" is the root for heart: *cor*.

For the final lesson in the series, "A Time to Celebrate," decorate the room as for a party: balloons, streamers, and the like. This study, from Esther 8 and 9, includes the origin of the Jewish celebration of Purim, the survival of the Jews in Persia.

The teacher with insight into how adults learn will look each quarter and each week for ways to reflect content and objectives in the very space where study will occur. Will learners come into a sterile, nondescript room? Or will they enter an "enriched learning environment"? The teacher decides.

Samuel: Dedicated to God

December 7
Lesson 1

DEVOTIONAL READING: 1 Samuel 1:9-18.

BACKGROUND SCRIPTURE: 1 Samuel 1:1–2:10; Luke 1:46-55.

PRINTED TEXT: 1 Samuel 1:20, 24-28; 2:1-8a.

1 Samuel 1:20, 24-28

20 Wherefore it came to pass, when the time was come about after Hannah had conceived, that she bare a son, and called his name Samuel, saying, Because I have asked him of the LORD.

. . . .

24 And when she had weaned him, she took him up with her, with three bullocks, and one ephah of flour, and a bottle of wine, and brought him unto the house of the LORD in Shiloh: and the child was young.

25 And they slew a bullock, and brought the child to Eli.

26 And she said, O my lord, as thy soul liveth, my lord, I am the woman that stood by thee here, praying unto the LORD.

27 For this child I prayed; and the LORD hath given me my petition which I asked of him:

28 Therefore also I have lent him to the LORD; as long as he liveth he shall be lent to the LORD. And he worshipped the LORD there.

1 Samuel 2:1-8a

1 And Hannah prayed, and said, My heart rejoiceth in the LORD, mine horn is exalted in the LORD; my mouth is enlarged over mine enemies; because I rejoice in thy salvation.

2 There is none holy as the LORD: for there is none besides thee: neither is there any rock like our God.

3 Talk no more so exceeding proudly; let not arrogancy come out of your mouth: for the LORD is a God of knowledge, and by him actions are weighed.

4 The bows of the mighty men are broken, and they that stumbled are girded with strength.

5 They that were full have hired out themselves for bread; and they that were hungry ceased: so that the barren hath borne seven; and she that hath many children is waxed feeble.

6 The LORD killeth, and maketh alive: he bringeth down to the grave, and bringeth up.

7 The LORD maketh poor, and maketh rich: he bringeth low, and lifteth up.

8a He raiseth up the poor out of the dust, and lifteth up the beggar from the dunghill, to set them among princes, and to make them inherit the throne of glory.

GOLDEN TEXT: For this child I prayed; and the LORD hath given me my petition which I asked of him: therefore also I have lent him to the LORD; as long as he liveth he shall be lent to the LORD. And he worshipped the LORD there.—1 Samuel 1:27, 28.

A Child Is Given
(Lessons 1-4)

Lesson Aims

After participating in this lesson, each student should be able to:

1. Tell how Hannah's devotion to God is seen in her prayerful request to the Lord for a son and in her faithfulness in carrying out her vow after the birth of Samuel.

2. State the importance of keeping spiritual commitments, no matter how difficult.

3. Suggest a specific commitment that he or she will fulfill in keeping with Hannah's example of faithfulness.

Lesson Outline

INTRODUCTION
    A. The Shirt Off His Back
    B. Lesson Background
 I. HANNAH'S PROMISE (1 Samuel 1:20, 24-28)
    A. The Lord Hears Hannah's Prayer (v. 20)
       Infertility
    B. Hannah Fulfills Her Vow (vv. 24-27)
    C. Samuel Is Dedicated to the Lord (v. 28)
       Letting Go
II. HANNAH'S SONG OF PRAISE (1 Samuel 2:1-8a)
    A. Hannah Rejoices (v. 1)
    B. God Is Exalted (v. 2)
    C. God Is Sovereign (vv. 3-8a)
CONCLUSION
    A. Hannah's Sacrifice Reforms a Nation
    B. Prayer
    C. Thought to Remember

Introduction

A. The Shirt Off His Back

In 1994, Alex Dovales was drifting toward Miami on a rickety boat with twenty-seven other Cubans. Two years later, Dovales saw fourteen exhausted, penniless Cuban rafters wash ashore on Key Largo and said, "I felt like I had just arrived here myself." The twenty-five-year-old dishwasher, who cleared $197 per week, walked home and gathered all the presents from under his Christmas tree. He gave the shirts and other clothing to the new arrivals. "They were wet and cold," explained Henry Paez, Dovales's roommate. "Alex took off his shirt and gave it to them."

The Old Testament book of 1 Samuel begins with an example of even greater selflessness. At this time of the year when we are eager to express our love and generosity in the giving of gifts, it is appropriate that we look to an example of one who gave out of her worship to the Lord. Hannah's dedication of her son, Samuel, to the service of the Lord is an act of devotion that still challenges believers today.

B. Lesson Background

"The period of the judges" lasted roughly three hundred and fifty years, from about 1406 to 1050 B.C. Samuel's prophetic ministry began during the latter part of those deplorable years; this was a time when Israel had no king (Judges 18:1; 19:1). This was also a time when moral conditions among the people were chaotic as "every man did that which was right in his own eyes" (Judges 21:25). Just before Samuel is born, a man named Eli holds a judgeship that ultimately lasts some forty years. But Eli's judgeship is a spiritual failure, largely because he allowed his sons to pervert worship at the tabernacle and to engage in blatant sexual immorality (1 Samuel 2:12-17, 22; 3:13, 14).

So God determined that new leadership was needed at the tabernacle. The birth of Samuel was God's answer to Israel's need. Samuel was to be God's leader who would bring Israel back to spiritual health. Things had to change!

In his transitional role, Samuel is sometimes referred to as "the last of the judges" (cf. 1 Samuel 7:6, 15-17) and "the first of the prophets" (cf. 1 Samuel 3:20; Acts 3:24; 13:20). One of Samuel's most important tasks would be to assist the people of Israel in their desire for a king (1 Samuel 8:4-22) even though Samuel did not think that was such a good idea (8:6). Not only would Samuel be the prophet to anoint Israel's first king, Saul (10:1), later Samuel would also anoint the second, namely King David (16:13).

But the story of Samuel's ministry begins with godly parents. Their faithfulness shows us how God often works out His will through ordinary, "blue collar" believers who struggle with the common issues of life. Hannah and Elkanah, Samuel's mother and father, were worshipers of the living God. When Hannah came to worship the Lord at the tabernacle in Shiloh (about twenty miles north of modern-day Jerusalem), she carried intense longings for a child. She understood, as so many modern believers do, that the deepest needs in life can find their answer only in the Lord of the universe. She trusted that the one true God would show His generosity to her, and she found Him to be ready to answer her prayers.

I. Hannah's Promise
(1 Samuel 1:20, 24-28)

The opening verses of 1 Samuel introduce us to Samuel's parents by mentioning several details that give us a good portrait of the couple. Elkanah is described as "a certain man" in 1:1, a phrase that gives no indication that he is of any rank or position. Apparently he is a common man. He is married to Hannah and they live in a town in the hill country of Ephraim. This is in the northern part of the spine of mountains that runs through Palestine. [See question #1, page 128.]

In addition to Hannah, who is childless, there is another wife named Peninnah. The two are rivals because Peninnah has borne children (1:2) and often uses this fact to embarrass Hannah (1:6, 7; cf. Genesis 16:1-6). In the bitterness of her soul Hannah carries her request for a child to the Lord during one of the family pilgrimages to the tabernacle for a feast day (1 Samuel 1:9, 10). As with other notable women of the Bible who faced the challenge of barrenness (Genesis 11:30; 25:21; 29:31; Judges 13:2), Hannah depends on the mercy of the Creator of life for this plea to be answered.

A. The Lord Hears Hannah's Prayer (v. 20)

20. Wherefore it came to pass, when the time was come about after Hannah had conceived, that she bare a son, and called his name Samuel, saying, Because I have asked him of the LORD.

Verse 19 tells us that the Lord is moved to answer Hannah's prayer uttered at the tabernacle. [See question #2, page 128.] After that prayer, she and her family return home and sometime later God's gift to Hannah becomes obvious. Verse 19 and the words *when the time was come about* indicate that the natural processes of conception and childbirth applied in the case of Hannah (contrast Luke 1:26-38). This would imply that Hannah goes home from Shiloh not knowing for sure how God will work out an answer to her prayer, even though Eli the priest had offered comforting words (1 Samuel 1:17).

When Hannah receives her precious gift from the Lord, she names him in such a way as to announce it to the world. The name *Samuel* contains within it the idea of the "name of God," and permits Hannah's play on words that this name is appropriate because she had *asked* for Samuel from God. [See question #3, page 128.]

INFERTILITY

When James and Carol Herget went to Jamaica in 1949, they went to do what most missionaries do: preach and teach. When they found that they would be childless, they adopted a little boy—

then a second, a third, a fourth, and a fifth. When they took in the sixth child, they learned that a private home could not take in more than six children. So they started the Jamaica Christian Boys Home. Over the years, fifty-eight orphaned boys found a home there.

After twenty-nine years in Jamaica the Hergets went to the more challenging field of Haiti. They used what they had learned in Jamaica to found Christianville, where today fifteen hundred students receive an education and two meals a day. They added a church, medical and dental clinics, and a nutrition center. When James died, Carol founded Village of Hope, where today more than four hundred children receive an education and two meals a day.

It is possible—in fact it is likely—that none of this would have happened had the Hergets not been childless. God used Hannah's situation in a marvelous way; He used the Hergets' situation also in a marvelous, but different, way. The Hergets' disappointment became His appointment. God always can use people to fulfill His plan, no matter what their life situations. Today, are you wallowing in self-pity because of some life circumstance, or are you looking for God's plan within that circumstance?   —R. C. S.

B. Hannah Fulfills Her Vow (vv. 24-27)

24. And when she had weaned him, she took him up with her, with three bullocks, and one ephah of flour, and a bottle of wine, and brought him unto the house of the LORD in Shiloh: and the child was young.

An infant's weaning period is three years, according to the non-Biblical account found in 2 Maccabees 7:27. No doubt Hannah treasures these short years with the son she has devoted to the Lord.

When the time comes for little Samuel to be taken to the tabernacle, we see no hesitation on Hannah's part. She makes the journey to *Shiloh* with the necessary sacrifice. More modern translations have the sacrifice as one three-year-old bull where the *King James Version* has *three bullocks*. If

---

How to Say It

ELI. *Ee*-lye.
ELKANAH. *El*-kuh-nuh or El-*kay*-nuh.
EPHRAIM. *Ee*-fray-im.
HANNAH. *Han*-uh.
MACCABEES. *Mack*-uh-bees.
PENINNAH. Peh-*nin*-uh.
SHILOH. *Shy*-low.
ZECHARIAH. *Zek*-uh-*rye*-uh (strong accent on *rye*).

the family is traveling with three bulls, the first may be for a special burnt offering, while the other two can serve as Elkanah's yearly sacrifice to the Lord (Numbers 8:8; 1 Samuel 1:3). If the phrase describes the age of the bull as three years, then they are sacrificing a bull in its prime. The *flour* and *wine* may serve as sustenance for the journey.

The note that *the child* is *young* dramatizes the sacrifice to which Hannah has committed herself, as well as the unusual nature of this decision that permits a young child to be given into the custody of the tabernacle service. Hannah fulfills her promise to the Lord even though it undoubtedly is painful to let go. In both the Old and New Testaments (unlike so often today), vows are not taken lightly (Judges 11:30-40; Proverbs 20:25; Ecclesiastes 5:4-6; Matthew 14:6-10; Acts 18:18).

25. And they slew a bullock, and brought the child to Eli.

Presenting the young boy to the tabernacle at this age is out of the ordinary: a Levite's son is usually not presented for such service until he has reached an age of about twenty-five. He would then continue in office until retiring at age fifty (Numbers 8:23-26). Samuel is beginning his life-long service some twenty-two years ahead of schedule!

26. And she said, O my lord, as thy soul liveth, my lord, I am the woman that stood by thee here, praying unto the LORD.

Hannah reminds the high priest Eli of the incident a few short years earlier when she *stood* before the tabernacle in prayer asking for a child (see 1 Samuel 1:11-18). The phrase *as my soul liveth* is a common oath formula (see 1 Samuel 17:55; 20:3; 25:26; 2 Samuel 11:11; 14:19).

Hannah's purpose in using this oath is to guarantee to Eli that whether or not his memory can effectively recall the incident in which she prayed for a child, she is speaking the truth about the matter. By the New Testament era, the religious leaders had perverted the practice of oath-taking (see Matthew 23:16-22). Oaths should be unnecessary for those who are always to speak the truth anyway (Matthew 5:33-37; James 5:12). Even so, the apostle Paul continued to take oaths in matters of extreme importance (see 2 Corinthians 11:31; Galatians 1:20).

VISUALS FOR THESE LESSONS

The visual pictured in each lesson (e.g., page 125) is a small reproduction of a large, full-color poster included in the *Adult Visuals* packet for the Winter Quarter. The packet is available from your supplier. Order No. 292.

---

27. For this child I prayed; and the LORD hath given me my petition which I asked of him.

Hannah intends that Eli understand that her prayer before the tabernacle was an authentic prayer (instead of drunkenness, as he concluded in 1 Samuel 1:14), and that the Lord had been gracious in answering that prayer. Her words to Eli are spoken so as to correspond with his own words to her in 1:17. [See question #4, page 128.]

C. Samuel Is Dedicated to the Lord (v. 28)

28. Therefore also I have lent him to the LORD; as long as he liveth he shall be lent to the LORD. And he worshipped the LORD there.

Hannah now expresses her intentions regarding the destiny of young Samuel: she will go home and leave him at the tabernacle in Shiloh. She will leave him there permanently as her way of giving back to the Lord who blessed her with a son. His role will be to serve in the tabernacle as one of the assistants to the priests (see 2:11). But his mother will not allow Samuel to escape her thoughts as he serves at the tabernacle. Each year she will produce clothing for him to wear as he serves, and she will deliver these items when she travels with her husband to Shiloh for annual worship (2:19). Nevertheless, Samuel will stay behind when the time comes for Hannah and her husband to return home.

The word "he" in the statement *he worshipped the Lord there* most likely refers to Samuel rather than Eli or Elkanah, since the immediate context addresses the ministry of young Samuel. Perhaps the statement conveys how Hannah's son quickly takes up his role in a very serious way (cf. 2:18). Hannah's unselfish dedication of her son begins to produce immediate results. [See question #5, page 128.]

LETTING GO

A lady said that when she was young there was in her family a vase that was a cherished heirloom. It had been handed down through the family. It occupied a place of honor in the living room. One day she broke it. Her mother came running. But there was no anger in the mother's eyes. "Are you hurt?" she asked as she picked up the child. Recalling that event the lady said, "That day I discovered that *I* was the family treasure."

Samuel must have known that he was the family treasure. He must have become aware at some time in his life that it had not been easy for his parents to keep his mother's vow and give him wholly to the Lord's service. Today's parents might not find it easy to see their adult children go off to the mission field—taking the grandchildren with them!—for years at a time. Unwed mothers do not find it easy to give up their children to adoptive parents who can do better for the child than they can. But when people put God's greater plans ahead of their personal desires and feelings, great things can happen.

In today's lesson a father and mother make the greatest possible sacrifice when they give Samuel to the Lord to grow up in the tabernacle. But their unselfish act was good for all concerned: for the family, for the child, and for the people of God. As a result, Samuel's godly influence reverberates through time and history. And it all began when two loving and faithful parents decided to honor a vow to God. What sacrifice is God asking you to make for Him today?—R. C. S.

UNIQUE BIRTHS OF SPECIAL CHILDREN

Child	Text(s)	How the Child Is Special	Life Accomplishment
Cain	Genesis 4:1	First human child	Cursed as the first murderer
Isaac	Genesis 18:1-15; 21:1-7	Mother old and barren, prophesied by an angel	Fathered Jacob, the father of Israel
Samson	Judges 13:2-24	Mother barren, announced by an angel	Championed Israel against the Philistines; died in shame
Samuel (Lesson 1)	1 Samuel 1:1-20	Mother barren; dedicated to God's service	As judge, prophet, and priest, anointed first kings of Israel
John the Baptist (Lesson 2)	Luke 1:5-25, 57-66	Mother old and barren; fulfillment of prophecy	Forerunner of the Messiah; herald of God's kingdom
Jesus (Lessons 3,4)	Matthew 1:18-25; Luke 1:26-35; 2:1-7	Father is God; born of a virgin	Messiah and Savior of all believers

Visual for lesson 1

Use this visual to illustrate how God chose people for His service from their earliest years.

II. Hannah's Song of Praise (1 Samuel 2:1-8a)

At such a moment Hannah expresses joy and adoration to the Lord as recorded in the verses that follow. We may compare her song with that of Mary after the birth of Jesus (Luke 1:46-55) and with the song of Zechariah at the birth of John the Baptist (Luke 1:67-79). See also the words of Moses and Miriam in Exodus 15:1-18, 21, the song of Moses in Deuteronomy 32:1-43, Deborah's song in Judges 5, and David's song in 2 Samuel 22. These show how Old Testament worshipers expressed their gratitude in joyful praise.

A. Hannah Rejoices (v. 1)

1. And Hannah prayed, and said, My heart rejoiceth in the LORD, mine horn is exalted in the LORD; my mouth is enlarged over mine enemies; because I rejoice in thy salvation.

Hannah directs her praises to *the Lord* by expressing the joy of knowing Him as a God of deliverance. Some commentators suggest that these words may be a quotation of a hymn that Hannah had learned at the tabernacle in Shiloh.

Whether Hannah learned these verses from someone else or wrote them herself, they are a richly descriptive tribute to the God who hears the prayers of the humble worshiper. She begins by proclaiming her gratitude for the Lord who brings us victory over our *enemies*, who are powerless when God moves to protect His people.

When Hannah refers to herself in this prayer, she speaks of her *heart*, her *horn*, and her *mouth* as the human instruments from which she offers praise. "Horn" is a poetic description of her "strength" (cf. 1 Samuel 2:10), since horned animals often raise their horns high in the air to prepare for battle and self-protection (as in Deuteronomy 33:17; Psalm 92:10). Hannah proclaims the Lord to be her *salvation* from defeat and humiliation.

Many men and women today understand the agony faced by Hannah. But these verses remind believers that the Lord is the source of victory for those who trust in Him.

B. God Is Exalted (v. 2)

2. There is none holy as the LORD: for there is none besides thee: neither is there any rock like our God.

In her praise Hannah carefully describes a God who deserves our worship exclusively. Hers is a world dominated by the pagan worship of innumerable gods and goddesses. Hannah's expression of the unique holiness and power of the Lord puts her firmly on the side of Old Testament teaching about God (Exodus 15:11; Psalm 99:3, 5, 9; Isaiah 5:16). She affirms that only the Lord deserves this praise. Referring to God as a *rock* is one of the most recognized ways of describing His protection for believers (see Genesis 49:24; Deuteronomy 32:4; Psalms 18:2, 31, 46; 95:1; Isaiah 17:10). When we sing "Rock of Ages cleft for me, let me hide myself in Thee," we also praise God as the rock of our protection.

C. God is Sovereign (vv. 3-8a)

3. Talk no more so exceeding proudly; let not arrogancy come out of your mouth: for the LORD is a God of knowledge, and by him actions are weighed.

In contrast to her praise for the Lord of our protection, Hannah now prays warnings upon those who take pride in their own strength. To what extent her prayer refers to the arrogant talk she has heard from her rival, Peninnah, cannot be determined (1:6). But Hannah's prayer takes aim at those who believe that their own strength and knowledge are sufficient. All human pride is useless (see Psalms 31:18; 138:6; Proverbs 16:18; Isaiah 5:15, 16).

4. The bows of the mighty men are broken, and they that stumbled are girded with strength.

Hannah now begins a series of contrasts that extend through verse 7. *Bows* are weapons of war often used by the powerful military forces that have dominated the earth. *Broken* bows, however, are useless for obtaining military victory. Thus God's power can humble the most powerful armed forces, while giving victory to those people who seem to stumble in weakness.

5. They that were full have hired out themselves for bread; and they that were hungry ceased: so that the barren hath borne seven; and she that hath many children is waxed feeble.

Two more contrasts describe the great reversals brought about by the Lord who protects the humble servant. The person who is *full* and well-fed becomes destitute to the point of needing to earn more money just to eat (e.g., 1 Samuel 2:36), while those without adequate food ultimately are supplied with plenty (2 Kings 7:3-8). Those, like Hannah, who have no children are given children by this God who cares for lowly people; on the other hand, *many children* will be no guarantee of strength and security (cf. Jeremiah 15:7).

6. The LORD killeth, and maketh alive: he bringeth down to the grave, and bringeth up.

Hannah's praise also extends to the Lord's power over life and death. In her own case the Lord had acted to make *alive* by bringing life to her childless womb. Meanwhile God's judgment can extinguish life for those who oppose Him, as ultimately occurs with Eli and his sons (1 Samuel 4:12-18; cf. 1 Kings 2:27).

7. The LORD maketh poor, and maketh rich: he bringeth low, and lifteth up.

This God, says Hannah, is powerful enough to determine and even reverse the fortunes of anyone. Perhaps Hannah is remembering the account of Joseph (Genesis 37, 39–50).

8a. He raiseth up the poor out of the dust, and lifteth up the beggar from the dunghill, to set them among princes, and to make them inherit the throne of glory.

The Lord can humble those who are rich and proud in this life, while lifting the poor person. He can lift a humble man like Saul as he hides among the luggage (1 Samuel 10:22) to be king over Israel; but God also brings about his downfall (1 Samuel 15:26-28; 31:1-6). Hannah's praise reflects adoration for the way that God extends mercy to those battered by the discouragements of this life.

So Hannah not only brings her son to dedicate him for the Lord's service, but also to open her heart to praise Him in vibrant worship. She is no reluctant promise-keeper. Hannah's praise of the living God shows that she fulfills her vow with gladness in her heart. She knows that she has been blessed with the gift of this child, and she considers it a privilege to be able to commit him to the Lord's service.

We could only hope and pray that such a spirit would be found within us when it comes time to fulfill promises that we have made to our God! Mothers and fathers who consider the example of Hannah will stand in awe of her devotion to give so much. But every believer who reflects on Hannah's single-minded dedication in carrying out fearlessly a bold and costly promise made in her hour of desperation will realize that in her actions lies an example for the church.

Conclusion

A. Hannah's Sacrifice Reforms a Nation

When Hannah dedicated Samuel to God's service, she unknowingly presented to Israel a powerful force for reform of the nation. She did it without knowing how God would use this future prophet to draw an entire people back to Him. She did it without knowing that Samuel would be the first prophet to foretell the days of Christ (Acts 3:24). What courage! What faith!

B. Prayer

Lord, we pray today that You will take our lives and let them be wholly consecrated to You. May we withhold nothing today that we have promised to give to You. In Jesus' name, amen.

C. Thought to Remember

Trust God to know "the bigger picture."

Home Daily Bible Readings

Monday, Dec. 1—Hannah Prays for a Son (1 Samuel 1:1-11)

Tuesday, Dec. 2—God Answers Hannah's Prayer (1 Samuel 1:12-20)

Wednesday, Dec. 3—Hannah Presents Samuel to God (1 Samuel 1:21-28)

Thursday, Dec. 4—Hannah Praises God (1 Samuel 2:1-5)

Friday, Dec. 5—The Lord Raises Up the Poor (1 Samuel 2:6-10)

Saturday, Dec. 6—Mary's Song of Praise (Luke 1:46-50)

Sunday, Dec. 7—He Has Helped His Servant Israel (Luke 1:51-55)

Learning by Doing

This page contains an alternative lesson plan emphasizing learning activities.
Classes desiring such student involvement will find these suggestions helpful.

Learning Goals

After participating in this lesson, each student will be able to:

1. Tell how Hannah's devotion to God is seen in her prayerful request to the Lord for a son and in her faithfulness in carrying out her vow after the birth of Samuel.

2. State the importance of keeping spiritual commitments, no matter how difficult.

3. Suggest a specific commitment that he or she will fulfill in keeping with Hannah's example of faithfulness.

Into the Lesson

As class members enter the classroom, have the following acrostic on vertical display: GOD ANSWERS PRAYER. Ask class members to write a word(s) for each letter that relates to the theme.

As the class begins say, "I want you to think about how God answers prayer requests." Then ask class members to move into groups of three to five and have them answer these questions:

1. What specific needs (or desires) have you ever prayed for God to meet?

2. What ultimatums (such as time frame or conditions) have you given God?

3. Why are diligence and fervor necessary for a healthy and fruitful prayer life?

Affirm, "God does answer all prayers, and it is important for us to be aware of His answers and how they fit into His big picture. Today we see Hannah as a picture of effective praying and responding to God's answer." Also, convey that prayer is an interactive process that often mirrors our relationship with our own friends. Point out that most of us never demand from friends what we do of God.

Into the Word

Ask the class members when, where, why, and how they pray. Note that we spend hours daily planning how to better ourselves at work, working out at the gym, watching TV, or spending time with our children, but only minutes a day in prayer. Ask the class, "How do environmental factors (such as location and time of day) influence your interaction with your children?" Then state, "If these factors influence other aspects of our lives, then why would they not influence our spiritual lives? To be successful in anything, one must plan, prepare, and execute efficiently and consistently. What can you do to provide more fervor to your prayer life?"

To integrate the above activity with the Scriptural text, consider presenting a mini-lecture on 1 Samuel 1:21–2:8a. Have the class turn to 1 Samuel 1 and 2 to follow along.

Along with the topics covered in the interactive phase of the lesson, it is important to emphasize prayer and the resultant blessings that sometimes come with sacrifices.

Say, "When the time came for Samuel to be taken to the tabernacle, there was no hesitation on Hannah's part. She journeyed to Shiloh with the necessary sacrifice. Hannah fulfilled her promise to the Lord even though it was painful." Move the class back to small groups to discuss, "What can we learn about prayer from Hannah?"

Make sure your class includes such principles as the following: (1) do not let circumstances preclude possibility—see 1:5; (2) do not let the doubts of others stifle hope in yourself—see 1:6; (3) acknowledge blessing in the midst of pain—see 1:8; (4) be willing to show to God the depth of emotion you feel—1:10; (5) though you cannot deal face-to-face with God, feel free to promise Him a response and do it—see 1:11, 28.

Examine other elements of Hannah's story for similar prayer principles. You may want to state these principles to your class orally and ask them to identify verses that reveal the truth in Hannah's life, or you may give each group a printed list and ask them to agree on how each truth is represented in Hannah's story.

Into Life

State: "Some people have called prayer 'a powerful tool'; however, this is a misnomer. To think of prayer as a tool assumes we have the control and the right to direct it as necessary. Instead, prayer is an attitude and act of communication—an interaction with a Friend, our Father and Creator. It is a source of inspiration, guidance, and empowerment." Say: "As we conclude our lesson time today, let's reflect on how we need to change our own prayer attitude and act to demonstrate the faith of Hannah."

After a few minutes of silent thinking, have all make a personal list of what they need to change, in two columns: ATTITUDES and ACTS. Suggest they keep their lists in an easily observable location for the next week or longer.

Let's Talk It Over

The questions on this page are designed to promote discussion of the lesson by the class and to encourage application of the lesson Scriptures. The answers provided are only discussion starters. Let your class talk it over from there.

1. What are some indicators in 1 Samuel 1 that a common faith strengthened the relationship of Elkanah and Hannah? How did this relationship help them in some of the tough decisions they had to face?

Elkanah and Hannah made sure that God was part of their relationship. They worshiped together (1:19). Elkanah encouraged Hannah to be faithful to her vow, although it meant personal sacrifice (1:23). When couples are united in their devotion to God, they have a common, living source of strength. They also have a common purpose. Their thoughts are not "What's in it for me?" but "How can we glorify God together?" For today, 2 Corinthians 6:14 notes that Christians are not to be "unequally yoked together with unbelievers."

2. What can we learn about the nature of God as He answers Hannah's prayer? What does He expect from those who benefit from His care? What could we expect to be the result of misusing God's gifts?

The Bible gives us many examples that show us that God listens to those who follow after Him (e.g., Deuteronomy 26:7; Judges 13:9; Acts 10:4). Perhaps He waits for us to show dedication and persistence before granting what He knows is best for us. Much like children, we may not fully appreciate the benefits of a gift until we are truly anxious and ready to receive it. It's safe to say that God expects us to use all His gifts for His glory.

We also know, however, that to receive a gift and then ignore God and His generosity can be ill-fated. Consider all the blessings the unfaithful Israelite nation could have received! Instead they were disciplined multiple times. An interesting contrast is to see how Cain and Abel responded to the gifts God had given them, and to see God's reaction in both cases (Genesis 4:1-7). Certainly, Hannah must have known that her promise was sacred and must be fulfilled.

3. Parents will readily acknowledge that the arrival of a child—especially the first—produces marked changes in their lives. How are the changes experienced by Hannah and Elkanah similar to or different from your own experiences or the experiences of parents you know?

The birth of a son in ancient cultures had implications of "birthright" for inheritance of family properties that we deal with differently today. And while the birth of a son to Hannah did not change the family's heritage (Elkanah's other wife, Peninnah, already had children), it spared Hannah the biting words that came from the woman who shared her husband. That, too, may be quite different from today!

A similarity we see is that the birth of a son in both ancient and modern culture helps "carry on the family name." Also, those who want children but are unable to conceive sometimes become bitter no matter what culture or age they live in.

4. In 1 Samuel in 1:27, Hannah refers to "the Lord." Eli, for his part, makes a broad reference to "the God of Israel" in 1:17 (not in our lesson text). Why might each have chosen to use his or her own specific reference?

The Scriptures provide us with many names for God and for the Christ. When making reference to God, the name we choose to use may reflect a characteristic we are attempting to describe, or it may reflect our personal relationship with Him. This seems to be the distinction between the references of Hannah and Eli. Perhaps Eli had grown distant from God, thus his use of "the God of Israel" rather than, say, "our God." Hannah, for her part, felt she had reason to focus on God's personal nature, since He had answered her private prayer.

5. In retrospect we are sometimes amazed to see how common occurrences fell into place as God achieved a complex plan. In the great scheme of history, who benefited when God answered Hannah's prayer for a child, and why?

Certainly Hannah herself benefited from God's answer to her prayer. Her reproach was lifted and her esteem was changed.

But Hannah's child was not just (or even primarily) for her benefit. The Israelite nation—which God was preparing to usher in the Messiah—was ready for a new type of leader. Here was a child dedicated to the Lord from birth who could redirect the people of Israel to God's plan. As the lesson text implies, Samuel truly becomes a "pivot point" in sacred history. Ultimately, all God's people who follow from the time of Samuel benefit from this birth.

John: Forerunner of Jesus

DEVOTIONAL READING: Isaiah 40:3-11.

BACKGROUND SCRIPTURE: Luke 1:5-80.

PRINTED TEXT: Luke 1:67-80.

Luke 1:67-80

67 And his father Zechariah was filled with the Holy Ghost, and prophesied, saying,

68 Blessed be the Lord God of Israel; for he hath visited and redeemed his people,

69 And hath raised up a horn of salvation for us in the house of his servant David;

70 As he spake by the mouth of his holy prophets, which have been since the world began:

71 That we should be saved from our enemies, and from the hand of all that hate us;

72 To perform the mercy promised to our fathers, and to remember his holy covenant;

73 The oath which he sware to our father Abraham,

74 That he would grant unto us, that we, being delivered out of the hand of our enemies, might serve him without fear,

75 In holiness and righteousness before him, all the days of our life.

76 And thou, child, shalt be called the prophet of the Highest: for thou shalt go before the face of the Lord to prepare his ways;

77 To give knowledge of salvation unto his people by the remission of their sins,

78 Through the tender mercy of our God; whereby the dayspring from on high hath visited us,

79 To give light to them that sit in darkness and in the shadow of death, to guide our feet into the way of peace.

80 And the child grew, and waxed strong in spirit, and was in the deserts till the day of his showing unto Israel.

GOLDEN TEXT: And thou, child, shalt be called the prophet of the Highest: for thou shalt go before the face of the Lord to prepare his ways.—Luke 1:76.

A Child Is Given
(Lessons 1-4)

Lesson Aims

After participating in this lesson, each student should be able to:

1. Tell how Zechariah saw that John's birth initiated the fulfillment of messianic prophecy.

2. List the various reasons for Zechariah's joy and praise to God.

3. Express praise and thanksgiving to God for the salvation that is ours through Jesus Christ.

Introduction

INTRODUCTION
    A. The Rescue Mission
    B. Lesson Background
 I. PRAISE FOR DELIVERANCE (Luke 1:67-75)
    A. Filled With the Holy Spirit (vv. 67, 68)
    B. God's Faithfulness to David (vv. 69-71)
    C. God's Faithfulness to Abraham (vv. 72-75)
    Promises, Promises
II. PREDICTION OF MINISTRY (Luke 1:76-80)
    A. Preparing the Way (v. 76)
    A Sense of Being Called by God
    B. Preaching Repentance (vv. 77, 78)
    C. Showing the Path (v. 79)
    D. Growing in Spirit (v. 80)
CONCLUSION
    A. Seeing God's Plan
    B. Prayer
    C. Thought to Remember

Introduction

A. The Rescue Mission

On March 5, 1994, a man armed with a bomb and a gun entered the Salt Lake City library and took numerous hostages. A deputy sheriff, who was dressed in "street clothes" and who just happened to be in the building at the same time, saw what was happening and voluntarily joined the group as the gunman herded them into a room. The deputy sheriff then waited . . . and waited. When time and circumstance were right, he made his move and shot the gunman to death. As a result, the hostages escaped unharmed.

A human parallel such as this can remind us—in a very small, inadequate way—of what God did to deliver us from the power of sin and the devil. The Gospels teach that God dressed Himself in "street clothes" and entered our world to bring about this rescue. But His was no spur-of-the-moment plan! He did not come unprepared, nor did He come as many expected. Today's lesson demonstrates how carefully God prepared the way for that rescue operation.

B. Lesson Background

Luke the physician was a missionary companion of the apostle Paul (Colossians 4:14; 2 Timothy 4:11; Philemon 24). He was not one of the twelve apostles and perhaps had no direct contact with either John the Baptist or Jesus during their ministries. But Luke had investigated carefully the facts about the "things which are most surely believed among us" (Luke 1:1). The Holy Spirit chose just the right person to document the facts of the birth and ministry of John the Baptist.

After introducing the purpose of his gospel (Luke 1:1-4), Luke begins his narrative with the Heavenly announcements of the coming births of both John (1:5-25) and Jesus (1:26-38), the details of those births (1:57-66; 2:1-38), and the poetic, worshipful praise of both Mary and Zechariah (1:46-55, 67-79). Luke describes Zechariah and Elisabeth as upright in their worship of the Lord, but Elisabeth was barren and they were praying for a son (Luke 1:5-7, 13). During his ministry in the temple as a priest, Zechariah saw an angel, who announced that Elisabeth would deliver a son. Because Zechariah had a difficult time believing this, the angel gave him a sign by striking him mute. [See question #1, page 136.]

Nevertheless, Elisabeth became pregnant in her advanced age. Zechariah, for his part, was unable to speak until the birth of his son, John the Baptist. When Zechariah finally spoke, his first words were a kind of hymn of praise including a prophetic announcement about his son. Zechariah's prophecy is often called the "Benedictus" after the word *blessed* in the Latin translation.

The prophecy falls into two main parts: Zechariah's praise for the deliverance that would come from the Messiah (1:68-75), and Zechariah's celebration of John's birth and prophecy about John's future ministry in relation to that of Jesus (1:76-79). Luke's description of Zechariah and Elisabeth presents certain parallels to Hannah and Elkanah in 1 Samuel 1 (see last week's lesson).

I. Praise for Deliverance
(Luke 1:67-75)

After John is born, Zechariah is again able to speak (1:57-64). The neighbors want to know, "What manner of child shall this be?" (1:66).

Zechariah responds with a prophecy that reveals some of God's plan of salvation.

A. Filled With the Holy Spirit (vv. 67, 68)

67, 68. And his father Zechariah was filled with the Holy Ghost, and prophesied, saying, Blessed be the Lord God of Israel; for he hath visited and redeemed his people.

As Elisabeth is *filled* with the Spirit in Luke 1:41, so now is *Zechariah*. In this way Zechariah is enabled to speak, as did the prophets of the Old Testament, the truth that God wants revealed (e.g., Jeremiah 2:1; Ezekiel 28:1; Hosea 1:2). The God whom Zechariah praises is called *the Lord God of Israel* because Zechariah knows very well that this God is the One who called that nation to usher in the Messiah. The terms *Israel* and *people* are parallel here, as Zechariah defines Israel as the people who belong to Him in a special way for a special purpose (see also v. 77). Zechariah's praise is directed toward the God who has taken action on behalf of His people—a nation that He chose from all the nations of the earth. [See question #2, page 136.]

Zechariah identifies two actions by God. First, God *visited* His people in that He comes to them with a remedy for their need (cf. Matthew 25:36, 43; James 1:27). Later in the ministry of Jesus some will repeat this idea when they see the power of Jesus' miracles and perceive that God has come to visit His people (Luke 7:16).

The second action is redemption. This concept extends back to the exodus in which God freed the Hebrew slaves from Egyptian bondage and then required the redemption of the firstborn (Exodus 12:1–13:16). Jesus' disciples will come to expect ultimate redemption to come through Jesus Himself (see Luke 24:21).

B. God's Faithfulness to David (vv. 69-71)

69. And hath raised up a horn of salvation for us in the house of his servant David.

The messianic emphasis of Zechariah's praise becomes clear as he praises God because He is fulfilling His ancient promise to King *David* (2 Samuel 7:11-16). Even though the promise takes almost ten centuries to reach this fulfillment, the Lord has remembered the deliverance He promised to David's royal dynasty.

The *horn of salvation* is a figure of speech from the world of agriculture and animal husbandry. See the discussion in last week's lesson concerning Hannah's prayer, page 125. Here the reference must be to Jesus and not to John, because Jesus is the One who traces His ancestry back through King David. See also Psalm 132:17.

70. As he spake by the mouth of his holy prophets, which have been since the world began.

The *holy prophets* refer to those whom God allowed to foresee, many hundreds of years earlier, the future ministry of the Messiah. The phrase *since the world began* can be translated more literally as "from of old." The first of these ancient prophets was Samuel (Acts 3:24), as we saw last week.

Examples of prophecies of Christ are found in Isaiah 42, 49, and 53. Those who will listen carefully to the teachings of the apostles will begin to see how such prophecies describe a Messiah who comes to restore Israel's spiritual awareness of God's will, and that this Messiah has to suffer and die in this cause (see Acts 2:22-37).

71. That we should be saved from our enemies, and from the hand of all that hate us.

In this context Zechariah uses the term *saved* to speak of political deliverance from *enemies* that may want to threaten the nation with intimidation or war (compare Psalm 2; 97:10; Acts 4:25-28). God has rescued His people in the past and will do so again! Verse 77 of Zechariah's praise blends spiritual themes of deliverance with this political one, and Zechariah is happy to praise the God of Israel for both blessings.

One of the failures of the church in industrialized nations today is that its members do not thank the Lord for the peace their nations have enjoyed. Unfortunately, the focus of many of those church members seems to be on political matters, being unduly concerned with candidates and governmental policies. We frequently neglect the admonition of Scripture to pray for "kings, and for all that are in authority" so that each believer may lead "a quiet and peaceable life in all godliness and honesty" (1 Timothy 2:2).

C. God's Faithfulness to Abraham (vv. 72-75)

72, 73. To perform the mercy promised to our fathers, and to remember his holy covenant; the oath which he sware to our father Abraham.

Zechariah's praise of God's faithfulness to David took us back to a time some one thousand years before Christ. Now Zechariah takes us back almost twice that far for another example of God's faithfulness. The *holy covenant* to which Zechariah refers is the promise God made to Abraham in Genesis 12:1-3; 17:2; and 22:16-18. God swore an oath that He would bless Abraham and make His descendants a mighty nation as numerous as the stars in the sky or the sand on the seashore. He also promised that through this nation all people on earth would be blessed.

Zechariah praises the Lord God of Israel because Zechariah has lived to see this promise of God unfolding before his very eyes! (Compare Simeon's praise in Luke 2:28-32.) Indeed, when we reach these two verses, we have come to the central point in Zechariah's praise. The poetic structure emphasizes the terms *covenant* and *oath*. As Zechariah portrays the arrival of John the Baptist (just born) and Jesus Christ (yet to be born), these events are not the basis for some new and unexpected religion that pops up without warning. Zechariah sees the births of Jesus, the Messiah, and His forerunner, John the Baptist, as the goal toward which the Old Testament faith was pointing from the beginning. God has taken great care to develop His plan for the salvation of His people.

PROMISES, PROMISES

Every time he got an offer for a new credit card, he accepted it. And every time he bought something, he charged it. His credit card debt soared. He promised to pay but he never did. He dismissed it by saying, "I'm the most promising young man in town. I promise to pay for this and I promise to pay for that."

The promises of people may not always be kept, but God's always are. He is in this sense "more promising" than we are. His promises are greater and His promises are sure to be kept. That's why when we sing that old song "Standing on the Promises," we note the last words of the refrain: we're "standing on the promises of God." Those are the only promises on which we can truly stand.

The promises of people often fail. You cannot stand on them. Some people never intend to keep their promises in the first place. Some intend to keep them but are prevented by circumstances beyond their control.

But God intends to keep His promises, and God has the infinite resources necessary to do so. Sometimes we dismiss the assurances that come from people and say cynically, "Promises!

Promises!" But no one can dismiss God's promises with such cynicism.

Today's lesson shows that it does not matter how old a promise is. God will keep it. You can see it in the Bible. You can see it in life. He may delay the keeping of the promise. He may keep it in a way we do not expect. But we may be certain God's promises will be kept. —R. C. S.

74, 75. That he would grant unto us, that we, being delivered out of the hand of our enemies, might serve him without fear, in holiness and righteousness before him, all the days of our life.

God's action does not imply that God's people now can be idle. If the Lord has granted His people deliverance from their *enemies*, then those people have a responsibility to *serve* before the Lord. The negative expression of this duty is the opportunity to serve *without fear*. The positive expression of this duty is service *in holiness and righteousness* (cf. Malachi 3:3). [See question #3, page 136.]

Thus Zechariah correctly summarizes God's will for all believers (see Ephesians 4:24). When believers join their worship together on Sunday, they should also join in their commitment to live by standards that far surpass those of an ungodly culture that is passing away. Singing praises to the God of all holiness includes pledging ourselves to living holy lives before Him (cf. Hebrews 12:14).

II. Prediction of Ministry
(Luke 1:76-80)

Zechariah turns now from praising the Lord to prophesying through the Spirit what the ministry of both John and Jesus will mean.

A. Preparing the Way (v. 76)

76. And thou, child, shalt be called the prophet of the Highest: for thou shalt go before the face of the Lord to prepare his ways.

Without being carried away with pride in his own son, Zechariah provides a sketch of what John's ministry will accomplish. His role will be a preparatory one. His mission will be *to prepare* for the coming of One greater than himself.

This preparation will be as one who arrives ahead of a traveling dignitary to make all necessary arrangements for that dignitary's visit to the town. Implied in this ministry is the kind of prophetic work Israel knew from earlier times when prophets like Hosea, Amos, Isaiah, and Jeremiah took up their own prophetic ministries. John will speak for the Lord by addressing the need of Israel to return to God. Such a picture is

---

How to Say It

AMOS. *Ay*-mus.

BENEDICTUS. *Ben*-eh-*dik*-tus (strong accent on *dik*).

CORNELIUS. Cor-*neel*-yus.

ELKANAH. *El*-kuh-nuh or El-*kay*-nuh.

EZEKIEL. Ee-*zeek*-ee-ul or Ee-*zeek*-yul.

HOSEA. Ho-*zay*-uh.

ISAIAH. Eye-*zay*-uh.

JEREMIAH. Jair-uh-*my*-uh.

MALACHI. *Mal*-uh-kye.

MESSIANIC. mess-ee-*an*-ick.

SIMEON. *Sim*-ee-un.

ZECHARIAH. *Zek*-uh-*rye*-uh (strong accent on *rye*).

consistent with the announcement of the angel of the Lord regarding John's birth, saying that John will "go before him in the spirit and power of Elijah" (v. 17) and will bring the people of Israel to "turn to the Lord their God" (v. 16).

About seven centuries earlier Isaiah had predicted that there would come a certain "voice of him that crieth in the wilderness, Prepare ye the way of the Lord, make straight in the desert a highway for our God" (Isaiah 40:3; cf. Luke 3:4). (This famous passage is also part of Handel's *Messiah*, which you may be privileged to hear this Christmas season.) Malachi 3:1 had foretold, "Behold, I will send my messenger, and he shall prepare the way before me" (see also Malachi 4:5; Matthew 17:10-13). Zechariah affirms that these prophecies present a description of John's ministry before the coming of the Messiah, Jesus Christ.

A SENSE OF BEING CALLED BY GOD

John was a man very well aware of his calling to be the prophet who would prepare the way for the Messiah. Not everyone grows up with a sense of calling like that, though some do. Rowan LeCompte is one. When he was fourteen years old, he visited the yet unfinished National Cathedral in Washington, D.C. Looking at the great edifice inspired him to work in stained glass. Eventually his dream came true and he designed more than forty-five stained glass windows for that magnificent structure.

A young man went to preach his first sermon in a little country church. After he had stumbled through it a man said, "Son, I believe that you are called to preach." Encouraged by those words, he kept trying and recently completed sixty years of preaching. Through more than half a century he was sustained by the confidence that God had called him to preach.

Some are not as fortunate in receiving a clear "call." They never seem to be sure what God has in mind for them to do or what the purpose of their lives is to be. Whatever calling they have is vague and indistinct. It may be that they will not know until they get to Heaven. Perhaps only then will they understand the part they played in God's plan. Often when people escape a serious accident or survive a serious illness they say, "I think God left me here for a purpose." Even if that purpose is never made quite clear, we serve God the best we can and leave the rest to Him. An old song says, "We'll understand it better by and by" (Charles A. Tindley, 1851–1933).   —R. C. S.

B. Preaching Repentance (vv. 77, 78)

77, 78. To give knowledge of salvation unto his people by the remission of their sins,

Thou, child, shalt be called the prophet of the Highest; for thou shalt go before the face of the Lord to prepare his ways.
— Luke 1/76

Visual for lesson 2

Use this artwork of Zechariah's praise song to illustrate today's Golden Text.

through the tender mercy of our God; whereby the dayspring from on high hath visited us.

At this point Zechariah's emphasis on salvation turns from the political theme (see v. 71, above) to the spiritual one. The phrase *knowledge of salvation* expresses the need for God's people not just to know "about" salvation, but to know it through experiencing it. This salvation or deliverance will permit God's people to escape *their sins.* Forgiveness of sins will characterize the message of John's ministry (cf. Luke 3:1-3). [See question #4, page 136.]

After Jesus' resurrection from the dead, He commissions His apostles to preach forgiveness of sins to the whole world (Luke 24:47). Peter continues this theme in his Pentecost sermon when he instructs the crowd to repent and be baptized "for the remission of sins" (Acts 2:38). Peter also proclaims the remission of sins to Cornelius as the Gospel extends to the Gentiles (Acts 10:43; see also Acts 13:38-48; 26:16-18).

The dayspring from on high refers to the rising sun; this is a figure of speech for Jesus Himself, the One whom John heralds. As that dayspring or rising sun, Jesus is the light who dawns on both Jew and Gentile (Isaiah 9:1, 2; 42:6; 49:6; 60:1-3; Matthew 4:16; Luke 2:32). The earlier reference to a "visit" from the Lord (Luke 1:68) gave us a vivid picture of God's personal attention to bringing about His program of salvation and redemption; now the figure of a rising sun communicates the bright hope of forgiveness that is granted from the Heavenly Father to a world stumbling in darkness.

In this connection Zechariah speaks of the *tender mercy of our God.* Without this mercy there would be no forgiveness of sins. Zechariah's magnificent words remind us that God's motivation for sending the Messiah and the forgiveness of sins that came through His ministry is the mercy of God's own heart. No better reason can be named for coming before the Lord in worship than to honor the merciful God who is moved to send to sinners a remedy for their sin. Here is the "God so loved the world" of Zechariah's prophecy. As believers sing the beloved carols of Christmas at this time of year, how appropriate that we raise our voices in praise to the merciful God who wants us to have this deliverance!

C. Showing the Path (v. 79)

79. To give light to them that sit in darkness and in the shadow of death, to guide our feet into the way of peace.

The rising sun provides *light* to those surrounded by *darkness* and brings guidance for their *feet* so that they do not fall to their destruction. The imagery is especially striking for those who lived in the time of Zechariah. With no streetlights, no automobile headlamps, and no flashlights for moving around at night, the darkness can seem overwhelming. This is especially true on nights when the sky is covered with clouds. The image of a town or village sitting in darkness, where walking along the paths can literally be fatal, is the picture presented by Zechariah's words. See verse 78 above for the Old Testament roots of this imagery.

Zechariah, however, is not thinking of the mortal danger in falling over a cliff while walking in the dark. He predicts that the coming Christ will shine such a light on those who believe that their feet will be guided *into the way of peace*. The theme of the peace brought by Christ is also the theme of the angels' song to the shepherds on the night of Jesus' birth (Luke 2:14). This peace describes the new relationship between people and God (Romans 5:1). It is a peace that consists of a new status with God as those pardoned from sin. How important, then, John's preparatory ministry will be!

D. Growing in Spirit (v. 80)

80. And the child grew, and waxed strong in spirit, and was in the deserts till the day of his showing unto Israel.

Even in his youth John's development toward the destiny predicted for him is apparent. [See question #5, page 136.] Becoming *strong in spirit* may refer either to John's determined willingness to conform to God's will, or it may describe the presence of the Holy Spirit in his young life. John's absence from the relative comforts of city life in Judea prepares him for the introduction of his ministry in Luke 3:2. See also the parallel statements about the early growth of Jesus in Luke 2:40 and 2:52.

When the time does come for John the Baptist to start his ministry, he begins preaching in the area of the Jordan River. He becomes the voice of one "crying in the wilderness" (Luke 3:4; cf. Isaiah 40:3). When crowds come, he charges them to turn their hearts to God in repentance and be baptized (Luke 3:7-18). We hear echoes of the tribute to the Messiah paid by John's father, Zechariah, when John says, "I indeed baptize you with water; but one mightier than I cometh, the latchet of whose shoes I am not worthy to unloose: he shall baptize you with the Holy Ghost and with fire" (Luke 3:16).

Conclusion

A. Seeing God's Plan

Though the story is old to us, Zechariah offers the praise of a believer whose heart has been moved by the freshness of seeing God's plan unfold. Believers today will be blessed by this Christmas season all the more if we can capture for ourselves the sense of surprise and thankfulness in Zechariah's reflections on God's decision to act by sending the Christ into the world. Zechariah's reflections on his son John's obedience can motivate our own obedience as well.

B. Prayer

Lord of my salvation, may I offer as much praise today as Zechariah offered, though he saw only the beginning of Your plan of redemption, and I have seen much more. May this make me humble and obedient. In Jesus' name, amen.

C. Thought to Remember

God had a plan for Zechariah, Elisabeth, and John—and God has a plan for you!

Home Daily Bible Readings

Monday, Dec. 8—Prepare the Way of the Lord (Isaiah 40:3-11)
Tuesday, Dec. 9—An Angel Appears to Zechariah (Luke 1:5-11)
Wednesday, Dec. 10—The Promise of a Son (Luke 1:12-17)
Thursday, Dec. 11—Elisabeth Conceives (Luke 1:18-25)
Friday, Dec. 12—John Is Born (Luke 1:57-66)
Saturday, Dec. 13—Zechariah Prophesies (Luke 1:67-75)
Sunday, Dec. 14—John Will Be God's Prophet (Luke 1:76-80)

Learning by Doing

This page contains an alternative lesson plan emphasizing learning activities. Classes desiring such student involvement will find these suggestions helpful.

Learning Goals

After participating in this lesson, each student will be able to:

1. Tell how Zechariah saw that John's birth initiated the fulfillment of messianic prophecy.

2. List the various reasons for Zechariah's joy and praise to God.

3. Express praise and thanksgiving to God for the salvation that is ours through Jesus Christ.

Into the Lesson

Last week we saw the power of prayer through the story of Hannah and Samuel. Today we study how the Lord guides the lives of the righteous as seen in the story of Zechariah and his son, John the Baptist (Luke 1:67-80). We see the great joy involved in being in the will of God and understanding the joy of redemption.

Display in large letters the word *JOY*. Have the letter *O* lined internally as if it were into jigsaw puzzle pieces. Ask your class, "What puts the 'O!' in joy? That is, what are the components of joy?" As class members suggest ideas, write them onto various "puzzle pieces." Expect such concepts as *happiness, delight, jubilation, deep emotion, contentment*. At the end ask the class to look for all of these components in today's text and context of Luke 1.

As an alternative introductory idea, display the phrase "A Song of Joy." Ask the class to help you make a list of songs of joy by singing a familiar line from a hymn or chorus about joy. As each is sung, write it into a list under the original title. Expect such musical pieces as "Joy to the World," "Ode to Joy," "I've Got the Joy, Joy, Joy, Joy Down in My Heart," and others. At the end, state, "Today's text is a song of joy from a very unlikely source: an old priest who recently had been a man of few words."

Ask class members to divide into their small groups. Ask each group to develop a word picture of the concept just discussed. Tell them to cut out words from magazines and newspapers you have provided that deal with the "Big Idea." They can paste these on a sheet of newsprint in such a way that they create a shape representing today's subject.

Into the Word

Direct the class to today's text, Luke 1:67-80, and affirm to them, "Zechariah had every reason to rejoice, for he could see in his newly born son the fulfillment of a host of God's promises to Israel." Show the following list of Old Testament Scripture references and ask the class to find them and write each one in at an appropriate point in Zechariah's song from Luke 1: Genesis 12:2, 3 (see v. 73); 2 Samuel 22:3 (v. 69); Ezra 7:27 (v. 68); Job 38:12 (v. 78); Psalm 83:18 (v. 76a); Psalm 136:24 (v. 71); Psalm 144:10 (v. 69); Isaiah 9:2 (v. 79); Haggai 2:9 (v. 79); Malachi 3:1 (v. 76b).

Note verse 67 of the text at the end of this matching exercise, noting that Zechariah is prophesying on the basis of being filled with the Holy Spirit, even as writers of the Old Testament were. God fulfills His promises.

Point out that both Mary's exclamation of verses 46-55 and Zechariah's in verses 67-79 are often labeled *Song*. Emphasize the joy each felt in being part of God's plan. Each was asked to give a son to God's will. Say, "Reflect on your commitment to and relationship with God and evaluate your ability to handle such difficult requests and expectations from the Lord."

Into Life

Those with children can understand the sacrifice both Zechariah and Mary displayed by allowing God's will to be done. Ask the class, "How were Zechariah and Mary able to do this?" Emphasize that each was filled with the Holy Spirit, allowing each one to see the larger picture and how a seemingly difficult experience was actually a blessing. As with last week's lesson, God continues to reemphasize our need to be open to His will in His time.

Say to your class, "Like Zechariah, let's write a brief song of praise to God using special event(s) in our own spiritual journey and relationship. Tell the group you are going to call out a phrase or affirmation from Zechariah's song, and that after each you would like someone to personalize it. For example, you say, "We should be saved from our enemies," and someone says, "My enemy death is nothing to be feared." Or, "Thou, child, . . . shalt give knowledge of salvation to his people," and someone responds, "Thank You, God, for (name), who taught me about salvation." Recommend that all do a personal journal this week on the truths of Zechariah's prophetic declaration.

Let's Talk It Over

The questions on this page are designed to promote discussion of the lesson by the class and to encourage application of the lesson Scriptures. The answers provided are only discussion starters. Let your class talk it over from there.

1. Zechariah, a highly educated and well-trained priest, was taken by complete surprise by the angel's message. What does Zechariah's experience teach us about God and ourselves?

God does not live in boxes created by people, whether those boxes are "physical" (cf. Acts 17:24, 25) or "mental." When we begin a thought with the words, "Surely, God would not . . . " then we start down a dangerous path of putting Him in one of those "mental boxes" we all are tempted to construct from time to time.

Even so, when we begin to learn more about God we may be able to recognize some ways that He definitely will *not* act just because it would be inconsistent with His holy nature. But we should be careful not to step beyond a certain point. Unless God makes a promise *never* to respond in a certain way—such as flooding the earth again—He maintains both the ability and the right to use whatever means He needs to accomplish His ends. When He does act, will we respond with more faith than Zechariah?

2. When Zechariah again was able to speak, he began immediately to praise God. How are Zechariah's reasons for praise similar to reasons why we should give praise today?

Zechariah felt blessed because he knew that God was keeping His promise to the Israelites just as He said He would. He also knew of the need of the Jewish nation and knew that this Promised One would fill this void. Redemption was coming and Zechariah was overwhelmed, although he undoubtedly didn't know all the implications of that coming redemption. Today we praise God for fulfilled promises as well—and we have much more information than Zechariah was privileged to have!

3. In Luke 1:74, Zechariah reminds the people that the deliverance promised to the Israelites comes with an expectation of service. What are some expectations that come as we begin our relationship with the One who has saved us from our sins? How do these change our lives?

One convenient way to sum up our Savior's expectations is with the three words "inreach," "upreach," and "outreach." Our "inreach" includes personal growth in faith and holiness

(1 Peter 1:15, 16), and the teaching of our fellow Christians (Romans 12:7). Our "upreach" is worship of God (John 4:24). Our "outreach" is evangelism (Matthew 28:19, 20) and mercy to others (Galatians 6:10). Living up to God's expectations means that we abandon our old lives and begin to "walk in newness of life" (Romans 6:4). That means a change in priorities, attitudes, relationships, and service.

4. For various reasons many first-century Israelites were hesitant to accept the "knowledge of salvation" from the lips of Jesus and John the Baptist. What are some roadblocks we should be prepared to overcome today as we spread the gospel to a skeptical world?

One big roadblock is simple indifference to the gospel message. Another roadblock is "postmodern" thinking that holds truth to be relative to each person. Still another roadblock is competition from cults and false religions. Yet another roadblock is the arrogance of those who refuse to listen to anything that challenges their set-in-concrete thinking patterns. There are other roadblocks as well!

Each type of roadblock requires a different, specific approach. But in a general sense we start to overcome each roadblock the same way that Jesus challenged wrong thinking in His day: with grace and truth (John 1:14). The historical, objective evidence of the miracles, fulfilled prophecy, and the resurrection of Jesus provide the truth. Our graciousness will be apparent in our gentle, humble approach.

5. We can only imagine the sense of obligation that Zechariah and Elisabeth must have felt as they assumed their parental duties for young John, the forerunner of the Messiah. In what ways have all Christian parents been given a similar responsibility?

All children today have the potential for becoming "priests" in God's kingdom (see 1 Peter 2:5-10). With such a potential, Christian parents must make sure that they model their own "priesthoods" in a godly fashion. Children are great imitators! When parents model God's own holiness (1 Peter 1:15, 16), their children are more likely to do so as well. Your learners can mention specific ways to do this.

Jesus: God With Us

DEVOTIONAL READING: John 14:6-14.

BACKGROUND SCRIPTURE: Matthew 1:18-25.

PRINTED TEXT: Matthew 1:18-25.

Matthew 1:18-25

18 Now the birth of Jesus Christ was on this wise: When as his mother Mary was espoused to Joseph, before they came together, she was found with child of the Holy Ghost.

19 Then Joseph her husband, being a just man, and not willing to make her a public example, was minded to put her away privily.

20 But while he thought on these things, behold, the angel of the Lord appeared unto him in a dream, saying, Joseph, thou son of David, fear not to take unto thee Mary thy wife: for that which is conceived in her is of the Holy Ghost.

21 And she shall bring forth a son, and thou shalt call his name JESUS: for he shall save his people from their sins.

22 Now all this was done, that it might be fulfilled which was spoken of the Lord by the prophet, saying,

23 Behold, a virgin shall be with child, and shall bring forth a son, and they shall call his name Immanuel, which being interpreted is, God with us.

24 Then Joseph being raised from sleep did as the angel of the Lord had bidden him, and took unto him his wife:

25 And knew her not till she had brought forth her firstborn son: and he called his name JESUS.

GOLDEN TEXT: Behold, a virgin shall be with child, and shall bring forth a son, and they shall call his name Immanuel, which being interpreted is, God with us.—Matthew 1:23.

A Child Is Given
(Lessons 1-4)

Lesson Aims

After participating in this lesson, each student should be able to:

1. Cite several ways in which Mary and Joseph demonstrated faith in trusting and obeying God.

2. Tell how believers can show trust in God as they make decisions about difficult life situations.

3. Make a commitment to take a risk in being obedient to the Lord.

Lesson Outline

INTRODUCTION
    A. When Trust Is Misplaced
    B. Lesson Background
  I. JOSEPH'S DILEMMA (Matthew 1:18, 19)
    A. Mary's Pregnancy (v. 18)
    B. Joseph's Decision (v. 19)
 II. GOD'S DIRECTION (Matthew 1:20-23)
    A. The Dream (v. 20)
    B. The Promise (v. 21)
      What's in a Name?
    C. The Prophecy (vv. 22, 23)
III. JOSEPH'S OBEDIENCE (Matthew 1:24, 25)
    A. He Takes Mary as His Wife (v. 24)
    B. He Names the Baby "Jesus" (v. 25)
      Taking the Christ Child Home
CONCLUSION
    A. Trusting the Lord
    B. Prayer
    C. Thought to Remember

Introduction

A. When Trust Is Misplaced

At ten minutes to midnight on June 1, 1999, the passengers on a flight to Little Rock, Arkansas, discovered that they had misplaced their trust. They came to this realization as the aircraft in which they were traveling careened off the end of the runway while landing in bad weather, causing eleven fatalities.

In the aftermath one question just wouldn't seem to go away: why did such a highly experienced flight crew exercise such bad judgment in attempting to land during a severe thunderstorm? The captain himself could not answer the question since he died in the crash. Nothing about his record as an airline pilot suggested him to be untrustworthy in either flying skills or judgment.

But our fellow humans can and will let us down from time to time—occasionally with deadly results. Curiously, many people who will continue to trust fallible airline pilots, air traffic controllers, etc., for their earthly destinies will hesitate when offered the chance to trust the infallible God for their eternity!

Although today's lesson features the birth of Jesus, we cannot help but notice the actions of Mary and Joseph, who were challenged to trust God in ways they never would have dreamed about. We not only celebrate this week the most important birth in history, we also keep our eyes on the faith that carried Mary and Joseph through the difficulties of their predicament. Their ability to trust in God's guidance will serve us well as we attempt to navigate through the thunderstorms of life ourselves.

B. Lesson Background

Even before Jesus' birth was announced, there was speculation everywhere in first-century Palestine about the coming Messiah—much of it misguided. Some Jews expected two different Messiahs, one a teacher and one a warrior. On more than one occasion pretenders incited Jewish enthusiasts to believe that the Messiah had come and it was time to march on the Romans (compare Acts 5:35-38).

But Matthew establishes that Jesus is no pretender. He alone has the credentials to sit on David's throne as the messianic promises foretold, and His ministry will proclaim the pure Word of God as would be expected of One truly sent from above.

After presenting a genealogy that establishes Jesus' credentials through the royal line of David, Matthew turns to the details of the birth of Jesus. The drama of the story is unfolded in such a way as to show clearly how the Lord God acted in this event to bring Jesus into the world and protect Him from the forces of evil that stood against Him.

I. Joseph's Dilemma
(Matthew 1:18, 19)

A. Mary's Pregnancy (v. 18)

18. Now the birth of Jesus Christ was on this wise: When as his mother Mary was espoused to Joseph, before they came together, she was found with child of the Holy Ghost.

Matthew's Gospel, unlike that of John, does not reflect on the preexistence of Christ in the presence of God before the beginning of the world (see John 1:1, 2). Instead, Matthew begins his account with an earthly genealogy of Jesus and a sketch of His *birth* in Bethlehem. Yet this is not a "natural" conception and birth—far from it! Matthew hints at this in 1:16 when he notes that Joseph is "the husband of Mary, of whom was born Jesus"; a typical genealogical statement might have said that Joseph was the father of Jesus.

That Joseph and Mary did not engage in sexual relations prior to Jesus' birth is clear. But at this point in the story no one but Mary herself knows the true source of her pregnancy (Luke 1:26-38). It is difficult to imagine the trauma that the statement *before they came together, she was found with child* implies for her life in her culture. Not only will she face stern disapproval from her family and neighbors, she also must have many questions about what is happening and how her role will play itself out.

Yet both the Gospels of Matthew and Luke indicate that Mary and Joseph meet their uncertainties with an unquestioning faith in God. Both set examples that remind modern believers that participating in the will of God does not always mean we will see clearly how God will use us for His purposes. Those whom God uses in His service must be willing to trust Him for the unexpected twists and turns that will come our way as a result. Anyone who insists that the Lord draw straight pathways to follow, where every step is fully illuminated and every objective is explained fully, cannot be used effectively in His service.

B. Joseph's Decision (v. 19)

19. Then Joseph her husband, being a just man, and not willing to make her a public example, was minded to put her away privily.

The fact that Joseph is *a just man* implies that he is concerned to meet the situation of Mary's pregnancy in accordance with his sense of duty before God. He realizes that he is unable to take Mary as his wife under the conditions of her pregnancy, since from his perspective she must have committed adultery with another man. He knows the regulations in Deuteronomy 22:23-27 require a death sentence for Mary. Even though Roman occupation of Israel prevents the Jews from exercising the death penalty, Joseph can still publicly humiliate Mary as an adulteress.

Instead, Joseph can present Mary with a bill of divorce in the presence of a few witnesses in accordance with Deuteronomy 24:1-4, since an engagement is as legally binding as a marriage. He chooses this more private course of action to meet his obligations before the law, while at the same time sparing Mary the public disgrace.

So Joseph must react to a situation about which he has neither been warned nor prepared. His

sense of obedience to God motivates him to respond to Mary's pregnancy in the most appropriate way he can think of. His knowledge of God's law and his desire to "do the right thing" by Mary serve as his guiding lights. But we can only guess at the inner turmoil that such events create within him. Nevertheless, Joseph's reaction allows us to gain some insight into how faith in our all-knowing God can be useful for times such as these.

II. God's Direction (Matthew 1:20-23)

A. The Dream (v. 20)

20. But while he thought on these things, behold, the angel of the Lord appeared unto him in a dream, saying, Joseph, thou son of David, fear not to take unto thee Mary thy wife: for that which is conceived in her is of the Holy Ghost.

Joseph is now permitted to see events from God's perspective. Joseph's experience corresponds to examples from the Old Testament in which angelic messengers reveal the will of God to His servants (e.g., Genesis 31:11).

The description of Joseph as *son of David* connects him to the preceding genealogy. This reinforces the theme of the royal ancestry of Jesus. But the main purpose in the message from the angel is to direct Joseph's course of action. Thus the angel commands him to *take* Mary home with him as his *wife,* offering the explanation that her pregnancy is the result of the work of the *Holy* Spirit rather than the adultery that Joseph has assumed.

The command to do this without *fear* could be a reference to Joseph's concern that he would be breaking God's law to marry a woman who had become pregnant out of wedlock. It is also possible that the fear has reference to the social pressures that will result from going ahead with the marriage.

How to Say It

AHAZ. *Ay*-haz.
BETHLEHEM. *Beth*-lih-hem.
DEUTERONOMY. Due-ter-*ahn*-uh-me.
GENTILE. *Jen*-tile.
HEROD. *Hair*-ud.
IMMANUEL. Ih-*man*-you-el.
ISAIAH. Eye-*zay*-uh.
JERUSALEM. Juh-*roo*-suh-lem.
JOSHUA. *Josh*-yew-uh.
MESSIAH. Meh-*sigh*-uh.
MESSIANIC. mess-ee-*an*-ick.
ZECHARIAH. *Zek*-uh-*rye*-uh (strong accent on *rye*).

B. The Promise (v. 21)

21. And she shall bring forth a son, and thou shalt call his name JESUS: for he shall save his people from their sins.

The message of the angel provides further details to Joseph about this birth, using terminology familiar in birth announcements in the Old Testament (see Genesis 16:11; 17:19; 1 Kings 13:2). The Greek name *Jesus* is a form of the Hebrew name "Joshua," which carries the idea that "the Lord is salvation" or "the Lord saves." This implies that the role of this *son* of Israel will be one of bringing the nation deliverance from the Day of Judgment. This sense of the name *Jesus* seems to be drawn from Psalm 130:8, which predicts that the Lord God "shall redeem Israel from all his iniquities."

Of course no details about how Jesus will accomplish this are revealed to Joseph. [See question #1, page 144.] But the rest of Matthew's Gospel will present astonishing facts about how the Messiah must redeem Israel by sacrificing His own life as a ransom (20:28) to save His people from their sins. Jewish expectations frequently promote the idea that the Messiah would free Israel from Roman tyranny and also purify His people. However, the notion that the Messiah would die a criminal's death is too much to accept for most of the Jewish faithful.

The full meaning of the phrase *his people* will unfold throughout Matthew's Gospel. These people are those who belong to the Messiah, whether they are from a Jewish or Gentile background; and being a Jew by birth will not mean being counted automatically as among the saved (Matthew 3:9, 10; 8:11, 12). Christians today can give thanks for the fact that Jesus' arms of mercy include people of many ethnic and national backgrounds!

WHAT'S IN A NAME?

Through a character in one of his plays William Shakespeare posed the question, "What's in a name?" (*Romeo and Juliet,* Act II, Scene 2). Most of the names we give to our children have meanings, but we rarely pay much attention to those meanings. We do not think of the fact that *Anna* means "grace" or that *David* means "beloved." We are not conscious of the fact that *Timothy* means "honoring God."

Unfortunately, we also do not always think about the meaning of the name *Jesus.* Certainly, people who use it in profanity do not think of its meaning. Neither do those who drop the name casually. But God thought it important enough to make doubly certain that that was the name given to our Lord. It is significant that the name *Jesus* means Savior. Of course, He would have

been our Savior no matter what His name. But surely it was for our benefit that God chose the name *Jesus.*

But we must also wonder if it did not have an effect on Jesus Himself! If your name is *Joy,* do you feel a need to be cheerful? If your name is *Faith,* does it affect your conduct? In Hebrew culture the giving of a name was always regarded as highly significant. If you are called a *Christian,* does it affect your life in some positive way—a way that others can see this Christmas season?   —R. C. S.

C. The Prophecy (vv. 22, 23)

22. Now all this was done, that it might be fulfilled which was spoken of the Lord by the prophet, saying.

The terms *fulfill* and *fulfilled* are very important in Matthew's Gospel. They appear numerous times to describe how Old Testament predictions are reaching fruition (e.g., Matthew 2:15, 17, 23). Matthew's theme of fulfillment makes it clear that the gospel message has its roots in Old Testament events and promises.

23. Behold, a virgin shall be with child, and shall bring forth a son, and they shall call his name Immanuel, which being interpreted is, God with us.

This prophetic quotation—more than seven hundred years old!—comes from Isaiah 7:14. The original context is the prophecy spoken by Isaiah to King Ahaz of Judah when he was threatened with attack. To defeat this attack, King Ahaz was considering asking for Assyrian help when the Lord commanded him (through Isaiah) to put his trust in the Lord instead. Isaiah offered King Ahaz a sign that would confirm that God would keep His promise that Jerusalem would go unharmed if the king would depend on the Lord. When King Ahaz refused to ask for a sign, Isaiah gave him one anyway, saying, *"Behold, a virgin shall* conceive, and bear a *son,* and *shall call his name Immanuel"* (Isaiah 7:14).

Naturally we may ask just how the prediction of the birth of a child to a virgin would have represented a sign to King Ahaz over seven hundred years earlier! We can answer this question by realizing that prophecies in the Old Testament can be understood either as "predictions that persuade people immediately" (as in Exodus 4:8, 9), or as sweeping statements to serve as "future confirmations" of something (as in Exodus 3:12).

In the case of King Ahaz the prophecy of Isaiah 7:14 fits the second of these two, since Ahaz will be long dead by the time Jesus is born. Isaiah in his day sees destruction coming not just to Ahaz in particular, but also for "the house of

David" in general (Isaiah 7:2, 13), resulting in the loss of the throne. Long after King David's dynasty has ended, it will be Jesus, born to a virgin and born of David's line, who comes to carry the government of God's people upon His shoulders (Isaiah 9:6). Jesus is the one for whom the nation waits. He is the "confirmation" of the truth of Isaiah's words. [See question #2, page 144.]

Those who faithfully await the arrival of the Messiah will gladly *call his name Immanuel . . . God with us.* What better blessing could one ask for than to know that God wants to dwell with His people? (See also Isaiah 60:18-20; Revelation 21:3.) Jesus made all of this possible for believers when He left His eternal glory to put on flesh and come to earth to die for our sins. He promises to include His people in a great banquet at the end of time when again He will be with us in glory (Revelation 19:6-9).

Visual for lesson 3

Use this poster to draw attention to today's Golden Text.

III. Joseph's Obedience (Matthew 1:24, 25)

A. He Takes Mary as His Wife (v. 24)

24. Then Joseph being raised from sleep did as the angel of the Lord had bidden him, and took unto him his wife.

Joseph's response to *the angel of the Lord* is immediate. As soon as he awakens *from sleep* Joseph moves with obedience to the Lord's command. The message that has been revealed convinces him that taking Mary to be *his wife* is exactly the Lord's will.

Here we see the beginning of a pattern of quick responses to the Lord's direction in the accounts of Jesus' birth. Later, in Matthew 2:12, the wise men quickly obey the divine instructions not to return the way they came because of Herod's intentions. When Joseph later receives a warning of Herod's intentions to murder the baby Jesus, he quickly obeys the message that he should take the infant and travel to Egypt (2:14). See also Matthew 2:21 and Luke 2:15, 16.

Throughout all of these incidents we see God's providential hand protecting this unique baby from those who oppose the program of salvation that has been announced from the Lord. Matthew's account as a whole also shows us the kind of believers, both Jewish and Gentile, whom God uses in the work of His kingdom. Joseph's example of trusting God when called upon to make risky decisions challenges us: how do we exercise our own faith when life throws unexpected curveballs? [See question #3, page 144.]

Though Joseph cannot see with unhindered vision all that God has in store for him in the birth of Jesus, he nevertheless answers each challenge with faithfulness. He does this by ap-

plying his understanding of God's will as revealed both in the Scriptures and in the dream, as well as his recognition of God's sovereignty over the events that confront him.

As Joseph moves through the surprising news of Mary's pregnancy and his own sense of what must be done, he does so with an ear tuned to how the Lord might next direct him. The dramatic message in the night convinces him that he must act upon this new insight into Mary's pregnancy and take her as his wife. Once that information is disclosed to him, his faith moves him again to act with decisiveness. We can compare Joseph's decisiveness with the hesitation and doubt of the highly educated priest Zechariah in Luke 1:18.

Each one of us faces moments in which our confidence in the Lord's plan for our lives will be tested. Today we cannot expect God to reveal His specific will for us in dreams (see Hebrews 1:1, 2). Rather, we will have to make decisions on the basis of our faith and our general knowledge of God's expectations of us as expressed in the pages of Scripture.

At times we will need to act with confidence that our best tool is our trust in God's ability to move us in the right direction. As with Joseph, we may find out during the unfolding drama that a change in course is necessary. When those times come, will we trust God to guide us through these adjustments? Of first importance is that we keep our hearts open for His direction. [See question #4, page 144.]

B. He Names the Baby "Jesus" (v. 25)

25. And knew her not till she had brought forth her firstborn son: and he called his name JESUS.

Joseph takes on his role of family patriarch in naming *Jesus* by His God-given name, and making Him his own son in the legal sense. The naming occurs at Jesus' circumcision, eight days after His birth. Some profound things happen at that time (see Luke 2:21-38).

Knew her not is Matthew's way of making it clear that the conception of this unique baby was not the result of any marital union between the parents. Joseph respects the initiative of God in the life of his spouse so much that even after their marriage is ceremonially inaugurated he delays the normal marital relationship with Mary. Thus Joseph brings Mary into his house, but continues to treat her sexually as if the relationship were in the premarital engagement phase until after the time of Jesus' birth. [See question #5, page 144.]

The word *till* is significant because it indicates a change that takes place after the birth of Jesus—the picture is that of Joseph and Mary in a normal married relationship, which includes a sexual relationship as God intends. Later Matthew will supply information about Joseph and Mary's other children, half-brothers and half-sisters to Jesus (Matthew 12:46). Matthew also includes the names of some of these—James, Joses, Simon, and Judas (13:55). There is no support in the Bible for the concept of the "perpetual virginity" of Mary as some today mistakenly believe.

TAKING THE CHRIST CHILD HOME

An American Indian pueblo in the western United States has an interesting custom. After the midnight service on Christmas Eve, one family takes the doll from the manger home with them. They keep the Christ child in their home for the twelve days of Christmas—until January 6. It is considered a great honor to be the family

chosen to do this. What a thought! They take the Christ child home with them!

Joseph and Mary took the Christ child home with them. In a sense every family attending church on Christmas Eve can take the Christ child home with them—and they should! If we are wise, we will not only take the Child home with us, but we will keep Him there throughout the year. Although we may lack the symbolism of the doll the Americans Indians use, ultimately we do not really need that symbolism. It is in our hearts we will take Him home, and He will remain in our hearts as well as our house.

Anyone who has brought home a baby knows that that moment changes everything. It did for Mary and Joseph as it does for every family. Spiritually, taking the Christ child home with us also "changes everything"—in the home and in the heart, for now and for eternity.   —R. C. S.

Conclusion

A. Trusting the Lord

The birth of Jesus came about in a most extraordinary way! But the parents of Jesus were ordinary people whose faith served them well in extraordinary circumstances. They were obviously not expecting to meet such challenges during those days when the happy couple planned together for sharing a lifetime of marriage. But their faith in the Lord was firm from the very start. As a result, their decisions could be made in a context of obedience to God's will as that will became progressively obvious to them.

Modern believers also face challenges as we make decisions about important issues. Mary and Joseph teach us to trust in the Lord to guide us even as we wonder what is coming next. What is really around the next corner—no one knows! But whatever it is the Lord has in store for us, we can submit ourselves to Him. We realize that our God "knows what He is doing." Often we will live to see how it all makes sense in light of God's bigger plans.

B. Prayer

All-knowing God, we ask forgiveness where our own blindness has prevented us from meeting new challenges with faith and obedience. Lead us through the surprises of life, and please pardon us where we fail to trust You. Empower us to meet those future challenges that await us. In the name of Your Son who saves His people from their sins, amen.

C. Thought to Remember

He will always show us "why"—if not in this life, then in the next.

Home Daily Bible Readings

Monday, Dec. 15—Believe in God, Believe in Christ (John 14:1-5)

Tuesday, Dec. 16—Know Christ, Know the Father (John 14:6-10)

Wednesday, Dec. 17—I Am in the Father (John 14:11-15)

Thursday, Dec. 18—Christ in God, We in Christ (John 14:16-20)

Friday, Dec. 19—Isaiah Prophesies Immanuel (Isaiah 7:10-17)

Saturday, Dec. 20—Jesus Is Born (Luke 2:1-7)

Sunday, Dec. 21—Prophecy Fulfilled (Matthew 1:18-25)

Learning by Doing

This page contains an alternative lesson plan emphasizing learning activities.
Classes desiring such student involvement will find these suggestions helpful.

Learning Goals

After participating in this lesson, each student will be able to:

1. Cite several ways in which Mary and Joseph demonstrated faith in trusting and obeying God.

2. Tell how believers can show trust in God as they make decisions about difficult life situations.

3. Make a commitment to take a risk in being obedient to the Lord.

Into the Lesson

This is Christmas Sunday. Begin by brainstorming the question, "What do you consider to be the operative word for the season?" Encourage everyone to contribute whatever he or she thinks without feeling that the ideas are going to be evaluated. Have someone take notes.

You may get secular responses like *Santa*, *presents*, or *family*, as well as religious responses such as *Christ's birth*. For continuity with the previous weeks, emphasize the concept of *faith*. Say, "Isn't faith what truly sets us apart as Christians?" Take a quick oral survey of how many members have lost faith in schools, the government, businesses, or another organization. No doubt you will get a wide show of hands. Ask, "How does this lack of faith affect your interaction with these groups?"

Make a transition by asking, "How many of you have had a prayer request go seemingly unanswered? How has this event affected your faith in God? It would not be unusual for it to affect your belief, at least slightly. In such tests, one solidly grounded in faith is able to differentiate himself/herself from others who are not."

Into the Word

Select and recruit three of your best oral readers and assign them these three "Christmas texts" respectively to read to the class as you begin: John 1:1-5, 14-18; Luke 1:26-38; 2:1-7; Matthew 1:18-25.

Provide each class member with writing materials. Ask the class to go through Matthew 1:18-25 and conduct his or her own Personal Checklist. Each one is to write down answers to the question: "What do these verses tell me about Mary, about Joseph, and about God?" Ask each class member to list in three separate columns everything he or she can find in about five min-

utes. Encourage each to star items that speak to him or her personally in current circumstances.

Ask learners to match the behaviors of Mary and Joseph to what God reveals and what they obviously believe about Him. For example, when God reveals Mary's "mysterious" pregnancy, in believing she affirms that God is able to set aside His universal controlling laws. When Joseph plans to do the right and gracious thing toward Mary, God suggests he do something even more righteously daring: marry her. He did.

Ask, "Are you ready and willing to do the same? What if God asked you to sacrifice your way of life to follow His will? How many of you would wait for *another* sign that would provide a loophole from the first?" After some discussion ask, "How was Mary's faith and Joseph's able to help them overcome their fears? What differentiates you from Mary and Joseph?"

Prepare and distribute copies of the following personal-evaluation activity labeled "Faith and Obedience":

(1) I believe God has spoken to me; therefore, I will. . . .

(2) I believe God has the power to do things I cannot imagine; therefore, I will. . . .

(3) I believe Jesus is the virgin-born child of Mary and Son of God; therefore, I will. . . .

(4) I believe that Jesus has honored the meaning of His name; therefore, I will. . . .

Into Life

To introduce this section, state: "As a year draws to a close, we often make resolutions we hope to keep: to lose weight, spend more time with our kids, enjoy life more, improve our walk with the Lord. What we really need to do is learn how to let go. God has a plan for personal success, and He has revealed it. Through faith, we can experience joy and achieve the goals God has for us."

Suggest that rather than preparing a list of "New Year's Resolutions," each class member instead prepare a list of "New Life Responses," honoring the faith and submission of Mary and Joseph. If you have access to a badge maker, prepare a badge for each, carrying the letters NYR and the universal prohibition vertical slash. Pin one on each, and tell the class to use it as a conversation starter on the true meaning of Christmas: faith and obedience.

Let's Talk It Over

The questions on this page are designed to promote discussion of the lesson by the class and to encourage application of the lesson Scriptures. The answers provided are only discussion starters. Let your class talk it over from there.

1. The Jews had heard others claim to be the Messiah or that there might even be two Messiahs. If you were in Joseph's shoes, what signs would have convinced you that this Child indeed was going to be the very One promised to "save his people from their sins"?

This is a difficult question since putting ourselves in Joseph's shoes means that we have to pretend that we lack the same knowledge that Joseph lacked. Certainly Joseph must have struggled with this issue and his lack of knowledge. Having an angel appear to confirm the story certainly helped! But even with this bit of "divine intervention," Joseph probably continued to struggle since God did not reveal the whole plan "up front."

Ultimately, what it takes to convince someone of the truth about Jesus is a very individual thing. Some of those whom Jesus met in His earthly ministry required very little convincing (e.g., John 1:48-50). Others may see Jesus perform even a resurrection and still act in unbelief (e.g., John 11:46). How amazing!

2. The prophecy from Isaiah 7:14 reveals God's patience in developing His plan over hundreds of years, even with a rebellious people. In what ways has God been patient with you?

Ask for volunteers to talk about rebellious periods in their lives, times when God was "right there" when they eventually decided to turn back to him (cf. 2 Peter 3:9). Caution your learners that we should take care not to interpret God's patience as "tolerance" in the modern sense that sees God as accepting all attitudes and behaviors as equally valid. The Bible makes clear that a day will come when God's patience with sinful humans will come to an end.

3. Joseph responded immediately to the angel's instructions. Is Joseph's reaction a model for us today? Why, or why not?

Some of your learners may object that Joseph is not a model for us because angelic appearances are so rare in the history of God's people. True enough! However, we have something Joseph did not: God's completed Word. Its pages are full of instructions that we should follow immediately.

Yet with all the clarity the Bible offers us, even the most devout Christian sometimes has trouble responding immediately to God's leading. We frequently think it best to weigh all options carefully, and consider the consequences for all involved. But a response to God's leading often demands immediate response (see also Matthew 2:14). Too often a delay can mean the complete loss of an opportunity—or worse.

4. Suppose Joseph and Mary had hesitated by asking God "why?" What kind of response could they have received? And what kind of answer can we expect when we ask "why?"

If Joseph and Mary had pestered God enough with "why?" He may simply have answered them as He answered Paul: "My grace is sufficient for thee" (2 Corinthians 12:9). Or He may have answered them as He answered Job: "Who is this that darkeneth counsel by words without knowledge?" (Job 38:2).

One of the most difficult things that Christians of all levels of maturity have to face is the fact that God doesn't have to explain His choices to us. His reasoning is perfect, His decisions are just, His timing is impeccable, and His authority is absolute. Even if Joseph and Mary had not known all the ancient prophecies (and they probably didn't), God was using this event to fulfill perfectly His promises and plan to save humanity from sin.

For Joseph, Mary, and us, it all comes down to *trust*. Do we trust God enough to say to Him, "I know that You have the bigger picture under control, and that You will explain it to me fully someday"?

5. Joseph's role in the drama of the coming of the Messiah required heroic decisions but garnered few accolades. What important lessons can we learn from Joseph in this regard?

The story of Jesus is "made human" by the way others reacted to His coming. In the case of Joseph, some lessons that we may learn are that (1) we must be open to the possibility that God's intervention can change our plans, (2) following God's plan is right even when we cannot foresee every outcome, (3) when God's plan is made clear we should act on it quickly, and (4) God will help us face even life's toughest challenges. Earthly accolades are not to be our goal; God will take care of all rewards in eternity.

Jesus: Growing in God's Favor

DEVOTIONAL READING: John 5:19-24.

BACKGROUND SCRIPTURE: Luke 2:40-52.

PRINTED TEXT: Luke 2:40-52.

Luke 2:40-52

40 And the child grew, and waxed strong in spirit, filled with wisdom; and the grace of God was upon him.

41 Now his parents went to Jerusalem every year at the feast of the passover.

42 And when he was twelve years old, they went up to Jerusalem after the custom of the feast.

43 And when they had fulfilled the days, as they returned, the child Jesus tarried behind in Jerusalem; and Joseph and his mother knew not of it.

44 But they, supposing him to have been in the company, went a day's journey; and they sought him among their kinsfolk and acquaintance.

45 And when they found him not, they turned back again to Jerusalem, seeking him.

46 And it came to pass, that after three days they found him in the temple, sitting in the midst of the doctors, both hearing them, and asking them questions.

47 And all that heard him were astonished at his understanding and answers.

48 And when they saw him, they were amazed: and his mother said unto him, Son, why hast thou thus dealt with us? behold, thy father and I have sought thee sorrowing.

49 And he said unto them, How is it that ye sought me? wist ye not that I must be about my Father's business?

50 And they understood not the saying which he spake unto them.

51 And he went down with them, and came to Nazareth, and was subject unto them: but his mother kept all these sayings in her heart.

52 And Jesus increased in wisdom and stature, and in favor with God and man.

GOLDEN TEXT: And Jesus increased in wisdom and stature, and in favor with God and man.—Luke 2:52.

A Child Is Given
(Lessons 1-4)

Lesson Aims

After participating in this lesson, each student should be able to:

1. List the details provided in today's text concerning the early years of Jesus' life, including His sense of His unique role as the Son of God.

2. Tell how the growth of Jesus in His knowledge of God and His interest in spiritual things reminds us of how essential it is for children to acquire a devotion for God at a young age.

3. Express a commitment to participate in helping area young people come to love the Lord.

Lesson Outline

INTRODUCTION
    A. The Youth of Today
    B. Lesson Background
  I. TO THE FEAST (Luke 2:40-42)
    A. Jesus Grows Up (v. 40)
    B. Jesus Observes the Passover (vv. 41, 42)
 II. ON THE ROAD (Luke 2:43-45)
    A. Parents Unaware (vv. 43, 44)
    B. Parents Frantic (v. 45)
III. IN THE TEMPLE (Luke 2:46-50)
    A. Jesus Astonishes the Scholars (vv. 46, 47)
      The Amazing Christ
    B. Jesus Puzzles His Parents (vv. 48-50)
IV. TOWARD HOME (Luke 2:51, 52)
    A. Jesus' Obedience (v. 51)
    B. Jesus' Growth (v. 52)
      "My, How You've Grown!"
CONCLUSION
    A. Jesus' Boyhood
    B. Prayer
    C. Thought to Remember

Introduction

A. The Youth of Today

Josh McDowell continues to challenge today's youth as he has done for more than thirty years. But in a 1997 interview with the *Dallas Morning News* he said that what he has seen happening to kids over the past several years disturbs him very much.

His chief concern is that young people do not believe in absolute truth. They may believe that God exists, but they don't connect that belief to the fact that there is a set of unchanging universal values established by that God. The modern notion of "tolerance" undermines young Christians' faith. And when a person accepts everything, he or she loses the ability to discern right from wrong.

The result is that instead of having morality we just have different opinions. Since much of today's theology and world outlook are based on emotional hurt rather than rational thought, children twelve or thirteen years of age are making life decisions and adult choices with adolescent emotions.

Sadly, Josh McDowell is right. The result is that many of our young people are virtually lost to the church today. He goes on to say that Christian parents must do more than teach the Bible to their children. They must practice what they preach. If they don't, their teens will be lost to a society that questions everything.

Luke's Gospel describes a young Person who had a different outlook on life from that of many of today's youth. His was a mind drawn very early to the Lord and the things of the Lord. Luke chooses one incident in the life of young Jesus to illustrate a point about the sense of duty to God that characterized Jesus from His youth. This account teaches us of the value of bringing to bear every noble spiritual influence upon all the young people we can reach for the gospel.

B. Lesson Background

Luke 2:40-52 is part of a longer unit within the early narrative of Luke's Gospel, a unit that encompasses all of chapter 2. The focus in this larger unit is Jesus' birth and early life. Throughout the passage Luke highlights events that show how Joseph and Mary conduct themselves before and after that birth.

Just after the birth, Luke shows us a picture of parents who are careful "to do for him after the custom of the law" (Luke 2:27; cf. Exodus 13:2, 12, 13, 15; Leviticus 12:3). Luke points out that the family of the young Jesus was serious in keeping the Passover in Jerusalem (Luke 2:41), and even though the law of Moses did not require women to go, Mary's presence will be carefully noted. This follows after the example of Hannah in 1 Samuel 1:7 and 2:19. Even Jesus' presence in Jerusalem as a young boy will be described as "after the custom of the feast" (Luke 2:42).

Luke notes this care again at the end of this earlier episode in the temple when commenting that Mary and Joseph "had performed all things according to the law of the Lord" (Luke 2:39). This emphasis finds expression in today's lesson text. Modern believers thus get a glimpse into the spiritual life of this dedicated family—a family where the oldest son happens to be the Son of God!

I. To the Feast
(Luke 2:40-42)

A. Jesus Grows Up (v. 40)

40. And the child grew, and waxed strong in spirit, filled with wisdom; and the grace of God was upon him.

Like bookends, Luke 2:40 and 2:52 enclose the narrative about the journey of Jesus' family to Jerusalem for the Passover feast. In addition, verse 40 provides us with a transition from the previous account of Jesus' dedication in the temple as a baby to the present episode twelve years later.

A brief note about the growth of *the child* Jesus—both spiritual and physical—begins Luke's account of this particular family journey to Jerusalem. Luke stresses that Jesus is *filled with wisdom* and the favor of God. The mention of wisdom prepares us to understand the incident that follows. [See question #1, page 152.]

Parents who lovingly chart the growth of their children in terms of height, weight, strength, athletic ability, academic progress, and social life are making a mistake if they do not also seek to encourage their children's spiritual development as well. From the young Jesus, to the young Timothy, to the young John and Charles Wesley, to the young Alexander Campbell, to the young Dwight Moody—these examples remind us that parents can bring a great influence to bear upon their children in spiritual matters. Modern parents must take every opportunity to shape the clay of their children's lives while it is still soft and pliable. (See Deuteronomy 4:9; 6:6, 7; 11:18, 19.) [See question #2, page 152.]

B. Jesus Observes the Passover (vv. 41, 42)

41. Now his parents went to Jerusalem every year at the feast of the passover.

Deuteronomy 16:16 establishes that "three times in a year shall all thy males appear before the Lord thy God in the place which he shall choose." That passage then goes on to list the three major Jewish celebrations of Unleavened Bread (Passover), Weeks (Pentecost), and Tabernacles (Booths) as those "three times."

The Feast of Unleavened Bread lasts one week and occurs immediately after the *passover* celebration; these two together (which, practically speaking, form one celebration) commemorate the deliverance of the Hebrew slaves from their bondage in Egypt. That deliverance included the powerful hand of the Lord that spared the firstborn of Israel (Exodus 12; Numbers 28:16, 17).

The Jewish historian Josephus implies that Jews were scattered so far from *Jerusalem* by the first century A.D. that many were fortunate to travel to that great city once in a lifetime. It is providential that Mary and Joseph live only seventy miles or so from Jerusalem.

Even so, this is not an easy trip for them to make in an age before automobiles. The fact that Mary and Joseph make this pilgrimage *every year* reveals to us their sense of duty to God. This sense of duty must be evident also to their young son and anyone who witnesses their annual trek out of Galilee and back home again. By mentioning this pattern, Luke gives us a snippet of family life in the home of Jesus. Are we surprised at God's choice of earthly parents for Him?

42. And when he was twelve years old, they went up to Jerusalem after the custom of the feast.

This is the point where Luke makes clear the specific age of Jesus. At the age of *twelve* Jesus is nearing a point in life where Jewish boys are expected to become aware of their duties before the Lord. Jewish literature outside the Bible states that the age of thirteen is the point at which Jewish boys become obligated to the law of Moses. But the following episode will illustrate that Jesus has advanced far beyond what is expected of other Jewish boys. [See question #3, page 152.]

II. On the Road
(Luke 2:43-45)

A. Parents Unaware (vv. 43, 44)

43. And when they had fulfilled the days, as they returned, the child Jesus tarried behind in Jerusalem; and Joseph and his mother knew not of it.

Galileans traveling to Jerusalem at feast times journey in large groups, perhaps as an extended family or clan. At His age, Jesus may be permitted to choose with whom He will travel. Under these circumstances, Mary and *Joseph* perhaps assume that Jesus is traveling with other members of the caravan—cousins, uncles and aunts, or neighbors from Galilee.

How to Say It

CORINTHIANS. Kor-*in*-thee-unz (*th* as in *thin*).

DEUTERONOMY. Due-ter-*ahn*-uh-me.

GALILEE. *Gal*-uh-lee.

JERUSALEM. Juh-*roo*-suh-lem.

JOSEPHUS. Jo-*see*-fus.

NAZARETH. *Naz*-uh-reth.

PHILIPPIANS. Fih-*lip*-ee-unz.

Nothing is said about whether Jesus remains *behind in Jerusalem* deliberately or simply gets "lost in the shuffle." In either case, He puts the time to good use while He is there, as we shall see.

44. But they, supposing him to have been in the company, went a day's journey; and they sought him among their kinsfolk and acquaintance.

A day's journey means that Joseph and Mary may have walked fifteen or twenty miles of the sixty-mile journey before realizing that young Jesus is missing. This probably corresponds to the end of a day's travel when the parents look for Jesus among the other relatives before making camp for the night.

Today we might think of parents who missed seeing their twelve-year-old child for eight to ten hours as negligent in their duties. But some of our assumptions are based on modern news stories about young people being abducted and brutally treated. Even the fictional adventures of Tom Sawyer in today's context make us wonder about whether Jesus' caretakers were negligent for letting Him roam so far and wide. But although travelers always face some degree of risk on this kind of journey (cf. 2 Corinthians 11:26), traveling in a large *company* reduces this risk significantly. Mary and Joseph trust those with whom they travel to be caretakers toward all of the younger people on the journey.

B. Parents Frantic (v. 45)

45. And when they found him not, they turned back again to Jerusalem, seeking him.

It is easy to imagine the fear and frustration that Mary and Joseph feel upon discovering that their son is missing. They probably didn't get much sleep that night before turning *back again!* Jesus' absence could mean that something terrible has happened.

As they set out at daybreak, they are undoubtedly scanning the road on both sides with each step, fearing that they might come upon their son's lifeless body. Perhaps they fuss and blame each other along the way, exchanging mournful "if onlys." Perhaps they make promises to each other as they walk along, saying that "something like this will never happen again."

Even wonderful parents can have regrets. It is always possible to say that "more could have been done" to care for any particular youngster. But doubtless Joseph and Mary are also conscious of the fact that every parent has limitations regarding what can be predicted about the events of life. If parents could have the kind of foresight that compares with their hindsight, parenting would be much easier indeed!

III. In the Temple
(Luke 2:46-50)

A. Jesus Astonishes the Scholars (vv. 46, 47)

46. And it came to pass, that after three days they found him in the temple, sitting in the midst of the doctors, both hearing them, and asking them questions.

The *three days* can be understood to include the day's journey away from Jerusalem of verse 44, the day it takes to travel back again, and one more day in Jerusalem locating Jesus. Looking for someone in a Passover crowd is a daunting task, since Jerusalem's "normal" population of between sixty and one hundred twenty thousand can swell five-fold during this time.

But one wonders whether Joseph and Mary may have a notion about where to look for Jesus, and thus perhaps they head straight for *the temple*. Even if they suspected that He would be there, it will be no small project to locate Him. The temple's complex of courts covers more than twenty-five acres!

Jewish literature indicates that during special feast days priests might come out from the temple sanctuary (where no "ordinary" worshiper can go) to mingle with the people in the various courts on the temple grounds and teach about the law. Perhaps it is in such a gathering that young Jesus stands listening to the teachers and *asking them questions*. We can barely tolerate not knowing what questions Jesus may be asking, but Luke is silent about this.

What is important to Luke is a portrait of a young Jesus completely captivated by God's truth. Even after being separated from His parents for days, His concentration is on those matters of God's will that believers find precious.

47. And all that heard him were astonished at his understanding and answers.

The spiritual maturity that Jesus displays amazes the crowd. It is not just that Jesus is able to ask deep questions (2:46), but that He also provides *answers* to questions—answers that reveal deep *understanding*. His knowledge and devotion to the Lord reflect a maturity beyond His twelve years. This certainly will not be the last time in Luke's Gospel that Jesus causes astonishment (see 4:22, 32, 36; 5:26; 9:43; 11:14).

THE AMAZING CHRIST

Before television became common, there was a popular radio program called *Quiz Kids* in the 1940s. Children under the age of sixteen would be asked to answer questions that most adults would find difficult. The program had a wide audience. People were amazed that children could have so much information.

Yet amazement with children did not start in the 1940s. The teachers in the temple long ago were startled at the knowledge and wisdom of Jesus. So are we. We have the added benefit of observing His whole life, not just a few hours. We share the wonder of Charles H. Gabriel (1856 –1932) who wrote, "I stand amazed in the presence of Jesus the Nazarene." Our amazement grows with each passing year. John Newton (1725–1807), the great preacher who wrote the song "Amazing Grace," once said, "I wonder that I do not wonder more!"

But some have lost their sense of wonder. They have "heard it all" and heard it so often that they no longer feel the full impact of the story of Christ. We need to sit again with those teachers in Jerusalem, with the disciples by the sea, and with the multitude on the mountain. We need to sit there long enough to recapture our amazement at the Christ who understood us so well, who loved us so much, and who saved us so freely.

Ultimately, there is nothing in the environment of Jesus that fully explains His wisdom. There is nothing in His ancestry to explain it. There is nothing in His life experience to explain it completely. The only truly satisfactory explanation is the one the Bible offers: He was the Divine Son of God. Those who do not stand amazed in His presence have closed their eyes to His genius.   —R. C. S.

B. Jesus Puzzles His Parents (vv. 48-50)

48. And when they saw him, they were amazed: and his mother said unto him, Son, why hast thou thus dealt with us? behold, thy father and I have sought thee sorrowing.

Luke permits us a glimpse of the emotions experienced by Joseph and Mary when they finally find their *son*. Their first reaction is amazement, which may be connected with the preceding scene (2:47) that astonished so many others in the crowd that day. Joseph and Mary, along with the others in their party, marvel as they witness their son as He sits with the teachers of Israel and communicates an impressive understanding of the Word of God.

But after their sense of amazement has settled a bit, they become aware again of the terrible sense of desperation they have felt in wondering what has happened to young Jesus. Mary is the one who takes the initiative in speaking to Jesus about this. She communicates the natural emotions of parents who have faced traumatic doubts about the safety of a child. It would be interesting to speculate why Joseph lets Mary do the talking!

49. And he said unto them, How is it that ye sought me? wist ye not that I must be about my Father's business?

ARE YOU ABOUT THE FATHER'S BUSINESS?

Visual for lesson 4

Use this illustration to challenge your learners to be about "the Father's business."

In reply to the question from His mother, Jesus gives an answer that encapsulates His mission as the Son of God. [See question #4, page 152.] Within this answer we notice that Jesus refers to the Lord God as His Father. This implies that Jesus is Son of God in a way that describes no one else. We also can wonder if by "my Father" Jesus intends to make a contrast with Mary's reference to "thy father" in Luke 2:48. [See question #5, page 152.]

50. And they understood not the saying which he spake unto them.

The words of Jesus present riddles to Joseph and Mary that they cannot solve. Why does their boy believe that He has to be in the temple? What does He mean by speaking of the Lord God Almighty as "my Father"? How could their own teachings at home have given Him the depth of understanding about the Lord that is evident in those conversations with the temple teachers? True, Mary and Joseph had been presented with certain facts about Jesus' birth and future ministry at the time of Jesus' conception (see Luke 1:30-33). Even so, it is obvious here that they have not been able to grasp the entire picture.

They should not be too ashamed. How could any parent understand completely what such a comment means? This same refrain will be heard more than once during the ministry of Jesus. Over and over those who witness His miracles and hear His words will be asking themselves what Jesus means by what He does or says (see Luke 4:22; 9:45; 18:34).

In all of these scenes, Luke will draw a sharp contrast between the wisdom of Jesus Christ and the slowness of those around Him. What we see before us and in Luke 2:40, 47, 52 is an opening emphasis on the wisdom of Jesus.

Home Daily Bible Readings

Monday, Dec. 22—A Branch Shall Grow (Isaiah 11:1-5)

Tuesday, Dec. 23—This Is My Son, My Chosen! (Luke 9:28-36)

Wednesday, Dec. 24—Here Is My Servant (Matthew 12:15-21)

Thursday, Dec. 25—I Am Well Pleased (Matthew 3:13-17)

Friday, Dec. 26—The Father Loves the Son (John 5:19-24)

Saturday, Dec. 27—Jesus Grew With God's Favor (Luke 2:40-44)

Sunday, Dec. 28—Jesus in His Father's House (Luke 2:45-52)

IV. Toward Home
(Luke 2:51, 52)

A. Jesus' Obedience (v. 51)

51. And he went down with them, and came to Nazareth, and was subject unto them: but his mother kept all these sayings in her heart.

The previous verses by themselves may leave the impression that Jesus is a defiant child. But Luke's comment here about Jesus' obedience to His parents cancels that possibility. Thus Jesus lives through His teenage years as a young man who shows respect toward His parents. He is a lad who demonstrates His godly life before the whole village of *Nazareth,* a town of only several hundred people. Sadly, these very people will be ones to show the least faith in years to come (see Matthew 13:53-58).

B. Jesus' Growth (v. 52)

52. And Jesus increased in wisdom and stature, and in favor with God and man.

Luke's brief and simple statement about Jesus' boyhood years carries none of the sensationalism of the invented, non-Biblical accounts of Jesus' life that come along a few years later. Instead, Luke fully represents the human nature of Jesus in this summary, as if to say that He experiences all the normal stages of human growth—whether physical, mental, or spiritual.

Although Christ came to earth "fully God," He voluntarily put on the limitations of human flesh (Philippians 2:7). Thus His increase *in wisdom* speaks to the growth in His "fleshly side." His growth *in favor with God and man* tells us that this growth is evident to all—that He is blessed by God and accepted by people around Him (cf. Proverbs 3:4). See again Luke's previous statement in Luke 2:40.

"MY, HOW YOU'VE GROWN!"

When going to visit grandmother after a long absence, every child knows exactly what she is going to say: "My, how you've grown!" And in many cases the child will be ushered to the kitchen where there are marks on the door frame. The child will stand up straight, back against the frame, and a new mark will be made. Both child and grandmother will be so proud to see how much the child has grown in stature.

The growth of the young Jesus was not just physical, but also in "wisdom" and "in favor with God and man." How sad it is if today a child's growth in stature is not matched by spiritual growth! How much sadder still if the child grows smaller spiritually while growing taller physically! Modern science teaches us that a child's physical stature is controlled by the pituitary gland and hereditary influences; thus there is little if anything we can do to make a child grow taller in stature (cf. Matthew 6:27). But we can do much to help a child grow in favor with God and people.

As adults we know we cannot govern our height. (As for our girth—that's another story!) But each of us definitely has the power to change our spiritual stature. Whether for children or adults, we want to be sure that spiritual growth is never taken for granted—that each of us "stands taller" each year. If God showed us the marks that chart our spiritual growth, would we be embarrassed to discover that we have not grown at all? Or that we have in fact shrunken in size?
—R. C. S.

Conclusion

A. Jesus' Boyhood

This incident from the boyhood of Jesus is all that the Gospels offer us regarding this stage in Jesus' life. It is obvious that the Gospel writers were selective in their choice of material! Yet this episode well demonstrates the remarkable nature of Jesus' early development and His awareness of His identity and mission. All this was nurtured when His godly parents created for Him the best spiritual environment possible.

B. Prayer

Please, Lord, lead me today to some young person who needs my encouragement to be in the house of our Heavenly Father. And may I not neglect my own spiritual growth in the process. In Christ I pray continually, amen.

C. Thought to Remember

What young person will you help today to grow in favor with God and people?

Learning by Doing

This page contains an alternative lesson plan emphasizing learning activities.
Classes desiring such student involvement will find these suggestions helpful.

Learning Goals

After participating in this lesson, each student will be able to:

1. List the details in today's text concerning the early years of Jesus' life, including Jesus' sense of His unique role as the Son of God.

2. Tell how the growth of Jesus in His knowledge of God and His interest in spiritual things reminds us of how essential it is for children to acquire a devotion for God at a young age.

3. Express a commitment to participate in helping young people come to love the Lord.

Into the Lesson

As we begin this section of Scripture, we get a glimpse of Jesus' youth. Assign pairs to discuss the following questions briefly:

1. Remember being someplace as a child when your parents didn't know where you were. Where were you and what were the consequences when you were reunited?

2. Recall an occasion when you were the only youth in the midst of an adult conversation, yet were free to participate in the conversation. What was being discussed? How did you fare?

Into the Word

Assign small groups and begin this activity by saying, "Read today's Scripture text and make a list of Jesus' character traits as revealed in this passage. As each is identified, discuss what each trait tells us about Jesus as a young boy."

After each group completes its assignment, allow each group leader to share one of the character traits identified. Continue in this process until every trait has been identified and explained as to the kind of child Jesus was. Write these traits where all can see them.

As an alternative way of looking at Jesus' characteristics, play a word-discovery game with your class. Have the following words on individual cards: *submissive, purposive, exceptional, child, inquisitive, astonishing, "lost."* Either have members of the class volunteer to give the stimulus clues or do it yourself. Do it in the order of words given. For example, for *submissive,* the clue could be, "One who yields to the will of another is being _____." For *purposive,* the clue could be, "Rather than living life aimlessly, without a goal, it would better to be _____." When all seven words are identified, attach the seven cards to the

wall or board one atop the other. When all are displayed, ask the class to note the word spelled by the first letters: *special.* Ask, "How is Jesus a special child and how is He not?" and "How is Jesus—and Mary and Joseph's rearing of Him—a pattern for successful growth?"

Following the character-traits discussion, pose these questions to the class:

(1) How does Jesus address His mission? (2) What benefit was it for Mary to keep all of this "in her heart"? (3) Describe the confidence Joseph and Mary placed in Jesus. Once they found Him, what was their attitude? (4) Explain whether Jesus was performing the role of teacher or student in the temple. Why was it important for Jesus to obey His parents? (See Exodus 20:12.) (5) How are the next eighteen years of Jesus' life summarized? If time permits, discuss why Luke included—at the Spirit's direction—this particular episode of Jesus' life.

Into Life

Whether your class members are prospective parents, parents of young or older children, or grandparents, the following discussion and decisions should prove to be valuable.

Ask, "What did Mary and Joseph do right in helping Jesus to increase 'in wisdom and stature, and in favor with God and man'?" *Answers may include acknowledging their great carefulness for His physical safety as an infant, their willingness to obey God's direction in all matters—including leaving home and family to make the annual pilgrimage to Jerusalem for the Passover—trusting Jesus to be responsible, their willingness to confront Jesus when they thought He had done wrong (even though they knew about His divine nature), and Mary's regular consideration (pondering) of who Jesus is in dealing with Him.*

Designate three groups to discuss and recommend answers to the following three questions: What can we as a class (or individually) do (1) to support the spiritual nurture of the children in our congregation? (2) to support parents in their godly rearing of their children? (3) to encourage the teachers who work in our children's ministry? Once the groups report and recommend, consider having the class select two or three projects to accomplish within the coming calendar year. Suggest that each one select a personal project as well.

Let's Talk It Over

The questions on this page are designed to promote discussion of the lesson by the class and to encourage application of the lesson Scriptures. The answers provided are only discussion starters. Let your class talk it over from there.

1. The text notes of Jesus that "the grace of God was upon him." In what ways has God extended His grace to you?

Hopefully, all Christians should realize that God's saving grace means rescue from sin. Beyond that, God is gracious to us in many ways; encourage your learners to share specific examples and incidents of God's grace in their lives.

2. How rare it is today to hear a child labeled as "wise"! What "markers of wisdom" would we have to see today to use "wise" to describe a twenty-first century child?

Educators are often gratified when their students are able to ask the right questions and use factual information to draw conclusions. It is such "critical thinking" that causes a person to analyze and synthesize materials in such a way as to form entirely new thoughts. Christian educators may refer to a child as "wise" who demonstrates a thirst for God's Word. Unfortunately, some young people think themselves to be truly wise when they are "wise in the ways of the world," or "street smart."

The young Jesus amazed the temple leaders with His questions. The questions must have shown intense introspection and insight uncommon to such a young lad. We can be certain that it was not "street smarts" that startled them.

3. Jesus' parents were diligent about observing the Passover. How can we make sure that observances of tradition today are not merely empty routine?

We live in a time when traditions are often treated as useless interruptions in our lives. To many, Christmas is a season to endure and "get through." When the need to attend a funeral canceled other plans, one man was heard to remark (only half-jokingly), "People die at the most inconvenient times!" But God entrusted the task of raising His only Son to a human couple who treated historical practices as something to be honored.

Even so, Jesus Himself would later criticize the Jewish leadership for their strict adherence to tradition (see Mark 7:1-13). We are quick to note, however, that it was the abuse of God's intended customs and belief systems that Jesus condemned in those leaders.

Today, we observe traditions established by God (e.g., the Lord's Supper) and traditions established by people (e.g., Thanksgiving). We avoid empty routine by continually asking ourselves, "How can I use this tradition to draw me closer to God?"

4. Instead of answering His parents directly, Jesus asked a question—suggesting a deeper meaning without becoming condescending or disrespectful. How can we use this technique in our interactions with fellow believers as well as with unbelievers?

Many of Jesus' responses to friend and foe during His ministry would come in the form of questions. This allowed Him to challenge His listeners or opponents to discover truth through personal reflection, or to provide understanding at a level that was appropriate to them. Those employed in sales and marketing careers today are trained to overcome objections by turning objections into questions. Remember: before we can arrive at the right answer, we have to ask the right questions.

5. Some people today have had to choose between pleasing their Heavenly Father and their earthly families. When have you seen people make the right choice in this regard, and when have you seen them make the wrong choice?

The responses to this question may turn out to be very emotional for some of your learners. Be prepared for some to recount tragic stories of estrangement from parents and siblings because of a decision to follow Christ. Rejection may take comparatively mild forms, such as being looked down on by family members as some kind of "religious nut." Estrangement may also take the severe form of being disowned outright—being unwelcome at family gatherings, etc.

You can encourage your learners by pointing out that Jesus also had to endure misunderstanding—perhaps we could even say rejection—by family members (see Mark 3:21). He understands! Jesus also predicted family discord because of our decision to follow Him (see Luke 14:26), so we are not to be surprised. As painful as these situations can be, our eternal reward will outweigh any loss (see Mark 10:29, 30).

Integrity in the Midst of Suffering

DEVOTIONAL READING: Romans 8:18-25.

BACKGROUND SCRIPTURE: Job 1:1–2:10.

PRINTED TEXT: Job 2:1-10.

Job 2:1-10

1 Again there was a day when the sons of God came to present themselves before the LORD, and Satan came also among them to present himself before the LORD.

2 And the LORD said unto Satan, From whence comest thou? And Satan answered the LORD, and said, From going to and fro in the earth, and from walking up and down in it.

3 And the LORD said unto Satan, Hast thou considered my servant Job, that there is none like him in the earth, a perfect and an upright man, one that feareth God, and escheweth evil? and still he holdeth fast his integrity, although thou movedst me against him, to destroy him without cause.

4 And Satan answered the LORD, and said, Skin for skin, yea, all that a man hath will he give for his life.

5 But put forth thine hand now, and touch his bone and his flesh, and he will curse thee to thy face.

6 And the LORD said unto Satan, Behold, he is in thine hand; but save his life.

7 So went Satan forth from the presence of the LORD, and smote Job with sore boils from the sole of his foot unto his crown.

8 And he took him a potsherd to scrape himself withal; and he sat down among the ashes.

9 Then said his wife unto him, Dost thou still retain thine integrity? curse God, and die.

10 But he said unto her, Thou speakest as one of the foolish women speaketh. What? shall we receive good at the hand of God, and shall we not receive evil? In all this did not Job sin with his lips.

GOLDEN TEXT: [Job] said . . . What? shall we receive good at the hand of God, and shall we not receive evil? In all this did not Job sin with his lips.—Job 2:10.

Lesson Aims

After participating in this lesson, each student should be able to:

1. Summarize the trials of Job and how he responded to them with integrity.

2. Indicate ways that Christians can hold on to hope during times of testing.

3. Express a commitment to respond to trials with the same integrity shown by Job.

Lesson Outline

INTRODUCTION
    A. The Test No One Wants to Take
    B. Lesson Background
I. GOD'S AFFIRMATION (Job 2:1-3)
    A. Satan's Appearance (vv. 1, 2)
      Is Satan Present Everywhere?
    B. God's Acknowledgment (v. 3)
II. SATAN'S ACCUSATION (Job 2:4-6)
    A. "Not Tough Enough" (vv. 4, 5)
      God Understands Us Better Than Satan Does
    B. God's Response (v. 6)
III. JOB'S INFIRMITY (Job 2:7, 8)
    A. Physical (v. 7)
    B. Spiritual (v. 8)
IV. JOB'S INTEGRITY (Job 2:9, 10)
    A. Questioned (v. 9)
    B. Confirmed (v. 10)
CONCLUSION
    A. "When the Going Gets Tough . . . "
    B. Prayer
    C. Thought to Remember

Introduction

A. The Test No One Wants to Take

How do you feel about taking tests? Some people enjoy tests, seeing them as an opportunity to prove their proficiency or expertise. Others agonize over approaching tests to the point of suffering paralysis or panic. Most of us fall somewhere between those two extremes.

There is one test, however, that we are certain no one wants to take. It is "The Job Test." Even though James 1:2, 3 tells us to consider testing a joyful experience, and even though James 5:11 holds Job up as a model, most Christians look at

Job's trials and hope they are never tested with such an intensely unpleasant experience.

But what would happen if Christians today faced real persecution? What if you lost what Job lost? It is difficult to even think about what Job experienced. Yet, there are lessons for us to learn from Job's experience. As you read and learn, question the depth of your faith and trust in God. Are you ready to be tested?

B. Lesson Background

The book of Job is layered with mysteries. There are more unanswered questions about Job than any book of the Bible (except perhaps Revelation). In most instances we know the authors, the approximate time frame, and the recipients of Bible books. Those facts influence our interpretation. With Job we are unenlightened about so many things!

We are certain, however, that Job was not a fictitious character (see Ezekiel 14:14, 20; James 5:11). He lived in "the land of Uz" (Job 1:1), which was in the territory of the Edomites, south of Palestine (Lamentations 4:21). Job was wealthy—perhaps the wealthiest man of his time (Job 1:3). Job was the head of a large family (1:2). Job was a man whose reverence for God caused him to lead a righteous life (1:1). Job lived sometime in the age of the patriarchs, between 1000 and 2000 B.C. There is no evidence that Job was aware of the Old Testament law.

The book of Job is one of the most profound writings in human history. Many people today who could not readily differentiate between the Old and New Testaments could, nevertheless, tell you what the book of Job is about. Its position as a literary classic can compromise its spiritual message, however. Job is about suffering, patience, faith, and trust. It is also about the righteousness and sovereignty of God.

In order to appreciate fully this week's lesson text, you must read Job 1 as background. There you learn about Job's character, position, and family (1:1-6). After that, a scene from Heaven is presented (1:7-12). Satan (whose name means "adversary") appears before God. God asks Satan if he has noticed the faithfulness of Job (1:8). Satan accuses God of offering such protection and prosperity to Job that he has no reason to be unfaithful (1:9, 10). Satan proposes that God strike Job down—then Job will curse God (1:11). Note that Satan proposed that God do this evil to Job. God refused, but gave Satan permission to test him (1:12). God's only restriction at this point was that Job not be harmed physically (1:12).

So Satan went to do his dirty work. A succession of messengers came to Job, telling him of the loss of his livestock and his servants (1:13-17).

Then, in what was surely the most devastating moment of his life, Job was told that a windstorm had demolished the house in which his children were gathered. All were dead (1:18, 19).

Despite Satan's dastardly deeds, Job remained faithful. He worshiped, blessed God, and refused to blame God (1:20, 21). In the midst of the unimaginable emotional anguish, Job did not sin (1:22). These events set the stage for this week's lesson and the three that follow in this unit of study.

I. God's Affirmation
(Job 2:1-3)

A. Satan's Appearance (vv. 1, 2)

1. Again there was a day when the sons of God came to present themselves before the Lord, and Satan came also among them to present himself before the Lord.

We are not told how much time elapses between the end of Job 1 and the beginning of Job 2. It may have been a relatively brief time, or it may have been years. Satan's scheme has not worked, but he is not ready to give up on Job.

Satan is mentioned by name fewer than twenty times in the Old Testament. The vast majority of those instances are in the book of Job. Here Satan is presented in a scene from Heaven, as in Job 1:6. *The sons of God* are angels (see also 38:7). They apparently are required *to present themselves before* God to give account of their activities.

We should remember that Satan is a fallen angel, a created being, who did not hold to the truth (John 8:44). Isaiah 14:12-14 and Ezekiel 28:12-15 clearly refer to earthly kings, but may also refer to Satan as the one who incited the evil actions of those kings.

How to Say It

Corinthians. Kor-*in*-thee-unz (*th* as in *thin*).

Edomites. *Ee*-dum-ites.

Ephesians. Ee-*fee*-zhunz.

Ezekiel. Ee-*zeek*-ee-ul or Ee-*zeek*-yul.

Hebrews. *Hee*-brews.

Isaiah. Eye-*zay*-uh.

Jeremiah. Jair-uh-*my*-uh.

Lamentations. Lam-en-*tay*-shunz.

Omnipotent. ahm-*nih*-poh-tent.

Omnipresence. *ahm*-nih-*prez*-ence (strong accent on *prez*).

Quid pro quo. kwid-pro-*kwoh*.

Thessalonians. *Thess*-uh-*lo*-nee-unz (strong accent on *lo*; *th* as in *thin*).

Is Satan Present Everywhere?

A retired preacher went to serve a little country church. There, in Sunday school, he was asked a question no one had ever asked him before. "Is Satan, like God, present everywhere? Or is omnipresence an attribute only of God and not of the devil?" Not only had he never been asked that before, he said he had never even contemplated such a question. So he delayed answering until he could give some thought to it.

He happened to be on the campus of a Bible college so he asked one professor, "Is Satan present everywhere?" The professor answered, "He's present everywhere I've been!" That was a good answer, but another professor gave him an equally good answer. When asked, "Is Satan present everywhere?" the second professor simply replied, "The doctrine of Satan is not fully developed in the Bible."

While the second professor's answer is more definitive, the first's may be more practical. We must *always* guard against temptation by assuming that Satan is constantly nearby. We never know when we will be attacked by our spiritual enemy. But judging from the book of Job, we may be certain that our experience is part of a larger drama, and that our struggle with sin and suffering a part of a much larger struggle (cf. Revelation 12:7). —R. C. S.

2. And the Lord said unto Satan, From whence comest thou? And Satan answered the Lord, and said, From going to and fro in the earth, and from walking up and down in it.

The Lord repeats His question from 1:6. God, of course, already knows where *Satan* has been and what he has been doing. But God's question is designed to start a conversation. In the New Testament era Satan's activities are more restricted (see Matthew 12:29; Luke 10:18; 11:21, 22; Revelation 20:1-3), but he is still quite dangerous. (e.g., 1 Thessalonians 2:18; 1 Peter 5:8; Revelation 2:13). Popular culture puts Satan in a red suit with horns and a trident. But he is far more subtle and devious than that (see 2 Corinthians 11:14). Satan is not omnipotent ("all powerful") like God, but we dare not underestimate his ability to deceive. [See question #1, page 160.]

B. God's Acknowledgment (v. 3)

3. And the Lord said unto Satan, Hast thou considered my servant Job, that there is none like him in the earth, a perfect and an upright man, one that feareth God, and escheweth evil? and still he holdeth fast his integrity, although thou movedst me against him, to destroy him without cause.

As in 1:8, God asks *Satan* if he has taken note of *Job*. It almost seems as if God is daring Satan to confront Him about this man. In the time that has passed between these two appearances it is obvious that Job's integrity has not waned. Can you imagine God mentioning your name to Satan? (Compare Luke 22:31.) Are you a person of such spiritual integrity that God could point to you as a model of righteousness? [See question #2, page 160.]

Notice that it is God's turn to make an accusation against Satan by reminding him that his (Satan's) accusation about Job (1:9, 10) is proven false. Job does not honor God just to receive God's blessing. Job's reverence for God is not a *quid pro quo* ("something for something") arrangement. That had been Satan's original accusation. Now God reminds the evil one that the facts as they have unfolded prove otherwise!

Why do you honor God? Is it because you think you will be blessed if you do? Is your faith a matter of "fire insurance," just making sure you do not go to Hell? It is easy to love and honor God when all is going well and you are "on top of the mountain." What about when all is not well and you are in "the valley"?

II. Satan's Accusation
(Job 2:4-6)

A. "Not Tough Enough" (vv. 4, 5)

4. And Satan answered the LORD, and said, Skin for skin, yea, all that a man hath will he give for his life.

One can almost sense the venom in Satan's response to God. The phrase *Skin for skin* is difficult to interpret. It may be a well-known proverb of the time. *Satan* may be complaining to God, "I've only taken off one layer of skin, so the test so far hasn't been fair!"

We can understand Satan's intent from the context: God has not permitted Satan to be tough enough on Job. Satan is accusing God of knowing that the limit for any *man* is his very *life*—that point at which he surely will curse God—but God has not allowed Satan to push Job to that limit.

5. But put forth thine hand now, and touch his bone and his flesh, and he will curse thee to thy face.

Satan again tries to get God to afflict Job. Although Job has suffered great emotional stress and personal loss, he has not yet suffered physically, since his own *bone and his flesh* have not been affected. Is God afraid to do this? Could it be that God knows that physical pain will be Job's breaking point? Satan's method changes, but not his goal. His goal is still to get Job to *curse* God and thus destroy their relationship.

This is Satan's goal even today. He works on Christians to get them to give up on God. He knows God will not give up on us, so the breaking of the bond between us has to be our doing. C. S. Lewis's classic book *The Screwtape Letters* provides marvelous insight into the deviousness of Satan. We must be aware of his schemes (2 Corinthians 2:11), and we must not let him succeed (Ephesians 6:11)!

GOD UNDERSTANDS US BETTER THAN SATAN DOES

The man was highly successful and highly respected in his profession. So it was a shock when his son was arrested and put in jail. Then the father suffered a stroke at an age when a stroke would not have been expected. Paralyzed on one side, unable to continue in his profession, he was unable to care for his own basic needs.

This brilliant and successful man sat all day long in front of his window, completely dependent on others. His minister remarked that it must be hard to deal with a stroke like that. "Oh," the man said, "this is easy compared with knowing that my son is in prison! That's much harder to face."

Every parent can understand that anguish. But you will notice that Satan "didn't quite get it." He thought that illness, pain, and physical suffering would be worse for Job than what he already had endured. But it was not. When Job's children died, Satan already had played his highest card; he already had done his worst. God knew Job as Satan did not.

It should comfort us to know that God understands us much better than Satan does. That is why God is able to help us and to strengthen us when we face either temptations or trials. There is a wonderful declaration in 1 John 4:4: "Greater is he that is in you, than he that is in the world." Not only is God greater, He is smarter. He knows us because He made us. We always will be better off to accept His directions for life and to reject Satan's!

—R. C. S.

B. God's Response (v. 6)

6. And the LORD said unto Satan, Behold, he is in thine hand; but save his life.

God's confidence in Job is astonishing. God will not bring evil upon Job, but He will permit *Satan* to escalate the level of Job's suffering.

Why does Satan think that afflicting Job physically will matter any more than the previous tragedies and losses? Perhaps Satan reasons that as long as Job is healthy, he knows he can replace what he once had. He can father more children. He can rebuild his financial empire. Satan's scheme goes beyond afflicting Job's health. He wants to disable Job completely and thus rob him of hope. This is consistent with Satan's desire for all our lives. He will work in every possible way to rob us of hope.

Think about how important hope is. Most people can endure a great deal if they think there is light at the end of the tunnel. Satan, the "prince of darkness," will do all he can to obliterate that light! People who live without hope will eventually give up on everything, including life itself.

The writer of the New Testament book of Hebrews calls our hope in God an "anchor of the soul" (Hebrews 6:19). Such hope helps us hang on through difficult times. There is a beautiful passage about hope in Lamentations. Jeremiah lost hope, but then his hope was renewed when he remembered the compassion and faithfulness of God (Lamentations 3:1-24).

Satan is a liar and a deceiver. He will try to rob you of hope. Do not let him succeed! Remember Job and Jeremiah. Renew your hope by remembering the character of God. He is loving. He is faithful. He keeps all His promises. Our ultimate hope is in Him and Him alone!

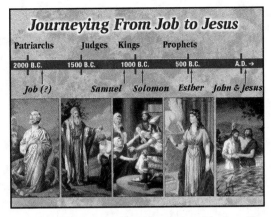

Visual for lessons 5 and 13. Use this time line to help your learners keep "the big picture" in mind.

III. Job's Infirmity
(Job 2:7, 8)

A. Physical (v. 7)

7. So went Satan forth from the presence of the LORD, and smote Job with sore boils from the sole of his foot unto his crown.

We now come to a section of Job that is graphic and painful to read. Most of us have suffered with some kind of physical malady. We, however, live in an age of powerful medications and painkillers. As you read these verses, remember that Job does not have a pharmacy just down the street.

Devious as he is, Satan chooses as his method of torture an affliction that God Himself promises (through Moses) to those who disobey; see Deuteronomy 28:35. Boils are extremely painful to the touch. Any pressure on them is excruciating. Imagine having them everywhere, even on your feet! (Deuteronomy 28:35 also promises that the extent of this affliction will be "from the sole of thy foot unto the top of thy head.") Whether sitting, lying, or standing, there is no relief.

We are not given a precise diagnosis of Job's condition. We can, however, describe some of the symptoms. He lost weight (Job 19:20). He has a constant fever, and his skin has turned black (30:30). His pain is constant (30:17, 27). Poor Job—he even has bad breath (19:17)!

His appearance is so disfigured that his friends will not even recognize him when they first see him (2:12). Long bouts of physical pain can

change a person's appearance. The toll on the body is reflected in the face.

Perhaps you have despaired because of physical pain. We speak of people who have high or low thresholds of pain. Some people deal with pain better than others. Most of us, however, have some means of lessening the pain. We may take medications or treatments, or we may even have surgery. For most people there is hope of the pain being decreased or completely relieved. Job, it seems, is without hope. There is no medicine, treatment, or surgery that will help. Death looms (10:20-22; 17:1).

B. Spiritual (v. 8)

8. And he took him a potsherd to scrape himself withal; and he sat down among the ashes.

Job's only means of temporary relief from the interminable pain and itching of the boils is scraping himself with the rough edge of a piece of broken pottery. We must note, however, where Job has chosen to suffer. He does not remain at home where he might have had some measure of comfort. He is outside sitting *among the ashes!*

In many ancient cultures, sitting in dust and ashes is a sign of mourning and/or repentance (Jonah 3:6; Esther 4:3). Job eventually makes it clear that sitting in ashes is an act of repentance for him (Job 42:6). That, of course, is at the end of the book, after God has chastised him.

When we first find Job sitting in the ashes, however, we may ask what he is repenting of. Has not God said of Job that he is "a perfect and an upright man" (1:8; 2:3)? Is Job repenting at first, or does he repent in chapter 42 only after God humbles him in chapters 38 and 39? Throughout most of the book Job contends that

17 my breath is offensive to my wife

he has not sinned. Is Job sitting in ashes at this point merely to mourn the deaths of his children? This is a question we cannot answer.

We can safely conclude, however, that Job is a man in spiritual turmoil. He is confused. Most people of Job's time directly connect their actions with God's blessings or His wrath in a "cause and effect" way (cf. John 9:1, 2). That, in essence, is the argument of Job's so-called friends. Job must have done something terribly wrong to incur such a ferocious outpouring of God's wrath. Are they right? Is Job right? Confusion rules the day!

IV. Job's Integrity
(Job 2:9, 10)
A. Questioned (v. 9)

9. Then said his wife unto him, Dost thou still retain thine integrity? curse God, and die.

Someone has lamented Job's situation by noting that all he had left was a nagging *wife!* But remember that Job's wife, too, has lost children and financial security. She has suffered tremendous loss. Perhaps she thinks that some sin of her husband is responsible. In any case, she cannot understand why Job does not just give up. Perhaps if Job would *curse God,* he would be struck dead. At least then he would be out of his misery! [See question #3, page 160.]

Some have seen a parallel between Eve and Job's wife. Both presented temptation to their husbands. Job's wife, however, was responding to the despair in her life. She lashed out at her husband and at God. She is like many who are willing to quit before the game is over. [See question #4, page 160.] Job's *integrity* means something to him. It apparently has little meaning to her.

Home Daily Bible Readings

Monday, Dec. 29—Compare Present Suffering With Future Glory (Romans 8: 18-23)

Tuesday, Dec. 30—All Things Work Together for Good (Romans 8:24-28)

Wednesday, Dec. 31—God Is for Us (Romans 8:29-33)

Thursday, Jan. 1—Nothing Can Separate From Christ's Love (Romans 8:34-39)

Friday, Jan. 2—Job Was Upright (Job 1:1-5)

Saturday, Jan. 3—Job Kept Integrity in Suffering (Job 1:13-22)

Sunday, Jan. 4—Job Would Not Curse God (Job 2:1-10)

B. Confirmed (v. 10)

10. But he said unto her, Thou speakest as one of the foolish women speaketh. What? shall we receive good at the hand of God, and shall we not receive evil? In all this did not Job sin with his lips.

Job rebukes his wife with stinging words. Her words are *foolish.* [See question #5, page 160.] Job's question about receiving both *good* and *evil* from God still rings in the human heart. At this point we should note that there are two kinds of evil: physical evil and moral evil. God does not inflict moral evil upon us (see James 1:13), and that is not what Job is talking about here. It is Satan who is responsible for offering us the moral evils that we at times so willingly embrace.

But God does cause and permit trouble and pain (which we could call "physical evil") to come into our lives. That seems to be what Job has in mind here. Sometimes God allows such evil to come about as a natural consequence of our own sin. Sometimes God sends these consequences specifically and intentionally (e.g., the plagues in Exodus 7–11). All pain and suffering can serve God's divine purposes in some way. Pain and trouble can cause us to understand our frailty and our need for God (cf. 2 Corinthians 12:7-10).

The "bottom line" here is that Job's integrity is confirmed. He refuses to curse God. He will not give up. He has faith in the ultimate goodness of God. Even when he does not understand God's ways, he acknowledges God's sovereignty and righteousness.

Conclusion
A. "When the Going Gets Tough . . . "

When life gets tough, what do you do? When the road of life gets rocky, are you tempted to take a detour? Job's integrity and trust in the face of adversity provide a powerful example for us. Remember that God knows our limits, and that He will not permit us to be tested beyond what we are able to bear (1 Corinthians 10:13). Satan loves quitters! God, on the other hand, loves those who hold on. Job did not understand everything about God, but he knew not to let go of God.

B. Prayer

Father, help us hold on to You! When we are weak and struggling, help us remember Job. Reinvigorate our faith. Increase our trust. Remind us that You are always with us, even in the midst of our struggles and pain. Help us rely on the Holy Spirit's power. In Jesus' name, amen.

C. Thought to Remember

Without God, what else is there?

Learning by Doing

This page contains an alternative lesson plan emphasizing learning activities.
Classes desiring such student involvement will find these suggestions helpful.

Learning Goals

After participating in this lesson, each student will be able to:

1. Summarize the trials of Job and how he responded to them with integrity.

2. Indicate ways that Christians can hold on to hope during times of testing.

3. Express a commitment to respond to trials with the same integrity shown by Job.

Into the Lesson

During the week, ask three class members to share a brief account of a painful experience from their lives. If you can and the individuals are able to talk of it, invite someone who has lost a child, someone who has experienced great financial loss, and someone who has dealt with debilitating health. Begin class by asking them to share what they have suffered.

Ask questions such as, "Why does God want us to know of Job's intense suffering? Can we learn about suffering from reading about Job, or do we have to experience suffering firsthand?"

Say, "Job not only suffered, but he did so with integrity." Ask why this is important to God and also to us.

Into the Word

Ask for seven volunteers to stand in the front of the class to hold a statement regarding Job's travails. All these will have to do is read aloud their statements when you direct. Have each of the following events written on separate sheets: (1) Sabeans attack, take Job's oxen and donkeys, and slay the servants in charge; (2) Fire from Heaven kills Job's sheep and the servants tending to them; (3) Chaldeans steal Job's camels and slay the attendant servants; (4) A strong wind destroys the house where Job's children are and kills them all; (5) Job is afflicted with sores (boils) from head to foot; (6) Job's wife challenges him to curse God and die; (7) Job's friends arrive to grieve with him (and to challenge his morality and ethics). Shuffle these so members stand randomly across the front. Have them read their statements left to right as they face the class. Once the random reading is accomplished, ask seated class members to look at chapters one and two of Job and tell, one at a time, cardholders to move and where to move to get these events in correct chronological order. When they are fin-

ished, have the statements reread and comment on the cumulative effect of Job's woes.

Next, have ten 8 1/2-by-11-inch sheets with the words from Job 1:22 on one side and the letters (and exclamation mark) of the word *INTEGRITY!* respectively on the reverse. The sheets will have these obverse/reverse pairings: *In—I; all—N; this—T; Job—E; sinned—G; not—R; nor—I; charged—T; God—Y; foolishly—!* As you Plasti-Tak™ each sheet—words showing—onto the wall, have the class join you in saying the word on each. After all ten are up, have the class read the whole in unison. Then say that you have letters on the backs of these sheets, and ask the class to guess. As a correct letter is guessed, turn the sheet over. When someone knows and says the word *INTEGRITY*, turn all the letters over. Save the exclamation mark until someone comments on the "leftover" sheet (!). At that point, turn it over and comment, "Job demonstrated integrity with an exclamation mark!"

Establish groups of three to five people. Give each group this same written statement: "Look for the 'Secrets of Hope in Difficult Times' as seen in Job's life and reactions to great stress and distress." Give each group a different example on their assignment sheet; for example, "Be in the right relationship with God before bad things occur" (see 1:1); "Begin each day early with a time of worship to God" (see 1:5); "Be such a good example of righteousness that even Satan notices" (see 1:9); "Realize that God sends rain (and storms) on the just and the unjust" (see 2:10); "Recognize and reject bad advice" (see 2:9, 10); "Count on your friends to comfort; hope that they will" (see 2:11-13). After a time, ask for the principles they have concluded. Write them for all to see.

Into Life

Give each of your learners a copy of the following prayer/commitment statement paralleling Job's trials and integrity. Make certain they understand the four in relationship to Job's life. Suggest they initial each line as they consider the implications for their own daily lives.

"God, give me grace to honor You

_____ in all family problems

_____ in financial difficulty

_____ in personal illness and weakness

_____ in social conflict."

Let's Talk It Over

The questions on this page are designed to promote discussion of the lesson by the class and to encourage application of the lesson Scriptures. The answers provided are only discussion starters. Let your class talk it over from there.

1. How do we apply to our lives the things we discover about God and Satan in the early verses of Job 2?

God and Satan certainly saw Job from very different perspectives! Job 2 reveals that God wanted to celebrate Job's strengths; Satan, on the other hand, was determined to expose some fault. It is reasonable to expect both of these patterns in the lives of Christians today.

The next time you are tempted to "kick yourself" over some miserable failure from your past, that may be Satan at work. If that attack succeeds, you will be a less effective servant in God's kingdom. You can begin to fight back by asking yourself this question: "If I'm so worthless, then why did Jesus bother dying for me?" Then you'll begin to take on God's perspective.

2. Job was a person of integrity. If you were to look for someone of integrity today, what markers would you use to verify that you had identified such a person?

Today we might identify such a person through how he or she approaches the "small things" in life. If the speed limit is fifty-five, does that person drive fifty-nine? Does this person conveniently "forget" to declare certain income on a tax return? Do you know someone who always seems to have a good reason to be someplace else when it come time to wash the dishes and clean up after the church pitch-in dinner?

A drill instructor told some recruits in basic military training that they could discover their true character and integrity in the things they did when they knew no one else was looking. Jesus tells us that those who are "faithful over a few things" will be entrusted with "many things" (Matthew 25:14-23). A person of such stature is one we can trust with family members. This is the type we want as a church leader, or as a counselor to whom we can go in time of trouble.

3. Why do some Christians continue to be positive while living in deplorable conditions while others seem to crumble at small inconveniences?

Those who are able to recognize that all earthly conditions are temporary are most likely to remain positive. They are the ones able to mean it when they sing the old hymn that goes, "We have an anchor that keeps the soul, Steadfast and sure while the billows roll." Is it not true that the most hopeful Christians you know keep returning to this constant in their lives?

If we are able to keep our priorities in life straight, then any other "thing" that might challenge our hope will seem insignificant in the long run. "Seek ye first the kingdom of God" (Matthew 6:33) is still good advice!

4. Satan loves to create confusion and wrong thinking, as we see in the attitude of Job's wife. How does Satan still use this technique today?

Finding examples of how Satan uses confusion today is not at all difficult—unfortunately! Consider the confusing mix of truth and untruth, of the important and the unimportant, that causes a church to split. When intense emotions are added to that mix, confusion is multiplied tenfold!

Also very dangerous is the subtle way in which Satan tries to convince modern society that multiple religions are okay—that all religions lead to God. Satan uses clever sounding ideas such as "open-mindedness" and "tolerance" to promote this idea. But lurking behind such noble-sounding concepts is a rejection of God's narrow way (Matthew 7:13, 14). This trick of Satan goes clear back to the Garden of Eden (Genesis 3:1-5).

5. How could the caustic remark by Job's wife have been especially damaging to his emotions?

We have to wonder if her comment was not just as painful to Job as his boils! Today, spouses who will not support the involvement of their partners in church activities can be particularly painful situations. Someone asked a friend how his son was doing. The reply was, "He's sad—sad because he knows what's right but he's not living it. I think he would like to do what is right, but his wife wants nothing to do with the church."

Unfortunately, this type of sadness invades many homes. Children who rebel against their parents' spiritual teachings and siblings who chide the faithfulness of brothers and sisters can cause real strain in a family. It's not unusual for one partner in a marriage to be weaker in faith and spiritual maturity than the other. That weakness will become very obvious during a time of trial, as we see with Job's wife.

Integrity in Seeking God

DEVOTIONAL READING: Psalm 26.

BACKGROUND SCRIPTURE: Job 9:21-35; 13:1-27; 19:2-29; 23:2-17.

PRINTED TEXT: Job 9:32-35; 13:20-24; 19:25-27; 23:10-12.

Job 9:32-35

32 For he is not a man, as I am, that I should answer him, and we should come together in judgment.

33 Neither is there any daysman betwixt us, that might lay his hand upon us both.

34 Let him take his rod away from me, and let not his fear terrify me:

35 Then would I speak, and not fear him; but it is not so with me.

Job 13:20-24

20 Only do not two things unto me; then I will not hide myself from thee.

21 Withdraw thine hand far from me: and let not thy dread make me afraid.

22 Then call thou, and I will answer: or let me speak, and answer thou me.

23 How many are mine iniquities and sins? Make me to know my transgression and my sin.

24 Wherefore hidest thou thy face, and holdest me for thine enemy?

Job 19:25-27

25 For I know that my Redeemer liveth, and that he shall stand at the latter day upon the earth:

26 And though after my skin worms destroy this body, yet in my flesh shall I see God:

27 Whom I shall see for myself, and mine eyes shall behold, and not another; though my reins be consumed within me.

Job 23:10-12

10 But he knoweth the way that I take: when he hath tried me, I shall come forth as gold.

11 My foot hath held his steps, his way have I kept, and not declined.

12 Neither have I gone back from the commandment of his lips; I have esteemed the words of his mouth more than my necessary food.

GOLDEN TEXT: Surely I would speak to the Almighty, and I desire to reason with God.—Job 13:3.

Lessons From Life
Unit 1: Job: Integrity in Times of Testing
(Lessons 5-8)

Lesson Aims

After participating in this lesson, each student should be able to:

1. Tell what Job said he wanted from God in the midst of his suffering.

2. Compare Job's need for a mediator with the need that is fulfilled by Jesus as our Mediator.

3. Praise God that we have Jesus Christ to make intercession for us.

Lesson Outline

Introduction

A. "Wait 'Til We Get to Court"

One of my sons-in-law is a police officer in a large city in Colorado. He has many interesting stories about his encounters with people who are breaking the law. When he was a rookie officer, he would often spend his days in a patrol car stopping people who were speeding. Because of his youthful appearance, many would try to intimidate him by promising to show up in court to present their cases. They would often say, "Wait 'til we get to court!" In very few cases did those folks actually appear to plead their cases. In this week's lesson we will find just the opposite in a man who desperately seeks the opportunity to appear before God and plead his case.

B. Lesson Background

Job was a figure of some note in his corner of the world (Job 1:3). Upon hearing of his unfortunate situation, three men who knew him decided to meet with him and attempt to console him (2:11). Job's physical condition alarmed his friends. They sat with him for a week before even beginning to speak (2:13). Finally Job spoke, pouring out his anguish in great torrents of despair (chapter 3). Job was overcome. He said he wished that he had never been born (3:3), or that he had died at birth (3:11). Job cried out that the thing he dreaded most in life had happened (3:25). He had no consolation—no peace (3:26).

At this point Job's friends began to speak. This starts a cycle of back-and-forth discussions. Eliphaz and Bildad, two of Job's friends, address him three times. Another friend by the name of Zophar addresses Job twice. Each of their arguments is countered by Job.

This week's lesson records Job's responses to four discourses from his friends. Two of the discourses are from Bildad, one is from Zophar, and one is from Eliphaz. We know virtually nothing of these men. They are not characters who appear in any other Biblical texts. They obviously cared about Job. They obviously thought they could help. Their "help," however, only deepened Job's despair and heightened his frustration (16:2).

I. Desire to Plead a Case
(Job 9:32-35)

As we come to Job 9, we find that Bildad has just accused Job of charging God with injustice (8:3). Bildad also contends that Job's children have lost their lives for their sins (8:4). This is fuel on the fire of Job's anguish. In this moment of great despair his friend essentially says, "Your kids got what they deserved." No loving father needs to hear something like that. Bildad insists that Job can right himself with God by becoming pure and blameless (8:6). This, of course, implies that Job has been otherwise. Now Job responds.

A. Thwarted by God's Nature (v. 32)

32. For he is not a man, as I am, that I should answer him, and we should come together in judgment.

Job already has argued against Bildad's theory that he (Job) has not been pure and blameless (see 9:21). The problem, as Job sees it, is that he cannot appear before God to present his case. There are many problems. The first is that God is not like a human judge. *He is not a man* who sits at a bench and dispenses justice. Job is distressed because he cannot find a courtroom in which to appear! Job understands that God is not confined to flesh and bone. Job knows that he and God are not equals. Job might have said, "If only God were a man so I could talk to Him face-to-face!"

B. Thwarted by Lack of an Intercessor (vv. 33, 34)

33. Neither is there any daysman betwixt us, that might lay his hand upon us both.

Job is not only frustrated by his inability to meet God face-to-face, he also is frustrated that there is no one to act as a judicial middleman. A *daysman* is an arbitrator or mediator who acts as an intercessor or "go-between" to help solve a dispute between two parties (cf. Deuteronomy 5:5; Galatians 3:20).

Job wants someone who can see his side of the story. Although unspoken, the idea of a mediator or arbitrator (some versions say "umpire") appeals to Job because such a go-between also can explain what has happened to Job from God's point of view. Job wants to give and receive information. But Job understands that no such mediator exists. The thought of someone placing his *hand upon* God and explaining His ways is, of course, ludicrous. Even so, that is Job's fervent hope (see also Job 16:19-21).

The great blessing of the Christian life is in knowing that the Mediator Job longs for has made Himself known. Jesus Christ is that Mediator (1 Timothy 2:5). Jesus is perfectly capable of representing us to the Father because Jesus is fully God (John 1:1; 10:30; 14:9-11).

Jesus is also uniquely qualified to be our High Priest because His sacrifice accomplished what the sacrifice of animals could not. His blood did not merely forestall God's judgment. His blood actually has the power to remove the stain of sin from the human soul (Hebrews 9:11-14).

We realize that no one stands before God as blameless. All people are sinners (Romans 3:23). No one meets God's standard of perfect righteousness. Thus, our view of our intercessor is different from that of Job. We do not need one who will present a call for justice on our behalf. Justice is precisely what we do not want! If justice were meted out to us, we would have no hope. Our Mediator is One who pleads our case as those who have been justified by His sacrifice on our behalf. His blood has covered our sin. His

death paid the penalty that God's righteousness demanded. Praise God for such a powerful and loving Mediator! [See question #1, page 168.]

34. Let him take his rod away from me, and let not his fear terrify me.

Job's frustration bubbles over into a cry of fear and dread. If there were an intercessor, he could explain Job's innocence. Surely then God would then quit punishing Job! But there is no such mediator or arbitrator. Does Job think God is continuing to punish him because He is unaware of Job's innocence? Whatever the case, Job is tired of living in *fear*.

From the beginning of time people have associated divine blessings and curses with their behavior. In last week's lesson, we noted John 9:1, 2 in this regard. Ancient people see things such as droughts or fires as divine punishment for evil. If one reads the entire book of Job, it seems that Job's friends are trying to persuade him that some evil in his life has brought about his suffering. Jesus opposed this kind of thinking in Luke 13:1-5.

We should also remember that while there are indeed built-in consequences for many sins, not everyone who sins will automatically suffer those consequences. Some people smoke and never get cancer. Indeed, Bible writers noticed that evil people seemed to prosper while decent people suffered (cf. Ecclesiastes 8:14; Jeremiah 12:1; Malachi 3:14, 15). This is all part of living in a fallen world where God has allowed free will.

The Bible does speak of God's correction or chastisement (Psalm 89:32; 94:12; Proverbs 3:11, 12; Lamentations 3:1). God's punishment can be an act of loving discipline (Revelation 3:19). Parents know that correcting children is not always easy, but is a necessary part of their upbringing. Repeating Proverbs 3:11, the writer of Hebrews 12:5 reminds us that we are not to take the Lord's

---

How to Say It

BILDAD. *Bill*-dad.

CORINTHIANS. Kor-*in*-thee-unz (*th* as in *thin*).

DEUTERONOMY. Due-ter-*ahn*-uh-me.

ECCLESIASTES. Ik-*leez*-ee-*as*-teez (strong accent on *as*).

ELIPHAZ. *El*-ih-faz.

GALATIANS. Guh-*lay*-shunz.

HEBREWS. *Hee*-brews.

ISAIAH. Eye-*zay*-uh.

JEREMIAH. Jair-uh-*my*-uh.

LAMENTATIONS. Lam-en-*tay*-shunz.

MALACHI. *Mal*-uh-kye.

ZOPHAR. *Zo*-far.

discipline lightly. God is not anxious to punish us. He is not "quick with the whip." His discipline and correction are for our benefit (Hebrews 12:6-11). It is to keep us from further damage and eternal harm.

But remember: Job is not being punished. However, Job thinks that that is what is happening. His incorrect assumption adds to his misery and frustration. Do we ever fall into this same trap?

LIVING IN FEAR

There is a section along the North Carolina coast called *Cape Fear*. There are several explanations offered for this unusual name. Some say the name was given because early settlers feared attack by Native American Indians. Some say that they feared the pirates who once roamed that coast. Others say it was a more generalized fear, that the broad estuary of the river left them vulnerable to invasion.

Today the only thing you have to fear is the traffic in Wilmington or sunburn on Wrightsville Beach! Perhaps the best explanation is that it was not originally named *Cape Fear* at all—that it was actually named *Cape Fair* and some mapmaker misread it.

Certainly it is true that those who decide to live in fear will do so no matter how fair the circumstances. Of course, we need a healthy respect for danger. Living without fear does not demand that we forget to be prudent and careful. But it does mean that we should never let fear dominate out lives. To fear God means that we respect Him and show Him reverence.

It has been said that Abraham Lincoln's Bible naturally fell open to Psalm 34, suggesting that he may often have turned there. Psalm 34:4 states, "I sought the Lord, and he heard me, and delivered me from all my fears." Of course, our love is

never perfect, but God's love *is* perfect. A loving God does not want us to live in fear.   —R. C. S.

C. Thwarted by Reality (v. 35)

35. Then would I speak, and not fear him; but it is not so with me.

Job has a bad case of the "if onlys." If only there were an intercessor! If only he were not so afraid! If only he could appear before God! If only he could *speak* to God face-to-face (cf. Exodus 33:11)! [See question #2, page 168.] Job knows, however, that these are pipe dreams. As much as he might wish these things to be true, they are *not* so. It seems, at least at this point, that it does not occur to Job that he can speak to God. Even from the middle of the city dump, he can cry out to God and be heard. Job incorrectly assumes that God is punishing him and is, therefore, unwilling to listen to him.

Incorrect assumptions about God still separate many people from Him today. That is why knowing and understanding the Bible is so important. When we study God's Word, we have knowledge, not assumptions. How spiritually priceless!

II. Desire to Preserve a Standing (Job 13:20-24)

In Job 12 and 13 we find Job responding to Zophar (Job 11). Zophar has been rather harsh with Job. Like the others, Zophar seemed to believe that if Job is suffering, he must have sinned. Zophar seemed to think Job has sinned so grievously that he is not being punished enough (11:6). He wondered why Job would think God should ignore his wickedness (11:11). He accused Job of being vain (11:12). He counseled Job to confess and repent of his wickedness (11:12-14). [See question #3, page 168.] Job's reply to this nonsense begins with sarcasm (12:2) and moves to issues of Job's fears.

A. Job's Fear of Fear (vv. 20, 21)

20. Only do not two things unto me; then I will not hide myself from thee.

Living in fear is stressful. Job lives in fear of continuing disasters. He wants to *hide* from God (cf. Job 6:4). With a slightly different understanding of a Hebrew vowel, the first *not* in this verse can be translated as "O God." With this translation, Job is saying that he wants God to grant him just *two things*. Then Job will come out of hiding and present himself to God. We will see what two things Job requests in the following verses.

21. Withdraw thine hand far from me: and let not thy dread make me afraid.

The first of two things Job wants God to do is simply to leave him alone. Fear does strange

---

Home Daily Bible Readings

Monday, Jan. 5—Vindicate Me, O Lord (Psalm 26:1-7)

Tuesday, Jan. 6—I Walk in My Integrity (Psalm 26:8-12)

Wednesday, Jan. 7—In Trouble I Call on You (Psalm 86:1-7)

Thursday, Jan. 8—Job Wishes to Speak to God (Job 9:32-35)

Friday, Jan. 9—Let Me Speak, and You Reply (Job 13:20-24)

Saturday, Jan. 10—I Know That My Redeemer Lives (Job 19:23-28)

Sunday, Jan. 11—He Knows the Way I Take (Job 23:8-12)

things to people. Job is *afraid* of continuing to live in such fear of God that he feels the need to hide (v. 20). President Roosevelt rallied the U.S. with his declaration, "The only thing we have to fear is fear itself." First John 4:18 says that fear is cast out by perfect love. Christians should have an appropriate respect for God, but not a paralyzing fear. Experiencing God's love removes fear.

B. Job's Fear of Silence (v. 22)

22. Then call thou, and I will answer: or let me speak, and answer thou me.

Job's second request is communication. He wants the opportunity to talk to God. If God will *call*, Job will *answer*. Anyone who has been maligned yearns for the opportunity to *speak* and clear the record. Job fears silence!

C. Job's Fear of Ignorance (vv. 23, 24)

23. How many are mine iniquities and sins? Make me to know my transgression and my sin.

Job argues that if God would just tell him what he has done wrong, he could make it right. Job desires a list with categories, dates, and places. Most of us do not have Job's problem. We are all too familiar with our *sins!*

24. Wherefore hidest thou thy face, and holdest me for thine enemy?

Job also fears that he has lost his standing with God. Job wants God to know that he is not His *enemy!* Even though he did not know the nature of his sin, whatever it might be it is not rebellion against God. And Job has not become God's enemy in response to his (Job's) travails. Job wants to preserve his standing before God. He does not want that standing diminished by fear, silence, or ignorance.

III. Desire to Preserve a Legacy (Job 19:25-27)

In Job 18 we find Job responding to a second discourse from Bildad. Bildad saw Job's rebuttals as refusals to acknowledge that he has been caught in his sins (18:8-10). Bildad has also referred to a man's legacy (18:17). In chapter 19 we see that Job is certainly one who does not want his legacy tarnished!

A. Job Believes in His Redeemer (v. 25)

25. For I know that my Redeemer liveth, and that he shall stand at the latter day upon the earth.

Some speculate that Job thinks he may die, and he wants to reaffirm his ultimate trust in God. No matter what has happened, Job's faith in God remains unshaken. Job believes God ultimately will vindicate him.

Have events in your life shaken your confidence in God? Do you believe Romans 8:28? Is your faith as solid as that of Job? What will your own spiritual legacy be?

A SOURCE OF COMFORT

When former British Prime Minister Winston Churchill died, he was not buried in Westminster Abbey as might have been expected. Certainly he was important enough to have been buried there with others who greatly influenced the nation. But he chose in advance to be buried in the little village cemetery at Bladon, near his birthplace and where his family members were buried.

One enters the cemetery through a covered archway called a *lych-gate*. The gateway is covered as a place for funeral processions to wait until the minister can come out of the church and lead the way. As one leaves the cemetery and passes again under the lych-gate, a quotation from the Bible is visible, engraved across the top of the arch. It is a verse from this lesson: "I KNOW THAT MY REDEEMER LIVETH."

What a comfort to any Christian family leaving the grave of one they loved! What a comfort to us! It is remarkable that Job had this confidence long before the promises of Jesus in John 14, long before Jesus Himself rose from the dead. If Job could believe it, with the limited information he had, surely we can believe it all the more.

The knowledge that our Redeemer lives is the basis for our confidence that we, too, shall survive the grave. It is not surprising that this grand text has found its way into sacred music and into many sermons. It is a glorious affirmation that gives us comfort when we grieve and gives us hope when we contemplate our own deaths.

—R. C. S.

B. Job Believes in Life After Death (v. 26)

26. And though after my skin worms destroy this body, yet in my flesh shall I see God.

In the Old Testament there are just a few affirmations of life after death, and this is one of them. Job not only believes in such life, he even indicates a belief in a bodily resurrection (cf. Isaiah 26:19; Daniel 12:2). The New Testament clearly establishes the promise of this resurrection (Acts 24:15; Romans 8:23; 1 Corinthians 15:12-55; etc.). Job's legacy is that of a man who believes God can do anything, including making the dead live again.

C. Job Believes His Longing Will Be Fulfilled (v. 27)

27. Whom I shall see for myself, and mine eyes shall behold, and not another; though my reins be consumed within me.

Job is convinced that he will one day *see* God face-to-face. That meeting will fulfill the longing of Job's heart. Job understands that he may not get to have that meeting with God right away, but he believes that God truly knows his heart. God will not condemn him unjustly. Most of all, Job simply yearns to see God. He wants people to remember that yearning. [See question #4, page 168.]

IV. Desire to Be Acknowledged (Job 23:10-12)

In chapter 22 we find Job confronting the arguments of Eliphaz. Eliphaz has accused Job of social injustice, of being rich and exploiting the poor (22:6-9). He also seems to accuse Job of treasuring his gold and silver more than he treasures God (22:23-26). [See question #5, page 168.]

A. Good as Gold (v. 10)

10. But he knoweth the way that I take: when he hath tried me, I shall come forth as gold.

Job turns Eliphaz's accusation on its ear. Job does not treasure precious earthly metal, but he wants to be seen as a treasured asset in God's eyes. Job knows that God treasures faith. Job may not understand why he is suffering, but he believes that God will, in the end, acknowledge his ultimate faithfulness.

B. On the Straight and Narrow (v. 11)

11. My foot hath held his steps, his way have I kept, and not declined.

The Bible often uses a road, path, or *way* metaphors for the godly life (e.g., Psalm 16:11; 119:105). Job knows that he has stayed on the right path. His footsteps have not wavered. He

My foot hath held his steps, his way have I kept. –Job 23:11

Visual for lesson 6

Use this visual to illustrate Job 23:11, challenging your learners to watch their own "feet."

has not taken any detours from God. He has not strayed from the path of righteousness.

Jesus speaks of two paths in Matthew 7:13, 14. One leads to life. The other leads to destruction. Have you chosen the path that leads to life? Are you leading others to that path?

C. Recognizing the Source of Life (v. 12)

12. Neither have I gone back from the commandment of his lips; I have esteemed the words of his mouth more than my necessary food.

Job continues to profess his innocence. He also acknowledges his complete dependence upon God. God's instruction is as necessary for Job's spiritual life as *food* is for his physical life.

In turn, Job wants God to acknowledge his faith—a faith that is completely dependent on God. Job is no longer acknowledged as wealthy and influential. He is no longer acknowledged as the father of a large family. But he clings to the hope of being acknowledged as God's faithful servant. This is one of the reasons the accusations of his friends wound him so grievously.

Some time later, God will tell Moses, "Man doth not live by bread only, but by every word that proceedeth out of the mouth of the Lord" (Deuteronomy 8:3). Jesus will repeat much the same thing (Matthew 4:4). Job understood this truth centuries before!

Conclusion

A. Doing Things the Right Way

Most people have heard the saying, "There is a right way and a wrong way to do everything." Job, as far as he is able, seeks God the right way. Job overwhelmingly upholds God as just, although we notice just a couple of places where Job begins to question that justice (see Job 19:7 and, for next week, 27:2). These can be explained as Job grasping for straws in the midst of his enormous pain. God will correct Job's slip-ups in His response (40:8), but overall God will praise Job for speaking "of me the thing that is right" (42:7). Even though Job complained to God, he did it with integrity.

B. Prayer

Father, increase our faith! Help us endure even when we do not understand. Help us remember your fairness, even when things seem unfair. When we are tempted to complain about life, remind us of the unfairness of Jesus' sufferings. May we trust you more. In Jesus' name, amen.

C. Thought to Remember

Life's trials must not compromise our integrity in seeking and acknowledging God.

Learning by Doing

This page contains an alternative lesson plan emphasizing learning activities.
Classes desiring such student involvement will find these suggestions helpful.

Learning Goals

After participating in this lesson, each student will be able to:

1. Tell what Job said he wanted from God in the midst of his suffering.

2. Compare Job's need for a mediator with the need that is fulfilled by Jesus as our Mediator.

3. Praise God that we have Jesus Christ to make intercession for us.

Into the Lesson

Before class get a large sheet of newsprint and felt-tip pens. Cut the newsprint into fairly narrow lengthwise sections to create a narrow strip of paper like a banner, suitable for display.

Assign class members to groups of three to five. Distribute banner paper and pens to each group. Pose the following questions for thought: "When do you feel the closest to God? When praying? When in church? When deeply hurt? When worshiping? When listening to music? When outdoors in nature? Why do you think that is?" Allow three minutes for the group members to jot down ideas on their banners and decorate them in any way they wish. Then have each group share some of their ideas or experiences. Display each banner in the classroom.

Next say, "In spite of all the negatives Job experienced, he never gave up. What a testimony!"

Into the Word

State: "The Scriptures in this lesson contain some of the most significant thoughts Job had regarding seeking the Lord." Establish four small groups to rewrite the following texts in their own words: Job 9:32-35; Job 13:20-24; Job 19:25-27; Job 23:10-12. Each group is to write descriptive conclusions of Job's feelings, what Job says about his friends, and what he asks from God.

As the leader, make sure each group includes the following ideas:

In Job 9, Job wished he could come to trial with God, so that he could prove his innocence. In Job 13, Job begged God to withdraw His terrifying hand and explain his sin or give him an opportunity to plead his innocence. In Job 19, Job affirmed that his Redeemer lives, with confidence that one day he would experience that truth (a clear Old Testament affirmation of life after death). In Job 23, Job reaffirmed that his testing would prove him to be faithful.

Upon completion of each group's paraphrase, allow each to share its completed section. Time permitting, allow discussion to continue.

Say to the class, "It has been said that 'The person who acts as his own lawyer has a fool for a client.' In a real sense, Job was in the difficult place of having to represent himself legally before God. (And any such representation has a built-in foolishness!) How is the Christian advantaged by having Christ to represent him or her before God?" Assign the following Scriptures to be read aloud. After each is read, ask, "What do you hear from this that gives us an advantage over Job and for which we need to praise God?" Scriptures: Matthew 3:16, 17; John 15:13-16; John 17:24; Hebrews 4:14-16; 1 Peter 3:21b, 22; 1 John 2:1, 2.

Into Life

This activity will help students relate Job's confession of faith in 19:25 to their own life situations. Write these instructions and show them:

Discuss this question: "Can you say with Job, 'I know my Redeemer lives'?"

Sing as a group the hymn, "Redeemed," especially verse three. Consider the meaning of the word *Redeemer*, and name an attitude or habit you want Christ to redeem you from right now.

Discuss the following: "If Job, from his perspective, could know with assurance that his Redeemer was alive, what is keeping you from the same assurance that your Redeemer can free you?"

Ask the groups who did the paraphrase activity to discuss these issues together. Provide every class member with paper or a 3 x 5 card for those who need them. Ask each one in the class to rephrase the paraphrase to show what his or her love for God has caused him or her to do.

Then ask each group to pray for the power of Christ to cover the current situations in their lives. Tell them you will lead them in directed prayer by using phrases from Hebrews 7:25-28. As you read the following phrases one at a time, pause to allow brief prayers of thanksgiving: (1) Jesus "is able . . . to save [us] to the uttermost"; (2) Our high priest is "holy, harmless, undefiled, separate from sinners, and made higher than the heavens"; (3) He "needeth not daily . . . to offer up sacrifice . . . for this he did once, when he offered up himself"; (4) Some advocates "have infirmity," but He is "consecrated for evermore."

Let's Talk It Over

The questions on this page are designed to promote discussion of the lesson by the class and to encourage application of the lesson Scriptures. The answers provided are only discussion starters. Let your class talk it over from there.

1. Job wanted to declare his case to the Judge of the universe. How is Christ similar to and different from a lawyer who presents a case before a judge on another's behalf?

A lawyer can be called upon to defend either the innocent or the guilty. How he or she chooses to defend a client may be built either upon whatever evidence exists or upon finding loopholes in the law. In our own case, we know that we are all guilty (Romans 3:23); it is the evidence that says so. And there are no loopholes in God's law!

For those who accept Jesus as Savior He becomes the One who pleads our case in God's court. Unlike most earthly defense attorneys, Jesus admits our guilt to the court. But then He points out that He already has paid the penalty at Calvary so we can go free.

2. Like Job, some people spend much time living in a theoretical world of "But what if . . . " or "If only. . . ." How do we help people move on to more productive thinking?

The "if only" kind of thinking is a natural emotional reaction for people who have suffered a tragedy. A person's mind gets stuck in this infinite loop when trying to cope. At the start, the most important thing a friend can do is simply to "be there" and not say too much. Don't run off at the mouth as Job's friends did! "In the multitude of words there wanteth not sin: but he that refraineth his lips is wise" (Proverbs 10:19).

After the time of the shock has passed—perhaps several months—the friend may still be stuck in "if only" thinking and talk. If so, then he or she probably is not functioning very well in other areas of life. When the time is right, you could gently say something like "I notice that you seem to be stuck in 'if only.' What can I do to help you move past this?" Notice that you are not "giving advice"!

3. Job's clumsy friends essentially said, "You got what you deserved." How do we sort out the punishment caused by sin, the testings that come because of Satanic attack, and sufferings from random occurrences? Why should we even try?

Often there is a direct correlation between certain types of sin and adverse consequences. We all know about the health problems that can

come from abusing our bodies with alcohol, tobacco, or food. On the other hand, we need to realize that bad things often happen to godly people because we live in a world filled with sin and everyone suffers the consequences.

Suffering that we can trace to intentional sin can show us an area where we need to confront someone. However, we should be very sure that we know the facts before we make accusations of sinful conduct! Confronting sinful behavior should be designed to protect the purity of the church (1 Corinthians 5) and restore the erring one to the faith (2 Corinthians 2:5-11). We must be careful to follow the Biblical plan of church discipline (Matthew 18:15-17, etc.). And, of course, we should make sure that we're not guilty of the same offense (Matthew 7:1-5).

4. If you were to write an autobiography, would a reader be able to say of you, "This person really lived life with eternity in mind!" Why, or why not?

Ideally, every aspect of our lives should be lived with "the afterlife" in view. We are always in the shadow of eternity!

We begin to develop an eternal perspective when we realize that so many things we do have eternal implications. Each day is full of choices, and the choices are not always clear as "good" and "bad." Sometimes the choices are more like "good," "better," and "best." Those having an eternal perspective will make different choices from those who don't. Even if we don't write an autobiography, people will be able to "read" our perspective in the choices we make.

5. Job's three friends were undoubtedly well-meaning in their counsel. What did they do wrong, and what could they have done better to ease Job's pain?

The friends started out on the right foot by simply "being there" and not talking too much (Job 2:13). But then they became masters in analysis—inaccurate analysis. Suggesting that Job's woes were caused by sin or a vain attitude toward his riches was a conclusion not based on any hard evidence. Wise counselors will listen and look at the facts before speaking. Job's friends would have been of much greater help if they had stuck with their original actions in Job 2:13.

Integrity in Everyday Life

DEVOTIONAL READING: Psalm 15.

BACKGROUND SCRIPTURE: Job 27:1-6; 31.

PRINTED TEXT: Job 27:2-5; 31:5-15, 24-28.

Job 27:2-5

2 As God liveth, who hath taken away my judgment; and the Almighty, who hath vexed my soul;

3 All the while my breath is in me, and the spirit of God is in my nostrils;

4 My lips shall not speak wickedness, nor my tongue utter deceit.

5 God forbid that I should justify you: till I die I will not remove mine integrity from me.

Job 31:5-15, 24-28

5 If I have walked with vanity, or if my foot hath hasted to deceit;

6 Let me be weighed in an even balance, that God may know mine integrity.

7 If my step hath turned out of the way, and mine heart walked after mine eyes, and if any blot hath cleaved to mine hands;

8 Then let me sow, and let another eat; yea, let my offspring be rooted out.

9 If mine heart have been deceived by a woman, or if I have laid wait at my neighbor's door;

10 Then let my wife grind unto another, and let others bow down upon her.

11 For this is a heinous crime; yea, it is an iniquity to be punished by the judges.

12 For it is a fire that consumeth to destruction, and would root out all mine increase.

13 If I did despise the cause of my manservant or of my maidservant, when they contended with me;

14 What then shall I do when God riseth up? And when he visiteth, what shall I answer him?

15 Did not he that made me in the womb make him? And did not one fashion us in the womb?

· · · · · · · · · · · · ·

24 If I have made gold my hope, or have said to the fine gold, Thou art my confidence;

25 If I rejoiced because my wealth was great, and because mine hand had gotten much;

26 If I beheld the sun when it shined, or the moon walking in brightness;

27 And my heart hath been secretly enticed, or my mouth hath kissed my hand:

28 This also were an iniquity to be punished by the judge: for I should have denied the God that is above.

GOLDEN TEXT: All the while my breath is in me, and the spirit of God is in my nostrils; my lips shall not speak wickedness, nor my tongue utter deceit.—Job 27:3, 4.

Lessons From Life
Unit 1: Job: Integrity in Times of Testing
(Lessons 5-8)

Lesson Aims

After participating in this lesson, each student should be able to:

1. Summarize Job's arguments that he had been falsely accused.

2. Explain how truth is the best defense against false accusations.

3. Give a specific example of how a person overcame accusations with the truth.

Lesson Outline

INTRODUCTION

    A. "Whatever You Want to Hear"

    B. Lesson Background

  I. THE TESTED MAN (Job 27:2-5)

    A. Speaking From Pain (vv. 2-4)

      Telling the Truth

    B. Admitting No Wrong (v. 5)

 II. THE TEFLON MAN (Job 31:5-15, 24-28)

    A. "Hypocrisy" Won't Stick (vv. 5-8)

    B. "Adultery" Won't Stick (vv. 9-12)

    C. "Injustice" Won't Stick (vv. 13-15)

    D. "Idolatry" Won't Stick (vv. 24-28)

      Gold or God?

CONCLUSION

    A. Resisting the Pressure

    B. Prayer

    C. Thought to Remember

Introduction

A. "Whatever You Want to Hear"

The proliferation of television cable channels has brought some great old movies to the small screen. Some of the cops-and-robbers movies have scenes in them that are very similar to one another. A suspect is brought into the police station for interrogation. The suspect is put under bright lights and given "the third degree." The policemen blow cigarette smoke in the suspect's face as they play "good cop, bad cop."

Finally, exhausted and desperate, the suspect blurts out, "Whatever you want to hear, I'll say it!" The movie plot then usually hinges on the truth or falsehood of the suspect's confession. Another very dramatic scene may play out in the courtroom when the suspect recants his confession and accuses his interrogators of coercion.

Job's friends were definitely guilty of coercion. They did not use bright lights and cigarette smoke to weaken Job's resolve, but their constant accusations take a toll. Can Job remain steadfast in pleading his innocence? Will Job maintain his integrity in the midst of such vile assaults on his character?

B. Lesson Background

The text for this week's lesson records portions of Job's final discourse to his three friends. After "The words of Job are ended" in Job 31:40, Job will not speak again until he addresses the Lord in chapter 42 (included in next week's lesson). Job has heard three discourses from Eliphaz, three discourses from Bildad, and two discourses from Zophar. These discourses, filled with accusation and acrimony, could have worn Job down. A lesser man might have simply thrown up his hands and said, "Okay. Okay. Whatever you say. I'm guilty." Not Job!

Job responded to Bildad's last discourse (Job 25) with a resounding acknowledgment of God's power (Job 26). Job's faith is intact. Job will not, however, capitulate to his friends' requests for confessions of guilt.

I. The Tested Man
(Job 27:2-5)

A. Speaking From Pain (vv. 2-4)

2. As God liveth, who hath taken away my judgment; and the Almighty, who hath vexed my soul.

Job now has had to endure three cycles of conversation with Eliphaz, Bildad, and Zophar—Job's "miserable comforters" (16:2). The oath "As God liveth," familiar in Eastern custom, is seen as an invitation for God to strike the speaker dead if he does not tell the truth. This is a desperate measure to persuade Job's accusers of the veracity of his denials. He's "had it" with them! They apparently get the message because after this response we hear no more from those three.

Job does not feel that he has been given his "day in court." He has been denied the appropriate opportunity for just judgment. He will not accuse God of some fault in finding him guilty.

Job does, however, call out to God and decry his lack of opportunity to defend himself. The God *who hath taken away my judgment* is the God whom Job believes has denied him justice (cf. 19:7).

Job does not deny that he is suffering and *vexed*. He cries out to know why he is suffering. He mistakenly attributes his suffering solely to God. It apparently does not occur to him that

Satan could be involved in bringing about such agony.

People still react as Job did. When something bad happens, they immediately question God. Why do people never give proper credit to Satan? He is the maker of mischief and sower of sorrow in people's souls. [See question #1, page 176.]

3. All the while my breath is in me, and the spirit of God is in my nostrils.

Job's steely resolve is expressed in these words. Even to his last *breath* he will remain steadfast in his denials. Job understands that God is his Creator (e.g., Job 26:7-14). It is God who has breathed into man and given life (Genesis 2:7; Job 12:10). Even though Job does not understand why God is permitting such evil to come to him, Job will acknowledge God as the One who created and sustained his life.

4. My lips shall not speak wickedness, nor my tongue utter deceit.

Job has not and will not lie! The irony of Job's situation is that in order to please his friends, he would have to tell lies. He would have to become what they falsely accuse him of being.

There are many ways for a person's speech to become wicked. The New Testament warns about the many evils of the tongue (James 3:1-12). Are you ever guilty of slander, gossip, or *deceit?* Is God honored in your language? Is it sometimes tempting to combat lies told about us by lying about the teller of those lies? Job staunchly refuses to commit evil by speaking that which is not true.

TELLING THE TRUTH

Not so long ago a very prominent American official admitted to lying under oath. Someone wrote to a newsmagazine defending him and said, "Let's be honest. Everybody lies." What an obviously self-contradictory statement!

The first half of the statement we can all agree with. We should be honest. We do not always have to be brutally frank, however—that could be hurtful. But we do have to be honest.

The second statement in the quotation is, of course, wrong. It is simply not true that everybody lies. It used to be said of an honest man, "His word is his bond." It meant that he did not have to swear to tell the truth—he always told the truth. He did not have to pledge a sum of money to guarantee that what he said was the truth.

We can depend on the truthfulness of Jesus who "did no sin, neither was guile found in his mouth" (1 Peter 2:22). We can depend on the truthfulness of His apostles. The world needs to be able to depend on the truthfulness of believers. We do it to be like Christ. We do it because

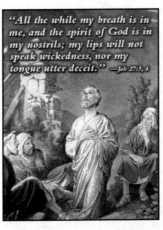

"All the while my breath is in me, and the spirit of God is in my nostrils; my lips will not speak wickedness, nor my tongue utter deceit." —Job 27:3, 4

Visual for lesson 7

This illustration of verses 3 and 4 will challenge your learners to consider their own loyalties.

we know the ultimate destiny of all liars (Revelation 21:8). We do it because we know that "lying lips are abomination to the Lord" (Proverbs 12:22). If Job in his day could keep his tongue from deceit, surely we who have both the example of Christ and the power of the Holy Spirit can do it, too.   —R. C. S.

B. Admitting No Wrong (v. 5)

5. God forbid that I should justify you: till I die I will not remove mine integrity from me.

The *you* in this verse is plural as Job addresses all three friends. They have not succeeded. Job will not admit that they are accurate in their portrayals of his character. They want Job to be contrite. Instead, he is stubborn. The more they accuse Job, the more vigorously he digs in his heels. He will "stick to his story" until he dies!

Some people admire Job's resolve, but question his pragmatism. Job can end the whole thing by saying, "Yeah, you guys are right!" Then they can leave the dump, go to Job's house for some pie and coffee, and Job can send them back home. At least he then will relieve himself of the suffering of listening to their harping. To do so, however, would compromise his *integrity.* Job is not that kind of fellow. Truth means more to him than convenience. Can that be said of you? [See question #2, page 176.]

II. The Teflon Man
(Job 31:5-15, 24-28)
A. "Hypocrisy" Won't Stick (vv. 5-8)

5, 6. If I have walked with vanity, or if my foot hath hasted to deceit; let me be weighed in an even balance, that God may know mine integrity.

Job's refusal to acknowledge any wrongdoing leaves him vulnerable to accusations of hypocrisy. How can anyone be so perfect? A character in Shakespeare's play *Hamlet* was suspicious of another who "doth protest too much." Often the more guilt a person bears, the louder he or she proclaims innocence. We know this is not the case with Job, however, because of what God says about him in Job 1:8.

So Job still defends his *integrity* with every attack. His "walk" with the Lord is true and unerring and he again pleads for the opportunity to prove that he is genuine in thought and action. Many goods today are preweighed on electronic scales. But in ancient times *balance* scales were part of everyday life. Several Old Testament passages note the Lord's view of honest scales, plus His own actions in weighing motives and value (see Psalm 62:9; Proverbs 11:1; 16:2; 20:23; 21:2; Isaiah 40:12). Job earlier alluded to balance scales in describing the depth of his agony (Job 6:2, 3).

Job wants the opportunity to vindicate himself by having God weigh him in an accurate scale to determine the genuineness of his life. He is not a hypocrite. His *integrity* is not an act! [See question #3, page 176.]

7. If my step hath turned out of the way, and mine heart walked after mine eyes, and if any blot hath cleaved to mine hands.

Even under intense cross-examination, Job has not "changed his story." He has walked the straight and narrow. He has not let his *heart* be led by his *eyes* (cf. Job 31:1). His friends have spoken abstractly about God's punishment of evildoers, but they haven't been able to point specifically to any area where Job's hands are sullied by the filth of corruption (6:24, 30). Job's moral résumé is pretty impressive!

Most of us know that we could not say what Job said. We have not always walked God's path. We may have been on God's path at one time, but we found lots of detours. Most of us have been enticed by things we have seen, and we

have let our desires run ahead of our discretion and dedication to God. Most of us have "dirty hands." The businessperson who sings loudly in church on Sunday and cuts under-the-table deals on Monday cannot make Job's claim. That businessperson is the poster child for hypocrisy. Job is ready to have all his actions weighed in whatever perfect balance scales God has.

8. Then let me sow, and let another eat; yea, let my offspring be rooted out.

In being willing to *let another eat* what he has sown, Job is ready to pay a heavy penalty if he is guilty of any of the offenses of verse 7. He offers what is equivalent to giving away a year's salary. Job, however, knows that he has nothing to worry about. He is not guilty of the offenses. He could make such an offer because he knows nothing is at risk. His conscience is clear.

Do not be confused by the reference to Job's *offspring* in this verse. Job is not talking about his children. They are all dead! Job is still talking about his crops. He is willing for all he has planted to be uprooted and ruined if he has been guilty of the sins of verse 7.

Job's offer reminds us of a similar offer by a man who met Jesus. Zaccheus was a wealthy tax collector who lived in Jericho (Luke 19:1, 2). Jesus met Zaccheus and went to his home (19:5, 6). Zaccheus's life changed that day. Expressing his commitment in terms most familiar to him, Zaccheus told Jesus that if he had cheated anyone, he would repay that person fourfold (19:8), in addition to offering half his goods to the poor. Was Zaccheus guilty of cheating people and trying to make that right by his offer? Or was Zaccheus like Job—confident that he was guiltless? Scholars debate the issue. The important point in both cases is that the offer was made. In Job's case, the offer is made because he knows that he can stand the scrutiny.

Try as they may, Job's friends cannot make the charge of hypocrisy stick. Job calls on God as his witness (Job 31:4). Job knows that God knows his heart. There is no pretense to Job. He does not fear examination. Hypocrites fear that someone will find out about the "other side" of their lives. Not so, Job!

B. "Adultery" Won't Stick (vv. 9-12)

9. If mine heart have been deceived by a woman, or if I have laid wait at my neighbor's door.

Job's friends do not make a specific accusation against him regarding his sexual purity. But since sexual temptation is so strong for men, Job may be addressing the matter just to "cover all the bases." For whatever reason, Job makes it clear that he is not guilty of sexual sin (again, see

---

How to Say It

ABADDON (Hebrew). Uh-*bad*-dun.

BILDAD. *Bill*-dad.

CORINTHIANS. Kor-*in*-thee-unz (*th* as in *thin*).

DEUTERONOMY. Due-ter-*ahn*-uh-me.

ELIPHAZ. *El*-ih-faz.

EPHESIANS. Ee-*fee*-zhunz.

ISAIAH. Eye-*zay*-uh.

ZACCHEUS. Zack-*key*-us.

ZOPHAR. *Zo*-far.

31:1). He has not lurked at his *neighbor's door* to get a peek at his neighbor's wife or perhaps to find a woman alone in the house. [See question #4, page 176.]

10. Then let my wife grind unto another, and let others bow down upon her.

Job's offer seems almost perverse. If he has been guilty of sexual sin, then he offers his wife in both the domestic sense (grinding grain) and the sexual sense *(bow down upon her)*. This may seem callous, but remember—Job knows that no charge can stand against him. Even though his wife offered him no comfort (2:9), he is not contemplating getting rid of her! He is not looking for another woman. This reveals the seriousness of Job's convictions and commitments.

11. For this is a heinous crime; yea, it is an iniquity to be punished by the judges.

To be guilty of sexual sin, especially the taking of another man's wife, is abominable. Most of the cultures of ancient times considered marriage to be sacred (unlike today). The breaking of the marriage bond through adultery is damaging to the individuals involved and to society as a whole (like today). One of the strongest threads in the fabric of any culture is the stability of the family unit. Jesus redefined adultery—moving beyond the act to include the desire of the heart as well (Matthew 5:27, 28). If Job is guilty of adultery, why has he not been judged?

12. For it is a fire that consumeth to destruction, and would root out all mine increase.

Job understands the insidious power of sexual temptation, even though it is very unlikely that he has access to Solomon's teaching in Proverbs 6:23–7:27. The word translated *destruction* is the Hebrew word *Abaddon*. In the Old Testament it refers to the world of the dead (Job 26:6; 28:22; Proverbs 27:20). Sexual sin is a killer! AIDS has made this true in the physical sense. It has always been true in the spiritual sense.

Job realizes the far-reaching effects of sexual sin. Were he guilty, even his prosperity will be forfeit. How many times have we seen such a scenario unfold before us? A man gets involved in an affair and before long he has lost his wife, his children, his job, his house, and eventually his life savings. Most seriously, that man also loses his relationship with God (cf. 1 Corinthians 6:12-20).

The charge of adultery will not stick to Job. He knows he is innocent. It is not merely that he has not been caught in sexual sin. He has, in fact, not committed sexual sin.

C. "Injustice" Won't Stick (vv. 13-15)

13. If I did despise the cause of my manservant or of my maidservant, when they contended with me.

Job's blameless behavior extends to the treatment of his servants. He has treated them justly, even when they had grievances against him personally. He has not been a tyrant with the people who worked for him.

Job apparently understands the important dynamic of social justice with those who are (in society's eyes) in an inferior position in life. While a grievous sin like adultery may have been readily noticed, the treatment of servants is of little social concern in Job's day. Despite that, Job knows that he has dealt with his servants justly; he also makes his claim knowing that three of his servants are still alive to contradict him if he is lying (Job 1:15-17).

14. What then shall I do when God riseth up? And when he visiteth, what shall I answer him?

Job understands that he is accountable to *God* for his treatment of others. This is not merely a matter between humans. God watches and knows how people in authority treat those in "lesser stations." Part of Job's motivation in treating others correctly is his realization of accountability to God.

The apostle Paul addresses the same issue in Ephesians 6:9. See also James 5:1-6.

15. Did not he that made me in the womb make him? And did not one fashion us in the womb?

Job shows remarkable humility. He understands that class positions in society are inventions of man, not God. God is the Author of all life, regardless of earthly position. All humanity is precious to God! Jesus provided a powerful reminder of this truth in Matthew 25:31-46. We should be very careful how we treat people who may be in a so-called "lesser station" in life.

Despite his prominence as one of the great men of his time (Job 1:3), Job does not mistreat those who are less fortunate. Job's servants even have remarked about his generosity to them (Job 31:31). The charge of injustice will not stick!

D. "Idolatry" Won't Stick (vv. 24-28)

24. If I have made gold my hope, or have said to the fine gold, Thou art my confidence.

Even though Job was very wealthy before his tragedy, he knew better than to make *gold* the center of his life. This is a direct refutation of an accusation made by Eliphaz (Job 22:23-25).

GOLD OR GOD?

The words "under God" appear in America's Pledge of Allegiance. The words "In God We Trust" appear on American coins. There have been "on again, off again" efforts in recent years to remove those words. (Political pundits say the issue "has no traction"!) But even with the words remaining, some have remarked that the sentiment is not accurate. Perhaps not, but they speak to America's ideals, goals, and hopes.

Others have said that if we were totally accurate we would replace "In God We Trust" on the coins with "In Gold We Trust." Let the word *gold* stand for materialism, wealth, and property, and you will probably agree that those living in prosperous societies trust more in gold than in God.

Job, however, did not. We must all look at ourselves honestly and ask, "Can I say what Job said? Would people who know me best agree that my trust is in God and not in gold?" The proof is in our actions and attitudes. Which gets us more riled up—politicians trying to delete references to God, or politicians messing with our various government-sponsored "entitlements"?

Those of us who live in the United States know that we live in a very materialistic society. How we respond to that materialism will communicate volumes to our children and grandchildren. What we must consciously communicate to them is that we know that ultimate security comes only from God, not from gold.　—R. C. S.

25. If I rejoiced because my wealth was great, and because mine hand had gotten much.

Job does not seem to have been the kind of man who paraded his *wealth* or sought to impress others with his possessions. He had been extremely wealthy, but he is not foolish enough to think that that wealth was of his own doing (cf. Luke 12:13-21).

26, 27. If I beheld the sun when it shined, or the moon walking in brightness; and my heart hath been secretly enticed, or my mouth hath kissed my hand.

Job also denies another form of idolatry: he is not a worshiper of any of the heavenly bodies.

Home Daily Bible Readings

Monday, Jan. 12—My Eyes Are Turned Toward You (Psalm 141:1-8)
Tuesday, Jan. 13—I Direct My Steps (Psalm 119:121-128)
Wednesday, Jan. 14—The Righteous Walk Blamelessly (Psalm 15:1-5)
Thursday, Jan. 15—Job Declares His Integrity (Job 27:2-6)
Friday, Jan. 16—Let God Know My Integrity (Job 31:3-8)
Saturday, Jan. 17—Job Defends Himself (Job 31:13-23)
Sunday, Jan. 18—Job Declares His Loyalty to God (Job 31:24-28)

Many in the ancient world worship the *sun, moon,* and other things they see in the sky (Jeremiah 7:18; 44:15-25; Ezekiel 8:16; Acts 7:43). However, the Old Testament law is quite specific in forbidding the worship of such things (Deuteronomy 4:19; 17:3). Job may have raised his hands to acknowledge and worship God, but he has never raised his hands in worship of the sun or moon.

28. This also were an iniquity to be punished by the judge: for I should have denied the God that is above.

Job fully grasps the gravity of idolatry. Even if Job is unaware of the Old Testament law forbidding idolatry (Exodus 20:3-5), there is a natural instinct within him that rules it out (Romans 1:19, 20).

Idolatry is a word often relegated to ancient times. We think of people bowing down to images of wood, stone, or metal. We should remember that idolatry takes many forms. Anything or anyone taking precedence over God in our lives becomes an idol to us. May we be like Job! As the charge of idolatry will not stick against him, may the same be said of us. [See question #5, page 176.]

Conclusion

A. Resisting the Pressure

What pressure Job was under! His tragedies, his unanswered questions, and his friends' accusations could have driven him to irrational, and even evil, retaliations. He could have given up and decided that living a righteous life was simply not worth the effort. He could have become a different man, emboldened to sin by the seeming lack of reward for doing good.

He did not do any of that. Perhaps he felt his integrity was all he had left. For him, that was enough. Would the same be true for you?

B. Prayer

Father, help us treasure our integrity—not as a cornerstone of self-righteousness, but as our means of showing You that we are truly devoted to living as You want us to live. When people falsely accuse us and knowingly lie about us, help us remember the example of Job. Help us remember that Your Word tells us to repay evil with good. Empower us to maintain our integrity in every situation. Strengthen us through the Holy Spirit's power within us. In Jesus' name we pray, amen.

C. Thought to Remember

We are to combat falsehood and ignorance with grace and truth.

Learning by Doing

This page contains an alternative lesson plan emphasizing learning activities.
Classes desiring such student involvement will find these suggestions helpful.

Learning Aims

After participating in this lesson, each student will be able to:

1. Summarize Job's arguments that he has been falsely accused.

2. Explain how truth is the best defense against false accusations.

3. Give a specific example of how a person overcomes accusations with the truth.

Into the Lesson

Put these two words on display, with several blank lines between them: INNOCENT and GUILTY. Tell the class, "I want you to do the old word game of changing one word to another by changing one letter per line to form an intervening word. Who has the first suggestion?" Someone very quickly will notice that these two words do not have the same number of letters and cannot be thus altered. When someone notes this, say, "You're right! The only way this could be done is if one ignores the rules of the game; that is, only if one cheats." Comment further that that's exactly what would have to happen for Job to be declared guilty. Truth affirms his claim of innocence; no one can change innocent to guilty.

As an alternative, have class members express words and phrases relating to the words, "NOT GUILTY" in an acrostic. Provide poster board or newsprint and a felt pen for putting a word to each letter vertically that relates to innocence. Tell them you'll "give them a bonus point" if they can relate their words to Job's story and the book of Job. Sample choices: *godly* for *G*, *undeserved* for *U*.

Into the Word

Invite a judge or lawyer to be present. Allow this legal professional to make a short address on the term Job continuously repeated: "Not Guilty."

Say, "Now, today, we are going to be judged by 'judge and jury.' Forgetting all the good things you have done, in a court of law what would be the most impressive thing you could tell the judge you have not done?"

Have each class member open the Bible to Job 31. Job had previously challenged God to meet him and either present His case or let Job speak (Job 13:20-24). Now he plays out his role as the accused, even though there is no evidence that God is paying any attention. He will take his solemn oath—his hand on the Bible so to speak—and protest his innocence.

Divide the class into groups of three to five; ask them to examine the entire text of Job 31 or assign the groups the following verses: 5-8; 9-12; 13-15; 24-28 to identify the supposed accusations and Job's responses to each. Give each group a sheet of paper or transparency with two headings: *Accusation* and *Plea*. Direct them to compile the list

As the groups complete their time together, ask each to report its findings on their transparency or simply orally and share with the rest of the class. Note, "Though Job is accused of a variety of serious offenses toward God, to each he could say, 'Not guilty!'"

Into Life

Lead everyone in meditating on Job 27:3, 4. Begin these activities by asking all to bow their heads in a spirit of meditation and reverence, as you lead them through the following. Indicate, "Now I am going to read the same list of charges made to Job. As I do, make your plea to God. If you must plea 'Guilty,' take this occasion to ask for God's forgiveness and to make a commitment to leave the sinful behavior behind." Pause after each "indictment" to allow reflection and response.

Read aloud verse three: "All the while my breath is in me, and the spirit of God is in my nostrils;" and then ask these questions, pausing after each: "What does this phrase mean in terms of my personal life? How do I feel about God knowing my way? What is one specific 'way' in my life I am assured He knows about me right now? Are there any areas in my life I would rather He didn't know about?"

Move to verse four: "My lips shall not speak wickedness, nor my tongue utter deceit." Share these questions for reflection: "What did Job mean in this verse? In what area in my life do I feel God is 'trying' me? What is He wanting to accomplish through this? Will I always be on trial before God? Who decides whether or not I'll come forth with integrity in my everyday life? How can I apply Job's principle of fighting accusations with truth? At home? At work? In every relationship?"

You may consider other verses from the text for a similar questioning and reflection.

Let's Talk It Over

*The questions on this page are designed to promote discussion of the lesson
by the class and to encourage application of the lesson Scriptures. The answers
provided are only discussion starters. Let your class talk it over from there.*

1. Insurance companies refer to natural disasters as "acts of God" in their insurance policies. Is this fair to God? Why, or why not?

For many, blaming God for almost any disaster just seems to be the easiest thing to do. Even blameless Job thought God solely to have been behind the "misfortunes" in his life.

But human suffering got its start when Adam and Eve voluntarily sinned in the Garden of Eden through the temptation of Satan (Genesis 3:1-19). And while God permitted a test of the faithfulness of His servant Job, God did not initiate the action or take pleasure in the pain caused by Satan. Too often God gets the blame for the pain caused in our world because simple thinkers do not stop to ponder the nature of God, the implications of sin, or the power of Satan. Your class can profit from a discussion regarding the contrasts between God and Satan.

2. Look at how Job "dug in his heels" in the face of an onslaught! If you had to face such a situation, how would you find the words and the strength to hold to the truth, even if you were "a minority of one"?

The accusations against Job are repeated so often and at such length that the temptation simply to give up must have been very strong. But if we have God on our side, we are not "a minority of one." We have the best majority we could ever have! (See 2 Kings 6:16, 17.)

One important thing to remember is not to respond too quickly when others accuse you unfairly. Your accusers may be trying to get you to play a "fast break"-type of game, with rapid back-and-forth questions and answers. You can slow things down by repeating their questions back to them. Start your responses with "I hear you saying. . . ." This will help keep your reponses measured and deliberate. It will also help you keep your temper. Remember that our ultimate source of strength at all times is the Holy Spirit who dwells within us.

3. Job was willing to "be weighed in an even balance" so God would know of his integrity. Would you be willing to have your integrity tested in this way? Why, or why not?

Personal motivation will be important in answering this question. God is certainly not impressed with any "look how good I am" attitudes, and He does not save us on the basis that our integrity "outweighs" our sins.

But a balance-scale approach can be useful as a personal check on our progress in spiritual maturity. If a person can see that his or her "fruit of the Spirit" (Galatians 5:22, 23) continues to gain ground against "the works of the flesh" (5:19-21), day by day, then that is a good thing indeed!

4. Job knew where the boundaries of sexual purity were. How have these lines been blurred today, and why should we care?

The lines get blurred when an "enlightened" culture views God's instructions as relics of a by-gone era. Personal freedom then becomes a license to do anything as long as it "doesn't hurt anyone else."

In America much of this thinking started with the so-called "sexual revolution" of the 1960s; this revolution also involved a rebellion against traditional authority. Groups such as COYOTE (which stands for "Call Off Your Old Tired Ethics") actively work to "promote the rights of all sex workers." Postmodern thinking, which sees truth existing only within each individual, makes the problem worse.

But sexual immorality does indeed hurt us. In a practical sense we all pay the bills for teenage pregnancies and sexually transmitted diseases. In an eternal sense sexual immorality is one of the most insidious of all sins (1 Corinthians 6:18).

5. In an attempt to prove his innocence, Job provides several benchmark examples. Why are some of these important markers of righteousness even today?

Many examples that Job mentions are included in the New Testament as well. Hypocrisy (Job 31:5-8; 1 Timothy 4:2), adultery (Job 31:9-12; James 2:11), social injustice (Job 31:13-15; Luke 20:47), and idolatry (Job 31:26, 27; Galatians 5:20) are some of these.

Our problem is that modern culture pays little attention to any of these standards. Just think of the types of jokes told on sitcoms, the moral laxness of public officials, and all the modern idols that people put ahead of God. Even so, God's Word is still the standard against which we are to check our morality.

Integrity in God's Presence

DEVOTIONAL READING: Isaiah 6:1-8.

BACKGROUND SCRIPTURE: Job 38–42.

PRINTED TEXT: Job 38:1-7; 40:6-9; 42:1-6.

Job 38:1-7

1 Then the LORD answered Job out of the whirlwind, and said,

2 Who is this that darkeneth counsel by words without knowledge?

3 Gird up now thy loins like a man; for I will demand of thee, and answer thou me.

4 Where wast thou when I laid the foundations of the earth? Declare, if thou hast understanding.

5 Who hath laid the measures thereof, if thou knowest? Or who hath stretched the line upon it?

6 Whereupon are the foundations thereof fastened? Or who laid the corner stone thereof;

7 When the morning stars sang together, and all the sons of God shouted for joy?

Job 40:6-9

6 Then answered the LORD unto Job out of the whirlwind, and said,

7 Gird up thy loins now like a man: I will demand of thee, and declare thou unto me.

8 Wilt thou also disannul my judgment? Wilt thou condemn me, that thou mayest be righteous?

9 Hast thou an arm like God? Or canst thou thunder with a voice like him?

Job 42:1-6

1 Then Job answered the LORD, and said,

2 I know that thou canst do every thing, and that no thought can be withholden from thee.

3 Who is he that hideth counsel without knowledge? Therefore have I uttered that I understood not; things too wonderful for me, which I knew not.

4 Hear, I beseech thee, and I will speak: I will demand of thee, and declare thou unto me.

5 I have heard of thee by the hearing of the ear; but now mine eye seeth thee:

6 Wherefore I abhor myself, and repent in dust and ashes.

Jan 25

GOLDEN TEXT: I have heard of thee by the hearing of the ear;
but now mine eye seeth thee.—Job 42:5.

Lessons From Life
Unit 1: Job: Integrity in Times of Testing
(Lessons 5-8)

Lesson Aims

After participating in this lesson, each student should be able to:

1. Summarize God's answer to Job, and tell how Job responded.

2. Tell why it was necessary for Job to recognize his own unworthiness and God's sovereign control.

3. Make a statement of submission to God's sovereignty.

Lesson Outline

INTRODUCTION
   A. "I Just Earned My Master's Degree"
   B. Lesson Background
 I. SOVEREIGN POWER (Job 38:1-7)
   A. Preparing for the Test, Part 1 (vv. 1-3)
   B. Taking the Test, Part 1 (vv. 4-7)
      Looking for Answers
 II. SOVEREIGN JUSTICE (Job 40:6-9)
   A. Preparing for the Test, Part 2 (vv. 6, 7)
   B. Taking the Test, Part 2 (vv. 8, 9)
III. SHAME AND SORROW (Job 42:1-6)
   A. God's Sovereignty (vv. 1, 2)
   B. Job's Ignorance (v. 3)
      A Biblical Drama
   C. God's Identity (vv. 4, 5)
   D. Job's Repentance (v. 6)
CONCLUSION
   A. The Essence of Faith
   B. Prayer
   C. Thought to Remember

Introduction

A. "I Just Earned My Master's Degree"

I once attended a seminar sponsored by a local university. Eighteen people gathered in a room to spend the day discussing the subject of adult education. A young lady breezed into the room about thirty minutes after the first paper had been read. She immediately injected herself into the discussion, even though she had heard only the last couple of minutes of the paper that had been presented. She continued to make comments throughout the discussion, even though it was apparent to everyone that she knew virtually nothing about the subject of the paper.

The second presenter read his paper, and about three minutes into his presentation, the young lady interrupted him with a comment. Those accustomed to having papers read in academic circles know that such an interruption is out of order. The lady moderating the seminar asked the young woman to hold all comments and questions until the paper had been read in its entirety. After the reading, the young woman continued to give her unsolicited opinion on a variety of subjects. To put it bluntly, she was unbearably obnoxious!

Finally, the moderator asked the young woman why she felt it necessary to comment on everything that was said. The young lady responded, "Well, I just earned my master's degree, and I thought I might help enlighten everyone." The moderator peered over the top of her glasses at the young woman and said, "Young lady, everyone in this room—except you—has a *doctorate* in some field of education." The young woman did not make any other comments that morning, and she did not return to the seminar after the lunch break.

In this week's lesson we will see know-it-all Job get his comeuppance. He had asked for a hearing before God—and he got it! Things did not, however, turn out quite the way Job expected.

B. Lesson Background

In last week's lesson we learned Job's responses to the accusations of his three friends. In the chapter preceding this week's lesson texts, another character had presented himself, a man named Elihu (Job 32–37).

Elihu's speech forms a potent preamble to God's response to Job. Elihu reminded Job of God's ultimate justice (Job 34). He reminded Job that he should speak to God humbly, carefully addressing his Creator (Job 35). He argued that Job should acknowledge God's sovereignty (Job 36). He called on Job to express his ultimate trust in God, regardless of his understanding of God's ways (Job 37). We have no record of any response from Job. The next voice we hear is that of God Himself (Job 38).

I. Sovereign Power
(Job 38:1-7)

God spoke to Job in the midst of a mighty wind storm. Some scholars have taken words in Job 37:21, 22 to mean that a storm was approaching as Elihu spoke. The storm would descend upon Job and his companions with an intense fury, and out of that fury Job would hear God speaking to him. Job gets what he requested. God is there, but God will speak while Job listens.

A. Preparing for the Test, Part 1 (vv. 1-3)

1. Then the LORD answered Job out of the whirlwind, and said.

Elihu's speech ended with a reminder that people fear (or revere) God because of His splendor, majesty, power, and justice (Job 37:22-24). Then God speaks. Job has wanted God to answer him (31:35). Now God is doing just what Job wants, but His voice does not come to Job in the midst of a moment of quiet contemplation. God's voice rises above the howling gale of a terrible storm. We might compare how God speaks here with how He speaks in passages such as Exodus 19:16-19; 1 Kings 19:9-12; and Ezekiel 1.

2. Who is this that darkeneth counsel by words without knowledge?

What an opening question! Imagine the scene: you are in the middle of a maelstrom, and suddenly you hear the voice of God. And God's voice is not comforting you—He is asking you why you are such a smart aleck.

In his presumption Job thinks he has God all figured out! The bad things that have happened came about because God did not have enough information. Job wants to talk to God to tell Him what He does not know. Job wants to argue.

As we consider Job's words, however, we recall that he "sinned not, nor charged God foolishly" (1:22), and that Job did not "sin with his lips" (2:10). The *words without knowledge* that God points out likely include Job's complaint—out of his very great pain!—that God has not heard his cry, thereby denying him justice (19:6, 7; 27:2). Even so, when all is said and done it is Job (and not Eliphaz, Bildad, and Zophar) who has spoken of God "the thing that is right" (42:7, 8). Whenever we question God's justice today we, too, speak foolish "words without knowledge."

3. Gird up now thy loins like a man; for I will demand of thee, and answer thou me.

God tells Job to get ready for a battle. To *gird up* the *loins* means to gather the outer garment into the belt or sash in order to be ready to run, fight, or work strenuously (2 Kings 4:29; 9:1; Job 40:7; Jeremiah 1:17). This is not to be a physical wrestling match as in Genesis 32:22-28, but Job will know that he has been in a battle when God is through questioning him.

Is Job prepared for this mental test (cf. 1 Peter 1:13)? Will he be able to defend himself on the charge of presumption? God is going to be a demanding Teacher—and Job had better be ready with good answers.

B. Taking the Test, Part 1 (vv. 4-7)

4. Where wast thou when I laid the foundations of the earth? Declare, if thou hast understanding.

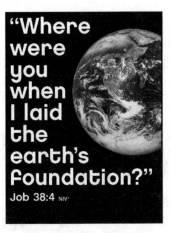

"Where were you when I laid the earth's foundation?" Job 38:4 NIV

Visual for lesson 8

This magnificent "space shot" will remind your learners of their relationship to the Creator.

God now begins a series of more than seventy questions to Job. The first question alone reminds Job of his proper place.

LOOKING FOR ANSWERS

William Temple (1881–1944) said that God minus the world would still equal God, but that the world minus God would equal nothing. If we eliminate God from our thinking, then there are too many questions without answers and too many puzzles without solutions. Certainly believers do not have all the answers, but they have better answers than those who do not believe.

Just the thought of a universe without God is depressing: a universe empty, lonely, friendless, and without purpose. But believers can look out into the vastness of space and know that we are not alone; we are not orphans. We are children. Like all children we keep asking questions. And like all children, we receive answers to some of them, but not to all of them. A child does not need to know all the answers, and we do not need to know all the answers. We have a Heavenly Father who does know all the answers, and we are to be content with that.

It is not wrong to ask questions. Job, Moses, and John the Baptist are among the many in the Bible who asked questions. But they asked them out of a heart of faith. Some think faith never asks questions, but they are wrong. Some think faith has all the answers, but they are wrong. Faith asks questions, accepts God's answers when they are given, and rests serenely when God withholds answers. The old song is right: "We'll understand it better by and by." —R. C. S.

5. Who hath laid the measures thereof, if thou knowest? Or who hath stretched the line upon it?

Picture a man using a measuring tape. He can hold one end and read the measurements, but he needs someone else holding the other end of the tape at the proper place. Did God need such a helper? If He did, was Job that helper? Given all the scientific knowledge we have today about the scope and dimensions of the universe, how much more humbled should we be by these questions than Job!

6. Whereupon are the foundations thereof fastened? Or who laid the corner stone thereof?

God asks Job an intriguing question: to what is the earth *fastened?* Job has indicated an elementary understanding of the fact that the earth is suspended in space (Job 26:7). So God's question to Job about the earth's *foundations* is, of course, figurative.

God is using the analogy of the earth as a building. Was Job present when earth's *corner stone* was laid? Does Job even begin to comprehend *who laid* that cornerstone? In 38:31 God will use some of Job's own words from 9:9 to make a similar point about stars. "Come on, Job. Do you know?"

7. When the morning stars sang together, and all the sons of God shouted for joy?

Stars could refer to the literal points of light in the sky as they declared God's glory by their very existence (cf. Psalm 19:1). It is also possible that *morning stars* refer figuratively to *the sons of God* (angels). In many Bible translations both Isaiah 14:12 and Revelation 22:16 use "morning star" to refer to living beings, so the exact usage here is hard to determine. In either case, Job was not there to hail God's creative powers as the morning stars were. Can Job possibly know how all these creation events occurred? [See question #1, page 184.]

II. Sovereign Justice
(Job 40:6-9)

Throughout chapters 38 and 39, God continues to question Job regarding his knowledge—or lack of knowledge—of the elementary workings of the systems of the earth and its creatures. Now in chapter 40 God switches themes as He begins to question Job about his accusations (Job 40:1, 2). It seems that Job is beginning to get the picture because he does not try to answer. He knows this is a time to keep his mouth shut (Job 40:3-5). Job's silence does not, however, silence God.

A. Preparing for the Test, Part 2 (vv. 6, 7)

6. Then answered the LORD unto Job out of the whirlwind, and said.

Amazingly, the storm has not abated. All of God's questions to Job have been voiced through *the whirlwind.* Poor Job—he finally gets to talk to God, but he has to do so in the midst of a tornado!

Job has admitted to God that he is "vile" or unworthy (Job 40:4). Perhaps he thinks that will put a stop to God's onslaught. It does not. God is going to continue to make His points.

7. Gird up thy loins now like a man: I will demand of thee, and declare thou unto me.

God repeats His warning from 38:3. Job's admission of his unworthiness is not sufficient. God has not declared Himself the winner of this battle of wits. He has scored enough points to win, but Job still has lessons to learn, and God is still willing to serve as Job's Teacher. So He again warns Job to prepare for battle.

B. Taking the Test, Part 2 (vv. 8, 9)

8. Wilt thou also disannul my judgment? Wilt thou condemn me, that thou mayest be righteous?

Job is now faced with a far more serious charge. God's questions have made it clear to Job that he is ignorant of His ways. Now, however, God directly confronts Job with Job's allegations of injustice in 19:6, 7 and 27:2.

We find many people today who are very willing to accuse God of injustice. They ask why God causes (or allows) natural disasters like floods, earthquakes, and hurricanes. They ask why little children die in the midst of wars. They, like Job, need to learn that we do not have the right to question God's justice. The prophet Habakkuk learned this lesson when God told him, in a nice way, "shut up!" (Habakkuk 2:20). God's sovereign justice prevails in His appointed time and fashion. [See question #2, page 184.]

God asks Job another penetrating question: does God have to be wrong in order for Job to prove himself right? Job has spoken against God, although the depths of Job's pain may make his "crossing the line" somewhat understandable. As noted before, in the end it is Job who has spoken right of God, and not his friends (Job 42:7, 8).

9. Hast thou an arm like God? Or canst thou thunder with a voice like him?

God reminds Job of his limitations. In his moment of greatest strength, Job could not accomplish what God can do in His moment of greatest weakness!

I am the proud father of a fifteen-year-old son. He will obtain his learner's permit in a few months and begin learning how to drive a car. Like most boys his age, he already thinks he knows how to drive. He thinks it perfectly appropriate to occasionally criticize my driving. That's when I turn to him and ask him how he gained such expertise. I do not instruct him in playing the trombone (which he does very well) or in diving off the high dive (which he also does very well). I do not do either of those things because he is our resident expert. When it comes to driving, however, I am the resident expert. Job has to be reminded that God is the One who is sovereign—the Resident Expert in all things! [See question #3, page 184.]

III. Shame and Sorrow
(Job 42:1-6)

We now hear Job speak. He has been inundated with questions he cannot answer. He has admitted that he is unworthy. Will God's questions lead Job to the proper conclusion? Will Job finally see the "big picture"?

A. God's Sovereignty (vv. 1, 2)

1. Then Job answered the LORD, and said.

Job's longing for the opportunity to speak with God has been fulfilled. He has listened to God's litany of rhetorical questions. Job has spoken much about God. Now he will speak to God.

2. I know that thou canst do every thing, and that no thought can be withholden from thee.

In his previous response to God, Job had admitted quickly that he was unworthy of the opportunity to speak with God. Then Job decided that the wisest course of action was to remain silent (Job 40:3-5). Silence, however, does not mean that Job has given up his contention that he has been dealt with unjustly. Job's admission simply may indicate that he knows he is overmatched. Job already had indicated that he knew he could not successfully argue with God (9:14). Job may be willing to be silent because he knows he cannot win such a debate. This does not rule out the possibility, however, that Job still thinks he is right!

Job has acknowledged God's sovereignty all along, so the admission *I know that thou canst do every thing* is nothing new. Job realizes now, however, that his insistence to have his case heard in God's court is foolish since God knows all thoughts anyway. The sovereign God who can do all things is the One who has been fully aware of Job's situation all along.

B. Job's Ignorance (v. 3)

3. Who is he that hideth counsel without knowledge? Therefore have I uttered that I understood not; things too wonderful for me, which I knew not.

Job seems to be crawling out from beneath his layers of self-defense as he uses the same words God has spoken against him (38:2). Job is saying, in essence, "Yes, God—You have me pegged." Job's attitude goes from that of a Mister Know-It-

All to one of humble admission. This is the kind of transformation that we could all use from time to time!

Realizing the limits of your knowledge and wisdom can be very liberating. It seems so with Job. He moves beyond his pride and finds the joy of honesty. He realizes that he has pondered on matters far beyond his intellectual capacity. He finally concludes that the wonderful and majestic ways and abilities of God are beyond his comprehension. He does not have God figured out, after all. And that is okay! It is not Job's responsibility to define God's path. That is a valuable lesson for all of us to learn. There is a limit to how much we can analyze God. Above all, He is there to be adored!

A BIBLICAL DRAMA

For many years Orlin Corey of Kentucky's Georgetown College has produced an outdoor drama entitled *The Book of Job*. Presented each summer at Pine Mountain State Resort Park near Pineville, Kentucky, the drama has received national attention because of Corey's unique "stained glass" makeup and costume design. It is regarded as a major event in American theater history.

Of course, the book is a natural for the stage. It *is* a drama. Just as the Bible contains poetry, history, and biography, so it contains drama. And just as Corey's theater production is unique, so the book and its message are unique.

The opening verses of the final chapter sum up this book and its message. G. K. Chesterton (1874–1936) said, "Great literature has always been allegorical. The *Iliad* is only great because all life is a battle. The *Odyssey* because all life is a journey, the Book of Job because all life is a riddle."

As believers we know the outcome of the battle, the end of the journey, the solution to the riddle. But "knowing the outcome" and "learning the lesson" are two different things! We must learn, as Job did, to be humble before God. God is wiser than we are. God is more powerful than

How to Say It
ABEDNEGO. Uh-*bed*-nee-go.
BILDAD. *Bill*-dad.
ELIHU. Ih-*lye*-hew.
ELIPHAZ. *El*-ih-faz.
MESHACH. *Me*-shack.
NEBUCHADNEZZAR. *Neb*-yuh-kud-*nez*-er (strong accent on *nez*).
SHADRACH. *Shay*-drack or *Shad*-rack.
ZOPHAR. *Zo*-far.

we are. It is worth reading through the whole book of Job to learn that. Nothing will serve believers better in facing life than a genuine humility. One of the world's greatest dramas can teach us one of God's best lessons.   —R. C. S.

C. God's Identity (vv. 4, 5)

4. Hear, I beseech thee, and I will speak: I will demand of thee, and declare thou unto me.

Again, Job quotes the Lord's words back to Him (38:3). God has instructed Job to listen, and Job has indeed heard. Job is beginning to understand God's true nature.

5. I have heard of thee by the hearing of the ear; but now mine eye seeth thee.

Previously, Job had known about God. Now he is actually getting to know God. Many people know about God. They, like Job, think they have God all figured out. They can quote Bible verses and recite church doctrine. But they have no personal relationship with God. How sad to know facts but not the Father! (See John 14:8, 9.) [See question #4, page 184.]

D. Job's Repentance (v. 6)

6. Wherefore I abhor myself, and repent in dust and ashes.

Job's new, correct view of God has changed his view of himself. This verse records a turning point of Job's life. His efforts at self-vindication cease. He stops looking at himself in his own mirror and starts looking at himself in God's mirror.

Job's experience in the presence of God reminds us of the experience of Isaiah. When Isaiah saw God, he also was overcome with a sense of his own unworthiness (Isaiah 6:5). As is the custom in that part of the world, Job's repentance is expressed visually by covering himself with

Home Daily Bible Readings

Monday, Jan. 19—My Soul Thirsts for God (Psalm 42:1-6)

Tuesday, Jan. 20—John's Vision of Christ (Revelation 1:12-18)

Wednesday, Jan. 21—Isaiah's Vision of God (Isaiah 6:1-8)

Thursday, Jan. 22—The Lord Speaks to Job (Job 38:1-7)

Friday, Jan. 23—God Calls for Job's Response (Job 40:1-5)

Saturday, Jan. 24—God Questions Job (Job 40:6-14)

Sunday, Jan. 25—Job Is Humbled by Seeing God (Job 42:1-6)

dust and ashes. He previously had covered himself in ashes to express sadness due to his suffering (Job 2:8). Now he covers himself in dust and ashes to express repentance. His arrogance has been an affront to God. His accusations have been false. His sense of God has been too low, his sense of self too high.

Spiritual arrogance is a destructive force in many churches today. God's Word instructs us to be humble (Matthew 18:4; Romans 12:3; James 4:10; 1 Peter 5:5). The humility God desires is exemplified in the life of Jesus. How many of us are truly like Him in that respect?

Job's integrity was his banner. He thought it unquestionable. He finally comes to the point of true integrity when he is willing to tell the truth about himself. He does not know everything. He does not have God figured out! He insisted on seeing God through a distorted lens, a lens that "must" be right. When Job finally talks to God, he is ashamed of himself. He is sorry not only for what he has done, but also for what he has been! [See question #5, page 184.]

Conclusion

A. The Essence of Faith

Many people think the book of Job is about suffering or patience. Those themes are part of the book, but more important is faith. What was the essence of Job's faith? Did he understand that God has the right to declare without explanation? God's sovereignty authorizes declaration, not explanation!

When Shadrach, Meshach, and Abednego refused to worship the image of Nebuchadnezzar, they were thrown into a fiery furnace. They believed God would deliver them from that fate, but their faith is expressed in this declaration: "but if not . . . we will not serve thy gods, nor worship the golden image" (Daniel 3:18). Even if God decided not to deliver them, it made no difference. The essence of faith is trusting God even when you do not understand what He is doing. Job finally learned that valuable lesson. How about you?

B. Prayer

Father, we thank You for being who You are. Help us learn to trust You more. May we remember Job when we are tempted to question Your ways or Your timing. Help us to follow the Spirit's leading in our lives when the way is not clear. In Jesus' name, amen.

C. Thought to Remember

"Though he slay me, yet will I trust in him" (Job 13:15).

Learning by Doing

This page contains an alternative lesson plan emphasizing learning activities.
Classes desiring such student involvement will find these suggestions helpful.

Learning Goals

After participating in this lesson, each student will be able to:

1. Summarize God's answer to Job, and tell how Job responded.

2. Tell why it was necessary for Job to recognize his own unworthiness and God sovereign control.

3. Make a statement of submission to God's sovereignty.

Into the Lesson

Option 1: Ask students to share a "foot-in-mouth" experience—a time when they spoke too soon, spoke out of ignorance, or made a humorous verbal blunder. Make the transition to Bible study by saying, "Job made a foot-in-the-mouth blunder demonstrating spiritual arrogance."

Option 2: Explain that God has spoken to people through a variety of unusual and unique media and in various environments. Write on a chalkboard or marker board the following open-ended sentences, and ask students to respond. A similar activity is included in *Adult Bible Class*.

1. "Some of the environments or media through which God spoke to people in the Old Testament include. . . ." *Examples: burning bush (Moses), still small voice (Elijah), whirlwind (Ezekiel), voice in the night (Samuel).*

2. "Some of the environments or media through which God spoke to people in the New Testament include. . . ." *Examples: dreams (magi, Joseph), angel (Mary), light from Heaven (Saul), vision (John).* Make transition to Bible study by saying, "God used a powerful medium to speak to Job—a tornado, a *whirlwind* in the text."

Into the Word

Give a brief lecture based on the Lesson Background (p. 178). Use a visual you have prepared with the heading "Elihu Reminded Job" through the entire Bible study. Under the heading write the following reminders. Chapter 34: God's ultimate justice; Chapter 35: Speak humbly to the Creator; Chapter 36: Acknowledge God's sovereignty; Chapter 37: Trust God, regardless of your understanding.

Below these chapter notes write a new heading, "God's Message to Job." Explain that we will discover that God takes His turn speaking to Job and has a powerful lesson for us.

Read Job 38:1-7. Ask groups to paraphrase verses 2 and 3. After allowing a few teams to share their paraphrases, tell the class that Job had a real problem with pride. God is addressing his spiritual arrogance. Next, ask two people to read aloud God's questions (vv. 4, 5), giving attention to the intonation and emphasis that God may have used to make His point. Then ask for an interpretation of God's meaning in verses 5 and 7. Finally, ask, "What is God's message to us in this passage?" Add to the chart, "Chapter 38," and note the student answers to, "What is God's message to us?" on that chart.

Ask a student to read Job 40:6-9, a text that continues God's peppering Job with tough questions. Ask, "What serious charge is God making to Job here?" Explain the background for this charge. Ask, "What is God's message to Job and to us?" On the visual write, "Chapter 40," and list the student responses to the last question.

Read Job 42:1-6, Job's response to God's tough questions. Add to the chart, "Chapter 42: Job's reply." List each of the following categories numbered below as you ask and discuss, "What did Job learn about (1) God's sovereignty? (vv. 1, 2); (2) Job's own wisdom? (v. 3); (3) knowing God? (vv. 4, 5)." Write the student responses to these questions on the visual. Use the lesson commentary to summarize Job's comments in verse 6.

Into Life

Testimonials: Remind the class that today's message to Job jolted him out of his spiritual arrogance and changed his attitude. Ask the class how their attitudes have been affected by God's revelation about His relationship to us. What probed their hearts and changed their values?

Prayer Circles: Hang four signs in the corners of the room. One is to read, "Spiritual Arrogance (I thought I had God pegged!)." Another: "Pride (Not enough humility)." A third: "God's injustice—failing to accept God's way." The fourth: "Unrelated and Unspoken Needs." As you hang the signs, explain that one may highlight a need or shortcoming class members have discovered in their own lives. Tell them to move to a sign appropriate to their needs, assuring them they will not have to reveal their need specifically. However, each group will ask for two or three people to pray for the needs of that group. Close by singing the chorus to the hymn "I Surrender All."

Let's Talk It Over

*The questions on this page are designed to promote discussion of the lesson
by the class and to encourage application of the lesson Scriptures. The answers
provided are only discussion starters. Let your class talk it over from there.*

**1. The best teachers help their students grow
in both understanding *and* character. How did
God's "test questions" help Job develop in both
areas as a student of the Almighty?**

Going to college can be a humbling experience: every new thing you learn makes you realize that there are ten other things you don't
know! Job thought he knew quite a bit about
God. But then God administered a test on Job's
ability to have sovereign power, to explain the
workings of all creation, and to know what it
means to be perfectly just in all circumstances.

As a result, Job will admit his inability to provide the answers. Such an admission helped develop humility! It was then that God gave Job the
best grade anyone of us can expect to receive in
this life—"I" for Incomplete but also a grade of
"A" for Accepted. Unlike the educational expectations we normally encounter, in God's Acad-
emy Job had to fail his test in order to succeed!

**2. When tragedy strikes, many today question
the justice of God as Job did (Job 19:6, 7). How
can Job 40:6-14 help us in rough times?**

Job 40:6-14 begins to help us when, above all,
we actually *read it!* What a priceless treasure this
passage is for teaching us about God's great
strength, His glory, and His ability to bring the
proud to their knees. This passage reminds us in
no uncertain terms that nothing that happens is
outside of God's sovereign control.

God doesn't make mistakes, and His understanding of "the big picture" is always complete
when ours is not. Now that Jesus has come and
we have the New Testament, we have more information than did Job. With so much more revelation, how can we not trust God?

**3. While speaking to Job, God reveals clues
about His nature. What are some of these and
why are they important?**

There are so many clues in Job 38–41 that it's
difficult to list them all! Among His characteristics God speaks about being in "command"
(39:27), being "Almighty" (40:2), and being pos-
sessor of everything (41:11). That certainly
doesn't allow room for any false competitors!

The more we learn about God the more humble it should make us. This is important because
an arrogant person can have a hard time being

used in God's service. The ability of the true God
to speak audibly while orchestrating a storm
must have impressed and humbled Job.

**4. In being able to speak directly with God,
Job experienced something very rare indeed!
Would you want to have a direct conversation
with God? Why, or why not?**

How we answer this question depends on personal motives. Many who would desire to talk
with God and have Him answer directly probably just want to argue about something. Those
who are more spiritually mature are willing to
wait until God calls them home before they anticipate having a direct conversation.

The toughest lesson we have to learn about
faith is that while we may not understand the
twists and turns in our lives, God does. God
doesn't have to give explanations since He is not
answerable to us.

But it's not God's egotism or play for power
that makes His reasons beyond understanding at
times. As Job learned, and as the spiritual heroes
mentioned in Hebrews 11 learned, we would be
unable to comprehend many of God's reasons
even if He did air them. But just as those heroes
were to trust God, so must we.

**5. Which lesson is more important to learn
from the book of Job: how to respond to adversity or the need to repent? Why?**

Often a person will begin to overcome adversity *by* repenting, so the two ideas actually are in-
tertwined. This is far different from pop
psychology and the daytime TV talk shows that
teach people to overcome adversity through
"mental wholeness." When a person repents, he
or she moves beyond being just a whiny "victim."

Sadly, we sometimes minimize the importance of having a repentant spirit in our efforts to
see how many can be added to the church. But
no matter how good we are, no matter how respected we may be, we still have weaknesses
that show up clearly as we place ourselves in the
shadow of the Almighty.

Brokenness is needed before God is truly able
to make anyone into what He wants him or her
to be. "The sacrifices of God are a broken spirit: a
broken and a contrite heart, O God, thou wilt not
despise" (Psalm 51:17).

A Time for All Things

DEVOTIONAL READING: Psalm 1.

BACKGROUND SCRIPTURE: Ecclesiastes 3.

PRINTED TEXT: Ecclesiastes 3:1-15.

Ecclesiastes 3:1-15

1 To every thing there is a season, and a time to every purpose under the heaven:

2 A time to be born, and a time to die; a time to plant, and a time to pluck up that which is planted;

3 A time to kill, and a time to heal; a time to break down, and a time to build up;

4 A time to weep, and a time to laugh; a time to mourn, and a time to dance;

5 A time to cast away stones, and a time to gather stones together; a time to embrace, and a time to refrain from embracing;

6 A time to get, and a time to lose; a time to keep, and a time to cast away;

7 A time to rend, and a time to sew; a time to keep silence, and a time to speak;

8 A time to love, and a time to hate; a time of war, and a time of peace.

9 What profit hath he that worketh in that wherein he laboreth?

10 I have seen the travail, which God hath given to the sons of men to be exercised in it.

11 He hath made every thing beautiful in his time: also he hath set the world in their heart, so that no man can find out the work that God maketh from the beginning to the end.

12 I know that there is no good in them, but for a man to rejoice, and to do good in his life.

13 And also that every man should eat and drink, and enjoy the good of all his labor, it is the gift of God.

14 I know that, whatsoever God doeth, it shall be for ever: nothing can be put to it, nor any thing taken from it: and God doeth it, that men should fear before him.

15 That which hath been is now; and that which is to be hath already been; and God requireth that which is past.

**Feb
1**

GOLDEN TEXT: To every thing there is a season, and a time to every purpose
under the heaven.— Ecclesiastes 3:1.

Lesson Aims

After participating in this lesson, each student should be able to:

1. Point out the contrasts that exist in the normal routines of life.

2. Express the comfort that comes from knowing that God is in control, even in the extremes of life.

3. Give a testimony of God's grace that sustained him or her through one of life's "extreme" periods.

Lesson Outline

INTRODUCTION
  A. Through a Glass
  B. Lesson Background
  I. DISCUSSION ABOUT TIME (Ecclesiastes 3:1-8)
    A. In Nature (vv. 1, 2)
       A Time to Die
    B. In Behavior (vv. 3, 4)
    C. In Business (vv. 5, 6)
    D. In Society (vv. 7, 8)
  II. FROM TIME TO ETERNITY (Ecclesiastes 3:9-15)
    A. God Allows Suffering (vv. 9, 10)
       Divine Irritation
    B. God's Works Are Beyond Understanding (v. 11)
    C. We Can Enjoy God's Gifts (vv. 12, 13)
    D. God Is Eternal, Beyond Time (vv. 14, 15)
CONCLUSION
  A. "Change and Decay"
  B. "Thou Who Changest Not"
  C. Prayer
  D. Thought to Remember

Introduction

A. Through a Glass

Glass is one of God's most remarkable gifts to mankind. Glass has been known and used for hundreds of years, but only in the past century or so have we become aware of its great versatility. We use it for windows, of course, and we also use it to package our food and beverages. We use it to insulate our houses, to make roofing materials, and to make fabrics to decorate our houses.

One of the most important uses of glass is in the field of optics. Perhaps you're reading this text through eyeglasses that sharpen your blurring vision. In the microscope and telescope we have fashioned glass into powerful lenses that open vistas beyond the range of even the sharpest eyes.

In a way, the microscope and the telescope symbolize two ways to look at life. The writer of Ecclesiastes uses the microscope to analyze life "up close" in its frustrating twists and turns. This gives us a sobering and sometimes pessimistic view of life. But the Scriptures also give us a telescopic view of life, allowing us to see beyond the confines of time and to catch a bit of God's purposes in eternity.

B. Lesson Background

The book of Ecclesiastes is not often studied in our churches and Sunday schools. As a result, we have missed many of the valuable lessons it has to teach us. In some ways it presents a rather pessimistic and even cynical view of life. Yet these very elements make it most worthy of study, for many of the views expressed in this book are as prevalent today as they were when Ecclesiastes was written three thousand years ago.

The Hebrew title of the book, *Qohelet,* is not clearly understood by modern scholars. The title we use today comes from the Greek translation *ekklesiastes,* which means "assemblyman," leading to translations of it as "Teacher" or "Preacher" (Ecclesiastes 1:1, 2; 12:8). The writer of the book identifies himself as "the Preacher, the son of David, king in Jerusalem" (1:1). This naturally leads us to believe that this king was Solomon. The tenor of the book certainly seems to fit the lifestyle of King Solomon, who started his reign so well but who enjoyed too many things too soon. As the years passed, he looked back on all his activities and began to feel the sense of emptiness expressed in verse 2 of the first chapter: "Vanity of vanities; all is vanity."

I. Discussion About Time (Ecclesiastes 3:1-8)

A. In Nature (vv. 1, 2)

1. To every thing there is a season, and a time to every purpose under the heaven.

This verse introduces a series of contrasts of things that may be observed in nature and in a variety of human activities. The seasons are not limited to the four seasons of the year, but apply to a whole range of activities that people are engaged in or observe.

2. A time to be born, and a time to die; a time to plant, and a time to pluck up that which is planted.

The first in this series of contrasts pairs the beginning of life with the end of life. Every person has experienced birth and, barring the return of the Lord, will experience death. Modern medicine has made it possible for premature babies to survive. Medicine is able to extend life expectancy, yet all of us will still experience the birth-death cycle.

All the other activities the writer uses fall between these two events. The first is a recognition that there is *a time to plant*. Those living in an agricultural economy are keenly aware of this, and that planting time is not the same for all crops.

There is also *a time to pluck up* those crops. Annual crops must be harvested or plowed under. Even trees that are set out have a definite life span depending upon the species, and in the cycle of life must eventually be cut down and disposed of.

Further, there is a time to plant and uproot in a nonagricultural sense (see Jeremiah 1:10; 4:3; Matthew 13:24-30). Knowing just when those times come requires spiritual wisdom.

A TIME TO DIE

Solomon was right: there is a time to die. There is a time when our bodies wear out. A faithful Christian with terminal cancer commented, "I'm ready to go. I know the Lord is waiting for me, and I'm so tired." This man was able to speak with calm assurance about his death because he had lived a faith-filled life. He was prepared and ready to die.

There is a time when we are alone. A 103-year-old Christian was only half joking when she said, "I need to hurry up and die or all of my friends in Heaven will think I went the other way." This woman had outlived her husband, her friends, her peers, and even her children. She was prepared and ready to be reunited with them.

There is a time when we no longer can serve, except perhaps through our prayers. A frail Christian in her eighties asked her young minister, "Why won't the Lord let me go to sleep and not wake up? I'm ready to die. I can't get out. I can't write letters. I can't hear people on the phone. I want to go home." There may be ways to serve we have not considered, but this woman was prepared and ready for death's release.

The acceptance of death is not the same as a reason to put innocent people to death; we do not have that right. But anticipating death is Biblical. The apostle Paul wrote, "I am now ready to be offered, and the time of my departure is at hand. I have fought a good fight, I have finished my course, I have kept the faith: henceforth there is laid up for me a crown of righteousness, which

Visual for lesson 9

This montage of life-event images will reinforce today's Golden Text.

the Lord, the righteous judge, shall give me at that day" (2 Timothy 4:6-8). Paul was prepared and ready to die.

The only time not to die is when you are unprepared to stand before the Lord. How are your preparations coming?   —J. D. J.

B. In Behavior (vv. 3, 4)

3. A time to kill, and a time to heal; a time to break down, and a time to build up.

Some commentators think the *time to kill* refers to war, but war is specifically mentioned in verse 8. This verse may refer to executions, as the Old Testament law specified. (See Genesis 9:6; Exodus 19:13; cf. Acts 25:11.)

A time to heal may have in mind the normal process through which one may experience the healing of a wound or the recovery from a serious illness. Or it might also extend to the healing of emotional wounds one has suffered or the repairing of broken relations between individuals.

To break down and *to build up* describe the process of destruction and construction. We today are familiar with urban renewal or highway construction where the old must be broken up and removed before the new and better can take its place. Those living in Solomon's day would have been quite aware of this process because of his many building projects.

4. A time to weep, and a time to laugh; a time to mourn, and a time to dance.

A person may *weep* for joy, but here the reference clearly is to weeping in sorrow (cf. Romans 12:15; James 4:9). Weeping occurs at the time of death or some other serious tragedy. Laughing and rejoicing normally occur when a child is born, when some important victory is gained, or during some other festive occasion.

The ancient Israelite people do not hesitate to display their emotions. Mourning over a death, for instance, often follows definite rituals that include hiring professional mourners as seen in Jesus' day (Mark 5:38-41). Dancing is often a part of a wedding ceremony. It can also be an act of religious devotion, as in the case of David when the ark of the covenant was returned to Jerusalem (2 Samuel 6:14).

C. In Business (vv. 5, 6)

5. A time to cast away stones, and a time to gather stones together; a time to embrace, and a time to refrain from embracing.

The most likely explanation for casting *away stones* refers to the practice of clearing a field prior to planting a crop or setting out vines. The land in ancient Israel is quite stony and much labor is required to prepare it for crops. The stones are gathered together and are used in the construction of houses, walls, or terraces. This process has to be done in a timely fashion, because obviously one cannot build walls until stone is first gathered.

6. A time to get, and a time to lose; a time to keep, and a time to cast away.

There is an appropriate time and manner in which one may acquire wealth. The first part of this verse seems to apply to many situations beyond one's control, while the second part seems to apply to conditions under which one consciously makes decisions. Success usually requires hard work, but we all know that outside factors can intervene. A farmer or a businessperson realizes that occasionally there are bad times, and these must be accepted. In our day we have experienced the wild gyrations of the stock market during the roaring 1990s when some made huge fortunes, and then during more recent years when these fortunes evaporated.

A couple may acquire a lot of things such as clothing, tools, mementos, and books that they eventually no longer use and merely clutter their closets. Then in retirement they move to smaller quarters and are faced with the painful task of disposing of all these accumulated things. Probably Solomon never had to make such decisions—he just built a bigger palace!

D. In Society (vv. 7, 8)

7. A time to rend, and a time to sew; a time to keep silence, and a time to speak.

The immediate reference may be to the rending of one's garment as an act of mourning (cf. Esther 4:1), but it certainly has wider applications. It can involve the tearing of a garment into smaller patches to be used to mend another garment. It could even apply to personal relationships (cf. Joel 2:13). Most of us on occasion have had to sever relationships with long-time friends, painful though this may be. For example, a recovering alcoholic sometimes has to give up his old drinking buddies if he is to recover from his addiction. [See question #1, page 192.]

Many of us have a problem of knowing when to *keep silence* (cf. Psalm 4:4; Amos 5:13). We sometimes speak harshly and in anger, intending to bring pain to others. At other times, even with good intentions, our words are hurtful. But in many situations "silence is golden"! (See Psalm 39:1.) Even so, there also are times to speak up (cf. Esther 4:12-14; Matthew 28:19, 20). Knowing which is which is an issue of spiritual maturity. [See question #2, page 192.]

8. A time to love, and a time to hate; a time of war, and a time of peace.

Drawing upon Old Testament law, Jewish teachers taught that there are times and situations when one is obligated *to hate* an enemy. Jesus challenged this concept in Matthew 5:43, 44. Even so, we are still to hate evil (Romans 12:9; Revelation 2:6).

Unfortunately, most of us are all too familiar with *war*. As the nineteenth century came to a close, many believed that the twentieth century would usher in an era of worldwide peace—some expected Utopia! After all, humanity had become "enlightened." Instead, the twentieth century turned out to be the bloodiest hundred-year period in history. World Wars I and II were fought by the most "educated" countries on earth. Numerous smaller conflicts and "ethnic cleansings" added to the death and misery.

As horrible as war is, there are times when it is preferable to an unjust *peace*. For example, if the Western allies had not adopted a policy of appeasement against Hitler in the 1930s, the Holocaust that murdered millions of innocent people might have been avoided. The events of September 11, 2001, remind us that terrible evil is still at work in our world in the twenty-first century. [See question #3, page 192.]

II. From Time to Eternity (Ecclesiastes 3:9-15)

A. God Allows Suffering (vv. 9, 10)

9. What profit hath he that worketh in that wherein he laboreth?

Some see in this verse an expression of the writer's despair. Since God is in complete control, there is nothing we can do to change the situation. Such a viewpoint can only lead to utter pessimism—why work, since there is no benefit in it? This possibility serves as a lead-in to the next verse.

10. I have seen the travail, which God hath given to the sons of men to be exercised in it.

The travail is the labor mentioned in the previous verse. As a result of humanity's fall, God pronounced a curse upon the ground, causing it to produce thorns and thistles (Genesis 3:18, 19). Although we have found ways to avoid the full burden of this curse, it still remains heavy upon the human race. We may escape the most tiring physical labor, but we often substitute for it the more demanding mental labor.

Even though we are still under this curse, God has given us the spiritual and mental resources that will allow us to find pleasure and satisfaction in our work. This allows us to escape the pessimism that comes from viewing verse 9 in isolation, as the following verse shows. [See question #4, page 192.]

DIVINE IRRITATION

A man picks up a Pinctada mollusk lying in a shallow ocean bay. He pries open the shell and cuts into the mollusk's inner flesh to insert a tiny object. He closes the shell and lays the mollusk back in the water. Inside, the creature secretes crystalline calcium carbonate to heal its wound. This mucous surrounds the tiny object lodged in the mollusk's skin. Month after month, layers of this nacre form around the tiny object and harden. After three years, a man picks up the oyster, pries open the shell, and removes a beautiful pearl.

Pearls grow only after an oyster is injured. But this injury must be precisely placed. If a mollusk is too young, or if the man handling it is not careful, the oyster will die. If the insertion is made improperly, a misshapen lump will develop or no pearl will grow. Experienced pearl growers know just how to irritate an oyster to produce beauty.

God knows just how to disturb people, too (cf. Hebrews 12:11). The Lord irritated Moses and produced a great leader. God bothered Isaiah and Jeremiah and developed courageous prophets. The Lord goaded Saul of Tarsus and produced an amazing apostle.

You may feel the Lord has laid an unwanted burden on your back, and you may be right. But as with the mollusk, only when God gets "under your skin" can He make something beautiful in His time. Endure irritations with patience for the Lord. Let God work in your life.   —J. D. J.

B. God's Works Are Beyond Understanding (v. 11)

11. He hath made every thing beautiful in his time: also he hath set the world in their heart, so that no man can find out the work that God maketh from the beginning to the end.

How to Say It

ECCLESIASTES OR EKKLESIASTES (Greek). Ik-*leez*-ee-*as*-teez (strong accent on *as*).
JEREMIAH. Jair-uh-*my*-uh.
JERUSALEM. Juh-*roo*-suh-lem.
QOHELET (Hebrew). Koe-*hel*-it.
SOLOMON. *Sol*-o-mun.

God has created a *beautiful* universe, hasn't He? [See question #5, page 192.] In the process of creating the universe, God also *set the world* in people's hearts. *World* means "eternity" in this context, as several other versions have it. Although we live under the burden of God's curse, He has planted in our hearts a glimpse of that eternity.

This inspires our hope that He has something better in store for us, and drives pessimism away. Yet this bit of eternity that we carry in our bosoms is but a hint of God's infinite wisdom since *no man can find out the work that God maketh from the beginning to the end.*

C. We Can Enjoy God's Gifts (vv. 12, 13)

12. I know that there is no good in them, but for a man to rejoice, and to do good in his life.

In certain contexts, it makes more sense to translate the Hebrew word for *good* as "better," and this is one of those cases. (The translators of the *King James Version* have done this very thing, for example, in Ecclesiastes 8:15.) While we're living with eternity in mind (v. 11), there is nothing "better" for us than *to rejoice, and to do good.*

Real joy and satisfaction come when we are actively involved in reaching out to help those who are in physical, emotional, or spiritual need. The testimony of the saints through the centuries gives ample proof of this.

13. And also that every man should eat and drink, and enjoy the good of all his labor, it is the gift of God.

Even though sin has brought upon the human race the curse of burdensome *labor*, God has also given us the insights to see labor as a *gift* from Him. Too often we try to avoid work by passing it on to someone else or looking for a government handout. But in so doing we deny ourselves the real joy that God wants us to have when we work. Food and *drink* always taste better when you've really earned it!

D. God Is Eternal, Beyond Time (vv. 14, 15)

14. I know that, whatsoever God doeth, it shall be for ever: nothing can be put to it, nor any thing taken from it: and God doeth it, that men should fear before him.

In the halls of Heaven there is no need of clocks or calendars. But human beings on planet Earth are confined by the boundaries set by time. As a result, we pay close attention to clocks and calendars, and there is no way that we can break out of these constraints in this world. God has granted us freedom on earth, but that freedom is always limited to a short bit of time and to a very small space. We can neither add to nor take away from His absolute sovereignty in this regard.

As a result we should *fear before him.* We should not understand this as the abject fear that motivates a pagan who bows down before idols. Rather, it is the reverential awe that we experience as we come to realize that He is a righteous God who has made ample provisions for our physical needs. He is also a loving God who will deal with us with justice tempered by grace.

15. That which hath been is now; and that which is to be hath already been; and God requireth that which is past.

The old saying, "History repeats itself" is true. Many things that are happening *now,* particularly sinful things, have happened before. They undoubtedly will happen again. But in requiring *that which is past,* God calls all of history to account.

Conclusion

A. "Change and Decay"

By our contemporary experiences, the decades before America's Civil War in the nineteenth century may seem like a relatively stable period in history. Yet when Henry F. Lyte wrote "Abide With Me" in 1847, he expressed a much different sentiment: "Change and decay in all around I see." How much more appropriate those words seem in our own times! The twentieth century was torn by wars, crime, oppressive governments, and violent ideologies. In more recent times we have witnessed the upsurge of terrorism that amounts to a strange, worldwide war. Are there any solid foundations left?

The study of history leads us to realize that times always have been unstable and threatening. The few brief periods of peace this old world has enjoyed seem only to be a prelude to greater violence. If this view seems pessimistic, then so be it; but that is the view we find expressed by the writer of Ecclesiastes.

If we look only at the things immediately around us, we are very likely to fall into dark despair. Indeed, we often run into people who are in these desperate straits. In spite of the fact that we enjoy the greatest prosperity the world has ever known and in spite of the fact that we have more things to cater to our comfort and pleasure, our suicide rates remain frighteningly high—a clear sign of despair.

B. "Thou Who Changest Not"

But Henry Lyte had an answer for all the change and decay he saw in the culture of his day. He appealed to God, "O Thou who changest not." Like the writer of Ecclesiastes, he knew that there was a God ruling over the universe who was present, always had been present, and would be present regardless of whatever else might change. How reassuring it is to know that amid all the confusion and chaos we see, God stands immovable.

But there is more. Our God is not some distant monarch who has no concern for us and doesn't even know that we exist. Rather, He is a loving Father. We do not see this viewpoint very clearly expressed in Ecclesiastes. But when we turn to the New Testament we learn that our God is a warm, personal God. He is the God who hears and answers our prayers.

Henry Lyte recognized this in the ending words of each stanza: "Abide with me." He had every reason to be assured that God would hear his plea. Indeed, God already answered that plea through His Son, Jesus Christ.

C. Prayer

Almighty God, although we live in a world that is wracked with decay and destruction, let us not fall into the throes of gloom and despair. Give us the vision to see beyond all these things. Remind us again that a day is coming in which You will set all things right. In Jesus' name, amen.

D. Thought to Remember

"The Lord is my rock, and my fortress, and my deliverer" (Psalm 18:2).

Home Daily Bible Readings

Monday, Jan. 26—God's Promise of Seasons (Genesis 8:15-22)

Tuesday, Jan. 27—Human Time as Nothing to God (Psalm 90:1-6)

Wednesday, Jan. 28—Teach Us to Count Our Days (Psalm 90:7-12)

Thursday, Jan. 29—Prosper the Work of Our Hands (Psalm 90:13-17)

Friday, Jan. 30—The Righteous Prosper, the Wicked Perish (Psalm 1:1-6)

Saturday, Jan. 31—A Season for Everything (Ecclesiastes 3:1-8)

Sunday, Feb. 1—God's Gift of Work (Ecclesiastes 3:9-15)

Learning by Doing

This page contains an alternative lesson plan emphasizing learning activities. Classes desiring such student involvement will find these suggestions helpful.

Learning Goals

After participating in this lesson, each student will be able to:

1. Point out the contrasts that exist in the normal routines of life.

2. Express the comfort that comes from knowing that God is in control, even in the extremes of life.

3. Give a testimony of God's grace that sustained him or her through one of life's "extreme" periods.

Into the Lesson

Choose one of the following activities to introduce this lesson.

Option 1. As class members arrive, give each a sheet of paper with a bold heading reading "I wish I had more time for. . . ." Ask students to write appropriate answers. After a few minutes allow students to share their answers. Make the transition to Bible study by noting that time is a quantity to be managed. What we do and when we do it are important in time management. State, "One book of the Old Testament has a strong philosophical flavor, and it has principles about time that can be helpful to us. However, it also teaches us that some events and happenings in life are simply in God's control."

Option 2. Prepare a large poster with a heading printed in bold letters, "A Discussion About Time." Ask the class this question: "If you could choose to discuss anything you wish about the concept of *time*, what would you choose?" Write their responses. Make the transition to Bible study by saying, "Time is an extremely important issue. There are many things we would like to talk about under this heading. One of the books of the Old Testament has a strong philosophical flavor, addresses this issue of time, and gives clues to God's control and grace in life's events."

Into the Word

Give a brief lecture about the author and purpose of this book. The Lesson Background will be helpful. Also you may wish to consult a Bible survey book or a commentary introduction to the book of Ecclesiastes.

Distribute copies of an activity sheet described below to groups of four to six. Each group will be working on identical tasks. (This activity is also included in the student book activity pages.) You may give each group a photocopy of the lesson commentary on verses 1-9. The sheet should have three columns: "Time," "The Concept," and "The Application." The rows below the first column should be IN NATURE (3:1, 2), IN BEHAVIOR (3:3, 4), IN BUSINESS (3:5, 6), IN SOCIETY (3:7, 8). Include space for writing below each line.

Ask the groups to discuss and summarize the concept of each Scripture, noting what God wants us to learn for life under "The Application" column. Encourage groups to work quickly. After they complete the task, ask groups to share their applications from each of the four passages.

Read verses 9-15. Ask the following discussion questions (also included in the student book's Learning by Doing section):

1. Are verses 9, 10 a statement of despair (see 2:17-26), or would you read this passage as a writer's device simply to stimulate thinking about the significance of toil? Why?

2. What is this passage saying about the relationship of work to life's joys and satisfactions? Why do you agree or disagree?

3. What does verse 15 say about God's concept of time? What does God want us to understand?

Into Life

Option 1. Allow the same groups that worked together earlier to do the following. Explain that we can apply these Scriptural concepts about time and life tasks every day. We can zero in on things we must face and do during specific times of our lives. Ask each group to write a new version of this Scripture (vv. 1-8) appropriate for one of the following people groups. Assign one people group to each activity group: college student, parents of young children, husband and wife (age forty), career mid-level manager, elderly couple, terminally ill woman. Allow each group to read its version to the entire class.

Option 2. Testimonial time. Remind the class of the variety of life's tasks that face us at different times of life. Sometimes those tasks or challenges are very difficult. Ask people to share times when life has been difficult, yet where they have seen God's sustaining power at work.

After a few testimonies, remind them that prayer was probably a very real part of God's work. Ask for prayer requests of people who are facing some of life's extreme tests. After each request, ask one person to pray for that need.

Let's Talk It Over

The questions on this page are designed to promote discussion of the lesson by the class and to encourage application of the lesson Scriptures. The answers provided are only discussion starters. Let your class talk it over from there.

1. The lesson writer suggests that "rending and sewing" may also be intended to apply to personal relationships. Was there ever a time when you had to break off a friendship because it was the right thing to do? If so, explain why.

The Scripture has a lot to say about appropriate relationships. These can be divided into two general categories: what to do regarding relationships that already exist, and what to do regarding relationships that don't yet exist but could. In the first category, for example, 1 Corinthians 5 talks about expelling an immoral brother from a church. Paul is also quite explicit in Titus 3:10 about breaking off relationships with people who cause division in the church.

For the second category, 2 Corinthians 6:14 warns believers against being "yoked together with unbelievers." The book of Proverbs also offers a great deal of instruction regarding relationships to avoid (e.g., Proverbs 1:10-19; 2:12-22; 6:23-29; 24:1, 2).

2. Ecclesiastes 3 is among of the most well-known pieces of literature in the Old Testament. In what ways have you seen its wisdom used—or misused?

This section of Ecclesiastes is so profound it has even influenced pop culture. In 1965 a singing group calling themselves "The Byrds" used Ecclesiastes 3:1-15 in a song they titled "Turn! Turn! Turn!" Released against the backdrop of the war in Vietnam, many found the lyrics to be haunting and poignant.

Some of your learners may note that a leader needs an understanding of the principles in Ecclesiastes 3 in order to be able to lead without frustration. For example, church leaders may be trying to decide whether or not to expand their church's facilities. Verse 3b may challenge them to determine which is more important: to preserve their heritage, or to "break down" and "build up" in order to serve better their church's current and prospective members.

A prudent leader will also consider the very sound advice in verse 7 about when to speak and when to be silent. This subject is important to churches of every era! For example, church leaders must "talk up" issues of doctrinal purity, but they may think it wise to remain silent concerning matters of expediency.

3. Ecclesiastes 3:8 speaks of proper times for love, hate, war, and peace. How do we recognize when times have changed, requiring that we shift our attitudes and our actions?

This is a difficult question! You may end up with as many different answers as you have learners in your class. Even so, there are some boundaries that all should be able to agree on.

First, Jesus' instructions in Matthew 5:38-44 cautions us to be careful never to engage in our own private little "wars" for personal vengeance. Second, Romans 12:9 tells us that the time is *always* right to hate evil and love good. Romans 13:3-5 and Revelation 2:6 can also add insight to the discussion.

4. How should Ecclesiastes 3:9, 10 influence our work ethic today, if at all?

We must be careful not to allow this passage, taken in isolation, to cause us to become cynical. Elsewhere, Solomon notes the importance of work (Ecclesiastes 3:22; Proverbs 14:23; 21:25). So does the apostle Paul (2 Thessalonians 3:10).

Work, properly approached, provides us with purpose and a sense of fulfillment. Our creative work benefits both others and ourselves. When Solomon asks, "What profit hath he that worketh in that wherein he laboreth?" we can answer *nothing!* if a person works merely for selfish, this-worldly purposes. But for a person whose work lays up "treasures in heaven" the "profit" is great indeed! (See Matthew 6:19-21.)

5. What are some things we find in life that are valuable and give us pleasure? How is the Christian's perspective on such things different from a non-Christian's?

The Christian's perspective is founded in remembering that we are created in God's image. Anything that is beautiful to Him should be beautiful to us, too. He desires our well-being and has given us creation to use and enjoy.

But although God "hath made every thing beautiful in his time," sinful people have a knack of turning that beauty into ugliness. For example, the beauty of certain plants is marred when sinners turn them into addictive drugs. Our hearts should grieve when we see how sin has introduced such corruption into the beauty of God's creation (cf. Romans 8:22).

A Time to Remember

DEVOTIONAL READING: Psalm 143:1-8.

BACKGROUND SCRIPTURE: Ecclesiastes 11, 12.

PRINTED TEXT: Ecclesiastes 11:7–12:8.

Ecclesiastes 11:7-10

7 Truly the light is sweet, and a pleasant thing it is for the eyes to behold the sun:

8 But if a man live many years, and rejoice in them all; yet let him remember the days of darkness; for they shall be many. All that cometh is vanity.

9 Rejoice, O young man, in thy youth; and let thy heart cheer thee in the days of thy youth, and walk in the ways of thine heart, and in the sight of thine eyes: but know thou, that for all these things God will bring thee into judgment.

10 Therefore remove sorrow from thy heart, and put away evil from thy flesh: for childhood and youth are vanity.

Ecclesiastes 12:1-8

1 Remember now thy Creator in the days of thy youth, while the evil days come not, nor the years draw nigh, when thou shalt say, I have no pleasure in them;

2 While the sun, or the light, or the moon, or the stars, be not darkened, nor the clouds return after the rain:

3 In the day when the keepers of the house shall tremble, and the strong men shall bow themselves, and the grinders cease because they are few, and those that look out of the windows be darkened,

4 And the doors shall be shut in the streets, when the sound of the grinding is low, and he shall rise up at the voice of the bird, and all the daughters of music shall be brought low;

5 Also when they shall be afraid of that which is high, and fears shall be in the way, and the almond tree shall flourish, and the grasshopper shall be a burden, and desire shall fail: because man goeth to his long home, and the mourners go about the streets:

6 Or ever the silver cord be loosed, or the golden bowl be broken, or the pitcher be broken at the fountain, or the wheel broken at the cistern.

7 Then shall the dust return to the earth as it was: and the spirit shall return unto God who gave it.

8 Vanity of vanities, saith the Preacher; all is vanity.

GOLDEN TEXT: Remember now thy Creator in the days of thy youth, while the evil days come not.—Ecclesiastes 12:1.

Lesson Aims

After this lesson each student should be able to:

1. Give reasons why it is better to remember the Creator in the days of youth rather than in old age.

2. Describe ways the church can do a better job of reaching out to young people.

3. Identify a young person and work for him or her to become a follower of Jesus Christ, or to grow in that relationship.

Lesson Outline

INTRODUCTION
    A. Ready, Aim—!
    B. Lesson Background
 I. ADVICE TO YOUTH (Ecclesiastes 11:7-10)
    A. Life in Perspective (vv. 7, 8)
    B. Life in the Shadow of Judgment (vv. 9, 10)
II. FRUSTRATION OF AGING (Ecclesiastes 12:1-8)
    A. Coming Storms (vv. 1, 2)
      In the Days of Youth
    B. Declining Health (vv. 3, 4)
    C. Growing Fears (v. 5)
    D. Looming Death (vv. 6, 7)
      Worn Headstones
    E. Closing Lament (v. 8)
CONCLUSION
    A. In the Days of Thy Youth
    B. Prayer
    C. Thought to Remember

Introduction

A. Ready, Aim—!

Few things are more awe inspiring than watching and hearing a battleship fire a broadside. With an earsplitting roar the huge sixteen-inch guns belch flame and smoke, hurling hundreds of pounds of steel and high explosives toward a target hidden beyond the horizon.

But if the shells are to hit their target, several involved calculations must be made. The range of the target must be determined either by sight or by radar. The powder charge must be accurately measured. The speeds of both the firing ship and the target must be taken into account. Allowance must be made for the pitch and roll of the ship. Even such things as temperature and humidity are important. When we think about all these factors, we are amazed that naval gunners ever succeed. When they do succeed, it is only because they exclude every other concern and concentrate on hitting the target.

Life is like this in some ways. When we pick out our "targets"—our life goals—we must concentrate upon them intensely. While Christians may have many short-term goals, our ultimate goal is Heaven. Often we miss many of our goals because we never really aimed at them. How tragic the life that wanders aimlessly about without any real goals! Sometimes we miss our goals because we do not take into consideration all the many factors involved—our abilities, opportunities, and preparation. Occasionally we must aim at a target that is out of sight, obscured by time and circumstances. Like the gunner, we must use our radar—our Christian faith—that allows us to aim at the target even when we cannot see it.

Ready, aim—AIM!

B. Lesson Background

Have you ever found yourself wishing that you could go back and relive your youth? Most of us have dreamed wistfully of those younger years at one time or another, especially when time begins to take its inevitable toll on our bodies. But most of us also have some reservations about going back. We would want to take with us the wisdom that years of experience have given us. That experience would help us avoid many of the foolish mistakes we made, mistakes that brought pain to others and to ourselves.

In today's lesson we can sense "the Preacher" (Solomon) going through that experience. He knew, of course, that he couldn't go back. But at least he could share some of the wisdom he had accumulated with future generations so that they could avoid some of the mistakes he had made. In these few verses he spells out the life cycle that all of us must travel—birth, childhood, adolescence, adulthood, middle age, old age, and death—if the Lord gives us enough years. He gives us a few general principles about attitudes concerning life rather than a list of specific moral teachings. As we study the book of Ecclesiastes, we can learn some valuable lessons from one who has "been there and done that."

I. Advice to Youth (Ecclesiastes 11:7-10)

A. Life in Perspective (vv. 7, 8)

7. Truly the light is sweet, and a pleasant thing it is for the eyes to behold the sun.

We may take *light* in its most obvious sense of physical light, especially the light of the sun. But the writer often uses figurative language that involves much more. He may very well have in mind here the whole sweep of life, and so light refers to the events and experiences that illuminate our time on earth. [See question #1, page 200.]

We feel sorrow for those who lack eyesight, because it is one of the most wonderful blessings God has given us. Our eyes allow us to do many things, including experiencing sweeping vistas of beauty. Light is indeed *sweet,* as it allows us to enjoy and use our eyesight even with glasses or after laser surgery. We who have our eyesight can scarcely imagine what it would be like to be blind.

Many of us, especially if we are "morning people," find it pleasant to see a bright *sun* rising to light a new day. The rising sun symbolizes the beginning of a new day of life with all the exciting potential that it holds.

8. But if a man live many years, and rejoice in them all; yet let him remember the days of darkness; for they shall be many. All that cometh is vanity.

Even as we enjoy life as it unfolds, we are given a solemn reminder to keep things in perspective. The *days of darkness* are old age (cf. Ecclesiastes 12:2, below). Those of us who have yet to experience the challenges of old age can nevertheless see its effects all around. Advancing years invite diseases such as Alzheimer's, Parkinson's, and osteoporosis. The nursing homes and long-term care facilities are not populated with young people! Younger adults today face the delicate problem of taking the car keys away from their elderly parents who no longer should be driving—a problem that didn't exist in Solomon's day.

This verse closes with the pessimistic warning that *all that cometh is vanity.* Perhaps it is best to think of this as a ploy to get our attention about how we ought to prepare ourselves for earthly life rather than a realistic appraisal of what life really is from an eternal perspective. Or perhaps this is indeed a realistic appraisal for the ungodly as they go through the seasons of life. Certainly life is not vanity (empty and meaningless) for a Christian.

B. Life in the Shadow of Judgment (vv. 9, 10)

9. Rejoice, O young man, in thy youth; and let thy heart cheer thee in the days of thy youth, and walk in the ways of thine heart, and in the sight of thine eyes: but know thou, that for all these things God will bring thee into judgment.

"The Preacher" (Solomon) continues to stress the importance of enjoying life, especially in one's youth. His suggestion that young people *walk in the ways* of their hearts sounds quite

contemporary on the surface—"whatever works for you." How frightening! Certainly Christian parents would not give this advice to their children. To give such advice to a teenager who is trying to cope with raging hormones and a desire to fit in with other teenagers is likely to be disastrous. Teen pregnancies, alcoholism, and drug addiction have exacted a terrible toll on young people who have followed their own impulses.

But Solomon is quick to establish boundaries for his advice in noting that *for all these things God will bring thee into judgment.* [See question #2, page 200.] This is a solemn warning that those who follow their own desires to the point of ignoring God's standards must face God's judgment, either here or hereafter. (See Ecclesiastes 3:17.) [See question #3, page 200.]

10. Therefore remove sorrow from thy heart, and put away evil from thy flesh: for childhood and youth are vanity.

The Hebrew word for *sorrow* also occurs in Ecclesiastes 1:18 and 2:23 where it is translated "grief." Sorrow and grief over the results of our actions can create anxiety. In our own times anxiety has become an epidemic, and people spend millions on counseling and medications to escape its debilitating effects.

This verse points the way to avoiding this sorrow: *put away evil from thy flesh.* When we do that we treat the actual cause of many sorrows, and not just the symptoms (cf. 1 Peter 2:11).

Years spent in *childhood and youth* can seem to be meaningless *(vanity)* because they are "fleeting," which is another way to translate this word. For teenagers eager to attain adult status, these years seem to drag. But to those who have reached maturity or beyond, those youthful years were all too brief.

II. Frustration of Aging (Ecclesiastes 12:1-8)

A. Coming Storms (vv. 1, 2)

1. Remember now thy Creator in the days of thy youth, while the evil days come not, nor the years draw nigh, when thou shalt say, I have no pleasure in them.

Deathbed confessions may, in some cases, be legitimate. But how much better it is when one makes a commitment to the *Creator* in his or her *youth!* [See question #4, page 200.] There are at least two good reasons why this is so. First, children and adolescents are less "set in their ways"; it is much easier for them to make that decision than for an adult whose life patterns have become increasingly rigid. Second, the younger that one is when joining the Lord's army, the more time he or she has to be involved in Christian ministry

Visual for
lesson 10

This visual will remind your learners of the responsibility they have to lead youth to God.

and enjoy all the blessings that result from a lifetime of service.

While the evil days come not gives the reason for remembering God in our youth. [See question #5, page 200.] Those evil days are the later years in life with their infirmities and pain. They seem especially evil to young people who rarely suffer such disabilities.

The writer himself has *no pleasure* in those closing years of life, although this sentiment is not universally shared by older people. Many have learned to cope with the problems of aging, and, freed from the pressures of jobs and rearing a family, they find a peace that earlier they could not enjoy.

IN THE DAYS OF YOUTH

A few years ago Barna Research discovered that people are most likely to come to Christ in their preteen years. Perhaps Solomon knew that faith commitments come easier in the earlier years when he wrote, "Remember now thy Creator in the days of thy youth" (Ecclesiastes 12:1). We must not overlook the importance of leading young people to the Lord!

Yet conversion at a young age has its dangers. Children can commit their lives to Christ without a clear understanding of what this commitment involves (cf. Matthew 13:6). Parents naturally fret about this. Is age seven too young to walk down the aisle and make a formal faith commitment? How about age ten? Children who are pushed too hard may become resentful and fall away from Christ later—in effect, they can become "inoculated" against faith.

Nevertheless, children need to be taught and encouraged to devote themselves to the Lord. Their hearts are open, they are eager to learn,

and, even before they become teenagers, they are capable of making decisions they will follow their entire lives.

You can help by volunteering in the children's ministry or youth ministry in your church. You can help by inviting neighborhood children to Bible study classes or other programs for them. You can help by praying for the young people in your congregation. And you can help by financially supporting your church's children's ministries and youth ministries. The days of youth can produce lifelong servants for the Lord, and you can help.   —J. D. J.

2. While the sun, or the light, or the moon, or the stars, be not darkened, nor the clouds return after the rain.

This verse and several that follow deal with some of the problems that the aging must face. The meanings of the figurative language used to describe some of these problems are not always clear, and not everyone agrees about the correct references. Yet there is no question that the writer is describing conditions that accompany advancing years.

B. Declining Health (vv. 3, 4)

3. In the day when the keepers of the house shall tremble, and the strong men shall bow themselves, and the grinders cease because they are few, and those that look out of the windows be darkened.

"The Preacher" (Solomon) describes the physical decline that accompanies advancing years in terms of the parts of a house. *The keepers of the house* probably refers to the hands and arms. They protect the house and care for it. As a person grows older, the hands and arms *shall tremble,* a common problem of older people suffering from various neurological afflictions or general physical weaknesses.

The strong men who *bow themselves* may refer to the legs and back that become bent by age. We now understand that many older people do not eat a balanced diet, or their bodies can no longer assimilate calcium, so their bones become weak. This causes their bodies to become stooped and sagging.

The grinders are, of course, the teeth. Older people in primitive societies are often toothless or nearly so. Today most older people living in cultures with advanced dentistry either have their own teeth or have dentures that work very well.

The windows of this figurative house are the eyes. There are not many people who escape the problem of failing eyesight. Moses was one of the few who avoided this weakness (see Deuteronomy 34:7).

4. And the doors shall be shut in the streets, when the sound of the grinding is low, and he shall rise up at the voice of the bird, and all the daughters of music shall be brought low.

Interpreting the symbolism in this verse is more difficult. One possible interpretation for *the doors* is as a reference to the ears. Ears can be thought of as doorways "into" a person in terms of being able to conduct a conversation. Physical problems may contribute to one's inability to converse, but older folks are often shut out of conversations because of poor hearing.

Helen Keller (1880–1968), perhaps the most well-known deaf and blind person of the twentieth century, is purported to have said that she would prefer to have the sense of hearing over eyesight, if given a choice. This was because lack of eyesight cuts us off from things, but lack of hearing cuts us off from other people. Modern culture has an advantage in this area with the marvel of hearing aids (although most of us know someone who is too stubborn to use one!). But modern culture also has a disadvantage of being very "noisy" (machinery, loud music, etc.), thus contributing to hearing loss.

The sound of the grinding is low probably refers to loss of teeth. With old age and loss of teeth come the inability to chew anything but mostly soft foods. The loss of teeth causes the cheeks to become sunken, making it more difficult to open the mouth. Again, modern dentistry can solve this problem, helping people avoid the look that once characterized many older people.

There are various interpretations to the statement *and he shall rise up at the voice of the bird.* It may refer to the fact that many elderly people are light sleepers and are readily aroused by the early morning call of birds, even with a loss of hearing. A few suggest that it refers to the possibility that an older person's voice can become high pitched and chirpy like that of a bird.

The phrase *the daughters of music shall be brought low* poses similar problems of interpretation. This may refer to the larynx and vocal cords, as they become enfeebled by age and thus almost silenced. Another possibility is that elderly people who have become hard of hearing no longer can take pleasure in the beauty of a woman's singing voice.

C. Growing Fears (v. 5)

5. Also when they shall be afraid of that which is high, and fears shall be in the way, and the almond tree shall flourish, and the grasshopper shall be a burden, and desire shall fail: because man goeth to his long home, and the mourners go about the streets.

To be *afraid of that which is high* may refer to the problems that older people have in climbing stairs or hills. Weak of limb and short of breath, they can find even a small ascent to be threatening. The *almond tree* in Palestine blooms in midwinter, perhaps pointing to the "winter" of a person's life—but with the important difference that there is no spring to follow. In the same way insects such as the *grasshopper* move very slowly when the weather is cold. This also is a picture of old age. It is at such a time that *desire shall fail* as interest in food and sex begin to fade away.

One's *long home* is his or her "eternal home." The last part of this verse looks to the end of life. The *mourners*, then, are professionals who have been hired to participate in the funeral ceremonies that surround a death.

D. Looming Death (vv. 6, 7)

6. Or ever the silver cord be loosed, or the golden bowl be broken, or the pitcher be broken at the fountain, or the wheel broken at the cistern.

The figures used in this verse all describe death. The *silver cord* suspends a lamp, the *golden bowl.* When the cord breaks, the lamp drops to the floor and the light is extinguished. Water is drawn from wells using clay vessels. Occasionally a pitcher would be dropped, shattering it and ending its useful existence.

The *wheel* refers to a device used to draw water from a deep well or *cistern.* When the wheel breaks, no more water can be drawn.

7. Then shall the dust return to the earth as it was: and the spirit shall return unto God who gave it.

God *formed* humanity from the *dust* of the earth (Genesis 2:7; 3:19). In death the physical body returns to the earth from whence it came, a quite dismal prospect.

But happily the verse does not end there because *the spirit shall return to God who gave it.* Here is one of the rare references to life after death in the Old Testament. "The Preacher" (Solomon) ultimately concludes that people do indeed have an advantage over the animals (cf. Ecclesiastes 3:18-21).

How to Say It

CISTERN. *sis*-turn.
DEUTERONOMY. Due-ter-*ahn*-uh-me.
ECCLESIASTES. Ik-*leez*-ee-*as*-teez (strong accent on *as*).
LARYNX. *lair*-inks.
SOLOMON. *Sol*-o-mun.

Home Daily Bible Readings

Monday, Feb. 2—I Have Beheld Your Power and Glory (Psalm 63:1-8)

Tuesday, Feb. 3—I Consider the Days of Old (Psalm 77:4-10)

Wednesday, Feb. 4—I Will Remember Your Wonders (Psalm 77:11-15)

Thursday, Feb. 5—I Think About All Your Deeds (Psalm 143:1-8)

Friday, Feb. 6—God's Work Is a Mystery (Ecclesiastes 11:1-5)

Saturday, Feb. 7—Youth Is Fleeting (Ecclesiastes 11:6-10)

Sunday, Feb. 8—Remember Your Creator (Ecclesiastes 12:1-8)

Worn Headstones

When was the last time you walked through a cemetery? We don't usually frequent such places. Even visiting www.findagrave.com on the Internet seems a little "creepy"! We generally visit cemeteries only for funerals or on Memorial Day.

But in graveyards there is wisdom for the seasons of our lives. One gravestone warns, "As you are now, so once was I. As I am now, so you must be, so prepare for death and follow me." My infant sister's gravestone says, "Asleep in Jesus," reassuring us that even though she is "absent from the body," she is "present with the Lord" (2 Corinthians 5:8).

Cemeteries remind us that we will return to dust no matter who we are. Cemeteries also remind us that we have value. We do not put markers in our gardens for deceased plants. Very few people make it a practice to honor their deceased pets with gravestones. Only humans regularly receive this honor in death. Perhaps it was God who put the drive to do this within us because we are made in His image. Even when people are gone, we erect these markers in the hope that they not be forgotten.

But headstones become worn with age. This reminds us that the relentless passage of time eventually wipes away our memories from planet Earth. Many gravestones that are one hundred years old or more are hardly legible. Only God remembers the people buried in such places.

You will die unless Jesus comes first. Yet you are valued because you bear God's image. Eventually, others will forget you, but you always will be precious to God. Devote yourself to Him now so that He will devote Himself to you for eternity.

—J. D. J.

E. Closing Lament (v. 8)

8. Vanity of vanities, saith the Preacher; all is vanity.

With these words *the Preacher* (Solomon) returns to the theme with which he began the book of Ecclesiastes: *Vanity of vanities* (1:2). This is certainly an appropriate conclusion to his discussion of physical life. Everything we accomplish on the earth eventually is left to others (2:18).

But life does not end at the grave. As Henry Wadsworth Longfellow (1807–1882) reminds us, "Dust thou art, to dust returnest, Was not spoken of the soul" (from "A Psalm of Life"). Thanks be to God for our resurrected Lord, through whom we have the hope of life eternal!

Conclusion

A. In the Days of Thy Youth

It may be more appropriate to speak of the *daze* of youth. Children and young people today are subjected to such a wide variety of threats and temptations that there is little wonder that many of them have distorted views of what life is really all about.

This puts a heavy responsibility on parents to provide guidance. Unfortunately, many parents cannot or will not provide this guidance. Thus a growing responsibility falls upon churches to fill this void.

This lesson ought to motivate your church to take a careful look at what is being done for its young people. Many churches today have youth ministers whose efforts are aimed at providing good teaching for teens. A few visionary churches have hired children's ministers for preteens. That's good!

But just hiring extra church staff can give church members the false sense of security that "we've got those bases covered." That's bad! Reaching our preadults for Christ takes more—it takes you. There is no higher calling than to help a young person develop a walk of Christian faith. What role will you play?

B. Prayer

Gracious Father, may this lesson remind us that this life is fleeting, that from a worldly point of view it is vanity. Give us the wisdom to look beyond the emptiness of life to see the opportunities for service You have for us and the hope we have for eternal life through Jesus Christ, through whom we pray, amen.

C. Thought to Remember

"For thou art my hope, O Lord God: thou art my trust from my youth" (Psalm 71:5).

Learning by Doing

This page contains an alternative lesson plan emphasizing learning activities.
Classes desiring such student involvement will find these suggestions helpful.

Learning Goals

After participating in this lesson, each student will be able to:

1. Give reasons why it is better to remember the Creator in youth rather than in old age.

2. Describe ways the church can do a better job of reaching out to young people.

3. Identify a young person and work for him or her to become a follower of Jesus Christ, or to grow in that relationship.

Into the Lesson

Option 1. Say, "We are going to play the 'What if' game." Display a poster that reads: "What if I could relive my high school or college years?" Continue, "Most of us would probably not actually want to relive those years; however, if we could change something about those years, what would it be? What would we do better? What would get more emphasis?" Allow each to share with one other person what he or she would change.

Remind the class that the Bible values the years of youth. God knows the value of formative years and how those years will affect later life.

Option 2. Find a large dartboard with a series of circles for a target and attach numerous balloons to it. Label the board "Goals of Youth." Ask the class members to cite what appears to be the center of focus for high-school students today. Use a marker to label the balloons with their answers. Cite a few examples: a car, sex, drugs, good grades, volunteering, worshiping God, starting a career, graduation, friends, popularity, Christian dates and relationships, computer gaming. When someone mentions a spiritual goal such as "serve or worship God," write that on the balloon in the center of the target.

Say, "Many things are tugging for the attention of youth in today's world. Unfortunately, some youth really don't have goals of significance. However, God's love for youth and for the lives they are beginning is demonstrated in today's text. He offers a very clear target for youth." Break the balloon in the center of the target.

Into the Word

Put the class into groups of four or five. Give each group one of the following assignments:

Task 1. Give groups with this assignment a copy of the lesson commentary on Ecclesiastes 11:7-10; 12:1. Also give them a work sheet with the heading and instructions: "Task Force 1: Discovering Lessons for Young People! Read Ecclesiastes 11:7-10; 12:1 and discover God's lessons for youth. Write your discoveries on this sheet. Assign someone to be ready to share your discoveries."

Task 2. Give groups with this assignment a copy of the lesson commentary on Ecclesiastes 12:1-8. Also give them a worksheet with the heading and instructions: "Task Force 2: Interpreting Lessons for Aging! Read Ecclesiastes 12:1-8 and discover God's lessons for aging. Write your discoveries on this sheet. Assign someone to be ready to share your discoveries."

After groups complete the assignment, ask the spokesperson from each to move to a group that did not study the same text. That person will read the text and share answers from his or her task force; thus, class members teach each other.

After this activity make a few comments about the significance of 12:8. See the lesson commentary for helpful information.

Into Life

Remind class members that the church has an opportunity and responsibility to encourage spiritual growth in youth. Ask them to brainstorm ways the church can do this effectively by building an acrostic using the letters of the words "Days of Thy Youth." Give an example by using the letter *O* as in *affirmatiOn*.

Next, challenge the class to become encouragers to at least one teenager. Bring a list of high school youth and their addresses to the class; ask each person to select the name of one in the congregation. Class members should not select the same person. For the remaining three weeks in the month each class member should send an anonymous weekly note of encouragement, appreciation, and promises of prayer for the young person chosen. No gifts should be given. Notes and cards—including a promise to pray for the teen, admiration of spiritual qualities or personal traits, prayers you have offered—should be sent to the young person's home address. (It would be best if men select boys and women select girls; husband and wife pairs can select either.)

Class members may reveal their names to their "secret pal" in their third and last note or by personally talking to the young person. As the teacher of the class, remind the class of this project for the next two weeks.

Let's Talk It Over

*The questions on this page are designed to promote discussion of the lesson
by the class and to encourage application of the lesson Scriptures. The answers
provided are only discussion starters. Let your class talk it over from there.*

1. What are some things that make life enjoyable no matter what our age? How are those things sometimes abused?

Notice how many times the Bible describes all God's acts of creation as "good" or "very good" in Genesis 1! He designed all of creation to be a pleasant environment for us. From the very beginning He intended for us to enjoy the discovery of His universe, to benefit from the wealth of His resources, and to delight in the beauty of relationships and love.

Sadly, sin has the tendency to turn our enjoyment into one of excess. In the excess of uncontrolled lust, people step outside the boundaries of their marriages to commit adultery. In their excess desire for more and more things, people become covetous. In an excess of indulgence, people "enjoy" food to the extent that they become obese and ruin their bodies. Often these excesses begin as habits in our youthful years.

2. Jeremiah 17:9 tells us that "the heart is deceitful above all things." Yet Solomon says in Ecclesiastes 11:9 to "walk in the ways of thine heart." How do we reconcile the two?

As Solomon tells us elsewhere, a cheerful heart is a good thing (Proverbs 15:13, 15). Acting or speaking with heartfelt conviction is generally also considered beneficial. If, however, we depend merely upon our heart—or, some would say, our conscience—to guide our every action, we are certain to fall. Acting only on our own personal perceptions of what is right or wrong is certain to end in disaster (cf. Romans 1:18-32).

Ecclesiastes 11:9 includes a valuable boundary that can be used to judge the desires of our heart: the reality of God's judgment. If our first love is our Savior, and we have studied God's Word carefully, then the guidance of our heart is more likely to be accurate as it considers the options of life.

3. Truly we live in the shadow of God's judgment. Why is it difficult to communicate this message to our culture?

This passage, as well as others in the Scriptures, points to judgment but does not put a timetable on it. God delays His ultimate judgment so that more people can be saved (2 Peter 3:9). Unfortunately, many interpret this delay to mean that there will be no judgment at all (cf.

2 Peter 3:3, 4). Some believe that God is "all love and no wrath" and will save everyone, or simply that there is no God, period. Once we understand these various viewpoints, we realize that a somewhat different approach is needed to confront each one.

Above all, we must make sure that we ourselves do not fall into any of these false viewpoints. We protect ourselves by remembering the many New Testament passages that speak of the wrath and judgment to come (e.g., Revelation 6:15-17). Solomon also helps us here by advising us to remember the Creator (Ecclesiastes 12:1). Such thoughts will help us push away those temptations to sin which offend our Maker.

4. The Scripture describes God in several ways. Why do you think Solomon chose to use the title "Creator" in his challenge to youth?

Perhaps Solomon wanted us to remember that God is the original Source of all that is good. Perhaps the reference reminds youth in particular that they are given life, but that it should not be taken for granted. (Youth sometimes think that they are invincible.)

The name also points to the fact that God has the ultimate power. In the New Testament era we realize that it is Jesus Himself who is the Creator (Colossians 1:16). He is also the One who makes us to be a new creation (2 Corinthians 5:17; Galatians 6:15). This makes the title "Creator" even more profound—if that's possible!

5. Imagine that you are writing an advice column for youth. What will you caution them to avoid?

This could be an opportunity for your learners to reflect on the experiences of life that have taught them valuable lessons. Some gems of wisdom will come immediately to mind from the Scriptures as well. The book of Proverbs helps us avoid the trap of multiple sex partners (chapters 5, 7). It also has advice regarding "friends" who have ulterior motives (14:20; 19:4, 6, 7).

Any type of excess or pride can rob us of many opportunities as they consume our lives and ruin our priorities. Peter may be including this idea when he refers to an "excess of riot" in 1 Peter 4:4. Your learners may mention various types of excesses they have succumbed to at times.

A Time for Love

February 15
Lesson 11

DEVOTIONAL READING: Jeremiah 31:1-5.

BACKGROUND SCRIPTURE: Song of Solomon 2:8-13; 7:10-12; 8:6, 7.

PRINTED TEXT: Song of Solomon 2:8-13; 7:10-12; 8:6, 7.

Song of Solomon 2:8-13

8 The voice of my beloved! Behold, he cometh leaping upon the mountains, skipping upon the hills.

9 My beloved is like a roe or a young hart: behold, he standeth behind our wall, he looketh forth at the windows, showing himself through the lattice.

10 My beloved spake, and said unto me, Rise up, my love, my fair one, and come away.

11 For, lo, the winter is past, the rain is over and gone;

12 The flowers appear on the earth; the time of the singing of birds is come, and the voice of the turtle is heard in our land;

13 The fig tree putteth forth her green figs, and the vines with the tender grape give a good smell. Arise, my love, my fair one, and come away.

Song of Solomon 7:10-12

10 I am my beloved's, and his desire is toward me.

11 Come, my beloved, let us go forth into the field; let us lodge in the villages.

12 Let us get up early to the vineyards; let us see if the vine flourish, whether the tender grape appear, and the pomegranates bud forth: there will I give thee my loves.

Song of Solomon 8:6, 7

6 Set me as a seal upon thine heart, as a seal upon thine arm: for love is strong as death; jealousy is cruel as the grave: the coals thereof are coals of fire, which hath a most vehement flame.

7 Many waters cannot quench love, neither can the floods drown it: if a man would give all the substance of his house for love, it would utterly be contemned.

Feb
15

GOLDEN TEXT: Set me as a seal upon thine heart, as a seal upon thine arm: for love is strong as death; jealousy is cruel as the grave.—Song of Solomon 8:6.

Lesson Aims

After participating in this lesson, each student should be able to:

1. Describe the affection portrayed between the beloved and the bride in the Song of Solomon.

2. Contrast the view of marital love in the text with contemporary sexual standards.

3. Commit to renewed sexual and relational purity and faithfulness.

Lesson Outline

INTRODUCTION
    A. "How Do I Love Thee?"
    B. Lesson Background
 I. THE BELOVED'S APPROACH (Song of Solomon 2:8-13)
    A. Joyful Anticipation (v. 8)
    Behold, He Cometh
    B. Timid Approach (v. 9)
    C. Appealing Invitation (vv. 10-13)
 II. THE BRIDE'S COMMITMENT (Song of Solomon 7:10-12)
    A. The Bride's Surrender (v. 10)
    B. The Bride's Sentiment (vv. 11, 12)
III. THE BOND OF LOVE (Song of Solomon 8:6, 7)
    A. Love Is Strong (v. 6)
    B. Love Is Unquenchable (v. 7)
    Love's Power
CONCLUSION
    A. The Sexual Revolution
    B. The Christian Response
    C. Prayer
    D. Thought to Remember

Introduction

A. "How Do I Love Thee?"

Elizabeth Barrett (1806–1861), a well-known poetess, was born into a well-to-do family and received a good education. Even as a child she began to write poetry that attracted attention. This brought her into contact with many of the literary luminaries of her day. But she suffered from such poor health that she was often bedridden, almost completely eliminating any chance she had of getting married. To compound the problem, her father, who ruled his family with an iron hand, forbade his children to marry.

Then Elizabeth met Robert Browning, a rising young poet, six years her junior. The two carried on a secret correspondence and eventually fell in love. But when Browning proposed to her, she turned him down, insisting that she didn't want to burden him with a sickly wife who could never have a normal life. Browning persisted, however, and they were secretly married. Her father was furious when he learned of it, and as a result the Brownings spent most of their married life in Italy, a life together that proved extremely happy.

In her *Sonnets From the Portuguese* Elizabeth poured out her love for her husband:

How do I love thee? Let me count the ways,
I love thee to the depth and breadth and height
My soul can reach, when feeling out of sight
For the ends of Being and ideal Grace.
I love thee to the level of everyday's
Most quiet need, by sun and candle-light,
I love thee freely, as men strive for Right;
I love thee purely, as they turn from Praise.
I love thee with the passion put to use
In my old griefs, and with my childhood's faith,
I love thee with a love I seemed to lose
With my lost saints,—I love thee with the breath,
Smiles, tears, of all my life!—and, if God choose,
I shall but love thee better after death.

We all know how much modern culture has emphasized sex. This has cheapened the physical aspects of love to the point that many cannot appreciate the type of love that overcomes all kinds of barriers and, most importantly, grows richer through the years!

B. Lesson Background

The Song of Solomon (or Song of Songs, or Canticles, as it is sometimes called) is one of the most controversial books in the Old Testament. Both Jewish and Christian commentators, put off by its erotic content, have often interpreted it in very figurative ways.

Some Jews see in the book a picture of God's love for His people expressed in physical terms. Some Christians similarly see in it Christ's love for the church. One of the reasons for taking this view is that at times both Jews and Christians have looked upon physical love as evil, permissible only for procreation. It was thus more acceptable to them to explain the obvious references to the physical aspects of love in figurative terms.

Perhaps the only good thing that has come out of the so-called sexual revolution of the past fifty years is that we can talk more freely and without embarrassment about sexual matters. Thus we can now begin to see the book as it was originally written—a beautiful and wholesome expression of the love between a man and a woman within the bonds of marriage.

Even within this viewpoint, however, scholars see this book in different ways. Many take it to be a collection of love songs to be sung at weddings, often by professional musicians. Such a view helps explain why it is so difficult to trace a clear pattern of continuity between the various parts of the book. Others see in this book a drama being played out in which there are three characters: King Solomon, the maiden, and her lover, who is a shepherd. According to this view, Solomon seeks to win the maiden, but she remains loyal to her true love. This view has some appeal, but the evidence is not all that clear.

Regardless of the approach one takes to the Song of Solomon, we can appreciate its poetic beauty and the many delightful glimpses it gives us of love and courtship. This book also reminds us that foundational human relations between men and women have not changed radically across the centuries.

I. The Beloved's Approach (Song of Solomon 2:8-13)

A. Joyful Anticipation (v. 8)

8. The voice of my beloved! Behold, he cometh leaping upon the mountains, skipping upon the hills.

We are not sure of the name of the young woman who is the heroine of this book. Some believe it was "Shulamite" (6:13), but this word probably designates her hometown. She seems to be recalling an earlier meeting with her lover. She eagerly awaits his arrival. As he approaches, he is not moving at a leisurely pace!

BEHOLD, HE COMETH

Many animals actively court their potential mates. Pacific tree frogs sing solos. Peacocks display spectacular plumage. Female moths produce perfume to attract a mate. Male bowerbirds build brightly decorated homes for their "brides." Male wolf spiders give their "dates" a gift of food wrapped in silk. Emphid flies spin balloons out of spider silk to give to their potential mates. Many animals go through elaborate courtships before they come together as mates.

Humans behave in similar fashion. Men and women dress up in "spectacular plumage." They put on cologne and perfume. People take their dates out to eat. Couples sing special songs together. We may bring each other wrapped gifts.

On a more intimate level, a person will hang on every word of a potential mate. We make time to spend together. We share our innermost thoughts and feelings. Through these experiences, we attract each other, we find a kindred soul, and we join our lives together.

Unfortunately, courtship often declines after marriage begins. Husbands and wives stop hanging on each other's words. They stop buying gifts or dressing up. They take each other for granted. Mates neglect to make time for each other once their beloved has already come "leaping upon the mountains" for them.

The apostle Paul has godly advice for both husbands and wives in Ephesians 5:22-33. Husband, will you love your wife enough to continue courting her? Wife, will you love your husband enough to continue responding to him? What will each of you do this week to keep your courtship alive?   —J. D. J.

B. Timid Approach (v. 9)

9. My beloved is like a roe or a young hart: behold, he standeth behind our wall, he looketh forth at the windows, showing himself through the lattice.

Although the lover hurries to meet the object of his affection, he becomes shy when he approaches her dwelling. As she watches his behavior, she compares him with *a roe or a young hart*. The roe is a small deer or antelope, and could also be translated as "gazelle." It is noted for its agility. *A young hart* is a young male deer or similar animal. However, we cannot precisely identify what this species is. At one time they roamed the hills of Palestine. They are considered extinct there today.

These animals are extremely shy, and this seems to be the idea the young woman wishes to express. Her lover conceals himself behind a wall, perhaps in the garden. But he is visible when he peers through the latticework of an opening. There doesn't seem to be any particular reason for the lover's shy behavior, except that lovers sometimes display such courtship rituals. Perhaps he is not quite sure that he has her approval for his efforts to woo her. [See question #1, page 208.]

C. Appealing Invitation (vv. 10-13)

10, 11. My beloved spake, and said unto me, Rise up, my love, my fair one, and come away. For, lo, the winter is past, the rain is over and gone.

How to Say It

CANTICLES. *Kan*-tih-kels.
DEUTERONOMY. Due-ter-*ahn*-uh-me.
POMEGRANATE. *pom*-ih-gran-it.
SOLOMON. *Sol*-o-mun.
SHULAMITE. *Shoo*-lam-ite.
ZEPHANIAH. Zef-uh-*nye*-uh.

The young woman recognizes the presence of her lover. As a result he overcomes his shyness and speaks, inviting her to join him outside the house.

The winter is past and the coming of spring has awakened nature, making his invitation an attractive one. Spring in Palestine is a beautiful time of the year. Most of the rainfall comes during the fall and winter. The rains end in the spring and the temperature becomes most pleasant.

12. The flowers appear on the earth; the time of the singing of birds is come, and the voice of the turtle is heard in our land.

The wild *flowers* are awakened from their slumber by the previous rains, and the hills become lovely blankets of color. It is a time made for courting, far better than the chilly, rainy days of winter.

The phrase *of birds* is not a part of the Hebrew text, and its inclusion represents the translators' opinion that it is birds that are doing the *singing*. Many commentators believe, however, that this passage refers to the singing of the workers as they go about their spring work.

The voice of the turtle refers to the plaintive cooing of the turtledove. A type of wild pigeon, the turtledove is normally a migratory bird in Palestine. However, some may remain to nest there, and their songs fill the warm spring air.

13. The fig tree putteth forth her green figs, and the vines with the tender grape give a good smell. Arise, my love, my fair one, and come away.

Figs are grown throughout ancient Israel. They can be dried and preserved, thus forming a stable part of the diet the year around (e.g., 1 Samuel 25:18; 30:11, 12). Many fig trees blossom and set fruit before they put out leaves. When the fig trees begin to set fruit, it is a good sign that

spring is near at hand. Occasionally a late freeze will destroy the early fruit, but the tree will produce new fruit later.

Grapes were widely grown by the Canaanites long before the Israelites took possession of the land. For example, the spies returned from Canaan with one cluster of grapes so large that it had to be carried on a pole between two men (Numbers 13:23). The grapes blossom in the early spring. The blossoms of many varieties give off a pleasant aroma, adding to the delight of the early spring days.

All these signs of the passing of winter and the arrival of spring offer the perfect opportunity for a courtship invitation. So the beloved suggests that the maiden join him in enjoying this pleasant environment. He has already extended the invitation earlier, but apparently she has coyly ignored it or rejected it. So a second invitation is necessary. [See question #2, page 208.]

II. The Bride's Commitment (Song of Solomon 7:10-12)

A. The Bride's Surrender (v. 10)

10. I am my beloved's, and his desire is toward me.

In the verses immediately preceding this verse we read an erotic description of some of the physical aspects of love, which some attribute to Solomon. Some students believe this verse portrays the young woman's rejection of the king's advances and her faithfulness to her shepherd lover. [See question #3, page 208.]

However, this passage might portray her acceptance of Solomon's descriptive words acclaiming his love for her. This verse echoes 6:3: "I am my beloved's, and my beloved is mine," indicating a surrender of each to the other. Mutual surrender is at the heart of marital bliss.

B. The Bride's Sentiment (vv. 11, 12)

11, 12. Come, my beloved, let us go forth into the field; let us lodge in the villages. Let us get up early to the vineyards; let us see if the vine flourish, whether the tender grape appear, and the pomegranates bud forth: there will I give thee my loves.

Perhaps feeling threatened and hemmed in by the city, the maiden invites her *beloved* to go with her *into the field*. There in the open countryside and the villages that dot the rural areas she feels they will have an opportunity to enjoy their affection for one another. This is a joy that the busy, noisy city conspires to deny. [See question #4, page 208.]

They find pleasure as they wander through the *vineyards*, checking the buds that begin to

---

Home Daily Bible Readings

Monday, Feb. 9—I Love You, O Lord (Psalm 18:1-6)

Tuesday, Feb. 10—A Commandment to Love God (Deuteronomy 6:4-9)

Wednesday, Feb. 11—Love Others as Christ Loves Us (John 15:8-12)

Thursday, Feb. 12—No Greater Love (John 15:13-17)

Friday, Feb. 13—God's Everlasting Love (Jeremiah 31:1-5)

Saturday, Feb. 14—A Song of Love (Song of Solomon 2:8-13)

Sunday, Feb. 15—Love Is Strong as Death (Song of Solomon 7:10-12; 8:6, 7)

turn green and will soon burst forth as leaves. This may be a symbol of their love that grows and develops with the passage of time. The buds are soon followed by the blossoms and then the *tender grape*.

Pomegranates bud in early spring, and their blossoms are orange-red in color. The fruit is about the size of an orange, and in the ancient world is considered a symbol of fertility and eternal life. Perhaps this is the reason that Solomon had pomegranates carved into beams in the temple (1 Kings 7:18, 20, 42). Along with grapes and figs, it is one of the most widely cultivated fruits in the ancient Near East.

III. The Bond of Love
(Song of Solomon 8:6, 7)
A. Love Is Strong (v. 6)

6. Set me as a seal upon thine heart, as a seal upon thine arm: for love is strong as death; jealousy is cruel as the grave: the coals thereof are coals of fire, which hath a most vehement flame.

In ancient times it was a common practice to authenticate a document with a seal pressed into moist clay or soft wax, rather than with a signature as today (cf. 1 Kings 21:8; Esther 8:8; Job 38:14). The beloved alludes to this practice as a guarantee of the steadfastness of their *love* (cf. 2 Corinthians 1:22; Ephesians 1:13). [See question #5, page 208.]

The young woman asserts that her love is just as certain as *death* and cannot for long be resisted. Death never releases its prey once it has been seized, and love is just as relentless.

The point of the statement *jealousy is cruel as the grave* is that the woman's love is exclusive and will not tolerate rivals. Jealousy is an incredibly powerful emotion. The Bible speaks of God as a jealous God; this is not jealousy in a petty or selfish sense, but the type that demands undivided loyalty of His followers (Exodus 20:5). Loyalty is what the young woman has in mind.

Jealousy is sometimes spoken of as a *flame* that burns relentlessly (cf. Deuteronomy 4:24; 6:15; Zephaniah 3:8). When jealousy is petty and selfish, it can be a consuming fire that destroys all the parties involved. We can hope that the beloved does not have such an attitude, but only a thin line separates this kind of jealousy from the type of jealousy that God has for His children.

B. Love Is Unquenchable (v. 7)

7. Many waters cannot quench love, neither can the floods drown it: if a man would give all the substance of his house for love, it would utterly be contemned.

"*Set me as a seal upon thine heart.*"
—Song of Solomon 8:6.

Visual for lesson 11. *Use this image to reinforce the first part of today's Golden Text.*

The young woman's *love* cannot be extinguished by water. It is as if one were to try to extinguish a river of hot lava with a garden hose. In this dramatic figure she reaffirms her devotion to her husband.

Even if *a man* would give all the substance of his house for love, it would be rejected or scorned *(contemned)*. This is an interesting statement in view of the fact that Solomon was the richest king Israel ever had. If the woman is saying to him that her love cannot be purchased, she is modeling true love! In Christian marriage ceremonies couples are asked to commit themselves to one another through health and sickness, in wealth and poverty. This affirms that love has its basis in something other than material possessions.

LOVE'S POWER

Love is so powerful! When a person is in danger of losing his life, he does not think of his boss, his neighbor, or his accountant. He thinks of his loved ones. Love has the power to cause a person to change careers and to forego wealth.

One man who discovered this was Edward VIII, King of England, who ascended to the throne on January 21, 1936. Less than a year later he announced, "I have found it impossible to carry the heavy burden of responsibility and to discharge my duties as king as I would wish to do without the help and support of the woman I love."

The woman King Edward referred to was twice divorced, and British law prohibited the monarch from marrying a divorced person. Therefore, Edward voluntarily gave up his crown and went into lifelong exile in order to marry Wallis Warfield Simpson.

Love is so powerful! King Edward was willing to give up prestige, popularity, and "perks" for the one he loved. What are you willing to give up for the people you love—a TV show, a nap, an evening in your garage, time on the computer? Show your loved ones you value them by giving your time, interest, and energy to them. When your life is done, you will be glad you did. For the greatest thing in life is love.   —J. D. J.

Conclusion

A. The Sexual Revolution

After World War II an assault began on the traditional standards of sexual morality, standards that were Biblically based and widely accepted. These standards were ridiculed as "prudish," "old-fashioned," "Puritanical," or "Victorian." We were told that more relaxed sexual standards would free us from old fears and superstitions. The open rejection of traditional standards on TV and in the movies has made adultery look attractive, desirable, and fun. "Live-in" arrangements and so-called "starter" marriages began to replace Biblical standards for marriage.

We now have had five decades of this new "freedom." Enough data is in to allow us to test just how things have worked out, and the results are appalling. In the early 1960s the divorce rate began to rise. Today, for every two new marriages in the United States there is about one divorce. Anger and bitter feelings are only a part of the satanic harvest from these failings. Children caught between warring parents are scarred, and many never fully recover from this trauma.

As the disdain for the institution of marriage grew, the number of births to unwed mothers skyrocketed. Along with an absence of shame came poverty as single mothers tried to hold families together without a husband in the picture. Live-in boyfriends just don't provide the income or the stability to build a solid home. Sexual "freedom" actually has become a kind of slavery. What was (and is) so enthusiastically proclaimed and practiced is now a merciless tyrant.

But sadly there is more. Sexual promiscuity has caused a substantial increase in the number of cases of sexually transmitted diseases. At one time many believed that powerful antibiotics would eliminate such diseases. But growing sexual promiscuity and the increased resistance of these diseases to treatment has dimmed this hope.

But the worst was yet to come. A little over two decades ago, AIDS burst upon the scene. Scientists have pinpointed its origins in Africa, where this terrible disease now decimates the population. Millions of dollars have been spent seeking a cure for this plague. But at best researchers have succeeded only in prolonging the lives of those who are HIV positive or have full-blown AIDS—and this only in nations that have access to the medications.

We pray that a medical cure for AIDS may soon be found. But to those looking for a "magic bullet" that will eliminate this disease we say that there already is one: it is the Biblical standard of morality.

B. The Christian Response

The home is the solid foundation for any stable society. Six thousand years of human history prove it. If our culture is to flourish, we must mount an active campaign to bolster the home. This includes Biblical teachings about sexual purity and true love. We must never mute or compromise this message. This is a message we must teach in our youth classes especially, because all too often their bodies are growing up more rapidly than their moral values.

The teaching can take different formats. Many churches hold special classes on developing strong homes and happy families. A great variety of printed and video materials is available. Many ministers serve as successful marriage counselors. Some churches use the skills of specially trained counselors to help their members. There is no shortage of ideas!

Yet it is not enough just to teach. Leaders of the church must demonstrate by their own lives that following God's standards for love and marriage brings life-long happiness and emotional security. We must do this despite the presence of high-profile examples of infidelity and the general acceptance of immoral behaviors and lifestyles.

This could be a good time to discuss with your class what your church is doing in this area. If your church is doing very little, your class can become a force to stimulate action. One does not have to be a prophet of gloom and doom to realize that the hour is late and the threat is serious. A church that is willing to take an active role in building stronger Christian homes is a church that will grow.

C. Prayer

Gracious Father, You have given us in the Scriptures very clear standards for sexual purity and for marriage. Give us the wisdom and the strength to live up to standards, and to teach them to our children and our friends. May we be bold in this, because eternity is at stake. In Jesus' name we pray, amen.

D. Thought to Remember

"Marriage is honorable in all, and the bed undefiled: but whoremongers and adulterers God will judge" (Hebrews 13:4).

Learning by Doing

*This page contains an alternative lesson plan emphasizing learning activities.
Classes desiring such student involvement will find these suggestions helpful.*

Learning Goals

After participating in this lesson, each student will be able to:

1. Describe the affection portrayed between the beloved and the bride in the Song of Solomon.

2. Contrast the view of marital love in the text with contemporary sexual standards.

3. Commit to renewed sexual and relational purity and faithfulness.

Into the Lesson

Early in the week, telephone married couples from the class and invite each to bring a picture of themselves from their dating days or from their honeymoon. Both persons should be in the photograph. Assure the couple they will get the picture back. As students arrive, ask them to attach the photos to a poster or bulletin board.

Give time to enjoy the photos. Tell them the class will talk about these later in the session. Also give each one a small adhesive colorful circle or dot. Ask the students to apply the colored circle near the statement that they believe is most accurate on a poster that reads: "God's purpose for including a sensual love letter (Song of Solomon) in the Bible is (a) God thought it would spice up His Bible; (b) it is symbolic of God's love for His people; (c) it is a collection of love songs sung at weddings; (d) it is intended to affirm the beauty of sexual and human love."

After all stickers have been placed, use the commentary's Lesson Background to prepare and deliver a brief lecture on the purpose of the book.

Into the Word

Distribute an activity guide to groups of four or five. Assign one of the activities to each group. The guide should have the heading, "A Model for Love and Sex." Include the following instructions:

Activity 1: Read 2:8-13. Then rewrite this scene of courtship, placing it in a contemporary setting of dating and courtship.

Activity 2: Read 7:10-12. Earlier verses in this chapter include an erotic declaration of physical love by the man or lover. Our text is the woman's response and commitment. (a) What is the key phrase in her response? *("I am my beloved's.")* Why is this statement significant in husband-and-wife relationships? (b) What does this text imply about the woman's role in the dance of love and

sexual behavior? (c) Paraphrase this text, putting it into contemporary words and setting.

Activity 3: Read 8:6, 7 and answer the following: (a) What is the significance of the *seal* in verse 6? (b) How or why is love as strong as death? (c) What does the woman mean saying, "Jealousy is cruel as the grave"? (d) The word *fire* is used not only by God to describe love; it is also used often in contemporary music. Why is *fire* so often used to describe love? What are the implications of this word as related to love?

Into Life

Write on a display board: "So what?" Tell the class we want this text to speak to believers in the year 2004. Ask the following questions: (a) What lessons about love and sex do you find in this love letter we've read today? (b) What disturbing variances from this beautiful snapshot of male and female relationships do you see in some contemporary views of love and sex? What dangers lie in some of those views? List these answers on the visual in two columns.

Point to the snapshots brought by married couples. Ask, "What potential problems endangering healthy sexual intimacy face couples today?" Then ask what messages this lesson has for single adults today. What values are implied?

Distribute the following commitment guide. One side should have the heading "Married Couples." The other side should have "Single Adults." (Tell them to check all that apply.) The side for married adults should read, "As a married adult, (a) I will be physically and emotional faithful to my spouse from this day forward; (b) within a week I will find one way (card, love letter, intimate conversation, or other) to express my love and commitment to my spouse and lover; (c) I will discuss a time with my spouse when we can retreat from life's hubbub for at least two days just to be together."

The side for singles should read, "Understanding the wonderful joy and intimacy God offers in marriage and to support these values, I will (a) respect God's boundaries about sexuality by controlling my desires and refrain from sexual intimacy unless I marry; (b) respect and honor marriage by rejoicing in other people's successful marriage relationships; and (c) respect and honor single adulthood by demonstrating faithfulness to my God and serving in His church."

Let's Talk It Over

The questions on this page are designed to promote discussion of the lesson by the class and to encourage application of the lesson Scriptures. The answers provided are only discussion starters. Let your class talk it over from there.

1. What suggestions would you offer to a young married couple about how to "keep the flame alive"? How would your suggestions differ from what secular culture seems to think is important in this regard?

The wide variety of responses—some even contradictory—will make this an interesting discussion. There is also a risk that this could turn into a "gripe session" as unhappy couples use this as an opportunity to snipe at one another, so be careful.

To make sure this begins on a positive note, you could encourage your married learners to share what first attracted them to their mates. Are these the same qualities that maintain a loving relationship later on?

2. Could it be that the location and time the two lovers met seemed ideal only because of their strong emotions? Explain how a loving relationship can affect our perceptions.

Most older married couples will acknowledge that their first house or apartment was quite modest when compared with their current accommodations. In almost the same breath, however, many will say that these were among the happiest times of life. Why? Often it is because intense love for the other person was far more important than things and possessions.

Revived love often comes about when couples regain their focus on one another. Unfortunately, secular culture often suggests that the best way to do this is to buy a certain product, to take a certain cruise, or to live life in a certain unbiblical way.

3. The text seems to indicate that this couple was completely devoted to one another. How does modern culture belittle the idea of exclusive devotion?

The concept of sacrificial love is under relentless attack today. Modern culture ridicules exclusive devotion by labeling it "psychological codependency." Instead, we are supposed to accept such clever-sounding ideas as "responsible nonmonogamy," "open marriage," and "multipartner relationships." The rights of the individual to do as he or she pleases is supposed to reign supreme, even within marriage, "just as long as it doesn't hurt anyone."

Verse 10, however, suggests that it is because the bride has surrendered herself to her lover that she has his continuing desire. Obviously this cannot be a one-directional pursuit. Does it sound too idealistic to suggest that the more one tries to attract the attention of a spouse, the less likely that other person is going to want to think about entering into another relationship?

A marriage partnership requires constant attention and effort, but it's worth it! Review the instructions of Ephesians 5:22-33 for additional help on this subject.

4. What kinds of circumstances can distract us from growing in our marital relationships? How does our text assist us in refreshing our marriages?

Broadly speaking, the vitality in our marriages can slip away when we allow "the urgent" to squeeze out "the important." There are so many urgent demands on our time these days—demands that rob us of time alone with our mates! There's that TV show that "we just can't miss." There's that holiday that "we just have to spend" with relatives. The list goes on.

The picture in verses 11 and 12 is valuable in this regard. At certain times it is important for couples to find times of retreat simply to enjoy one another's company. These times of separation from other responsibilities and concerns can help us rediscover our joy in each other.

5. The text speaks of a "seal" upon the heart. What are some things we use today as "marriage seals"? Why are they important?

As noted in the lesson, the seal referred to in the text draws upon the idea of a stamp used to authenticate official documents. It is a symbol of a guaranteed and steadfast love.

Today, we use a variety of things to indicate being "sealed" to another person: wedding rings, marriage licenses, unity candles, and a public exchange of vows are just a few. Some of these are important in a legal sense. But more important is the sense of commitment before God that they convey. We can keep our eyes from wandering toward another by glancing down at our wedding rings and remembering what they signify: I made a promise before God to be steadfastly devoted to one particular person.

A Time for Courage

DEVOTIONAL READING: Psalm 27:1-8.

BACKGROUND SCRIPTURE: Esther 3, 4.

PRINTED TEXT: Esther 3:1-6; 4:7-16.

Esther 3:1-6

1 After these things did king Ahasuerus promote Haman the son of Hammedatha the Agagite, and advanced him, and set his seat above all the princes that were with him.

2 And all the king's servants, that were in the king's gate, bowed, and reverenced Haman: for the king had so commanded concerning him. But Mordecai bowed not, nor did him reverence.

3 Then the king's servants, which were in the king's gate, said unto Mordecai, Why transgressest thou the king's commandment?

4 Now it came to pass, when they spake daily unto him, and he hearkened not unto them, that they told Haman, to see whether Mordecai's matters would stand: for he had told them that he was a Jew.

5 And when Haman saw that Mordecai bowed not, nor did him reverence, then was Haman full of wrath.

6 And he thought scorn to lay hands on Mordecai alone; for they had showed him the people of Mordecai: wherefore Haman sought to destroy all the Jews that were throughout the whole kingdom of Ahasuerus, even the people of Mordecai.

Esther 4:7-16

7 And Mordecai told him of all that had happened unto him, and of the sum of the money that Haman had promised to pay to the king's treasuries for the Jews, to destroy them.

8 Also he gave him the copy of the writing of the decree that was given at Shushan to destroy them, to show it unto Esther, and to declare it unto her, and to charge her that she should go in unto the king, to make supplication unto him, and to make request before him for her people.

9 And Hatach came and told Esther the words of Mordecai.

10 Again Esther spake unto Hatach, and gave him commandment unto Mordecai;

11 All the king's servants, and the people of the king's provinces, do know, that whosoever, whether man or woman, shall come unto the king into the inner court, who is not called, there is one law of his to put him to death, except such to whom the king shall hold out the golden sceptre, that he may live: but I have not been called to come in unto the king these thirty days.

12 And they told to Mordecai Esther's words.

13 Then Mordecai commanded to answer Esther, Think not with thyself that thou shalt escape in the king's house, more than all the Jews.

14 For if thou altogether holdest thy peace at this time, then shall there enlargement and deliverance arise to the Jews from another place; but thou and thy father's house shall be destroyed: and who knoweth whether thou art come to the kingdom for such a time as this?

15 Then Esther bade them return Mordecai this answer,

16 Go, gather together all the Jews that are present in Shushan, and fast ye for me, and neither eat nor drink three days, night or day: I also and my maidens will fast likewise; and so will I go in unto the king, which is not according to the law: and if I perish, I perish.

GOLDEN TEXT: So will I go in unto the king, which is not according to the law: and if I perish, I perish.—Esther 4:16.

Lesson Aims

After participating in this lesson, each student should be able to:

1. Tell how the Jews in Esther's day were threatened, and how Esther was persuaded to take action to avert the danger.

2. Compare the challenge to Esther's faith with some challenge he or she is facing.

3. State how he or she will confront a specific challenge to personal faith in the coming week.

Lesson Outline

INTRODUCTION
  A. When God Picks Up the Pen
  B. Lesson Background
I. HAMAN (Esther 3:1-6)
  A. Honor and Refusal (vv. 1-4)
  B. Anger and Plot (vv. 5, 6)
    Righteous Rebellion
II. MORDECAI (Esther 4:7-9)
  A. Message Sent (vv. 7, 8)
  B. Message Received (v. 9)
III. ESTHER (Esther 4:10-16)
  A. Esther's Problem (vv. 10-12)
  B. Mordecai's Challenge (vv. 13, 14)
  C. Esther's Response (vv. 15, 16)
    Prayer Partners
CONCLUSION
  A. "For Such a Time As This"
  B. A Time of Decision
  C. Prayer
  D. Thought to Remember

Introduction

A. When God Picks Up the Pen

On October 8, 1871, a great fire began to sweep across the city of Chicago. As the fire burned day after day, homes, factories, and businesses were consumed. Thousands were left homeless and destitute. In the midst of the confusion an old Quaker, whose home and business had been burned, seemed not the least perturbed. Someone said to him, "Don't you realize what this means? We're finished! This is the last chapter for us!" The old man smiled as he replied, "God begins to write anew when men lay down the pen."

Through the machinations of evil Haman, King Ahasuerus had signed a decree that meant death to the Jews in his domain. Wicked men were writing the last chapter for the Jews. But godly Mordecai was not quite ready to accept this. When he challenged Esther with these words, "Who knoweth whether thou art come to the kingdom for such a time as this?" he was in effect saying, "It is now time for God to begin to write."

B. Lesson Background

King Ahasuerus, who ruled the Persian Empire from 486 to 465 B.C., is also known as Xerxes, the name the Greeks gave to him. The Book of Esther opens by mentioning a feast that took place in the third year of his reign (Esther 1:3). At this time more than fifty years have elapsed since the first wave of Jewish exiles had returned to their homeland in Judah (2 Chronicles 36:22, 23), but the time of Ezra and Nehemiah is still some twenty-five years in the future.

Some believe that the king's feast is an occasion to rally his leaders for an attack on Greece. (This attack, which took place in 480–479 B.C., resulted in a Greek victory.) This feast proved to be an occasion of unrestrained drunkenness (Esther 1:5-8). When Queen Vashti was ordered to appear before the revelers, she refused (1:10-12). This refusal came at the cost of her position! The plot of the story that follows is both involved and intriguing.

I. Haman
(Esther 3:1-6)

As the search for a new queen begins, we are introduced to "fair and beautiful" Esther; she is an orphan who was reared by a close relative named Mordecai (Esther 2:7). As the result of a long and involved beauty contest, Esther becomes the new queen (2:8-18). During this whole process Esther keeps her Jewish heritage a secret (2:10, 20). Next, the evil Haman enters the picture.

A. Honor and Refusal (vv. 1-4)

1. After these things did king Ahasuerus promote Haman the son of Hammedatha the Agagite, and advanced him, and set his seat above all the princes that were with him.

Haman is an *Agagite,* which may indicate his lineage from King Agag of the Amalekites (see 1 Samuel 15:7-33). We are not told why Haman is elevated to a position that is *above all the princes.* No doubt Haman is a man of some ability. But as the story unfolds, it will also be obvious that he is a clever operator—someone who takes every opportunity to advance his own career.

Samuel + Saul anointed 1 Samuel 15

2, 3. And all the king's servants, that were in the king's gate, bowed, and reverenced Haman: for the king had so commanded concerning him. But Mordecai bowed not, nor did him reverence. Then the king's servants, which were in the king's gate, said unto Mordecai, Why transgressest thou the king's commandment?

In Oriental courts it is a common practice for *servants* and even officials to bow or prostrate themselves before their superiors. We wonder, then, why *the king* has to issue a special order that *Haman* be honored this way. Perhaps Haman has been elevated over other officers that he had served formerly, and thus needs the king's command in order to receive the new treatment that is "due" him.

But Mordecai refuses to bow before Haman. Is Mordecai just being stubborn, or is something deeper involved? Perhaps he is inspired by the prophet Daniel's behavior more than fifty years previously (Daniel 6). [See question #1, page 216.]

4. Now it came to pass, when they spake daily unto him, and he hearkened not unto them, that they told Haman, to see whether Mordecai's matters would stand: for he had told them that he was a Jew.

It does not take long for *Mordecai's* behavior to attract the attention of his companions. Perhaps out of concern for Mordecai's well-being, they speak to him about his actions. But Mordecai *hearkened not unto them.* We can almost hear them pleading with him *daily!*

There are times when we need to listen to the advice of others; but there are other times when we must take our stand and refuse to go along with the crowd. For Mordecai this is one of those times.

To bow down out of respect for an earthly king or superior is not wrong if it's merely a sign of respect or honor (Genesis 27:29; 2 Samuel 14:4; 1 Chronicles 21:21). But as a devout *Jew* Mordecai knows there is a line he must not cross. Perhaps *Haman* sees all this bowing as worship. Or perhaps Mordecai's refusal stems from his knowledge that Haman is descended from an ancient enemy of the Jews (again, 1 Samuel 15:7-33).

In either case, Mordecai refuses to heed the advice of his companions. Perhaps they do not understand his Jewish beliefs, or they may harbor antagonism toward Jews. In any event, they reported Mordecai's actions to Haman.

B. Anger and Plot (vv. 5, 6)

5. And when Haman saw that Mordecai bowed not, nor did him reverence, then was Haman full of wrath.

Haman makes a point to observe Mordecai's behavior. When he sees that *Mordecai* is not bowing and scraping before him, he is furious. Like many people who feel inferior or inadequate, he vents his feelings against those who raise any question about his authority.

RIGHTEOUS REBELLION

At the end of 1941, Lieutenant Damon Gause fought in the hopeless battle for the Philippines. When the Japanese overran Bataan, Gause was captured. He made a dash for freedom and swam to Corregidor Island. When the Japanese took Corregidor, Gause swam back to Bataan and hid in the mountains. Eventually, with the help of courageous Filipinos, Gause and another American sailed over three thousand miles to Australia in a twenty-foot skiff.

Lieutenant Gause could have given up hope on Bataan, on Corregidor, or any number of times thereafter. After he reached Australia and was flown back to the United States, Gause could have retired from the fighting. But Lieutenant (later Major) Gause rejoined the war until he died in a training accident in England.

Wars are terrible, but sometimes a just war is better than an unjust peace. Had Gause and thousands of men like him been unwilling to fight, who knows how we might all be living today!

And sometimes we have to fight alone, at least in the beginning. When Martin Luther nailed his ninety-five theses to the Wittenberg church door in 1517, he stood alone. Luther fought against wrongs he saw in the church. Eventually, he was excommunicated. But he stood up for what was right according to Scripture.

How to Say It

AGAGITE. *Ay*-guh-gite.

AHASUERUS. Uh-haz-you-*ee*-rus.

AMALEKITES. *Am*-uh-leh-kites or Uh-*mal*-ih-kites.

CORREGIDOR. Ko-*ree*-guh-door.

EZRA. *Ez*-ruh.

HAMAN. *Hay*-mun.

HAMMEDATHA. Ham-med-*day*-thuh.

HATACH. *Hay*-tak.

MORDECAI. *Mor*-dih-kye.

NEHEMIAH. *Nee*-huh-*my*-uh (strong accent on *my*).

PERSIAN. *Per*-zhun.

SHUSHAN. *Shoo*-shan.

SUSA. *Soo*-suh.

VASHTI. *Vash*-tie.

WITTENBERG. *Vit*-ten-burg.

XERXES. *Zerk*-seez.

Mordecai stood up, both literally and figuratively, for what was right. He would not stoop to Haman despite this powerful man's wrath. You may not be challenged to bend your body to a human, but you will be challenged to bend your will to Satan. Sometimes you have to stand up for what is right. "Wherefore take unto you the whole armor of God, that ye may be able to withstand in the evil day, and having done all, to stand" (Ephesians 6:13).   —J. D. J.

6. And he thought scorn to lay hands on Mordecai alone; for they had showed him the people of Mordecai: wherefore Haman sought to destroy all the Jews that were throughout the whole kingdom of Ahasuerus, even the people of Mordecai.

Haman's immediate thought is to seize *Mordecai* and have him imprisoned or executed. But when he learns that Mordecai is a Jew, all of Mordecai's *people* became a target of his rage. [See question #2, page 216.]

II. Mordecai
(Esther 4:7-9)

Haman sets the plan in motion "in the twelfth year of King Ahasuerus," or about 474 B.C. (Esther 3:7). Esther has been queen for five years (2:16) by the time Haman goes to the king with the charge that "a certain people" do not keep the king's laws and that it would be in the king's best interest to eliminate them (3:8, 9).

Ahasuerus goes along with the proposal. The appropriate documents were drawn up and dispatched to the far reaches of his empire (3:12-15), with the massacre scheduled to be carried out on a set day. It is to include "all Jews, both young and old, little children and women" (3:13). The king apparently does not know that his decree is a death sentence for his own wife as well!

When Mordecai hears the news he goes into mourning. He rends his clothes and puts on sackcloth and ashes (4:1). There is similar mourning by Jews across the empire (4:3). When Esther learns of Mordecai's distress, she sends him new clothes so that he can enter the king's court. But he refuses to accept them (4:4). Then she sends "one of the king's chamberlains," Hatach, to inquire of Mordecai what is troubling him (4:5).

A. Message Sent (vv. 7, 8)

7. And Mordecai told him of all that had happened unto him, and of the sum of the money that Haman had promised to pay to the king's treasuries for the Jews, to destroy them.

Mordecai gives Hatach all the bad news, mentioning the large *sum* of *money* Haman has *promised to pay* the king to allow the Jews to be slaughtered. There is nothing at this point to suggest that Hatach or anyone else in the king's court knows that Esther is Jewish.

It may seem surprising to us that Esther knows nothing about Haman's plot to kill her people. But we need to keep in mind that the harem of an Oriental potentate is virtually isolated from the world of politics and from most other activities as well.

8. Also he gave him the copy of the writing of the decree that was given at Shushan to destroy them, to show it unto Esther, and to declare it unto her, and to charge her that she should go in unto the king, to make supplication unto him, and to make request before him for her people.

Since Mordecai is not allowed to enter the harem compound, he has to rely upon a third party. This person is Hatach, who as a "chamberlain" is probably one of the eunuchs keeping watch over the harem.

To carry out his task, Hatach has some specific things to do. His first task is to take a *copy* of the *decree* and *show it* to *Esther*. The decree has been issued in *Shushan* (also known as Susa), which is the winter capital of the Persian Empire. This city is located about two hundred miles east of Babylon (cf. Nehemiah 1:1; Daniel 8:2). Then Hatach is to *declare* (explain) it to her. Finally, he is to *charge* Esther to go before the king to plead on behalf of *her people*.

B. Message Received (v. 9)

9. And Hatach came and told Esther the words of Mordecai.

Hatach faithfully carries out his part of the plan. Now, as we say, "the ball is in Esther's court." She can, of course, ignore Mordecai's request. At first glance this would seem to be the safest course. But to ignore his request might not actually be all that safe. There is always the possibility that her heritage would eventually be revealed, a fact that Mordecai mentions to her (4:13, below). But more important than doing the *safe* thing is doing the *right* thing.

III. Esther
(Esther 4:10-16)

Esther had been obedient as a child (2:10). This is a character trait that proves to be of great significance for what follows.

A. Esther's Problem (vv. 10-12)

10, 11. Again Esther spake unto Hatach, and gave him commandment unto Mordecai; All the king's servants, and the people of the king's

provinces, do know, that whosoever, whether man or woman, shall come unto the king into the inner court, who is not called, there is one law of his to put him to death, except such to whom the king shall hold out the golden sceptre, that he may live: but I have not been called to come in unto the king these thirty days.

Even if Esther chooses to do as Mordecai asks, she has a big problem. Anyone who approaches the king in *the inner court* without being called faces the death penalty. This seems like a very severe law, but Oriental rulers are surrounded with all kinds of intrigue and plots against their lives (cf. 2 Kings 12:19-21; 15:10, 25, 30; 21:23). Under such conditions this severe rule seems to be a reasonable precaution. Indeed, we see one assassination plot already has been foiled in Esther 2:19-23. (The king's precautions do not prevent his murder in 465 B.C., however.)

There is one exception to the death penalty of the king: if the person seeking an audience finds favor in his sight, the king will extend his *golden sceptre* and the law will be suspended. But Esther has another problem. She has not been called into the presence of the king for *thirty days*. Such a lengthy period of time may make Esther wonder if she has fallen out of favor with the king. [See question #3, page 216.]

12. And they told to Mordecai Esther's words.

Does Esther hope that her situation will relieve her of further responsibility in the matter? Or does she hope that the king will call her on his own? Of course, if she waits until he calls it could be too late. Or does she hope that *Mordecai* will come up with another plan that has a better chance of succeeding?

B. Mordecai's Challenge (vv. 13, 14)

13. Then Mordecai commanded to answer Esther, Think not with thyself that thou shalt escape in the king's house, more than all the Jews.

Most of us try to avoid situations where we have to make hard decisions, but sometimes in life they are unavoidable. *Mordecai* reminds *Esther* that she cannot hope to find safety in the *king's* palace. Hatach already knows that she is Jewish and sooner or later others will find out, sealing her fate along with that of her people.

14. For if thou altogether holdest thy peace at this time, then shall there enlargement and deliverance arise to the Jews from another place; but thou and thy father's house shall be destroyed: and who knoweth whether thou art come to the kingdom for such a time as this?

Mordecai's plan seems like the best idea at the time. But even if Esther does not cooperate, he firmly believes that God will deliver His people

Visual for
lesson 12

A Time for Courage

Use this artwork to stress the need for courage in the service of God in all situations.

in some other way. He knows enough history to understand that in times past God had delivered His people in various ways and can do so again.

Although God works through people in His plan for human redemption, He is not limited to one person or a small group of people to carry out that plan. This is true for your own life situation as well. There are things that God "wants done" where you live. Will He work through you or will He have to find someone else? [See question #4, page 216.]

C. Esther's Response (vv. 15, 16)

15, 16. Then Esther bade them return Mordecai this answer, Go, gather together all the Jews that are present in Shushan, and fast ye for me, and neither eat nor drink three days, night or day: I also and my maidens will fast likewise; and so will I go in unto the king, which is not according to the law: and if I perish, I perish.

Esther is determined not to "go it alone" once she has made her decision. Knowing that *all the Jews* of *Shushan* are joining her in a three-day *fast* will provide moral support. Although prayer is not specifically mentioned, we can be certain that those fasting hours were filled with numerous requests offered up to God for deliverance (cf. 9:31). [See question #5, page 216.] Once she has made her decision Esther faces the consequences with an unwavering resolve: *if I perish, I perish.*

PRAYER PARTNERS

"Irene has been taken to the hospital. She may have had a stroke. Please pray she will recover." Our prayer chain was on the line to each other and to God. Urgent requests start the prayer chain. Members pause to pray and then dial the next link in the chain. In this way we can call more than twenty-five households to prayer within an hour.

Around a candle in a darkened room, four young men kneel. They begin with confession—owning up to sins in their actions and attitudes. They move to requests for God's help in their lives. Finally, they intercede for friends they know to be in need. This prayer time together is the highlight of their week. It refreshes them and restores their sense of purpose for Christ.

In place of plates heaped with food sat cups of apple juice. Instead of a pitch-in dinner, the missions ministry invited people to a time of fasting at a prayer banquet. One by one, missionaries and their needs were lifted to God. Those who gathered recognized that their prayers were reaching all around the world. And they gave thanks for the opportunity to "pray ye therefore the Lord of the harvest, that he will send forth laborers into his harvest" (Matthew 9:38).

Esther asked all the Jews of Susa to fast with her for three days; no doubt they also prayed. Prayer chains, prayer partners, or special prayer events continue to call us to God. If your church has a prayer group, join it. Prayer groups help us make time for prayer. Invite a friend or two to pray with you. "For where two or three are gathered together in my name, there am I in the midst of them" (Matthew 18:20). Sincere prayer helps God's kingdom to come and God's will to be done on earth as it is in Heaven.   —J. D. J.

Conclusion

A. "For Such a Time As This"

Esther is the only book in the Bible that does not mention God. Yet imbedded in Mordecai's challenge to Esther is a profound Biblical truth, a truth based upon the belief that God is active in human lives. Mordecai believed that God had been preparing Esther all of her life for this major crisis. That she grew into a beautiful young woman who was chosen to become the queen to the powerful Persian king was no accident of history! She came to be in a crucial position at just the right time because God had planned it that way.

This reminds us of a somewhat similar situation centuries earlier when Joseph confronted his brothers in Egypt. Previously, they had sold Joseph into slavery. In a fit of jealousy they had taken action to rid themselves of him.

But when the brothers were finally reunited years later, Joseph was a ruler in Egypt. He had access to food during a time of severe famine. Joseph was thus able to save his family from starvation. Joseph saw God's hand at work and did not seek revenge. Instead, he said, "Now therefore be not grieved, nor angry with yourselves, that ye sold me hither: for God did send me before you to preserve life" (Genesis 45:5).

We may not always be where God wants us to be. We are, after all, free to rebel against Him and His purpose for us. But one of the joys of a Christian life is looking back at crucial points and seeing how God has providentially used us.

B. A Time of Decision

Most of us live out our lives in quiet routine, free of heroic choices such as Esther had to make to save her people. And yet God calls each of us to decisions that are spiritually heroic, even though they will never make the front page of the newspapers.

The most important decision we ever make, obviously, is to become a Christian. But there are many other important decisions as well. Will we be regular in our church attendance (Hebrews 10:25)? Will we resist the lure of illegal drugs? Will we avoid becoming involved in sexual immorality? The list could go on. The decision we make in each one of these situations can involve great courage. But our decisions will go a long way toward determining our eternal destiny—and, perhaps, the destinies of others.

C. Prayer

Gracious Father, we pray for help in the decisions we must make in life. Give us wisdom to make decisions that will be pleasing to You, and the courage to carry out those decisions even when they are painful. In the name of our Lord and Savior we pray, amen.

D. Thought to Remember

Know the times, live your convictions.

Home Daily Bible Readings

Monday, Feb. 16—Council Sees Disciples' Boldness (Acts 4:13-22)

Tuesday, Feb. 17—A Prayer for Boldness (Acts 4:23-31)

Wednesday, Feb. 18—Whom Shall I Fear? (Psalm 27:1-8)

Thursday, Feb. 19—Mordecai Will Not Bow (Esther 3:1-6)

Friday, Feb. 20—Mordecai Grieves for His People (Esther 4:1-5)

Saturday, Feb. 21—Esther, Called Upon to Show Courage (Esther 4:6-11)

Sunday, Feb. 22—Esther Prepares to Plead the Cause (Esther 4:12-17)

Learning by Doing

This page contains an alternative lesson plan emphasizing learning activities.
Classes desiring such student involvement will find these suggestions helpful.

Learning Goals

After participating in this lesson, each student will be able to:

1. Tell how the Jews in Esther's day were threatened and how Esther was persuaded to take action to avert the danger.

2. Compare the challenge to Esther's faith with some challenge he or she is facing.

3. State how he or she will confront a specific challenge to personal faith in the coming week.

Into the Lesson

Option 1. Give each class member a three-by-five index card. Ask each to identify and write on the card one of the challenges he or she faces in maintaining or developing a relationship with the Lord or with another person—a personal habit, a desire, an individual, a relationship, a task to do. No one will be asked to share this information.

They are to put the cards away until needed. Make the transition to Bible study by telling the class, "Sometimes we need a model or an example to show us how to face life's challenges. Today we will begin a two-lesson study of one of the Old Testament's greatest heroines, who may give us encouragement to face what we need to face and to make heroic decisions."

Option 2. Ask the class to name individuals who significantly influenced the course of history—and how they did it. List these on a poster or marker board. Make the transition to Bible study by saying, "We will look at one of history's great heroines. A woman who changed Jewish history and gives us a great model for facing life's tough moments has an entire Bible book dedicated to recording her experience: Esther."

Into the Word

The following activities may be done in small groups, pairs, or as a class. Give each a copy of the work sheet described below. Allow learners to read through the text and complete the work sheet. (These are included in the student book.)

The work sheet will have two sections. The first section heading is "Leading Characters in Esther's Drama." Under the heading have three columns. The headings for the columns are "Character or Place," "Position or Role," and "Activity or Event." Under the first heading include the names Haman, Mordecai, Hatach, Shushan, Esther, and Ahasuerus. Leave space for class members to write answers in the second and third columns.

In the second column ask the groups or class to identify the position or role each of the characters (or place) plays. In the third column they are to jot a brief note about what that person did (or what happened in a place). When the groups are reporting (or during the class discussion), ask the following questions or make comments: Haman—"Why did Haman have such power and influence with the king?" "What were Haman's character flaws as seen in this drama?"; Mordecai—"What other Old Testament hero faced a similar challenge?" *(Daniel);* Hatach—"Few people have ever heard of Hatach; fewer still have any idea how important he was in this plan. How was he important, and what were his tasks?"; Shushan—Simply tell the class the significance of this place; Esther—"What was the tension in the decision Esther had to make?" "What makes her decision heroic?"; Ahasuerus—Explain the significance of the golden sceptre.

The second work sheet heading should read "The Story Line of Esther's Drama." The story of Esther is complicated, so this activity will help sort out the events leading up to Esther's decision. On this section they should note the story's events as they occur in the drama.

Into Life

Remind the class that most of us live lives in a quiet routine, never having to make such a heroic choice as Esther. However, we do make decisions heroic in the sense that they benefit other people or our own character. Give examples, such as making a decision that no matter what sexual temptation comes, one will be faithful to a spouse. Brainstorm heroic decisions people make for everyday life.

If you did *Option 1* of Into the Lesson, remind class members of what they identified on their cards. Ask them to take their cards in hand. Stress that life's challenges often require personal heroic decisions, decisions usually sacrificial and benefiting someone else. Ask them to identify the "heroic" parts of their decisions and write them on the cards. Challenge each to take the first step in meeting this life challenge this week.

If you did not do *Option 1* at the beginning of this lesson, do so here. Then complete the task in the preceding paragraph.

Let's Talk It Over

The questions on this page are designed to promote discussion of the lesson by the class and to encourage application of the lesson Scriptures. The answers provided are only discussion starters. Let your class talk it over from there.

1. First Peter 2:17 requires that we show proper respect to those in authority. But Mordecai refused to honor Haman. How do we know which example or precept to follow?

The New Testament helps us to recognize some situations where we should render honor. See Ephesians 6:2 (parents); 1 Timothy 5:17 (elders); and 1 Peter 2:17 (governing authorities).

We do not know all the reasons why Mordecai refused to bow to Haman. But "proper respect" to an earthly authority is never to involve what could be taken as *worship*, whether in New Testament or Old Testament times.

Perhaps Mordecai knew of Haman's murderous character. Mordecai as a righteous man may have refused to honor someone that he knew God Himself would not honor.

2. As a result of Mordecai's refusal to bow, Haman became a man "full of wrath." How are the causes and results of Haman's anger similar to effects you've observed?

The anger that results from personal "slights"—real or imagined—often leads to a thirst for revenge. Thoughts can escalate in a person's mind until "molehills become mountains." Haman's anger focused itself first on Mordecai and how to destroy him. Then he reasoned that hurting Mordecai was best accomplished by destroying his people. Imagine it: a plan for mass murder simply for a refusal to bow!

Such anger often does more damage to the hater than to the hated. That was true in Haman's case. Hatred creates a blindness that diminishes one's ability to sort through the good and the bad. Perhaps that's one reason the Scriptures warn us against taking revenge (cf. Romans 12:19).

3. Esther was called upon to make a choice: obey the legal expectations of the king or attempt to make a plea for her people. Why was the one she chose the more noble—the "greater good"?

Those who promote "situation ethics" would suggest that either choice would have been equally appropriate, depending on what one wants to accomplish. Those of us who believe in ethical absolutes, however, know that we must dig deeper. One choice usually will be more pleasing to God than the other, and His will is our guiding principle in making our decisions.

In the case at hand, one choice meant yielding to the laws of an earthly authority; this could have protected the life of one person (Esther's, although Mordecai had good reason to doubt that she would truly be safe). The other choice meant Esther voluntarily risking her own life for the possibility of saving many thousands of innocents. Stated this way, the proper choice is beyond doubt.

4. "Who knoweth whether thou art come to the kingdom for such a time as this?" is a question that confronts all of us. What has God called you to do through the special circumstances of your own life?

You may need to ask this question a week in advance to give your learners a chance to think through their answers. Some may even be willing to share stories of defeat—about times when they did not "rise to the occasion" as they should have.

Each of us, like Esther, needs to consider whether the skills and opportunities that God has provided us place us in unique positions of responsibility in the service of His kingdom. When we see a variety of factors "come together" in our own lives in an unusual way, we should stop and consider whether God may be selecting us for a special task in His larger plan.

5. Esther made certain preparations before she presented herself to the king with her request. How could this be an example for us?

There is a very fine line to walk here! Spending too much time on preparation can indicate an overreliance on our own ability and a lack of faith in God. Spending too little time in preparation, however, may disregard God's desire that we use the abilities He has given us for their intended purposes.

Esther demonstrates the right balance. Her fasting and prayer show God her devotion to His cause. Gathering others to join in a supportive network strengthens that devotion. The three-day delay gives her time to strengthen her resolve and prepare her thoughts. Nehemiah will go through a similar preparation a few years later (see Nehemiah 1:4). How different life would be if all Christians chose to incorporate these elements into their God-honoring decision making!

A Time to Celebrate

February 29
Lesson 13

DEVOTIONAL READING: **Psalm 98.**

BACKGROUND SCRIPTURE: **Esther 8, 9.**

PRINTED TEXT: **Esther 8:3-8; 9:17-23.**

Esther 8:3-8

3 And Esther spake yet again before the king, and fell down at his feet, and besought him with tears to put away the mischief of Haman the Agagite, and his device that he had devised against the Jews.

4 Then the king held out the golden sceptre toward Esther. So Esther arose, and stood before the king,

5 And said, If it please the king, and if I have found favor in his sight, and the thing seem right before the king, and I be pleasing in his eyes, let it be written to reverse the letters devised by Haman the son of Hammedatha the Agagite, which he wrote to destroy the Jews which are in all the king's provinces:

6 For how can I endure to see the evil that shall come unto my people? or how can I endure to see the destruction of my kindred?

7 Then the king Ahasuerus said unto Esther the queen and to Mordecai the Jew, Behold, I have given Esther the house of Haman, and him they have hanged upon the gallows, because he laid his hand upon the Jews.

8 Write ye also for the Jews, as it liketh you, in the king's name, and seal it with the king's ring: for the writing which is written in the king's name, and sealed with the king's ring, may no man reverse.

Esther 9:17-23

17 On the thirteenth day of the month Adar; and on the fourteenth day of the same rested they, and made it a day of feasting and gladness.

18 But the Jews that were at Shushan assembled together on the thirteenth day thereof, and on the fourteenth thereof; and on the fifteenth day of the same they rested, and made it a day of feasting and gladness.

19 Therefore the Jews of the villages, that dwelt in the unwalled towns, made the fourteenth day of the month Adar a day of gladness and feasting, and a good day, and of sending portions one to another.

20 And Mordecai wrote these things, and sent letters unto all the Jews that were in all the provinces of the king Ahasuerus, both nigh and far,

21 To establish this among them, that they should keep the fourteenth day of the month Adar, and the fifteenth day of the same, yearly,

22 As the days wherein the Jews rested from their enemies, and the month which was turned unto them from sorrow to joy, and from mourning into a good day: that they should make them days of feasting and joy, and of sending portions one to another, and gifts to the poor.

23 And the Jews undertook to do as they had begun, and as Mordecai had written unto them.

GOLDEN TEXT: The Jews had light, and gladness, and joy, and honor.—Esther 8:16.

Feb 29

Lessons From Life
Unit 2: Wisdom for the Times of Our Lives
(Lessons 9-13)

Lesson Aims

After participating in this lesson, each student should be able to:

1. Summarize the events that led to the beginning of the Jewish festival of Purim.

2. Discuss the importance of celebrating special events in his or her Christian life to help strengthen faith.

3. Plan a church or family celebration to commemorate a specific milestone or victory.

Lesson Outline

INTRODUCTION
    A. Holidays
    B. Lesson Background
  I. THE JEWS RESCUED (Esther 8:3-8)
    A. Plea Offered (v. 3)
    B. Plea Honored (v. 4)
    C. Wish Stated (vv. 5, 6)
       Native Missionaries
    D. Decree Issued (vv. 7, 8)
 II. THE FEAST OF PURIM ESTABLISHED (Esther 9:17-23)
    A. Day of Celebration (vv. 17-19)
    B. Letter to the Jews (vv. 20, 21)
    C. From Sorrow to Joy (vv. 22, 23)
       Gifts to the Poor
CONCLUSION
    A. Memories and Memorials
    B. Prayer
    C. Thought to Remember

Introduction

A. Holidays

Festivals and holidays are an important part in the life of Christianity. They help give us an identity and bind us together. For example, Christians around the world observe many holidays, but the most important are Christmas and Easter. This is rightly so, for they mark the two most significant events in the life of our Lord—His birth and His resurrection.

Festivals and holidays are important to nations as well. Citizens of the United States observe Independence Day (July 4) as an important date in their history—the signing of the Declaration of Independence in 1776. France observes Bastille Day on July 14, marking an important event that occurred in the French Revolution in 1789.

Other holidays are not considered to be "major" celebrations, although they may commemorate important events. How much attention is given to such observances varies widely. For example, many in Britain and parts of the Commonwealth observe Guy Fawkes Day on November 5; Fawkes was a conspirator who attempted (and failed) to blow up the king and Parliament in the infamous Gunpowder Plot of 1605. Columbus Day in the United States, however, often passes without much notice.

Likewise, the ancient Jews had what we could call both "major" and "minor" feasts and celebrations. The major feasts, such as Passover, Unleavened Bread, and Pentecost, are well known to most Christians today. But along the way—particularly after the exile—the ancient Jews added other festivals. One of these was Purim, which celebrated their deliverance from the efforts of Haman to exterminate them. Our two lessons from the Book of Esther show us the origins of this feast.

B. Lesson Background

The book of Esther reads like a thriller that Hollywood would dream up—except it isn't fiction, it is history. In last week's lesson we saw Haman's hatred of Mordecai. This hatred led Haman to seek revenge, so he secured a decree from King Ahasuerus (also known as Xerxes) to exterminate all Jews in the Persian Empire. Then Mordecai prevailed upon Esther to intervene.

In the text not included in either of our two lessons, Esther makes her appeal at a banquet she hosts for the king and Haman (Esther 7). Before that banquet, however, Haman had ordered a huge gallows to be built upon which to execute the Jew Mordecai (Esther 5:14). Yet at about the same time, and without Haman's knowledge, the king decided to honor Mordecai for foiling an assassination plot earlier (2:19-23; 6:1-3).

The supreme irony came when the king asked Haman (who had just arrived to request the death of Mordecai) how to reward "the man whom the king delighteth to honor" (6:6a). Haman, thinking that he himself was the one to be rewarded, replied that such a man should be dressed in the finest clothes and be paraded through the streets, mounted on a fine horse led by a leading citizen (6:6b-9). Imagine Haman's chagrin when he learned that Mordecai was the one to be honored and that he (Haman) was the one to lead the horse!

During the banquet that followed, Esther told the king about the plight of her people (7:1-6). In another great irony the king ordered Haman hanged on the gallows that Haman had built for Mordecai (7:9, 10). The closing chapters of the book tell how the king issued a new order allowing the Jews to defend themselves against their enemies. The time of their deliverance came to be celebrated with feasting and rejoicing from that day forward.

I. The Jews Rescued (Esther 8:3-8)

As we join the narrative, Haman has just been executed (7:10). Further, the king has given Haman's estate to Esther that same day (8:1), and Mordecai receives the honor that previously belonged to Haman (8:2). Even so, Esther realizes that there is work yet to do.

A. Plea Offered (v. 3)

3. And Esther spake yet again before the king, and fell down at his feet, and besought him with tears to put away the mischief of Haman the Agagite, and his device that he had devised against the Jews.

One would suppose that Mordecai could revoke the decree that called for the death of his people. We might think this because of the fact that he now possesses the king's signet ring that Haman had used to issue that decree in the first place (3:10-12; 8:2). But such is not the case. Among the Medes and Persians a decree once issued cannot be withdrawn. It is set in stone. (See Daniel 6:8, 12, 15.)

For this reason Esther once more has to step forward to save her people. Emboldened by her earlier success, she approaches *the king* a second time. This time she falls prostrate before him *with tears* to plead for protection against the scheme Haman has devised to destroy her people. [See question #1, page 224.]

B. Plea Honored (v. 4)

4. Then the king held out the golden sceptre toward Esther. So Esther arose, and stood before the king.

Esther must realize that she is in the good graces of *the king*, and her judgment is correct. He extends his *sceptre* again (cf. Esther 5:2), indicating that he understands her plea and is willing to take some action in regard to it. Thus she arises and stands *before* him. The problem now is how to revoke a law that cannot be revoked!

C. Wish Stated (vv. 5, 6)

5. And said, If it please the king, and if I have found favor in his sight, and the thing seem right before the king, and I be pleasing in his

eyes, let it be written to reverse the letters devised by Haman the son of Hammedatha the Agagite, which he wrote to destroy the Jews which are in all the king's provinces.

Like a lawyer pleading a case, Esther carefully lays out her argument point by point. Her first appeal is a personal one: *if I have found favor*. Of course, she has clear evidence that she has found favor in the king's sight. But a reminder won't hurt. [See question #2, page 224.]

The phrase *and the thing seem right before the king* is Esther's appeal to the king's sense of justice. Unfortunately, justice is not an absolute thing among human beings. Without the Word of God to control our thinking, one person's justice is another person's crime. For example, certain Muslim radicals today believe that murdering a non-Muslim (an "infidel") is a righteous act. Most of us are horrified by such a concept of justice.

On the other hand, Esther understands the concept of self-defense when she appeals to the king's sense of right and wrong. Like most ancient rulers, he is at times brutal and heavy-handed. But he comes through as reasonably decent when compared with others of his time.

In requesting that the king *reverse the letters devised by Haman*, Esther places the blame for the evil decree on Haman rather than on *the king*. All rulers, even those today, rely on close advisors and others who work under them to provide the information needed to make decisions. This is especially true in a kingdom as vast as the ancient Persian Empire, where communications were not as swift and as readily available as they are today. Obviously, no ruler can be wise enough to understand every issue in every village in every province. Rulers need advisors for this.

So King Ahasuerus had trusted Haman completely. Consequently, when the schemer presented the king with a decree to destroy the Jews,

How to Say It
AGAGITE. *Ay*-guh-gite.
AHASUERUS. Uh-haz-you-*ee*-rus.
ASSYRIAN. Uh-*sear*-e-un.
HAMAN. *Hay*-mun.
HERODOTUS. Heh-*rod*-uh-tus.
JOSEPHUS. Jo-*see*-fus.
MACCABEES. *Mack*-uh-bees.
MEDES. Meeds.
MORDECAI. *Mor*-dih-kye.
PERSIANS. *Per*-zhunz.
PURIM. *Pew*-rim.
SHUSHAN. *Shoo*-shan.
SUSA. *Soo*-suh.
XERXES. *Zerk*-seez.

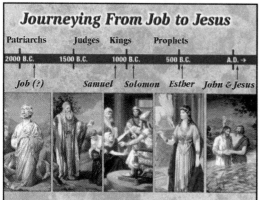

Journeying From Job to Jesus

Patriarchs   Judges   Kings   Prophets

2000 B.C.   1500 B.C.   1000 B.C.   500 B.C.   A.D. →

Job (?)   Samuel   Solomon   Esther   John & Jesus

Visual for lessons 5 and 13. *Use this time line to help your learners keep "the big picture" in mind.*

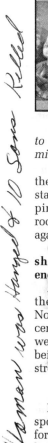

the king had "bought off on it" with the understanding that it would be beneficial to his empire. Little did he realize that the decree was rooted in Haman's personal desire to get revenge against Mordecai for a personal slight.

6. For how can I endure to see the evil that shall come unto my people? or how can I endure to see the destruction of my kindred?

At the time he had approved the death decree, the king had no idea that Esther was Jewish. Now, of course, he realizes the impact that it is certain to have on her. We can feel sorrow when we read of thousands of people in a foreign land being massacred; but we will feel it much more strongly if the victims are friends and relatives.

NATIVE MISSIONARIES

In the heat and squalor of one of the poorest spots on earth, a "native missionary" ministers for Christ. He works with people who have very little education and even less money. He battles daily with superstition, unsanitary conditions, violence, and abject poverty. It is hard work, but he continues to serve.

This missionary does not have to stay where he is. With his earned Master's degrees he could be serving in affluent North America, where he studied. He could live in an upscale home and drive an expensive car. He could work with college-trained church members and a well-paid staff. But like many others, this man chose to leave these advantages behind. He chose to go home, back to his native land to serve his people.

Every year men and women from all over the globe come to North America to train for ministry. When they arrive, they often enter a new world. Wealth, convenience, safe drinking water, electricity every day, smooth roads, and easy access to health care surround them. Luxuries we take for granted leave these Christians wide-eyed with wonder. Like Esther in the king's palace, it is easy to forget about their heritage. It is very easy to find a reason to stay. Many do.

But many also echo the words of Esther: "How can I endure to see the evil that shall come unto my people? or how can I endure to see the destruction of my kindred?" So they go home as "native missionaries" to bring the message of eternal life.

Encourage such folks whenever you can! Ask about international students at a Bible college or a campus ministry near you. Support their education. Welcome them into your home. Pray for them. Warn them of the dangers of the affluent culture to which they temporarily belong. Caution them with the example of Demas (2 Timothy 4:10). In short, be a Mordecai! Perhaps God has "raised you up" to do just that.   —J. D. J.

D. Decree Issued (vv. 7, 8)

7. Then the king Ahasuerus said unto Esther the queen and to Mordecai the Jew, Behold, I have given Esther the house of Haman, and him they have hanged upon the gallows, because he laid his hand upon the Jews.

Ahasuerus realizes that he has been tricked by *Haman*, so he takes steps to rectify the problem. He begins his response by reminding both *Esther* and *Mordecai* about Haman's fate. Although the king's swift action against Haman has settled that part of the problem, the evil decree still stands.

8. Write ye also for the Jews, as it liketh you, in the king's name, and seal it with the king's ring: for the writing which is written in the king's name, and sealed with the king's ring, may no man reverse.

Once the king understands the situation, he wastes no time in providing a remedy. He turns to Mordecai and gives him the authority to *write* a decree as he sees fit. The king places his trust in Mordecai to do the right thing. The king's trust in Haman had been misplaced. Now the king seems certain that Mordecai can be trusted. He has good reason for this conclusion because it was Mordecai who earlier had reported the conspiracy against the king, quite possibly saving the king's life (Esther 2:19-23). [See question #3, page 224.]

Although the first decree cannot be rescinded by any *man*, its effects can be nullified by another decree granting the Jews the right to defend themselves if attacked. Mordecai is the one to write this second decree. It will circulate under the authority of the king, bearing his seal. In matters of state the king's word is final—*may no man reverse* it. He doesn't have to worry about legislatures or courts overriding it as is the usual process in a democracy.

II. The Feast of Purim Established (Esther 9:17-23)

In the verses between 8:8 and 9:17 we learn that Mordecai loses no time in using the king's authority to carry out his plan to save his people. The first thing he does is to call in scribes to make copies of the new decree that will be dispatched to the most remote corners of the Persian Empire. The empire consists of one hundred twenty-seven provinces, stretching from India to Ethiopia. Many different languages are spoken throughout the empire. The scribes thus not only copy the royal decree, they also translate it into the language appropriate to each province (8:9).

Once the translations are made and sealed, Mordecai dispatches them to the far reaches of the realm. The Persians have one of the best postal systems in the ancient world, and they quickly and efficiently deliver their messages (8:10, 14). The Greek historian Herodotus (485–425 B.C.) described this postal service in these words: "Neither snow nor rain nor heat nor gloom of night stays these couriers from the swift completion of their appointed rounds." (This statement is inscribed today on the New York City General Post Office building.) Getting the message out swiftly is essential, because the Jews need time to prepare for their defense.

Many may be willing to attack Jews who are defenseless, but most will have second thoughts about challenging those who are armed and organized. Some, however, do attack the Jews out in the provinces, and thousands of the attackers are killed (Esther 9:5, 16). In Shushan (Susa) the capital city, the Jews kill about eight hundred over two days (9:12-15).

A. Day of Celebration (vv. 17-19)

17. On the thirteenth day of the month Adar; and on the fourteenth day of the same rested they, and made it a day of feasting and gladness.

These bloody conflicts occur mainly on two days—the *thirteenth* and *fourteenth* day of *Adar* (this month corresponds to late February or early March). The time that had been set for the destruction of the Jews becomes, instead, days of salvation for them—a time of rejoicing and *feasting*. The plan by which the enemies of the Jews hoped to destroy them becomes an event that binds them closer together across the empire.

18, 19. But the Jews that were at Shushan assembled together on the thirteenth day thereof, and on the fourteenth thereof; and on the fif-

teenth day of the same they rested, and made it a day of feasting and gladness. Therefore the Jews of the villages, that dwelt in the unwalled towns, made the fourteenth day of the month Adar a day of gladness and feasting, and a good day, and of sending portions one to another.

The *Jews* in different parts of the empire have different experiences in defending themselves. As a result, they apparently do not all observe this special event on the same day. How Mordecai handles this difference is the subject of the next verse.

B. Letter to the Jews (vv. 20, 21)

20, 21. And Mordecai wrote these things, and sent letters unto all the Jews that were in all the provinces of the king Ahasuerus, both nigh and far, to establish this among them, that they should keep the fourteenth day of the month Adar, and the fifteenth day of the same, yearly.

It would seem that there is some disagreement about when the feast should be observed—some want to celebrate on *the fourteenth* and some want to celebrate on *the fifteenth*. Because of his work in saving the Jews from Haman's scheme, *Mordecai* has become the recognized leader of the Jewish people wherever they may live in the empire. Thus he is the one who settles the issue: instead of celebrating on a single day, the Jews will have two days to celebrate. This is a wise decision because it easily includes both points of view—and no one will object to having an extra day for celebration! [See question #4, page 224.]

C. From Sorrow to Joy (vv. 22, 23)

22, 23. As the days wherein the Jews rested from their enemies, and the month which was turned unto them from sorrow to joy, and from mourning into a good day: that they should make them days of feasting and joy, and of sending portions one to another, and gifts to the poor. And the Jews undertook to do as they had begun, and as Mordecai had written unto them.

This joyous festival becomes known as "Purim." This term comes from the Assyrian word *pur*, which means "lots." It indicates that in some way Haman cast lots to eliminate the Jews (Esther 3:7; 9:24; cf. John 19:24; Acts 1:26).

Second Maccabees 15:36, which describes some events that happen about one hundred and sixty years before Christ, calls it "Mordecai's Day." The Jewish historian Josephus also mentions this festival. [See question #5, page 224.] But this festival is not mentioned in the New Testament, perhaps because it is not one of the major Jewish feasts, and, being celebrated only locally, is not a factor in the ministry of Jesus.

Home Daily Bible Readings

Monday, Feb. 23—The Lord Sets the Prisoners Free (Psalm 146:1-9)

Tuesday, Feb. 24—A Song of Praise Is Fitting (Psalm 147:1-5)

Wednesday, Feb. 25—Sing to God With Thanksgiving (Psalm 147:6-11)

Thursday, Feb. 26—Praise Your God, O Zion! (Psalm 147:12-20)

Friday, Feb. 27—God Has Brought Victory (Psalm 98:1-9)

Saturday, Feb. 28—Esther Saves the Jews (Esther 8:1-8)

Sunday, Feb. 29—The Jews Celebrate Their Deliverance (Esther 9:18-23)

GIFTS TO THE POOR

Every November a volunteer army rises up to provide Thanksgiving dinners for needy people. Businesses offer food and equipment. Warehouses reserve space for supplies. Donations flow from individuals throughout the community. Public schools open their cafeterias to cook and serve the meals. And hundreds of workers stay up through the night to roast turkeys, peel potatoes, bake pies, and mix dressing.

You may have something similar in your community. At Thanksgiving, Christmas, or on other occasions throughout the year, people volunteer their time, effort, and resources to provide such "gifts to the poor." This is a way to celebrate God's goodness.

The apostle Paul wrote, "Being enriched in every thing to all bountifulness, which causeth through us thanksgiving to God. For the administration of this service not only supplieth the want of the saints, but is abundant also by many thanksgivings unto God" (2 Corinthians 9:11, 12). When we help people in need in the name of Christ, we bring joy to them. We also provide a reason for them to give thanks to God.

As Mordecai urged the Jews in Persia, so we can help the poor on our own "days of feasting." God's own Son saved us from wrath and destruction, so how can we not help the poor celebrate right alongside us? The Jews were to treat the poor among them as God had treated them—with grace.

This remains a wonderful way to celebrate God's goodness to us. What can you do to celebrate by serving? Do you have a special day or a special achievement coming up? Mark this milestone with the joy of helping someone in need. Then your celebration will honor both God and humanity.   —J. D. J.

Conclusion

A. Memories and Memorials

Memories are a vital part of our personalities. In fact, we are largely defined by our memories. All of us have hundreds of memories, some painful, some pleasant, that have shaped us into the kind of people we are and the kind of people we will be. Psychologists tell us that a person may be scarred permanently by the memories of a violent or discouraging childhood.

Many of us have had the painful experience of visiting an old friend who is in the advanced stages of Alzheimer's disease. Her memory is gone. She no longer knows who she is. Her life is lived out in a gathering gloom.

Families can suffer a similar fate. Parents and their children share many common memories. But then grandchildren and great-grandchildren lose these "memory ties" that bind them together. Over the years they drift apart. The common values they once cherished gradually erode and disappear.

Institutions can suffer a similar fate. They lose sight of their original purpose. They eventually dissipate their energies, becoming involved in activities that are quite foreign to their original "reason for being." The church has not completely escaped this trap. (See Galatians 1:6; Revelation 2:4.)

God, knowing the human tendency to forget, has left us some important "memorial markers." Those markers He allowed the ancient Jews to have eventually were to give way to those He established for the church. Every time we witness a baptism, we are reminded of His sacrifice for us (Romans 6:1-11). The bread and fruit of the vine of the Lord's Supper remind us of His body, broken for our sins, and His blood, poured out for us. Each time we participate, our minds are stirred again to remember His sacrifice for us (1 Corinthians 11:23-25).

God gave (or allowed) the ancient Hebrews various feasts and holy days to remind them of His providential care for them. So also He has given us these memorials lest we forget.

B. Prayer

All-loving God, we thank You that across the centuries You have given guidance and protection to Your people, leaving memorials to remind them of Your goodness. Give us the faith we need to see that in our day You have not left us but are ever present to lead and protect. In the name of our Savior we pray, amen.

C. Thought to Remember

Whenever you celebrate, don't forget why!

Learning by Doing

This page contains an alternative lesson plan emphasizing learning activities.
Classes desiring such student involvement will find these suggestions helpful.

Learning Goals

After participating in this lesson, each student will be able to:

1. Summarize the events that led to the beginning of the Jewish festival of Purim.

2. Discuss the importance of celebrating special events in his or her Christian life to help strengthen faith.

3. Plan a church or family celebration to commemorate a specific milestone or victory.

Into the Lesson

Have a class member give a brief report on the Jewish feast of Purim, which originated in Esther's bravery. The focus should be on the reason for the celebration, when Jews celebrated, and how they celebrated down through the centuries since Esther.

Your reporter will need resources. Early in the week give this individual a photocopy of the lesson commentary on Esther 9:22, 23. Also give the reporter a Bible dictionary with the pages marked that tells about this feast. Of course, the Internet is also a valuable tool for doing historical research.

After the presentation say, "Holidays are an important part of every religion and nation." Ask the class to name the major national and Christian holidays, and list these for later use.

Into the Word

Activity 1: Begin with a brief lecture on the Lesson Background, summarizing last week's study. Make a visual of the story line from last week's lesson to summarize Esther's story right up to the time she made her dramatic decision.

Activity 2: Call three class members during the week and ask them to do a brief dramatization of Esther 8:1b-8. The characters will be Ahasuerus, Esther, and Mordecai. Ask them to meet about fifteen to twenty minutes before class and rehearse, putting the text into contemporary words. Simple props may include a crown, a ring, a cane or umbrella for a sceptre, and large name tags to wear around the neck.

Following the drama, read the printed text and ask the following discussion questions:

(1) Remember that to enter the king's throne room without an invitation meant death—unless the king offered his sceptre as an expression of pardon. Esther did not wait for the king to offer his sceptre before she made her appeal. Why did she jump right in before the king could decide whether or not to make the offer?

(2) The challenge was how to revoke a law that could not be revoked, for the king's word was irrevocable law. What was Esther's plan?

Activity 3: Ask someone to read the remainder of Chapter 8 to the class. Ask three class members to be a "listening team," ready to summarize a small portion of the text. Ask one to note especially where the edict went. A second is to summarize the edict. A third will report the reactions of the Jews and other nationalities.

Activity 4: Tell the class that the next portion of the text is the very first celebration of the feast of Purim. Then read the printed text, Esther 9:17-23. Highlight a few of the remarks made by your reporter in the lesson introduction.

Into Life

As you point to the list of national and religious holidays made earlier, note that there is value to holidays. Ask the class to identify the values. Write their remarks on another poster. Answers may include the values of teaching history, teaching ethics, teaching God's will or purpose, building family relationships, or others.

Form groups of three to five, and give each a large piece of poster board and a marker. Each group is to brainstorm how to make one of the following holidays effective and meaningful for families or individuals, especially how we can teach God's values and priorities in these holidays. Choose from the holidays or events listed in the Into the Lesson activity to assign to the groups. Allow each group time to compile its suggestions and then to report its suggestions with its poster on display.

Ask the entire group to focus on the next major Christian holiday, Easter. Suggest that the group do something together to celebrate Christ's resurrection. Ask the class for ideas and suggestions. Appoint a team to make the preparations.

Conclude the class by asking members to complete a commitment card. The card will have two statements to complete and a simple commitment to sign: "The next holiday or celebration in my family or life is. . . . The value and opportunities this event or holiday present include. . . . I will make this event or holiday teach Christ's values and priorities. Signed _____"

Let's Talk It Over

The questions on this page are designed to promote discussion of the lesson by the class and to encourage application of the lesson Scriptures. The answers provided are only discussion starters. Let your class talk it over from there.

1. Esther's plea was one filled with genuine emotion. When is it proper to vent our emotions, and when should we control (or suppress) them?

Your learners' answers will depend largely on individual personalities. Some are afraid of emotions. Their assumption may be that only weak and/or manipulative people display tears when rational discussion is to be greatly preferred. But in those same people there is often a lack of passion that can hinder their effectiveness in attacking problems.

Emotions are God-given expressions. Emotions flow when they come in contact with our "hot buttons," our priorities, and our purpose for living. Jesus, for example, wept on a sobering occasion (John 11:35).

It is indeed possible to use emotions out of wrong motives (e.g., 1 Kings 18:28). But we must not suppress them at a time when the suppression can be interpreted as a lack of real concern. Esther's emotional response was appropriate because it demonstrated that her first priority was for her people—not retaliation against a single enemy.

2. In what ways had Esther earned the king's approval prior to presenting her "case"? How is this important to family relationships today?

Some will assume that because Esther was his wife the king obviously would favor her. Few, however, can doubt that it is the attitude of a wife toward her husband that determines how readily he will listen. In this very serious situation Esther had chosen to approach the matter with careful planning and respect for the position of her husband. Almost any man will respond better if these are the attitudes of his spouse! Compare the nagging of Delilah in Judges 16:16. See also the discussion of how husbands and wives are to treat each other in Ephesians 5:22-33.

3. Mordecai's character must have marked him as a different kind of advisor than Haman. What were some of Mordecai's strengths that evoked a high level of trust by the king? How can we emulate these today?

Certainly the first qualification of a trusted companion is determined by the level of commitment that he or she demonstrates. Remember that Mordecai had saved the king's life earlier (Esther 2:19-23). Beyond that, Mordecai had demonstrated his astuteness as he had advised Esther. Certainly the king must have benefited by aligning to himself a man whose fame was beginning to spread among a significant part of the king's constituents.

One important way we emulate Mordecai is being careful of our motives in all situations. Mordecai ended up being very well off (Esther 8:15), but that was never his motivation. As a result of all this, Mordecai became "next unto" the king (Esther 10:3).

4. Mordecai made everyone happy by his compromise to hold the celebration over two days' time instead of one. When is compromise a good idea, and when is it not? Explain.

First of all, we should never compromise on our core Bible doctrines. No matter what the world wants us to do in order to be "relevant," we are here to please God first. The apostle Paul was exasperated on more than one occasion because churches were compromising doctrine.

But sometimes it can be a good idea to reach a compromise solution on a matter of expediency, as Mordecai's case shows. A good question to ask is, "Will the gains outweigh the losses in the compromise we're considering?" This will not always be an easy question to answer. Sometimes a compromise of two plans will be more of a monstrosity than either plan would be on its own! We must be careful about compromising just so that "everyone ends up with something."

5. What was an occasion that for you "turned . . . from sorrow to joy, and from mourning into a good day"? Why did it happen, and what was it about such an occasion that helped you grow spiritually and strengthen your faith?

The answers to these questions will be highly individual. You may have to ask these questions a week in advance in order to give your learners a chance to think about them before the lesson is presented. If you feel the need to "prod" people's memories, you might suggest certain types of occasions such as a funeral for a Christian believer, reconciliation with a child who had been something of a "prodigal," or the healing of a division within the church.

Spring Quarter, 2004

Special Features

Lessons

Jesus Fulfills His Mission

Unit 1: Road to the Cross

Unit 2: Victory Through Death

Living Expectantly

Unit 1: Preparing for the Lord's Return

Unit 2: Visions of Hope

About These Lessons

Our Christian faith is anchored in the fact that Jesus' death and resurrection secure our eternity. Historical reality and "future history" work together to tell us how to live today. Past, present, and future—it's all here!

Mar
7

Mar
14

Mar
21

Mar
28

Apr
4

Apr
11

Apr
18

Apr
25

May
2

May
9

May
16

May
23

May
30

Quarterly Quiz

The questions on this page may be used in several ways: as a pretest at the beginning of the quarter; as a review at the end of the quarter; or as a review after each lesson. The questions are based on the Scripture text of each lesson (King James Version). **The answers are on page 228.**

Lesson 1

1. The chief priests, scribes, elders of the people, and the high priest were all involved in the plot to kill Jesus. T/F *Matthew 26:3, 4*

2. According to Jesus, what was the reason the woman poured ointment on His head? (to anoint Him as king, to prepare for His burial, to comfort Him?) *Matthew 26:12*

3. What clue did Jesus give to the identity of His betrayer? *Matthew 26:23*

Lesson 2

1. Which two disciples did Jesus send to prepare the Passover? *Luke 22:8*

2. When Jesus broke the bread He said, "This is my _____ which is given for you." *Luke 22:19*

Lesson 3

1. What was Jesus' mood as He prayed in Gethsemane? *Matthew 26:37*

2. Judas was accompanied by a few men from the chief priests, who came to arrest Jesus. T/F *Matthew 26:47*

Lesson 4

1. For what alleged crime was Jesus condemned to death? *Mark 14:63, 64*

2. Who questioned Jesus and asked Him, "Art thou the King of the Jews?" (Caiaphas, Pilate, Herod?) *Mark 15:2*

3. When Pilate asked the crowd what he should do with Jesus, they shouted, "_____ _____." *Mark 15:12, 13*

Lesson 5

1. The sign on the cross identified Jesus as "the King of the Jews." T/F *John 19:19*

2. What did the soldiers who crucified Jesus do with His seamless coat? *John 19:23, 24*

Lesson 6

1. What occurred when the angel rolled back the stone from the door of Jesus' tomb? (a thunderstorm, total darkness, a great earthquake?) *Matthew 28:2*

2. After hearing the angel's message that Jesus was alive, what two emotions did the women experience? *Matthew 28:8*

3. The soldiers who guarded the tomb were bribed to lie and say Jesus' _____ stole His body. *Matthew 28:12, 13*

Lesson 7

1. The Thessalonians were examples to believers in _____ and _____. *1 Thessalonians 1:7*

2. Paul prayed night and day to see the believers at Thessalonica again. T/F *1 Thessalonians 3:10*

Lesson 8

1. Where will those who are alive meet the Lord when He returns? (on earth, in Heaven, in the air?) *1 Thessalonians 4:17*

2. Children of light are instructed to _____ and be _____. *1 Thessalonians 5:5, 6*

Lesson 9

1. What negative experiences were part of the Thessalonians' lives? *2 Thessalonians 1:4*

2. Paul was concerned that the Thessalonians would not do what he had commanded them. T/F *2 Thessalonians 3:4*

Lesson 10

1. Who was the only one worthy to open the book and loose the seals? *Revelation 5:2, 5*

2. What do the "golden vials full of odors" represent? *Revelation 5:8*

3. Those singing praise to the Lamb were made _____ and _____ unto God. *Revelation 5:10*

Lesson 11

1. What were the four angels on the four corners of the earth holding? *Revelation 7:1*

2. How were those from the great tribulation able to make their robes white? *Revelation 7:14*

Lesson 12

1. The angel announced that which city had fallen? (Babylon, Rome, Jerusalem?) *Revelation 14:8*

2. How were those who worshiped the beast identified? *Revelation 14:9, 11*

3. A voice from Heaven said that those who die in the Lord are blessed. T/F *Revelation 14:13*

Lesson 13

1. In the last days what will happen to the first heaven and the first earth? *Revelation 21:1*

2. When God dwells with His people, there will be no more tears, death, sorrow, or pain. T/F *Revelation 21:4*

3. Who will be allowed to live in the holy city with God? *Revelation 21:27*

In the Stream of History

by Ronald L. Nickelson

"THE PROBLEM WITH MOST PEOPLE," one observer lamented, "is that they live their lives as if history began on the day they were born."

The sad result of such an outlook is what we might call tunnel-vision living. Without a larger sense of history, people tend to see only their immediate situations, living only for the present moment. History becomes irrelevant because, after all, "that was then; this is now."

But the Bible assures us that history is indeed important. The birth, death, and resurrection of Jesus Christ were events that occurred at specific times and places. Each has its own meaning as determined by God. All other points along God's time line of salvation-history either *lead up to* the occurrence of these events, or *build upon* them as established facts.

And what a stream of history this is! From our twenty-first century vantage point we have the privilege of marveling at how God has brought about His plans over thousands of years. Fulfilled prophecy proves Christianity to be the only true religion. Fulfilled prophecy is the firm basis upon which Christians stand in the here-and-now as we look confidently toward future fulfillment. How tragic it is to see people live their lives day by day with no sense of God's movement in history!

The lessons of this quarter invite us to stand in this stream of history and look both ways. We will begin by looking two thousand years into the past. There in the gospel accounts we will see Jesus fulfill the sobering requirements of God's plan for our eternal salvation.

As our lessons move forward, our gaze ultimately will shift to "future history"—to the time (if we can use that term) when we are in our eternal home. That eternal home (Heaven) will be for those who have repented because they recognize what the God of all history has done for us *in* history through Jesus Christ.

Jesus Fulfills His Mission

Unit 1: Road to the Cross

Lesson 1: Love and Betrayal. Our first lesson opens to us the final week of Jesus' earthly ministry as depicted in Matthew's Gospel. As we see people react to Jesus with the extremes of love and hatred, we realize that it is unlikely that anyone involved in this drama (other than Jesus Himself) understood what roles they were playing in the grand sweep of history. The two thousand years of hindsight that we have on the lives of these people should give us pause: do we live out our own lives for Christ with a sense of how our behavior may affect others many years—even centuries—hence?

Lesson 2: Loaf and Cup. This lesson from Luke's Gospel could also be titled "In the Eye of the Hurricane," since this is a period of calm in the midst of Jesus' hectic final week. The tumult of the triumphal entry and temple confrontation are past at this point, while arrest and crucifixion are yet future. It is within these few hours that Jesus shifts the course of history in an entirely new direction: Lord's Supper observances have begun, and Passover celebrations are to be no more. Whenever we participate in the Lord's Supper, do we have the sense of history that we need to understand the importance of this shift?

Lesson 3: Prayer and Arrest. The calm that is in the eye of the hurricane is about to come to an end as we move back to Matthew's Gospel. In His hour of crisis, Jesus is all alone. His disciples are nearby in a physical sense, but in an emotional or supportive sense they are very much absent. The reason is simple: they don't understand the critical importance of this brief moment in history. Do we?

Lesson 4: Trial and Sentence. This lesson from Mark shows us Jesus on trial before people who are caught up in their personal agendas and sense of self-importance. These individuals include members of the Jewish Sanhedrin plus the Roman Governor, Pontius Pilate. Their arrogance and "situation ethics" blind them to the sobering roles they are playing in history. They don't have a clue!

Even so, history is still moving inexorably toward its conclusion. On that great, final day when God concludes history, these leaders will find the roles reversed: they will be the ones standing for judgment before the One whom they judged unjustly. When that day comes, where will *we* be standing?

Unit 2: Victory Through Death

Lesson 5: Jesus' Crucifixion. The Gospel of John portrays the reality of Jesus' death for us. At His crucifixion, Jesus' friends and disciples asked themselves, "How could this possibly be happening?" At the same time, Jesus' enemies gloated, "We have finally stopped him!" But in the final analysis it was only Jesus' Himself who had the correct sense of history. It was only Jesus who had a true sense of the importance of what was really happening.

The truth was that Jesus' death was neither tragic accident nor the triumph of an earthly foe. Rather, it was Jesus' voluntary, intentional payment of sin's price. Do we have the right view of history to understand this today?

Lesson 6: The Empty Tomb. Jesus' triumph over death was disbelieved by both friend and foe, and Matthew's Gospel shows us a small part of these reactions. Even though the initial disbelief of the disciples quickly gave way to amazement, their reactions revealed misconceptions. They had been taught personally by the Lord for more than three years, and they still did not understand. With the completed Bible in our hands, God has given us the capability of interpreting this vital historical event correctly. Have we?

Living Expectantly

Unit 1: Preparing for the Lord's Return

Lesson 7: Faithful in His Service. With the writing of 1 Thessalonians, time has moved forward some twenty years from the crucifixion and resurrection. The Thessalonians have demonstrated through their faith and service a proper understanding of those historical facts. With all

---

**Answers to Quarterly Quiz
on page 226**

Lesson 1—1. true. 2. to prepare for His burial. 3. the one who dipped his hand with Him in the dish. **Lesson 2**—1. Peter and John. 2. body. **Lesson 3**—1. sorrowful and very heavy. 2. false (a great multitude). **Lesson 4**—1. blasphemy. 2. Pilate. 3. "Crucify him." **Lesson 5**—1. true. 2. cast lots for it. **Lesson 6**—1. a great earthquake. 2. fear and great joy. 3. disciples. **Lesson 7**—1. Macedonia, Achaia. 2. true. **Lesson 8**—1. in the air. 2. watch, sober. **Lesson 9**—1. persecutions and tribulations. 2. false. **Lesson 10**—1. Jesus, the Lion of Judah. 2. the prayers of saints. 3. kings, priests. **Lesson 11**—1. the four winds of the earth. 2. washed them in the blood of the Lamb. **Lesson 12**—1. Babylon. 2. they received his mark. 3. true. **Lesson 13**—1. they will pass away. 2. true. 3. those who are written in the Lamb's book of life.

---

the additional information we have today through completed revelation, will we understand as well as the Thessalonians did?

Lesson 8: Ready for His Return. What an interesting blend of past, present, and future we see in this lesson! Jesus died and rose again (past), and He is coming again (future). These past and future events affect how we are to live in the present, as Paul stresses in his counsel to the Thessalonians. Will we accept Paul's instructions to them as our marching orders as well?

Lesson 9: Reflecting His Glory. Having firmly established the importance of both past and future events regarding the Christ, we are ready in this lesson from 2 Thessalonians to view Paul's focus on the present. History, which has revealed the power, glory, and goodness of God, *must* shape how we live our lives day by day. Do people see us living out our calling by His power?

Unit 2: Visions of Hope

Lesson 10: Worshiping the Lamb. With the final four lessons in this quarter our attention shifts decisively to future history as depicted in the book of Revelation. The events we will read about can indeed be called "future history" because the probability that they will happen is 100 percent. The certainty of these blessed promises should cause us to worship. Does it?

Lesson 11: Receiving God's Salvation, and **Lesson 12: Enduring With the Saints.** Every Christian suffers. Some suffer more than others. Some Christians suffer even to the point of martyrdom, yet they remain steadfast in their faith. How do they do it? There is only one way: they focus on the eternal reward that awaits them. Are you one of these?

Lesson 13: Dwelling With God. The first act of history was creation itself (Genesis 1:1). The climactic acts that bring down the curtain on history will be the return of Christ, final judgment, and the unveiling of the new creation. But the new creation (with its new Jerusalem) is only for those who have renounced the depravity and decay of the old creation and who have Jesus Christ as their Savior. Are you one of these?

This quarter's lessons are just what we need to keep a perspective on past and future history. And what a breathtaking stream of history we stand in! What a marvelous future awaits us!

Even so, many today are so blinded by the allures and distractions of this world that they cannot (or will not) see that eternal destruction is their sobering destiny. We reach these people for Christ by sharing with them what Christ did for us some two thousand years ago. But telling the story isn't enough. We must live it as well.

The City of Jerusalem

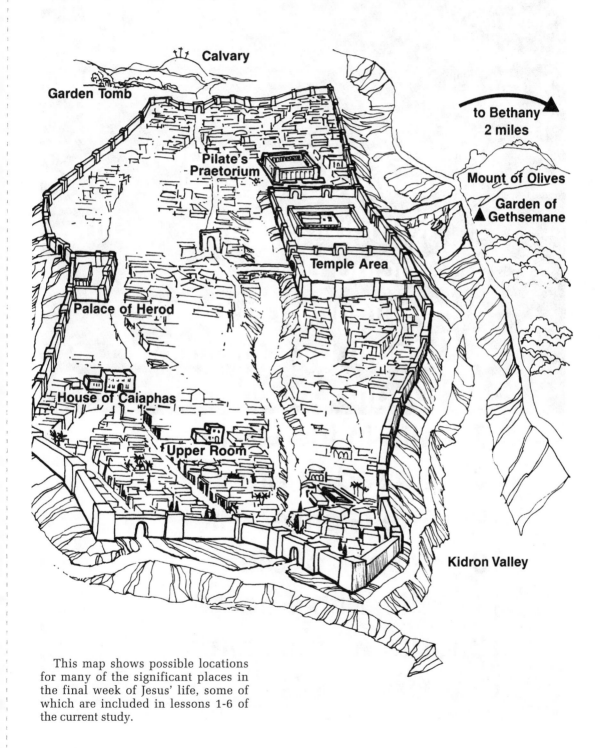

Calvary

Garden Tomb

Pilate's
Praetorium

to Bethany
2 miles

Mount of Olives

Garden of
Gethsemane

Temple Area

Palace of Herod

House of Caiaphas

Upper Room

Kidron Valley

This map shows possible locations
for many of the significant places in
the final week of Jesus' life, some of
which are included in lessons 1-6 of
the current study.

Jesus' Victory Over DEATH—
Jesus' Death Gives Us LIFE

Lesson	Theme
1	Prepared for Death; Betrayed to Death
2	Remembering His Death
3	Facing Death
4	Sentenced to Death
5	Death by Crucifixion
6	Death Conquered
7	Life in the Lord
8	Raised to Life
9	The Glorified Life
10	A Book of Life
11	Life With God
12	Life After Death
13	Eternal Life

Something More

Imagery and Incompletions

by Ronald G. Davis

Teachers and learners alike have much to anticipate in the series of studies in this quarter. Moving from the love of Christ implied in His death on the cross, to the power and hope in His resurrection, to the marvelous images of eternal life given in the letters to the Thessalonians (and to us!), to John's grand and glorious Revelation of the future reality—what could be more exciting? The most important "teacher tip" for the series may be: "Get excited, and show it!"

More practically, the teaching ideas, as usual, need to reflect in some way the basic content. A quick preview of the two units reveals two key truths: (1) simple objects take on deep, emotional significance as life is lived, and (2) waiting for completion and fulfillment is tolerable when the anticipated outcome is good.

The first lessons in the series are filled with key objects that carry deep and provocative imagery and emotion. The later lessons all carry the sense of waiting—waiting for something good to happen.

Special Things

Those who watch the popular PBS® show *Antiques Roadshow™* see an interesting phenomenon. Owners of the articles under evaluation reflect two varying attachments: some seem to have only a monetary interest in their prize; others, because of some family connection with their object, display a love and emotion well beyond a dollars-and-cents tag. Viewers can hardly resist speculating as to which individuals will likely sell their items. Intense feelings can be stirred, for a variety of reasons.

Through the Bible revelation, God uses simple things as "thought provokers" for His people. Imagine Noah and his sons, after the flood, seeing a rainbow without recalling the stormy days afloat on a covered, dead world and without rejoicing in God's grand promise (see Genesis 9:12-17). Imagine Peter, at the end of his life, seeing (or hearing) a rooster without remembering his dark and ugly sin of denying he knew Jesus (see Matthew 26:33-35, 69-75). Every dawn would spur Peter to say, "Never again, Lord."

Consider the significant objects in the first six lesson texts on the death and resurrection of Christ:

Lesson 1—A container of rich anointing perfume becomes a memorial to the woman who poured it out on Jesus' head; thirty silver coins becomes a sign of infamy forever.

You can offer attenders a "squirt" of (fragrance-free—for the hypersensitive) hand lotion as they arrive, or give each one a shiny dime as he or she leaves. Either offers a relational reminder for this week's study. The lotion given as members arrive and the coin given as they leave will represent the correct sequence of the events.

Lesson 2—The simplest elements of the Passover meal take on the most profound meaning granted to any element of God's creation: the unleavened bread is Christ's body of death; the pure juice of the vine is Jesus' blood poured out at Calvary for sins. Simply having a cup or tray of juice and a plate of bread present as learners arrive will immediately foreshadow the study.

Lesson 3—A sign of deepest love (a kiss) becomes a stigma of despicable treachery.

Handing out a chocolate kiss (or if your class would appreciate the symbolism, a pair of candy wax lips) to each member would be a useful reminder of lesson truths.

Lesson 4—Having all the accoutrements of judicial power does not ensure justice will be done. Few things represent the courtroom better than a judicial gavel. The sound of wood on wood has the sound of finality and authority. A judge's robe, if one can be obtained, may carry the symbolism as well.

Lesson 5—The cruel and unusual Roman execution technique of crucifixion yields an image worn with pride and honor by many Christians.

For each learner have an envelope containing the pieces of a tangram-like puzzle made from a cut-out cross that has been further cut into three to five pieces (see sample on the next page). Ask the group to assemble their pieces into a recognizable shape. Read 1 Corinthians 1:23, "We preach Christ crucified, unto the Jews a stumblingblock, and unto the Greeks foolishness." Note that to many the cross is a true puzzle, but to God it is both power and wisdom.

Lesson 6—Something empty (Jesus' tomb) fills the world for all time with endless hope.

For each class member have a small, unadorned empty box. (If necessary, visit a packaging, shipping store where small [jewelry-sized]

SAMPLE CUT LINES
FOR "CROSS" PUZZLE

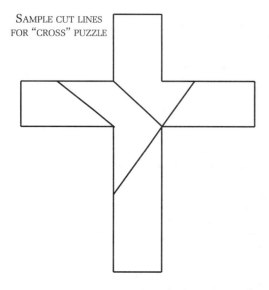

boxes can be bought inexpensively.) Put one on each seat before students arrive. Curiosity will drive many to open their boxes, discovering that they are empty. When some moan or joke about disappointment, note that, "Some empty things terminate hope; one empty thing gives hope!"

God is the Master of the symbolic. From the "mark upon Cain" (Genesis 4:15) to the beautiful stones of the wall of the "great city, the holy Jerusalem" (Revelation 21:10, 19, 20), God provides the imagery that catches the eye and fills the mind. The wise teacher will attempt to do the same.

Expecting Completion

A predictably successful way to stimulate initial thinking as learners arrive for class is simply to display a completion statement. Few can read a partial, incomplete statement without mentally (if not orally) finishing it.

Consider the following statements—based on the texts—for lessons seven through thirteen:

7. One Christian or church that brings a smile to my face is ____. 8. One of my Christian friends (or family) who has died and whom I am looking forward to seeing in Heaven is ____. 9. Reflecting the glory of God is most difficult for me when ____. 10. My favorite hymn/song of worship of Christ is ____. 11. I have the most difficulty living a holy life when ____. 12. Believing in Hell motivates me to ____. 13. The kinds of people I see going to Hell are ____. (Did you find yourself finishing each statement as you read it?)

If your class has available a marker board or chalkboard, displaying "pieces" of words is sure to get a learner response. Writing key words from a lesson text and then erasing top halves or bottom halves or simply "swirling" an eraser through the words will have the viewers "filling in the blanks." (Be certain not to erase too much.) Consider some of the following words for the lessons in this unit. *Lesson 7*—thankful, prayers, hope, work; *Lesson 8*—wrath, salvation, ignorant, trump; *Lesson 9*—glory, sanctification, traditions, evil; *Lesson 10*—Lamb, worthy, book, seals; *Lesson 11*—angel, multitude, Shepherd, tears; *Lesson 12*—Babylon, judgment, voice, beast; *Lesson 13*—new, his, Jerusalem, no. The same can be done with whole ideas (sentences), such as the "Thought to Remember" in each lesson.

What's Missing?

A similar effect can be achieved with a "What's Missing?" activity. This can be accomplished in a verbal activity in which statements are correct, and yet there is a key word or words missing. The challenge for the learner is to supply a missing word or words that maintain the truth of the statement in keeping with the context. Present the statements and say, "Each of these sentences is true. What word or words can be added to each that keep them true? What word or words will reflect today's lesson text?"

For example, for lesson 7 one could give the following statements (offered here with possible missing word in brackets) from 1 Thessalonians:

"Before Paul preached to the Thessalonians, they were [idol] worshipers" (1:9); or "Paul prayed [night and day] to see the Thessalonians" (3:10); or "Paul told the Thessalonians he was remembering their work [of faith] and labor [of love] and patience [of hope]" (1:3).

For lesson 8, the teacher could use the following statements, also from 1 Thessalonians:

"When the Lord returns from Heaven, the dead [in Christ] will rise first" (4:16); or "Christians who are alive on the earth when the Lord comes will meet Him [in the air]" (4:17).

Each text can lend itself to such an approach.

Jigsaw Puzzles

Consider writing, in large print from edge to edge, a key verse from a lesson or a key truth on a piece of poster board. Cut the poster into twelve to sixteen approximately equal pieces in a jigsaw puzzle form. Hand out the pieces randomly as members arrive. At the appropriate point in your time of study, invite those who hold pieces to come to the front and stick their pieces on the wall or board (masking tape or Plasti-Tak® should work) and arrange them correctly as they do. If you have an artistic class member, you might ask her or him to draw a relevant image on poster board and do the same as with the verses/ideas.

Love and Betrayal

March 7
Lesson 1

DEVOTIONAL READING: Psalm 55:12-22.

BACKGROUND SCRIPTURE: Matthew 26.

PRINTED TEXT: Matthew 26:3-15, 20-25.

Matthew 26:3-15, 20-25

3 Then assembled together the chief priests, and the scribes, and the elders of the people, unto the palace of the high priest, who was called Caiaphas,

4 And consulted that they might take Jesus by subtilty, and kill him.

5 But they said, Not on the feast day, lest there be an uproar among the people.

6 Now when Jesus was in Bethany, in the house of Simon the leper,

7 There came unto him a woman having an alabaster box of very precious ointment, and poured it on his head, as he sat at meat.

8 But when his disciples saw it, they had indignation, saying, To what purpose is this waste?

9 For this ointment might have been sold for much, and given to the poor.

10 When Jesus understood it, he said unto them, Why trouble ye the woman? for she hath wrought a good work upon me.

11 For ye have the poor always with you; but me ye have not always.

12 For in that she hath poured this ointment on my body, she did it for my burial.

13 Verily I say unto you, Wheresoever this gospel shall be preached in the whole world, there shall also this, that this woman hath done, be told for a memorial of her.

14 Then one of the twelve, called Judas Iscariot, went unto the chief priests,

15 And said unto them, What will ye give me, and I will deliver him unto you? And they covenanted with him for thirty pieces of silver.

20 Now when the even was come, he sat down with the twelve.

21 And as they did eat, he said, Verily I say unto you, that one of you shall betray me.

22 And they were exceeding sorrowful, and began every one of them to say unto him, Lord, is it I?

23 And he answered and said, He that dippeth his hand with me in the dish, the same shall betray me.

24 The Son of man goeth as it is written of him: but woe unto that man by whom the Son of man is betrayed! it had been good for that man if he had not been born.

25 Then Judas, which betrayed him, answered and said, Master, is it I? He said unto him, Thou hast said.

GOLDEN TEXT: And as they did eat, he said, Verily I say unto you, that one of you shall betray me. And they were exceeding sorrowful, and began every one of them to say unto him, Lord, is it I?—Matthew 26:21, 22.

Jesus Fulfills His Mission
Unit 1: Road to the Cross
(Lessons 1-4)

Lesson Aims

After participating in this lesson, each student should be able to:

1. List the ways, both good and bad, that people reacted to Jesus in today's text.

2. Tell how the same reactions are expressed today.

3. Suggest one concrete way that the believer can imitate Mary's example of showing extravagant love for Christ.

Lesson Outline

INTRODUCTION
  A. Diversity
  B. Lesson Background
 I. PREMEDITATED TREACHERY (Matthew 26:3-5)
  A. Leaders Meet (v. 3)
  B. Leaders Plot (vv. 4, 5)
    Dark Nights and Dark Deeds
 II. PRECIOUS GIFT (Matthew 26:6-13)
  A. Gift Given (vv. 6, 7)
  B. Gift Criticized (vv. 8, 9)
  C. Gift Honored (vv. 10-13)
III. PERSONAL BETRAYAL (Matthew 26:14, 15, 20-25)
  A. Betrayer's Contract (vv. 14, 15)
    Conspiracy Theories and a Real Conspiracy
  B. Betrayer's Charade (vv. 20-22)
  C. Betrayer's Exposure (vv. 23-25)
CONCLUSION
  A. Varied Responses
  B. Prayer
  C. Thought to Remember

Introduction

Are you basically a "meat-and-taters" person, the consummate "I'll try anything once" connoisseur, or something in between? People differ in tastes, but the differences from person to person run much deeper in importance than that.

A. Diversity

As humans we share much in common, yet no one questions our diversity of thought patterns and behavioral styles. Some researchers conclude that people can be categorized broadly in terms of how they approach a task. One person

just wants to get the job done as quickly as possible. Another wants to do the job while interacting with people. One person wants to do the job in a way that keeps the peace. Yet another wants to do the job correctly above all else. Each will take a different approach to the same job.

Similarly, with our diversities of race, religion, education, socioeconomic standing, gender, worldviews, and personal agendas, it should not surprise us to see different people react differently to the same person or situation. In today's lesson we observe people reacting in four different ways to Jesus. The Jewish leaders, a loving woman, the apostles as a group, and Judas in particular all display differing responses to the Lord.

B. Lesson Background

The final week of Jesus' ministry left the world changed forever. Jesus' normal base of operation when in Judea was Bethany, a village about two miles southeast of Jerusalem (see Matthew 21:17; Mark 11:1-11). His dear friends Mary, Martha, and Lazarus lived there (John 11:1, 2), as well as Simon the leper (see below).

Our text today picks up after Jesus has spent some intense days in Jerusalem. After a triumphal entry, Jesus had driven money changers out of the temple, had verbally jousted with the enemies who wanted to trap Him, had denounced their hypocrisy, had warned His disciples of the coming destruction of Jerusalem, had challenged them to be prepared for the final judgment, and had reminded them once again that He would be betrayed and crucified (Matthew 21:1–26:2). And the week was far from over!

I. Premeditated Treachery (Matthew 26:3-5)

First we consider the reaction of the Jewish leaders. They have opposed Jesus for most of His ministry, but now events take a particularly ominous turn.

A. Leaders Meet (v. 3)

3. Then assembled together the chief priests, and the scribes, and the elders of the people, unto the palace of the high priest, who was called Caiaphas.

This assembly constitutes an informal gathering of the Sanhedrin, Israel's "supreme court." This is an unscheduled meeting to carry out a sinful, misguided agenda. Yet Jesus Himself had just predicted His death in Matthew 26:1, 2! Jesus' death ultimately is in His own hands, and not in the hands of *the chief priests, and the scribes, and the elders of the people* (Matthew 26:53, 54; John 10:18).

B. Leaders Plot (vv. 4, 5)

4. And consulted that they might take Jesus by subtilty, and kill him.

Only one item appears on the agenda. In consultation, they plot to *take Jesus* into custody as an enemy of the state. And their treachery is evident. Rather than arresting Jesus boldly and openly, they opt to use *subtilty* (stealth) to do so.

Jesus' arrest, however, is only the first step toward their real objective: they want to *kill him.* Without His death their plan will be incomplete. An informal meeting to plot the execution of a man who has not yet been tried or convicted violates Jewish law (John 7:51). Yet the presumed spiritual leaders of Israel have fallen into such corruption that they are willing to set aside the law to have Jesus eliminated. [See question #1, page 240.]

DARK NIGHTS AND DARK DEEDS

During Russia's Bolshevik revolution, Czar Nicholas II and the royal family were taken captive. Their captors transferred them to a private residence in the town of Ekaterinburg. Shortly after midnight on July 17, 1918, the family was awakened and taken to a basement room on the pretext that it was for their protection.

Soon a team of assassins burst into the room and killed the family. Still under the cover of night, conspirators took their bodies by truck to an abandoned mine pit and burned them. Acid was poured on the remains to cover the atrocity. A legend grew up around the event to the effect that Princess Anastasia had been spared and remained alive until late in the twentieth century.

Compare this story with the events surrounding Jesus' arrest and crucifixion. The Jewish leaders also chose the cover of night as they prepared to secure Jesus' death. Darkness enabled them to keep their evil deeds from the common people. As for the survival of Anastasia—whose name, ironically, means "resurrection"—this legend was an act of grasping at the proverbial straw of hope during the dark night of Communism's reign over Russia. Jesus' resurrection, on the other hand, was attested by hundreds of eyewitnesses (1 Corinthians 15:6). Our hope is real!

But the point of our text is that evil people choose darkness (both physical and spiritual) to cover the darkness of their hearts and deeds. They still do so in the twenty-first century. Praise God for the light we have that defeats that darkness (John 1:5). —C. R. B.

5. But they said, Not on the feast day, lest there be an uproar among the people.

Jesus' popularity with the masses poses a real threat to the power of the Jewish leaders (John 11:48). To arrest Jesus openly could spawn a riot among the sympathetic populace. The "normal" population of Jerusalem is probably somewhere between sixty thousand and one hundred twenty thousand. This figure may temporarily swell fivefold during the Passover!

Overcrowding during such a *feast day* means that tempers sometimes run short. The populace is already worked up over Jesus' triumphal entry and teaching. A riot over having Jesus falsely arrested can result in Roman intervention, jeopardizing the Jewish leaders' standing with Rome. To keep the peace and maintain their own political clout, the Jewish leaders seek an opportune time to seize Jesus.

II. Precious Gift (Matthew 26:6-13)

Next we contrast the hatred the religious elite have for Jesus with the extravagant love of a woman whose story has endured through the ages.

A. Gift Given (vv. 6, 7)

6. Now when Jesus was in Bethany, in the house of Simon the leper.

Bethany is about two miles southeast of Jerusalem. *Simon,* a man apparently healed by Jesus, opens his home to friends to prepare a meal in the Lord's honor. Mary, Martha, and Lazarus are there as well as Jesus' disciples (Mark 14:3; John 12:2, 3).

John 12:1, 12 specifically place this event before the triumphal entry, and thus earlier than what we have just read in Matthew 26:3-5. This means that Matthew places this event where he does in his text in order to achieve a certain dramatic effect. When we compare the reason the Jewish leaders are assembled in Matthew 26:3-5

How to Say It

ANASTASIA. An-ah-*stay*-shuh.
BETHANY. *Beth*-uh-nee.
BOLSHEVIK. *Boll*-shuh-vick.
CAIAPHAS. *Kay*-uh-fus or *Kye*-uh-fus.
DEUTERONOMY. Due-ter-*ahn*-uh-me.
EKATERINBURG. Eh-*kah*-ter-in-berg.
ISAIAH. Eye-*zay*-uh.
JERUSALEM. Juh-*roo*-suh-lem.
JUDAS ISCARIOT. *Joo*-dus Iss-*care*-e-ut.
MESSIAH. Meh-*sigh*-uh.
SANHEDRIN. *San*-huh-drun or San-*heed*-run.
ZECHARIAH. Zek-uh-*rye*-uh (strong accent on *rye*).

with the reason for the assembly at Simon's house, the contrast is startling indeed!

7. There came unto him a woman having an alabaster box of very precious ointment, and poured it on his head, as he sat at meat.

John informs us that it is Mary, the sister of Lazarus and Martha, who is the *woman* who anoints Jesus' *head* with *precious ointment* or perfume (John 12:3). It is customary to anoint the heads of important guests, but this act is extraordinary in more than one respect. The *alabaster box,* or jar, probably is a cherished family heirloom. The *precious ointment* is worth a great deal of money (John 12:5).

Mary not only pours the perfume *on* Jesus' *head* while He is having supper, she also anoints his feet, wiping them with her hair (John 12:3). Generally it is considered immodest for a woman to loosen her hair in mixed company, but Mary defies a prevailing cultural norm in expressing her devotion. [See question #2, page 240.] She is willing to give up a family treasure and her own reputation among those who value tradition over truth in order to show her love to the Lord.

B. Gift Criticized (vv. 8, 9)

8, 9. But when his disciples saw it, they had indignation, saying, To what purpose is this waste? For this ointment might have been sold for much, and given to the poor.

Judas is the spokesman who raises concerns about the proper use of the perfume (John 12:4, 5). His motives are based in personal greed (John 12:6). But He couches the argument in such a way that the disciples are easily swayed to His point of view. Judas's counterproposal sounds spiritual to the rest of the disciples. None of them really seems to understand where these events are leading (Matthew 16:21-28; 26:40, 43, 45).

C. Gift Honored (vv. 10-13)

10. When Jesus understood it, he said unto them, Why trouble ye the woman? for she hath wrought a good work upon me.

Before *Jesus* responds, Mary must feel as if "no good deed goes unpunished." She has honored the Lord in a profound way, but one that still probably falls short of the Lord's worth in her

---

VISUALS FOR THESE LESSONS

The visual pictured in each lesson (e.g., page 237) is a small reproduction of a large, full-color poster included in the *Adult Visuals* packet for the Spring Quarter. The packet is available from your supplier. Order No. 392.

---

own eyes. The disciples should be applauding rather than criticizing the selfless and generous nature of her love. [See question #3, page 240.]

11. For ye have the poor always with you; but me ye have not always.

Many of Jesus' teachings contain a "startle factor" that grabs attention. This is one of them. On the surface it would appear that Jesus is minimizing the concern we are to have for the *poor.* But actually He is reaffirming Deuteronomy 15:11. Jesus' recognition that the poor will *always* be among us indirectly acknowledges our need to minister to them. That will not change until the Lord returns.

We should also recognize that some service opportunities are timeless, while others are narrowly time bound. When the window of opportunity to serve in the time bound cases is shut, it is permanently lost. When Jesus says that they will *not always* have Him with them, He reveals that the opportunity for His followers to honor Him in the final tragic hours of His earthly ministry is severely limited. On the stage of history, Mary seizes the opportunity of a lifetime.

12. For in that she hath poured this ointment on my body, she did it for my burial.

As Mary anoints Jesus with the *ointment,* does *she* realize that she is doing it for His *burial?* We cannot be certain that Mary does indeed realize this, but Jesus Himself certainly sees the deeper meaning. This incident provides the Master with yet another opportunity to teach.

13. Verily I say unto you, Wheresoever this gospel shall be preached in the whole world, there shall also this, that this woman hath done, be told for a memorial of her.

Jesus makes a bold prediction that history confirms. Though she wants nothing more than the privilege of honoring her Lord, Jesus guarantees that Mary herself would receive a *memorial.* The very fact that we study this story today establishes the truthfulness of Jesus' prediction. [See question #4, page 240.] Like Mary, we also can seize those unique moments in which we demonstrate that we "would rather have Jesus than silver or gold."

III. Personal Betrayal (Matthew 26:14, 15, 20-25)

How much the disciples "get the idea" at this point we don't really know. The one definite exception is Judas. The lure of cold hard cash leads him down the path of ultimate infamy.

A. Betrayer's Contract (vv. 14, 15)

14. Then one of the twelve, called Judas Iscariot, went unto the chief priests.

Judas's previous greed and theft are indications that he has already turned away from the Master in an appreciable way. However, going to *the chief priests* to deal with Jesus constitutes a total rejection of the Lord. This is treason!

15. And said unto them, What will ye give me, and I will deliver him unto you? And they covenanted with him for thirty pieces of silver.

As an insider, Judas has exact knowledge of the whereabouts and movements of Jesus. Consequently, he knows where and when the authorities can arrest Him secretly, without fear of a riot. Jesus came to earth to deliver Judas from sin to eternal life; Judas goes to the chief priests to *deliver Him* from life *unto* death.

As a result, the Jewish leaders "put out a contract" on Jesus' life. The *thirty pieces of silver* is no more than what the Old Testament requires as compensation for the death of a slave (Exodus 21:32). What a low value Judas and the Jewish leaders placed on the life of the King of the universe! (See also Zechariah 11:12.)

We do not know if Judas has motives other than greed. Speculation abounds as to what could make such a close companion of Jesus turn so drastically. Possibly Judas has become disillusioned because Jesus isn't quite the type of Messiah that Judas expects. Maybe Jesus' stinging rebuke in Matthew 26:10-13 has pushed Judas over the edge. All we know for sure is that a heart once drawn to accept the call to apostleship now sets into motion the wheels of ultimate betrayal.

CONSPIRACY THEORIES AND A *REAL* CONSPIRACY

Some people simply insist on getting things all wrong. One example is *The Horrifying Fraud*, the English title of a best-selling French-language book written by Thierry Meyssan and published early in 2002. Meyssan is a conspiracy-theorist who conjured up this scenario for what "really" happened on September 11, 2001: the terrorist attacks were carried out by U.S. government officials for economic and military reasons to allow America to attack Afghanistan and Iraq; the story we all got from the news media was a "loony fable"; no plane really struck the Pentagon—the explosion was triggered on the ground; the planes that struck the World Trade Center were flown by remote control and guided by navigational beacons in the towers.

This bizarre nonsense devalues the lives of all who died in those attacks. It also demonstrates that the author has much in common with Judas and those Jews whose conspiracy to kill Jesus devalued the life of the Son of God.

There is another similarity: just as Thierry Meyssan was unable to see the reality of "9-11," neither Judas nor the Jewish leaders could accept

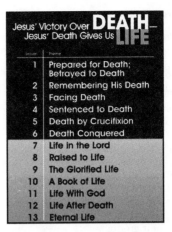

Visual for
lesson 1

Leave this chart posted to highlight the Death and Life emphases of this quarter.

the truth about the real nature of Jesus' mission. It simply didn't fit their own ideas of who they thought the Messiah "should" be. As a result, they constructed a terribly misguided version of reality. How many today continue to construct untruths about Jesus because the truth He confronts them with is too uncomfortable? —C. R. B.

B. Betrayer's Charade (vv. 20-22)

20. Now when the even was come, he sat down with the twelve.

The scene now shifts to the evening of Jesus' final Passover observance with His disciples. Judas already has agreed to the contract on Jesus' life, but none of the disciples know that. Therefore, *when the even was come* for them to share the Passover, it is easy for Judas to sit *down* as one of *the twelve* with his plan undetected.

21. And as they did eat, he said, Verily I say unto you, that one of you shall betray me.

After Peter's confession of Jesus as the Son of God, the Lord had begun to reveal that He would be rejected by the Jewish leaders, suffer, and be killed (Matthew 16:21; Luke 9:22). This is the first time, however, that they have heard Him say *one of you shall betray me.*

22. And they were exceeding sorrowful, and began every one of them to say unto him, Lord, is it I?

Jesus' comments hit the group with maximum force. They are extremely distressed, exceedingly *sorrowful.* They never dreamed that the cancer of betrayal could infiltrate their group. Judas conducts his charade so flawlessly that no one suspects him.

Out of emotional anguish and with personal urgency each asks, *Lord, is it I?* Each man trusts the others, so the only place to look is inward.

Each one wonders if some fatal character flaw will be exposed to his own shame and disgrace. [See question #5, page 240.] And all the while Judas acts as if he is as distressed as the others in the room.

C. Betrayer's Exposure (vv. 23-25)

23. And he answered and said, He that dippeth his hand with me in the dish, the same shall betray me.

Jesus' answer at this point is still somewhat general. *He that dippeth his hand with me in the dish* could refer to anyone in the room, for all of them are sharing in that activity during the evening meal. By saying *the same shall betray me,* Jesus reemphasizes that the betrayal will indeed come from within their group.

24. The Son of man goeth as it is written of him: but woe unto that man by whom the Son of man is betrayed! it had been good for that man if he had not been born.

Jesus acknowledges His willing intent to fulfill God's plan *as it* has been *written of Him* in the Old Testament (cf. Isaiah 53). He never dodges the work of giving His life to pay sin's price for our eternal salvation.

But Jesus sternly warns that His betrayer will not be allowed to dodge the consequences of his rebellion either. In the terrible judgment he will face, Judas will not be able to argue, "Well, I wasn't warned." (See also Acts 1:15-20.)

25. Then Judas, which betrayed him, answered and said, Master, is it I? He said unto him, Thou hast said.

Judas maintains his charade of loyalty to the very end. Knowing full well that he is the one, he still asks *Master, is it I?* In true prophetic fashion Jesus throws off the cover to reveal Judas's wicked betrayal. If Judas thinks he has success-

fully hidden his evil work, he finds out what he should have known all along: nothing can be hidden from the Lord.

But the Lord's reply falls on deaf ears. Although Jesus makes it clear to Judas that He knows about the nefarious plan, Judas will betray Him anyway.

Conclusion

Love and betrayal step to center stage in today's lesson text. But they do not stand there alone. Hatred and lack of discernment make their appearances as well.

A. Varied Responses

The hatred of the Jewish leaders for Jesus demonstrates the depths of corruption to which people in power can sink. The very people who should have accepted the message were the ones who resisted it by all means possible. The same is true today.

The extravagant love of Mary for Jesus challenges us to love Him just as completely. If she had to break a conventional norm to anoint Jesus' feet, or if she needed to let go of a family treasure to satisfy her longing to serve Christ, she just did it. May we do the same.

The disciples allowed themselves to get caught up in what seemed like a pious position, only to discover their own lack of discernment. How important it is that we evaluate all sides of an issue and then reach a conclusion with spiritual insight! To do otherwise causes us unintentionally to devalue our Lord.

And then there is Judas. How tragic that a man who had been invited into such close fellowship with the Son of God could turn so completely! While we take great pleasure in our relationship with Christ, we should never take it for granted. What will we do when we find ourselves in situations where we ask, "Will it be I who betrays the Lord?" Instead of running toward Christ's enemies, let us decide right now that in every circumstance, regardless of the cost, we will run full speed to the Lord of glory!

B. Prayer

Dear Father, we marvel at how the Lord Jesus still loved in the face of hatred, His disciples' lack of discernment, and the betrayal of one so close. Give us grace to be extravagant in loving You, for You are worth everything we have to give. In Jesus' name, amen.

C. Thought to Remember

Let the extravagance of our love for Him reflect the extravagance of His love for us.

Home Daily Bible Readings

Monday, Mar. 1—The Psalmist Mourns a Friend's Betrayal (Psalm 55:12-17)

Tuesday, Mar. 2—A Friend Violates a Covenant (Psalm 55:18-22)

Wednesday, Mar. 3—Zeal for Your House (Psalm 69:6-14)

Thursday, Mar. 4—A Woman Pours Ointment on Jesus (Matthew 26:1-13)

Friday, Mar. 5—Judas Agrees to Betray Jesus (Matthew 26:14-19)

Saturday, Mar. 6—Jesus Announces Upcoming Betrayal (Matthew 26:20-25)

Sunday, Mar. 7—Peter Promises Not to Desert Jesus (Matthew 26:31-35)

Learning by Doing

This page contains an alternative lesson plan emphasizing learning activities.
Classes desiring such student involvement will find these suggestions helpful.

Learning Goals

After this lesson each student will be able to:

1. List the ways, both good and bad, that people reacted to Jesus in today's text.

2. Tell how the same reactions are expressed today.

3. Suggest one concrete way that the believer can imitate Mary's example of showing extravagant love for Christ.

Into the Lesson

To begin thinking about how individuals respond differently to different things, hold a Popularity Poll. Prepare a list of things, events, and/or people. As you read the items, ask class members to indicate how much they like/dislike each. Begin with selections that will create friendly feuds: foods (pizza, chocolate, etc.), activities (bowling, skydiving, etc.), favorite sports teams (Green Bay Packers, New York Yankees, etc.), or style of music (classical, bluegrass, etc.). Move to people, perhaps beginning with political figures. Maybe even let the class cheer or boo as each name is mentioned.

As you take the vote, ask for reasons why learners like or dislike each one. Use this to introduce the idea that as one looks at the life of Jesus, he or she will find differences of opinion about Jesus, ranging from extravagant love to intense hatred. The attitudes are generally not stated directly, but demonstrated by actions. Describe how individuals in today's lesson would answer the opinion poll about Jesus. (If you would like to get your class members thinking about the lesson, consider sending the list home with them the week before, or send an e-mail for them to complete and bring to class.) This same pattern is repeated in future lessons as well, as every aspect of Jesus' life and ministry drew widely varying responses from people.

Into the Word

Examine the four different responses to Jesus discussed in this lesson. Place the following headings on columns on a board: *Person or Group, Scripture, Response to Jesus, Contemporary Example.* The last column will list individuals or groups who demonstrate the same response to Jesus today. Under the *Person or Group* heading, write the following below each other; *Jewish Leaders, Mary, Apostles* (in general),

and *Judas* (in particular). Review their specific actions, and summarize the attitudes reflected. *(Jewish leaders were antagonistic, planning to kill Jesus, Matthew 26:3-5; Mary demonstrated extravagant love, willing to show her love publicly, in costly, humbling, even potentially embarrassing ways, Matthew 26:6, 7; John 12:3-5; the apostles, including Judas, were indignant at first, seeing this act of worship as extreme waste, Matthew 26:8, 9.)* Come back and complete the Judas line later, as Judas responded very differently from the other apostles to Jesus' words.

Jesus provided His personal commentary on the extravagant actions of the woman described in this story: He explains that her acts came from a heart overflowing with love, prompting her to express her love for the Savior publicly (Matthew 26:10-14). He also notes that her actions will be recounted by future generations when the gospel is told, leaving a living legacy to this special tribute. Complete the column regarding the *Response to Jesus*, contrasting Judas with the other apostles. The other apostles seemed to get the point. There is no further record of their arguing this way, and they are identified as followers of Jesus later in the Gospels and other places in the New Testament. Judas, however, shows that he would not accept the teaching of Jesus; instead, Judas approaches the chief priests and offers to betray Jesus for thirty pieces of silver (Matthew 26:14-16). Discuss the difference between those who first respond wrongly but then listen and change, versus those who become hardened in their resistance to Jesus.

Into Life

Finish the last column, *Contemporary Example.* As a class, list people or groups today that demonstrate the same response to Jesus as each of the four you have been examining. Discuss what these attitudes look like today (antagonism; extravagant love; misguided, but teachable; or greedy and selfishly resistant). Judas and Mary have become famous for their actions, leaving a legacy we still remember. If Jesus provided commentary, as He did regarding Mary, what would you want Him to say was the significance of your life? What steps do you need to take this week to build such a pattern in your life and to prepare yourself for unique events that could be the lasting moment remembered about you?

Let's Talk It Over

The questions on this page are designed to promote discussion of the lesson by the class and to encourage application of the lesson Scriptures. The answers provided are only discussion starters. Let your class talk it over from there.

1. Events leading to the crucifixion of Jesus brought out character defects in the Jewish leaders, in Pontius Pilate, and even in Jesus' own disciples. How do we recognize and overcome such flaws in our own lives?

Try as we may, we cannot be completely objective about our own behavior. That is the reason many Christian leaders recommend having an accountability partner. This may be a formal arrangement or an informal one, but we need to have someone who can challenge us when we get off track and suggest some other course. This person is someone whom we trust, and we know that he or she has our best interest at heart.

Whether we have such a partner or not, we need to spend much time in the Word, and we need to examine ourselves (2 Corinthians 13:5) as objectively as possible. We need to pray for wisdom (James 1:5) and discernment to be sure we are being doers of the Word and not hearers only (James 1:22). And we thank God for His continuing forgiveness for sin (1 John 1:9).

2. Mary defied prevailing cultural norms to demonstrate her devotion to the Lord. What are some cultural norms we must defy today? How do we do this properly?

Today's postmodern culture is one of "diversity." As that term is generally understood, it demands we accept any point of view as equal with any other. To insist that one religious system is better than another violates this expectation. Thus, trying to win people to Christ defies "prevailing cultural norms." To call any behavior a sin is equally "intolerant" in the world's view. Any discussion of immorality, whether criticizing illicit relations between a man and woman or criticizing homosexual behavior, is labeled as bigoted and inappropriate.

The world says Christians are free to believe what they want, but they are to keep it to themselves. But Jesus says we are to share it! We do this recognizing our obligation to obey God above all (Acts 5:29). Our witness for Christ is to be undergirded with gentleness, respect, and good behavior (1 Peter 3:15, 16).

3. Suppose you were to do something out of good motives but, unlike Mary, your actions turned out to be misguided despite your good intentions. How would you handle the criticism that may follow?

Almost anything done in the name of Christ can draw criticism (cf. 2 Corinthians 8:19-21). When we are criticized, we need to accept the evaluation calmly and give it serious consideration. Assume that the critic is acting in good faith and compare his or her remarks with what the Scripture says. If the critic is right, you can adjust your behavior. If the critic is wrong, you can graciously decline the advice. Then you will have the added peace of mind of knowing that you have given careful consideration to your behavior and still believe it is in harmony with God's will.

4. Jesus said that Mary's act of devotion would be remembered throughout time. For what will you be remembered? Why do you think so?

Your learners might list many specific things. It will be important, however, to stress a bigger picture: we will be remembered for those things that characterize our lives. Therefore, if we want people to remember us as followers of the Lord, then we need to be sure we demonstrate that. We cannot rewrite the scripts of our lives after we have lived them. We must give ourselves now to that kind of service.

Stress to your learners the importance of having right motives in their answers. We must be careful not to do our good deeds "before men, to be seen of them" (Matthew 6:1). We will be remembered as phonies in that case!

Ultimately, we must give ourselves to the Lord wholeheartedly, and not worry about how others will remember us. Mary was completely unselfconscious when she anointed the Lord. But her story is told even twenty centuries later.

5. To their credit, each of the disciples asked, "Lord, is it I?" and not, "Is it him?" How can we develop a pure, godly attitude that resists pointing fingers?

Jesus said, "Seek ye first the kingdom of God, and his righteousness" (Matthew 6:33). When we do that, we are concerned about our own service in the sight of God and not someone else's (cf. John 21:20-23). We are to advance the Lord's purposes above all. Paul's entire ministry was an example of service before self.

Loaf and Cup

DEVOTIONAL READING: John 13:1-15.

BACKGROUND SCRIPTURE: Luke 22:7-30.

PRINTED TEXT: Luke 22:7-23.

Luke 22:7-23

7 Then came the day of unleavened bread, when the passover must be killed.

8 And he sent Peter and John, saying, Go and prepare us the passover, that we may eat.

9 And they said unto him, Where wilt thou that we prepare?

10 And he said unto them, Behold, when ye are entered into the city, there shall a man meet you, bearing a pitcher of water; follow him into the house where he entereth in.

11 And ye shall say unto the goodman of the house, The Master saith unto thee, Where is the guest chamber, where I shall eat the passover with my disciples?

12 And he shall show you a large upper room furnished: there make ready.

13 And they went, and found as he had said unto them: and they made ready the passover.

14 And when the hour was come, he sat down, and the twelve apostles with him.

15 And he said unto them, With desire I have desired to eat this passover with you before I suffer:

16 For I say unto you, I will not any more eat thereof, until it be fulfilled in the kingdom of God.

17 And he took the cup, and gave thanks, and said, Take this, and divide it among yourselves:

18 For I say unto you, I will not drink of the fruit of the vine, until the kingdom of God shall come.

19 And he took bread, and gave thanks, and brake it, and gave unto them, saying, This is my body which is given for you: this do in remembrance of me.

20 Likewise also the cup after supper, saying, This cup is the new testament in my blood, which is shed for you.

21 But, behold, the hand of him that betrayeth me is with me on the table.

22 And truly the Son of man goeth, as it was determined: but woe unto that man by whom he is betrayed!

23 And they began to inquire among themselves, which of them it was that should do this thing.

GOLDEN TEXT: This is my body which is given for you: this do in remembrance of me. . . . This cup is the new testament in my blood, which is shed for you.
—Luke 22:19, 20.

Jesus Fulfills His Mission
Unit 1: Road to the Cross
(Lessons 1-4)

Lesson Aims

After participating in this lesson, each student should be able to:

1. Summarize the events of Jesus' last supper with His disciples and the institution of the Lord's Supper.

2. Articulate the significance of the emblems of the Lord's Supper.

3. Recommit himself or herself to faithfulness to the Lord Jesus Christ and His church.

Lesson Outline

Introduction

A. Priceless Times

A major credit card company capitalized on how important special times are. In its TV ad everything was priced, except one—tickets to the game, sixty dollars; game program, ten dollars; hot dogs and drinks, fifteen dollars; autographed baseball, forty dollars; an evening with your son, priceless!

There are indeed times that have infinite meaning. A chaplain once told me that the great-est fear of a child facing death is that Mom or Dad might not be there. With Mom or Dad there, a child can face the most threatening time confidently. Times together are priceless.

Jesus had looked forward to one of those priceless times with His disciples. In the face of terrible danger He longed to be with the men in whom He had invested so much of Himself. He also longed for one final time to provide instruction and guidance.

B. Lesson Background

God commanded the Jewish people to observe the Passover feast in memory of their dramatic deliverance from bondage in Egypt (Exodus 12:1-32). As a result, Passover became a national spiritual holiday that called on God's people to remember their birth as a nation. God had commanded it to be celebrated in Jerusalem on the fourteenth day of the first month (Leviticus 23:5). This was the month of "Nisan" (formerly called "Abib") in the Hebrew calendar, which is late March and early April. It was an event that the spiritually minded anticipated with enthusiasm.

Jesus knew that His whole life pointed to a final Passover that would be the most eventful of all. This particular Passover would not be merely an act of faithful observance, but one of ultimate obedience. He would be preparing Himself to fulfill His mission as the perfect Passover Lamb (John 1:29; 1 Corinthians 5:7; Revelation 5:12; 13:8) in giving His life in sacrifice for the sins of humanity. One last Passover with His closest friends would mark the beginning of a new Lord's Supper that galvanizes Christian worship to this day.

I. Supper Preparation
(Luke 22:7-13)

A. The Disciples' Question (vv. 7-9)

7. Then came the day of unleavened bread, when the passover must be killed.

Technically, the feasts of *unleavened bread* and Passover are separate festivals, with Passover occurring on the fourteenth of Nisan, and the Feast of Unleavened Bread running from the fifteenth to the twenty-first (Leviticus 23:5, 6; Numbers 28:16, 17). Because these celebrations occur back-to-back, the Jews naturally think of them as one (e.g., 2 Chronicles 35:17).

When the *day* to begin the celebration comes, there is much to be done. The phrase *the passover* in this specific context refers to the Passover lamb itself, and families need to secure a lamb to *be killed*. Part of the process involves sending a representative to the priests to have it slaughtered in the temple that afternoon, then returning with the meat that will feed the entire family that night. In addition to the lamb, many other preparations will have to be made (see v. 13, below).

8. And he sent Peter and John, saying, Go and prepare us the passover, that we may eat.

The disciples have asked Jesus where He wants them to *prepare* the *passover* meal (Mark 14:12). Jesus knows that Judas is looking for a time and place to report His whereabouts to the authorities, but Jesus undoubtedly doesn't want His Passover celebration interrupted (we shall see why later). So He delegates the work of securing a place to *Peter and John,* two leading men among His disciples He knows He can trust.

9. And they said unto him, Where wilt thou that we prepare?

Sometimes the opportunity to show one's true colors comes through a willingness to take care of the details. Peter and John express their desire to do just that. Moreover, their devotion to the Lord and sensitivity to His desires cause them to seek His leading even in the small things. "We should always ask the Lord of all, to lead in everything, big and small!" [See question #1, page 248.]

B. The Lord's Directions (vv. 10-12)

10. And he said unto them, Behold, when ye are entered into the city, there shall a man meet you, bearing a pitcher of water; follow him into the house where he entereth in.

Jesus' deity reveals itself again as He gives the disciples a sign. *A man . . . bearing a pitcher of water* will certainly stand out, even in a large crowd. Women, not men, almost always carry such jars. Even more telling is the fact that Jerusalem is flooded with visitors at Passover. That the disciples will meet this man at an exact place and time in such a crowd points to Jesus' divine guidance. Thus Jesus gives Peter and John what they need to know, without providing Judas an exact address where he can report the Lord's whereabouts to the Jewish authorities.

11. And ye shall say unto the goodman of the house, The Master saith unto thee, Where is the guest chamber, where I shall eat the passover with my disciples?

The goodman is the owner *of the house.* Jesus apparently has made previous arrangements with this man for the use of *the guest chamber,* where Jesus can *eat the passover with* His *disciples.* In speaking to this owner, the disciples are to use certain words—*the Master saith*—to indicate to him that they come from Jesus. The disciples have given up everything to follow Jesus, acknowledging Him as their Master. The owner is expected to accept the news that the Master is asking about the room. This indicates that this man, too, is one of Jesus' devoted followers.

12. And he shall show you a large upper room furnished: there make ready.

At the mere mention of the Master, this nameless follower will be ready to assist the disciples. Many of us today will never serve in positions of great prominence like the apostles, but we can be ready to support those who do with our willing cooperation. [See question #2, page 248.]

The fact that this man's house has an *upper room* large enough to accommodate thirteen men indicates that the owner probably is well-to-do. We are encouraged to note how this wealthy man shares the use of His possessions with the Lord. We should never assume that riches in and of themselves will corrupt the human heart. When the wealthy make Jesus the Lord of life, they display humble generosity and unselfish sharing of their possessions for godly purposes.

THE IMPORTANT THING

The land called Israel has not known much peace since the modern nation was founded in 1948. Occasionally, the land has been peaceful enough for tourists to travel there safely. In such times, a typical tour of Jerusalem includes a visit to "the Upper Room." If the tour guide were honest, he would inform the tourists in his charge that the room was only "similar to" the one we read about in our text today, since the room Jesus used ceased to exist long ago.

The upper room the visitors see is like most other "holy" sites on the modern tour: it is either an uncertain location, is at an archeological level above the original site, or is obscured completely by a structure built upon it many centuries later.

The upper room in which Jesus kept the Passover with His disciples was like other sites in His ministry: each is significant, not in itself, but in the fact that a very important act of God took place in that location. That particular upper room was no more holy than any other upper room in the city of Jerusalem that evening.

What was significant is what Jesus did there: He established the table of the Lord as a memorial to the offering of His life on the following day. We honor Him more by our participation in the Lord's Supper each time it is served than by any number of pilgrimages to Jerusalem.   —C. R. B.

C. Just as He Said (v. 13)

13. And they went, and found as he had said unto them: and they made ready the passover.

Are we surprised that Peter and John find everything just as Jesus *had said unto them?* More personally, are we surprised to find things in life as Jesus has told us they will be, including His gracious provision for us?

[handwritten in left margin, rotated: ① Deuteronomy 16 for 7days at unleaved bread]

How to Say It

ABIB. *A*-bib.
DEUTERONOMY. Due-ter-*ahn*-uh-me.
JERUSALEM. Juh-*roo*-suh-lem.
JUDAS. *Joo*-dus.
LEVITICUS. Leh-*vit*-ih-kus.
NISAN. *Nye*-san.

Even with Jesus' promise, however, the disciples have their own work to do. The room is "furnished" (v. 12), but this probably refers only to the presence of a low table surrounded by pallets for reclining. The furnishings do not include food, which the disciples will have to provide.

To make *ready* the food for *the passover* will involve preparing or purchasing several things: the Passover lamb, which would take some time to kill and roast; unleavened bread—meaning bread made with no yeast—to remind them of the haste of the departure from Egypt; a bowl of salt water to remind them of the Red Sea; bitter herbs as a reminder of their bitter experience as slaves; a paste or sauce made of a mixture of fruit and nuts; and fruit of the vine to drink. All this preparation has to be finished on the fourteenth of Nisan within the space of just a few hours (see Exodus 12:6; Numbers 9:3; Deuteronomy 16:6). *[handwritten: Tabernacle]*

II. Supper Fellowship
(Luke 22:14-18)

A. Jesus' Desire (vv. 14, 15)

14. And when the hour was come, he sat down, and the twelve apostles with him.

The hour occurs at sunset. When that time arrives, He sits *down*, reclining with His friends. Couches (for reclining while eating) line perhaps three sides of the table. At the most important time in His life Jesus surrounds Himself with the people with whom He has shared so many memorable experiences.

This occasion also gives Jesus valuable last-minute opportunities for continued training of His disciples. This is something He takes seriously to the end—even while dying (e.g., John 19:25-27).

15. And he said unto them, With desire I have desired to eat this passover with you before I suffer.

Jesus' strong yearning to share this meal with them is apparent in the emphatic language *with desire I have desired.* Jesus knows He soon will *suffer* agony at the hands of His enemies, and this Passover prefigures His own death as the perfect lamb of God (John 1:29).

The Jewish people have long anticipated a "new exodus" in which God will deliver them

from their political oppression (cf. Acts 1:6). They are looking forward to a new, messianic Moses. What God provides instead is the perfect sacrificial Lamb. The Lamb will die in their place, paying the price that God's wrath demands for sin, thereby granting deliverance from eternal condemnation (Romans 3:21-26; 5:9). With so much at stake, Jesus longs for fellowship with His chosen few.

B. Jesus' Prediction (vv. 16-18)

16. For I say unto you, I will not any more eat thereof, until it be fulfilled in the kingdom of God.

Jesus predicts that this will be the last Passover they will *eat* together, while also indicating that in some way there will be "a next time" (cf. Matthew 8:11; Revelation 19:9). Today we celebrate the Lord's Supper "till he come" (1 Corinthians 11:26). It is when that great event occurs that *the kingdom of God* will be *fulfilled* in its ultimate sense.

17. And he took the cup, and gave thanks, and said, Take this, and divide it among yourselves.

The Passover celebration normally follows a set order. After the opening prayer comes the first of four cups of fruit of the vine and a dish of bitter herbs and sauce. The Passover story is recited, Psalm 113 is sung, and the second cup is introduced.

Grace is then offered and the participants eat the main course of roast lamb and unleavened bread. Next comes another prayer followed by the third cup, called "the cup of blessing." After singing Psalms 114–118 (cf. Matthew 26:30), participants drink the fourth cup. *[handwritten: Sang a Hymn]*

We can't be certain exactly which of the four cups Jesus takes at this point in the narrative, but it is probably "the cup of blessing." When Jesus gives *thanks* and instructs the disciples to *divide it among* themselves, He is providing them with a lifelong reminder to strengthen their faith (see v. 20, below). *[handwritten: went to mount of olives]*

18. For I say unto you, I will not drink of the fruit of the vine, until the kingdom of God shall come.

By declaring this to be the last time He would share *the fruit of the vine,* Jesus offers a solemn farewell to the Old Testament Passover ceremony. The Passover celebration is temporary and now gives way to something better. Jesus' death on the cross will make that Old Covenant obsolete (Hebrews 8:6-13). After Jesus' resurrection and ascension the church will find the living Christ, not in the old Passover feast, but in the new Lord's Supper (1 Corinthians 11:23-26). See also comments on verse 16, above. [See question #3, page 248.]

III. Supper Institution
(Luke 22:19, 20)

A. Jesus Remembered (v. 19)

19. And he took bread, and gave thanks, and brake it, and gave unto them, saying, This is my body which is given for you: this do in remembrance of me.

The Passover meal is nearly complete. With the Old Covenant within hours of passing away, Jesus is inaugurating the supper that will symbolize the New Covenant. Receiving the *bread* of Communion calls for prayers of *thanks* yet today as we remember what Christ has done for us.

As Jesus breaks the bread and gives it to the disciples, He does all He can to communicate its spiritual and symbolic import. With Jesus physically present, the bread is symbolic for His *body*. The bread of Communion will be a tangible symbol of that fact and a concrete *remembrance* of the death of Christ for our sins from this time forward. His body will not be taken against His will; rather, it is *given* freely for our salvation.

B. New Covenant Ratified (v. 20)

20. Likewise also the cup after supper, saying, This cup is the new testament in my blood, which is shed for you.

The *cup* Jesus returns to *after supper* is packed with so much significance! A *testament* or "covenant" refers to a formal, solemn, and binding agreement. Here the agreement has the force of a will, which can be ratified only at death, or as Jesus said, by the shedding of His *blood* (see Hebrews 9:14-26).

This reminds us of the prophecy of the Lord's suffering "servant" who poured out "his soul unto death" and "bare the sin of many" (Isaiah 53:12). The horrible prospect of a violent, lingering, unjust death cannot stop Jesus from dying in our place. Through the power of His blood we discover the forgiveness of sins (Romans 3:25; 5:9; Ephesians 1:7; Colossians 1:20; Hebrews 9:22; 13:20; 1 Peter 1:18, 19; 1 John 1:7; Revelation 1:5; 5:9). The result is that we can relate to God on the basis of the New Covenant of grace revealed in the New Testament. [See question #4, page 248.]

IV. Supper Warning
(Luke 22:21-23)

A. General Warning (v. 21)

21. But, behold, the hand of him that betrayeth me is with me on the table.

Luke reminds us of the prelude to Jesus' betrayal. The unthinkable is that *the hand of him that betrayeth* is reclining with His *on the same*

"This do in remembrance of me." Luke 22:19

Visual for lesson 2

Use this elegant yet sobering imagery to reinforce today's Golden Text.

table. Ancients would have considered this extreme treachery. They view hospitality and the sharing of table fellowship as creating a close bond. To betray such a bond is scandalous, indeed! See Psalm 41:9.

B. Specific Warning (v. 22)

22. And truly the Son of man goeth, as it was determined: but woe unto that man by whom he is betrayed!

God's sovereign plan had *determined* that *the Son of man* must go to face unjust trial, persecution, and crucifixion. The preaching of the first-century church recognized God's foreknowledge and predetermined plan that led to Jesus' betrayal (Acts 2:23). It was important to let the world know that the events of Jesus' death, burial, and resurrection are not mere coincidence or freak accidents of history.

Even so, God's plan never overrode Judas's free will. He *betrayed* the Lord by choosing freely his sinful path. In a final effort to turn him around, Jesus warned Judas of the *woe* to come—God's extreme displeasure and hellish penalty that Judas would suffer (Acts 1:25). But Judas refused to listen.

C. Group Inventory (v. 23)

23. And they began to inquire among themselves, which of them it was that should do this thing.

On this same evening the disciples bicker over who is the greatest, and who will get the chief seats in God's kingdom (Luke 22:24). Here they find themselves doing the opposite—wondering who is the worst among them. But even as Judas carries out his sinful charade, nothing in his behavior makes them suspect him over anyone else

(John 13:27-29). *This thing* thus results in both history's greatest injustice and the gateway to our eternal life.

COULD *I* POSSIBLY DO SUCH A THING?

Out of the horrors of the terrorist attacks on September 11, 2001, came many tales of heroic action. For example, several passengers on a flight to San Francisco learned that terrorists had crashed three other planes into the World Trade Center towers and the Pentagon. Their plane had also been hijacked and turned back east. With terrorists at the controls, there was no doubt that they faced a similar fate.

However, the brave souls on that flight did not consider a few more minutes of life for themselves to be more precious than the lives of those who would surely be killed when their plane crashed into the White House or Capitol. So they joined forces and overpowered the terrorists, forcing the plane to crash in a field in western Pennsylvania.

The heroes on board that plane have been memorialized in many ways. One of them was Tom Burnett. After a street was named for him in the town where he lived, his widow said, "Twenty years from now, children will know a wonderful story of an American hero is connected with that name."

Whether the act we are contemplating is noble, as this one was, or like the despicable act Judas would soon be committing, the question of the other disciples is one worth asking: could *I* possibly do such a thing? Do I have the moral courage to avoid evil actions? Would I do good in spite of the cost? Is there anything in my character that would tempt me to deny my Lord by word or deed? Those who follow us will surely know the answer! —C. R. B.

Home Daily Bible Readings

Monday, Mar. 8—Disciples Prepare the Passover Meal (Luke 22:7-13)

Tuesday, Mar. 9—Jesus Eats With Disciples (Luke 22:14-18)

Wednesday, Mar. 10—Do This in Remembrance of Me (Luke 22:19-23)

Thursday, Mar. 11—Jesus Washes the Disciples' Feet (John 13:1-5)

Friday, Mar. 12—Peter Protests (John 13:6-10)

Saturday, Mar. 13—Jesus Sets an Example (John 13:11-15)

Sunday, Mar. 14—Jesus Teaches About Greatness (Luke 22:24-30)

Conclusion

A. A Priceless Memorial Celebration

Some parents, in wanting their children to have the very best, fail to give them what is truly priceless. How can you put a price tag on love expressed, encouragement offered, instruction supplied, faith modeled, and time given? The most important things seldom have a price attached to them.

Jesus opted to give us something more valuable than money. It was something upon which the core of our souls can feast, regardless of life's circumstances. The psalmist anticipated a memorial feast wherein both rich and poor would satisfy their souls (Psalm 22:26-29).

When Jesus instituted the Lord's Supper as a regular observance in worship, He gave us exactly what we need. In Communion we remember His sacrificial death. In that moment we also rely on *Him* to help us fulfill our destiny as witnesses of His love and great salvation.

We marvel that the Lord designed this event in which He invites us corporately into His presence. The Guest of honor wants the honor of our presence. What a great reminder of how many ways He loves us!

Moreover, the bread that represents His broken body and the cup that signifies His blood call us to cherish our participation in a New Covenant. The Old Covenant, for all of its strengths, could never have broken the stranglehold of sin nor delivered us from eternal judgment. The loaf and cup remind us that we are the recipients of grace through a death that satisfied God's wrath. This in turn motivates us to greater service for Jesus Christ. [See question #5, page 248.]

For centuries millions have discovered the power and importance of this loaf and cup. The only price we can put on this priceless spiritual feast is the one that Jesus Himself paid in dying for our salvation.

B. Prayer

Father, we praise Your holy name for the love You have shown us in Your Son Jesus Christ. When He poured out His blood for our forgiveness, He also poured on us His love. Lord, we ask You to form in us an unending desire to fellowship weekly with You and Your people during the Supper that You have given us. For this divine Communion with You, Your Son, Your Spirit, and Your people, we give thanks! In Jesus' name, amen.

C. Thought to Remember

Participate faithfully in the loaf and cup, priceless reminders of Christ's sacrificial love.

Learning by Doing

This page contains an alternative lesson plan emphasizing learning activities.
Classes desiring such student involvement will find these suggestions helpful.

Learning Goals

After participating in this lesson, each student will be able to:

1. Summarize the events of Jesus' last supper with His disciples and the institution of the Lord's Supper.

2. Articulate the significance of the emblems of the Lord's Supper.

3. Recommit himself or herself to faithfulness to the Lord Jesus Christ and His church.

Into the Lesson

Ask class members to share experiences that taught them significant, life-changing lessons (illness, job change, war experience, mission trip, etc.). Ask, "What lessons learned from the experience still influence you today? What do you do to help remember those lessons?"

Ask for and discuss traditions that class members and their families have. Are there certain ways they celebrate particular holidays? Are there certain traditions they maintain when they have reunions? What are the benefits of such traditions? Say, "Today we will explore a tradition at the heart of the Christian family experience, one instituted and explained by Christ Himself."

Into the Word

Watch a short clip from a video that recounts the first Passover in Exodus 11:1–12:36. (For information about licensing the use of copyrighted videos, contact *Christian Video Licensing International* at 888.771.2854 or www.cvli.org.) Use this as a tool to prompt your class members to look more closely at Scripture and examine the story. After viewing the clip, discuss how the events were portrayed. In what ways did it recount the Biblical story accurately? Were there aspects that contradicted the Bible? How are the details that the Bible doesn't explain dealt with in the video clip? Is the tone created by the film appropriate?

Compare the key elements of the Passover as observed in the Old Testament and the meaning of the Lord's Supper in the New Testament. Consider these questions: What did it commemorate? *(Being spared from death and receiving freedom from bondage in Egypt; the introduction of the New Covenant, where Jesus, the Passover Lamb, is sacrificed to spare us from eternal death and free us from bondage in sin.)* What was the significance of the bread? *(Unleavened bread, as well*

as *eating while dressed ready to travel, reminded them of leaving Egypt in haste, while the bread in the last supper represents Jesus' body, broken for sinners.)* What was the significance of the blood? *(In the Old Testament, blood from the sacrificed lamb was sprinkled on the doorpost to remind of God's protection from the death plague when they sacrificed in the way He prescribed; in the New Testament, it represents the blood of Jesus Christ, offered as payment for our sin.)*

Ask, "How much did the apostles get the point of the lesson?" Consider the things they talked about during the meal: Who would betray Jesus? (Luke 22:23); Who is the greatest? (Luke 22:24-27). Notice the focus on themselves rather than on Jesus' teaching about Himself.

Then ask, "What can be done to avoid this self-centered attitude and remain open to what God wants us to learn? What situations make you, as a learner, most impressionable? When are you most ready to listen to someone give you direction? What are areas where you miss (or resist) God's message to you because your focus is on other things?"

Into Life

In 1 Corinthians 11:17-34, Paul gave us a key to understanding and assessing our current practice of this memorial to Jesus Christ. It involves all aspects of our lives: past, present, and future.

Past—Does the commemoration focus on the work of Jesus and remind us of what He has done to make payment for our sin?

Present—Does our observance demonstrate the common bond and resulting love we share because of our commitment to Jesus Christ? Read chapter 11 and highlight the ways lack of love and fellowship with each other actually desecrated the observance (allowing others to go hungry, being drunk, participating individually and ignoring others and the corporate experience).

Future—Does the observance remind us that this is a temporary command, to be fulfilled "till he come"? (See 1 Corinthians 11:26.)

Discuss ways you can keep these aspects—Christ's work on the cross, our current fellowship with other believers, the anticipation of Christ's return for us—current and fresh in your heart and life, so that you are prepared for the Lord's Supper each time you observe it together with fellow believers.

Let's Talk It Over

The questions on this page are designed to promote discussion of the lesson by the class and to encourage application of the lesson Scriptures. The answers provided are only discussion starters. Let your class talk it over from there.

1. We see in the disciples a willingness to take care of details. Why is this still important, even in an age of advanced technology?

Our parents used to tell us, "Anything worth doing is worth doing right!" That is especially true in our church programming. It's tempting to lean on technology as a crutch—eye-catching PowerPoint® presentations, mesmerizing music videos, etc. But these things will be superficial if they are used as a substitute for true preparation. When planning an outreach program, a special worship service, a class for children, etc., we need to give careful attention to the details.

But sometimes we get careless; we plan in generalities and then "wing it" when time comes for the actual event. Sometimes that seems to work, but often we sweat through it and run frantically to-and-fro trying to keep the program together. How much better to plan ahead and then execute a well-designed plan to give to the Lord that which is excellent. Remember, "Holy shoddy is still shoddy!"

2. The "goodman" was expected to make his guest chamber available to the Master. Beside monetary gifts, what can we offer the Lord to demonstrate our devotion to His cause?

There are many ways we can imitate this unnamed "goodman"! We can offer our own homes for meeting places for small groups or youth meetings. A couple whose children are grown and gone may have a spare bedroom that can become a temporary church office for a new church that meets for worship in a rented facility.

We have other assets we can use as well. Perhaps we can let a visiting missionary use one of our cars while he is in town (our good car, not the junker with the broken air conditioning). Or we can prepare a meal for a family in need. Perhaps we have some skill that we can share. An auto mechanic, for example, can offer to check cars or even do minor repairs for church members or the community. Or that same mechanic could teach young people how to do routine maintenance. But we must make sure that we do all things in the name of Christ, and not under a vague notion that we are "giving back to the community."

3. The disciples must have been startled when Jesus' Passover words were not what they were used to hearing. What changes in the normal worship routine make you uncomfortable? Which do you accept? Why?

Answers to these questions will be highly individual. But you might note that as a general rule adults get increasingly comfortable with routine as they age. Thus, the older your group, the more they will find change uncomfortable. Younger adults sometimes embrace change just for the sake of change.

With each specific item mentioned, try to get your learners to measure the change by Scripture and not by personal preference only. If a change violates the Word of God, then believers ought to resist it. But if the possible change is in harmony with God's Word, then the church ought to consider whether implementing it can help to reach out to others and lead them to Christ.

4. What do you find most significant about the observance of the Lord's Supper? Why?

"In remembrance of me," Jesus' own words, will be most meaningful to some. These words are inscribed on many Communion tables to cause us to think about His sacrifice. Some will mention the idea of Communion itself, suggesting a fellowship with Christ and His church. This is a major theme in 1 Corinthians 11. Some find great significance in the fact that the Lord's Supper also looks forward to the time when Jesus will come back (1 Corinthians 11:26).

Whatever particular details your learners bring up, look for the Scriptural basis. Take note of how the Bible supports each aspect, and be sure your learners are clear on each point.

5. If you could plan a special Communion service, what would you include? Why?

Music is a powerful worship act, so your learners are sure to mention this. Drama is also a useful tool to illustrate Christ's sacrifice. Perhaps some would like to include a multimedia presentation including still pictures or video of a dramatic portrayal of the crucifixion.

Distribution of the bread and fruit of the vine may also be done in different ways. If your church normally shares in the emblems as they are passed, someone might suggest that they be taken in unison. Discuss the significance of the proposed changes.

Prayer and Arrest

DEVOTIONAL READING: John 12:27-36.

BACKGROUND SCRIPTURE: Matthew 26:36-50.

PRINTED TEXT: Matthew 26:36-50.

Matthew 26:36-50

36 Then cometh Jesus with them unto a place called Gethsemane, and saith unto the disciples, Sit ye here, while I go and pray yonder.

37 And he took with him Peter and the two sons of Zebedee, and began to be sorrowful and very heavy.

38 Then saith he unto them, My soul is exceeding sorrowful, even unto death: tarry ye here, and watch with me.

39 And he went a little further, and fell on his face, and prayed, saying, O my Father, if it be possible, let this cup pass from me: nevertheless, not as I will, but as thou wilt.

40 And he cometh unto the disciples, and findeth them asleep, and saith unto Peter, What, could ye not watch with me one hour?

41 Watch and pray, that ye enter not into temptation: the spirit indeed is willing, but the flesh is weak.

42 He went away again the second time, and prayed, saying, O my Father, if this cup may not pass away from me, except I drink it, thy will be done.

43 And he came and found them asleep again: for their eyes were heavy.

44 And he left them, and went away again, and prayed the third time, saying the same words.

45 Then cometh he to his disciples, and saith unto them, Sleep on now, and take your rest: behold, the hour is at hand, and the Son of man is betrayed into the hands of sinners.

46 Rise, let us be going: behold, he is at hand that doth betray me.

47 And while he yet spake, lo, Judas, one of the twelve, came, and with him a great multitude with swords and staves, from the chief priests and elders of the people.

48 Now he that betrayed him gave them a sign, saying, Whomsoever I shall kiss, that same is he; hold him fast.

49 And forthwith he came to Jesus, and said, Hail, Master; and kissed him.

50 And Jesus said unto him, Friend, wherefore art thou come? Then came they, and laid hands on Jesus, and took him.

GOLDEN TEXT: [Jesus] fell on his face, and prayed, saying, O my Father, if it be possible, let this cup pass from me: nevertheless, not as I will, but as thou wilt.—Matthew 26:39.

> ## Jesus Fulfills His Mission
> Unit 1: Road to the Cross
> (Lessons 1-4)

Lesson Aims

After participating in this lesson, each student will be able to:

1. Tell of Jesus' experiences in Gethsemane, both in His prayers and in His betrayal and arrest.

2. Suggest some times of temptation during which disciples may be called on to imitate their Master's resolve.

3. State a plan of action to make prayer a consistent and effective weapon against temptation.

Lesson Outline

INTRODUCTION
  A. Big Prayers Before Big Actions
  B. Lesson Background
I. THE PASSIONATE PRAYER (Matthew 26:36-44)
  A. Need for Prayer (vv. 36-38)
    Hello? Is Anyone There?
  B. Subject of Prayer (v. 39)
    Is There Any Way Out of This?
  C. Exhortation to Prayer (vv. 40, 41)
  D. Tenacity in Prayer (vv. 42-44)
II. THE AWFUL ARREST (Matthew 26:45-50)
  A. Jesus Complies (vv. 45, 46)
  B. Judas Betrays (vv. 47-49)
  C. The Guard Arrests (v. 50)
CONCLUSION
  A. The Power of Prayer
  B. Prayer
  C. Thought to Remember

Introduction

A. Big Prayers Before Big Actions

It can be foolish to act before praying, but there is also a time to change your prayer into action. When Moses and the Israelites were pinned against the shore of the Red Sea with the Egyptian army rapidly approaching, that was a big problem. God asked Moses, "Wherefore criest thou unto me? speak unto the children of Israel, that they go forward" (Exodus 14:15). Moses had already prayed. Now it was time to act.

After Jesus' resurrection, Peter and John were brought before the Jewish authorities and sternly warned not to preach in Jesus' name (Acts 4:18). The church faced the prospect of persecution if they did. How could they maintain courage and boldness with the threat of punishment hanging over their heads? That was a big problem. Yet those in the early church knew that they must offer big prayers when facing big problems. After praying, the church went into action (Acts 4:31).

When Jesus went to Gethsemane, He faced the biggest problem any human ever would. The impending reality of betrayal, unjust conviction, savage beating, and brutal crucifixion would be enough to make even the bravest cower in fear. In addition, Jesus would carry the sins of the whole world, tasting the full fury of God's wrath. But Jesus knew that if He brought big prayers to the biggest problem of all, He would have the ultimate victory.

B. Lesson Background

At the conclusion of their final Passover meal together, after the institution of the Lord's Supper, Jesus and His disciples sang a hymn together (Matthew 26:30; Mark 14:26). Then they made their way to Gethsemane, a garden just outside of Jerusalem on the western slope of the Mount of Olives. Most likely this was the usual place of retreat for Jesus and the disciples following the Passover each year.

As we saw last week, Jesus had not allowed Judas to know the exact address of their last Passover meal together because of the need for uninterrupted time with His disciples. Judas, however, had full knowledge of the usual post-Passover meeting place that Jesus liked to use (John 18:1, 2). It was just a matter of time until the betrayer, intent on his evil plot, showed up with an armed guard to take Jesus into custody. Jesus refused to face the most challenging few hours in human history without intensely seeking His Heavenly Father's help.

I. The Passionate Prayer (Matthew 26:36-44)

A. Need for Prayer (vv. 36-38)

36. Then cometh Jesus with them unto a place called Gethsemane, and saith unto the disciples, Sit ye here, while I go and pray yonder.

Gethsemane means "oil press," which tells us what this hillside area is used for. Here *Jesus* brings the entire band of *disciples*, minus one. The human side of Jesus shines through this moment, as He desires the companionship of His closest friends. He does not want to go through this agony alone.

Even so, there is also a need for solitude and space, allowing Him the freedom to wrestle in private prayer. Thus Jesus has the disciples *sit* at the entrance of the garden *while* He goes to *pray yonder*. [See question #1, page 256.]

"HELLO? IS ANYONE THERE?"

For nearly forty years, a telephone booth sat in the middle of California's Mojave National Preserve—fourteen miles from the nearest paved road—for the benefit of an occasional miner who needed to contact the "outside world." In 1997, a desert wanderer found the booth and put a story about it on the Internet.

People who read his story started calling the number. Most of the time no one answered. However, occasionally someone would monitor the phone. Rick Karr, a Texan, was one such person. He said, "The Holy Spirit told me to go out there and answer the phone."

Karr spent thirty-two days there and answered more than five hundred calls from all over the world. Why call? Why answer? One caller said, "Someone answers, a person you have absolutely no connection with. You exchange names and talk about the weather. What a thrill!" In other words, lonely people were reaching out for a "friend" to talk to. (The phone was removed in March, 2000, because all the traffic was destroying the environment.)

Compare this foolishness to Jesus' experience in the Garden of Gethsemane. That garden was also a deserted place—especially at night—when Jesus went there. But He went *with* friends, not searching *for* them. He *was* seeking to make a connection, but He wasn't in doubt. He talked frequently with the Father, and so He could always expect "someone to answer when He called." Perhaps our prayer lives could profit from such regularity.   —C. R. B.

37. And he took with him Peter and the two sons of Zebedee, and began to be sorrowful and very heavy.

Undoubtedly, Jesus has a powerful relationship with the crowds. Deeper still is His relationship with the Twelve. His deepest relationship is with *Peter and the two sons of Zebedee,* namely James and John. These three are the only ones allowed to witness Jesus' raising of Jairus' daughter from the dead (Mark 5:35-42). Jesus selects these three to accompany Him on the mountain of transfiguration (Matthew 17:1-13). Now He desires their companionship in this hour of extreme distress.

Jesus' distress is captured in the words *sorrowful and very heavy.* Overwhelming sadness and deep anguish flood His heart and mind as He begins to focus on what lies ahead.

38. Then saith he unto them, My soul is exceeding sorrowful, even unto death: tarry ye here, and watch with me.

Communication is a key to any relationship and situation. Some make the mistake of assuming that those around them should know what they are feeling or what to do in a difficult time. [See question #2, page 256.] Jesus does not make that mistake. He tells the disciples clearly and specifically how He is feeling and what His expectations are for them.

Moreover, Jesus tells His disciples exactly how they can be of comfort when He says *tarry ye here.* Jesus plans to move on ahead of them just far enough to get some comfortable space, and He wants them to wait nearby.

Yet He is not asking them to be passive as they wait. He calls them to stay awake, to be alert, and to *watch* with Him. He asks them to take note of His passion, feel His pain, and offer prayers for their own trials and temptations that are just around the corner (Luke 22:40). As they observe Him wrestling with the weight of the world, He expects them to be ready to offer help and consolation. His agonizing in prayer will at one point cause Him to sweat drops like blood (Luke 22:44).

Even without the benefit of hearing Jesus' voice inflection or seeing His body language, we can sense the urgency of His appeal to His friends. His anguish penetrates to the deepest part of His being, and He needs their comfort. Jesus' words are very similar to parts of Psalms 42 and 43.

B. Subject of Prayer (v. 39)

39. And he went a little further, and fell on his face, and prayed, saying, O my Father, if it be possible, let this cup pass from me: nevertheless, not as I will, but as thou wilt.

A little further is about a stone's throw according to Luke 22:41. There is no one acceptable position for prayer, but the position we take can

"*Yet not as I will, but as you will.*"
— *Matthew 26:39, NIV*

Visual for lesson 3

This captivating artwork makes vivid the Golden Text of this lesson.

speak volumes about the depth of our emotion. Jesus does indeed go to His knees (again, Luke 22:41), but that's just the start of falling prostrate—*on his face*—as He throws His total being into this prayer.

Jesus begins His prayer as He taught the disciples to begin theirs in Matthew 6:9: *O my Father.* The closeness Jesus has known with God the Father from before the foundation of the world now serves as the rock on which He leans.

The *cup* Jesus fears is a figure of speech for the terrible ordeal He is about to experience at the hands of sinful people. But even worse than that, this cup stands for the wrath of the Father that Jesus will bear as He dies to pay sin's terrible price. "Cup" frequently stands for God's wrath in the Old Testament (see Psalm 75:7, 8; Jeremiah 25:15, 16; Ezekiel 23:31-34).

Given the pain and suffering of the cross that lies just ahead—physically and especially spiritually—it is natural for Jesus to look for an alternative that will allow the cup to *pass* from Him. Could there possibly be a "Plan B"?

Of course, there is no "Plan B." Jesus' prayer helps prepare Him to set aside His own *will* and self-interests to do as God wills. To accomplish the eternal plan for saving humanity remains Jesus' uncompromised priority. Although He seeks to find a way other than the cross, *nevertheless* He decides that nothing can keep Him from obeying God, loving us, and completing His mission. There are no shortcuts, as Satan had tried to offer Him at least twice before (Matthew 4:1-11; 16:21-23). [See question #3, page 256.]

IS THERE ANY WAY OUT OF THIS?

Most of us have been in situations that seemed to be so difficult that we could see no clear or satisfying way to deal with our circumstances. This brings to mind a fable about an old, decrepit mule that fell into a well. The farmer decided the well was too shallow, and was also a danger to passersby. Further, the mule was too old to be any good, so the farmer called in his neighbors and said, "Help me fill in this well and bury my mule at the same time."

The mule panicked as the first shovelful of dirt hit his back, but he quickly noticed that the dirt was falling off his back and down into the bottom of the well. So he accepted the pain from the clods and occasional rock that hit him, and kept on stepping on the dirt as it dropped to the bottom. It wasn't too long before the well was filled and the mule stepped right out onto level ground. He did what he had to do!

Jesus' prayer to be able to avoid what He knew to be ahead of Him was a very human prayer. Over an extended period of time that night Jesus prayed for release. But also each time He stated His commitment to God's will.

Sometimes we simply have to do what we know must be done and trust God for the outcome. He is faithful and will grant eternal deliverance for those who trust him. As the poet Robert Frost has said, "The best way out is always through."

        —C. R. B.

C. Exhortation to Prayer (vv. 40-41)

40. And he cometh unto the disciples, and findeth them asleep, and saith unto Peter, What, could ye not watch with me one hour?

Although Jesus speaks directly to *Peter,* the word *ye* is plural in the Greek, so the message is for all three disciples (v. 37, above). This is neither the first nor last disappointment Jesus experiences with the disciples during this trying time.

Even so, Jesus does not get angry, ranting and raving over their failure. He knows that people get sleepy after a heavy meal, and that the disciples really don't have much of a clue as to what is about to happen. A simple *what* leads the question that registers His disappointment.

41. Watch and pray, that ye enter not into temptation: the spirit indeed is willing, but the flesh is weak.

The disciples had already proven that they were susceptible to *temptation.* Previously that evening they had bickered over who was the greatest (Luke 22:24), and Judas has already set the wheels of betrayal into motion.

The next few hours and days will be fraught with opportunities to fall into even more temptation. These temptations could lead them into momentary setbacks (such as Peter's denial of Christ), or irreversible rejections of Christ (like Judas's). It is crucial that the disciples seek God's strength for such dangerous times. Thus the need to *watch and pray.* [See question #4, page 256.]

In the midst of His own agony, Jesus shows amazing concern for others. Jesus refuses to play the blame game, questioning the intentions or genuineness of His disciples. In spite of all their

---

How to Say It

EPHESIAN. Ee-*fee*-zhun.

EZEKIEL. Ee-*zeek*-ee-ul or Ee-*zeek*-yul.

GETHSEMANE. Geth-*sem*-uh-nee (G as in get).

JEREMIAH. Jair-uh-*my*-uh.

JERUSALEM. Juh-*roo*-suh-lem.

JUDAS. *Joo*-dus.

MOJAVE. Mow-*hah*-vee.

RABBI. *Rab*-eye.

ZEBEDEE. *Zeb*-eh-dee.

shortcomings, He knows their hearts are in the right place. Therefore, He offers His personal vote of confidence and His compassion by saying that *the spirit indeed is willing*. He knows they are spiritually minded men who want to do the right thing. This is one occasion when the disciples do not do the good they know they should do (see Romans 7:15). Jesus understands.

The very fact that *the flesh is weak* is the very reason the disciples need to heed Jesus' exhortation to watch and pray. Exhausted or not, there are times to rise above human weakness to tap into God's strength. This is one of those times.

D. Tenacity in Prayer (vv. 42-44)

42. He went away again the second time, and prayed, saying, O my Father, if this cup may not pass away from me, except I drink it, thy will be done.

Except for matters of style, there is no addition or subtraction in the content of Jesus' *second* prayer. The issues and concerns have not changed. He knows His strength for the crisis at hand can come only from the *Father*. The reality of impending ultimate suffering causes an earthquake in His soul that finds Him contemplating some other way to save the world. However, if the only way to achieve God's eternal purpose for us is for Jesus to *drink the cup of suffering and death*, then drink it He will!

43. And he came and found them asleep again: for their eyes were heavy.

Jesus had hoped that these three would muster the strength to watch and pray, but sadly this is not to be. Yet once again the Lord proves His own empathy and restraint. In this critical hour He could have "blown a fuse" or "gone off" at them in anger because of their apparent lack of concern. Although He had hoped for more, He understands their weakness.

44. And he left them, and went away again, and prayed the third time, saying the same words.

Jesus' example in prayer during the biggest crisis of His life can save us from misconceptions in our own prayer lives. First of all, we should realize that repeating a prayer does not automatically place it in the category of vain or meaningless repetition that we see condemned in Matthew 6:7. That passage refers to pointless and mindless babble such as the pagan world used in praying to their imaginary gods; likewise, when we memorize certain formulas and repeat them without thinking, our prayers are meaningless.

Also, some mistakenly draw the conclusion that if we have faith, we should pray about something only once, trust God with its outcome, and leave it at that. To do otherwise is a lack of faith, they claim. But here Jesus demonstrates the error in that thinking. He prays about the same urgent matter over and over. No one can accuse Jesus of lacking faith! Satan wants Jesus to convince Himself that He can find God's "Plan B." Jesus fights off the temptation to avoid God's one-and-only plan by using the same prayer of surrender over and over.

When an issue is heartfelt, we can pray about it in many different ways as we rely on our need for God's help. Our prayers may be short and repetitive (as Jesus' prayer here is); our prayers may last "all night" (Luke 6:12); and they may be persistent (Luke 18:1-8).

II. The Awful Arrest
(Matthew 26:45-50)

A. Jesus Complies (vv. 45, 46)

45. Then cometh he to his disciples, and saith unto them, Sleep on now, and take your rest: behold, the hour is at hand, and the Son of man is betrayed into the hands of sinners.

As Jesus completes His third cycle of prayer, His *disciples* are again asleep. His words can be construed as sad irony, as if to say *"Sleep on now, and take your rest,* because I have won the prayer battle without your help." Or these words may constitute a sad question: "Are you still sleeping and resting? The opportunity to join me in the prayer battle has passed you by."

In any case, they have missed an important chance to pray, and Jesus knows that *the hour* for *the Son of man* to be *betrayed* has come. It is now time to change prayer into action.

46. Rise, let us be going: behold, he is at hand that doth betray me.

Whether He hears them coming, sees the torches in the distance, or senses divinely that the enemies are on their way, Jesus implores His disciples to *Rise, let us be going*. The word "going" in the overall context does not suggest resignation or retreat, but a courageous advance to meet the enemy. [See question #5, page 256.]

Jesus knows that the one leading the approaching band is *he . . . that doth betray* Him. Judas, called to follow, seeks to force events down a path of his own choosing. This one, who could have been sent into the world with a message of hope, now sends his Master on a journey of death. A man who was once known as Jesus' friend now wears for eternity the label "betrayer."

B. Judas Betrays (vv. 47-49)

47. And while he yet spake, lo, Judas, one of the twelve, came, and with him a great multitude with swords and staves, from the chief priests and elders of the people.

Betrayal, under any circumstance, is bad business. For it to come from *one of the twelve* takes our breath away! From the standpoint of *the chief priests and elders of the people*, this is the moment they have been looking for: the opportunity to arrest Jesus in secret, far from the unpredictable mobs that might come to His defense.

They take no chances, arriving with an armed detachment of the Roman guard (John 18:3, 12). If there is to be resistance from this messianic revolutionary named Jesus, they are prepared for it. Such action, however, shows that the Jewish leaders, to the very end, understand neither Jesus nor the nature of His mission.

48. Now he that betrayed him gave them a sign, saying, Whomsoever I shall kiss, that same is he; hold him fast.

Recognizing people in the dark is difficult. This is especially true in an age before electric lights. There is no photography either, so few would know what Jesus looks like even in broad daylight. Thus the need for a prearranged *sign*—a *kiss*. In ancient culture, as in some cultures today, the kiss is a traditional form of greeting.

49. And forthwith he came to Jesus, and said, Hail, Master; and kissed him.

Upon arrival, Judas wastes no time. His unassuming *Hail, Master* (or "Hello, Rabbi") is filled with treachery as he kisses *Jesus.* The term *kissed* is the same as that used of the Father's reaction to the prodigal son (Luke 15:20), and that of the Ephesian elders at Paul's farewell (Acts 20:37). Judas gushes over Jesus in a sickening, ostentatious display.

C. The Guard Arrests (v. 50)

50. And Jesus said unto him, Friend, wherefore art thou come? Then came they, and laid hands on Jesus, and took him.

Home Daily Bible Readings

Monday, Mar. 15—Jesus Is the Good Shepherd (John 10:7-13)
Tuesday, Mar. 16—I Lay Down My Life (John 10:14-18)
Wednesday, Mar. 17—Father, Glorify Your Name (John 12:27-31)
Thursday, Mar. 18—When I Am Lifted Up . . . (John 12:32-36)
Friday, Mar. 19—Jesus Prays in Gethsemane (Matthew 26:36-41)
Saturday, Mar. 20—Your Will Be Done (Matthew 26:42-46)
Sunday, Mar. 21—Judas Betrays Jesus With a Kiss (Matthew 26:47-54)

Jesus takes the high road by addressing Judas as *Friend.* The purpose of the question *wherefore art thou come?* is to expose Judas's intentions while refusing to accept his show of affection as genuine.

This is the point where the authorities step in. When they lay *hands on Jesus*, they set in motion a chain of events that will never be paralleled in the annals of history.

Conclusion

A. The Power of Prayer

Over the years I have talked to several people whose greatest fear is that some day, through a bizarre set of circumstances, they will be falsely accused of a crime they did not commit and find themselves in prison, or even on "death row." What a nightmare!

That nightmare became a reality for Jesus. Even so, His unwarranted arrest was a part of the predetermined plan of God. There was no escape, short of disobeying the Father. But Jesus would be obedient to the end.

We marvel at Jesus' determination to "stay the course," to teach His followers to the end, to treat the most heinous betrayal with civility, to love mankind so extravagantly, and to obey the Heavenly Father regardless of the cost.

Where can we find such power to obey? Where Jesus did! The fact that He threw Himself so completely into His prayer is a witness to us. But turning to God in prayer—the kind of prayer where He wrestled repeatedly over the same issue, and where He totally surrendered to God's will—He found the power to overcome even the worst nightmare and the most painful reality.

But Jesus also found the power to act when the time for prayer had passed. This heroic example shines brightly for us as well, even two thousand years later!

B. Prayer

Dear Father, we thank You from the bottom of our hearts for Jesus' unwavering commitment to You! His inexhaustible love for us leaves us stunned and amazed. Lord, help us to overcome the weakness of the flesh and to be responsive always to Your will. Shield us from ever committing an act of betrayal against You.

Father, also teach us to rely on prayer as Jesus did. Teach us to act as well. We surrender our lives to Your leading, and we thank You for the blessings that result. In Jesus' name, amen.

C. Thought to Remember

Surrender your all to God in prayer.
Then act.

Learning by Doing

This page contains an alternative lesson plan emphasizing learning activities.
Classes desiring such student involvement will find these suggestions helpful.

Learning Goals

After participating in this lesson, each student will be able to:

1. Tell of Jesus' experiences in Gethsemane, both in His prayers and in His betrayal and arrest.

2. Suggest some times of temptation during which disciples may be called on to imitate their Master's resolve.

3. State a plan of action to make prayer a consistent and effective weapon against temptation.

Into the Lesson

Make a list of difficult situations caused by other people (for example, a coworker lies on your personnel evaluation, a neighbor's dog keeps digging in your flower bed). Ask class members to rank them in order of difficulty to handle. Make suggestions of how *not* to handle the situation, then ideas for how to respond appropriately. State, "We will see a pattern for how to respond to such situations by examining how Jesus dealt with the most difficult situations."

Into the Word

Jesus was "sorrowful and very heavy." Ask the class to list reasons why. *(He had confronted the bickering of the disciples over who was the greatest; He knew He was about to face Judas' betrayal, false arrest and imprisonment, Peter's denial, beatings, the disciples' abandonment, crucifixion, and punishment for sin; see 2 Corinthians 5:21; 1 Peter 2:24.)*

Discuss what a normal response might be. *(Possibilities include seeking revenge, fleeing, fighting back, and blaming other people to save self.)* Consider Jesus' response as a pattern for us to deal with adversity.

Prayer—Immediately following the last supper Jesus left for Gethsemane to pray. Have the class compare Jesus' prayer with other New Testament passages regarding prayer (for example, Acts 4:23-30; 1 Timothy 2:1-3) or explain how to respond when facing persecution (see Philippians 1:19-26; James 5:7-11; 1 Peter 3:8-16; 4:12-16). Ask, "What instructions do these passages give about responding to suffering?" *(Some possible answers: standing for Jesus and righteousness, recognizing the value in suffering, seeking strength to endure, and concentrating on having the ability to stand for Christ rather than focusing on eliminating the persecution).*

Support from friends—Observe that Jesus brought the apostles with Him and kept Peter, James, and John near. We think of strength as the ability to stand alone and be independent. At Jesus' hour of greatest need, He showed that it is natural to need people and request their support. He explained not only His need, but also the way He wanted His followers to help. *(To wait, to watch, and to be ready to offer help, comfort, and consolation.)* Ask the class to consider lessons from these men. What ways do we most often fail others in need? What could we do to assist when others face spiritual battles?

Repeated prayer—Read Matthew 6:7, 8 and Luke 18:1-8. Ask, "How do you reconcile these passages?" *(God answers prayer that comes honestly from a hurting heart seeking Him, but He does not respond to prayer that we believe will be answered simply because of repetition.)* What in the prayers of Jesus on this night help us differentiate repetitive prayers to avoid from repeated prayers that are encouraged? *(As Jesus repeated the same request, He demonstrated the appropriateness of echoing our requests to the Father when done in a right spirit; Matthew 26:39, 43).*

Surrender to the Father's will—Note that this is not the first time Jesus has been confronted with a challenge to avoid the Father's plan and remove Himself from difficulty. When tempted to avoid hunger, He chose to submit to the Father (see Matthew 4:3, 4). Now in His darkest hour, about to face the punishment for our sin, He again submits Himself to the will of the Father.

Persevere through trials—In spite of the intense agony of this experience, Jesus faithfully fulfilled the will of the Father. This obedience was necessary to secure our salvation (Romans 5:18, 19; Hebrews 10:5-10).

Into Life

Ask the class to share difficult situations they are facing. Determine how others in the class can pray for them and other practical ways to provide encouragement and support throughout the week. Ask church leaders or the missions committee for specific difficult situations some of your missionaries are facing, and commit yourselves to pray specifically for them to have endurance and faithfulness. Send a card from the class letting them know of your continued commitment.

Let's Talk It Over

The questions on this page are designed to promote discussion of the lesson by the class and to encourage application of the lesson Scriptures. The answers provided are only discussion starters. Let your class talk it over from there.

1. Jesus wanted His closest friends nearby even as He took time alone with His Father. When has the presence of brothers and sisters in Christ been most helpful to you, and why?

Answers to this question will be highly individual. Members of your class undoubtedly have faced serious problems in their families or have lost loved ones. Perhaps some have had difficulty standing up for the Lord at the workplace, or they have been seriously challenged at the university. As each one tells his or her story, affirm the value of a group of supportive friends.

There should be no disagreement that it is good to have others pray with us and for us when we face difficulty. Perhaps your class can work on a plan to organize a team or teams of prayer warriors to be with, and to pray with, church members who are in distress.

2. Why do some people "make the mistake of assuming that those around them should know what they are feeling or what to do in a difficult time"? How should we respond when someone becomes upset with us for that reason?

No two people will handle the same situation in exactly the same way. Nor does anyone know all the inner turmoil that another person is experiencing. It is almost always a mistake to say, "I know how you feel." Nor can we expect that others will know exactly how we feel.

Often, however, a spouse or other loved one will expect us to "know" what he or she is feeling. The person who is in pain may say something like, "If you really loved me, you'd know how I feel." Such a person is already feeling badly, so we need to respond with gentleness in a way that affirms the person. It is easy to get defensive because the person is really making an unreasonable demand.

If we realize, however, that issues of low self-esteem may be involved, then we can give that person the freedom to work through it without adding to his or her problem. This is all part of bearing one another's burdens (Galatians 6:2) without adding to those burdens.

3. When have you had to pray, "not as I will, but as thou wilt"? How did God answer? If His will was different from what you wanted, how did you accept that fact?

Most of your learners have faced situations where they prayed for healing of loved ones who were ill. Many have faced times when God did not heal their loved one, but death came instead. Others may have prayed for an opportunity to change jobs or to preserve their financial condition, only to find out that God's will was different. Those who accept these situations gracefully are those who trust God to have the "bigger picture" in view that we cannot see. While we would like to see things go our way, we are sometimes made better—or God Himself is glorified—in the midst of our sorrow and stress.

4. What difference would it have made if the disciples had stayed awake and prayed with Jesus before the arrest?

It would not have made any difference as far as Jesus' arrest and crucifixion were concerned. That was part of God's plan for our redemption. Still, it could have made a big difference for the disciples themselves. Perhaps they would not have scattered and run. Perhaps Peter would have been bolder and not denied Jesus. (Though these things were prophesied, they were predicted based on how things really were going to be; the prophecy would have been different if the disciples had been bolder due to wakefulness and prayer.)

Also, if the disciples had been more consistent in prayer, perhaps they would have been more in tune with God's plan. Then they would have been less fearful after Jesus' death. They may even have anticipated Jesus' resurrection. This has something to say about our own "wakefulness" as we anticipate Jesus' return.

5. Jesus gained ultimate victory by yielding to the arrest. How does that encourage us when we face difficult, seemingly no-win circumstances?

From a human standpoint it appeared that Jesus had lost when He surrendered to the mob. The disciples thought so, and they fled. The rulers thought so, and they were glad. But in God's timing these events were part of a greater victory. When we face trials and hardships, sometimes we feel the outcome has not been positive. But if we remain faithful to the Lord and His purposes, we are part of a greater plan (see the example of Joseph in Genesis 45:5-8). More than yielding to a mob, Jesus yielded to the Father.

Trial and Sentence

DEVOTIONAL READING: John 10:22-30.

BACKGROUND SCRIPTURE: Mark 14, 15.

PRINTED TEXT: Mark 14:53, 55-64; 15:1, 2, 12-15.

Mark 14:53, 55-64

53 And they led Jesus away to the high priest: and with him were assembled all the chief priests and the elders and the scribes.

. . . .

55 And the chief priests and all the council sought for witness against Jesus to put him to death; and found none.

56 For many bare false witness against him, but their witness agreed not together.

57 And there arose certain, and bare false witness against him, saying,

58 We heard him say, I will destroy this temple that is made with hands, and within three days I will build another made without hands.

59 But neither so did their witness agree together.

60 And the high priest stood up in the midst, and asked Jesus, saying, Answerest thou nothing? what is it which these witness against thee?

61 But he held his peace, and answered nothing. Again the high priest asked him, and said unto him, Art thou the Christ, the Son of the Blessed?

62 And Jesus said, I am: and ye shall see the Son of man sitting on the right hand of power, and coming in the clouds of heaven.

63 Then the high priest rent his clothes, and saith, What need we any further witnesses?

64 Ye have heard the blasphemy: what think ye? And they all condemned him to be guilty of death.

Mark 15:1, 2, 12-15

1 And straightway in the morning the chief priests held a consultation with the elders and scribes and the whole council, and bound Jesus, and carried him away, and delivered him to Pilate.

2 And Pilate asked him, Art thou the King of the Jews? And he answering said unto him, Thou sayest it.

. . . .

12 And Pilate answered and said again unto them, What will ye then that I shall do unto him whom ye call the King of the Jews?

13 And they cried out again, Crucify him.

14 Then Pilate said unto them, Why, what evil hath he done? And they cried out the more exceedingly, Crucify him.

15 And so Pilate, willing to content the people, released Barabbas unto them, and delivered Jesus, when he had scourged him, to be crucified.

GOLDEN TEXT: Again the high priest asked him, and said unto him, Art thou the Christ, the Son of the Blessed? And Jesus said, I am.—Mark 14:61, 62.

Jesus Fulfills His Mission
Unit 1: Road to the Cross
(Lessons 1-4)

Lesson Aims

After participating in this lesson, each student should be able to:

1. Summarize the events of Jesus' trials and condemnation.

2. Tell how God's will was carried out through the noble acts of Jesus and in spite of the contemptible acts of the Sanhedrin and Pilate.

3. Express a commitment to working in harmony with the purposes of God.

Lesson Outline

INTRODUCTION
 A. The Case of Richard Jewell
 B. Lesson Background
 I. JESUS BEFORE THE SANHEDRIN (Mark 14:53, 55-64)
  A. Condemned by Lies (vv. 53, 55-61a)
  B. Convicted by Truth (vv. 61b-64)
  An Innocent's Death; An Outpouring of Mercy
 II. JESUS BEFORE PILATE (Mark 15:1, 2, 12-15)
  A. Jesus' Bold Confession (vv. 1, 2)
  B. Pilate's Cowardly Concession (vv. 12-15)
  Respect for the Word of God
CONCLUSION
 A. God's Interest vs. Self-Interest
 B. Prayer
 C. Thought to Remember

Introduction

A. The Case of Richard Jewell

At about 1:20 A.M. on July 27, 1996, a bomb exploded in an Atlanta park during a celebration for the Olympic games. The explosion killed one woman and injured many other bystanders. The casualties likely would have been much worse but for the swift action of security guard Richard Jewell, who discovered the suspicious-looking green backpack and alerted the authorities. Jewell and the other authorities were in the process of evacuating the park when the bomb exploded.

Initially, Richard Jewell was hailed as a hero. But a few days later several media outlets named him as the primary suspect in the bombing itself. Their information was based on leaks from the FBI.

Several months later the FBI formally cleared Jewell of any wrongdoing. He indeed was a hero, he indeed had helped to save many lives, and he was innocent of every accusation. But great damage had already been done. Jewell lost his job, was abandoned by many of his friends, became burdened by huge debts, and found his reputation in ruins.

We would like to think that false accusations and judicial error—including those of "the court of public opinion"—are the stuff of repressive regimes. Some people and some judicial systems are flawed in spite of good intentions. Some are flawed, however, because of self-interest, character defects, and "political realities."

B. Lesson Background

Untrue accusations, unjust imprisonment, and unfair punishment make up the story of our lesson today. Jesus is on trial for His life. It has been only a few hours since He sat at the table with His disciples, sharing with them the Passover. He has just been brought from the garden where He had been praying. God had answered Jesus' prayer to remove the cup from Him; the answer was "No," and it was delivered by a mob led by Judas Iscariot.

In our text today we see Jesus standing in two different courts. The first is a religious tribunal. The Sanhedrin, which was the ruling council of religious leaders, had a strong interest in preserving its own power and influence (John 11:47, 48). In the council's eyes, this rabble-rouser Jesus was gathering support from the people and had to be removed.

The other court is a political tribunal with a similar set of interests. Pontius Pilate, the Roman governor in Jerusalem, wanted to maintain his position. To do that he had to keep the peace.

Each of these tribunals needed the other. The Sanhedrin could not legally execute a prisoner (John 18:31). Only the Romans could do that. But Pilate did not have the support of the people he governed. His success in governing depended on the support of the Sanhedrin. Thus, their common self-interest focused on one innocent figure: Jesus.

I. Jesus Before the Sanhedrin (Mark 14:53, 55-64)

A. Condemned by Lies (vv. 53, 55-61a)

53. And they led Jesus away to the high priest: and with him were assembled all the chief priests and the elders and the scribes.

Our text picks up the story immediately after Jesus' arrest in the Garden of Gethsemane. Of interest is the fact that the religious leaders are already *assembled.* This demonstrates that Jesus' arrest is not simply a whim motivated by opportunity, but rather is a well-planned and executed plot.

According to Matthew 26:57, this *high priest* is Caiaphas, the son-in-law of another high priest by the name of Annas. Little is known of Caiaphas other than his role in Jesus' crucifixion. Apparently he is greatly influenced by his father-in-law, for John 18:13 tells us that Annas takes the lead in questioning Jesus (cf. Acts 4:6).

John also tells us, "Now Caiaphas was he, which gave counsel to the Jews, that it was expedient that one man should die for the people" (John 18:14). The counsel of Caiaphas is especially significant because, as John explains, it was a prophetic utterance in keeping with Caiaphas's role as high priest (11:51, 52).

Caiaphas undoubtedly understood his words to mean that Jesus should die rather than continue to cause trouble for the authorities. God, however, puts His own "spin" on the message of the high priest. Caiaphas is right: one man is to die for the people. But Caiaphas is far more right than he knows, for Jesus is to die not only for the Jewish people of His time, but for all people at all times who call upon the name of the Lord.

55. And the chief priests and all the council sought for witness against Jesus to put him to death; and found none.

The Greek word translated as *witness* can refer to either individuals who testify or to the evidence found within the testimony that they bring. The latter seems to be the better understanding here, since the next verse tells us that *the council* indeed has witnesses who are willing even to perjure themselves. It appears that this assembly of religious leaders has reached its conclusion even before hearing any testimony. [See question #1, page 264.]

56. For many bare false witness against him, but their witness agreed not together.

We can only imagine the frustration of those religious leaders who seek an airtight legal case against Jesus. Even within this sham procedure they cannot get enough testimony to convict Him. Deuteronomy 17:6 requires more than one *witness* for the death penalty. If these leaders cannot get more than one witness to testify to a capital offense in their own hearing, then they will not be able to bring their case before the Roman authorities.

57-59. And there arose certain, and bare false witness against him, saying, We heard him say, I will destroy this temple that is made with hands, and within three days I will build another made without hands. But neither so did their witness agree together.

According to John 2:19 this testimony is partly accurate. Speaking against the *temple* is a capital offense (see Jeremiah 26:1-19). But Jesus had been speaking "of the temple of his body" (John 2:21). Obviously these witnesses have no idea what exactly Jesus had been talking about. [See question #2, page 264.] And once again the witnesses are unable to coordinate their testimony. Whether they differ in their interpretation of Jesus' intent or in the wording of His statement, their testimony is regarded as unreliable even in this biased court.

60. And the high priest stood up in the midst, and asked Jesus, saying, Answerest thou nothing? what is it which these witness against thee?

We sense a bit of desperation that *the high priest* is feeling at this point. His witnesses have failed to convince anyone—even those who came into the trial with their minds already made up! They are preaching to the choir and the choir is not persuaded. The modern prohibition against self-incrimination that does not require a person to testify against himself or herself does not apply, however. So the high priest hopes that the accused will say something useful.

61a. But he held his peace, and answered nothing.

Jesus' lack of reaction is quite surprising to those of us who are used to "standing up for our rights." The prophet Isaiah describes the coming Messiah "as a sheep before her shearers is dumb, so he openeth not his mouth" (Isaiah 53:7). This is fulfilled prophecy.

We can look at this trial before the religious authorities from two perspectives. First, we can focus on the tragedy of an innocent man being framed for crimes He did not commit. This view looks at Jesus as victim, carried along by forces beyond His control to a fate He did not choose.

How to Say It

BARABBAS. Buh-*rab*-us.
CAIAPHAS. *Kay*-uh-fus or *Kye*-uh-fus.
DEUTERONOMY. Due-ter-*ahn*-uh-me.
GETHSEMANE. Geth-*sem*-uh-nee (G as in *get*).
JOSEPHUS. Jo-*see*-fus.
JUDAS ISCARIOT. *Joo*-dus Iss-*care*-e-ut.
KOSOVO. *Koh*-so-voh or Koh-*so*-voh.
LEVITICUS. Leh-*vit*-ih-kus.
MERITA SHABIU. Meh-*ree*-tah Shah-*bee*-ooh.
MESSIAH. Meh-*sigh*-uh.
PHILO. *Fie*-low.
PONTIUS PILATE. *Pon*-shus or *Pon*-ti-us *Pie*-lut.
SANHEDRIN. *San*-huh-drun or San-*heed*-run.

But rather than seeing Jesus as a passive victim of oppressive justice, we should see Jesus as being fully in control of the situation. He is not silent before the false accusations because of fear or because of a hope that He may be able to escape the fate His accusers plan for Him. He is silent before the false accusers because He wants everyone to know exactly who He is: the Christ, the Son of the Living God. It is Jesus' silence that draws the high priest's question to bring this out (next verse).

B. Convicted by Truth (vv. 61b-64)

61b. Again the high priest asked him, and said unto him, Art thou the Christ, the Son of the Blessed?

Suddenly the dynamic of the trial changes. Up to this point, Jesus has been asked to respond to untruths and half-truths. False witnesses have borne inconsistent testimony, failing to convince even those who desperately want to see Jesus convicted. But continued silence after the question *Art thou the Christ, the Son of the Blessed?* could be taken as a denial. It is time to affirm the truth.

62. And Jesus said, I am: and ye shall see the Son of man sitting on the right hand of power, and coming in the clouds of heaven.

We could say that Jesus at this point has "thrown down the gauntlet" to history. Clearly this passage indicates that He believes Himself to be God's Son, the predicted Messiah. See Daniel 7:13. [See question #3, page 264.]

63. Then the high priest rent his clothes, and saith, What need we any further witnesses?

The reaction of *the high priest* proves that he understands exactly what Jesus is claiming. What all of his *witnesses* have failed to do Jesus

J Am!

Visual for lesson 4

Display this powerful image to reinforce Jesus' answer to the high priest in verse 62.

Himself does with one statement. The tearing of *clothes* is a reaction intended to show the intensity of emotions (cf. 2 Kings 18:37; Acts 14:14).

64. Ye have heard the blasphemy: what think ye? And they all condemned him to be guilty of death.

Blasphemy involves almost any speech that defames God. According to Leviticus 24:16, the punishment for blasphemy is death (cf. John 5:18; 10:33). In the minds of the religious leaders, Jesus' "defamation" is that a mere man would equate himself in any way with God. [See question #4, page 264.]

AN INNOCENT'S DEATH;
AN OUTPOURING OF MERCY

On January 13, 2000, eleven-year-old Merita Shabiu disappeared from her village in Kosovo. She had been abducted, assaulted, murdered, and then buried in a snowbank by a U.S. Army staff sergeant who was part of the peacekeeping force in that country. Her body was discovered by other Americans after the Army private who had helped bury the body admitted the truth about what had happened.

The private's truthful, but belated, witness was an important component in bringing the criminal to justice. (He's now serving a life term without parole.) The response of the perpetrator's fellow soldiers in some measure atoned for the evil deeds. Many of them attended Merita's funeral; an Army Reserve doctor took ten soldiers on a two-hour mission to the Shabiu home, where they apologized for the crime. The doctor helped the family design a grave marker, then paid for it. American troops collected four thousand dollars to be used for humanitarian purposes in Merita's name among the citizens of Kosovo. The worst action by an American also brought out the best in other Americans.

In a sense, we see a similar sequence in the first century. The one who betrayed Jesus, those who presented false testimony, the leaders who "set up" Jesus' crucifixion—they all represented the worst in human nature. But the unjust execution that resulted set in motion an amazing chain of events that brought an outpouring of mercy upon the human race: the possibility of eternal salvation from sin. What a God we serve!

—C. R. B.

II. Jesus Before Pilate
(Mark 15:1, 2, 12-15)

A. Jesus' Bold Confession (vv. 1, 2)

1. And straightway in the morning the chief priests held a consultation with the elders and scribes and the whole council, and bound

Jesus, and carried him away, and delivered him to Pilate.

The religious leaders have accomplished the first part of their goal in getting Jesus to "confess." In their minds He is clearly guilty of blasphemy. No longer do they need the unreliable witnesses who tried to profit from perjury. Now they themselves are the witnesses. In their presence Jesus has claimed to be the Son of God.

The next scene of Jesus' legal drama moves from the residence of Caiaphas (Mark 14:54) to the presence of the local Roman governor (or, more exactly, "prefect") named Pontius *Pilate.* Although the Jewish religious leaders can enforce religious law and punish offenders, they are not allowed to execute anyone. The Roman authorities have to authorize any executions. Thus, the religious leaders need Pilate in order to carry out their plans.

Pilate is an intriguing character for the religious leaders to be relying upon. Descriptions of him by the Jewish historian Josephus and the Greek-speaking Jew Philo are quite unflattering. They portray him as greedy, cruel, and willing to do almost anything to remain in power. Luke 13:1 refers to an incident where Pilate mingled the blood of certain Galileans with their own sacrifices, but no further details are recorded by history. Pilate is no friend of the Jews!

2. And Pilate asked him, Art thou the King of the Jews? And he answering said unto him, Thou sayest it.

In some ways this is the high point of this entire passage. Pilate's plainspoken question *Art thou the King of the Jews?* evokes a response that is equally plain. There is no doubt in the mind of Pilate or anyone else hearing it that Jesus is indeed claiming to be some kind of king, although Jesus is quick to explain the spiritual nature of this kingdom in John 18:36.

When confronted with Jesus' answer, each of us must ask ourselves this question: Was Jesus telling the truth or not? Our answer affects where we spend eternity. It also determines how we live our earthly lives in anticipation of eternity. If Jesus is my King, how does that affect the way that I treat my neighbor? If Jesus is my King, how does that affect the way I talk about my coworker? If Jesus is my King, can anyone tell that I am subject to Him?

B. Pilate's Cowardly Concession (vv. 12-15)

12. And Pilate answered and said again unto them, What will ye then that I shall do unto him whom ye call the King of the Jews?

We know from the other Gospel accounts that *Pilate* believes Jesus to be innocent of any crime deserving death (Luke 23:4; John 18:38). But Pi-

late is unwilling to upset the community. He has established a tradition of releasing a prisoner each year as a sort of "Passover gift" to the people, so he assumes that the crowds will insist upon Jesus' release rather than someone else's. Pilate knows that it is from envy that the chief priests have arrested Jesus in the first place (Mark 15:10).

13. And they cried out again, Crucify him.

This cry of the crowd, inspired by the religious leaders (Mark 15:11), is shocking for at least four reasons. The first is, of course, the innocence of Jesus. Clamoring for the death penalty for someone who has stood for peace and humility, who has healed the sick and raised the dead, is an unspeakable horror.

The second reason this is so shocking is the swiftness with which the tide of public opinion has turned against Jesus. Less than a week earlier the crowds had hailed His coming. Now they call for His execution. The support that had seemed so unshakable only days before has turned into something quite different. The crowds now prefer the political rebel Barabbas (v. 15, below).

Third, we are startled to see the crowd's bloodthirsty desire to inflict the terrible cruelty of death by crucifixion. Victims of crucifixion die slowly of suffocation, shock, exposure, and infection while enduring excruciating pain for hours (and perhaps days) on end. Eagerly desiring such a death for anyone—let alone a fellow Jew—staggers the imagination.

Finally, the cry of the crowd is shocking because not only is crucifixion a cruel death, it is an accursed death (Galatians 3:13; cf. Deuteronomy 21:22, 23). The crowd not only wants Jesus dead, they also want His death to send a message to all Jews: this man is accursed by God!

RESPECT FOR THE WORD OF GOD

What is the best-selling book in history? The Bible? You're right! Think of its effect on Western culture: inspiration for countless works of art, for great writers such as William Shakespeare and C. S. Lewis, and for freedom movements such as the American Revolution and the abolition of slavery. The English language is indebted to the Bible for some choice idioms: "the salt of the earth" and "Woe is me!" are just two.

But, ironically, the Bible may well be less read than many other books. Barna Research Group does frequent scientific polls on things religious. This group has discovered, for example, that two-thirds of Americans don't read the Bible regularly and don't know the names of the four Gospels. It seems that acknowledgment of the Bible as the Word of God does not radically affect how people actually live!

All of this should not surprise us, since the Word of God who came in the flesh (John 1:14) met with similar treatment. One day the crowds were hailing Jesus; a short time later they were calling for His death. But as we denounce their fickleness, we may also be passing judgment on ourselves. To what extent do we also give lip service to the Word of God—either the Word living or the Word written—but do not match it with our lives?   —C. R. B.

14, 15. Then Pilate said unto them, Why, what evil hath he done? And they cried out the more exceedingly, Crucify him. And so Pilate, willing to content the people, released Barabbas unto them, and delivered Jesus, when he had scourged him, to be crucified.

So we see the convergence of motivated self-interests. The religious officials want to get rid of a troublemaker who has a knack for stepping on toes and attracting followers. Pilate wants to keep the peace and maintain his position. In between these two parties stands one expendable man. [See question #5, page 264.]

But we should not think of Jesus as a helpless victim. He is the one figure in this entire drama who is not motivated by His own interests. Rather, Jesus is the one who voluntarily "humbled himself, and became obedient unto death, even the death of the cross" (Philippians 2:8). When He did, He took our place. This is the very heart of the Christian message!

Conclusion

A. God's Interest vs. Self-Interest

Were we part of this drama, where would we have stood? Would we have pursued motives of profit and power? Would we have been swept up in the emotion of the crowd? We move toward an answer when we examine honestly "what motivates us"—is it God's interest, or our own?

The way we treat others is a direct reflection of our motives. Ask yourself, "Have I ever spoken badly of a coworker, seeking to lift myself up at her expense?" "Have I ever fudged the figures on my expense report or my taxes?" "Have I ever had some 'roast preacher' for lunch?" "Have I ever failed to speak up for what I knew was right because I feared what others might say?" Dig deeply enough, and each of us will find a piece of Caiaphas and of Pilate within our own hearts.

Yet we do not have to continue making the same mistakes they made. God's grace is great enough for anyone—whether high priest, Roman governor, or assembly line worker. Repentance and baptism lead us into God's forgiveness (Acts 2:38). Within His grace we can realign our priorities so that our interests coincide with God's purposes.

But those stuck in self-interest need to be warned: people cannot frustrate the designs of God. Caiaphas thought he was acting to remove a troublemaker. Pilate thought he was acting to appease the people. Both were acting for personal reasons to achieve personal goals.

But the end result was something far beyond either party's comprehension. God used their self-interests to achieve His ultimate goal: the eternal salvation of all who would accept it. Just as in the Old Testament, where God used the swords of pagans and the hubris of a Pharaoh to achieve His ends, so in the New Testament God uses the personal goals of a corrupt priest and a contemptible politician to achieve the ultimate of all goals. Joseph recognized the power of God to do such things when he said to his brothers, "But as for you, ye thought evil against me; but God meant it unto good, to bring to pass, as it is this day, to save much people alive" (Genesis 50:20).

B. Prayer

Lord, we pray that our interests would be Your interests. We pray that You would use us as Your tools, Your hands, Your feet. We recognize that Your will can be fulfilled in spite of us as easily as it can be fulfilled through us. We confess that far too often we are guilty of acting out of our own self-interests rather than seeking Your interests. Forgive us for going our own way, and draw us into Your plans so that we become willing participants in unfolding Your will on earth as it is in Heaven. In Jesus' name, amen.

C. Thought to Remember

God will achieve His purposes either *through* you or *in spite of* you. It's your choice!

Home Daily Bible Readings

Monday, Mar. 22—Jesus Is Arrested, Disciples Desert (Mark 14:46-52)

Tuesday, Mar. 23—Jesus Is Taken to the High Priest (Mark 14:53-59)

Wednesday, Mar. 24—Jesus Declares He Is the Messiah (Mark 14:60-65)

Thursday, Mar. 25—The Father and I Are One (John 10:22-30)

Friday, Mar. 26—Jesus Goes Before Pilate (Mark 15:1-5)

Saturday, Mar. 27—The Crowd Wants Barabbas Released (Mark 15:6-10)

Sunday, Mar. 28—The Crowd Shouts for Jesus' Death (Mark 15:11-15)

Learning by Doing

This page contains an alternative lesson plan emphasizing learning activities.
Classes desiring such student involvement will find these suggestions helpful.

Learning Goals

After this lesson, each student will be able to:

1. Summarize the events of Jesus' trials and condemnation.

2. Tell how God's will was carried out through the noble acts of Jesus and in spite of the contemptible acts of the Sanhedrin and Pilate.

3. Express a commitment to working in harmony with the purposes of God.

Into the Lesson

Find and jot down a few of the more bizarre headlines from tabloids. Read these to the students one at a time, and ask whether they believe the stories to be true or false. Then have the class pretend to be editors of a first-century Jerusalem tabloid. Mention an event from Jesus' life, and have them write a headline they would give the story. Let class members work with partners or in teams. Stories you might use include raising a child from the dead, bringing Lazarus back to life after being in the grave several days, or Jesus' teaching that the meek will inherit the earth. Finish with Jesus' teaching that He is the promised Messiah and His claim to be King of the Jews. Have several headlines read aloud. Ask, "How might people in Jesus' day have responded to these headlines? Why?" Today's lesson will examine the responses different people made to the claims of Jesus when He was on earth.

Into the Word

Review how the story in today's text affirms that Jesus was completely innocent of any crime. The Jewish tribunal needed evidence for the Roman court to justify the sentence against Jesus. They were unable to find two witnesses who could agree in their testimony against Jesus, even when lying (Mark 14:56). This group could not muster enough evidence even for them to consider it credible (Mark 14:56, 59).

Write on the board the two critical questions answered by Jesus. The religious leaders asked, "Art thou the Christ, the Son of the Blessed?" (Mark 14:61). The political leader with responsibility to ensure justice asked, "Art thou the King of the Jews?" (Mark 15:2). Jesus answered both questions affirmatively. If His claims are true, they demand submissive worship and obedience. Consider together the responses of the different characters in this story to Jesus. Discuss how each person or group responded to Jesus and what their motivations were.

The religious leaders: How did the religious leaders respond to Jesus? *(They looked for evidence that would allow them to kill Jesus; Mark 14:55.)* Why did the leaders hate Jesus so much? *(He had a growing following, had attacked and embarrassed them publicly, had disrupted their market in the temple, etc.)* What motivated them to act this way? *(They were protecting their own power and influence; even Pilate recognized they were motivated by envy; see Mark 15:10.)*

Pilate: How did Pilate respond to Jesus? *(He did not release Jesus, but had Him scourged; Pilate ultimately passed sentence of crucifixion; Mark 15:15.)* What motivated Pilate to respond this way? *(He was more concerned about satisfying people and keeping peace than about justice; Mark 15:15.)*

The crowds: How did the crowds respond to Jesus? *(We need to ask, "Which day of the week?" Less than a week earlier, the crowds in Jerusalem had shouted, "Hosanna; Blessed is He that cometh in the name of the Lord" in Mark 11:9. Now, at the urging of the chief priests, the crowd shouts, "Crucify him!" in Mark 15:14. Note that this response was influential in prompting Pilate to release Barabbas and have Jesus flogged and sentenced to be crucified in Mark 15:15.)* What motivated the crowds to respond this way? *(While the Scriptures do not clearly answer this question, we learn how easily people can be influenced by others and by circumstances, and we know that here some chose to follow the religious leaders instead of Jesus.)*

Sadly, there is no record of anyone in the crowd standing up for the innocence of Jesus. It seems His closest followers had all deserted Him. Even though the injustice was evident, no one was willing to risk speaking on His behalf.

Into Life

Jesus has answered two critical questions in the affirmative: He is the Christ, and He is the King. Ask, "How does your life show that you believe His answers to be true? If other people were reading the story of your life, what would they say is your response to Jesus? Consider the answers from work, play, and home. What changes need to be made for others to see you responding affirmatively to these claims of Jesus?"

Let's Talk It Over

*The questions on this page are designed to promote discussion of the lesson
by the class and to encourage application of the lesson Scriptures. The answers
provided are only discussion starters. Let your class talk it over from there.*

1. How should a Christian defend himself or herself before a group that already "has its mind made up"?

When opponents of Christianity use slander and misrepresentation to attack a believer, one sometimes can appeal to decency and the facts of the case to preserve his or her reputation. When Jesus faced the Sanhedrin, however, He "answered nothing" (Mark 14:61). If no one in earshot is interested in the truth, it may be best to keep quiet. Then one's attitude and personal dignity speak up. That may speak louder than any human voice. (See also Amos 5:13.)

Perhaps some of your learners have faced such a situation, either on the job, at the university, or even among unbelieving family members. How did they deal with it? What would they do differently if they could repeat the experience? Keep in mind we want to glorify God first—our own reputations come second to that.

2. The witnesses twisted Jesus' words, either intentionally or unintentionally, regarding the temple. How should we respond when someone twists our words to make a false accusation?

False accusations may arise in circumstances noted in question 1. False accusations also may arise in situations where the accuser hopes to sway the opinion of someone who has authority over the one being falsely accused. In such cases we need to follow in Jesus' steps, as noted by the apostle Peter in 1 Peter 2:21-23. See also Peter's instructions in 1 Peter 3:16, 17.

3. Suppose a coworker says to you, "Jesus was a great teacher, but that's all. He never even claimed to be any more than that. His disciples made up that stuff about His being the Son of God after His death." How would you respond?

History tells us that most of Jesus' original twelve disciples went on to die the deaths of martyrs. People will willingly die (1) for truth and (2) for a lie that they believe to be true. People will not willingly die, however, for an untruth that they know to be an untruth. That's why it makes no sense to think that Jesus' disciples would make up a lie and then willingly die for that lie.

In verses 61, 62 Jesus clearly declares His divinity. Encourage the class to use concordances to locate other passages where Jesus identifies

Himself as more than merely a "good teacher." Consider Matthew 16:16 (and note Jesus' reply in verses 17-19); John 1:49 (again, note Jesus' response in verses 50, 51); 5:17, 18; 9:35-38.

4. The charge of using God's name in an improper way (blasphemy) could bring the death penalty in the first century. In what ways today do we not take the name of God as seriously as we ought? How can we do better?

Profanity is much more accepted in modern culture than it used to be. Even those who do not use bad language often find it tolerable. We say a movie was good even if it had some bad language in it. Using God's name as a curse word is "not so bad" if the rest of the movie is good.

In a different sort of way, even well-meaning believers may be guilty of misusing God's name. We sometimes say much too easily that the Lord "told" us this or "led us" to that. In reality, it may be simply our own opinion. We may be completely convinced that we are acting in harmony with God's will, but we ought to be careful not to ascribe to the Lord that which is not His work. A group of elders met to consider an issue. When consensus seemed to form, one of them said, "I believe it is the Spirit at work leading us to this decision." The very next day new information came to light, and the elders completely reversed their decision! In good faith they had acted in what they believed to be God's will. But they did not have all the information, as God always does, so they ultimately decided that God's will was just the opposite of what they had attributed to the Spirit just a day before.

5. Pilate sentenced Jesus to death, knowing His innocence. Why are people sometimes unwilling to stand up for what they believe? Where does the courage to do so come from?

People without a strong moral compass will go whichever way seems to be most advantageous to them at the time. That describes Pilate, and it describes postmodern thought today as well. Taking a stand requires that one believe in something strongly enough that defending it is "worth the cost." The apostles ultimately decided that standing up for Christ was worth any cost—even their lives. They found the courage to take that stand in their faith in the living Christ. See 1 Corinthians 15:14-19.

1 Peter 3 — our lives are you called.) 3—Keeping a clear conscience (Peter 3:16 — Bring in word. The water Baptism.) 16—it is better if God will... the doing good... suffer for doing good.) 31—suffer for doing good.

Jesus' Crucifixion

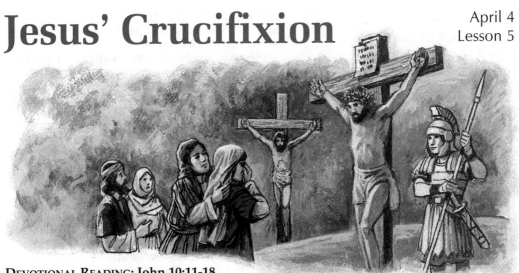

DEVOTIONAL READING: **John 10:11-18.**

BACKGROUND SCRIPTURE: **John 19:16b-42.**

PRINTED TEXT: **John 19:16b-24, 26-30.**

John 19:16b-24, 26-30

16b And they took Jesus, and led him away.

17 And he bearing his cross went forth into a place called the place of a skull, which is called in the Hebrew Golgotha:

18 Where they crucified him, and two others with him, on either side one, and Jesus in the midst.

19 And Pilate wrote a title, and put it on the cross. And the writing was, JESUS OF NAZARETH THE KING OF THE JEWS.

20 This title then read many of the Jews; for the place where Jesus was crucified was nigh to the city: and it was written in Hebrew, and Greek, and Latin.

21 Then said the chief priests of the Jews to Pilate, Write not, The King of the Jews; but that he said, I am King of the Jews.

22 Pilate answered, What I have written I have written.

23 Then the soldiers, when they had crucified Jesus, took his garments, and made four parts, to every soldier a part; and also his coat: now the coat was without seam, woven from the top throughout.

24 They said therefore among themselves, Let us not rend it, but cast lots for it, whose it shall be: that the Scripture might be fulfilled, which saith, They parted my raiment among them, and for my vesture they did cast lots. These things therefore the soldiers did.

· · · · · · · · · · · ·

26 When Jesus therefore saw his mother, and the disciple standing by, whom he loved, he saith unto his mother, Woman, behold thy son!

27 Then saith he to the disciple, Behold thy mother! And from that hour that disciple took her unto his own home.

28 After this, Jesus knowing that all things were now accomplished, that the Scripture might be fulfilled, saith, I thirst.

29 Now there was set a vessel full of vinegar: and they filled a sponge with vinegar, and put it upon hyssop, and put it to his mouth.

30 When Jesus therefore had received the vinegar, he said, It is finished: and he bowed his head, and gave up the ghost.

GOLDEN TEXT: And they took Jesus, and led him away. And he bearing his cross went forth into a place called the place of a skull, which is called in the Hebrew Golgotha: where they crucified him.—John 19:16b-18.

Jesus Fulfills His Mission
Unit 2: Victory Through Death
(Lessons 5, 6)

Lesson Aims

After participating in this lesson, each student should be able to:

1. Recount the details of Jesus' crucifixion as described in John's Gospel.

2. Discuss reasons why it was necessary for Jesus to die on the cross.

3. Pledge to live in a sacrificial manner to serve the One who died for him or her.

Lesson Outline

INTRODUCTION
  A. "I Surrender All"
  B. Lesson Background
 I. DESPISED AND REJECTED (John 19:16b-24)
  A. The Man Crucified (vv. 16b-18)
  B. The Men Crucifying (vv. 19-24)
    What's in a Name?
 II. A MAN OF SORROWS (John 19:26, 27)
  A. Concern for a Mother (v. 26)
  B. Commitment of a Disciple (v. 27)
    Acquainted With Grief
III. POURED OUT . . . UNTO DEATH (John 19:28-30)
  A. Human Thirst (vv. 28, 29)
  B. Divine Quenching (v. 30)
CONCLUSION
  A. Dying for Change
  B. Prayer
  C. Thought to Remember

Introduction

A. "I Surrender All"

All to Jesus I surrender,
  All to Him I freely give;
I will ever love and trust Him,
  In His presence daily live.
I surrender all,
  I surrender all.
All to Thee, my blessed Savior,
  I surrender all.
      —Judson W. Van DeVenter (1855–1939)

The decade of the 1890s was a heady time in America. Ellis Island was open to immigration, new inventions such as telephones and movies were making inroads, and the importance of the automobile ("horseless carriage") was asserting itself. It was in the midst of all this prosperity

and promise that Van DeVenter wrote, "I Surrender All" in 1896. Could it be that he recognized a danger that we have yet to see?

Those of us who have grown up in the church, especially churches with a more traditional worship style, probably have known and sung this hymn for decades. But what exactly is it that we have surrendered to Jesus in the midst of our prosperity? Precisely how have our lives changed because we have indeed surrendered "all" to Jesus? Can you make a list right now of five things you have surrendered—meaning sacrificed or given up—so that you will not be distracted from following Jesus?

Unfortunately, most of us are much better at singing about surrender than we are at practicing it. Too often we content ourselves with fairly minor sacrifices: I will surrender watching the sporting event on TV to attend the church potluck; I will sacrifice "sleeping in" on Sunday morning to attend church; I will give up my old clothes for the missions project; I will use a week of vacation to work at church camp.

But are these really the sorts of sacrifice that Paul had in mind when he told us to "present your bodies a living sacrifice, holy, acceptable unto God, which is your reasonable service" (Romans 12:1)? What exactly can we sacrifice that truly honors Jesus—things that recognize the commitment He made to us while dying on the cross?

B. Lesson Background

Crucifixion was an incredibly brutal, painful, and dehumanizing way to die. Roman crucifixion typically was reserved for non-Roman political and military enemies of the state, and for those guilty of various heinous crimes. Runaway slaves were also subject to the cross.

As we peer at the scene before us on Golgotha, we see various related activities going on simultaneously. In the center our attention is drawn to Jesus, nailed to the cross—enduring the scorn of His contemporaries, the sins of humanity, and the wrath of His Father.

Near the cross are various clusters of bystanders. A group of soldiers is kneeling, engaged in a game of chance to divide Jesus' clothes. Another cluster is mostly women, friends of Jesus who came to mourn and to give Him whatever support they had to offer. Still another group, whose numbers fluctuate with the passing hours, is there to gawk and deride. Farther away, we notice the religious officials and Pilate once again meeting, this time arguing over the wording of the sign above Jesus' head.

Those who acknowledge Jesus as the Messiah cannot help but hear the echoes of Isaiah 53 throughout Jesus' crucifixion. The outline for today's lesson takes its main points from Isaiah's prophecy. But the promise for all of us is also found in the prophet's words: "But he was wounded for our transgressions, he was bruised for our iniquities: the chastisement of our peace was upon him; and with his stripes we are healed" (Isaiah 53:5). In today's lesson we see Jesus surrender His very life—for us.

I. Despised and Rejected
(John 19:16b-24)

A. The Man Crucified (vv. 16b-18)

16b. And they took Jesus, and led him away.

Pilate is finished with *Jesus*. He has washed his hands of the matter—literally (Matthew 27:24). Although he found Jesus to be innocent, Pilate chooses to please the mob and condemn Jesus to die. *They* undoubtedly refers to the Roman soldiers (cf. John 19:23, below).

17. And he bearing his cross went forth into a place called the place of a skull, which is called in the Hebrew Golgotha.

John's description of the actual crucifixion is brief and to the point. He omits many details that the other Gospel writers include. Much of the detail in the other accounts focuses on Christ's suffering. Although John also discusses Christ's suffering at points, this Gospel writer seems very intent to stress the overall plan of the Father and the Son's obedience within that plan.

Golgotha is a Hebrew (or Aramaic) word that John translates for his readers as *the place of a skull*. The Latin word *calvaria* also means "skull," and this is where we get our well-known word *Calvary*. Perhaps this place gains its name from the skulls of executed criminals that could be found there. Or perhaps something about the terrain has the appearance of a skull. No one knows for sure. In any case, the place is likely very near a major road, as the Romans want their crucifixions to serve as public deterrents to sedition.

18. Where they crucified him, and two others with him, on either side one, and Jesus in the midst.

Critics of Christianity sometimes accuse Jesus of manipulating events to appear to be fulfilling prophecy. In a way, that actually is not such bad theology: Christians also believe that God is orchestrating events to align with the prophecies He has given!

But certainly some prophetic fulfillments are beyond mere human ability to coordinate. This is one of them. Hundreds of years previously the prophet Isaiah foretold that the Messiah would be "numbered with the transgressors" (Isaiah 53:12). [See question #1, page 272.] If Jesus were

Visual for lesson 5. *Use this stark visual of nails and rough wood to reinforce the sobering reality of today's Golden Text.*

merely a man, He could have had no way of making sure that others would be crucified alongside Him. [See question #2, page 272.]

B. The Men Crucifying (vv. 19-24)

19. And Pilate wrote a title, and put it on the cross. And the writing was, JESUS OF NAZARETH THE KING OF THE JEWS.

What an intriguing inscription! Before the Romans execute a prisoner, they prepare a sign detailing the person's crimes. That sign precedes the prisoner to the place of execution, informing everyone of the reason for the punishment. The sign is nailed above the criminal's head to reinforce the nature of the crimes.

In this case, no truer sign was ever posted! Jesus is indeed being crucified for who He claimed to be rather than for anything He did.

20. This title then read many of the Jews; for the place where Jesus was crucified was nigh to the city: and it was written in Hebrew, and Greek, and Latin.

Following Roman practice, Pilate makes sure that everyone knows what the "crime" of Jesus is. The sign is worded in the three major languages of the area so that anyone who can read will know why this man is being killed. But more than that, Pilate wants to humiliate the Jewish leaders who have manipulated him, as the next two verses show.

21. Then said the chief priests of the Jews to Pilate, Write not, The King of the Jews; but that he said, I am King of the Jews.

This is not a small point that *the chief priests* make. There is quite a difference between someone who actually *is* the *King of the Jews* and someone who merely *claims* to be the King of the Jews. The religious leaders want Jesus dead, after

How to Say It

ARAMAIC. *Air*-uh-*may*-ik (strong accent on *may*).
CALVARIA (Latin). kal-vuh-*ree*-uh.
GOLGOTHA. *Gahl*-guh-thuh.
ISAIAH. Eye-*zay*-uh.
MESSIAH. Meh-*sigh*-uh.
NAZARETH. *Naz*-uh-reth.
PILATE. *Pie*-lut.

all, because of statements like that. Pilate is now giving the world the very message that Jesus' death is supposed to silence.

WHAT'S IN A NAME?

Have you ever heard the argument over how the *Baby Ruth*® candy bar got its name? One story has it that the name came from Babe Ruth, the famous home-run hitter. The bar was first marketed in 1921, and as Babe Ruth's fame increased, he began signing his autograph on *Baby Ruth*® wrappers. The Curtiss Candy Company (maker of the confection) claimed it was named for "Baby Ruth," the daughter of U.S. President Grover Cleveland.

Eventually, Babe Ruth asked the Curtiss Company to pay him royalties since he was helping to sell their product. The company declined, so Ruth gave his permission to another company to use his name, and they produced the *Babe Ruth Home Run Bar*. The whole issue went to court, and the Curtiss Company won the lawsuit.

If the American legal system had existed in Jesus' time, the Jewish leaders would undoubtedly have taken Pilate to court for putting the title "King of the Jews" on Jesus' cross. They may have claimed this was "trademark infringement" on something that belonged only to God. They certainly had already convicted Jesus in court on equating Himself with God!

But Jesus' execution wasn't enough for them. These leaders also sought to strip Jesus of the wording on a small piece of wood that sarcastically revealed His true identity—even as Roman soldiers were stripping him of his most basic worldly possessions. Many who reject Jesus today do so by denying that Jesus is King. They also attempt to deny others their right to claim Him as their King. The more things change . . . !

—C. R. B.

22. Pilate answered, What I have written I have written.

With this answer *Pilate* takes his revenge on the religious leaders who have manipulated him. Pilate's sign mocks Jesus, but it mocks the Jewish leaders even more! Pilate sees through their pretended allegiance to Caesar (John 19:15), and now declares the dying Jesus to be their king. But in so doing, Pilate also unknowingly speaks the truth: the crucified One is indeed the King of the Jews!

23. Then the soldiers, when they had crucified Jesus, took his garments, and made four parts, to every soldier a part; and also his coat: now the coat was without seam, woven from the top throughout.

A squad of four *soldiers* usually attends Roman crucifixions (cf. Acts 12:4). They handle the details of the execution, prevent any escape or rescue attempt, and keep the mobs away from the condemned.

An apparent side benefit for soldiers conducting an execution is being able to claim at least some of the possessions of the condemned—his clothing in particular. We can assume that Jesus' clothes are fairly plain and common for His time. Likely His clothing includes a tunic, a belt, a head covering, sandals, and an outer robe or *coat*. To keep things "fair," these soldiers divide this clothing into *four* roughly equal *parts*. The only thing of enough value to create any conflict among the soldiers is the *coat*.

24. They said therefore among themselves, Let us not rend it, but cast lots for it, whose it shall be: that the Scripture might be fulfilled, which saith, They parted my raiment among them, and for my vesture they did cast lots. These things therefore the soldiers did.

Psalm 22:18 is the backdrop for this verse. Those who are crucified must give up some or perhaps all of their personal possessions to their executioners. Dignity dies when the beaten prisoner is marched through the crowds. Emotions explode as the condemned dies slowly in the presence of loved ones and enemies. Nothing can be held back, nothing can remain hidden, nothing can stay personal. Crucifixion robs its victims of everything they have accumulated during life—finally stealing life itself. John uses Psalm 22:18 to show fulfillment of God's plan in a very sobering way. [See question #3, page 272.]

II. A Man of Sorrows
(John 19:26, 27)

A. Concern for a Mother (v. 26)

26. When Jesus therefore saw his mother, and the disciple standing by, whom he loved, he saith unto his mother, Woman, behold thy son!

We can only imagine the intensity of emotions contained in this brief exchange between three people who love each other deeply. In the fog of pain, blood, and sweat, Jesus' eyes are clear enough to see *His mother* and John, one of His dearest disciples (cf. John 13:23; 20:2). They are standing together, part of a group that Luke describes as "a great company of people, and of women, which also bewailed and lamented him" (Luke 23:27). Years earlier Simon had warned Mary, "A sword shall pierce through thy own soul also" (Luke 2:35). No doubt those words echoed in her heart long after witnessing Jesus' crucifixion.

Jesus captures in this moment the essence of being part of this world while being part of the kingdom of God. Who could fault Him if, while consumed by His own pain and suffering, He would pay no attention to His surroundings? Yet not only does He see those around Him, Jesus reaches out to them and makes sure that His mother will be taken care of (next verse). [See question #4, page 272.] As the oldest child, it would have fallen to Jesus to care for His mother after the death of Joseph. Although Jesus has siblings (Matthew 12:46; John 2:12), they apparently are not part of the gallery (and might not even be in Jerusalem at the time).

B. Commitment of a Disciple (v. 27)

27. Then saith he to the disciple, Behold thy mother! And from that hour that disciple took her unto his own home.

All of the disciples had fled when Jesus was arrested—but at least one has returned. John now stands with Mary and others who lament Jesus' impending death. Even as Jesus is dying, He faces the burden of caring for His mother as she ages.

Neither John nor Mary have yet reached fullness in their Christian faith (see John 20:8, 9), and this is undoubtedly their darkest *hour*. Yet it is in this very hour that John proves he still can accept instructions from His Lord. We can assume that John cared for Mary as well as any son would care for his own *mother*.

ACQUAINTED WITH GRIEF

On April 9, 2002, the British people laid to rest the remains of the "Queen Mum," mother of Queen Elizabeth. The Queen Mum's experiences over her life of one hundred one years were proof that wealth, power, and acclaim do not protect people from grief. Refusing the safety of exile, she stood with her husband, George VI, encouraging the British people during the long nights of bombardment in World War II. Her husband died in 1952, and she buried her daughter Margaret just two months before her own death.

We can only guess at the grief she endured in watching her grandchildren mock the dignity of the royal family by their disastrous personal lives. Yet, in spite of the sins of her descendants, she carried to her grave a sense of dignity and an openness to her people that made her a beloved figure.

Jesus, of course, was alone in the incalculable burden of grief that He carried over lost humanity. But He also endured sorrow for the frailties of His "descendants"—people He had created. These included family members who would not recognize Him and disciples who doubted, denied, and even betrayed Him. Even so, His compassionate life, courageous death, and miraculous resurrection have made Him loved by billions of people from every nation and tongue. Devotion to all earthly leaders pales by comparison.
—C. R. B.

III. Poured Out . . . Unto Death (John 19:28-30)

A. Human Thirst (vv. 28, 29)

28. After this, Jesus knowing that all things were now accomplished, that the Scripture might be fulfilled, saith, I thirst.

Crucifixion provides many physical reasons for Jesus' *thirst*. Blood loss, exposure to the hot sun, pain, and labored breathing can individually parch one's throat. Taken together, these mean that Jesus suffers terribly from dehydration.

The fulfillment of *Scripture* that is in view is Psalm 69:21: "They gave me also gall for my meat; and in my thirst they gave me vinegar to drink." (See also the use of Psalm 69 in John 2:17; 15:25.)

29. Now there was set a vessel full of vinegar: and they filled a sponge with vinegar, and put it upon hyssop, and put it to his mouth.

This wine *vinegar* is probably the inexpensive drink favored by the soldiers themselves. Jesus earlier had refused a wine mixture that would have dulled his pain (Mark 15:23); He chose, instead, to drink the full cup of agony from His Father.

Now thirst compels the Lord to request and accept the offer of drink (cf. Mark 15:36). If the solders intend to prolong Jesus' agony by slaking His thirst, then theirs is not an offer of compassion but one of additional torture.

B. Divine Quenching (v. 30)

30. When Jesus therefore had received the vinegar, he said, It is finished: and he bowed his head, and gave up the ghost.

The relief the *vinegar* cannot provide, death does. Relief is not to be found in this world. But from Jesus' words to the thief next to Him we know that He was looking forward to being in Paradise that very day (Luke 23:43). Burning with a fever that could not be cooled, parched with a thirst that could not be quenched, Jesus finally finds refreshment at the table set for Him in that place.

As cruel as this entire experience is, Jesus' suffering is comparatively brief. Those condemned to death by crucifixion often remain alive for two or even three days. The physical agony experienced by Jesus for several hours could easily have gone on for a much longer period of time. Mark 15:44 tell us that Pilate was surprised that Jesus was already dead.

Even so, Jesus' suffering is long and severe enough to fulfill the Father's plan. We see this fulfillment when Jesus says *It is finished.* This is the victory cry of One whose work is complete—it is not the cry of defeat. Jesus had spoken previously of the work He came to carry out (John 17:4), but the disciples hadn't understood it. And they still don't understand. It will be only after the crucifixion and resurrection that understanding will come. [See question #5, page 272.]

The Gospel descriptions help us understand, too, the depths of the terrible price Jesus took upon Himself to pay in dying for our sins. There is the obvious physical price—the torture and agonizing death of an innocent man. Much worse, however, is the spiritual torture of bearing our sins (Hebrews 9:28). This is the greater part of the punishment—a punishment that rightly belongs to us!

And Jesus did indeed suffer on our behalf. It was our sins that nailed Jesus to the cross. It was our sins that caused Him such agony. He sacrificed Himself to pay the penalty for our failures. "Forasmuch then as the children are partakers of flesh and blood, he also himself likewise took part of the same; that through death he might destroy him that had the power of death, that is,

the devil; and deliver them, who through fear of death were all their lifetime subject to bondage" (Hebrews 2:14, 15).

Jesus sacrificed Himself so that we could be reconciled to God. He took upon Himself the sins of the world, accepting the punishment (death) due to each of us, so that we may have eternal life (Romans 3:21-26).

Conclusion

A. Dying for Change

In a phrase, "dying for change" is exactly what Jesus did. He died for a change in us. He died that our relationship with God could change. Before Jesus' death, humanity was alienated from God. After His crucifixion, alienation changed into the possibility of reconciliation. Before His death, humanity was under a death sentence. After His crucifixion, the certainty of our death changed into the possibility of eternal life. The price that the holiness and justice of God demanded to be paid was indeed paid (Romans 3:25; 1 John 4:10).

"Dying for change" also describes much of the world outside the walls of our churches. Think of your neighbors, your friends, your family members, your coworkers—think of the waitress in your favorite restaurant, the checker at the grocery store, the cop on patrol, the executive in her office. All are dying for change—and without a change they will die eternally.

Jesus sacrificed Himself so that they could be saved. But how will they hear? How will they know? That is up to us. What will we sacrifice to bring them the message of the cross? Will we risk personal rejection and humiliation by talking to them? Will we risk careers, ambitions, even our very lives to reach the lost? A disgraced figure hanging on a cross hopes that we will take those risks.

But those aren't the only risks we are asked to take. Will we give sacrificially to fund missions and new church plants? A dying man watches soldiers gamble over the scraps of cloth He once wore and He prays that we will not focus on the goods of this world in such a way. Will we?

B. Prayer

Father, we stand in awe at the price Jesus paid for us. But we also stand in sorrow as we think of the lost. Change our hearts so that we will pay any price to reach them with Your love. You paid the highest price for us—may we share Your values. In Jesus' name, amen.

C. Thought to Remember

Jesus has done His part. Have we?

Home Daily Bible Readings

Monday, Mar. 29—Isaiah's Prophecy of the Suffering Servant (Isaiah 53:1-6)
Tuesday, Mar. 30—He Bore the Sins of Many (Isaiah 53:7-12)
Wednesday, Mar. 31—Jesus Is Crucified (John 19:16-20)
Thursday, Apr. 1—The King of the Jews (John 19:21-25a)
Friday, Apr. 2—It Is Finished (John 19:25b-30)
Saturday, Apr. 3—The Spear Pierces His Side (John 19:31-37)
Sunday, Apr. 4—Joseph and Nicodemus Take Jesus' Body (John 19:38-42)

Learning by Doing

This page contains an alternative lesson plan emphasizing learning activities.
Classes desiring such student involvement will find these suggestions helpful.

Learning Goals

After participating in this lesson, each student will be able to:

1. Recount the details of Jesus' crucifixion as described in John's Gospel.

2. Discuss reasons why it was necessary for Jesus to die on the cross.

3. Pledge to live in a sacrificial manner to serve the one who died for him or her.

Into the Lesson

Begin the class by considering the costs involved in different activities. Place the activity on the board, and let the class list and add up the costs, including costs other than money. You might consider such an activity as taking a camping trip *(equipment, vehicle travel, lot permits, food, bugs, sleeping on hard ground, cold or heat, rain)*. Use an activity that interests several in your class. Note that there are costs involved with everything, even beyond the sticker price. Discuss what it means to have "hidden" (unanticipated or surprising) costs.

Then say, "We all attempt to calculate what something costs, and then decide whether it is worth that expenditure of finances, time, and effort, as well as the sacrifice from other parts of our lives. Today we look at what it cost Jesus to secure salvation for us and then ask what price we should be willing to pay as a follower of Jesus."

Into the Word

Many films and videos reenact the life of Jesus. (See page 247 for information on the use of copyrighted film clips.) Watch clips from one or two concerning how they depict His time of suffering. Discuss the following: In what ways is the clip accurate? What is missing? Does each create a tone and atmosphere that captures the essence of these events in a realistic, memorable way? What new questions are raised? What does it teach you that you had not considered before? What forgotten truths does it remind you of?

Read aloud the passages describing the suffering of Jesus (Matthew 27:27-37; Mark 15:16-26; Luke 23:26-43; John 19:16-30). Ask people what images stand out most to them. Pray, thanking God for the sacrifice made by His Son, Jesus.

Select several hymns or favorite songs that speak of the suffering and death of Jesus. Distribute hymnals with pages of those songs marked, or provide copies of the words from contemporary songs (only songs in the public domain or those for which your church has obtained permission). The following songs could be used: "At the Cross"; "Alas! And Did My Savior Bleed?"; "And Can It Be?"; "Behold the Lamb"; "Hallelujah, What a Savior"; "When I Survey the Wondrous Cross"; and "There Is a Redeemer." (More will be listed in the topical section of your hymnal's index or by those who lead worship in your church.)

Divide the class into small groups. Provide each group with the words to two songs and ask members to analyze the words: What aspect of Christ's suffering do those songs emphasize? Is it an accurate portrayal? Overall, how does music help in highlighting and emphasizing the things that Scripture emphasizes? What part can music play in encouraging from us an appropriate response to Jesus' suffering?

Observe that John records the inscription that Pilate had attached to the cross: JESUS OF NAZARETH THE KING OF THE JEWS (John 19:19). It was posted in three different languages so that all would know the crimes. The chief priests asked Pilate to change the inscription, but he would not. While such a sign was a common means for posting the crime of the person being crucified, the inscription reflects the truth that Jesus was crucified for who He was rather than anything He did.

Discuss why Jesus would suffer these things. *(He died for our sins, Isaiah 53:5, 6 and 1 Peter 2:24; He is the good Shepherd who laid down His life for us, John 10:11).* We have considered the great price paid or the "cost" to Jesus. Jesus fully knew what He was facing (no "hidden" costs) and He still paid the price as He willingly let Himself be the sacrifice for our sins (Hebrews 2:14, 15). Discuss ways to remind each other on a daily basis this week about the great sacrifice Jesus made to save us from our sin.

Into Life

Ask students to list five things it "costs" a person to follow Jesus. Say, "In each of these five matters/elements, what sacrifices have you made for being His follower? Are there ways you know you should intensify your commitment or increase your personal sacrifice? What holds you back from that commitment?"

Let's Talk It Over

The questions on this page are designed to promote discussion of the lesson by the class and to encourage application of the lesson Scriptures. The answers provided are only discussion starters. Let your class talk it over from there.

1. Combining our text with Matthew 27:44 and Luke 23:39-43, we learn that one of the thieves had a change of heart after first having taunted Jesus. Why this change? How can we influence people to have a similar change of heart?

We can only guess at the reason for the thief's change of heart, but it could have come about because of the regal way Jesus faced death. Just as the centurion also noticed something divine about Jesus (Mark 15:39), so did this thief.

This speaks volumes about the importance of our own example, especially as we face difficult circumstances. If people of the world see that our faith in Jesus makes a difference, they will be more attracted to Him. Perhaps some of your learners can give specific examples of times when they saw the power of example change people's hearts.

2. Some writers and speakers go into great detail to describe crucifixions. They paint gruesome word pictures that evoke tears and gasps from their audiences. The Bible, however, is quite brief in this regard. Why? How should this brevity influence the amount of detail we use in describing Jesus' crucifixion today?

One reason for the Bible's brevity is that the original readers, like everyone else in the Roman Empire, knew what a crucifixion was. The very word called up horrible mental pictures for anyone who actually had seen one. Details would not have added to understanding.

Today's reader does not have the same knowledge of crucifixion or other first-century practices. It helps modern readers for someone to do research into those practices and explain them.

Even so, details that simply evoke emotional responses and do not add to understanding are not necessary. We ought to follow the example of Scripture and give only what is necessary for faith (Romans 10:17; cf. John 20:30, 31). We certainly are not to manipulate people's emotions.

3. We cringe at the callous behavior of the soldiers, gambling for Jesus' clothes while He hung dying above them. How is the same cold-hearted spirit displayed today? What similar guilt do Christians share?

Human life was cheap to those soldiers, and in many ways it is cheap to modern culture. Abor-

tion on demand and assisted suicide are two examples of this attitude. The idea of "terminating" the life of unborn children or the elderly simply because those lives inconvenience others is every bit as chilling as the attitude displayed by the soldiers. Perhaps your learners can cite additional examples.

Many issues deal with our temporary, earthly lives only, however. Are we even more callous than the soldiers when we refuse to share the message of eternal life simply because it is not convenient?

4. Jesus was concerned for others in the midst of His own pain. Have you known people who could demonstrate concern even when experiencing hardship? What gives people that kind of outward focus? How can we duplicate it?

We can attribute this concern to a sense of duty (cf. Luke 17:7-10). Some people understand that we all have a responsibility to care for others, and that that responsibility is not dimmed by personal suffering.

We can also see this concern as an act of love. Some people have such a love for others that they are able to look past their own situations to feel and respond to the pain of others. Certainly it is an expression of discipleship; these folks are trying to imitate the Master. Answering Jesus' call to total commitment is a key to duplicating His concern for others.

5. Right to the end Jesus had His mission in mind. How can we have such a sense of mission, of knowing that our lives are fulfilling a great purpose for the Lord?

Paul said, "Therefore, my beloved brethren, be ye steadfast, unmovable, always abounding in the work of the Lord, forasmuch as ye know that your labor is not in vain in the Lord" (1 Corinthians 15:58). When we have given ourselves completely to the Lord, then we, too, can have confidence that our lives have meaning and purpose. As we give ourselves over to fulfilling the Great Commission (Matthew 28:19, 20), then we share in accomplishing Jesus' mission.

Ask your learners, "If you were to die tonight, could you say with confidence, 'It is finished'? Why, or why not?" You can also use Paul's reflections on his own life as found in 2 Timothy 4:7.

The Empty Tomb

DEVOTIONAL READING: Luke 24:1-12.

BACKGROUND SCRIPTURE: Matthew 28:1-15.

PRINTED TEXT: Matthew 28:1-15.

**Apr
11**

Matthew 28:1-15

1 In the end of the sabbath, as it began to dawn toward the first day of the week, came Mary Magdalene and the other Mary to see the sepulchre.

2 And, behold, there was a great earthquake: for the angel of the Lord descended from heaven, and came and rolled back the stone from the door, and sat upon it.

3 His countenance was like lightning, and his raiment white as snow:

4 And for fear of him the keepers did shake, and became as dead men.

5 And the angel answered and said unto the women, Fear not ye: for I know that ye seek Jesus, which was crucified.

6 He is not here: for he is risen, as he said. Come, see the place where the Lord lay.

7 And go quickly, and tell his disciples that he is risen from the dead; and, behold, he goeth before you into Galilee; there shall ye see him: lo, I have told you.

8 And they departed quickly from the sepulchre with fear and great joy; and did run to bring his disciples word.

9 And as they went to tell his disciples, behold, Jesus met them, saying, All hail. And they came and held him by the feet, and worshipped him.

10 Then said Jesus unto them, Be not afraid: go tell my brethren that they go into Galilee, and there shall they see me.

11 Now when they were going, behold, some of the watch came into the city, and showed unto the chief priests all the things that were done.

12 And when they were assembled with the elders, and had taken counsel, they gave large money unto the soldiers,

13 Saying, Say ye, His disciples came by night, and stole him away while we slept.

14 And if this come to the governor's ears, we will persuade him, and secure you.

15 So they took the money, and did as they were taught: and this saying is commonly reported among the Jews until this day.

GOLDEN TEXT: And the angel answered and said unto the women, Fear not ye: for I know that ye seek Jesus, which was crucified. He is not here: for he is risen, as he said. Come, see the place where the Lord lay.—Matthew 28:5, 6.

Lesson Aims

After participating in this lesson, each student should be able to:

1. List the aspects of Matthew's resurrection account that support the reality of the resurrection.

2. Explain why a literal bodily resurrection of Jesus is believable and, in fact, vital.

3. State at least one benefit he or she enjoys because Jesus rose from the dead.

Lesson Outline

Introduction

A. Positive Negatives

Sometimes the best news is the news of what is not there. "Your tests show there is no cancer"; "We found no signs of an intruder"; "The flood waters will not affect your property"; "Your daughter was not in the house when it caught fire." The American idiom that something is "found missing" sums up this type of news. The absence of the terrible can be quite wonderful!

B. Lesson Background

The best news ever of something "found missing" was the body of Jesus. The women went to the place of Jesus' interment expecting to find a corpse. Instead, they found an angel and an empty tomb. They found Jesus' body missing!

Two wealthy and influential followers took possession of Jesus' body after His death (Matthew 27:57-60; John 19:38-42). As an executed "criminal," Jesus' body likely would simply have been thrown into a pit with those of the other two convicts, or according to Roman custom the bodies would have been left on the crosses to rot.

However, the Jewish religious leaders approached Pilate with a request. It was the Day of Preparation—the day before a special Sabbath, in this case, the Passover Sabbath—and the religious leaders did not want dead bodies left out during this special time (John 19:31). Therefore, they asked Pilate's permission to have all of the bodies removed from the crosses and disposed of. Joseph of Arimathea and Nicodemus, members of the Sanhedrin (Luke 23:50; John 3:1; 19:38, 39), were the ones who took Jesus' body and hastily prepared it for burial before sundown, the beginning of the Jewish Sabbath.

The two men anointed the body with a great quantity of spices (John 19:39), but their preparations had to be done quickly because of the coming sunset. With some exceptions, Jewish days were typically reckoned from sunset to sunset. Needing to be home before sundown, they had hurriedly placed Jesus' body in a nearby tomb owned by Joseph (Matthew 27:60; John 19:42).

I. Quest and Declaration (Matthew 28:1-7)

A. Angel's Announcement (vv. 1-3)

1. In the end of the sabbath, as it began to dawn toward the first day of the week, came Mary Magdalene and the other Mary to see the sepulchre.

Burial preparations typically are done by family members or close friends. Undoubtedly *Mary Magdalene and the other Mary* want to add their own resources to those provided by Joseph and Nicodemus. All four Gospels agree that the women came to the tomb in the earliest hours of the morning of *the first day of the week*.

There are several women named Mary mentioned in the New Testament, and we find two of them here. The word *Magdalene* simply means "from Magdala," a fishing village on the southwest shore of the Sea of Galilee. Luke 8:2 tells us that this Mary was one "out of whom went seven devils"—demons cast out by Jesus. She is privileged to be the first to learn of Jesus' resurrection.

Matthew 27:56 helps us discover that "the other Mary" is "the mother of James and Joses." She may also be "the wife of Cleophas" (John 19:25), but this is not certain. What *is* certain is that these two Marys know exactly where Jesus had been buried (see Mark 15:47).

2. And, behold, there was a great earthquake: for the angel of the Lord descended from heaven, and came and rolled back the stone from the door, and sat upon it.

Only Matthew mentions this *earthquake* in addition to the earlier one that accompanied Jesus' death (Matthew 27:51, 54). Quite possibly these were more significant to the Jewish writer Matthew than to the Gentile writers Mark and Luke, as earthquakes were sometimes associated with appearances of God on the earth in the Old Testament (e.g., 1 Kings 19:11-13; Isaiah 29:6).

Typically the tombs of wealthy men (like Joseph of Arimathea) are small caves hewn out of rock. A large, circular stone is placed in front of the opening in an inclined groove. This makes the stone fairly easy to roll into place but extremely difficult to move away. Mark 16:4 describes this stone as being "very great." Normal circumstances would require several men working with levers to move it.

But these are not normal circumstances, and the stone is moved easily by divine action. An important point to note is that the tomb is already empty when the angel arrives. The stone is not moved to let Jesus out—the stone is moved to let the women in! [See question #1, page 280.]

3. His countenance was like lightning, and his raiment white as snow.

According to Mark 16:5, the angel, or messenger from God, looks like "a young man." Apparently some kind of light emanates from his face, and his clothing is unnaturally *white*. Given the dustiness of the Judean environment, purely white clothing is undoubtedly an unusual sight —unusual enough to be noted by three of the four Gospel writers (cf. Acts 1:10). Luke tells us that there were two angels, but it is common for writers to focus on only one figure when more than one are actually present.

B. Guards' Reaction (v. 4)

4. And for fear of him the keepers did shake, and became as dead men.

The keepers, or guards, are frightened out of their senses. The shock of the angel's appearance sends them into a dead faint. Perhaps we would react the same way!

The chief priests had requested guards from Pilate for the purpose of keeping the disciples from stealing the body (Matthew 27:62-66). Most likely these are Roman guards that serve as part of the temple police, a cadre of soldiers who maintain order in the temple. They serve the wishes of the religious officials at the permission of Pilate. This would explain why the members of this team of guards report back to the chief priests initially, and not to Pilate (Matthew 28:11-15, below).

C. Women's Rejoicing (vv. 5-7)

5. And the angel answered and said unto the women, Fear not ye: for I know that ye seek Jesus, which was crucified.

The sudden appearance of *the angel* had caused the guards to pass out. His presence also puts fear into the hearts of *the women*. Angels tend to have this effect on humans; often an angel's first words to a person are *fear not* (cf. Daniel 10:12; Luke 1:13, 30; 2:10).

The angel knows why these women have come: they are looking for the body of *Jesus*. What is just as true, but unspoken, is the fact that the women are not looking for or expecting a risen Christ.

WHAT A MIXTURE OF EMOTIONS!

For seventy-seven hours in July, 2002, fear held the town of Quecreek, Pennsylvania, in its grasp: nine coal miners were trapped two hundred forty feet below ground in a flooded mine shaft. They managed to find an air pocket, but then had to wait and wonder in cold, wet, depressing darkness.

Workers above drilled an air shaft, and the miners' hopes rose. Hope was strengthened again as they heard the rescue shaft being bored toward them. But then despair came as the noise stopped for eighteen hours—the drill bit had broken, halting the rescue effort. The men vowed to live or die together and wrote out their wills, putting them into a lunch box.

But drilling resumed, and when the new drill broke through, despair turned to hope. Then, as the miners were brought to the surface one by one, hope turned to joy for the miners, their families, their rescuers, and literally an entire nation that had been watching on TV.

Visual for lesson 6

This exciting visual will remind your learners of the good news of the Easter season.

On the morning Jesus arose from where He had been entombed, there was a similar mixture of fear, despair, and joy. The guards were "frightened to death"—as the saying goes—by the sight of the angel. The women's own fear was mixed with despair that someone had stolen His body. But that despair would soon give way to joy when they heard that Jesus was alive. How blessed we are: because of their testimony we have no cause for fear or despair, only unmitigated joy!   —C. R. B.

6. He is not here: for he is risen, as he said. Come, see the place where the Lord lay.

Jesus had predicted His resurrection on more than one occasion (see Mark 8:31, 32; 9:31; 10:32-34). Even the enemies of Jesus knew about this prediction (again, Matthew 27:63). The angel reminds the women of Jesus' own words, then invites them to *see* some (but not yet all) of the proof for themselves. The tomb is empty—the cave that had never been used as a tomb before is no longer being used as one now.

7. And go quickly, and tell his disciples that he is risen from the dead; and, behold, he goeth before you into Galilee; there shall ye see him: lo, I have told you.

Matthew 26:32 records Jesus' prediction at the last supper that He would "go before you into Galilee" after His resurrection. Jesus will indeed meet them there (Matthew 28:16; John 21), but some important events in and around Jerusalem will intervene first (John 20:19-31).

II. Appearance and Conspiracy (Matthew 28:8-15)

A. Jesus' Appearance (vv. 8-10)

8. And they departed quickly from the sepulchre with fear and great joy; and did run to bring his disciples word.

Completely overwhelmed by the angel's news, the women begin running to meet the *disciples*. It takes little imagination to understand their mix of emotions. *Joy* and *fear* are natural reactions for such news! The appearance of the angel alone engendered fear; combined with the news the angel bears, these women have a front-row seat for the greatest demonstration of God's power since the creation. For them and for all of humanity, this is the most important demonstration of God's grace ever.

ACCEPTING A NEW ROLE

"Rosie the Riveter" was a determined-looking woman who wore a work shirt rolled up above her elbows and a kerchief tied about her head. She was flexing her biceps and saying, "We can do it!" Of course, Rosie was a fictional character who appeared on posters across America during World War II, encouraging women to work in the factories building machines and munitions while American men were on the battle lines fighting for freedom.

Rosie symbolized a role that women of that time were unaccustomed to playing: factory workers. They were asked to do everything men had previously done in the manufacturing processes. Without the women "manning" the factories, the men in the armed forces would not have had the materiel necessary to win the war. When the war was over, many of the women enjoyed the irony of being asked to tell the returning soldiers how to do the jobs they were coming back to!

It is highly unlikely that the women who came to the tomb on the morning of Jesus' resurrection were expecting the unaccustomed role that would soon be thrust upon them. Nevertheless, when the angel charged them with the task of announcing the resurrection to the rest of Jesus' disciples, they rose to the occasion and became the first heralds of the greatest news ever told! Are you prepared to accept whatever role God calls you to fill? *Go & Tell*   —C. R. B.

9. And as they went to tell his disciples, behold, Jesus met them, saying, All hail. And they came and held him by the feet, and worshipped him.

As the women are running to tell the *disciples*, suddenly *Jesus* Himself appears to them. What shock they must feel upon hearing Jesus' simple greeting! Jesus has just risen from the dead, the women have just talked to an angel, and Jesus starts this conversation by saying, in essence, "Hello!"

Now it all begins to come together for the women. Recognizing Jesus for who He is, they fall at His *feet* and worship Him. What more appropriate reaction can there be? No doubts remain in their mind about Him: truly He is the Christ, the Son of the Living God.

10. Then said Jesus unto them, Be not afraid: go tell my brethren that they go into Galilee, and there shall they see me.

No one can have a close encounter with the power of God and not be *afraid*. [See question #2, page 280.] When one encounters the living God, Creator of Heaven and earth, Ruler of the entire universe, it is a terrifying experience. Moses met regularly with God, as friends might meet. After those meetings Moses' face shone, likely in a way similar to that of the angel's face in our account. The result was that the Israelites wanted Moses to wear a veil to hide his face, for they were terrified of the power of their own God (Exodus 34:28-35).

When we harmonize the accounts of the four Gospels, it seems likely that the disciples did not believe the women's story. John tells us that he and Peter went to the tomb to check it out and found it empty as Mary Magdalene had told them. But even then they did not have the answers. Thomas is faulted for his refusal to believe until he can see the risen Christ with his own eyes, but all of the apostles acted in a similar manner. And although the women were told (both by the angel and by the Lord Himself) to send the disciples to *Galilee*, it will eventually take a personal appearance by the Lord to the disciples to get them moving in the right direction.

The fear felt by the disciples gives us greater confidence in the reality of the resurrection. Consider that in just the few weeks between Passover and Pentecost the disciples make a transition from cowering in locked rooms (John 20:19) to preaching fearlessly and openly in Jerusalem (Acts 2:14-41). Only the confidence given by the risen Savior can explain this dramatic turnaround.

B. Guards' Report (v. 11)

11. Now when they were going, behold, some of the watch came into the city, and showed unto the chief priests all the things that were done.

We have already discussed who the guards (the *watch*) were and why they were posted at the tomb (see v. 4, above). We cannot know exactly what *some of* them say *unto the chief priests*. But when these soldiers report *all the things that were done*, they undoubtedly include the earthquake, the angel, and the empty tomb. The guards probably did not see the risen Lord; we should not assume that these were non-Christian witnesses to the resurrection.

C. Priests' Plan (vv. 12-15)

12. And when they were assembled with the elders, and had taken counsel, they gave large money unto the soldiers.

This report by the guards creates a great deal of consternation among the religious leaders. They quickly gather together to cook up another plan. This plan involves bribing *the soldiers*.

The fact that it takes a *large* amount of *money* to pull this plan off indicates the stakes involved. The priests want this matter dealt with decisively. The story of an angel appearing would throw great doubt upon their role in Jesus' crucifixion. The chief priests and elders had declared during the crucifixion, "If he be the King of Israel, let him now come down from the cross, and

we will believe him" (Matthew 27:42). Now is their chance to realize the truth and make good on this pledge.

Truth, however, is not important to these leaders. What matters is the expediency of keeping the peace and keeping their own positions of power and influence. [See question #3, page 280.] *They* prayed for a Messiah, then rejected Jesus because He was not the kind of Messiah they wanted or were expecting. They could not believe, because they thought they knew what to expect from God.

But how often do we ourselves see the hand of God at work and refuse to believe it? We are not so different from those religious leaders at times. We pray for the healing of those in the hospital, then credit the doctors when the healing occurs. We pray for newcomers for our church, then credit our fine preaching or beautiful singing for packing them in. We pray for a new job, then credit our excellent résumé or fine interviewing skills for landing the position. We pray for rain, then complain when showers ruin our picnic.

We all need to be careful about putting God into a box of our own design. Solomon said, "But will God indeed dwell on the earth? behold, the heaven and heaven of heavens cannot contain thee; how much less this house that I have builded?" (1 Kings 8:27). If Solomon's temple could not contain God, what makes us think that the "temples of expectations" that we erect will be any more successful?

13, 14. Saying, Say ye, His disciples came by night, and stole him away while we slept. And if this come to the governor's ears, we will persuade him, and secure you.

Roman soldiers who are derelict in their duty can be executed (cf. Acts 12:18, 19). Members of

---

How to Say It

ARIMATHEA. *Air*-uh-muh-*thee*-uh (*th* as in *thin*; strong accent on *thee*).

CLEOPHAS. *Klee*-o-fus.

COLOSSIANS. Kuh-*losh*-unz.

CORINTHIANS. Kor-*in*-thee-unz (*th* as in *thin*).

JOSES. *Jo*-sez.

JUDEAN. Joo-*dee*-un.

MAGDALA. *Mag*-duh-luh.

MAGDALENE. *Mag*-duh-leen or Mag-duh-*lee*-nee.

NICODEMUS. *Nick*-uh-*dee*-mus (strong accent on *dee*).

PILATE. *Pie*-lut.

SANHEDRIN. *San*-huh-drun or San-*heed*-run.

THESSALONIANS. *Thess*-uh-*lo*-nee-unz (strong accent on *lo*; *th* as in *thin*).

the temple police are under the control of the Sanhedrin, however. With the right "connections," they may be able to escape such harsh punishment. The guards want to avoid this punishment just as much as the religious leaders want to maintain their own positions. So all agree on an "explanation" that *His disciples came by night, and stole him away while we slept.* [See question #4, page 280.]

Obviously there is no fingerprint evidence, no crime-scene investigators, no video surveillance to contradict this lie. But even without such modern investigative techniques, this is a curious lie to tell and is easily exposed. If the guards were asleep, how would they really have known what happened? If one of the soldiers had been awake and saw the disciples, why didn't he awaken the rest of the group? The obvious weaknesses in this fabrication reflect both the haste in which it is created and the desperation felt by the religious leaders.

Furthermore, we can hardly imagine the disciples being able to muster the courage to steal Jesus' body. The disciples had fled when Jesus was arrested, Peter had denied he even knew Jesus, and perhaps only John was present at His execution. We see no evidence that any of the Eleven plays a part in His burial, and they do not accompany the women on their trip to the tomb. Even after Jesus' resurrection they kept "the doors . . . shut where the disciples were assembled for fear of the Jews" (John 20:19).

In passing we should note that the chief priests seem to have paid more attention to Jesus' words than did His own disciples, for the Jewish leaders recalled that Jesus had said, "After three days I will rise again" (Matthew 27:63). [See question #5, page 280.] The women and the Eleven did not comprehend this, for it was not until after the resurrection that they understood Jesus' promises.

15. So they took the money, and did as they were taught: and this saying is commonly reported among the Jews until this day.

Matthew's Gospel is most likely written for a Jewish audience. Therefore it is quite natural that he would address a story that was circulating among the *Jews.* Rather than going into any great detail, Matthew simply reports what actually happens—Christ arises from the dead—and reports that the guards have to be bribed to tell their fabricated story.

Conclusion

A. The Power of the Resurrection

Around the time of Easter every year, various magazines and talk shows focus on the person of Jesus. I listened in dismay to one radio program in March, 2002, where three scholars (two of whom claimed to be Christian) agreed that it did not really matter if Jesus rose from the dead. To them if the "spirit" of Christ (meaning His character and His attributes) lives in our hearts, a physical resurrection is unnecessary.

Yet Jesus invited the disciples to touch and confirm the reality of His living, physical, resurrected body (Luke 24:37-39; John 20:27). The apostle Paul makes it clear that the resurrection is at the heart of Christian doctrine. He goes so far as to pin our entire faith on the truth of the resurrection: "and if Christ be not risen, then is our preaching vain, and your faith is also vain" (1 Corinthians 15:14).

Regardless of what false teachers today might say, it matters greatly whether Christ rose from the dead. If He is still in the grave, then we are still in our sins. Paul associates the resurrection with our justification (Romans 4:24, 25), with our baptism (Romans 6:4; Colossians 2:12), and with our own expectation of resurrection and eternal life (1 Thessalonians 4:14). Christ's resurrection is the centerpiece of Christianity. We can have confidence in Matthew and the other Gospel writers when they tell us what they saw: Jesus Christ is risen indeed!

B. Prayer

Lord, thank You for taking our sins on the cross. And thank You again for giving us new life—eternal life. We rely on Your power that raised Jesus from the dead, and we trust in You, the God and Father of our Lord Jesus Christ. In Jesus' name, amen.

C. Thought to Remember

Christ's resurrection guarantees ours!

Home Daily Bible Readings

Monday, Apr. 5—I Am the Resurrection (John 11:20-27)

Tuesday, Apr. 6—The Stone Is Rolled Away (Luke 24:1-5)

Wednesday, Apr. 7—The Women Remembered Jesus' Words (Luke 24:6-12)

Thursday, Apr. 8—Jesus Has Been Raised (Matthew 28:1-6)

Friday, Apr. 9—Go Quickly and Tell (Matthew 28:7-15)

Saturday, Apr. 10—Jesus Stood Among the Disciples (John 20:19-23)

Sunday, Apr. 11—Death No Longer Has Dominion (Romans 6:4-11)

Learning by Doing

This page contains an alternative lesson plan emphasizing learning activities. Classes desiring such student involvement will find these suggestions helpful.

Learning Goals

After participating in this lesson, each student will be able to:

1. List the aspects of Matthew's resurrection account that support the reality of the resurrection.

2. Explain why a literal bodily resurrection of Jesus is believable and, in fact, vital.

3. State at least one benefit he or she enjoys because Jesus rose from the dead.

Into the Lesson

Ask learners how families and churches annually celebrate Jesus' resurrection. Are special services held? Are certain songs sung? Do families have special traditions? Are certain foods eaten at the Sunday meal? Do these traditions place the focus appropriately? What traditions have members observed that they believe help people remember and celebrate the resurrection?

Into the Word

Provide the following information as background: Jesus had clearly predicted His resurrection (Matthew 20:19; Mark 8:31; 10:34; Luke 18:33). The chief priests seemed to have understood Him, for they cited His prediction as the reason to provide a guard for the tomb (Matthew 27:62-66). They simply rejected His teaching, calling Him a "deceiver" and suggesting that His followers might try to steal the body. The disciples themselves still did not understand this, even when they were confronted with the empty tomb (John 20:9).

Ask the class to consider the different responses from people as they were confronted by the empty tomb. Provide a handout to assist the students in this assignment. Read each of the following passages and describe the reactions of each to this news.

The Women: Matthew 28:8 *(they were afraid, yet filled with great joy).* **The Disciples:** John 20:3-9, 24-29 *(disbelief, confusion, and doubt, that disappeared only after meeting with the risen Christ).* **The Chief Priests:** Matthew 28:11-14 *(they rejected the possibility of the resurrection, deceitfully devised a cover story to mislead others, and bribed the soldiers to lie).* **The Guards:** Matthew 28:15 *(accepted bribe money to keep quiet, possibly out of fear for their own lives because they had failed in their duty, at least from their perspective).*

Discuss evidence you would present to members of each of these groups to confirm that Jesus truly had risen from the dead.

At times, adults study the Bible so intently for details and new information that they overlook the power and simplicity of the story. The following activity can rehearse the simple story, as well as give ideas to parents for sharing the story with their families. Gather as many of the following objects as you can: a silver coin, a thorny branch (rose stem), a large spike, a strip of linen/cotton cloth, a round flat rock, a jar of spices, an empty/full Dawn™ bottle, a plastic or paper snowflake, a small angel figurine, a map of Galilee, a watch, a large play money bill, and a small, sealed but empty box. Display the objects (either all at one time or one at a time, and ask the class to identify the item's relationship to the resurrection events as presented by Matthew and the other Gospel writers.

Into Life

Challenge the learners to repeat this object lesson to at least one person this week. Parents can go through the story with their children, showing one object each night at bedtime, reading the corresponding Scripture, discussing what happened, and expressing thanks to God for these events.

Finish class by praying together. Explain the traditional Christian greeting in which one says, "He is risen!" and the class responds in unison by saying, "He is risen indeed!" Instruct them that as you pray, whenever they hear you say, "He is risen," they should affirm their belief in this truth by saying together the response, "He is risen indeed!" Then pray aloud, looking at the past, the present, and the future. (*Past*—gratitude for the truth of the story that Jesus died in our place, paid the penalty for our sins, and then rose victoriously from the dead; *Present*—we serve a living Savior who serves as our High Priest, interceding for us and opening the way for us to come into the Father's presence in prayer [Hebrews 4:14-16]; *Future*—the resurrection of Jesus is the foundation of our hope that the dead in Christ will rise, and we can look forward to the return of Jesus and an eternity with Him [1 Corinthians 15:12-26; 1 Thessalonians 4:13-18]). As you conclude each section of your prayer, echo the phrase, "He is risen!" with " He is risen indeed!" Remind all that this is our hope.

Let's Talk It Over

The questions on this page are designed to promote discussion of the lesson by the class and to encourage application of the lesson Scriptures. The answers provided are only discussion starters. Let your class talk it over from there.

1. How would you respond to a coworker who says, "Why worry about whether Jesus rose from the dead? If His life makes you a better person, that's what's important."

The person offering this viewpoint sees only a here and now value to religion—to make people "better." If that were all there was to it, then Jesus' resurrection would make no difference. Christianity then would be just one good religious choice among other good choices.

But Jesus claimed to be the one and only way to the Father (John 14:1-6). Preparing the way for us to be with the Father required a perfect sacrifice to pay sin's price (thus, Jesus' death) and a victory over death (thus, His resurrection). Your students will find more information to help them answer this question in 1 Corinthians 15.

2. The lesson writer says, "No one can have a close encounter with the power of God and not be afraid." If that is true, how ought we to demonstrate that reality in our lives?

One expression of this fear, or reverence, is the use of our language. Certainly we will not profane the name of God, either through what is typically recognized as profanity or even with such casual references as "the Man upstairs."

Our lifestyles ought to reflect our reverence for the awe inspiring God we serve. Commenting on the end of the world (a dramatic display of God's power), Peter says we should take heed to "what manner of persons ought [we] to be in all holy conversation and godliness" (2 Peter 3:11). The careless manner in which many people live—living only for the here and now, paying no attention to eternal matters—demonstrates they do not appreciate the power and holiness of God. They need to be reminded of what the writer of Hebrews says: "It is a fearful thing to fall into the hands of the living God" (Hebrews 10:31).

3. The Jewish leaders are amazing! They have evidence of a supernatural event, and their plan is to cover it up. How could they harden their hearts in the face of such evidence? How can we reach people like this today?

The simple fact of the matter is that we will never reach some people. Jesus Himself couldn't reach everyone, and neither will we. The Jewish leaders continued to oppose God's truth, perse-

cuting the apostles and other Christian leaders, for many years.

But some of the priests actually did change (Acts 6:7). A consistent witness by life and by word can, over time, lead people to consider the gospel claims. That can lead to opportunities to study the Word of God with them, and they may come to faith. The hardness of some people's hearts is never an excuse to fail to witness for the Lord Jesus.

4. Matthew reports on the lie about the disciples stealing Jesus' body. What lies are commonly reported in our own day? How can we convince people of the truth in these areas?

Many lies are accepted as truth in modern culture. One of the biggest lies is that there is no truth, that nothing is absolute. (And the people who hold that lie believe it to be absolutely true!) Based on that lie, many others abound. One example is the lie "you only go around once" (denying the reality of life after death) and "it's your body and you can do with it as you please."

Rejecting such lies requires a shift in one's worldview to recognize that there is a Creator, and we are accountable to Him. Such a shift will not come easily. We need to demonstrate genuine concern for people and great patience as we testify to the truth. As opportunities arise, we can plant and water some seeds of truth and pray that God may give the increase (1 Corinthians 3:6).

5. The chief priests seemed to have understood Jesus' predictions of resurrection better than the disciples did. How could that be? How can modern disciples avoid the type of blindness that infected the first-century disciple?

Jesus' disciples were blinded by their own preconceived ideas about what the Messiah's kingdom would be (Acts 1:6). Death simply did not figure into the matter for them, so resurrection did not fit either. Peter, for his part, flatly rejected the idea (Matthew 16:21, 22). Perhaps the others thought that Jesus was speaking figuratively.

Whenever we read the Bible with preconceived ideas, we can suffer from the same blindness. Of course we cannot merely ignore the interpretations we have already accepted. But the more we can let the Bible interpret itself, the more harmony we will have among believers.

Faithful in His Service

DEVOTIONAL READING: 1 Thessalonians 2:13-20.

BACKGROUND SCRIPTURE: 1 Thessalonians 1–3.

PRINTED TEXT: 1 Thessalonians 1:2-10; 3:6-10.

1 Thessalonians 1:2-10

2 We give thanks to God always for you all, making mention of you in our prayers;

3 Remembering without ceasing your work of faith, and labor of love, and patience of hope in our Lord Jesus Christ, in the sight of God and our Father;

4 Knowing, brethren beloved, your election of God.

5 For our gospel came not unto you in word only, but also in power, and in the Holy Ghost, and in much assurance; as ye know what manner of men we were among you for your sake.

6 And ye became followers of us, and of the Lord, having received the word in much affliction, with joy of the Holy Ghost:

7 So that ye were ensamples to all that believe in Macedonia and Achaia.

8 For from you sounded out the word of the Lord not only in Macedonia and Achaia, but also in every place your faith to Godward is spread abroad; so that we need not to speak any thing.

9 For they themselves show of us what manner of entering in we had unto you, and how ye turned to God from idols to serve the living and true God;

10 And to wait for his Son from heaven, whom he raised from the dead, even Jesus, which delivered us from the wrath to come.

1 Thessalonians 3:6-10

6 But now when Timothy came from you unto us, and brought us good tidings of your faith and charity, and that ye have good remembrance of us always, desiring greatly to see us, as we also to see you:

7 Therefore, brethren, we were comforted over you in all our affliction and distress by your faith:

8 For now we live, if ye stand fast in the Lord.

9 For what thanks can we render to God again for you, for all the joy wherewith we joy for your sakes before our God;

10 Night and day praying exceedingly that we might see your face, and might perfect that which is lacking in your faith?

GOLDEN TEXT: We give thanks to God always for you all, making mention of you in our prayers; remembering without ceasing your work of faith, and labor of love, and patience of hope in our Lord Jesus Christ, in the sight of God and our Father.—1 Thessalonians 1:2, 3.

Living Expectantly
Unit 1: Preparing for the Lord's Return
(Lessons 7-9)

Lesson Aims

After participating in this lesson, each student should be able to:

1. Summarize Paul's commendation of the Thessalonian Christians for their active, faithful service despite difficulties.

2. Tell how faithfulness in serving God leads to victory over one's own difficulties and encourages others to be faithful as well.

3. Identify one specific way in which to serve actively and faithfully despite difficulties.

Lesson Outline

INTRODUCTION
    A. Feeling Abandoned
    B. Lesson Background
I. ACTIVE FAITH (1 Thessalonians 1:2-10)
    A. Paul's Prayer (vv. 2, 3)
      Super Movers
    B. Thessalonians' Status (vv. 4, 5)
    C. Thessalonians' Actions (vv. 6-10)
      Imitating the Master
II. GROWING FAITH (1 Thessalonians 3:6-10)
    A. Timothy's Report (v. 6)
    B. Paul's Encouragement (vv. 7-9)
    C. Paul's Longing (v. 10)
CONCLUSION
    A. The Eye of Faith
    B. Prayer
    C. Thought to Remember

Introduction

A. Feeling Abandoned

My mother told me that she would be back in just a few minutes. I was to wait quietly by the shopping carts while she went to the service desk to correct a cashier's mistake. She walked around to the other side of a cubicle and out of sight of her five-year-old son.

I knew my mother's instructions: wait quietly. I also knew that she would never abandon me. Certainly she was not away from me more than the few minutes that she promised. But those minutes felt like hours to a child who could not see his mother. I began to cry.

Soon a clerk came along and brought my mother to me. As I saw her reappear around the corner I realized that my fears were unfounded. I had never been left alone.

B. Lesson Background

Before receiving 1 Thessalonians, the readers probably felt like they had been left alone. They had faced the hardships of rejection by friends and family who did not accept their new faith (cf. 1 Thessalonians 2:14). Some may have faced economic hardships when those suspicious of the new religion took their business elsewhere. Government officials also may have questioned their loyalty to the local gods or the emperor.

Adding to the distress was the fact that the founder of the new Thessalonian church, the apostle Paul, had been forced to leave town suddenly (Acts 17:5-10). Paul's hasty departure under cover of darkness undoubtedly made some people wonder whether he was just another fast-talking, fast-moving religious con man—a figure just as common in the Roman Empire as in this age of cable television.

Paul devotes much of the first three chapters of 1 Thessalonians to assuring those Christians that neither God nor he had abandoned them. He urges them to look beyond the negative circumstances to see the signs of God's presence with them. Their faithfulness to the gospel has been matched at every step by God's power at work in their lives. In the end, Christ's return will show that God has been in control at every step and that He has been faithful to His faithful people.

I. Active Faith
(1 Thessalonians 1:2-10)

Paul's letters, like many other letters written in his day, generally begin with a statement of thanksgiving to the deity for blessings received. The deity to Paul is, of course, the one true God. In 1 Thessalonians 1, Paul uses this thanksgiving to announce a major message of his letter: the authenticity of the Thessalonians' faith is linked to the spread of the gospel. The gospel has not only spread *to* the Thessalonians, but *from* them.

A. Paul's Prayer (vv. 2, 3)
2. We give thanks to God always for you all, making mention of you in our prayers.

Paul begins many of his letters by mentioning his *prayers* of *thanks* for the people to whom he writes. Whatever else Paul has to say to the Thessalonians, prayer comes first! And the word *we* shows us that he is not alone in his prayers—Silvanus and Timothy are with him in prayer (1:1). Prayer is at the center of Paul's life. [See question #1, page 288.]

3. Remembering without ceasing your work of faith, and labor of love, and patience of hope in our Lord Jesus Christ, in the sight of God and our Father.

Paul now explains exactly what he gives thanks for. Christians are accustomed to thinking of *faith, hope,* and *love* because of 1 Corinthians 13:13. However, this trio appears in many other passages as well. (See Romans 5:1-5; Galatians 5:5, 6; Ephesians 4:2-5; Colossians 1:4, 5; 1 Thessalonians 5:8; Hebrews 6:10-12; 1 Peter 1:21, 22.)

Paul is giving thanks for more than just "armchair virtue." Faith, love, and hope provoke constant activity, like Paul's constant prayer. Elsewhere Paul sharply distinguishes faith and works to stress that salvation is not earned by what we do, but is given freely by God to those with faith in Christ. Here he stresses the other side of the faith equation: real faith always produces real works (cf. Ephesians 2:8-10; James 2:26). [See question #2, page 288.]

Labor of love builds on the work of faith. Paul has in mind the way that Christians, prompted by God's love, put love into action by sacrificing time, energy, and money for others. Genuine love is more than saying, "You were always on my mind." Like genuine faith, it produces action.

In the New Testament, *hope* is more than just an optimistic wish for the future, as in "I hope that the weather gets better soon." Rather, hope expresses a confident expectation about the future, based on trust in God's promises. Paul connects hope to *patience*, meaning steadfastness or endurance (2 Thessalonians 1:4). Our confidence that God always delivers His people makes any problem something that we can endure.

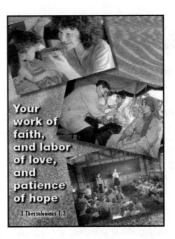

Visual for lesson 7

Use this series of images of Christians at work to illustrate today's Golden Text.

These "super movers" share a common faith in their very specialized equipment, love for their work, and an abundance of patience. In a sense, their job is an example of what we Christians are called to be: super movers! With faith in the moral and spiritual "equipment" God has given us—with love for our task of being God's reconciling agents to the world, patient assurance in God's calling, and reliance on prayer—we count ourselves to be "super movers" to accomplish, through His power, the movement of His will in human affairs (Matthew 17:20). May it be so until the Lord returns! —C. R. B.

SUPER MOVERS

The coastline near the Cape Hatteras lighthouse had been battered by the sea relentlessly. The survival of the lighthouse was threatened, so it was moved in 1999 to a safer site some twenty-nine hundred feet inland. For Jerry Matyiko, president of Expert House Movers in Sharptown, Maryland, moving the multi-million-pound tower was just another day's work (sort of). On July 9, 1999, he and his workers completed the move that took just twenty-three days.

Matyiko's company is one of just six such "super movers" worldwide. Another moved Howard Hughes's "Spruce Goose," one of the largest airplanes ever built, by barge to McMinnville, Oregon, from Long Beach, California. Yet another company moved a two-hundred-ton autoclave—twenty feet in diameter and nearly as long as a football field—eight hundred miles from an aircraft factory in Los Angeles to a military base in Ogden, Utah.

B. Thessalonians' Status (vv. 4, 5)

4. Knowing, brethren beloved, your election of God.

As he gives thanks for their faithfulness, Paul assures his readers that, by receiving the gospel, they have genuinely become God's people. Not only are they now Paul's *brethren,* they are *beloved.* They are the objects of God's favor, like Old Testament Israel (e.g., Psalms 60:5; 108:6).

Election is a term that has incited much doctrinal controversy! When placed alongside other Scriptures such as Acts 10:43 and Ephesians 1:4, 5, our best interpretation is that all who respond with genuine faith to the gospel and its plan of salvation are the chosen people of God. God's "elect" do not believe because they were chosen; rather, they are chosen because they believe. God has foreknown our belief from eternity past. That's how He can decide in advance who will be in Heaven, and who won't.

5. For our gospel came not unto you in word only, but also in power, and in the Holy Ghost, and in much assurance; as ye know what manner of men we were among you for your sake.

Paul now summarizes the evidence that the Thessalonian Christians are among God's chosen. They could easily have believed a false religious message. Their world was full of competing religions and philosophies, and not all of them could be true. But Paul reminds the Thessalonians that, by believing the *gospel*, they received something else: the *power* that comes only from God's Spirit.

Perhaps Paul also is referring to miracles that he performed in Thessalonica when he mentions "power." Although Acts 17:1-10 does not speak of any miracles in Thessalonica, Paul's ministry is commonly marked by visible demonstrations of God's power (Romans 15:18, 19). Those miracles were not ends in themselves. Rather, they are visible signs of something even greater: the eternal salvation that God was working invisibly through the gospel of Christ.

The same Holy Spirit who enabled Paul to do these acts of power now is living in the Thessalonian Christians. Although they should not necessarily expect to do miracles as the apostle did, the same Holy Spirit power works in them to make their lives consistent with the gospel. When Christians look carefully, they will see the same evidence of the Spirit's power that Paul had: living the new life that God intended, the life that produces the fruit of the Spirit (Galatians 5:22, 23).

The fact that Paul's preaching has come to the Thessalonians *in much assurance* is probably his way of speaking of his own deep conviction. Paul is not the kind of preacher who is all words and no deeds. He has shown himself to be utterly sincere and completely sold out for Jesus, and the Thessalonians can remember that. Paul's genuineness is another source of confidence that the gospel is for real.

C. Thessalonians' Actions (vv. 6-10)

6. And ye became followers of us, and of the Lord, having received the word in much affliction, with joy of the Holy Ghost.

Now Paul stresses how his readers are living out the gospel and fulfilling God's purpose in the world. Since he imitates Christ, Paul often urges Christians to imitate him (1 Corinthians 4:15, 16; 11:1; Ephesians 5:1; Philippians 3:17; 1 Thessalonians 2:14; 2 Thessalonians 3:7-9). Here he is especially stressing that the Thessalonian Christians have imitated him in accepting hardships that have come because of their faith.

The core of the gospel is Jesus' willing death on the cross in submission to God. Jesus' followers will face hardships that call for similar faithfulness (John 15:20). If we understand the cross, we realize that following Jesus will mean accept-

ing hardship, daily carrying our own crosses (Luke 9:23, 24).

That life would sound bleak except for the important fact that despite *affliction*, the Holy Spirit brings *joy* to the Christian. If we can keep our eyes on the ultimate prize of eternal life, we, too, shall have this joy despite all temporary hardship.

7. So that ye were ensamples to all that believe in Macedonia and Achaia.

As Paul has been a model of Christlikeness to the Thessalonians, so now they have become the same to others. *Macedonia* is the region of northern Greece in which Thessalonica is found. *Achaia* is the region of Greece just to the south of Macedonia that includes the important cities of Athens and Corinth. It is as if Paul is saying that the Thessalonians were known far and wide, in their own state and in the adjoining one. This really means something when we consider the rudimentary methods of communication available at the time. [See question #3, page 288.]

IMITATING THE MASTER

While grade school kids played with yo-yos and teenagers were trying the Hula Hoop® in the 1950s, their parents were "painting by the numbers." It was a time when President Eisenhower and Winston Churchill were being celebrated as amateur painters. So in America, where the culture says anyone can aspire to greatness, why not imitate the President and the Prime Minister?

Not everyone has an eye for color, composition, and form, so painting by numbers was a help to many would-be artists. Strangely enough, the idea for this genre of pop art came from the great Leonardo da Vinci! He had left numbered sections of his paintings for his assistants to fill in. Centuries later, Dan Robbins and Max Klein of the Palmer Show Card Paint Company hit upon the idea that could make anyone an artist. So for the purchase price of two dollars and fifty cents, you, too, could imagine yourself to be assistant to one of the great Masters! Today, some of those 1950s paintings are on display in a museum (a nineteenth-century townhouse in Brooklyn) devoted to the genre.

Paul told the Thessalonian Christians they were doing the right thing in imitating him and Christ. In so doing, they were also providing others with an example of how to live. It is a principle that still works today: when we follow Christ, we make it easier for others to make their lives into works of art.   —C. R. B.

8. For from you sounded out the word of the Lord not only in Macedonia and Achaia, but also in every place your faith to God-ward is spread abroad; so that we need not to speak any thing.

Now Paul draws the circle even more widely. The Thessalonian Christians may feel like a small, insignificant group of persecuted people, but from God's perspective they are powerful examples of what He wants us to be doing.

9. For they themselves show of us what manner of entering in we had unto you, and how ye turned to God from idols to serve the living and true God.

Paul now helps the Thessalonians understand the wider significance of their conversion to Christ. He does this by expressing his amazement that *they themselves*—meaning the inhabitants of places mentioned in verses 7, 8—are speaking of the reception Paul enjoyed when he preached to the Thessalonians. The Thessalonians had received his message with enthusiastic faith that brought obvious change to their lives.

In turning to Jesus Christ, the Thessalonians renounced false gods to serve the true God. The Thessalonians' world is filled with idolatry. Every region has its own local god. Even trade guilds and businesses have patron deities that they worship. Most people in Paul's day believe that if worshiping one god is good, then worshiping several is better.

The Scriptures, however, teach otherwise. There is only one true God. The pagan world is in rebellion against Him. That rebellion is most obvious in the worship of idols. But the true God promises that ultimately He will make Himself known to all the nations (Isaiah 2:2-4; 42:6; Micah 4:1-3; Zechariah 8:20-23).

This means that the Thessalonians' conversion is not just important to them personally. Through the spread of the gospel God is genuinely doing what He promised: He is making Himself known to the nations in the end time. The Thessalonians may feel insignificant, but they are at the very center of God's work in the world.

10. And to wait for his Son from heaven, whom he raised from the dead, even Jesus, which delivered us from the wrath to come.

Coming to know the true God means knowing Him through His *Son.* The Thessalonians are not just converts to Judaism, as some in the Greco-Roman world had been. They now believe that the God of Israel has fulfilled His promises through *Jesus,* who entered into human history as a man, suffered death, and rose *from the dead.*

Jesus has indeed fulfilled God's promises. But there is more fulfillment to come. As long as sin continues in the world, God's purpose is not complete. The gospel is turning the world around, but that turning will be complete only when Christ returns. Paul reminds these suffering Christians that they still look forward to God's final victory.

So where is Jesus now? Paul says that He will come *from heaven.* This means that right now Jesus is in the position of universal authority. Though He cannot be seen, Jesus rules over all the world from His heavenly position. His return will make His rule final, complete, and visible to all.

When He comes, Jesus will rescue the people of God from God's *wrath.* God's wrath can seem difficult to square with His love. How can God love the world and still have wrath? Sometimes we confuse the inconsistent, selfish anger that we see in humans with the holy wrath of God. If He is holy and just, He must abhor and punish sin. Otherwise, there would be no hope for justice in our unjust world. But how can God still love sinners and show mercy? The cross supplies the answer. In Jesus' death, God took on Himself the punishment for our sin. In this way Jesus rescues His people from *the wrath to come.*

This has been God's purpose from the beginning: to reverse the effects of sin in the world, to crush the head of the tempter (Genesis 3:15). So by believing and faithfully living out the gospel, Christians share in the fulfillment of God's promises, even in hard times.

II. Growing Faith
(1 Thessalonians 3:6-10)

In the verses between 1 Thessalonians 1:10 and 3:6 Paul recounts his labors among the Thessalonians and summarizes the circumstances that have kept him from returning. He stresses the example of his own faithfulness, the reality of hardship for God's people, and God's ongoing work in the midst of that hardship.

Recent events help Paul make his point. Concerned for the welfare of the Thessalonian

---

How to Say It

ACHAIA. Uh-*kay*-uh.

ATHENS. *Ath*-unz.

COLOSSIANS. Kuh-*losh*-unz.

CORINTH. *Kor*-inth.

CORINTHIANS. Kor-*in*-thee-unz (*th* as in *thin*).

EPHESIANS. Ee-*fee*-zhunz.

GALATIANS. Guh-*lay*-shunz.

LEONARDO DA VINCI. Lee-uh-*nard*-oh duh *Vin*-chee.

MACEDONIA. Mass-eh-*doe*-nee-uh.

MATYIKO. Mah-*tie*-eh-koh.

SILVANUS. Sil-*vay*-nus.

THESSALONIANS. *Thess*-uh-*lo*-nee-unz (strong accent on *lo*; *th* as in *thin*).

ZECHARIAH. *Zek*-uh-*rye*-uh (strong accent on rye).

church, Paul sent Timothy to visit those Christians. Timothy has now returned to Paul with an encouraging report (Acts 18:5).

A. Timothy's Report (v. 6)

6. But now when Timothy came from you unto us, and brought us good tidings of your faith and charity, and that ye have good remembrance of us always, desiring greatly to see us, as we also to see you.

Timothy's report is specific: the Thessalonians continue in the *faith* and love *(charity)* that Paul commended in 1 Thessalonians 1:3. These are indeed *good tidings!* [See question #4, page 288.]

As an example of that love, Paul mentions that the Thessalonians continue to remember him fondly. Despite his hasty departure from their city, the Thessalonians continue to regard Paul as God's ambassador. In fact, they look forward to renewing their fellowship when they are reunited, as Paul does also. Those who have experienced Jesus' love—love that binds people together despite differences and distances—can understand that the love of which Paul speaks comes only from the work of God Himself.

B. Paul's Encouragement (vv. 7-9)

7. Therefore, brethren, we were comforted over you in all our affliction and distress by your faith.

Previously Paul had been concerned about the Thessalonians. He felt the burden of separation from them as much as they did from him. Elsewhere Paul speaks of the burden that he felt for all the churches (2 Corinthians 11:28), a burden of concern for their growth and welfare. [See question #5, page 288.] Timothy's visit had encouraged the Thessalonians, and now Timothy's report encourages Paul.

Home Daily Bible Readings

Monday, Apr. 12—Paul Remembers Thessalonians' Faith (1 Thessalonians 1:1-5)

Tuesday, Apr. 13—You Have Become an Example (1 Thessalonians 1:6-10)

Wednesday, Apr. 14—Paul's Coming Was Not in Vain (1 Thessalonians 2:1-8)

Thursday, Apr. 15—You Received God's Word (1 Thessalonians 2:9-13)

Friday, Apr. 16—You Have Suffered for Christ (1 Thessalonians 2:14-20)

Saturday, Apr. 17—Timothy Sent by Paul to Encourage (1 Thessalonians 3:1-5)

Sunday, Apr. 18—Timothy Brings Back Good News (1 Thessalonians 3:6-13)

8. For now we live, if ye stand fast in the Lord.

Paul's language here seems extreme, but in fact it is very reasonable. His burden of concern is like death to him, so receiving a good report about the Thessalonians is like new life. Now that he knows of their faithfulness, he counts his joy as an example of the new life that Christians have (2 Corinthians 4:10-18). That joy will grow as the his readers continue steadfastly in faithfulness.

9. For what thanks can we render to God again for you, for all the joy wherewith we joy for your sakes before our God?

God's grace is always so great that His people can never repay it. Paul reflects on that truth now as he thinks of his *joy* because of the Thessalonians' faithfulness. The people of *God* know that the greatest joy is seeing God at work in His people. For Paul this joy is almost like the joy of Heaven!

C. Paul's Longing (v. 10)

10. Night and day praying exceedingly that we might see your face, and might perfect that which is lacking in your faith?

Paul longs to be reunited with the Thessalonians. Christians naturally feel a "holy restlessness" to be reunited when separated from their spiritual family. The great reunion is in Heaven, of course, but God gives us a foretaste of that reunion whenever we gather as His people.

Although the Thessalonians have been faithful, they have not "arrived." True Christians are always growing Christians, and Paul wants to contribute to the Thessalonians' growth—to *perfect* their faith. Do you think you have "arrived" in your Christian life, or do you admit that you have growing to do as well?

Conclusion

A. The Eye of Faith

In a world where sin seems to hold sway, God's people can easily feel lonely and discouraged. But the eye of faith sees more than just outward appearances. It sees God's work going forward in the lives of God's people. It sees past the hardships and disappointments, and recognizes the victories. It looks forward to the final victory. Seeing those things, it yields a life of faithful service: faith, love, and hope put into action.

B. Prayer

Father, help us to walk in the faithful path of the Thessalonians, now long gone. And may others walk in our faithful path, long after we are gone. In Jesus' name, amen.

C. Thought to Remember

"Be thou faithful unto death" (Revelation 2:10).

Learning by Doing

This page contains an alternative lesson plan emphasizing learning activities.
Classes desiring such student involvement will find these suggestions helpful.

Learning Goals

After participating in this lesson, each student will be able to:

1. Summarize Paul's commendation of the Thessalonian Christians for their active, faithful service despite difficulties.

2. Tell how faithfulness in serving God leads to victory over one's own difficulties and encourages others to be faithful as well.

3. Identify one specific way in which to serve actively and faithfully despite difficulties.

Into the Lesson

Choice One: Neighbor Nudge. Ask class members to turn to the persons next to them and describe difficulties that prevent them from serving Christ actively and faithfully. Encourage all to be as specific as possible. What situations discourage them? What fears do they have that prevent them from serving actively and faithfully?

Allow about five minutes for this activity to introduce the lesson. After about two minutes, say, "If your partner has not started to share yet, wrap it up quickly and let him or her begin."

Call for three volunteers to tell their difficulties to the whole class. After they do, say, "All of us have difficulties that discourage us from serving Christ actively and faithfully. Keep these in mind as we look at today's text and watch for answers to our difficulties." (This activity is in the student book.)

Choice Two: Brainstorm. Ask the class to help you compile a list of difficulties that that prevent Christians today from actively and faithfully serving Christ. The purpose of brainstorming is to create a list that is as long as possible, so ask people to call out their responses quickly. Direct class members not to comment or evaluate during the listing.

Make a list so that the entire class can see it. Use an overhead projector, a marker board, or a large piece of paper taped to the wall.

After you have a long list, read through it. Ask class members to raise their hands when you read a topic that is difficult for them. Put stars by the ones that receive many votes.

Make the transition to the lesson by saying, "All of us have difficulties that discourage us from serving Christ actively and faithfully. Let's keep these problems in mind as we look at the text and watch for answers to our difficulties."

Into the Word

Choice One: Marginal Markings. Ask your class to put marks in the margins of their Bibles or class books. Put one of these symbols beside each verse:

"**C**"—Something for which Paul commended the Thessalonians.

"**?**"—I have a question about what this verse means.

"**E**"—A verse with a source of encouragement for me and other Christians.

Then take a poll, verse-by-verse, as to which verses were marked with question marks; take time to discuss answers to the questions learners ask. (The commentary will help.) Discuss the verses that received the other marks.

Choice Two: Praise List. Ask your class members to list the things for which Paul commended the Thessalonians. For example, he commended them for their work of faith, labor prompted by love, and endurance inspired by hope (1:3). Or he said they had been models of service in the face of difficulties (1:7). Learners should be able to find something in almost every verse. (This activity is included in the student book.)

Into Life

Choice One: Prayer of Thanks. Ask class members to write a prayer for a young Christian, based on how Paul prayed for the Thessalonians. Or they might paraphrase the text and make it a prayer. For example, "Dear God, I am always thanking you for Charles, mentioning him by name in all my prayers. I thank you for his work produced by faith, his labor prompted by love, and his endurance inspired by hope." (This activity is included in the student book.)

Choice Two: Hymn Study. Many songs and hymns encourage believers to be faithful in the face of difficulties. Have groups of students look at such hymns or songs together and compare each with the encouragement Paul gives in today's text. For example, "His Eye Is on the Sparrow" (by Civilla D. Martin) says the believer can sing because he or she is happy. This is like 1 Thessalonians 1:6, where Paul says we can have joy given by the Holy Spirit in spite of severe suffering. Or verse two from "God Will Take Care of You" (also by Martin) says, "Beneath his wings of love abide." This parallels 1 Thessalonians 1:4 where Paul says we are loved by God.

Let's Talk It Over

The questions on this page are designed to promote discussion of the lesson by the class and to encourage application of the lesson Scriptures. The answers provided are only discussion starters. Let your class talk it over from there.

1. Paul constantly prayed for his new converts. Why is it important that we do the same? What methods can we use?

Satan likes to attack Christians at their most vulnerable times. "Babes in Christ" are his prime targets. Prayer not only helps keep Satan away, it also reminds us of our need to help in tangible ways.

Some churches promote prayer by publishing names of new Christians in bulletins and church newsletters. Such churches might do this for up to a year so that all members can be praying for them. (Do this only with the person's permission, however.) Every leader of the church should have the names and needs of new Christians recorded in personal prayer journals.

2. Discuss some specific ways that we can move from "armchair virtue" to real virtue. What "works" will show our faith, and what "labors" will show our love?

This will be a freewheeling discussion since there are thousands of ways to demonstrate our faith and love. Point out that both types of virtues are like calories: they can't actually be seen, only their results can.

"Armchair virtue" makes itself known when we merely focus on what we don't do: sinful thoughts and behavior, etc. That's okay as far as it goes, but real virtue is more active. Among the many ways we demonstrate active faith is in church attendance, a willingness to speak of our Savior to friends and peers, and in acts of mercy. Brainstorm specific "labors" of kindness your class could do for such groups as single mothers, the elderly, unbelieving neighbors, the poor, the grieving, recent converts, our enemies, etc.

3. Paul notes how a seemingly insignificant people became powerful examples of faith to others. How have you been influenced by such people? How have you passed this influence on to others?

Answers will be highly individual. Many will speak of parents who, though just "ordinary" people, showed day in and day out how to live with faith through trials, fears, and tears. Some will mention seemingly "no-name" preachers, teachers, youth leaders, and church members whose steady examples, steadfast interest, words of encouragement, cheerful spirits, considerate and thoughtful deeds, and regular prayers made (and make) profound differences in how they live.

With the power of the Holy Spirit within us, there is no reason all of us "ordinary" Christians cannot have extraordinary influence on the people around us. There are many opportunities to do kind deeds to hurting people, and we have no excuse for not making a lasting impact on someone's life.

4. Thinking about Timothy's encouraging news, how might one of your previous ministers be encouraged (or discouraged) by news of the progress (or regress) of your church since he's been gone?

We can evaluate progress (or lack thereof) partially in terms of numbers: attendance trends, baptisms, and transfers of membership are examples. Attitudes such as enthusiasm, love for one another, and harmony are more difficult to measure, but are no less vital. Which areas your learners mention will reveal what each thinks is relatively more important.

It is important not to allow this discussion to turn into a negative gripe session. To keep the conversation constructive, you can suggest to your learners that they think in terms of where the church should be six months from now, and what your church should start doing right now to ensure that that report would be an encouraging one. Then get to it!

5. In their excitement some Christians overstate how "rosy" the new life in Christ is. What can we do to avoid misleading new or potential believers in this way?

Honesty is important. That means we must make an effort to give a realistic picture of the Christian life. We can emphasize several things. First, trials and suffering are common to every human being, including believers. Second, some trials (persecution, slander, etc.) will come *because* we are Christian. Third, God uses hardships to improve our character and make us stronger. Fourth, God also promises us strength to see us through our trials and provides an eternal hope that makes our temporary suffering bearable. (See Romans 5:3, 4; 8:17, 18; James 1:2-4; 1 Peter 1:6-9; 4:13-17; 5:10.)

Ready for His Return

DEVOTIONAL READING: 1 Thessalonians 5:12-24.

BACKGROUND SCRIPTURE: 1 Thessalonians 4, 5.

PRINTED TEXT: 1 Thessalonians 4:13-18; 5:2-11.

1 Thessalonians 4:13-18

13 But I would not have you to be ignorant, brethren, concerning them which are asleep, that ye sorrow not, even as others which have no hope.

14 For if we believe that Jesus died and rose again, even so them also which sleep in Jesus will God bring with him.

15 For this we say unto you by the word of the Lord, that we which are alive and remain unto the coming of the Lord shall not prevent them which are asleep.

16 For the Lord himself shall descend from heaven with a shout, with the voice of the archangel, and with the trump of God: and the dead in Christ shall rise first:

17 Then we which are alive and remain shall be caught up together with them in the clouds, to meet the Lord in the air: and so shall we ever be with the Lord.

18 Wherefore comfort one another with these words.

1 Thessalonians 5:2-11

2 For yourselves know perfectly that the day of the Lord so cometh as a thief in the night.

3 For when they shall say, Peace and safety; then sudden destruction cometh upon them, as travail upon a woman with child; and they shall not escape.

4 But ye, brethren, are not in darkness, that that day should overtake you as a thief.

5 Ye are all the children of light, and the children of the day: we are not of the night, nor of darkness.

6 Therefore let us not sleep, as do others; but let us watch and be sober.

7 For they that sleep sleep in the night; and they that be drunken are drunken in the night.

8 But let us, who are of the day, be sober, putting on the breastplate of faith and love; and for a helmet, the hope of salvation.

9 For God hath not appointed us to wrath, but to obtain salvation by our Lord Jesus Christ,

10 Who died for us, that, whether we wake or sleep, we should live together with him.

11 Wherefore comfort yourselves together, and edify one another, even as also ye do.

Apr 25

GOLDEN TEXT: For God hath not appointed us to wrath, but to obtain salvation by our Lord Jesus Christ.—1 Thessalonians 5:9.

Living Expectantly
Unit 1: Preparing for the Lord's Return
(Lessons 7-9)

Lesson Aims

After participating in this lesson, each student should be able to:

1. Tell what Paul said about Christ's return and how Christians ought to live in anticipation of it.

2. Explain how hope in Christ's return brings comfort, even when loved ones die before that event.

3. Evaluate his or her feelings about the Lord's return and express them verbally or artistically.

Lesson Outline

INTRODUCTION
    A. Two Views of Death
    B. Lesson Background
  I. REUNION AT CHRIST'S RETURN (1 Thessalonians 4:13-18)
    A. Assurance of God's Promise (vv. 13, 14)
      Reunions
    B. Particulars of Christ's Return (vv. 15-17b)
      A Long-Awaited Return
    C. Results of God's Faithfulness (vv. 17c, 18)
 II. LIFE UNTIL CHRIST'S RETURN (1 Thessalonians 5:2-11)
    A. Expecting the Unexpected (vv. 2, 3)
    B. Living in the Light (vv. 4-8)
    C. Fulfilling God's Purpose (vv. 9-11)
CONCLUSION
    A. The Hope of His Return
    B. Prayer
    C. Thought to Remember

Introduction

A. Two Views of Death

Cemeteries tell stories. In some cultures, people were buried with important objects from their lives. In America of a bygone era, gravestones often listed the relatives and accomplishments of the deceased. Today the practices may be different, but the messages persist. To one gravestone mourners attach a deck of cards, a bottle of whiskey, and a pack of cigarettes—mementos of a life of hopeless indulgence. Beside it stands another marker with the simple inscription, "In hope of the resurrection of the dead."

How we look at death determines how we look at life. If death is the end of our existence, then at best life is, as one writer put it, "the unpleasant interruption of nothingness."

But the Bible teaches something different. God is faithful to His people even in death. Death for the Christian is not the end. It means being with Christ in an even greater way than we have been in this life. And at Christ's return, all of His people, those who have died and those who are still alive, will be reunited. The sting of death is gone!

B. Lesson Background

Acts 17:1-10 tells us that Paul was forced to leave Thessalonica because of persecution. As a result it appears that he did not have the time to instruct the church thoroughly in the gospel's implications. It appears that after Paul left, some in the church were troubled by the ongoing reality of death. Perhaps the death of some member of the church prompted a crisis of faith for those who remained. What would happen to a Christian who died? How would God fulfill His promises to a person if that person were no longer alive?

Likewise, it appears that the Thessalonian Christians struggled to understand Christ's return. Those who knew the Old Testament understood its promise of a coming Messiah. Christians understood that Jesus is that Messiah. But the idea that the Messiah would ascend to Heaven and return a second time was new. What did this mean for His people on earth? What could it mean for those who had died?

These are the kinds of questions that Paul addresses in this passage. Properly understood, the promise of the Lord's return radically changes our idea of life and death.

I. Reunion at Christ's Return (1 Thessalonians 4:13-18)

The foundation of the New Testament's teaching on Christ's return is God's faithfulness. As things stand, sin and evil are still rampant in the world. God's people suffer all kinds of evil, including the final evil, death. Will God abandon them to this situation? God answers this question with an unqualified *no*. When Jesus returns, He will bring the final defeat of evil. He will reverse the effects of sin, including death. All of His people, living and dead, will be reunited with Him and will remain with Him forever.

A. Assurance of God's Promise (vv. 13, 14)

13. But I would not have you to be ignorant, brethren, concerning them which are asleep, that ye sorrow not, even as others which have no hope.

In Paul's day it is common to refer to death politely as sleep (cf. John 11:11-14; Acts 7:60;

13:36). This figure of speech is suggested by the similarity in appearance between sleeping people and dead bodies. It does not imply that the dead have no consciousness beyond the grave, what some call "soul sleep." Paul will make that clear in verse 14 and in other passages (2 Corinthians 5:1-10; Philippians 1:20-23).

Paul's remark about *sorrow* must be carefully understood. He does not criticize the Thessalonian Christians for the natural sadness that they feel over the death of fellow Christians (cf. Philippians 2:27). Rather, their grief is not to be like that of the pagans, who *have no hope* of ever seeing their deceased loved ones again. When Christians lose a fellow Christian to death, they will grieve the loss as they feel the void that has been left in their lives. But their grief will be tempered by the assurance that God will reunite them. [See question #1, page 296.]

14. For if we believe that Jesus died and rose again, even so them also which sleep in Jesus will God bring with him.

The foundation of this hope is Jesus' own resurrection from the dead. By raising Jesus from the dead, God began to fulfill His promise to raise His people from the dead as well (Isaiah 26:16-19). Jesus' resurrection therefore can be compared with a down payment or guarantee that God will complete His promise by raising all His people (1 Corinthians 15:20-23).

Furthermore, Paul says, Christ's resurrection means the defeat of death. It gives us the assurance that He will bring the dead in Christ *with him* when He returns. Christians who die are with Christ in Heaven and will continue to be with Him when He returns. [See question #2, page 296.]

REUNIONS

Every year since 1947 the "Doolittle Raiders" have met to remember their comrades who died in an April, 1942, air raid on Japan that was America's first hopeful news since Pearl Harbor. Lieutenant Colonel Jimmy Doolittle had led sixteen B-25 bombers in a response ordered by President Roosevelt to show America's resolve to win a war it didn't want to fight.

A carrier take-off in B-25s had never been done in battle; it was impossible to land them back on the carrier. The pilots hoped they could fly on to China, but they suspected they might not make it that far. Jacob DeShazer was one of the crew members who had to bail out over Japan.

DeShazer later said that as interrogation, torture, and the executions of his comrades were causing him to lose hope, his captors gave him a Bible. He relates how the Bible's message of salvation caused him to "feel free and ready to die

or to do whatever God wants me to do." His hope in Christ carried him through more than three years in prison camp. After the war was over, he soon returned to Japan as a missionary to share the hope he had experienced!

The number who attend the annual gatherings of these aged comrades-in-arms is shrinking every year. But DeShazer knows a greater reunion is ahead of him. That is the kind of hope Paul was trying to get us to experience—a hope that is assured in its outcome because of our faith in Christ.   —C. R. B.

B. Particulars of Christ's Return (vv. 15-17b)

15. For this we say unto you by the word of the Lord, that we which are alive and remain unto the coming of the Lord shall not prevent them which are asleep.

Paul now begins to describe what Jesus' return will entail. His purpose here is not just to satisfy curiosity or to stimulate speculation. Rather, he aims to supply those details that will make a meaningful difference in the lives of his readers.

He begins by indicating that those who *are alive* when Christ returns will have no advantage over those who have died. In the antique English of the *King James Version* the word *prevent* means "precede" or "go before." This is probably not so much a statement of the chronology of events (which would matter little) as it is of the quality of events. Both the living and the dead in Christ will participate fully in the joy of His return.

16. For the Lord himself shall descend from heaven with a shout, with the voice of the archangel, and with the trump of God: and the dead in Christ shall rise first.

Shouts and trumpet blasts—what a celebration at Christ's return as *the voice of* a mighty *archangel* proclaims the victory! Christ's victory will be complete with the unfolding of this great event, and no one will be able to mistake it.

Again assuring readers that all Christ's people will participate fully in His return, Paul stresses that *the dead in Christ shall rise first.* They will not miss out on the celebration.

How to Say It

AMOS. *Ay*-mus.
AZERBAIJAN. Ah-zer-bye-*shahn*.
EPHESIANS. Ee-*fee*-zhunz.
ISAIAH. Eye-*zay*-uh.
RAPERE (Latin). rap-*ear*.
THESSALONIANS. *Thess*-uh-*lo*-nee-unz (strong accent on *lo*; *th* as in *thin*).
THESSALONICA. *Thess*-uh-lo-*nye*-kuh (strong accent on *nye*; *th* as in *thin*).

Of course, Paul had just spoken of Christ bringing the dead "with him." So in what sense will they then "rise"? Many believe that the spirits of the faithful live without bodies in the presence of Christ until His return; at that time, their spirits come with Christ to take possession of their new bodies—bodies fit for the life of eternity. Others believe the dead have "spiritual bodies" until the time of Christ's return; at that time those bodies will be glorified in various degrees.

17a, b. Then we which are alive and remain shall be caught up together with them in the clouds, to meet the Lord in the air.

What a magnificent "reunion" this will be! *Caught up* implies a sudden, dramatic action. (The Latin translation here is *rapere* and is the basis for the expression "rapture.") *Clouds* sometimes appear in Scripture to depict the powerful presence of God (Exodus 13:21; Daniel 7:13; Acts 1:9). Meeting together in the clouds and the air suggests that God will gather people in the midst of His glorious presence, sharing in His victory. [See question #3, page 296.]

A LONG-AWAITED RETURN

In a ceremony at the U.S. Customs House in July, 2001, fifteen million dollars' worth of artwork by Rembrandt and Dürer were returned to representatives of Germany's Bremen museum. The masterpieces had hung there for a century before being hidden during World War II. At the end of the war, Soviet troops took them as booty. The KGB then sent them to a museum in Azerbaijan.

Later, the art works were again stolen. Years passed, and somehow the paintings and drawings were smuggled into America. A former Olympic wrestler from Japan teamed up with a counterpart from Azerbaijan, and together they tried to sell the art to raise money for a kidney transplant. Finally, authorities tracked the art to a Brooklyn, New York, apartment in 1997. There it was recovered and the perpetrators arrested.

This string of incidents reminds us that when something of great value has been missing for a long time, there is still hope for its return. God's most valuable gift to humanity—the one Person who has been the subject of more artistic works than any other in history—has been "missing" for twenty centuries. But Jesus left His followers with the promise that He would return. Paul informs us of some details of His return, but more importantly, Paul assures us of the *fact* of Jesus' return. We serve a God who keeps His word! —C. R. B.

C. Results of God's Faithfulness (vv. 17c, 18)

17c. And so shall we ever be with the Lord.

Paul now draws out the key implication of his description: God will not abandon His people. At Christ's return, God will reunite all His people fully in His presence. They will never be separated from Him or from each other.

This teaching is not just a vague "whispering hope" that gives mild comfort. God's purpose in creation is to make for Himself a people who will belong to Him, living in fellowship with Him and with each other for eternity. God will see His people through to that goal!

18. Wherefore comfort one another with these words.

The passage has now turned full circle. Having begun with the objective that the readers not grieve hopelessly (v. 13), Paul now urges that they use this teaching to encourage and *comfort one another*. [See question #4, page 296.] That encouragement and comfort will come from the assurance that death does not mean final separation from the fellow Christians whom we love, or any separation from the Lord who loves us.

What a comfort it is indeed to serve such a God! As long as we do not drift away of our own accord (Hebrews 2:1-3), nothing can separate us from His love, not even death itself (Romans 8:38, 39). In the end, He will gather the multitude of His people (Revelation 21:3, 4). He is with us "till we meet again . . . at Jesus' feet."

II. Life Until Christ's Return
(1 Thessalonians 5:2-11)

The New Testament's teaching about Jesus' return revolves around two poles. One is that Jesus could return at any time. The other is that His return may take longer than His people expect or hope. Both of these ideas appear in the passage before us. Together, they urge Christians to live with expectancy and endurance. [See question #5, page 296.]

A. Expecting the Unexpected (vv. 2, 3)

2. For yourselves know perfectly that the day of the Lord so cometh as a thief in the night.

Paul has just stated that he has no need to teach the Thessalonians about "the times and the seasons" (5:1). By this he does not mean that they know the time of the Lord's return or can figure it out (cf. Matthew 24:36). Paul's whole discussion insists that the time of Jesus' return is unknown. Rather, he is stressing that they should be able to understand that the times and seasons call for alertness, a sense of urgency, and a readiness to remain faithful through difficulties.

Jesus Himself compared His return with the coming of *a thief in the night* (Matthew 24:43; Luke 12:39; see also 2 Peter 3:10; Revelation 3:3; 16:15). Two observations should be made about this statement. First, His arrival will occur at a time that is unexpected. Some have understood the "thief" to arrive and depart secretly (as in the so-called "secret rapture"), but this is not the point of these texts.

Second, Jesus comes as a "thief" only for those who are unprepared. Jesus' return is a disaster only for those who do not believe in Him and do not await Him expectantly. Believers, ready for His return at any time, welcome Him because He brings blessing. In Jesus' return, Christians have everything to look forward to and nothing to fear.

Paul refers to Jesus' return as *the day of the Lord.* This is an Old Testament expression that was used to refer to any action of God that brought great blessing or judgment (see Isaiah 13:6-16; Joel 1:15; Amos 5:18-20). Any such action can be "the day of the Lord," but the Scriptures anticipate a final "day"—God's final act of blessing and judgment. Jesus' return means God's final victory, the ultimate fulfillment of His purpose for creation.

3. For when they shall say, Peace and safety; then sudden destruction cometh upon them, as travail upon a woman with child; and they shall not escape.

Here we see the grave mistake of unbelievers who do not expect the day of the Lord. For them life seems to have peace. However, Paul teaches that real peace is available only through Christ (Romans 5:1; 1 Thessalonians 1:1; 5:23). So instead of safety, unbelievers face destruction—the complete ruin of their confidence and comfort—when Jesus returns.

Like labor pains, this event will happen suddenly and without the possibility of escape. In keeping with the context, we should not conclude that one can calculate in advance the approximate time of Jesus' return as an expectant mother can calculate the approximate time of her delivery. The comparison of Jesus' return to labor pains implies only that it is sudden and inescapable.

B. Living in the Light (vv. 4-8)

4. But ye, brethren, are not in darkness, that that day should overtake you as a thief.

Now Paul says openly what he has been implying previously. The fearful aspects of Jesus' return exist only for unbelievers. For believers, Jesus comes not as an unexpected *thief* who brings disaster, but as an expected deliverer bringing salvation.

Paul will now develop another aspect of His comparison. For unbelievers, Jesus comes as a thief in the night. Yet Christians are not people of the night but of the day. The contrast between a life in the darkness and a life in the light will make clear what it means to expect Jesus' return at any time.

Visual for lesson 8. *Use this powerful visual to remind your learners that the "sunset" of earthly life will give way to the "sunrise" of eternal life.*

5. Ye are all the children of light, and the children of the day: we are not of the night, nor of darkness.

The Bible commonly associates *light* with God. God's first words in Scripture are "Let there be light" (Genesis 1:3). God's truth is often compared with light (Psalm 27:1; Proverbs 4:18, 19; Isaiah 9:2; Matthew 5:14; 1 John 2:8). In a figurative usage in the Bible, to be *children of* something means to be characterized by that thing. So Christians are to be characterized by the light of God's truth.

The life *of darkness,* on the other hand, is a life centered on satisfying the self. In contrast to such a self-centered life, the gospel teaches a life of self-control and of being submissive to the will of God. The cross of Christ is one pillar of this new life: in the cross we see the horror of sin and the wonder of God's love. Another pillar is Jesus' return: He comes to bless His people and judge unbelievers. Supported by these pillars, who would want to have anything to do with the sin that God forgives through Jesus' death and judges at His return?

6, 7. Therefore let us not sleep, as do others; but let us watch and be sober. For they that sleep sleep in the night; and they that be drunken are drunken in the night.

Paul continues to expand on the comparisons that he has made earlier. People who do not reckon with Jesus' return are like those who *sleep* or get drunk at *night.* They are insensitive to and unconscious of spiritual truth. They are unresponsive to the stern reality of God's coming judgment.

8. But let us, who are of the day, be sober, putting on the breastplate of faith and love; and for a helmet, the hope of salvation.

God first words in scripture Let there be light

In contrast to those who live as if asleep or drunk, Christians are to live as faithful soldiers on sentry duty. They are alert, watchful, and prepared. *Sober* here means much more than just avoiding the intoxicating influence of alcohol. It means being self-controlled in all matters. Such self-control comes only when a person submits in faith to the God who will bring judgment. *Putting on* the armor of God is how the submissive believer becomes self-controlled. Paul compares God's provision for the Christian with armor in Romans 13:12 and Ephesians 6:10-17 as well.

The means to godly self-control are the three great Christian virtues of *faith, love,* and *hope* (see also 1 Thessalonians 1:3). *Faith* directs the believer to submit to God's truth, confident that God is right in all that He says. *Love* directs us to act to benefit others rather than to indulge our selfish desires. *Hope* enables us to endure the hardships that faith and love entail, knowing that God will bring *salvation* in the future. "Hope of salvation" is not just a belief that we have "a chance" to be saved, but is a confident expectation that God will certainly fulfill His promise to save.

C. Fulfilling God's Purpose (vv. 9-11)

9. For God hath not appointed us to wrath, but to obtain salvation by our Lord Jesus Christ.

God's holiness demands that He judge and punish sin. Even so, He does not delight in punishing sinners but seeks to forgive them. Yet such mercy cannot be taken for granted. It is awful to treat God's grace as something cheap by continuing to sin because of the promise of forgiveness. Rather, if sin makes God's *wrath* necessary, we must recoil from it. We must live according to the purpose for which God *appointed us:* not to be punished, but to be saved.

Likewise, we must understand the reality of God's judgment from the vantage of His gracious purpose to save. Final judgment is real, and the danger of "falling asleep" and being surprised by judgment like an unbeliever is also real. But God has given us every protection because He intends to save us, not judge us. We can therefore be confident, not anxious and worried.

10. Who died for us, that, whether we wake or sleep, we should live together with him.

When we speak of God's purpose, we should remember what He did to accomplish it: He gave His Son in death to save undeserving sinners. When Jesus died *for us,* He became a substitutionary sacrifice: He died in place of the people who deserved to die. If God will do that to save sinners, surely He will provide everything they need to come to the goal of their salvation!

Paul continues to speak of waking and sleeping here, but now he has returned to the comparison between death and *sleep* that he used in 1 Thessalonians 4:13-15. He repeats his earlier point that God will be faithful to His promise. Even death cannot keep Him from saving His people and uniting them in His presence forever.

11. Wherefore comfort yourselves together, and edify one another, even as also ye do.

Just as he does in 4:18, Paul tells his readers to remind each other of the practical value of understanding Jesus' return. For the believer, it is a source of joy, encouragement, and motivation. It shows us what He created us for and how we need to live out His purpose in the world. So Paul tells us to use this message constantly with each other, so that God's saving purpose can be fulfilled in all of us.

Conclusion

A. The Hope of His Return

As it is sometimes presented, Jesus' return can seem strange and fantastic, like science fiction. For many Christians, it seems frightening. When we really see what Paul says in this passage, we understand that it is neither. Jesus' return is the purposeful end of everything God has done, the climax of His program. For the believer it means the fulfillment of our fondest hopes and healing of our deepest hurts. It changes life from hopeless self-indulgence to hopeful, purposeful service.

B. Prayer

Father, bring to our minds again the hope to which we have been called. Empower us to live in light of that hope! In Jesus' name, amen.

C. Thought to Remember

God's future determines my present.

Home Daily Bible Readings

Monday, Apr. 19—Live to Please God (1 Thessalonians 4:1-7)

Tuesday, Apr. 20—Live Quietly (1 Thessalonians 4:8-12)

Wednesday, Apr. 21—The Lord Will Return (1 Thessalonians 4:13-18)

Thursday, Apr. 22—He Will Come as a Thief (1 Thessalonians 5:1-5)

Friday, Apr. 23—Be Alert (1 Thessalonians 5:6-11)

Saturday, Apr. 24—Encourage the Fainthearted (1 Thessalonians 5:12-18)

Sunday, Apr. 25—Prayer for Blamelessness at Christ's Coming (1 Thessalonians 5:19-28)

Learning by Doing

This page contains an alternative lesson plan emphasizing learning activities.
Classes desiring such student involvement will find these suggestions helpful.

Learning Goals

After participating in this lesson, each student will be able to:

1. Tell what Paul said about Christ's return and how Christians ought to live in anticipation of it.

2. Explain how hope in Christ's return brings comfort, even when loved ones die before that event.

3. Evaluate his or her feelings about the Lord's return and express them verbally or artistically.

Into the Lesson

Choice One: Agree/Disagree. Ask your class to respond to the following agree/disagree statements designed to encourage class members to express what they understand about, and their feelings associated with, the return of Christ. Say, "I will read each statement and then count to three. On *three*, indicate your response by raising your right hand if you agree with the statement, your left hand if you disagree." (This activity is included in the student booklet.)

1. The idea of Christ's return causes me to be afraid.

2. The Scriptures tell us the approximate time of the return of Christ.

3. When a Christian dies, his or her soul sleeps until Jesus comes again.

4. Signs will precede the return of Christ.

5. The concept of the return of Christ should cause people to be alert and ready.

6. Christians will be surprised at the return of Christ.

7. Anticipating the return of Christ is a source of encouragement and joy for me.

Choice Two: Write a Letter. Read the letter printed below to your class. Then ask, "How would you respond to Erica's questions?" Allow class members to give possible responses.

"Dear Friend, I am really confused about the second coming of Christ. Some books I have read are so dogmatic about details of the return of Christ. Is it possible to know when Jesus will return? What signs will precede the return of Christ so that Christians will be ready? What passages in the New Testament can I read to find answers? Please help. —Your friend, Erica." (This is included in the student booklet.)

Make the transition to the lesson by saying, "Today's lesson text looks at the questions posed to 'Erica' that we have been trying to answer. As we study today's lesson, watch for answers for Erica."

Into the Word

Choice One: Bible Quiz. Have class members write a Bible quiz on today's text, trying to write a question for each verse. Assign this to be done in pairs, or have the whole class work together, as you write the questions for all to read.

A sample question from 1 Thessalonians 4:13: "True or False—Christians grieve at the death of a loved one just like anyone else." Or 1 Thessalonians 5:8 may suggest, "What three things should Christians do in anticipation of the second coming of Christ?" (This activity is included in the student booklet.)

Choice Two: Guest Speaker. Many congregations have a "resident expert" on the second coming. Ask your preacher or an elder to suggest a guest speaker. Your "expert" will enjoy the opportunity to expound on this oft-misunderstood topic; the class will enjoy hearing someone else.

Into Life

Choice One: Write a Letter. Ask class members to write a letter to "Erica" (see "Into the Lesson," above) and answer her questions from today's lesson. Provide paper and pens. Or have your class members write encouragement and joy to someone (such as a missionary, military personnel, or someone incarcerated) based on the text. Have addresses, envelopes, and postage ready.

Choice Two: Responsive Reading. Lead your class in a responsive reading, using ideas from today's text. Since Paul uses the phrase, "Comfort one another" twice in the text, use the phrase, "Comfort one another with these words," as a refrain after each verse in the style of Psalm 136. A reading might read like this:

"I would not have you to be ignorant, brethren, concerning them which are asleep, that ye sorrow not, even as others which have no hope."

"Comfort one another with these words."

"We believe that Jesus died and rose again, even so them also which sleep in Jesus will God bring with him."

"Comfort one another with these words."

Continue through the entire text in this manner. Suggest that all use these words this week to provide personal comfort.

Let's Talk It Over

*The questions on this page are designed to promote discussion of the lesson
by the class and to encourage application of the lesson Scriptures. The answers
provided are only discussion starters. Let your class talk it over from there.*

1. What inspirational sayings or epitaphs have you read in cemeteries? What would you want on your tombstone as a testimony to your faith? Explain.

For nearly two thousand years Christians have "out-died" pagans. We have a long history of deathbed testimonies and tombstone inscriptions that express peace, faith, and hope.

On our own tombstones we may prefer to express how we honored Christ in life. One Christian teacher said he would like his epitaph to describe him as "a servant of the church" (like Phoebe in Romans 16:1). Or perhaps we would prefer to emphasize the afterlife hope we have in Christ—something like, "Now in Heaven with her Lord, soon to return for her new body."

See how creative, powerful, and (especially) Christ-honoring the suggestions can be. You could also ask your learners to share some of the best epitaphs they've seen.

2. If Christians have such a wonderful after-death hope, why is it most of us don't want to die? And why do we so often cry at funerals?

Death is still our enemy even though Christ has overcome its worst consequences. Death won't be completely vanquished until Christ's return (1 Corinthians 15:25, 26). Death is still an unnatural rending apart of soul from body, and loved one from loved ones; it creates physical and emotional pain.

We should not be made to feel guilty when we shed tears as a result of these hurts, but we must balance our grief with hope. We know that our Lord Jesus Christ will reunite our spirits and our bodies, and will reunite us with loved ones who have died in the Lord. Although death is followed by judgment, we know the Lord has already taken our sins upon Himself, so the "sting of death" (1 Corinthians 15:55-57) and the "fear of death" (Hebrews 2:14, 15) have been removed. The horrors of death are mitigated only for believers, however.

3. Many Christians seem to think the study of the end times is pointless. They say, "The subject is too hard," or "God will work things out whether I understand them or not." How would you convince them that at least a basic understanding is necessary?

Paul commands the Thessalonians (and us) to encourage one another with his teachings about the end (1 Thessalonians 4:18; 5:11). That is impossible to do if we don't know the Bible's foundational teachings about death, the Second Coming, resurrection, judgment, rewards, punishments, and the new heavens and earth that await.

Understanding God's ultimate plan is crucial in keeping our perspective (every choice seen in light of eternity and judgment), our priorities (earthly *vs.* eternal things), our excitement about His coming, our purity (are we ready?), our power to persevere (hope produces endurance), and our urgency about evangelism (everyone will spend eternity somewhere!).

4. Does the unrelenting stream of Christian books and movies about "the end times" help or hinder our efforts to prepare people for the Lord's return? Explain.

Certainly the massive distribution of books, tapes, charts, movies, T-shirts, etc., on the subject has created a tremendous interest. Thousands are being brought to the Lord by these materials and by sermons and lessons on the topic.

However, many of the more popular works contain departures from traditional Christian teachings and must be read or viewed with much caution. We always must test everything by Scripture, even when writers tell us their works are "guaranteed to be theologically correct." Theories that teach multiple second comings of Jesus, for example, might be better "left behind."

5. Suppose someone came into your Sunday school class and claimed to have knowledge that Jesus would return on July 18 in the year 3198. What would be the danger in having such knowledge, even if it were true?

God wants us, as the lesson writer says, to live with both expectancy and endurance. "Expectancy" means that we will be ready if He comes today or tomorrow. "Endurance" means that we will keep serving faithfully for the long haul, being ready every day as long as it takes until Jesus returns.

If we thought Jesus was coming for us tomorrow, we could fail in our long-term plans for service. If we thought He wasn't coming for centuries, we might be slack in remaining ready.

Reflecting His Glory

DEVOTIONAL READING: Ephesians 1:3-14.

BACKGROUND SCRIPTURE: 2 Thessalonians 1–3.

PRINTED TEXT: 2 Thessalonians 1:3, 4, 11, 12; 2:13–3:4.

2 Thessalonians 1:3, 4, 11, 12

3 We are bound to thank God always for you, brethren, as it is meet, because that your faith groweth exceedingly, and the charity of every one of you all toward each other aboundeth;

4 So that we ourselves glory in you in the churches of God, for your patience and faith in all your persecutions and tribulations that ye endure.

. . . .

11 Wherefore also we pray always for you, that our God would count you worthy of this calling, and fulfil all the good pleasure of his goodness, and the work of faith with power:

12 That the name of our Lord Jesus Christ may be glorified in you, and ye in him, according to the grace of our God and the Lord Jesus Christ.

2 Thessalonians 2:13-17

13 But we are bound to give thanks always to God for you, brethren beloved of the Lord, because God hath from the beginning chosen you to salvation through sanctification of the Spirit and belief of the truth:

14 Whereunto he called you by our gospel, to the obtaining of the glory of our Lord Jesus Christ.

15 Therefore, brethren, stand fast, and hold the traditions which ye have been taught, whether by word, or our epistle.

16 Now our Lord Jesus Christ himself, and God, even our Father, which hath loved us, and hath given us everlasting consolation and good hope through grace,

17 Comfort your hearts, and stablish you in every good word and work.

2 Thessalonians 3:1-4

1 Finally, brethren, pray for us, that the word of the Lord may have free course, and be glorified, even as it is with you:

2 And that we may be delivered from unreasonable and wicked men: for all men have not faith.

3 But the Lord is faithful, who shall stablish you, and keep you from evil.

4 And we have confidence in the Lord touching you, that ye both do and will do the things which we command you.

May 2

GOLDEN TEXT: But we are bound to give thanks always to God for you, brethren beloved of the Lord, because God hath from the beginning chosen you to salvation through sanctification of the Spirit and belief of the truth.
—2 Thessalonians 2:13.

Lesson Aims

After participating in this lesson, each student should be able to:

1. Summarize Paul's description of how the Thessalonians would glorify God by living by and growing in their faith.

2. Tell why it is important for believers to reflect God's glory in the way that they live.

3. State one specific action he or she can take this week to reflect God's glory.

Lesson Outline

INTRODUCTION
    A. Practice What You Preach
    B. Lesson Background
I. THANKSGIVING AND PRAYER (2 Thessalonians 1:3, 4, 11, 12)
    A. Faith for Trials (vv. 3, 4)
      Dying for One's Faith
    B. Prayer for Christ's Glory (vv. 11, 12)
II. SAVED AND SANCTIFIED (2 Thessalonians 2: 13-17)
    A. Remembering the Initial Call (vv. 13, 14)
    B. Holding Fast to the Teachings (v. 15)
      The Cost of Tradition
    C. Counting on God's Provision (vv. 16, 17)
III. MESSAGE AND DELIVERANCE (2 Thessalonians 3:1-4)
    A. Pray for the Message (v. 1)
    B. Pray for Deliverance (vv. 2-4)
CONCLUSION
    A. Reflecting His Glory
    B. Prayer
    C. Thought to Remember

Introduction

A. Practice What You Preach

The story made the nightly news as one of those "would-you-believe-it?" segments at the end of the show. A jewelry company named "Love Your Neighbor" was suing a homeless charity called "Love Thy Neighbor" for trademark infringement. The similar names, said the jewelry company, confused customers. The company demanded that the charity pay monetary damages for lost sales and stop using the "trademarked" name.

We can laugh or shake our heads at such outrageous tales. But we all know too many examples of people whose claim to godliness is contradicted by their actions.

B. Lesson Background

Paul knew of such examples, too. As he wrote his second letter to the Thessalonians, he realized that these infant Christians were far from perfect. Yet he saw in them evidence of the Lord's work in their lives. They were the genuine article—not perfect people, but people whose lives gave glory to the Lord who had saved them.

After Paul's first letter to the Thessalonians, many things seemed to have become worse in their lives. They had faced persecution, but now it seemed to become more intense. Such experiences probably prompted some to doubt. If Christians were being persecuted, was God still faithful to them? Furthermore, some of the problems that Paul had addressed in his first letter were still continuing. In particular, some Christians who had been taking advantage of others' generosity still refused to work when they were able. Paul wrote 2 Thessalonians largely to correct these ongoing problems.

But a church with problems is not a failure. Whatever needed correcting in their beliefs and actions, the Thessalonian Christians were still showing the glory of God through lives transformed by the gospel. So Paul offers commendation to them and thanks to God for their lives, even as he prays that they (and he) will continue to glorify the Lord Jesus until He returns.

I. Thanksgiving and Prayer
(2 Thessalonians 1:3, 4, 11, 12)

A. Faith for Trials (vv. 3, 4)

3. We are bound to thank God always for you, brethren, as it is meet, because that your faith groweth exceedingly, and the charity of every one of you all toward each other aboundeth.

In 1 Thessalonians 1:2, 3, Paul had commended the church for its active faith, love, and hope. Here he repeats his commendation of their *faith* and love *(charity)*. The measure of their growth in these two areas is impressive because it comes despite hardships that the church has faced. The church may have been discouraged by its struggles, but Paul sees its growth as all the more significant because of it. When we understand that the gospel begins with the message of the cross, we realize that God's work in our lives will take place in the midst of hardship rather than apart from it.

For all this, Paul believes that he is *bound* or "ought" *to thank God.* Thanksgiving is not just something that Christians do when they feel like it. Those belonging to the body of Christ, who understand the cross of Christ, are obliged to thank God for His work in Christians' lives even when circumstances seem less than joyful. [See question #1, page 304.]

4. So that we ourselves glory in you in the churches of God, for your patience and faith in all your persecutions and tribulations that ye endure.

When Paul says *we ourselves glory in you in the churches of God* he means he is boasting about the Thessalonians to other churches. This is not self-glorifying boasting, but God-glorifying boasting (see Romans 3:27; 2 Corinthians 10:17). Paul is sharing the good news that God's work is continuing among His people.

To do such boasting in the midst of suffering takes a keen eye of faith. Paul's eye of faith focuses on the Thessalonians' *patience* or perseverance, an active quality that endures difficulty with firmness. He also commends their *faith*—not just the faith that they had when they first believed in Jesus, but their ongoing faith that has remained firm in trials that have come since. Real faith under trial always demonstrates staying power based on trust in God.

Suffering through *persecutions* from others along with various *tribulations* (trials) has become the soil in which the Thessalonians' faith has taken root. Such difficulties could have been a threat to their faith. Instead, suffering has made their faith grow stronger. Compared to their difficult circumstances, their faith stands out all the more! God is often best glorified in circumstances that seem most difficult.

The Thessalonians' suffering prompts Paul to remind them of something: God promises to punish those who refuse to repent of their opposition to Him and His people (see 2 Thessalonians 1:5-10, not in today's text). But God's judgment is not His only response to His people's suffering. His other response is His promise to strengthen them. Paul counts on that promise as he explains his prayers for the Thessalonian Christians in verses 11, 12 (next).

DYING FOR ONE'S FAITH

Most Christians in Western Europe and North America really don't know much about persecution. We talk about being "persecuted" when an atheist tries to get prayer out of schools or sues to have a cross removed from a public square, or when a movie or TV show portrays Christians in a less-than-complimentary light.

It's a far different picture elsewhere in the world. The church was repressed for decades in Communist countries, sometimes with deadly violence. More recently the persecution has been in Muslim countries in Africa, Asia, and the Middle East. In the aftermath of America's response to Muslim terrorists, Christians' lives have been at risk in many nations that have a strong Islamic presence.

Take Pakistan, for example. In that country sixteen worshipers at a Catholic church died in gunfire on October 28, 2001. Five were killed at a Protestant service on March 17, 2002. On August 5, 2002, two Christians were murdered in an attack on a Christian school. Four days later, four nurses at a Christian hospital were killed as they left a prayer service. Ironically, most of their patients were poor Muslims.

This puts persecution in a different light! In Thessalonica as in threatening places today, true Christians respond with renewed faith and commitment to the Lord, who gave His life for them. How do you suppose Western Christians would respond if pressed in similar circumstances?
—C. R. B.

B. Prayer for Christ's Glory (vv. 11, 12)

11. Wherefore also we pray always for you, that our God would count you worthy of this calling, and fulfil all the good pleasure of his goodness, and the work of faith with power.

Paul's constant prayer for these Christians is that what God has begun in them He will by His faithfulness bring to completion. The Thessalonians, like all Christians, had been called by God through the good news of Jesus to belong to Him forever (see 1 Thessalonians 2:12). Persecution and suffering might make believers think that God had abandoned them since they had received their *calling*. But Paul knows that God does no such thing. God's purpose is to make His people His forever. He will see that purpose through to its end.

Like most Christians, the Thessalonians may be troubled by their own sense of failure and unworthiness. Paul prays not that they actually will *be* worthy of God's call (which is impossible), but that God will *count* them *worthy*. God's favor does not come by merit, and no one can earn it. But by His grace God promises to treat those

---

How to Say It

COLOSSIANS. Kuh-*losh*-unz.

CORINTHIANS. Kor-*in*-thee-unz (*th* as in *thin*).

EPHESIANS. Ee-*fee*-zhunz.

HAVASUPAI. Ha-vuh-*soo*-pie.

THESSALONIANS. *Thess*-uh-*lo*-nee-unz (strong accent on *lo*; *th* as in *thin*).

with faith in Christ as if they are worthy, despite the fact that they are sinners. Being counted worthy is the foundation of all of God's work in the lives of His people.

12. That the name of our Lord Jesus Christ may be glorified in you, and ye in him, according to the grace of our God and the Lord Jesus Christ.

What happens when Christians cooperate with God in what He is doing in their lives? *Christ* is *glorified*. When Christ returns, His glory will be seen by all (2 Thessalonians 1:10). In the meantime, His glory is to be seen in the lives of people transformed in His image and living out their calling by His power. [See question #2, page 304.]

II. Saved and Sanctified
(2 Thessalonians 2:13-17)

A. Remembering the Initial Call (vv. 13, 14)

13. But we are bound to give thanks always to God for you, brethren beloved of the Lord, because God hath from the beginning chosen you to salvation through sanctification of the Spirit and belief of the truth.

In 2 Thessalonians 2:1-12 (not in our text for today), Paul has been discussing the ongoing problem of evil in the world. Now he shifts gears to focus again on the people of God, who have been saved from that evil. He repeats his thanksgiving from the beginning of the letter, again saying that he has an obligation to thank God despite what seems like bad circumstances. Those circumstances do not lessen Christ's love for His family, even though they sometimes make His love difficult to see.

Being loved by Christ and being *chosen* by God are different expressions of the same essential idea in this verse. Both mean that Christians belong to God and can depend on His power to see them through to the end. However, it is important to understand the relationship between our faith and God's choosing. God does not choose people and then cause them to believe as a result of being chosen. Rather, it's the other way around: He chooses people to be with Him for eternity because they believe. We are saved through *belief in the truth.*

God's choosing means that Christians receive the blessings of *salvation*. In this regard, Paul stresses the work of the Holy Spirit. The Holy *Spirit* brings *sanctification*, that is, making believers to be the holy people of God. When the Holy Spirit enters a person's life, the Spirit identifies or marks that person as one who belongs to God. But that identity carries the need to imitate the holiness of God—to become holy in thought and behavior as well as in identity. Saved people can never stay the way they were before. When they live out their holy identity by imitating God's holiness, they reflect His glory in the world. [See question #3, page 304.]

14. Whereunto he called you by our gospel, to the obtaining of the glory of our Lord Jesus Christ.

The message of the *gospel* calls people to all that Paul has mentioned: belonging to God's people, being saved from judgment, being made holy by the Holy Spirit—all based on faith in the message of Christ. The gospel "call" is not a mysterious experience. It is the summons of the gospel message that addresses our deepest needs and most difficult problems. We hear it when we listen to the message that Jesus, the Son of God, died and rose for our sins.

God's purpose in the gospel call is that by believing in Christ we should share in Christ's own *glory*. Part of the wonder of the gospel is that God willingly shares His glory with His people. They participate in His victory in the world and enjoy the benefits of it. That is true both in the present and in the future. In the present we enjoy the blessings of life in the Holy Spirit and fellowship with each other as God's people. We may suffer in this age, but so did the Christ whose glory we share.

When Jesus returns, His glory will be fully revealed. We will be gathered to Him at that time and will be known to all as His people. In the meantime, we are to live in a way that demonstrates His glory to the world.

B. Holding Fast to the Teachings (v. 15)

15. Therefore, brethren, stand fast, and hold the traditions which ye have been taught, whether by word, or our epistle.

Therefore sums up what Paul has just written. If the gospel calls Christians to reflect the glory of God, then they must remain firm in that calling to see it through to its goal. They need to be firm because of the opposition that they will continue to face as God's people in a hostile world. If they fail to remain firm, they are working against the purpose of God.

The word *traditions* has negative connotations for many Christians today. We tend to think of traditions as the things that the church has done for a long time without good, Scriptural reasons. Traditions in this context, however, means the teachings about Christ that the Thessalonian Christians had learned by *word* of mouth from Paul and his associates in ministry, or by letters such as 1 and 2 Thessalonians.

So to remind Christians to remain true to the traditions is to tell them to remain true to the original gospel that they had received. As we think about our lives and practices, we need to know the difference between Biblical teaching—the original, authentic tradition—and our own customs, habits, and preferences.

THE COST OF TRADITION

A few hundred people live in a Havasupai village in a remote branch of the Grand Canyon. This village is seventy-five miles by road from Peach Springs, and then eight miles by mule path. Residents have a few modern comforts, such as electricity and telephones. But the U.S. Mail still comes in its traditional way: by mule train, as it has for more than one hundred years. Everything the Havasupai use or eat comes to their village in this way.

Such mail delivery is expensive! For example, postage for fresh water costs more than the water itself. A typical shipment of five hundred cases of soda costs two thousand six hundred dollars. Food, clothes, wheelbarrows, computers, the usual letters and cards, and even Christmas trees get "mailed" into the village by mule.

It costs a lot to maintain tradition. To the Havasupai, it's apparently worth it. But what is the value of tradition to Christians? It depends on what traditions we're talking about. The "traditions" Paul referred to were the core teachings of the gospel, not "the way we've always done things," as we think of tradition. "Tradition" can be a positive and necessary identifying link to the past. Or, in the form of "tradition-*alism*," it can make the gospel an irrelevant vestige of bygone days. We must be wise enough to discern the difference. The future of the church depends on it! —C. R. B.

C. Counting on God's Provision (vv. 16, 17)

16, 17. Now our Lord Jesus Christ himself, and God, even our Father, which hath loved us, and hath given us everlasting consolation and good hope through grace, comfort your hearts, and stablish you in every good word and work.

"Holding fast" is a tough assignment when the world is filled with evil. So Paul moves quickly from his command to hold fast to a confident prayer for God's help to overcome in the struggle.

Paul begins this prayer by mentioning *Christ* emphatically. Doing so helps us understand how God helps us hold fast. If Christ endured the cross for our salvation, He can certainly provide what we need to endure opposition and hold firm to the gospel. Further, Christ is the *Lord* of glory (see verse 14). That means He has unlimited power to help His people.

Paul also refers here to God as *Father*, underlining what we can expect from Him. As Father,

That the name of our Lord Jesus Christ may be glorified in you.
2 Thessalonians 1:12

Visual for lesson 9

Let this simple visual remind your learners that God is glorified even in our "small" services.

He gives His children exactly what they need (see Luke 11:11-13). He is the God who has already given His people *everlasting consolation and good hope through grace.* The word *consolation* in the *King James Version* may sound like the lesser prize for second place, but it really means something more like "encouragement" or even "help." Because that help comes from God, it can never end.

Comfort represents the same root word as "consolation." It includes reassurance in difficult times, but it goes beyond that sense to include encouragement and help to overcome difficulties and to move forward. To comfort the heart means more than consoling the feelings; it means strengthening the believer's will to act on what is right and true.

We can understand the rest of these two verses in the same way. To *stablish* or "strengthen" means to make believers firm in their convictions. This leads them to say and do what is right and good. God certainly will see His purpose through to its end at Christ's return. Until then, He will enable believers to live as His people. We will bring Him glory in our words and works, as we live holy lives, until His glory is fully revealed.

III. Message and Deliverance (2 Thessalonians 3:1-4)

A. Pray for the Message (v. 1)

1. Finally, brethren, pray for us, that the word of the Lord may have free course, and be glorified, even as it is with you.

In several of his letters Paul not only speaks of his prayers for the readers, but also asks for their prayers for him (Romans 15:30-32; Ephesians

6:18-20; Colossians 4:3). Here he asks in a way that means not just praying once but praying repeatedly. Such prayer expresses the reliance on God that the gospel demands.

He asks for prayer first that the gospel can move forward rapidly *(have free course)* toward God's goal of salvation for all. Paul also desires prayer that the gospel will *be glorified.* The gospel runs forward and is glorified when it is believed and obeyed. This is what has happened with the Thessalonian Christians. Though they have faced discouragements and problems, their life in the gospel has glorified the gospel. This reminds us again of the glory of Christ, revealed at present in His people and in its fullness at His return. [See question #4, page 304.]

B. Pray for Deliverance (vv. 2-4)

2. And that we may be delivered from unreasonable and wicked men: for all men have not faith.

Paul describes his readers' opponents as *unreasonable.* This word suggests something that is not fitting or appropriate. Opponents of Christianity probably insisted that Christians did not fit with the established social order. They did not worship the established gods or follow the established customs. Paul turns this language around. Christians may not seem to fit the established social order, but opponents of the gospel do not fit God's established order.

Lawlessness and evil will oppose God's work until Christ returns. Then they will be defeated utterly. But God is already overcoming them as the gospel goes forward. So Paul asks for prayers that God would continue to overcome his opponents as they opposed Paul. In effect, Paul says, "Continue to pray 'Deliver us from the evil one' on my behalf." [See question #5, page 304.]

Home Daily Bible Readings

Monday, Apr. 26—We Have an Inheritance in Christ (Ephesians 1:7-14)
Tuesday, Apr. 27—Your Faith Is Growing (2 Thessalonians 1:1-5)
Wednesday, Apr. 28—Christ Glorified by His Saints (2 Thessalonians 1:6-12)
Thursday, Apr. 29—Called to Obtain Glory (2 Thessalonians 2:13-17)
Friday, Apr. 30—The Lord Will Strengthen You (2 Thessalonians 3:1-5)
Saturday, May 1—Imitate Us (2 Thessalonians 3:6-10)
Sunday, May 2—Do Not Be Idle (2 Thessalonians 3:11-18)

---

3. But the Lord is faithful, who shall stablish you, and keep you from evil.

Confidence in prayer comes from knowing the faithfulness of God. Many people do not have faith, but God is always *faithful.* He will always deliver His people and see His purpose through to its end.

Paul expresses this confidence in a way that reminds us how God proves Himself faithful. He will *keep* His people *from evil,* not by removing them completely from its presence (until Christ returns), but by enabling them to overcome evil by His strength.

4. And we have confidence in the Lord touching you, that ye both do and will do the things which we command you.

Paul has good reason to be confident about the Thessalonian Christians. Despite persecutions, they have held to their faith.

But Paul's ultimate confidence is in God Himself. God has been at work in the Thessalonian Christians in the past, strengthening them to bring Him glory. He has been with Paul in the past, enabling him to proclaim the gospel and bring God glory. He was faithful to His Son, Jesus Christ, raising Him from the dead. He has always been faithful to all of His people. We can count on Him now. We can count on Him in the future. We can count on Him forever.

Conclusion

A. Reflecting His Glory

The story of God's people often reads like a story of failure. Our faith sometimes fails. We struggle with sin. Some believers succumb to the pressures of the world and forsake the Lord altogether. Demas was just such a one—he even went to Thessalonica! (See 2 Timothy 4:10.)

Yet God is glorified when His people live out their faith, even imperfectly. He continues to change them and strengthen them so that they reflect His glory more and more. At Christ's return, He will glorify them with His Son. When we know what God is doing and where He is taking us, we will be ready to reflect His glory more clearly until Christ comes again.

B. Prayer

Dear Father, help us to *hang on!* When the world distracts us, teach us to lift our gaze to eternity. May we be Yours forever. In Jesus' name, amen.

C. Thought to Remember

"The sufferings of this present time are not worthy to be compared with the glory which shall be revealed in us" (Romans 8:18).

Learning by Doing

This page contains an alternative lesson plan emphasizing learning activities.
Classes desiring such student involvement will find these suggestions helpful.

Learning Goals

After participating in this lesson, each student should be able to:

1. Summarize Paul's description of how the Thessalonians would glorify God by living and growing in their faith.

2. Tell why it is important for believers to reflect God's glory in the way that they live.

3. State one specific action he or she can take this week to reflect God's glory.

Into the Lesson

Choice One: Case Study. Read the following case study to your class to introduce the lesson. Or ask a class member in advance to read it to the class.

"David and Beverly have been church members for several years. They attend church regularly, but it does not seem to affect the way they live. Beverly is a self-confessed gossip. Dave's language at work and his ribald jokes make him popular with the guys, but where is his influence for Christ? Doesn't God and shouldn't we expect more from Beverly and Dave?" (This activity is also included in the student book.)

Make the transition to the lesson by saying, "What does God expect from believers in regard to our lifestyle? As we look at our text today, watch for what God expects from believers."

Choice Two: Debate. Ask two students in advance to prepare a debate. One will affirm the proposition, "God expects Christians to glorify Him by the way they live." The other will refute the proposition, arguing that since every person sins and falls short, the pressure to conform is too powerful; and besides, God does not need us to glorify Him—He is altogether glorious already.

Into the Word

Choice One: Group Discussion. Divide your class into four groups to discuss the four sections in today's text. Assign each group to develop a list of ways that God is glorified through the lives of believers. Each group is to select a leader and a recorder who will list the group's findings. Ask each group to share its list.

Choice Two: Interview. Conduct an "interview with the apostle Paul," as you would if he visited your class. Prepare the questions and discuss as a group how he might answer them. Study each verse and frame a question that

might be suggested by the content. For example, 3:1 can suggest the question, "What are your personal feelings about the people in the church at Thessalonica?" Paul could answer, "I am always thanking God for each one of them. I am so pleased that their faith and love are both increasing." (This activity is included in the student book.)

Choice Three: Acrostic. Write the words *Glorify God* vertically down the left edge of a page of newsprint with a large black marker. Then ask your class to list things that glorify God that can be tied into the phrase. For example, "Good deeds" could be written next to a "G." (This activity is included in the student book.)

Into Life

Choice One: Write a Prayer. In his epistles Paul records many of his prayer concerns for people. Write and pray a Paul-like prayer for a young Christian. For example, based on 1:3, 4 you might pray, "Lord, I thank You for (Harold) because his faith is growing more and more and his love for all the brothers is increasing. All the leaders are proud of his perseverance and faith in all the persecutions and trials he is facing." (This activity is included in the student book.)

Choice Two: Brainstorm. Lead your class in a brainstorming session to compile a list of ways that Christians can glorify God today. Paul makes general statements in the text like, "every good purpose," "every act prompted by your faith," and "every good word and deed." What you want to create is a list of specific and practical ways of giving glory to God. Tell your class that the purpose is to generate as many ideas as possible, so you will not stop to evaluate or discuss ideas. Encourage them to call out things as rapidly as they can be written down. Have two people ready with markers and large pieces of paper taped to the wall.

After the brainstorming period, go back and put stars beside the items your class thinks are the most plausible and realistic projects. Then select one that your class can do together that would give glory to God. For example, your class might list "Feed the hungry." One way to accomplish this would be to open a soup kitchen. Or perhaps your class could raise funds for an existing soup kitchen and then volunteer as a group to staff a specific meal each month.

Let's Talk It Over

The questions on this page are designed to promote discussion of the lesson by the class and to encourage application of the lesson Scriptures. The answers provided are only discussion starters. Let your class talk it over from there.

1. Thinking about Paul's example, what obligation do we have to thank and praise our fellow Christians? How might their growth depend on our doing those two things?

Everyone should be recognized and honored for his or her faithful service, especially children and new Christians. We can have a tremendous ministry of encouragement to other believers by well-timed words of gratitude and praise.

At times, ingratitude can be not only bad manners, but sin (cf. Luke 17:16-18; 2 Timothy 3:2). A lack of feedback, especially from church leaders, can lead others to think their service doesn't really matter. On the other hand a spirit of thanks and praise from church leaders will serve to channel the Christian growth of others as it says, "This is what is important."

2. If the deeds of God's people are to reflect His glory and character, what lies have you "told" about God lately by your behavior? How can you correct this?

When our traits are not reflective of God's, we repulse people from Him rather than attract them to Him (Matthew 5:13-16). When His children "stretch the truth," folks question whether God's Word can be trusted. When we selfishly act in our own interests or act in a hateful way to our neighbors, observers may have a hard time understanding that "God is love." God's mercy and patience may be doubted when we are temperamental; His warmth and compassion can't be seen when we are distant and uncaring.

Even if we praise God with our lips, we will deny Him by sinful and careless deeds (Titus 1:16). Encourage your learners to find a few new ways to "tell the truth" about God this week through their behavior.

3. The lesson writer says, "Saved people can never stay the way they were." But we all know people who show little or no difference after their conversion. Why do some Christians make such dramatic changes for the better while others fail?

The Christian life should be a continuous story of change. Immediately after conversion, some major changes are mandatory. Some have to take big steps—away from crime, drugs, drink, sexual immorality, etc. Even "good, moral people" must still make major shifts in priorities and choices.

But even after major changes the genuine disciple learns more of God's will regarding what he or she must do concerning lifelong "necessary adjustments." He will not be satisfied with laziness, selfishness, or a temper. She will work on her unseen sins of jealousy and pride. Failure comes from being satisfied with the flaws we have. The one who is not changing for the better is changing for the worse—there is no standing still.

4. Again, we see the importance of prayer for Paul. If we don't pray for our church leaders, church members, and church programs, then how much of the blame is ours when they fail?

We do bear at least some guilt when a church leader, member, or program fails if we haven't prayed for the person or function. Prayer for people and programs is not the last step but the first. Leaders make better decisions, teachers teach better lessons, and programs run more smoothly when they are lifted up in prayer. Prayer recognizes that there is a God, and we need His help. Perhaps our first prayer right now could be one that asks for forgiveness in failing to pray!

5. Describe times when you have not fit in with the world's established gods and customs. In what ways did you turn (or could you have turned) those times into opportunities to demonstrate "God's established order"?

Every temptation and trial is an opportunity for a testimony. From school-age years (when we were offered smokes, beers, or cheat sheets), to our work years (when we are pressured by peers to join them in altering time cards, sharing dirty stories, or pilfering company property), we have fared best when we've taken an immediate stand as Christians.

Our peers and friends need to know why we won't participate in their customs and habits. In discussions of current events, we must find a way to explain how the Bible has shaped our opinions about abortion, homosexuality, "living together," and other hot issues. Rather than living in the world's culture without protest, we must resolve to introduce worldly people to God and His order of things however we can.

Worshiping the Lamb

May 9
Lesson 10

DEVOTIONAL READING: Revelation 4:1-11.

BACKGROUND SCRIPTURE: Revelation 4, 5.

PRINTED TEXT: Revelation 5:1-10.

Revelation 5:1-10

1 And I saw in the right hand of him that sat on the throne a book written within and on the backside, sealed with seven seals.

2 And I saw a strong angel proclaiming with a loud voice, Who is worthy to open the book, and to loose the seals thereof?

3 And no man in heaven, nor in earth, neither under the earth, was able to open the book, neither to look thereon.

4 And I wept much, because no man was found worthy to open and to read the book, neither to look thereon.

5 And one of the elders saith unto me, Weep not: behold, the Lion of the tribe of Judah, the Root of David, hath prevailed to open the book, and to loose the seven seals thereof.

6 And I beheld, and, lo, in the midst of the throne and of the four beasts, and in the midst of the elders, stood a Lamb as it had been slain, having seven horns and seven eyes, which are the seven Spirits of God sent forth into all the earth.

7 And he came and took the book out of the right hand of him that sat upon the throne.

8 And when he had taken the book, the four beasts and four and twenty elders fell down before the Lamb, having every one of them harps, and golden vials full of odors, which are the prayers of saints.

9 And they sung a new song, saying, Thou art worthy to take the book, and to open the seals thereof: for thou wast slain, and hast redeemed us to God by thy blood out of every kindred, and tongue, and people, and nation;

10 And hast made us unto our God kings and priests: and we shall reign on the earth.

May
9

GOLDEN TEXT: Worthy is the Lamb that was slain to receive power, and riches, and wisdom, and strength, and honor, and glory, and blessing.
—Revelation 5:12.

Living Expectantly
Unit 2: Visions of Hope
(Lessons 10-13)

Lesson Aims

After participating in this lesson, each student should be able to:

1. Describe the unique position of the Lamb as the One who is worthy of worship.

2. Explain why the focus of one's worship and life must be on the Lamb.

3. Express worship to the Lamb who is worthy.

Lesson Outline

INTRODUCTION
  A. Into the Presence of God
  B. Lesson Background
I. WHO IS WORTHY? (Revelation 5:1-5)
  A. Sealed Book (v. 1)
  B. Important Question (v. 2)
  C. Deep Grief (vv. 3, 4)
    Unworthy!
  D. Vital Answer (v. 5)
II. HE IS WORTHY! (Revelation 5:6-10)
  A. The Lamb Comes (v. 6)
  B. The Lamb Acts (v. 7)
  C. The Lamb Worshiped (vv. 8-10)
    A New Song
CONCLUSION
  A. The Lamb's Presence and Power
  B. Prayer
  C. Thought to Remember

Introduction

A. Into the Presence of God

Have you ever had trouble worshiping and serving in the church? On Sunday morning, do you find it difficult feeling or believing that you're really in the presence of God? Today the book of Revelation will give you the opportunity to come into His presence in a unique way!

When we are aware of God's presence, we can worship and serve profoundly in spirit and in truth. And Revelation is indeed a book of truth! Here we can learn more about the relationship of Father, Son, and Spirit to one another. The book of Revelation teaches us truth about Jesus, who is given many identifying titles: the faithful witness, the first begotten of the dead, the prince of the kings of the earth, Alpha and Omega, the beginning and the ending, the first and the last. In addition to the titles there are many actions picturing what Jesus has done for all Christians, His servants, so that they can know the blessings of being in a relationship with Him.

Whatever helps we may use in our worship services—worship leader, praise team, words on a screen, songbooks, musical instruments of all sorts—cannot be substituted for a real sense of the presence of God. And bringing us into God's presence is where the book of Revelation truly shines! No other book in the Bible can kindle the mind and heart of the Christian for worship better than the book of Revelation.

B. Lesson Background

To understand any passage of Scripture properly, we must get an overview of the context in which it stands. This is especially important for passages in the book of Revelation because the author (the apostle John) develops a vocabulary to be used throughout, and the message of the book builds upon this vocabulary.

John makes clear from the outset that this is a message revealed by Jesus Christ Himself (Revelation 1:1, 5). But not only is the message *from* Him, it is also *about* Him. We see Christ in the midst of the seven golden candlesticks in 1:20, which are identified as the seven churches of Asia. Christ is the One who knows the circumstances of the seven churches—their strong points, their weak points, everything! He challenges them (and us) to be overcomers of those things that would destroy a proper relationship with Him.

There is blessing for the overcomers, but judgment for the failures. The form of the message carries a likeness of the Old Testament prophets. Those prophets proclaimed God's message for the people to repent. Their message was conditional. If the people repented, then there would be blessing from God. If not, God must pronounce judgment—penalty for rejecting His word.

With each of the letters to the churches is the closing command that they must heed what the Spirit says. The reader thus becomes aware that the Holy Spirit's ministry is a part of this whole matter. When the Spirit is called the "seven Spirits" of God (Revelation 1:4; 3:1; 4:5; 5:6), we do not count Spirits, but rather we consider His "sevenfold" potential to convict and encourage the faithful Christian.

In chapter 4 we move to a vision of the throne room of God. The focus of attention is on the One seated upon the throne. John indicates that he himself was brought right into God's presence so that he could see things from God's vantage point. It became John's responsibility to present the facts so that his readers would understand. We come to greater understanding when we identify with John by being where he is, as well as seeing and hearing the things he does.

One important thing John discovers in chapter 5 is the existence of a sealed book. This book does not exist for its own benefit—rather, it points to Christ.

I. Who Is Worthy?
(Revelation 5:1-5)
A. Sealed Book (v. 1)

1. And I saw in the right hand of him that sat on the throne a book written within and on the back side, sealed with seven seals.

As chapter 5 opens, our attention falls upon *the book,* or scroll, that is in God's *right hand.* This book is entirely filled with a message. The fullness is indicated by the description of being *written within and on the back side.* It is also heavily *sealed* under someone's authority. John uses the word *seven* more than fifty times in the book of Revelation. Very frequently, "seven" shows us "the full value" of what is under discussion. Hence, the reader desires to know this full message, but only the One of proper, full authority can open it.

B. Important Question (v. 2)

2. And I saw a strong angel proclaiming with a loud voice, Who is worthy to open the book, and to loose the seals thereof?

To open the book and *to loose the seals thereof* are two ways of saying the same thing. To do one is to do the other. The *strong angel* in charge for the moment kindles our anticipation, for not just anyone dare open it. The call of this angel is able to reach to the farthest limits in seeking someone of proper office before God. Is it possible to find someone with sufficient authority?

C. Deep Grief (vv. 3, 4)

3, 4. And no man in heaven, nor in earth, neither under the earth, was able to open the book, neither to look thereon. And I wept much, because no man was found worthy to open and to read the book, neither to look thereon.

Although the shattering call of the angel rings through every corner of the universe, no answer comes back. There is no response, at least at first. This fact causes John *much* grief because he apparently senses that the message of the sealed *book* can give him help and hope for his needs. John instinctively knows that the sealed message is vital. So he gives in to despair since no one immediately steps forward claiming the right *to open* this book.

UNWORTHY!

It was an amazing decision: at the height of the 1996 college football season, Robert Carothers, President of the University of Rhode Island, suspended all seventy-two players, thus forfeiting an upcoming game with rival University of Connecticut. The reason? Six team members had rushed into a fraternity house and beat up three residents while twenty-five teammates surrounded the house to ensure that no one escaped.

The National Collegiate Athletic Association said that in its long history no team had ever forfeited a game for such a reason. Some complained because the action jeopardized the team's playoff chances. But the president became a hero to many who had been saddened and sickened by the attitude of many sports "heroes" who thought themselves immune to the requirement of decent conduct. "This is not about football," Carothers said. "This is about character." President Carothers's suspension of the team said, in effect, that the team was not worthy to carry the university's name and colors onto the field.

When we talk in terms of human worthiness before God, we always must conclude, "No one is worthy." Not one of us is worthy to carry the "name and colors" before Him. Sin has made this tragically so. Does this fact make you weep as it did John?

—C. R. B.

D. Vital Answer (v. 5)

5. And one of the elders saith unto me, Weep not: behold, the Lion of the tribe of Judah, the Root of David, hath prevailed to open the book, and to loose the seven seals thereof.

Revelation 4:4 mentions twenty-four *elders* in the throne room. One of the elders serves as the spokesman for God, or as a "master of ceremonies" to give encouragement at this critical situation. This elder announces that there is indeed One who is worthy *to open the book.* [See question #1, page 312.] This worthiness is indicated first by two messianic titles: *the Lion of . . . Judah* (cf. Genesis 49:9) and *the Root of David* (cf. Isaiah 11:1, 10; Jeremiah 23:5; 33:15). These titles are coupled with the action of prevailing or overcoming. The next verse tells us why.

How to Say It

ASIA. *Ay*-zhuh.
EPHESIANS. Ee-*fee*-zhunz.
ISAIAH. Eye-*zay*-uh.
JEREMIAH. Jair-uh-*my*-uh.
JUDAH. *Joo*-duh.
MESSIANIC. mess-ee-*an*-ick.
PHILIPPIANS. Fih-*lip*-ee-unz.

II. He Is Worthy!
(Revelation 5:6-10)
A. The Lamb Comes (v. 6)

6. And I beheld, and, lo, in the midst of the throne and of the four beasts, and in the midst of the elders, stood a Lamb as it had been slain, having seven horns and seven eyes, which are the seven Spirits of God sent forth into all the earth.

The *elders* of Revelation 4:4 and the *four beasts* of 4:6b-8 are still in the throne room, but now the focus of attention now shifts to *a Lamb.* [See question #2, page 312.] This is the first of more than thirty uses of "Lamb" in Revelation. The apostle John (who writes the book of Revelation) is already aware of the application of this term to Jesus (see what this apostle wrote earlier in John 1:29, 36).

The fact that this Lamb *had been slain* brings to mind the suffering servant of Isaiah 53. Even so, He is now standing alive and ready to act. The Lamb has *seven horns* of power. No literal lamb has horns, so this is a figure. A lamb is normally thought of as a docile, meek animal, but these horns of power are very fitting in the midst of God's throne room. There seems to be a bit of a paradox as power and submissive sacrifice are coupled together. [See question #3, page 312.]

Besides having the horns of power, the Lamb has *seven eyes.* These are equated with *the seven Spirits of God,* which we have already discussed in the Lesson Background. This sevenfold Spirit communicates with *all the earth,* not just with the seven churches of Asia in chapters 2 and 3. This verse shows us that the Lamb has a tie with God who sits on His throne, as well as with the Spirit who functions on behalf of people. The entire Godhead (Father, Son, and Holy Spirit) is united in the redemptive work. Even so, the achievement of the Lamb draws our attention and our praise here. The Lamb is worthy of our worship! He is ready to act (again) on our behalf.

B. The Lamb Acts (v. 7)

7. And he came and took the book out of the right hand of him that sat upon the throne.

Anticipation heightens. Hope is about to become fulfilled. There is no question as to the Lamb's relationship with *him that sat upon the throne.* Neither is there any question as to the Lamb's right to *the book.* Its message will assist John and all other suffering servants. This includes us, even though at this point the "suffering" aspect may not seem personal. It is, however, very personal for John, who is in exile on the island of Patmos "for the word of God, and for the testimony of Jesus Christ" (Revelation 1:9).

C. The Lamb Worshiped (vv. 8-10)

8. And when he had taken the book, the four beasts and four and twenty elders fell down before the Lamb, having every one of them harps, and the golden vials full of odors, which are the prayers of saints.

When the Lamb receives the sealed *book* from the hand of God, the conduct of the *beasts* and the *elders* is that of worship. It is proper for John and the readers to join in with them. The *harps* are for praise, and the *golden vials full of odors* (or incense) are equated with *the prayers of saints.* Passages such as Ephesians 1:1 and Philippians 1:1 remind us that all Christians are "saints." This means that the prayers of saints are our prayers, too!

As yet it is not apparent what the prayers of the saints have to do with the message of the sealed book. We will have to wait until the fifth seal is opened in Revelation 6:9, 10. There we will see that the message concerns those who were "slain for the word of God, and for the testimony which they held." The suffering of the faithful servants called forth God's vengeance on the wicked, and the servants are given the means to sustain themselves through suffering. See also the opening of the seventh seal in Revelation 8:1-4.

9. And they sung a new song, saying, Thou art worthy to take the book, and to open the seals thereof: for thou wast slain, and hast redeemed us to God by thy blood out of every kindred, and tongue, and people, and nation.

Many folks who have been to church for years don't like to learn any new songs. They're content to stick with their "old favorites"! But in God's Heavenly throne room we see those gathered singing *a new song* (see also Revelation 14:3).

The word "new" doesn't just mean "different." Rather, it signifies a "changed quality" of songs that have been sung before. See also the changed quality of the "new name" in Revelation 2:17 and the "new Jerusalem" in 3:12. [See question #4, page 312.]

This song of praise expresses appreciation of a person's relationship with God under the new covenant. That changed relationship has been brought about by the saving work of Christ in forgiving sin through *blood,* making righteousness available. It is the providing Christ—the "Rock" of 1 Corinthians 10:4—who will disclose the message of the sealed book, a message designed to preserve this relationship that we have with God through Christ. No other relationship can equal it, regardless of how strong human bonds may be.

Robert E. Coleman is right when he adds that "It is called 'a new song' because that which Christ has accomplished is wholly different and superior to the old covenant; nothing like it has ever existed before. New works of grace call forth new songs of praise" *(Songs of Heaven).*

A New Song

New musical idioms often seem strange and (sometimes) shocking. The twentieth century saw the advent of jazz and rock 'n' roll. Perhaps strange at first, both are now well-established forms of musical expression.

However, one of the strangest "new songs" in secular music was John Cage's "4'33"." It was first performed for a gathering of modern, cutting edge artists at Woodstock in 1952, and it was too outrageous even for them to accept. Some walked out during the performance.

The piece lasted for four minutes and thirty-three seconds (hence the name). The pianist played nothing, but merely closed and opened the piano keyboard lid and turned several pages of blank musical score while timing it all with a stopwatch. Even stranger is one reviewer's comments: "4'33" wasn't at all easy for Cage to write. Although it was initially conceived in 1947, the piece wasn't written until 1952, and then only after long and careful deliberation."

Late in the twentieth century, we saw Christian music metamorphose from hymns and gospel songs to the "praise music" of contemporary worship services. Dismay and disdain not unlike the response to John Cage's "4'33"" characterize the reaction of many Christians to the new music.

But the "new song" of which the apostle John writes is new more for its message than for its style: out of all who have ever lived, One has finally been found who is worthy to open the book of life. That One is our Lord Jesus Christ who has brought redemption to reality. This is a song worth singing throughout eternity! —C. R. B.

10. And hast made us unto our God kings and priests: and we shall reign on the earth.

This verse, a part of the "new song," also presents the blessings of this relationship with God. To be made *kings and priests* is similar to Revelation 1:6, which tells us what Jesus Christ has achieved in making "us kings and priests unto God and his Father." [See question #5, page 312.]

The king-kingdom idea carries throughout the Bible. For Christians, our position in God's kingdom is a present reality that has eternal significance; it reaches its fulfillment in Heaven itself. What a privilege it is to have God's provision and protection in His kingdom! We allow this protection to become a reality when we show our submission to Him and depend on Him.

Yet this privilege, as others, holds a corresponding responsibility: we are *priests* to minister for God on behalf of our needs and the needs of others (1 Peter 2:5, 9). What access, what protection, what relationship, what responsibility! Praise the Lord!

Also, we know what it is to *reign* with Christ. We have become united in the likeness of His death and His resurrection, and thus live and reign with Him (cf. Romans 6:3-7). John discusses this idea again in Revelation 20:6. What assurance it is knowing that our relationship with Him includes reigning with Him! Praise the Lord again!

And Christ is indeed praiseworthy. The ground of praise is Christ's death and resurrection, and the blessings thereby brought to those who accept His redemptive work. He has met our need. He is the One who has the answer to the problems of His people, His suffering servants.

The fifth chapter of Revelation closes with the picture of God's triumphant jubilation as coming from the four beasts, the twenty-four elders, the thousands of angels, and the inhabitants of the universe. The great act of homage closes as it began: with the response of the central characters. God shows that He is worthy of worship. And all those of us who view this scene now add our "amen." Worthy is the Lamb to receive our worship! Amen! Come, Lord Jesus!

Conclusion

A. The Lamb's Presence and Power

The throne room scene has enabled us as readers to have further revelation of Jesus Christ. We have seen Christ on the throne as overcomer, having accomplished His task.

This kind of Lamb sees and knows (seven eyes) the situation of the saints (all Christians). He has the power and authority (seven horns) to act. He stands ready to move into action. He understands our suffering, and He cares and acts on our behalf.

As we consider the visions that God provided John, it is important to note what one sees and what one hears. When we put these elements together, we should have a clear understanding of what the visions mean. The visions are not intended to be mysterious or vague or subject to anyone's opinion. They are revelations from God, who allowed John to remove the "cover" so that we can see and understand.

If we can think of today's lesson text as a scene in an act of a drama, we will instinctively realize that it is essential that all parts be kept in their proper sequence. In that way we will be able to understand the author's intent. As we meditate on the scene, we realize that the dominant figure is the Lamb. His description gives us an insight into His nature, His role, and His relationships.

As we find ourselves drawn into the scene, we identify with John in sensing the meaning of all the imagery. We are reassured and comforted to be in the presence of the Lamb, who cares about our need and can act to meet that need. This need and the desire for assistance is brought into focus as we consider what the message of the sealed book might be.

Our anticipation is heightened, for we know that only the Lamb has the right to open the seven-sealed book. This book holds an assuring message for John and all the rest of the suffering servants—then and now (see Revelation 6:1–8:5). Christians, praise the Lamb!

Are you hurting today because things do not seem to be going well at church, even though you are serving faithfully? Do you wonder whether anyone understands how desperate you feel, knowing your spouse is terminally ill? Are you grief stricken because your position has been cut at work? A great number of circumstances that bring us hurt cause us to cry out, "It's just not fair!"

True, it may not be fair. But we are not promised that situations and events in this life will always be fair. What we are promised is that the Lamb (whose own death wasn't "fair") is present to provide what we need at such an hour. It is especially comforting to remember that He will be with us in the hour of our death, as we journey to His arms. Hence, we can sing "the new song" of praise to the Lamb—our Lamb!

During the past two decades, there has been an ongoing discussion and debate in many churches as to style of music to be used in worship. The emphasis has been such that some Christians could conclude that music is the central feature of our assemblies and our worship. Such an issue is not only divisive in the church, but it is also taking our focus away from what the vital matter is in worship.

The real matter is not hymn or praise choruses, guitars, pianos, or organs, padded pews or chair arrangements, worship ministers or song leaders—or all the various helps we want to emphasize. Today's lesson teaches us that the foundational requirement is a real sense of the presence of the Lamb, an understanding of who He is, and a perception of our relationship with Him. It is He who is worthy of praise!

When we let things that we have incorporated into our worship services take our minds and hearts away from the Lamb, we need to repent and return to the worship of the One who is worthy of our devotion. In this way we will not withhold our commitment and service to Him. If we repent, then there is blessing. If we do not, the result is judgment.

B. Prayer

Almighty, loving Father, thank You for the book of Revelation. Thank You for the encouragement it gives us to see how You have provided for us through Your saving work as Jesus, the Lamb. We know He is aware of our suffering and all our situations. We struggle in many ways to stay faithful and committed to You. We thank You for such portions of Your Word as the text of our lesson that make the presence of the Lamb so real. Because of Him we worship and praise Your name, amen.

C. Thought to Remember

He is real and He is ours.

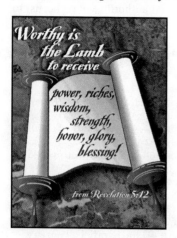

Visual for lesson 10

This calligraphy will help reinforce today's Golden Text. Who is worthy? He is worthy!

Learning by Doing

This page contains an alternative lesson plan emphasizing learning activities.
Classes desiring such student involvement will find these suggestions helpful.

Learning Goals

After participating in this lesson, each student will be able to:

1. Describe the unique position of the Lamb as the one who is worthy of worship.

2. Explain why the focus of one's worship and life must be on the Lamb.

3. Express worship to the Lamb who is worthy.

Into the Lesson

For these activities you will need the following: (1) a long sheet of paper with a ribbon to be wrapped around it as a scroll; (2) a "special" chair (throne) that is different from the rest of the chairs in the room; (3) a sheet of paper with the words *Perfect Person* written on it; (4) a tape or CD copy of the song "Watch the Lamb" by Ray Boltz.

Before the class arrives, prepare the scroll with the words of the songs found in Revelation 5:9, 10, 12, and 13. Set the special chair apart from the other furniture in the class. Attach the sheet of paper with the words *Perfect Person* to this chair. Wrap the scroll with a ribbon and place it on the seat of the chair.

As you begin the class, say, "Write the name of the person in the class who is most worthy to sit in this special chair." This will likely result in some discomfort for the students because there is not a person in the class who is "perfect" or even "most worthy."

Say, "Obviously, not one of us could be seated in this chair as a perfect person. There is only one Person who could sit here."

Into the Word

As a volunteer reads Revelation 5:1-10, tell the class to listen carefully for the word used to designate the One who is worthy. Ask, "Why is the word *Lamb* used of Jesus?" Allow the students time to respond and discuss possibilities. Say, "This word *Lamb* is used extensively in the book of Revelation, beginning with chapter 5. It is a special designation set aside for the One worthy to open the book."

Form small groups and assign the following texts: *Group 1*—Exodus 12:1-14; *Group 2*—Luke 22:7-16; *Group 3*—Revelation 6:16; 12:10-12; Revelation 17:12-14; and Revelation 21:22-27. Tell the students to make a list of characteristics and purposes of the lambs or Lamb based on these texts.

Have a member of each group report their findings. The first two groups have texts that focus on the idea of a lamb as sacrifice in the Passover. The Revelation texts provide several characteristics, such as wrathful (6:16), conqueror, King of kings (17:14), and dwelling place (21:22).

Ask, "Given these characteristics and purposes of the Lamb, why is He and He alone to be worshiped?" The response should mirror the characteristics and purpose: He should be worshiped because He is Lord of lords; He is our dwelling place; He provides the perfect and final sacrifice.

If you have time, you can enhance your discussion by being ready to note how the Scriptures refer to Jesus as the Lamb in other passages. Isaiah 53:7 and 1 Peter 1:19 are examples.

Into Life

Have the students return to their groups. Say, "List ways our focus in worship are often diverted away from the Lamb." After a short time, ask a representative from each group to present the ways a person may be distracted in worship. These may include such distractions as food and drink in the sanctuary, style of music, family conflict on the way to church, anticipation of activities following church. As each is presented, identify how it may affect a person's worship.

Note that worship does not occur only in the church building. The image of a slain Lamb standing recalls the image of the living sacrifice mentioned in Romans 12. Worship is a way of life, and our way of life, our worship, is to be directed toward the Lamb.

Encourage students to write down one issue that distracts them from worship in the assembly and one issue that distracts them from a life of worship. Ask them to write the words, "Not Worthy" across this sheet of paper as if voiding a check. Open the scroll placed on the chair and read the words aloud to the class. As the song "Watch the Lamb" by Ray Boltz plays, have the students pray for wisdom in worshiping the Lamb without distraction. If this song is not accessible, sing a hymn or chorus focused on worshiping the Lamb (e.g., "Thou Art Worthy").

Finally, say, "We will leave this chair with the opened scroll to remind us of the focus of the book of Revelation throughout the remaining three weeks."

Let's Talk It Over

The questions on this page are designed to promote discussion of the lesson by the class and to encourage application of the lesson Scriptures. The answers provided are only discussion starters. Let your class talk it over from there.

1. How much of a gap is there between the Lamb's worthiness to open the scroll and that of "the best of the rest" of the universe? Why is that important to you?

Beside the Father and the Holy Spirit, no one has ever came close to equaling Christ's power and wisdom. No being in any realm has ever surpassed His feat of creating then redeeming by the sacrifice of His uncreated self. None in Heaven (angels, godly heroes from the past), or on earth (kings, presidents, heroes from the present), or under the earth (Satan, demons, unsaved conquerors from the past) even remotely approaches the character or the deeds of Jesus. The gap between Him and them is infinite.

These facts should both comfort and humble us. Our comfort comes from the fact of Jesus' love for us and His victory over sin. Our humility comes from realizing that "we are not He."

2. Verse 6 places the spotlight on the Lamb. What are some ways we can put the spotlight on the Lamb in everything we do?

Our church services should center on Christ by being saturated with reminders of Him as Creator, Redeemer, and the One who will return. Songs and sermons should be Christ-centered, and visitors should always be told how to accept Christ and be encouraged to do so.

Our homes should be places where Jesus is mentioned often. At work, our coworkers should know without a doubt—by our words, our character, and by what they see on our desks—that we are in love with Jesus. Our witnessing should focus less on our church, our preacher, prominent members, and our own stories, and focus most on the story of Jesus—who He is and what He has done to deserve the spotlight!

3. The lesson notes "a bit of a paradox as power and submissive sacrifice are coupled together" in Jesus as both Lion and Lamb. How can we exhibit a similar "paradox" in our lives of service?

The key is what church leaders model to their church's members. Church leaders are to follow the model of Christ in having a blend of strength and humble service. The church leader must be strong in moral character, family, faith, the Word, and work ethic (1 Timothy 3; Titus 1).

There must be strength in fulfilling the shepherding duties of ruling, teaching, disciplining, and encouraging the church.

But another key job of the church leader—and any Christian—is to give oneself in humble service to the Lord and to His flock. Christian leaders do not powerfully "lord" it over them, but humbly set an example of Christian living (1 Peter 5:3, 4), expending themselves in service (2 Corinthians 12:15). God expects strength (Ephesians 6:10) and a life of sacrifice (Romans 12:1) from every Christian.

4. How has the "song" you have sung as a Christian been "new"?

Shame on us if there is no noticeable difference between the old us and the new us! If we have really been rescued from sin, Satan, death, worry, and eternal torment, how can that not be reflected on our faces and in our entire way of life?

Whether we're actually singing aloud or just singing on the inside, others should see peace, joy, fulfillment, optimism, satisfaction, and security. We are confident in Christ without being arrogant. The new concern for others and interest in more important things ought to leap out at folks who have known us a while. Let the world sing the same old tune; we have a new song!

5. Now that we have become "priests," how can we live out our priestly calling in the coming week?

Unlike Old Testament priests, we do not offer blood sacrifices for sin. We have a Great High Priest who already has done that (Hebrews 4:14–5:10). Praise God!

But if it's true that blessing brings responsibility, then God must expect certain things from us as His newly appointed priests. We perform our priestly duties when we teach people about God and Christ. We pray for them. We offer ourselves and our possessions as sacrifices (Romans 12:1; Philippians 4:18; 2 Timothy 4:6). We serve the people of the church, whose bodies are God's temple (1 Corinthians 3:16).

How we perform our priestly duties daily is highly individual, and your learners will have many different ideas. Remind your learners that there is no retirement from our priestly service!

Receiving God's Salvation

DEVOTIONAL READING: Revelation 3:7-13.

BACKGROUND SCRIPTURE: Revelation 7.

PRINTED TEXT: Revelation 7:1-3, 9, 10, 13-17.

Revelation 7:1-3, 9, 10, 13-17

1 And after these things I saw four angels standing on the four corners of the earth, holding the four winds of the earth, that the wind should not blow on the earth, nor on the sea, nor on any tree.

2 And I saw another angel ascending from the east, having the seal of the living God: and he cried with a loud voice to the four angels, to whom it was given to hurt the earth and the sea,

3 Saying, Hurt not the earth, neither the sea, nor the trees, till we have sealed the servants of our God in their foreheads.

· · · · · · · · · · · ·

9 After this I beheld, and, lo, a great multitude, which no man could number, of all nations, and kindreds, and people, and tongues, stood before the throne, and before the Lamb, clothed with white robes, and palms in their hands;

10 And cried with a loud voice, saying, Salvation to our God which sitteth upon the throne, and unto the Lamb.

· · · · · · · · · · · ·

13 And one of the elders answered, saying unto me, What are these which are arrayed in white robes? and whence came they?

14 And I said unto him, Sir, thou knowest. And he said to me, These are they which came out of great tribulation, and have washed their robes, and made them white in the blood of the Lamb.

15 Therefore are they before the throne of God, and serve him day and night in his temple: and he that sitteth on the throne shall dwell among them.

16 They shall hunger no more, neither thirst any more; neither shall the sun light on them, nor any heat.

17 For the Lamb which is in the midst of the throne shall feed them, and shall lead them unto living fountains of waters: and God shall wipe away all tears from their eyes.

May
16

GOLDEN TEXT: For the Lamb which is in the midst of the throne shall feed them, and shall lead them unto living fountains of waters: and God shall wipe away all tears from their eyes.—Revelation 7:17.

Lesson Aims

After participating in this lesson, each student should be able to:

1. Tell how the believer's relationship with the Lamb provides protection, salvation, and comfort.

2. Relate the blessings of this relationship to the trials one faces in life, and describe the victory that results.

3. Identify a personal trial for which he or she will seek the Lord's help and comfort.

Lesson Outline

INTRODUCTION
    A. What Salvation Costs
    B. Lesson Background
  I. RESTRAINT AND SEAL (Revelation 7:1-3)
    A. Angels Protect the Church (v. 1)
       Protection From the Wind
    B. Angels Seal the Church (vv. 2, 3)
 II. MULTITUDE AND PROCLAMATION (Revelation 7:9, 10)
    A. Appearance of Many (v. 9)
       The Changing "Face" of the Church
    B. Ascent of Praise (v. 10)
III. IDENTITY AND SERVICE (Revelation 7:13-17)
    A. John Questioned (vv. 13, 14a)
    B. Elder Replies (vv. 14b-17)
       Return of Stolen Property
CONCLUSION
    A. God's Presence in Suffering
    B. Prayer
    C. Thought to Remember

Introduction

A. What Salvation Costs

Robert E. Coleman tells a story of a traveler who was always on the lookout for unusual things in each city he visited. In one particular town, he noticed a curious spire atop a public building. Upon closer inspection the man noticed that the wall bore a stone figure of a lamb about two-thirds of the way up. Upon inquiry, the traveler discovered that the replica marked the spot where a workman had lost his balance and had fallen while the building was under construction.

But the worker wasn't killed, as a local resident related. When the mason fell, he providentially landed on a lamb that was on its way to slaughter along with several others. The lamb's body provided enough "cushioning" to break the man's fall and save his life (at the cost of the lamb's own life). The builder was so impressed with the event that he had the image of a lamb placed there as a lasting tribute. If you had been that traveler, what would your reaction have been? [See question #1, page 320.]

B. Lesson Background

When we saw the Lamb in Revelation 5, we saw Him standing, ready to act. We also saw an image of the Lamb having been slain. The reality of the Lamb's suffering was obvious. Both His suffering and readiness to act were for our benefit.

As the story unfolded, the Lamb began to act as He took the sealed book in order to open it and reveal its desired message (Revelation 5:5, 8). The book held an assuring message for John and all the rest of us who are suffering servants "for the word of God, and for the testimony of Jesus Christ" (1:9).

In the first five messages of the sealed book the reality of suffering is obvious. But more than that, the reader understands that the suffering church in her faithfulness asks for judgment upon sin. All the aspects of the throne room scene combine to assure us that God and the Lamb will execute this righteous judgment. That judgment is only on the wicked who have not repented. The message of the sixth seal emphasizes just how serious this judgment shall be (6:12-17).

In the series of images, the reader is aware that the entire message is building to a climax. As we cross into chapter 7, we realize that it is "intermission time" in this act of the play we are watching. During this intermission, the reader can reassess his or her relationship with the Lamb, knowing His salvation and His protection.

Here in John's "theater" is a scene that will help to strengthen our patience. The sixth seal left us with a scene that was quite bleak; but as happens so often in this book, the scene changes when the picture looks the bleakest. The scene of chapter 7 is a refreshing interlude, for the reader is given a graphic pledge of God's protection for His church through her trials.

Unless the Lamb's salvation and protection are real, Christians may break under the stress of their trials. We can learn much from the scene, understanding that tribulation does not come from God. We comprehend the protection and the strength provided by the Lord. The reader, along with John, becomes involved in the scene so that he or she knows the personal and practical nature of what is seen and what is heard.

I. Restraint and Seal
(Revelation 7:1-3)

A. Angels Protect the Church (v. 1)

1. And after these things I saw four angels standing on the four corners of the earth, holding the four winds of the earth, that the wind should not blow on the earth, nor on the sea, nor on any tree.

The opposition for the people of God is pictured as *the four winds of the earth*. This fourfold nature of the wind creates a kind of "fullness of opposition" as the four horses and their riders did in the opening of the first four seals of the sealed book (Revelation 6:1-8).

God's protection is seen as *four angels standing*, ready to serve God and His people. To make the picture all-inclusive, they are positioned at *the four corners of the earth*. It is not stated in this fashion to convey the idea that the earth is flat. Rather, the figure shows a full defense from all directions.

The series of the potential recipients of the wind seems somewhat unusual: the *earth*, the *sea*, and *any tree*. In identifying the realm where people live, John probably uses this series so that the reader will not be tempted to take it too literally and try to cite a particular geographical location at a certain time in history. A tree is a natural object to select for observing the reality of opposition, the wind. Do not we do the same thing if someone asks us if the wind is blowing, or how strong it is? We look to the nearest tree to check the movement of the leaves or the branches. Thus, the use of *tree* helps us to know the expression is figurative, but *real*.

It is the ministry of the angels to hold back the wind. Hence, the Christian perceives that there is no way any opposition need destroy one's relationship with Christ. It is foolish to ask what would happen if the angels were to let go. We know that God is in control, and the four angels will not weaken.

What assurance this is for all Christians, realizing God's power is greater than that of the opposition! This imagery should remind us that things are not always what they seem to be. Even though Christians know what it means to hurt as they go about their day-to-day encounters, they must know also that the reality of the suffering is not a sign that God has abandoned them. There are two sides to the Christian experience. The security must be as real as the suffering. The scene helps to get this point across.

PROTECTION FROM THE WIND

The wind: sometimes it is a refreshing, gentle breeze; sometimes, the destructive frenzy of a tornado or hurricane. Even between these two extremes it can have amazing power. You may have seen film clips of the collapse of "Galloping Gertie," a suspension bridge across Tacoma Narrows in Washington State. Gentle winds through the Narrows would cause the bridge to rise and fall several feet so that drivers would lose sight of cars ahead of them.

Then, early in the morning of November 7, 1940—just four months after its completion—winds reaching forty-five miles per hour began to twist the roadway over a twenty-eight-foot arc from side-to-side—a ninety-degree movement. For thirty minutes the bridge twisted violently before collapsing into the waters below.

It is this destructive power of the wind that John alludes to when he notes that the four angels are holding back the metaphorical winds that could bring suffering to the people of God. The forces of evil—whether natural, human, or demonic—may twist the surface of life beneath us and toss us violently from side to side. But it is only to a limited degree and for a limited time. John assures us that the power of God is a stabilizing force, our ultimate protection and our hope for eternal refuge. It is a protection available to the Christian, and no one else.   —C. R. B.

B. Angels Seal the Church (vv. 2, 3)

2. And I saw another angel ascending from the east, having the seal of the living God: and he cried with a loud voice to the four angels, to whom it was given to hurt the earth and the sea.

The spotlight now falls on another angel, who comes *from the east*. This phrase could be translated more literally as "from the rising of the sun." This is another expression for the radiance of God's glory. The angel's *loud voice* relays instructions to *the four angels* seen holding back the four winds from the servants of God. There is no mistaking the commanding nature of this voice. The next verse helps us understand the meaning of *the seal of the living God*.

3. Saying, Hurt not the earth, neither the sea, nor the trees, till we have sealed the servants of our God in their foreheads.

When we read *Hurt not the earth, neither the sea, nor the trees*, our thought is not on "place," but on "people," as the context indicates. This

---

How to Say It

CORINTHIANS. Kor-*in*-thee-unz (*th* as in *thin*).

EPHESIANS. Ee-*fee*-zhunz.

EZEKIEL. Ee-*zeek*-ee-ul or Ee-*zeek*-yul.

ISAIAH. Eye-*zay*-uh.

"hurt" or "harm" is delayed until God's *servants* can be *sealed* and protected. The idea of sealing the people of God is a figure found in the Old Testament (cf. Song of Solomon 8:6; Ezekiel 9:4).

Sealing is also a figure used in the New Testament of the presence of the Holy Spirit (cf. 2 Corinthians 1:22; Ephesians 1:13; 4:30). It is a mark of ownership, and thus provides authentication, security, and protection. [See question #2, page 320.] Revelation 9:4 shows us God's wrath against those who are not sealed.

II. Multitude and Proclamation (Revelation 7:9, 10)

A. Appearance of Many (v. 9)

9. After this I beheld, and, lo, a great multitude, which no man could number, of all nations, and kindreds, and people, and tongues, stood before the throne, and before the Lamb, clothed with white robes, and palms in their hands.

Following the "sealed servants" of Revelation 7:3 and the "144,000" of 7:4-8 (not in today's text), the reader is shown another identification for God's people: *a great multitude.* When we place these three values together we see John's way of indicating "kind" or "quality" of those in the scene.

Whether we think of this group as "numbered" (144,000) or "without number," we should not miss John's intent to show us the bigger picture: twenty-first-century Christians are just as much a part of this group as those in John's day. When we read the messages to the seven churches in Revelation 1:9–3:22, for example, we understand that the apostle's intent is for the message to be for all churches of all time (including our time).

For this multitude, nationality and language are irrelevant! As we see them *before the throne, and before the Lamb,* they are ready to worship. Part of being ready for this festive celebration is wearing the right clothes (cf. Matthew 22:11, 12). To be dressed in *white* is a common characteristic of those who overcome through Christ (Revelation 3:4, 5, 18; 6:11; 7:13, 14). Their actions involve having *palms in their hands.* Palm branches are often a part of a scene of festive joy (John 12:13). They are appropriate for the expression of praise and worship that follow.

THE CHANGING "FACE" OF THE CHURCH

As the early church expanded, Christianity became primarily a white, Western religion, and it remained so for centuries. But after World War II the church began to break out of this small box. What amazing changes are taking place today! Consider, for instance, that of the world's esti-

mated four hundred million evangelical Christians, 70 percent are non-Western, living in Africa, Asia, Oceania, and Latin America.

In 1960, more than half of all who claimed to be Christians lived in North America and Europe. Around 1970, Christianity's "center of gravity" began moving south and east. By 1990, only 38 percent of all Christians lived in Western nations. That figure is now down to only about 30 percent!

The church is growing at a much slower rate in the Western nations than elsewhere in the world. To put it another way, the "face" of Christianity is changing. No longer is it white and Western; now it is brown, black, and yellow.

As the affluent and self-satisfied West has turned its back on Christian values, the rest of the world has found the answer to the soul's deepest needs. Today the church looks more and more like the picture John paints for us in our text for today, with members from "all nations, and kindreds, and people, and tongues." May we continue to spread the gospel to the uttermost parts of the world!   —C. R. B.

B. Ascent of Praise (v. 10)

10. And cried with a loud voice, saying, Salvation to our God which sitteth upon the throne, and unto the Lamb.

When Christians see what their relationship with *God* and *the Lamb* really means, the natural reaction is praise and worship. The Lamb has provided our salvation, which includes forgiveness, righteousness, and assurance with the presence of the Holy Spirit. He provides all we need. What do we have to worry about? [See question #3, page 320.]

III. Identity and Service (Revelation 7:13-17)

A. John Questioned (vv. 13, 14a)

13, 14a. And one of the elders answered, saying unto me, What are these which are arrayed in white robes? and whence came they? And I said unto him, Sir, thou knowest.

Now John finds himself personally involved in the vision. As *one of the elders* asks him to identify those dressed *in white robes,* John has not forgotten the previous scenes. In those scenes he saw Christ dressed in white, the overcomers promised robes of white, and the twenty-four elders on twenty-four thrones with their robes of white and their crowns of gold. As John now ponders the great multitude dressed in white robes, he undoubtedly also remembers the slain saints under the altar, satisfied with their white robes and their rest for a little time.

The question that the elder asks of John means that John is being challenged to draw "the bottom line" and comprehend the meaning. When John replies to the elder *Sir, thou knowest,* the implication is something like "you know that I understand."

B. Elder Replies (vv. 14b-17)

14b. And he said to me, These are they which came out of great tribulation, and have washed their robes, and made them white in the blood of the Lamb.

The reply of the elder, who serves as spokesman in the scene, then reinforces the meaning for the reader. The ones clothed in white *robes* are overcomers. The *great tribulation* is a "trial" they have experienced or are experiencing as their faith is tested. They are clothed in righteousness in God's presence because of their faith in the salvation provided by Christ. In casting their allegiance with Him, they have *washed their robes* in the *blood of the Lamb.* What availing faith! What white-robed overcomers!

Daniel 12:1 speaks of a great "time of trouble," and Matthew 24:21 warns of "great tribulation." These passages may refer to specific periods in history. But before we get carried away with too much speculation of "when" and "where," let us remember that all Christians are tested. Each of us goes through some kind of *great tribulation.* Each of us has personal struggles in a sin-sick world, as John had in his day. But those struggles will come to an end, as we see in the next verse.

15. Therefore are they before the throne of God, and serve him day and night in his temple: and he that sitteth on the throne shall dwell among them.

The uncountable multitude from verse 9 is observed standing ready to *serve* before the *throne.* This service is *day and night*—a picture of continued service, growth, and appreciation of the presence of God.

What blessings there are in that presence! We are learning in the scenes to appreciate this presence and relationship in the here and now, especially in the ministry of the Holy Spirit. If people do not enjoy being in God's presence now and serving Him continually in the church, they surely could not enjoy Heaven. Unless Christians come to an understanding of the presence of God, they will make a sham of faith and the church. Our faith is not real if we do not know the blessings of His presence. The more we overcome in this life through His power, the greater will be our comfort in the life to come.

16. They shall hunger no more, neither thirst any more; neither shall the sun light on them, nor any heat.

This verse sets forth figures that express the reality of hurt, trials, or suffering common to Christians. The very necessities of physical life can be the occasion for trial. Food, water, clothing, shelter—all are basic.

There are times when it may seem that we don't have much assurance of these physical necessities. In such times we can find ourselves put to the test as to whether we will stay faithful amidst our suffering and lack. When we hurt, the presence and the protection of the Lamb can seem far away and not quite real. The image from our next verse gives us something to hold on to in such times.

17. For the Lamb which is in the midst of the throne shall feed them, and shall lead them unto living fountains of waters: and God shall wipe away all tears from their eyes.

The figure that we have become familiar with from chapter 5 onward is the metaphor of Christ as *the Lamb.* In a way, it may seem paradoxical that the Lamb is also a Shepherd who *shall feed them.* But remember that when we first saw the Lamb in last week's lesson He stood ready to minister even though He appeared to have been slain. The hurt brought to the Lamb may have caused the onlooker to wonder whether there might be someone greater than He.

But being able to overcome His own ordeal means that He is the very One who has the power to help us in our time of trial. The Lamb's ability to help us is no assurance that we shall bypass trial and suffering. It *is* a guarantee, however, that we shall triumph because of our relationship with the Lamb.

Because He lives, we live. Heaven has already started for the Christian. [See question #4, page 320.] Eternal life (the Lamb's kind of life) began

Visual for lessons 11, 13

God shall wipe away all tears.
~ Revelation 21:4

Use this visual to remind your learners that God is the Great Tear-Wiper.

for the new Christian when he or she became united with Christ and was raised to "walk in newness of life" (Romans 6:3-5). As a result, Christians know what it is to live and reign with Christ even now.

Many Old Testament passages speak of God's provisions (e.g., Psalm 23; Isaiah 49:10, 11; Ezekiel 34:23). In the New Testament we see Christ Himself providing for our needs. This fact comes alive when we see Him in the midst of the seven golden candlesticks of Revelation 1, as the Lamb with seven horns and seven eyes in Revelation 5, and as the Good Shepherd protecting the flock of God in John 10. In the verse before us we have a chance to see His gracious provision made more vivid than anywhere else in Scripture. We share His tent, His food and water, and His supply for all our needs.

When we realize "where we are," somehow we are not as threatened and the pain is not as severe. The stubbed toe of the child somehow seems less painful in the security of the parent's arms. In like manner, God is the Great Tear-Wiper! What love and security in His presence! [See question #5, page 320.]

RETURN OF STOLEN PROPERTY

In 1960 Audrey Wheeler left her purse at a restaurant. It contained her ID card, several pictures of her family, a copy of Psalm 23 from her father's funeral, and her pay envelope with a week's pay in cash. A thief took the money and left the rest, which somehow ended up in the kitchen wall of the café. It was found forty years later when the building was demolished.

When Wheeler recovered her purse at the police station, it was in surprisingly good condition considering the time and the place where it had been hidden. As she pulled out each of the lost treasures, she and her sisters spent several hours talking about the memories that each item brought forth. The women agreed that the memories triggered by the pictures were far more important than the lost cash, although at the time it had been a lot of money.

The innocence of the human race was stolen in the Garden of Eden. Our relationship with God that was lost in the fall was far more valuable than anything Adam and Eve hoped to gain. We still suffer from their mistaken quest today.

But John tells us about a new Heaven. There everything that has been stolen by sin shall be renewed in the presence of God. All our hurt and misery shall be wiped away. In fact, through the work of Christ God already is giving us a taste of the new Paradise that He is preparing for us. With such a great gift at hand, does it make any sense to continue in sin? —C. R. B.

Conclusion

A. God's Presence in Suffering

Because of God's salvation provided in the Lamb, Christians have the assurance of a right relationship with God. His dwelling place brings protection; throne or tent are essentially the same. Where God is and what results from His presence are the necessary things to understand.

All this means is that we need not worry about why Christians suffer, or the timing of the Lord's return and the end of the world. Our relationship with God is restored and real *right now*, and any trial is temporary and bearable. His presence makes it that way!

We shall not, and dare not, let anything interrupt this relationship. Thus, our hearts are kindled for praise, and we echo the words of the great multitude: "Salvation to our God which sitteth upon the throne, and unto the Lamb!"

B. Prayer

Thank You, God, for being the loving, caring Father that You are. Because of the Lamb we know You have seen our needs and are able to meet those needs. And because of the Lamb we are never alone, no matter what kind of situation tests our faith.

Father, it is because of the Lamb that we understand both sides of our Christian experience: our hurting and our protection. We know that testing is very real, but we are thankful that Your provision strengthens us. Because of Christ we smile amidst our tears. In the name of the Lamb we pray, amen.

C. Thought to Remember

Our hurt is real, but so is the Lamb's power.

Home Daily Bible Readings

Monday, May 10—Deliverance Belongs to the Lord (Psalm 3:1-8)

Tuesday, May 11—The God of My Salvation (Psalm 25:1-5)

Wednesday, May 12—My Rock and My Salvation (Psalm 62:1-6)

Thursday, May 13—On God Rests My Deliverance (Psalm 62:7-12)

Friday, May 14—Through Jesus Is Forgiveness of Sins (Acts 13:32-39)

Saturday, May 15—Salvation Belongs to Our God (Revelation 7:1-10)

Sunday, May 16—Before the Throne of God (Revelation 7:11-17)

Learning by Doing

This page contains an alternative lesson plan emphasizing learning activities.
Classes desiring such student involvement will find these suggestions helpful.

Learning Goals

After participating in this lesson, each student will be able to:

1. Tell how the believer's relationship with the Lamb provides protection, salvation, and comfort.

2. Relate the blessings of this relationship to the trials one faces in life and describe the victory that results.

3. Identify a personal trial for which he or she will seek the Lord's help and comfort.

Into the Lesson

Ask several students to name the person from whom they have experienced the most helpful shepherding. This person does not have to be living. Students may indicate people such as a parent, close relative, classmate from high school, close friend, elder, spouse, or an employer. Ask, "What characteristics of this person make him or her so helpful?" List these characteristics for all to see.

Ask, "When you have faced difficult times in your life, what has this person provided?" Write responses on the board. After taking all of the responses, identify each as either (1) helping through providing comfort or (2) helping through providing protection. Examples of comfort responses include crying with the person, coming to visit, or simply being available. Examples of protection responses include standing up for someone in the presence of criticism, making sure the person was not in the same situation again, providing the basics of life—food, clothing, shelter.

Say, "The Lamb as our Shepherd provides us with both the ultimate comfort and absolute protection, regardless of the severity of the trials we face as Christians."

Into the Word

Say, "This particular section of Revelation is quite involved, and students often miss the point in the details." Tell the students to read through Revelation 7:1-8, focusing on every detail they can find. After they have finished reading, ask students to list these details aloud while you write them. *(Details will include four angels, four corners, four winds, angel from the east, seal on foreheads, 144,000, and 12,000 from each of the twelve tribes.)* Ask, "Give some examples of times you have heard or seen any of these details used

as the focus of a study or presentation of Revelation." You can provide an initial example of the focus of Jehovah's Witnesses on 144,000 people who are saved. When examples are stated, do not let students pursue them in detail.

Say, "Often people stop at the details and completely miss what this text is intended to be: a very encouraging text." Have students read Revelation 7:9-17 with a view to the "big picture." When they have finished, have each student write a short summary of this section. Ask for volunteers to read their summaries. A sample summary is: "People of every background who have experienced severe trials will receive salvation and rest, ultimately standing before the Lamb in worship."

Into Life

Read from the commentary, "Daniel 12:1 speaks of a great 'time of trouble,' and Matthew 24:21 warns of 'great tribulation.' These passages may refer to specific periods in history. But before we get carried away with too much speculation of 'when' and 'where,' let us remember that all Christians are tested. Each of us goes through some kind of *great tribulation*. Each of us has personal struggles in a sin-sick world, as John had in his day. But those struggles will come to an end."

Say, "In reviewing this text we see the inevitability of trials and the assurance of victory." Have each student recall, without dwelling on the details, several of the most difficult trials he or she has faced throughout life, writing each one on the left side of a sheet of paper. On the right side each should then write how his or her relationship with the Lamb has affected the experience of this trial. An example of a difficult trial might be extended unemployment. A strong relationship with Christ during this period could include trust in God's provision. Ask volunteers to report on how they have faced difficulties within the context of a relationship with Christ. Ask some to volunteer experiences they have had in dealing with trials outside of a relationship with Christ. Have each student write down one current trial that needs to be addressed by completing this sentence: A great trial in my life is ____.

After reading from the scroll (from lesson 10), ask students to write a prayer to the Lamb concerning this specific trial. Encourage the students to seek the Lord's help and comfort through prayer and through God's people in the days ahead.

Let's Talk It Over

The questions on this page are designed to promote discussion of the lesson by the class and to encourage application of the lesson Scriptures. The answers provided are only discussion starters. Let your class talk it over from there.

1. In what ways can we pay "a lasting tribute" to the Lamb who saved our lives, as the appreciative mason did? Following that, what do we do to prepare for the reaction of others?

Grateful believers show appreciation to Jesus in many creative ways. Some put Christian bumper stickers on their cars. Some place banners of the Lord's Prayer on their front lawns. Some put miniature nativity scenes on their desks at work during Christmastime.

Sometimes, however, these can be mere token expressions of a rather shallow appreciation. Probably the best tribute we can pay to our Savior is in lives characterized by purity, faithfulness, and service. To suffer (1 Peter 4:14), to discipline ourselves to purity (2 Timothy 2:21), or to do a deed of kindness in His name (Matthew 10:42) ultimately may be better tributes. In addition, we prepare ourselves to answer everyone who asks about the hope to which these tributes point (1 Peter 3:15).

2. Knowing that you have been "sealed," how secure and protected do you feel? How do we manage those times of trial when God seems distant?

Feelings are deceptive! In our Christian understanding of suffering we must realize that God is there even when we don't feel His presence. Through our sufferings He is working things to our good (Romans 8:28), refining us (1 Peter 1:6, 7), and making us better (James 1:2-4). Perhaps we should tape these Scriptures on our mirrors!

God has promised to deliver us from the trial (2 Corinthians 1:10), to give us strength to endure the trial (1 Corinthians 10:13), or to use the trial to bring us to the ultimate safety of Heaven (2 Timothy 4:18). Security and suffering are the "two sides to the Christian experience," as the lesson writer noted in commentary on 7:1. God has us covered, whether we feel like it or not.

3. What strategies might we use to ensure that in our next affliction we will have a song instead of (or along with) a tear?

The Bible suggests that the way to have joy through trials is to appreciate the benefits they bring. These benefits include strong character (Romans 5:3, 4; James 1:2-4), increased rewards

and glory (Matthew 5:10-12; 2 Corinthians 4:17), increased empathy and ability to comfort other sufferers (2 Corinthians 1:4), dissatisfaction with this earthly life, an anticipation of Heaven, and increased dependence on God, to name a few.

Earlier lessons have shown that hope is the key to endurance; so the more precise our hopes are, the more courageous and cheerful we can be in facing suffering. Strategies might be to memorize some of the Scriptures above, to read regularly from Job and 1 Peter, or to keep contact with an older Christian who has, by experience, learned the secrets of singing in the pain.

4. Do you have trouble believing that "Heaven has already started for the Christian"? In what ways is this really true in your personal life?

The Bible does indicate that we've already received a "taste" of Heaven and of God's grace (Hebrews 6:4, 5; 1 Peter 2:3). Think about it: we have been saved, delivered, and sanctified; we have new life; we are in God's kingdom; He is present with us; Satan has lost power over us; death is no longer a fear; we are under God's protection; and He is meeting our every need.

We show this reality by living lives of holiness. It works the other way, too: when we live lives of holiness, we tell the world that we trust what the Bible has to say about the taste of Heaven we have now and that which is yet to come.

5. What are some ways that the Lamb has been a "Shepherd" and a "Great Tear-Wiper" in your life? What "great tribulation" are you feeling right now that needs His tender, loving care?

We may not face the same kinds of persecution that the early Christians did, but every believer has struggles in this life (John 16:33; Acts 14:22; 1 Thessalonians 3:3). And our trials come in many varieties (1 Peter 1:6).

Your learners can share some of the crises they've experienced—perhaps related to death, health, finances, relationships, and disappointments—as well as how the Lord has protected them, rescued them, and dried their tears. Those who are willing to share current trials should be encouraged and reminded of the Good Shepherd's care for them. Following this sharing, ask them how the rest of the class can help and pray.

Enduring With the Saints

DEVOTIONAL READING: 2 Timothy 2:3-13.

BACKGROUND SCRIPTURE: Revelation 14.

PRINTED TEXT: Revelation 14:6-13.

Revelation 14:6-13

6 And I saw another angel fly in the midst of heaven, having the everlasting gospel to preach unto them that dwell on the earth, and to every nation, and kindred, and tongue, and people,

7 Saying with a loud voice, Fear God, and give glory to him; for the hour of his judgment is come: and worship him that made heaven, and earth, and the sea, and the fountains of waters.

8 And there followed another angel, saying, Babylon is fallen, is fallen, that great city, because she made all nations drink of the wine of the wrath of her fornication.

9 And the third angel followed them, saying with a loud voice, If any man worship the beast and his image, and receive his mark in his forehead, or in his hand,

10 The same shall drink of the wine of the wrath of God, which is poured out without mixture into the cup of his indignation; and he shall be tormented with fire and brimstone in the presence of the holy angels, and in the presence of the Lamb:

11 And the smoke of their torment ascendeth up for ever and ever: and they have no rest day nor night, who worship the beast and his image, and whosoever receiveth the mark of his name.

12 Here is the patience of the saints: here are they that keep the commandments of God, and the faith of Jesus.

13 And I heard a voice from heaven saying unto me, Write, Blessed are the dead which die in the Lord from henceforth: Yea, saith the Spirit, that they may rest from their labors; and their works do follow them.

May
23

GOLDEN TEXT: Here is the patience of the saints: here are they that keep the commandments of God, and the faith of Jesus.—Revelation 14:12.

Living Expectantly
Unit 2: Visions of Hope
(Lessons 10-13)

Lesson Aims

After participating in this lesson, each student should be able to:

1. Contrast the punishment of the wicked with the blessings of the faithful.

2. Explain how God's judgment for sin gives Him glory and avenges the faithful.

3. Praise God for His justice and mercy.

Lesson Outline

INTRODUCTION
 A. Our Most Precious Possession?
 B. Lesson Background
 I. EVERLASTING GOSPEL (Revelation 14:6-8)
 A. Message to Everyone (vv. 6, 7)
 B. Message of Judgment (v. 8)
  The Mighty Always Fall
 II. EVERLASTING PUNISHMENT (Revelation 14:9-11)
 A. Identity of the Condemned (v. 9)
 B. Fate of the Condemned (vv. 10, 11)
  "Pomobabble"
 III. EVERLASTING REWARD (Revelation 14:12, 13)
 A. Obedient and Faithful (v. 12)
 B. Labor and Rest (v. 13)
CONCLUSION
 A. Understanding Both Sides
 B. Prayer
 C. Thought to Remember

Introduction

A. Our Most Precious Possession?

In his book *Songs of Heaven* Robert E. Coleman passes along a story from Henri Nouwen about a Lutheran bishop who was sent to a Nazi concentration camp during World War II. While there, an SS officer tried to force a confession from the man by beating him. Although the intensity of the torture increased, it could not break the man's silence. The infuriated officer, pounding his victim even harder, finally shrieked, "But don't you know that I can kill you?" The man looked in the eyes of his torturer and said, "Yes, I know—do what you want—but I have already died."

Instantly, as though paralyzed, the officer could no longer raise his arm. It seemed as though power over the man had been taken from that officer. All the cruelties had been based on

the assumption that the man's physical life was his most precious possession. But it wasn't.

B. Lesson Background

The book of Revelation strengthens Christians to be victorious over all those forces that oppose them and attempt to destroy their relationship with the Lamb. This divine drama—properly seen, understood, and applied—blesses the viewer or reader. The drama begins by showing us Christ in the midst of the churches (Revelation 1–3). The church as a whole asks for judgment on the sin that causes her to suffer (4–11). After that comes the climax of victory for the faithful, and God's wrath for the wicked (12–22).

Throughout this drama we are reminded that there is a "greater reality" beyond that of our temporary earthly existence. This "Revelation of Jesus Christ" (Revelation 1:1) reminds us of God's glory and power. He is present with faithful Christians. He is willing and able to protect us for eternity. But God is also able to bring judgment on the ones who deserve it. That judgment is sure and full; none of the wicked will escape it.

Chapter 14 presents both the reality of that judgment and God's protection of Christians. God is faithful to His Word. He will not abandon His own.

As an expression of His active relationship with us, the Lamb is standing in God's dwelling place. God's people (by the figure "144,000," the same sealed group of chapter 7) are identified by having the Father's name on their foreheads (14:1). The sights and sounds of the scene are reinforced by the "new song" of the faithful because of what is made possible by virtue of their relationship with the Lamb (14:3). They are in the protective presence of the throne.

These who are purchased or redeemed are introduced to the reader as "the firstfruits unto God and to the Lamb" (14:4). The Old Testament offering of the firstfruits was a trusting experience in faith. Through this faith experience the worshiper would learn what God is like. The worshiper believed God would supply a full harvest. The firstfruits belonged to God just as the whole harvest did. The faithful, like the firstfruits offering, belong to God. They have faith that God will provide all that they need—for eternity.

I. Everlasting Gospel (Revelation 14:6-8)

A. Message to Everyone (vv. 6, 7)

6. And I saw another angel fly in the midst of heaven, having the everlasting gospel to preach unto them that dwell on the earth, and to every nation, and kindred, and tongue, and people.

The scene now changes to focus on a series of angels and their messages. We need not try to identify these angels concerning whether or not they already have had a ministry in connection with the Revelation of Jesus Christ. After all, God has a great host of angels to assist in His purposes. Remember that Jesus, on the night He was betrayed, said that He could call on "twelve legions" of angels (Matthew 26:53).

The series of angelic messages has to do with *the everlasting gospel*. In Revelation 14:3, 4, just before our text begins, we can see what this gospel means for those who have been redeemed "from the earth" and "from among men." These are the ones who sing the "new song," knowing the quality of life with the Lamb. Their faithfulness is one side of the gospel. The flip side is the judgment of the unfaithful. This is something of a repeat of the opening of the fifth seal in Revelation 6:9-11. There we see the protected position of the slain servants under the altar, calling out for the judgment of the wicked. (See also Matthew 12:41, 42 and 2 Thessalonians 1:4-10.)

The gospel message of the glorified Christ is a two-edged sword (Revelation 1:16; 2:12), even for Christians; the gospel corresponds with the message of "the little book" that to John was both sweet and bitter (10:9-11). Throughout the book of Revelation we have occasion to see both sides of the gospel in the lives of the faithful: it means both protection and suffering for God's people. The suffering is brought by sin, which comes from various directions.

But the gospel requires also that this suffering not go unavenged. This message before us shows the just recompense in the everlasting gospel. This is a message to all *that dwell on the earth*.

7. Saying with a loud voice, Fear God, and give glory to him; for the hour of his judgment is come: and worship him that made heaven, and earth, and the sea, and the fountains of waters.

Those hearing the message must worship God. They must *Fear God, and give glory to Him*. He is Almighty God, the powerful Creator (Exodus 20:11; Psalm 146:6). Christians gladly worship Him. God's enemies, however, prefer to worship "the beast" of Revelation 13. They stubbornly resist the truth, even though they must be aware of the certainty of the judgment of God for their evil deeds.

B. Message of Judgment (v. 8)

8. And there followed another angel, saying, Babylon is fallen, is fallen, that great city, because she made all nations drink of the wine of the wrath of her fornication.

The second angel in this series now speaks his judgment message. This message centers on the figure of Babylon. This is a term that kindles in the minds of those first readers a picture of a mighty foreign power that had brought captivity to the people of God (2 Chronicles 36:20). In the first century A.D., *that great city* no longer existed in its literal, historical sense. Yet the hurt that the Babylonian Empire caused in centuries past still could serve as a figure of speech for the enemies of God's people (cf. 1 Peter 5:13).

The angel qualifies "Babylon the great" as *fallen* (cf. Isaiah 21:9). All prestige of the past is seen as sham. The proud lie prostrate under the judgment of God. Nothing is hidden from Him.

There is no question that what the wicked receive is their just due, for they have *made all nations drink of the wine of the wrath of her fornication* (cf. Jeremiah 51:7-9; Revelation 18:2, 3). Judgment has come as a consequence of their debauchery before God. They willingly received what they were offered. It tasted so good and felt so good at the time—sin is like that—yet it ended in wrath. What an aftertaste! [See question #1, page 328.]

THE MIGHTY ALWAYS FALL

Darius the Great was one of the most powerful emperors in the ancient world. From 522 to 486 B.C., he ruled over an empire that stretched from the Indus River in what is now eastern Pakistan, west to what is now Turkey, and south to the area covered by modern Egypt. He built the royal city of Persepolis (in what is modern Iran), built a road system that is still in use, and established a postal system that was far ahead of its time.

In October 1971, Iran's Shah Reza Pahlavi held an opulent celebration in Persepolis to commemorate the founding of the Persian Empire some twenty-five centuries previously. Of course, it was a celebration that commemorated

---

How to Say It

BABYLON. *Bab*-uh-lun.
CORINTHIANS. Kor-*in*-thee-unz (*th* as in *thin*).
CYRUS. *Sigh*-russ.
DARIUS. Duh-*rye*-us.
HERCULANEUM. Her-ky-*lay*-nee-um.
ISAIAH. Eye-*zay*-uh.
JEREMIAH. Jair-uh-*my*-uh.
JEZEBEL. *Jez*-uh-bel.
NICOLAITANS. Nik-o-*lay*-ih-tunz.
PERSEPOLIS. Pur-*sep*-puh-lis.
POMPEII. Pom-*pay*-ee.
SHAH REZA PAHLAVI. Shaw *Rez*-ah Puh-*lav*-ee.
THESSALONIANS. *Thess*-uh-*lo*-nee-unz (strong accent on *lo*; *th* as in *thin*).
VESUVIUS. Veh-*soo*-vee-us.

the Shah's reign as well! But only eight years later, that reign was over when radical Islamic clerics took control. The Shah was forced to flee into exile with what little he could salvage of his tattered claims to imperial glory.

Cyrus, a predecessor of Darius, had conquered Babylon in 539 B.C. The remains of that city were a part of Darius's empire. But as Babylon had fallen to a Persian conqueror, so also the time came for the Persian Empire to fall to Alexander the Great. Centuries later, the Shah's time came as well. And so it goes!

John uses *Babylon* as a symbol of the arrogance of power and opposition to God. The fates of Darius, the Shah, and a thousand others teach us that all earthly kingdoms are temporary. God will use the nations of the world as He wills, and He will condemn those who oppose Him. Rulers and nations neglect these truths at their peril. God still writes on the pages of history. —C. R. B.

II. Everlasting Punishment (Revelation 14:9-11)

A. Identity of the Condemned (v. 9)

9. And the third angel followed them, saying with a loud voice, If any man worship the beast and his image, and receive his mark in his forehead, or in his hand.

The third angel now declares the wicked to be those who worship *the beast and his image*. The repetition reassures the reader that unrepentant sinners cannot escape the wrath of God. Revelation 7:3 and 9:4 tell us that Christians are "sealed" to receive God's protection. The wicked are, in a sense, also "sealed"—they are marked folks, doomed to destruction (Revelation 16:2). To worship the beast and his image is idolatry, pure and simple (cf. 13:12-17; 14:11).

B. Fate of the Condemned (vv. 10, 11)

10. The same shall drink of the wine of the wrath of God, which is poured out without mixture into the cup of his indignation; and he shall be tormented with fire and brimstone in the presence of the holy angels, and in the presence of the Lamb.

God's *wine of . . . wrath* will be *poured out* on *the same*, meaning the condemned of verse 9. The images of pouring and *fire and brimstone* may remind John's readers of the volcanic eruption of Mt. Vesuvius, which had destroyed the cities of Pompeii and Herculaneum in A.D. 79. That destruction does not compare, however, with the expression of God's righteous anger for sin that is to come.

There is to be blessing for the faithful and dire penalty for the wicked. The wrath poured out

without mixture means that God's judgment is not watered down. The wicked will receive no less than what they deserve. Their sin has doubled back on them. [See question #2, page 328.]

When we imagine the pungent smell of burning sulfur and the pain that fire causes, we sense the full dimensions of the scene. The wicked are not punished off in a corner somewhere, but receive their punishment *in the presence of the holy angels, and in the presence of the Lamb*. The wicked are not in fellowship with the righteous—their unrighteousness is clear for all to see. This makes them worthy of God's wrath.

Those attracted to the world are going to perish with the world. Anyone who chooses to serve the devil must expect to suffer the consequences that the devil will suffer (Revelation 20:10, 13-15; 21:8).

11. And the smoke of their torment ascendeth up for ever and ever: and they have no rest day nor night, who worship the beast and his image, and whosoever receiveth the mark of his name.

Another dimension of the doom for the wicked is pictured as fire sending up *smoke* as evidence of the consuming power that is present; however, this fire never runs out of fuel. This fiery punishment lasts "for ever and ever" (Revelation 20:10).

We are cautioned, therefore, to be on guard so that the temptations confronting us daily do not have an overpowering appeal. They may come from peer pressures—no age is exempt. Our pride may be the stumbling block. Prestige in the community may seem to be more important than the moral issues involved. In our day all kinds of sins are so common that we are tempted to think that if "everyone is doing it," then it must not be so bad. After all, this is the twenty-first century —aren't we "enlightened"?

If we are drawn back into sin, we must realize what group we are becoming part of: the opposers of God's people and God's work. In such a situation we are subject to the wrath of God if we do not repent and change our lifestyle. Sin unforgiven calls forth due judgment.

"POMOBABBLE"

John Leo, a commentator on the social and political peculiarities of Western society, has come up with the term *pomobabble*. The term refers to postmodern explanations of right and wrong that, in reality, explain *away* the existence of ultimate truth. Postmodernism says truth doesn't exist and all values are simply a way for those in power to stay there.

Fortunately, some people are beginning to see through the haze. Writing satirically to point out the logical holes in such folly, Alan Sokal, a physicist at New York University, wrote a pomobabble article arguing that gravity is simply a "social construct"—that is, a value society has accepted because it is useful. *Social Text* magazine did not realize the article was a hoax and printed it. Professor Sokal then wrote to the editors and said that anyone who believes gravity to be a "social construct" should come to his apartment and jump out the window—from the twenty-first floor (*U.S. News & World Report,* March 15, 1999).

One of the most dangerous forms of pomobabble is seen in the area of morality. For quite some time now we have been told that morality is merely what society has agreed upon, nothing more nor less. But the fires of Hell are not a "social construct." Those whose "smoke of their torment ascendeth up for ever and ever" will be the ones to find this out the hard way. Make sure you're not one of them. —C. R. B.

III. Everlasting Reward (Revelation 14:12, 13)

A. Obedient and Faithful (v. 12)

12. Here is the patience of the saints: here are they that keep the commandments of God, and the faith of Jesus.

This verse provides us a key for interpreting not only this series of angelic messages, but also the entirety of this Revelation of Jesus Christ. Revelation 13:10 offered a similar encouragement: *"Here is the patience and the faith of the saints."*

In the everyday activities of life, we find our faith and our relationship to Christ tested. It is not always easy to make the right choices, especially in unanticipated or unique circumstances. The appeal is strong; the test so real. To assist us in having the patience we need to endure, we have the everlasting gospel hidden in our hearts. It is a ready resource. Since we are aware of "both sides," we want to do whatever it takes to maintain our all-important relationship with Christ.

In a way, we need to set our minds on considering an active plan in dealing with the hard choices and tests. An active plan begins with backing up to get a full view of what is happening. Is it of God, of the devil, or of my own selfishness? Will my choice strengthen my relationship with Christ or weaken it? How will the results of my choice affect the ones who look to me as an example? It takes active resistance on our part to develop patience. We are resolved to do whatever it takes to stay faithful.

Many of life's difficulties can be linked to a lack of will and a failure to consider the outcome. We are thankful that God does not permit us to be tempted beyond what we are able to bear (cf. 1 Corinthians 10:13). The devil cannot really make us do the wrong thing. God is for us, and His Spirit is all-powerful. But we must yield our spirit to His. It takes an act of our will.

Also, our overview enables us to consider the final outcome. If we join the enemy by foolish choices, we can expect due penalty. [See question #3, page 328.] We can know blessing only when we are willing to do "all that it takes" to keep our relationship with the Lamb. Only then can we anticipate the time when there will be no more tests.

In overcoming the obstacles that stand in the way of holiness, we need proper motivation—that motivation is eternal life. To gain that prize we have to continue to *keep the commandments of God* and hold on to *the faith of Jesus.* We are strengthened in these when we participate in godly endeavors in the church and in relationships with those who provide insight, encouragement, and accountability. All in all, we must resolve to do whatever it takes to endure with the saints. We can win with Christ!

We are also strengthened by the sure fact that judgment will come for the wicked. There will not be anything lacking in God's vengeance when He repays. Patience is that ability to hold up under a burden with active resistance. We cannot be passive, only observing. We are "in the game" for keeps—and it's no mere game!

B. Labor and Rest (v. 13)

13. And I heard a voice from heaven saying unto me, Write, Blessed are the dead which die in the Lord from henceforth: Yea, saith the Spirit, that they may rest from their labors; and their works do follow them.

Visual for lesson 12

This visual illustrates both the sobering reality and marvelous comfort of Revelation 14:13.

The *voice* that John hears *from Heaven* is comparable to the voice "from the throne" (Revelation 16:17; 19:5). Either expression indicates it is God's voice, and this message is to be heard and heeded. This fact is strengthened as John is told to *Write*. It is not that John has to be told this because he is old and absentminded, but rather because there is significance to the message that must not be missed.

One side of the message that has been presented is the assurance of due judgment of the wicked. The other side of the everlasting gospel, the counterpart, is the reward of the righteous. This reward is not in dollars and cents. Neither is it based on any of our "merits." All is by God's grace through relationship with the Lamb.

This reward will mean the absence of those things that bring toil and trouble. It is truly *rest from* the *labors* of "the sweat of thy face" (Genesis 3:19). The effect of such rest does not mean that our *works* are forgotten. Quite the contrary! Christians have the assurance that their godly *works do follow them* into eternity (Luke 19:11-19). [See question #4, page 328.]

We do well to remember, though, that not all works of service done in the name of Christ are of equal value before God (see 1 Corinthians 3:10-15). It is even possible to get so careless in our Christian walk that we "lose it all." Apostasy was very real in the first century—the devil used every tool he could. Whether the occasion was the Nicolaitans, false apostles, the prophetess Jezebel, or any other false teacher, people were being drawn away from the truth (Revelation 2:14-16, 20-23). [See question #5, page 328.]

Prosperity and persecution also are very real to John's audience. The devil uses those tools as well. Exile on the island of Patmos is an occasion of testing for John (Revelation 1:9). Therefore, it was very helpful for John to receive the Revelation of Jesus Christ so that he would know things are not what they seemed to be.

It is possible to be an overcomer with the Lamb! We do well to identify with John in this scene, as well as in the kinds of choices John makes. Only then can there be a proper sense of security, assurance, and confidence of our relationship with God.

Conclusion

A. Understanding Both Sides

The message of Christ is indeed "a sharp two-edged sword" (Revelation 1:16). There are two sides. The one is God's protection, and the other is the reality of hurt. The message of the "slain souls under altar" (6:9) has two sides. These faithful servants of God know the reality of suffering. But they are also very much alive, knowing God's presence and protection "under the altar."

The everlasting gospel of Revelation 14 gives us another opportunity to consider both sides. We are protected, yet we still suffer. But our suffering is temporary since there is sure punishment for the wicked opposers of God and His people. As a result, the faithful are rescued from their great trials. The punishment is personal; each one who deserves it receives fully what is due. The blessing is also personal; each faithful servant will know rest from trials since each one has demonstrated patient endurance.

Faithful servants are overcomers. Overcomers are ones who know the strengthening afforded by God's presence. Even in this life we know something of what Heaven is like. Even when we are experiencing opposition, we can lift up our eyes to catch a glimpse of Heaven where trials are no more. Even now we know the presence of the Lamb. He provides and protects, even though we are not yet entirely shielded from hurt. His grace is sufficient for us to be overcomers!

B. Prayer

Thank You, God, for the clarity of Your Word. Its light makes it possible for us to have a full view of Your work. We are so grateful that that work includes us. We know that our lives will not always be easy. But we are thankful for the help of Your Holy Spirit and the Lamb. May we be able and willing to assist fellow Christians when they, too, are tempted. Because of the Lamb and in His name we pray, amen.

C. Thought to Remember

"The Lamb shall overcome them: for he is Lord of lords" (Revelation 17:14).

Home Daily Bible Readings

Monday, May 17—In the World You Face Persecution (John 16:29-33)

Tuesday, May 18—Endure to the End (Matthew 10:16-22)

Wednesday, May 19—Many Will Fall Away (Matthew 24:9-14)

Thursday, May 20—Be Faithful to the Task (Matthew 24:45-50)

Friday, May 21—Our Hope in the Risen Lord (1 Corinthians 15:12-20)

Saturday, May 22—We Have Victory Through Christ (1 Corinthians 15:54-58)

Sunday, May 23—A Call for Endurance (Revelation 14:6-13)

Learning by Doing

This page contains an alternative lesson plan emphasizing learning activities.
Classes desiring such student involvement will find these suggestions helpful.

Learning Goals

After participating in this lesson, each student will be able to:

1. Contrast the punishment of the wicked with the blessings of the faithful.

2. Explain how God's judgment for sin gives Him glory and avenges the faithful.

3. Praise God for His justice and mercy.

Into the Lesson

As students arrive, ask them to write on the board major events throughout history that would be considered terrible trials or "tribulations." These may include the fall of Jerusalem, the Crusades, various wars, the Great Depression, the Holocaust, the spread of totalitarian regimes, "ethnic cleansing," and the attacks on the World Trade Center. Ask, "How does a person suffering through any of these events endure such trauma?" Limit the answers to this question so that they remain in the context of the terrible trials mentioned at the beginning of class.

Say, "Viktor Frankl, a survivor of the Nazi death camps and a psychiatrist, found that spiritual life could deepen even in the midst of the trauma of a concentration camp. He discovered that those people who could remain focused on some meaning beyond the severe trials of the camps tended to survive longer and be less affected by the trauma than those without any such meaning. In his classic book, *Man's Search for Meaning,* he reported realizing that he had to learn and teach despairing men that 'it did not really matter what we expected from life, but rather what life expected from us.'"

Say, "By substituting the word *God* for *life,* in this quote, we find a capsule of the message of our text for today and, perhaps, the book of Revelation itself: It did not really matter what we expected from God, but rather what God expected from us." Display this statement for the students.

Into the Word

Form two groups. Tell the first group to read Revelation 14 and determine how a faithful person is identified. *(Among the characteristics of these people are these: they were not defiled, they were pure, they followed the Lamb, and they did not speak falsehood.)* The other group should read the same text and determine ways by which a wicked person is identified. *(These are charac-*

terized as worshiping the beast and the image of the beast and receiving the mark of the beast.) Ask both groups to report.

After this first reading, the first group will read the text again, recording all of the blessings that the faithful will receive. *(These include the ability to sing a new song and to rest from their labors.)* Tell the other group to read the same text a second time and record all the punishments the wicked will receive. *(These include torment and no rest.)* Ask both groups to report.

Have both groups compare their findings from the Revelation text with what is presented in Matthew 25:31-46 by answering the following questions: How do the faithful and wicked compare with the sheep and goats? How are the faithful and wicked identified in Matthew as compared with Revelation? How does keeping or obeying God's commandments in Revelation 14:12 fit with the King's response to the righteous in Matthew 25:40? Using the students' comparisons, clarify that the Matthew and Revelation texts together provide the image of Jesus as Judge. Point out that the faithful are characterized by their response of obedience based on faith.

Into Life

Say, "It is not unusual for people to claim they believe in Heaven but not in Hell. This text is clear that there are two very different destinations for people. God has expectations for us, and how we respond to those expectations will be factored into God's righteous judgment."

Ask students to state expectations that God has for every individual according to His Word. A general example would be to live in a way that is worthy of the gospel (Philippians 1:27). A more specific example would be to watch what one says (James 1:26). Write these for all to see.

Ask students to consider these and privately note any in which they have not been obedient. Say, "If God judged us without any mercy, we all would be lost. Yet, God has demonstrated His mercy in providing His Son as the Lamb. The faith we have in the Lamb of justice and mercy allows us to endure."

Read the the scroll used in lesson 10. Lead the class in a corporate prayer praising God for His justice and His mercy, especially toward those who believe. Read James 5:7-11 as a conclusion to the time of corporate prayer.

Let's Talk It Over

The questions on this page are designed to promote discussion of the lesson by the class and to encourage application of the lesson Scriptures. The answers provided are only discussion starters. Let your class talk it over from there.

1. Why is it that sin "tastes good" at the time, but leaves a bitter "aftertaste"? What was a time that you experienced both?

Most sins entail a certain amount of temporary excitement and pleasure, and, of course, that is their allure. Sexual sin seems to promise the most pleasure, but it often brings the most pain and tragedy. A sobering example is King David's adultery and the deadly results of that sin (2 Samuel 11:1–12:23; Psalm 51).

Some of your learners may be willing to share times when they experienced both the taste and aftertaste of sin, and some won't. In any case, remind them that unforgiven sin ends in God's eternal wrath. Even forgiven sins may result in consequences in the here and now. (Some believe that forgiven sin also robs us of some of our eternal rewards.) The "bottom line" is that whether or not our earthly justice system punishes us for our sins, God never overlooks the unrepentant.

2. How does it affect you to read about God's vengeance—His "boiling anger," ready to erupt like a volcano?

On the one hand, the certainty of God's wrath ought to make us sad that some people will actually experience that unbearable vengeance. On the other hand, it ought to comfort us that God will execute justice on behalf of all our brethren who have suffered unimaginable cruelties through the centuries.

The certainty of His wrath also should motivate us to remain faithful despite hardships. Nothing can compare with the pain that God can inflict, so His wrath is to be feared above any human's (Matthew 10:28). We appreciate the awe-inspiring justice of God. But at the same time we are to feel a great urgency to help others escape this threatening "downside" of justice.

3. Do you agree with the lesson writer that our sins are "foolish choices"? Why, or why not?

When it comes right down to it, we commit sin when we think we know better than God. How foolish!

Most sins are committed with the mistaken notion that the selfish benefits of a wrong act will outweigh the negative consequences of that act. Many seem perpetually willing to keep "giving it a chance" to make them happy.

But only fools refuse to accept the lessons of life and of Scripture, and choose to live in Satan's world of illusion and unfulfilled promises. Even so, we recognize that on rare occasions we seem to have to choose between "the lesser of two evils" because we live in a fallen world. Praise God for His forgiveness! (See 1 John 1:9.)

4. What do you think happens to those who "die in the Lord" but who have no labors to rest from, and no works to follow them? Or is such a situation even possible? Explain.

This could be a controversial question, so tread carefully and graciously! Be prepared for someone to say, "Well, we're not to judge." (See Matthew 7:17-20 for a response to this.)

We may tentatively propose that the only time a person might "die in the Lord" with no Christian works would be in the case of a deathbed conversion (which itself is probably quite rare). All other Christians would at least have *some* godly labors and works. As a person remains in Christ for even a few weeks, love should compel him or her to toil, sacrifice, and perform deeds of service to the glory of the Savior. Those who think that they can be Christians without Christian works are fooling themselves (see James 2:14-26).

5. The lesson writer notes that "Apostasy was very real in the first century—the devil used every tool he could." What tools do you see Satan using in your own life to try to draw you into apostasy? How do you stay on guard?

Satan has some tools now that did not exist in John's day. The Internet is just one example of a tool that can be used for evil. Since the visual images of modern media provide such a tempting inroad to sin, we can be on guard by practicing "eye control" (Psalm 101:3).

Even with modern technology, however, we do well to keep in mind that human nature itself has not changed over the centuries. So although Satan has new *tools,* his fundamental *lures* are pretty much the same. Sexual temptation has always been with us. Modern-day cults with their false Christs, prophets, and teachers frequently just "repackage" the false doctrine from of old. We resist these lures by being firmly grounded in the Word of God (Psalm 119:11).

Dwelling With God

DEVOTIONAL READING: Revelation 22:1-5.

BACKGROUND SCRIPTURE: Revelation 21:1–22:5.

PRINTED TEXT: Revelation 21:1-7, 22-27.

Revelation 21:1-7, 22-27

1 And I saw a new heaven and a new earth: for the first heaven and the first earth were passed away; and there was no more sea.

2 And I John saw the holy city, new Jerusalem, coming down from God out of heaven, prepared as a bride adorned for her husband.

3 And I heard a great voice out of heaven saying, Behold, the tabernacle of God is with men, and he will dwell with them, and they shall be his people, and God himself shall be with them, and be their God.

4 And God shall wipe away all tears from their eyes; and there shall be no more death, neither sorrow, nor crying, neither shall there be any more pain: for the former things are passed away.

5 And he that sat upon the throne said, Behold, I make all things new. And he said unto me, Write: for these words are true and faithful.

6 And he said unto me, It is done. I am Alpha and Omega, the beginning and the end. I will give unto him that is athirst of the fountain of the water of life freely.

7 He that overcometh shall inherit all things; and I will be his God, and he shall be my son.

.   .   .   .

22 And I saw no temple therein: for the Lord God Almighty and the Lamb are the temple of it.

23 And the city had no need of the sun, neither of the moon, to shine in it: for the glory of God did lighten it, and the Lamb is the light thereof.

24 And the nations of them which are saved shall walk in the light of it: and the kings of the earth do bring their glory and honor into it.

25 And the gates of it shall not be shut at all by day: for there shall be no night there.

26 And they shall bring the glory and honor of the nations into it.

27 And there shall in no wise enter into it any thing that defileth, neither whatsoever worketh abomination, or maketh a lie: but they which are written in the Lamb's book of life.

GOLDEN TEXT: And I heard a great voice out of heaven saying, Behold, the tabernacle of God is with men, and he will dwell with them, and they shall be his people, and God himself shall be with them, and be their God.—Revelation 21:3.

Living Expectantly
Unit 2: Visions of Hope
(Lessons 10-13)

Lesson Aims

After participating in this lesson, each student should be able to:

1. Identify the rewards for the righteous that are associated with Heaven.

2. Give reasons to support the idea that being with God is the best part of Heaven.

3. State one way that he or she will become more aware of living daily in God's presence.

Lesson Outline

INTRODUCTION
    A. The Big Stuff
    B. Lesson Background
 I. IN A NEW SITUATION (Revelation 21:1-7)
    A. New Creation (vv. 1, 2)
      "No More Sea"
    B. New Relationship (vv. 3, 4)
    C. New Assurance (v. 5)
    D. New Inheritance (vv. 6, 7)
      As Much as We Want, and It's Free!
II. IN THE PRESENCE OF GOD (Revelation 21:22-27)
    A. Temple and Lamb (vv. 22, 23)
    B. Nations and Gates (vv. 24, 25)
      Bringing the Nations Together in Peace
    C. Glory and Honor (vv. 26, 27)
CONCLUSION
    A. Assurance for the Faithful
    B. Prayer
    C. Thought to Remember

Introduction

A. The Big Stuff

"Don't sweat the small stuff!" more than one person has advised. "And it's *all* small stuff," someone else added. There is a lot of truth in those two observations. Everything in this world that is temporary is "small stuff." This fact becomes amazingly clear when we have an eternal perspective or outlook on our earthly lives.

But that same eternal perspective reminds us that there is some "big stuff" as well. That "big stuff" includes everything that God thinks is important: love, holiness, righteousness, forgiveness—the list goes on!

The ultimate "big stuff" for every human being is his or her eternal destiny. How sad to see so many people drifting unconcerned in their quagmires of sin. Today's lesson challenges us to lift our gaze to the future, our eternity. When we do, we can find it surprisingly easy to let go of the temporary pleasures of sin. What a blessing God has prepared for His faithful people!

B. Lesson Background

The "future realities" for both the righteous and the unrighteous come across vividly in the book of Revelation! Those marked by the Lamb receive full blessing. Those opposed to God, who are marked by the beast, receive full judgment. Beyond any doubt the reader must know that he or she needs to maintain a right relationship with the Lamb.

That relationship is not based on what we see in our lifetimes, but on the full revelation of Christ. The scenes of the book of Revelation and their messages fortify our faith and reassure us that we will be able to handle any present suffering. The divine power that is with us is much greater than the demonic power that is against us.

We see the end result of demonic power in Revelation 20:11-15, just before today's text. There the spotlight falls upon the wicked, who receive the Judge's condemnation. The fact that unrepentant people deserve their judgment is shown by the record of the works of their lives as recorded in "books." These books of God's knowledge are thorough and contain no mistakes.

This part of the victory scene of Revelation 20 may seem sad to us. We cannot picture the victory of the faithful, however, without also being aware of the flip side: the judgment of the unrighteous and the unfaithful. Sin demands judgment. We see in the Revelation of Jesus Christ what it means to be in fellowship with the Lamb, as well as what it means to be His opponent. It is not hard to choose to be an overcomer with the Lamb. He is our great resource of strength. With Him by our side we, too, shall be victorious! Whether that victory is a long time in coming or is to arrive soon doesn't really matter. It's the ultimate, eternal victory that counts.

Our challenge today, then, is to be as faithful as John wanted his first-century readers to be. If we are, then our lives will demonstrate godliness to this generation and to the next. If we are not, then judgment awaits.

The book of Revelation makes all this clear to us. The closing scenes of this book bring this message to a climax and motivate us to faithfulness. Rather than seeking more revelation, as some today foolishly do, may we devote ourselves to understanding and applying the revelation that God has already given us. When we do, rich blessings surely await.

I. In a New Situation (Revelation 21:1-7)

A. New Creation (vv. 1, 2)

1. And I saw a new heaven and a new earth: for the first heaven and the first earth were passed away; and there was no more sea.

The transition *and I saw* juts forth in the text. This phrase extends as a point to hang our hope upon, as nails fastened in a sure place (cf. Ezra 9:8; Ecclesiastes 12:11; Isaiah 22:23). Throughout the book of Revelation we have been alert both to what is seen and what is heard, for the message is the combination of these two.

This scene here is that of *a new heaven and a new earth* in contrast to *the first heaven and the first earth*. In John's vision of the future, the old situation has *passed away*. This will be a realization of Isaiah 65:17.

This present world has been good, but it is not sufficient for the eternal structure. [See question #1, page 336.] It groans under the weight of sin (Romans 8:22). In 2 Peter 3:10, 12, the apostle tells us how this physical world will be destroyed. Even the Garden of Eden was not complete enough to provide the fullness of relationship that God has in view for His people. The word *new* emphasizes quality.

We see another contrast between the old and the new creations with the image *there is no more sea*. The sea was a figure of great threat in the minds of ancient people. The sea separates John from his loved ones as he is exiled on the island of Patmos (Revelation 1:9). It is from the sea that "the beast" of Revelation 13:1 comes with his purpose to overcome the saints. For John and his contemporaries, the sea is the epitome of evil, of all things bad and harmful.

Thus the situation that John pictures is one in which all opposition is gone—anything that would trouble the servants of God or anything that would separate them from God. The relationship in "a new heaven and a new earth" is realized in its fullness without "sea."

"NO MORE SEA"

In May 2002, Richard Van Pham sailed from Long Beach, California, toward Catalina Island, usually visible just twenty-six miles off the coast. Pham was tired and went below deck to sleep—not normally a good idea since his route would cross a busy shipping channel. But it was an even worse idea on that particular evening.

When Van Pham awoke in the morning, he discovered that the wind had changed, a storm had broken his mast and torn his sails, and he was drifting far off course. Neither his outboard motor nor his two-way radio were working. He spent the next three-and-one-half months adrift, surviving on fish, sea turtles, and sea gulls. (His verdict on the taste of sea turtle meat was "excellent!" and sea gulls "taste like chicken.")

The U.S. Navy discovered Van Pham drifting about two hundred fifty miles west of Costa Rica, or about twenty-five hundred miles from home. Inadequate preparation for the journey, inattention, and rough weather turned the sea, which had been his friend, into an enemy that almost took his life.

For John, the island of Patmos was not a romantic place where one could watch the day fade away as the sun sank picturesquely into the sea. No, the sea for John separated him from fellow Christians. When he rejoices that "there was no more sea," he uses the sea partly as a symbol of his loneliness that will be destroyed in Heaven's glorious reunion of the saints. Both "seafarers" and "landlubbers" can look forward to that reunion. —C. R. B.

2. And I John saw the holy city, new Jerusalem, coming down from God out of heaven, prepared as a bride adorned for her husband.

The scene of "renewal" continues in such a marvelous way! John's first-century readers know about old *Jerusalem*, of course, with all its unholiness and injustice. Even now in the early twenty-first century we can see that earthly Jerusalem is a place torn by violence and fear.

What a refreshing contrast it is, then, to anticipate the *new Jerusalem!* (See also Revelation 3:12.) Abraham hoped to see this *city* (Hebrews 11:8-10, 16).

Not only is the city new, it is also *holy* and *prepared as a bride adorned for her husband.* The text expresses the rejoicing there is in the climax of the marriage. Faithfulness has been pledged and tested. The beautiful result is that

---

How to Say It

ALPHA. *Al*-fa.

CORINTHIANS. Kor-*in*-thee-unz (*th* as in *thin*).

ECCLESIASTES. Ik-*leez*-ee-*as*-teez (strong accent on *as*).

EZEKIEL. Ee-*zeek*-ee-ul or Ee-*zeek*-yul.

GALATIANS. Guh-*lay*-shunz.

HEBREWS. *Hee*-brews.

ISAIAH. Eye-*zay*-uh.

LEVITICUS. Leh-*vit*-ih-kus.

OMEGA. O-*may*-guh or O-*mee*-guh.

PATMOS. *Pat*-muss.

ZECHARIAH. *Zek*-uh-*rye*-uh (strong accent on *rye*).

bride and husband are thus to dwell together forever. The resulting fellowship is worth all earthly struggles! (See also Revelation 19:7.)

This new city affords protection and security as contrasted with the fear of the sea (21:1). It is God's doing. The bride portrays the blessed response to God's gracious action: a prepared people brought into an eternal relationship because of their faithfulness to the Lamb and what He has done. God's action and our response unite to form a blessed, secure relationship. It is a relationship greater than that which has ever been known. [See question #2, page 336.]

B. New Relationship (vv. 3, 4)

3. And I heard a great voice out of heaven saying, Behold, the tabernacle of God is with men, and he will dwell with them, and they shall be his people, and God himself shall be with them, and be their God.

When we read of the *tabernacle of God,* an Old Testament background comes to mind. We recall the tent of meeting in Moses' day, God's presence, the system of sacrifices, and all that God provided to cause people to desire a relationship with Him. The twelve tribes of Israel in the Old Testament did indeed learn something of what it meant to be the people of God (Leviticus 26:11, 12).

However, it is only the true Israel (cf. Romans 9:6; Galatians 6:16) that will know the fullness. It is only in Christ that people have become able to comprehend the real meaning of the kingdom of God, a meaning that was beyond the grasp of the Old Testament kings and prophets. We in Christ have learned the meaning of submission to the King and the benefit of His protection. We will learn still more when Christ returns.

4. And God shall wipe away all tears from their eyes; and there shall be no more death, neither sorrow, nor crying, neither shall there be any more pain: for the former things are passed away.

John emphasizes the fullness of God's care by stressing the removal of *all* tears. God Himself wipes away our tears (Isaiah 25:8; Revelation 7:17). No comforting parent can rival Him!

Not only does John picture the removal of tears, but he also lists more things from our experience that indicate the hurts we have felt from our struggle with opposition. The words *death*, *sorrow*, *crying*, and *pain* bring to mind issues of suffering and separation. But the time is coming when "the enemy" that brought us such things is no more! All those *former things* that belong to the first heaven and the first earth *are passed away.* Those things were temporary, but the "new" are eternal.

Visual for lessons 11, 13

God shall wipe away all tears.

Use this visual to illustrate verse 4 of the lesson text.

C. New Assurance (v. 5)

5. And he that sat upon the throne said, Behold, I make all things new. And he said unto me, Write: for these words are true and faithful.

The source of the message—*he that sat upon the throne*—underscores the extreme importance of what is said. What is *new* implies a contrast with what was "first." This is an important fact regarding what it means for God to be with His people. The old creation will not just be "fixed up." It is even more than a restoration of the Garden of Eden. [See question #3, page 336.] It is *new!* At that time "our vile body" will be "fashioned like unto his glorious body" (Philippians 3:21). Those who know the "new life" (cf. 2 Corinthians 5:17) can become the "new Jerusalem" (cf. Galatians 4:25, 26; Hebrews 12:22-24).

The message gives divine assurance. There may not yet be all the answers concerning "how" and "when," but we know "for whom" this message is given. It is for the overcomers, those who triumph over suffering.

As we have heard along with John the command to *write,* we know the value and the usefulness of the message. Just as the One who gave them is "Faithful and True" (cf. Revelation 19:11), so also are His words.

D. New Inheritance (vv. 6, 7)

6. And he said unto me, It is done. I am Alpha and Omega, the beginning and the end. I will give unto him that is athirst of the fountain of the water of life freely.

Again we see titles used to identify the glorified Christ of Revelation 1. He who is the "faithful witness" (1:5) is also the *Alpha and Omega* (1:8; 22:13)—the first and last letters of the Greek alphabet. His identification as *the beginning and the end* is very similar to "the first and the last" in 1:17. He is the source of life, both earthly and eternal. Many of the titles throughout the book of Revelation keep the reader aware of the reality. Everything is assured—*It is done!*

However, the protection of Christ is only for those who take their thirst to *the fountain of the water of life.* People feel longings for various things and they often attempt to satisfy those impulses in sinful ways. Those unrepentant people are not included here. It is only God's true people who will receive this benefit. Some benefit already has been realized—we are experiencing it right now. The Eternal One who has spoken is the One who has invited us to share this water of life.

The idea of "water" as a figure of God's care is not new. See Psalm 65:9; Isaiah 41:17, 18; 55:1; Jeremiah 2:13; Zechariah 13:1; John 4:13, 14; 7:37, 38. This figure is also found in Revelation 7:17 at the close of a grand scene depicting God, His people, and the absence of all opposition. In our present context we have opportunity to have this theme amplified as we view the city in all its beauty. Amidst the imagery we must not forget we are viewing God with His people.

AS MUCH AS WE WANT, AND IT'S FREE!

Years ago, a small midwestern town put in a municipal water system. Water meters seemed to be a needless expense; citizens numbered only a few hundred, and the town had its own lake. But soon it was discovered that someone, disgruntled with local politics, was entering vacant houses and turning on the faucets so that they would run continuously. Water meters soon followed!

That petty act was a symbolic precursor to the water problems the world is now facing. The world's population boom increases the need for irrigation water if that population is to be fed. Next, throw in the need for green lawns and golf courses so desert cities in affluent cultures will seem like "home" to people moving there from wetter climes. All this translates into growing demands on the supplies of water.

But the water problem for the less affluent parts of the world is more basic: one in five people in the world do not have access to safe drinking water! In China and the Indian subcontinent, the two most populous regions in the world, the rivers are polluted to the point of endangering health and life.

However, John's promise regarding Heaven is that the pure water of life will be free to all for eternity. He uses water—the very stuff of life itself—as a symbol of the magnificence of the preparations God is making for us. And there won't be any water meters!   —C. R. B.

7. He that overcometh shall inherit all things; and I will be his God, and he shall be my son.

We must stress again that the result we see is only for those *that overcometh* through the power of the Lamb. Not all will accept or keep a place in God's family as Christians, the church. It is noteworthy to check the listing in Revelation 21:8 of those whose end is the second death. Their end is eternal separation from God—the opposite of the inheritance of the faithful, God with His people (cf. 2 Corinthians 6:16).

II. In the Presence of God (Revelation 21:22-27)

A. Temple and Lamb (vv. 22, 23)

22. And I saw no temple therein: for the Lord God Almighty and the Lamb are the temple of it.

The focal point of Old Testament worship was the *temple*. God put His glory there (1 Kings 8:11), but also took that glory away because of wickedness (Ezekiel 10). The laying anew of the temple's foundation in Ezra's day was a time of great joy and weeping (Ezra 3:10-13). The completion of the second temple in 515 B.C. was also a time of high emotion (Ezra 6:13-18).

But no temple experience of the Old Covenant can match what is being described here! The fullness of the picture gives us God and the Lamb. From Revelation 4 and 5 and following we were made conscious of the vital role of the Lamb to make our relationship with God possible. There is no "curtain" to separate God from people as in the old temple. The Lamb has removed it (cf. Mark 15:38). This is the great worship experience we desire—all barriers are gone. Now we are in the very presence of God.

23. And the city had no need of the sun, neither of the moon, to shine in it: for the glory of God did lighten it, and the Lamb is the light thereof.

The Old Testament experience was good, but it was not complete. When we see *the city* of God now, we see it in its wholeness. God provided lights to benefit us in this world (Genesis 1:16). Yet what they provided in part is now seen in fullness (cf. Isaiah 60:19, 20; Revelation 22:5). Here is the eternal safety and security!

B. Nations and Gates (vv. 24, 25)

24. And the nations of them which are saved shall walk in the light of it: and the kings of the earth do bring their glory and honor into it.

Try to imagine all the dignity, power, and greatness of all the mighty rulers of all time. If you can do that, you might have something of a composite picture to help you understand the *glory* of God. The phrase *the nations* does not refer to everyone who has ever lived. Rather, it refers to the faithful ones who will share the presence of God and His glory. (The phrase *of them which are saved* does not appear in the original Greek, but the idea is certainly right.)

BRINGING THE NATIONS TOGETHER IN PEACE

In 1899, the International Peace Conference was held in The Hague to develop a forum for settling international disputes peacefully. Fifteen years later, World War I erupted. The League of Nations was founded in 1919 at the end of that war, but less than twenty years later World War II had begun.

The world tried again in 1945. That was the year that delegates from fifty nations met in San Francisco to sign the charter for the United Nations. Since then, world leaders have addressed the UN, but often with a spirit of belligerence. One of the most famous examples of this occurred in a 1960 session of the UN, attended by U.S. President Eisenhower, Britain's Macmillan, the Soviet Union's Khrushchev, Cuba's Castro, India's Nehru, Yugoslavia's Tito, Egypt's Nasser, and many others. The session is remembered for Khrushchev's act of pounding his shoe on the desk in rage.

When the kings of the earth bring their glory to Heaven's gathering of which John writes, it will be in a far different spirit. All people there— whether great or humble—will give honor to the Lamb of God. The Prince of Peace will, at last, have brought the world together. Come again, Lord Jesus!   —C. R. B.

25. And the gates of it shall not be shut at all by day: for there shall be no night there.

How dark a city often was in ancient times! City *gates* would be *shut* securely at *night* lest enemies plunder the defenseless inhabitants under cover of darkness. Our scene reminds us that the threat of enemies is gone for people in the presence of God. He offers constant light and complete protection. It is eternal day with God and His people. (See Isaiah 60:11; Zechariah 14:7; and Revelation 22:5.) [See question #4, page 336.]

C. Glory and Honor (vv. 26, 27)

26. And they shall bring the glory and honor of the nations into it.

Rays of *glory* seem to stream in from all sectors. Because of the Lamb, all *the nations* have been blessed. Salvation has reached unto the uttermost part of the earth (cf. Acts 1:8). Grace given to the faithful returns from them as praise and *honor* and *glory* for the Lamb upon the throne, for He is "King of Kings and Lord of Lords" (Revelation 19:16). God shows Himself as God by achieving His purposes in bringing us to Himself. Here is glory!

27. And there shall in no wise enter into it any thing that defileth, neither whatsoever worketh abomination, or maketh a lie: but they which are written in the Lamb's book of life.

The holy city has nothing unclean or unholy. All things are pure and holy as God and redeemed humanity live together (Isaiah 52:1). It is the Lamb who has made such conditions possible. There is complete separation from the wicked. Those whose names are *written in the Lamb's book of life* (cf. Philippians 4:3) gain the promise of Revelation 21:7: "He that overcometh shall inherit all things." These are those who know full relationship with God. [See question #5, page 336.]

Conclusion

A. Assurance for the Faithful

All the details of "the city" have helped us as Christians to comprehend what it means to be "the wife of the Lamb." We have no doubts about God's protection and provision. We desire to enter into the city to dwell with Him forever. Knowing the result, we are equipped to handle the present tests to our faith. We are ready to worship and to serve the Lamb.

B. Prayer

Father, Your glory is beyond description! We have a better grasp of it as we see the goal of our faith in this lesson. We long to be home with You. But right now, Father, we want to share the message so that we can bring others with us. Help us to do so in the name of the Lamb, amen.

C. Thought to Remember

Heaven makes it all worthwhile!

Home Daily Bible Readings

Monday, May 24—The Lord Almighty Reigns (Revelation 19:6-10)

Tuesday, May 25—A New Heaven and Earth (Revelation 21:1-7)

Wednesday, May 26—John Sees the Holy City (Revelation 21:9-14)

Thursday, May 27—God's Glory Is Its Light (Revelation 21:22-27)

Friday, May 28—There Will Be No More Night (Revelation 22:1-5)

Saturday, May 29—I Am Coming Soon! (Revelation 22:6-10)

Sunday, May 30—I Am the Alpha and Omega (Revelation 22:12-17)

Learning by Doing

This page contains an alternative lesson plan emphasizing learning activities. Classes desiring such student involvement will find these suggestions helpful.

Learning Goals

After participating in this lesson, each student will be able to:

1. Identify the rewards for the righteous that are associated with Heaven.

2. Give reasons to support the idea that being with God is the best part of Heaven.

3. State one way that he or she will become more aware of living daily in God's presence.

Into the Lesson

Prior to today's class session take an informal survey of several children, asking them, "What is Heaven like?" Record some of the responses either with video or audio.

At the beginning of class ask students to complete this sentence: "My vision of Heaven is ___." After the students have completed this activity, share with them the responses you have received from the children you asked in preparation for this class. Then ask several class members to relate their "visions."

Say, "There are almost as many different human ideas of Heaven as there are human beings, it seems. The idea of what awaits us has occupied the thoughts of writers and filmmakers for many years. In fact, *Newsweek's* August 12, 2002, cover was entitled 'Visions of Heaven.'" (If you have access to that issue, consider sharing what is included.) "To separate fact from opinion and imagination, let's see how Heaven is presented in Revelation 21."

Into the Word

Have the students read Revelation 21:1-7, 22-27 in order to complete the sentence, "The vision of Heaven presented in Revelation 21 is _____." Students may summarize how Heaven is described in this text or write a single word that captures the essence of the text. As students respond, direct their attention to these concepts: (1) Heaven has some rewards such as the ceasing of pain, sorrow, and death; (2) Heaven, as presented in Revelation 21, is not quite as tailored to each individual as many of us tend to think, since the idea of God residing with people (21:3) is a key concept in this text; (3) Heaven does not have the physical boundaries we have come to associate with life and living, such as a temple (21:22), celestial bodies for light (21:23), and night (21:25).

Ask, "What is the focus of Revelation 21:22, 23?" This is an opportunity to revisit the previous points. God and the Lamb are the temple. God and the Lamb provide the light. The focus in these verses is on God and the Lamb. Mention that this focus on God, coupled with the idea of God residing with people (21:3), demonstrates the value of God's presence in a Biblical concept of Heaven. Though moving from pain and suffering into rest (see Hebrews 4) is often the focus of a human concept of Heaven (and even mentioned in Scripture; see Revelation 21:4), the everlasting presence of the eternal God and the Lamb are what should truly draw the believer's gaze Heavenward.

Into Life

Say, "It is difficult for a finite person to describe something that is eternal. That is what we try to do with Heaven." Remind the students of the concept of dwelling with God in Heaven. Ask students to provide occasions and experiences in which they have been aware of God's presence. These may include such Biblical history as the Exodus or the Incarnation, but it may include personal history, as well. Identify ways in which we can know that God has been present in the examples provided.

Ask, "If God is indeed present in this world and not only a distant God who has removed Himself from us, how can we become more aware of His presence?" Have students work in pairs to brainstorm ideas. *(Possible ideas include waking up with the first thought on one's mind being a prayer, noticing the handiwork of God's creation more intentionally and verbalizing it, and seeing contacts with people as opportunities to do ministry—service, evangelism—for God.)* Have one of each pair volunteer what he or she considers a particularly good idea of his or her partner.

Say, "Revelation 21 concerns eternity and begins to give us an idea of the value of dwelling with God. Yet, we remain here on earth in anticipation of that eternity." Ask students to review the ideas suggested earlier concerning how to be more aware of God's presence. Instruct each student to select and write down one way in which he or she will commit to becoming more aware of living in God's presence. Conclude the lesson by once again reading the verses from the scroll used in lesson 10.

Let's Talk It Over

The questions on this page are designed to promote discussion of the lesson by the class and to encourage application of the lesson Scriptures. The answers provided are only discussion starters. Let your class talk it over from there.

1. Thinking about the statement, "This present world has been good," what are some of the best things in this earthly life? How will they be improved in Heaven? What joy of Heaven are you most anticipating?

Because this world does offer many wonderful experiences—after all, it is God's creation—we sometimes get too attached to it and have no desire to leave. We enjoy the physical pleasures brought through our five senses, sharing lives with family, worshiping God with a loving congregation, and the sense of accomplishment from our work and service.

But earthly joys are only a small fraction of the joys of Heaven. Our bodies will be perfected and capable of even greater things, our relationships will be deepened and expanded, all our hopes will realized, and our worship of and union with God will be heightened as we live in His very presence for all eternity.

2. Which figure in this lesson presents to you a more powerful image of the church: the figure of "the bride" or the figure of "the city"? Why?

A good case, of course, can be made for either answer. Most of us probably are more drawn to the touching bridegroom image. But both images suggest the same essential facts about the church. In both cases we see beauty: the beautiful bride "adorned" for her Groom, plus the brilliant city of precious stones and gems (Revelation 21:11, 18-21). We also see purity: the virgin bride prepared for her Groom, plus the holy city where no unclean person or thing is allowed (21:2, 8, 27).

We also see a close relationship: the bride at long last finally in perfect union with her Groom, plus the city's divine "Mayor" taking personal interest in each resident (21:3, 4, 7). We can also see security: the Groom as Protector of His bride, plus the city with strong foundations and thick walls (21:12-17).

3. The lesson writer says that our eternal home is "even more than a restoration of the Garden of Eden." What improvements over the Garden of Eden do you most anticipate? Why?

In a sense, Heaven will be "Paradise Regained" (including the "tree of life"; see Revelation 2:7; 22:1, 2). But we will experience vast improve-ments over the old Garden of Eden. We can start with the fact that there will be no devil and no temptations in Heaven. God wants the universe to be forever finished with sin (20:7-15). This means that there will be no "probation period" (as Adam and Eve had) during which we are tested, with the possibility of failure and loss of blessing.

Thus there is no chance that we could be "cast out" of our new Paradise. Our eternal home and our eternal blessings are just that—eternal. Our bodies and our spirits will be perfected, incapable of any future sin or death. And, most importantly, God will not come and go, visiting us only periodically as in the Garden of Eden. Instead, He will dwell and fellowship with us perpetually.

4. Will you feel secure in the "gated community" of Heaven if the gates are never closed? Why, or why not?

The lesson writer is right: "The threat of enemies is gone." The open gates will be a constant reminder that every threat has been removed. Anything corrupt that could possibly enter the city to tempt or hurt us will have been destroyed (Revelation 20:7-15). Only that which adds to the glory of God and the well-being of His people will be allowed (21:23-27).

These prospects are so different from the constant vulnerability that we experience in this life that we wonder if it will take some time to adjust to it! Sometimes it can seem like our lives revolve around locks and keys for protection—car keys, house keys, office keys, etc. But under God's protection and by His power we truly will be invulnerable!

5. Christians have their names written in the "book of life," even though we have done sinful things. What will you have to say about such things when you meet your Savior face-to-face?

Here again is the good news of the gospel. Yes, we have sinned and done "abominable" things, but Christians have been forgiven (Revelation 1:5; 5:9; 14:3, 4). It is the Lamb who has made all this possible, and we will undoubtedly fall down before Him in thanks and worship. We need not fear the Lamb's condemnation. That will be only for the unrepentant. (See Romans 1:32; 1 John 3:6.) Such people have not been cleansed of sin by the blood of the Lamb.

Summer Quarter, 2004

Special Features

Lessons

Hold Fast to the Faith
(Hebrews)

Unit 1: Encouraged to Be Faithful

Unit 2: Strengthened to Be Faithful

Guidelines for the Church's Ministry
(1, 2 Timothy; Titus)

About These Lessons

Championship sports teams are very skilled at playing both defense and offense. Our summer lessons offer us a great mix of these two concepts for the Christian life. We will learn how to remain faithful (defense) while making sure the church is ready to light the world (offense). Join the training!

Jun 6
Jun 13
Jun 20
Jun 27
Jul 4
Jul 11
Jul 18
Jul 25
Aug 1
Aug 8
Aug 15
Aug 22
Aug 29

Quarterly Quiz

The questions on this page may be used in several ways: as a pretest at the beginning of the quarter; as a review at the end of the quarter; or as a review after each lesson. The questions are based on the Scripture text of each lesson (King James Version). **The answers are on page 340.**

Lesson 1

1. In time past God spoke by the ____; in the last days He spoke by His ____. *Hebrews 1:1, 2*
2. God the Father said to the Son, "Thy throne, O God, is for ever and ever." T/F *Hebrews 1:8*
3. What is it that we dare not neglect? *Hebrews 2:3*

Lesson 2

1. How was Jesus, the captain of our salvation, made perfect? *Hebrews 2:10*
2. Jesus did not take on the nature of angels, but of the seed of ____. *Hebrews 2:16*
3. Because Jesus was God's Son, He never experienced being tempted. T/F *Hebrews 2:18*

Lesson 3

1. The Israelites who died in the wilderness did not enter God's rest because of what sin? (idolatry, sexual immorality, unbelief?) *Hebrews 3:18, 19*
2. What is quick, and powerful, and sharper than any two-edged sword? *Hebrews 4:12*

Lesson 4

1. Two qualities we will find at God's throne in time of need are ____ and ____. *Hebrews 4:16*
2. Jesus was a high priest forever after whose order? (Melchizedek, Aaron, Levi?) *Hebrews 5:5, 6*

Lesson 5

1. The writer of Hebrews praised the Christians for being mature and able to teach others. T/F *Hebrews 5:12, 13*
2. What two offenses are committed against Jesus by believers who fall away? *Hebrews 6:6*

Lesson 6

1. What did God do for the Israelites when He established the first covenant with them? *Hebrews 8:9*
2. In the new covenant with Israel, God puts His laws into their ____ and writes them in their ____. *Hebrews 8:10*
3. For those of the new covenant God will no longer remember their sins. T/F *Hebrews 8:12*

Lesson 7

1. Which of the following did not see death: Abel, Cain, or Enoch? *Hebrews 11:5*
2. What is the one quality we must have to please God? *Hebrews 11:6*

3. Who believed God's promise and was able to conceive in her old age? *Hebrews 11:11*

Lesson 8

1. Where should we be looking as we run the race set before us? (at the cloud of witnesses, at the goal, at Jesus?) *Hebrews 12:1, 2*
2. God chastens us for our profit so that we may be partakers of His ____. *Hebrews 12:10*

Lesson 9

1. A bishop should not be a novice so that he does not fall into which sin? (greed, pride, envy?) *1 Timothy 3:6*
2. A person must be proved before being given the office of deacon. T/F *1 Timothy 3:10*
3. Elders who rule well, especially those who teach, are to be given ____ honor. *1 Timothy 5:17*

Lesson 10

1. Paul encouraged Timothy to wait until he was older before trying to be an example to others. T/F *1 Timothy 4:12*
2. Timothy was told not to rebuke an elder but to entreat him as what? (a father, a son, a brother?) *1 Timothy 5:1*

Lesson 11

1. Timothy was told to endure hardness as a good ____ of Jesus Christ. *2 Timothy 2:3*
2. Why is Paul willing to endure all things for the elect's sake? *2 Timothy 2:10.*
3. If we study to show ourselves approved to God, then we need not be ashamed. T/F *2 Timothy 2:15*

Lesson 12

1. What should we do when we encounter men who are proud, unholy, fierce, traitors? (withstand them, preach to them, turn away?) *2 Timothy 3:1-5*
2. All Scripture is given by inspiration of God. T/F *2 Timothy 3:16*
3. Timothy was to do the work of a/an ____. *2 Timothy 4:5*

Lesson 13

1. Since Christ has redeemed us and purified us, what should we be zealous for? *Titus 2:14*
2. God our Savior saved us not by works of ____ but according to His ____. *Titus 3:4, 5*

Faithful in Doctrine and Life

by John W. Wade

THIS QUARTER'S LESSONS provide an interesting mix. With Scripture texts from Hebrews, 1 and 2 Timothy, and Titus, we will find several studies dealing with important doctrinal issues while others deal with the practical application of doctrine to life situations.

Our overall theme for June and July will be "Hold Fast to the Faith." During these two months, we will discover doctrinal foundation for our faith as we see the writer of Hebrews comparing and contrasting certain points of the Mosaic covenant with the new covenant. An understanding of Jewish worship practices in the tabernacle and the temple will be helpful in understanding and teaching these lessons. For August we move to "Guidelines for the Church's Ministry." These lessons are drawn from what are commonly called "the Pastoral Epistles," namely 1 and 2 Timothy and Titus.

Hold Fast to the Faith

As genuine books of the New Testament came to be recognized in the early church, the book of Hebrews was somewhat controversial. The controversy was not due to its content, but rather to the fact that no one knew for certain who had written the book. Unlike other New Testament epistles, we do not know the author or the destination of Hebrews.

Many scholars today believe that Hebrews was written to Jewish Christians who were being tempted to return to their former Jewish faith. A central theme of the epistle is to convince the readers that Christianity is now God's one and only plan. The old covenant is passing away, the new is here! Judaism has fulfilled its purpose. It is now to be left behind. God intends Christianity for all peoples.

Unit 1: Encouraged to Be Faithful

Lesson 1 begins the quarter on a high note. In the past God spoke through the prophets. That earlier revelation culminated in the revelation brought by God's Son. Once He had provided cleansing for sin, He sat down at the right hand of God. The Son is superior to the angels, and the revelation He brought is better than that under the old covenant. With all that God has done for us, how can we not be "Faithful to the Son"?

While the first lesson sets forth Christ's unique relationship with God, **Lesson 2** sets forth Christ's humanity. He was made "a little lower than the angels" in His incarnation so that He would "taste death" for all (Hebrews 2:9). Although He shared with God in the creation of the physical world, at the same time He could be tempted by the things of that world. This kinship with the human race gave Him an appeal that none other could possibly have. What could be more important than "Following the Author of Our Salvation"?

Lesson 3 begins with an exhortation for the first-century Jewish Christian readers to remain faithful to their commitment. They are reminded of the tragic example of the Israelites who were delivered from slavery in Egypt. Through faith they had followed Moses into the desert, but their disobedience showed their lack of faith and led to their death. Christianity promises rest and the blessings of Heaven, but in order to receive this great blessing, they must remain faithful to the end. Shall we not be "Faithful Through Obedience" as well?

Lesson 4 concludes the first unit of the quarter by emphasizing Christ's work as our great high priest. He is the One who intervened for us, offering us the ultimate sacrifice of His own life to pay sin's penalty. He can empathize with us because He faced the same temptations we face. Yet He was without sin! Because of this unique situation, shall we not approach the throne of grace boldly with the assurance that we will be helped by "Jesus: The Great High Priest" in our own time of need?

Unit 2: Strengthened to Be Faithful

Lesson 5 provides us an opportunity to stress the need for Christians to continue to learn about the intellectual content of their faith. Some of the Hebrew Christians were still content to survive as babies on the "milk" of the gospel message. Sadly, they were not yet at the point where they could grow on its "meat."

This is a vital lesson for those modern Christians who may have a strong emotional attachment to Christianity, but understand little about what the Bible actually teaches. How can we be "Faithful to Teaching" when we don't know what the teaching really is?

Lesson 6 reminds us that in the Christian era God deals with us through a new covenant. The Mosaic covenant was weak toward the flesh and the people could not keep it. The new covenant, however, is not based on our efforts but those of Christ. This covenant is not written on tablets of stone but on the minds and hearts of the people.

Within a short time of the writing of Hebrews, the Romans destroyed the temple. That naturally brought an end to the worship and sacrifices there. With that event the last vestige of the old covenant passed away. Now God calls all peoples to be "Faithful to the New Covenant."

Lesson 7 affords an opportunity to study one of the great passages of the Bible, namely Hebrews 11. This is sometimes called the Bible's "faith chapter." It briefly reviews the exploits and troubles of some of the great heroes of the faith.

While those heroes were not sinless or perfect, the author holds them up as examples for us because they were faithful. The early readers needed these models to help them avoid the danger of abandoning their Christian faith in times of trouble. Will we be counted in the "Roll Call of the Faithful" on God's great, final day?

Lesson 8 causes us to consider God's discipline in our lives. This is a study much needed in pleasure-driven cultures. We don't like to think about pain and suffering, and we go to great lengths to avoid discomfort.

Yet the writer of Hebrews is quick to point out that God chastens and disciplines us to prepare us for the race of life. In serving the Lord we must learn to lay aside the weight of sin that besets us. We are to run our race with patience and discipline, realizing that "we also are compassed about with so great a cloud of witnesses" (Hebrews 12:1). With eternity before us, how can we not be "Faithful and Disciplined" in the here and now?

Answers to Quarterly Quiz on page 338

Lesson 1—1. prophets, Son. 2. true. 3. so great salvation. Lesson 2—1. through sufferings. 2. Abraham. 3. false. Lesson 3—1.unbelief. 2. the Word of God. Lesson 4—1. mercy, grace. 2. Melchizedek. Lesson 5—1. false. 2. they crucify Him afresh, and put Him to an open shame. Lesson 6—1. led them out of the land of Egypt. 2. mind, hearts. 3. true. Lesson 7—1. Enoch. 2. faith. 3. Sarah. Lesson 8—1. at Jesus. 2. holiness. Lesson 9—1. pride. 2. true. 3. double. Lesson 10—1. false. 2. a father. Lesson 11—1. soldier. 2. so they may obtain the salvation which is in Christ Jesus. 3. true. Lesson 12—1. turn away. 2. true. 3. evangelist. Lesson 13—1. good works. 2. righteousness, mercy.

Guidelines for the Church's Ministry

Our lessons for August will give you and your learners the opportunity to apply some of the lessons from June and July. If the church is to be effective in carrying out its missions to both believers and unbelievers, it is vital that we follow the New Testament in matters of both faith and practice.

Lesson 9 begins our unit with Paul's instructions to Timothy, his younger colleague in ministry, regarding selection of elders and deacons. Those are the two offices that are most clearly established in the New Testament for leadership and service in local congregations. If we fail to "Select Good Leaders," how can the ministry of our churches have any credibility?

Lesson 10 reminds us that while physical exercise has some value, training in godliness provides benefits both in this life and the life to come. Paul urged Timothy to put his spiritual gifts to good use, and not to allow his youthfulness to stand in the way of employing these gifts. If our leaders neglect their gifts, how can they "Be Ministers of Godliness"?

In a time when the teaching of God's Word is often rejected, neglected, or distorted, we need Lesson 11! Here Paul warns Timothy about what is and isn't useful in a Christian leader's life and in the teaching process. How can the gospel move forward if we do not "Handle God's Word Rightly"?

In Lesson 12 Paul warns Timothy that in the last days many people would become unholy and rebellious. To protect his people from being led astray by false teachers, Timothy must remain patient and persistent in his ministry. This challenge rings just as true for us today. What will we say to God on the Judgment Day if we do not "Remain Faithful" to our callings?

Lesson 13 winds up our summer studies with a lesson from the short book of Titus. Paul reminds his colleague that, among other things, God's salvation is intended for everyone. Titus is therefore to urge the people to give up their evil ways and surrender to God's will. Their faith will show in their godly actions. If we fail to "Do Good Works," can we really claim to be part of the body of Christ?

We pray that the Lord will bless you as you share the lessons of this quarter with your learners. There is much solid doctrinal teaching in here, but this is not just doctrine for the sake of doctrine. Sound doctrine should always result in changed lives that glorify the Lord. This should be your goal as you invite your learners to apply these lessons to their lives.

A Merciful and Faithful High Priest

LEVITICAL PRIESTS	JESUS AS PRIEST
Many	One
Of the tribe of Levi	Of the tribe of Judah
Offered animal sacrifices (over and over)	Offered Himself (once)
In the order of Aaron	In the order of Melchizedek
Sacrificed for their own sins and the sins of others	Sacrificed for the sins of others; He was sinless
Served only for a limited time	Serves eternally
Served only as priests	Serves as both Priest and King
Served in a physical, temporal tabernacle	Serves in a spiritual, eternal tabernacle
Functioned under a weak and terminal covenant	Serves in a strong and endless covenant

OLD COVENANT BY MOSES	NEW COVENANT IN JESUS
temporary	eternal
national	universal
priests from the tribe of Levi	priests from all in the covenant
sinful men as high priests	Jesus as only and sinless high priest
sealed by the blood of animals	sealed by the blood of the Lamb of God
repeated sacrifices necessary	a single and final Sacrifice
high priest enters into Holy of Holies for the people	High Priest enters Heaven to welcome the people
written on stones by the hand of God	written on hearts by the Spirit of God

Lots of Questions

Mastering the Master's Art

by Ronald G. Davis

JESUS WAS A MASTER OF QUESTIONS. Some of His questions were designed to elicit statements of faith. Some were designed to force thinking. Others were intended to put the one questioned on the spot. And though He could know the answer by divine insight, Jesus asked questions to "check on" the accomplished level of understanding in His learners.

Jesus asked Nathanael, "Because I said that I saw you under the fig tree, do you believe?" (paraphrased from John 1:50). Jesus challenged His mother's assumption with the question, "What have I to do with this wedding need?" (John 2:4). Nicodemus was humbled by the query: "Are you a teacher in Israel and don't know basic spiritual truths?" (John 3:10). To the man ill for thirty-eight years, He curiously asked, "Do you want to be well?" (John 5:6). To the Jews who challenged His authority for healing on the Sabbath, Jesus simply questioned and observed: "If you don't really believe Moses' words, how can you believe mine?" (John 5:47). And to Philip—as the multitude approached in the wilderness of Galilee—He posed a stumper: "Where shall we buy bread for these thousands to eat?" (John 6:5). Poignantly He would have to ask the Twelve, "Will you go away just like the multitude of disciples?" (John 6:67). And His purpose was always to elicit the highest level of learner activity possible: thinking!

Questions may initially have only a review and reinforcement purpose. On a much deeper level they force learners to compare, contrast, evaluate, analyze, synthesize, and apply. The perceptive teacher—in imitation of the Master—will ask questions and stir learner questions of all levels.

Tests as Questioning Activity

Though some Christian teachers resist the idea of testing (and sometimes defer because "they don't have enough time"), Jesus gave His learners tests. That is exactly what He was doing with Nicodemus when he arrived with commendation (John 3:1, 2) and with Philip by the Sea of Galilee as the crowd arrived with anticipation (John 6:1-6). (Both failed the test!) A wholesale rejection of all testing shows a misunderstanding of the concept of instruction. Testing is a part of the teaching-learning phenomenon.

And the classroom teacher can use tests for all the right reasons: to discover or verify learners'

levels of understanding, to make the learners curious as to answers they do not have and to initiate their exploratory behavior toward finding answers, to review and reinforce facts and conclusions already studied, and to evaluate the learners' understanding after instruction. (And any who use tests will choose to avoid all the wrong reasons: to show learners how ignorant they are, to compare student with student, to encourage pride in the highly successful, and a host of other wrong motives.)

All the traditional testing devices can be used: true-false statements, matching series, multiple-choice, fill-in-the-blank, and open-ended questions. A simple fill-in-the-blank "test" could be an effective introduction to this whole series of lessons. Consider this emphasis on Hebrews 1:1-3 (lesson 1) as the keynote verses for the writer's whole epistle: in the upper third of a sheet to be copied and given to each learner, print these verses with key words omitted; for example,

> "God, who at _____ times and in _____ manners spake in times past unto the fathers by the _____, hath in these _____ days spoken unto us by his _____, whom he hath appointed _____ of all things, by whom he made the _____; who being the _____ of his glory, and the _____ image of his person, and upholding all things by the _____ of his _____, when he had by himself _____ our _____, sat down on the _____ hand of the _____ on high."

On the lower third of the sheet print the verses without omissions. Fold the bottom third up over the middle and tape the flap to keep it from easily falling open. As students arrive, hand them copies of the sheet and direct them to fill in the blanks as best they can—without using Bibles. As class begins (and as they are finished with the fill-in), direct them to untape the lower flaps and check their own tests. This will give you an effective focus toward introducing the key truth of the lessons for the first eight lessons of the series, all from texts in the epistle to the Hebrews: Jesus is God's final revelation, and He is superior in every way to God's earlier revelations of Himself.

A simple multiple-choice series could offer a useful introduction to a Bible book about to be studied. Again, the epistle to the Hebrews could be introduced with questions such as the following (with answers in bold):

(1) As we have it divided, the book of Hebrews has ___ chapters. (A) 7, (B) 9, (C) 11, **(D) 13,** (E) 15

(2) One Old Testament person not given significant attention in Hebrews is (A) Aaron, (B) Abraham, (C) David, **(D) Joseph,** (E) Moses.

(3) Which of the following best characterizes the epistle to the Hebrews? (A) a summary of Old Testament history, with a messianic emphasis; (B) an extended appeal to Gentile Christians not to revert to paganism; **(C) a careful presentation of the superiority of Christ and the church over the Mosaic system;** (D) a collection of proverbs and wise sayings; (E) a refutation of arguments presented by first-century Judaizers.

(4) Melchizedek is the name of (A) an opponent of early Christianity in Rome, **(B) a high priest of God introduced in Genesis,** (C) the angel who revealed the message of this book to its writer, (D) the only person who is greeted at the end of the book, other than Timothy; (E) an unidentified book to which this epistle refers several times.

(5) Which of the following grand truths is from the epistle to the Hebrews? (A) "Contend earnestly for the faith," (B) "From a child thou hast known the Holy Scriptures," (C) "Godliness with contentment is great gain," **(D) "How shall we escape, if we neglect so great salvation?"** (E) "Our citizenship is in Heaven."

(6) Which of the following places is named in the epistle? (A) Assyria, (B) Corinth, **(C) Egypt,** (D) Galatia, (E) Rome.

(7) In the chapter giving examples of outstanding faith, which of the following women is named? (A) Deborah, (B) Eve, (C) Miriam, (D) Rachel, **(E) Rahab.**

An occasional test will add variety to the classroom and will allow the teacher to accomplish various goals that are difficult to attain in any other activity.

Oral Interrogatives

Asking questions aloud to learners is not as simple as it seems. Whole books have been written as pedagogical studies on the "simple" use of questions in the classroom. Teachers tend to make three recurring mistakes: (1) they ask only factual questions that elicit little thought (these are matters of either-or for the individual learner; either the learner knows the answer or does not); (2) they expect immediate answers, and from an anybody-who-knows respondent; and (3) they word questions clumsily and elicit only the response thought from learners: "What does the teacher want?"

Adult students need questions that they can mull over and manipulate. They need questions that call for personal evaluation and judgment.

Adults need time to ponder a reasonable response. (If the question is worth asking, it is worth fifteen to thirty seconds of thought time!) Adult learners need questions they do not have to recast as "Do you mean . . . ?" before they respond.

Teachers need to involve learners in the questioning process, not simply the answering process. Asking questions may well show as much cognitive behavior as answering questions. Consider a "Circle of Questions." Put learners into a general circular configuration, assign each a verse or verses of the study text(s), and ask each to word a question based on his or her assigned content. Then proceed around the circle, letting each ask a question to the person to the left. (If your group could handle the consequence, don't let a learner ask a question until he or she has answered a question—to the satisfaction of the asker.) Continue around the circle until all questions are handled.

You could "prime" the group by distributing prepared questions. Consider Lesson 9, "Select Good Leaders," as a study that lends itself to such a procedure. If you were distributing questions to learners, these could be useful:

First Timothy 3:1—"If *desire* is a true qualification for one becoming a 'bishop,' how does the church establish such desire?" 3:2—"What does it mean for a bishop to be *blameless?"* 3:3—"Does the expression 'not given to wine' preclude any consumption of alcoholic drink?" 3:4, 5—"What is there about 'having his children in subjection' that has to do with being qualified for church leadership?" 3:6—How long does one need to be a confessed Christian before he is no longer a 'novice'?" 3:7—"How can the church establish that a candidate for the office of 'bishop' has 'a good report of them which are without'; that is, non-church people? 3:8—"How would a servant-leader with a 'double tongue' create problems within the local body of believers?" 3:9—"What does this verse/this trait actually mean?" 3:10—"How does one prove himself worthy to be a deacon?" 3:11—"How is it fair to a man to expect certain traits in his wife before he is considered for office?" 3:12—"What does being the 'husband of one wife' require: marriage? monogamy? no history of divorce? disqualification of widowers?" 3:13—"Why would the Spirit add a note on motivation and reward to a list of qualifications for the deacon?" 5:17—What does it mean to have 'double honor'?" 5:18—"Why would you say that a 'paid eldership' is a practice to be considered (or not considered)?" 5:19—"What implications for 'how the church is run' are implied by the requirement in this verse?"

Asking questions is a time-honored strategy for successful teaching. Ask away!

Faithful to the Son

DEVOTIONAL READING: Colossians 1:14-20.

BACKGROUND SCRIPTURE: Hebrews 1:1–2:4.

PRINTED TEXT: Hebrews 1:1-9; 2:1-4.

Hebrews 1:1-9

1 God, who at sundry times and in divers manners spake in time past unto the fathers by the prophets,

2 Hath in these last days spoken unto us by his Son, whom he hath appointed heir of all things, by whom also he made the worlds;

3 Who being the brightness of his glory, and the express image of his person, and upholding all things by the word of his power, when he had by himself purged our sins, sat down on the right hand of the Majesty on high;

4 Being made so much better than the angels, as he hath by inheritance obtained a more excellent name than they.

5 For unto which of the angels said he at any time, Thou art my Son, this day have I begotten thee? And again, I will be to him a Father, and he shall be to me a Son?

6 And again, when he bringeth in the first-begotten into the world, he saith, And let all the angels of God worship him.

7 And of the angels he saith, Who maketh his angels spirits, and his ministers a flame of fire.

8 But unto the Son he saith, Thy throne, O God, is for ever and ever: a sceptre of righteousness is the sceptre of thy kingdom.

9 Thou hast loved righteousness, and hated iniquity; therefore God, even thy God, hath anointed thee with the oil of gladness above thy fellows.

Hebrews 2:1-4

1 Therefore we ought to give the more earnest heed to the things which we have heard, lest at any time we should let them slip.

2 For if the word spoken by angels was steadfast, and every transgression and disobedience received a just recompense of reward;

3 How shall we escape, if we neglect so great salvation; which at the first began to be spoken by the Lord, and was confirmed unto us by them that heard him;

4 God also bearing them witness, both with signs and wonders, and with divers miracles, and gifts of the Holy Ghost, according to his own will?

GOLDEN TEXT: Who being the brightness of his glory, and the express image of his person.—Hebrews 1:3.

Hold Fast to the Faith
Unit 1: Encouraged to Be Faithful
(Lessons 1-4)

Lesson Aims

After participating in this lesson, each student should be able to:

1. List the reasons why Jesus is superior to all others in revealing God to us.

2. Explain the honor that is due Jesus as God's Son, the author of our salvation.

3. Make a statement of faith in Jesus as the Son of God.

Lesson Outline

INTRODUCTION

   A. "How Shall We Escape?"

   B. Lesson Background

 I. GOD HAS SPOKEN (Hebrews 1:1-9)

   A. Through the Prophets (v. 1)

   B. Through His Son (vv. 2, 3)

     "The Eagle Has Landed"

   C. Superiority of His Son (vv. 4-9)

     The Only Leader Worthy of Worship

II. WE MUST LISTEN (Hebrews 2:1-4)

   A. Importance of Heeding (v. 1)

   B. Punishment for Disobedience (vv. 2, 3)

   C. Evidence to Believe (v. 4)

CONCLUSION

   A. Facing Our Problems

   B. Prayer

   C. Thought to Remember

Introduction

A. "How Shall We Escape?"

Just outside the town where I grew up, a big barn sat near one of the main roads. Painted on its side in large letters visible to all who drove by were these words from Hebrews 2:3: "How shall we escape, if we neglect so great salvation?"

Through the prophets and others chosen to lead the Israelites, God began to prepare the way for His fuller revelation through His Son. Through His Son, God opened the very gates of Heaven, making salvation possible for all who will hear our Lord and heed Him. For those who foolishly reject Him "there remaineth no more sacrifice for sins, but a certain fearful looking for of judgment and fiery indignation" (Hebrews 10:26, 27). This may not be what sinners want to hear, but it is certainly unambiguous!

There is a sequel to this story. Recently I drove by the barn and noticed that all the words had been painted over. No longer were those who passed by challenged to give thought to their spiritual status. Perhaps this is a modern parable on the condition of the spirituality in our times. The secular world no longer worries or even cares about its relationship with God. And worse, even many who call themselves Christians show little real concern about God's uncompromising demands that His followers live pure and holy lives. But painting out words on a barn will not obliterate His timeless commandments.

B. Lesson Background

The first eight lessons of this quarter are based on the epistle to the Hebrews. Commentators have suggested that this epistle "begins like a treatise, proceeds like a sermon, and closes like a letter." Although some controversy has surrounded this book, it occupies a crucial place in the New Testament.

The main controversy about Hebrews deals with its authorship. In the past many have ascribed this book to Paul. However, there are some serious problems with attributing it to that great apostle. Unlike the epistles that bear Paul's name, the letter to the Hebrews is unsigned. Nor can we give an exact date for the writing of this book. It seems obvious, however, that it was written before A.D. 70. The Romans destroyed Jerusalem and the temple in that year, ending the worship services that had been conducted. Had Hebrews been written after that date, the writer almost certainly would have mentioned it because of the book's subject matter at various places.

We are not told of the specific destination of this epistle. But clearly it seems to be aimed at ~~Jewish Christians~~, specifically those then living in Palestine. The purpose of the letter was to encourage them to remain faithful in spite of the persecutions they had endured. The writer seems concerned that they might be tempted to abandon Christianity and return to Judaism. For that reason *better* is a key word throughout the letter. Christ is better than the fathers who had spoken in the past or the angels. Further, Christians have a better hope (7:19), a better covenant based on better promises (8:6), a better sacrifice (9:23), and in Heaven a better inheritance (10:34).

I. God Has Spoken
(Hebrews 1:1-9)

A. Through the Prophets (v. 1)

1. God, who at sundry times and in divers manners spake in time past unto the fathers by the prophets.

A fundamental proposition of both Judaism and Christianity is that God has spoken to the human race. Our God is not some remote, obscure deity who observes our activities from afar with little or no involvement. How reassuring, and at the same time sobering, to realize that He is not just "out there," but is also here with us.

The fact that God has spoken *at sundry times* means that He has never locked Himself into a predictable timetable for His numerous revelations. But one thing is sure: He always has revealed Himself when humanity has needed it. *In divers manners* suggests the great variety of ways through which He has spoken. He has, of course, used people *(the prophets)*—sometimes speaking to them in an audible voice, at other times through dreams or visions. But He has also used other means of getting His message to the *fathers.* He revealed His will through a burning bush (Exodus 3:2), through a pillar of fire and a pillar of cloud (Exodus 40:38), and even through a donkey (Numbers 22:22-35).

B. Through His Son (vv. 2, 3)

2. Hath in these last days spoken unto us by his Son, whom he hath appointed heir of all things, by whom also he made the worlds.

These last days may refer to the closing days of the old covenant that, with the coming of Christ, was no longer binding on the people. It seems best, however, to take this as referring to the new covenant, which ushers in the final stage of God's dealings with sinful humanity. Although nearly two thousand years have passed since these words were written, we need to keep in mind that God doesn't count time as we do, for "one day is with the Lord as a thousand years, and a thousand years as one day" (2 Peter 3:8).

Combining verses 1 and 2, we see a clear contrast between God's previous revelations and His revelation through *His Son,* Jesus Christ. That contrast was made quite clear on several occasions during Jesus' earthly ministry. On the mount of transfiguration, for example, Moses (representing the law) and Elijah (representing the prophets) appeared with Jesus. Both the law and the prophets were important parts of God's revelation. But in conclusion God spoke, "This is my beloved Son, in whom I am well pleased; hear ye him" (Matthew 17:5).

The importance of the Son's message is affirmed when we see that the Father has *appointed* Jesus to be *heir of all things.* Jesus is "firstborn of every creature" (Colossians 1:15). The "all things" that Jesus has created according to John 1:3 certainly includes *the worlds.* Jesus affirmed His own preexistence when He stated, "Before Abraham was, I am" (John 8:58). God's main purpose for

speaking to "the fathers by the prophets" through the centuries was to prepare for the coming of His Son. [See question #1, page 352.]

"The Eagle Has Landed"

The words from July 20, 1969, are still burned in my memory: "Houston, Tranquility Base here. The Eagle has landed." My astonishment and elation as a fourteen-year-old knew no limits when, six hours later, Neil Armstrong descended a ladder to become the first human in history to set foot on another celestial body.

The twenty-one hours those adventurers spent on the surface of the moon came back to us in grainy black-and-white, but we could see it all: the lunar module sitting proudly upon the surface, an astronaut coming down the ladder from the module, the panoramic views—so many images! Astronaut Edwin "Buzz" Aldrin called the view one of "magnificent desolation."

The astronauts didn't make it to the moon simply in the lunar module, however. Many years of planning and building had produced the Saturn V booster rocket. After launch, that rocket would shed successive stages until it was gone—leaving only the command, service, and lunar modules. The booster rocket existed for a specific purpose, and it performed its job well.

Judges, prophets, and kings all made their appearance before Christ arrived. They were the successive "stages" over the centuries that pointed to His coming. But they've served their purpose and have dropped away. Now it is Christ alone to whom we look—the One who is "on the right hand of the Majesty on high."

When the Son of God set foot on planet earth, we can imagine that what He saw around Him was a picture of "magnificent desolation." It was

The **Son** *is the* **radiance** *of* **God's glory.**

Hebrews 1:3, NIV

Visual for lesson 1

This glorious visual will remind your learners of the majesty of their Savior.

magnificent because "He came unto his own," but desolate because "his own received him not" (John 1:11). As we look to Him today, may we remember that there are many in our world of magnificent desolation who still need Him.

—R. L. N.

3. Who being the brightness of his glory, and the express image of his person, and upholding all things by the word of his power, when he had by himself purged our sins, sat down on the right hand of the Majesty on high.

This verse summarizes some of the more important aspects of the relationship between the Father and the Son. First of all, the Son is like the Father in *the brightness of his glory*. John 1:14 affirms this same idea: "We beheld his glory, the glory as of the only begotten of the Father."

Second, the Son shares with the Father the *power* to uphold *all things*. That is, Christ is involved in the power that sustains all created things. Third, He has *by himself purged our sins*. Through His death on the cross He has paid the price required by God's holiness and justice (Romans 3:21-26). Finally, He *sat down on the right hand of the Majesty on high*, indicating His eternal reign with the Father. (See also Hebrews 8:1; 10:12; 12:2; Revelation 3:21.) There is no glory or power greater than Jesus.

C. Superiority of His Son (vv. 4-9)

4. Being made so much better than the angels, as he hath by inheritance obtained a more excellent name than they.

The recipients of Hebrews were being tempted to return to the Judaism that they had left to become Christians. One of the main thrusts of this letter was to encourage them to hold fast in their new faith. One argument that the writer uses is to show that the Son is superior to *the angels*. During the centuries between the Old and New Testaments, Jewish writers created much speculation about the work of angels. Although angels are Heavenly beings and are messengers for God, they are inferior to the Son because they have not received His *more excellent name*, that is, Son of God. The next several verses give us more reasons for the Son's superiority.

VISUALS FOR THESE LESSONS

The visual pictured in each lesson (e.g., page 347) is a small reproduction of a large, full-color poster included in the *Adult Visuals* packet for the Summer Quarter. The packet is available from your supplier. Order No. 492.

---

5. For unto which of the angels said he at any time, Thou art my Son, this day have I begotten thee? And again, I will be to him a Father, and he shall be to me a Son?

The writer demonstrates the superiority of the Son over the angels by using a series of quotations from the Old Testament. The writer knows that the Christian readers of Jewish background accept these Scriptures as God's authoritative Word.

The first quotation is from Psalm 2:7 (also found in Acts 13:33 and Hebrews 5:5). This psalm is widely recognized both in Judaism and in Christianity as being messianic. *Thou art my Son* was not spoken to the angels, but only to the Christ.

The second quotation is from 2 Samuel 7:14, which is identical to 1 Chronicles 17:13. This prediction originally applied to future–King Solomon, but the writer of Hebrews now applies it to Jesus as well. Solomon was in the line of David, as is Jesus (Matthew 1:1, 6).

6. And again, when he bringeth in the first-begotten into the world, he saith, And let all the angels of God worship him.

First-begotten does not refer to some hypothetical remote period when the Son did not exist (indeed, He has existed from eternity past). Rather, it refers to the incarnation, when the baby Jesus was born in Bethlehem. *And let all the angels of God worship him* is from Deuteronomy 32:43 in the Septuagint, the ancient Greek translation of the Old Testament, which doesn't read the same way either in the earlier Hebrew or in English versions. (Perhaps your copy of the *King James Bible* explains this in a footnote.) Luke 2:14 confirms for us that angels said, "Glory to God in the highest" at the birth of Jesus.

THE ONLY LEADER WORTHY OF WORSHIP

Today is the sixtieth anniversary of the D-Day invasion, which led to the defeat of Adolf Hitler and his henchmen. Hitler grew up a penniless vagabond on the streets of Vienna, Austria. After serving as a soldier in World War I, he came into contact with the National Socialist German Workers' Party (Nazis) while living in Germany.

The Nazis were a handful of malcontents and radicals on the fringe of society. Hitler asserted himself into their leadership and transformed the Nazis into a political force. Through political scheming and his considerable ability as an orator, Hitler campaigned so effectively that he eventually enlisted about a third of Germany under the Nazi banner.

By March 23, 1933, Hitler was dictator of Germany. On May Day of that year, he held a rally of one hundred thousand workers and delegates from German labor unions at Tempelhof airport in Berlin. With the help of Nazi symbols, special lighting effects, and Hitler's fiery oratory, the cheering workers were mesmerized. Hitler was, in effect, worshiped as a type of "savior." The sobering and deadly events over the course of the next twelve years would make the error of this adulation plain to all.

Human leaders are fallible and will always disappoint us—perhaps not on the scale of a Hitler, but they will disappoint us nevertheless. Only Jesus is worthy of worship. Following the example of angels, we should worship no one but God (Revelation 19:10; 22:8, 9). Jesus Christ is God, and He will never deceive us. He will never disappoint us. Only He can show us the way to eternal life.   —R. H.

7. And of the angels he saith, Who maketh his angels spirits, and his ministers a flame of fire.

This quotation is from Psalm 104:4. This verse shows the contrast between Jesus, whom God calls His "Son" (in verse 5), and the *angels*, who are ministering *spirits* (cf. Hebrews 1:14). The Son is to be worshiped (verse 6), but the angels are to serve.

8, 9. But unto the Son he saith, Thy throne, O God, is for ever and ever: a sceptre of righteousness is the sceptre of thy kingdom. Thou hast loved righteousness, and hated iniquity; therefore God, even thy God, hath anointed thee with the oil of gladness above thy fellows.

These two verses are a quotation from Psalm 45:6, 7. There the psalmist praises the glory and might of *God*. The writer of Hebrews, inspired by God, takes these verses and applies them quite appropriately to *the Son* of God.

Since the throne of the Son is *for ever and ever*, it is secure, eternal, and can never be threatened. Because God is holy, He, on the one hand, loves *righteousness* and, on the other hand, must hate *iniquity*.

Being *anointed* with *oil* is a majestic picture of the Son's position *above* His *fellows*. See Exodus 28:41; 1 Samuel 10:1; and 1 Kings 19:16 for Old Testament examples of anointing someone to an office of high service.

II. We Must Listen
(Hebrews 2:1-4)

A. Importance of Heeding (v. 1)

1. Therefore we ought to give the more earnest heed to the things which we have heard, lest at any time we should let them slip.

The word *therefore* is crucial in this epistle. It is often used to mark a conclusion that logically follows arguments or statements that have preceded it. Thus when we see the word, we ought to be alert to the practical applications that follow.

In this verse the writer exhorts his readers to give *heed to the things* that they have *heard*. These things include the gospel message that they had received and responded to while they were still Jews living under the law. Also included are sermons and lessons they have heard that have helped them grow toward maturity in the faith.

While many of the Jewish Christians had suffered persecution because of their faith, this does not seem to be the problem addressed here. The author apparently is not concerned that the readers will openly and dramatically renounce Christianity and return to Judaism. The real danger is that the readers will carelessly, little by little, *slip* away.

That danger remains as real today as it was in the first century. Rarely does a Christian publicly renounce his or her faith. He or she is much more likely to drift away slowly. We see it when a person who once attended worship services every Sunday begins to attend only once or twice a month (cf. Hebrews 10:25). Eventually that person shows up only for special occasions, such as Christmas and Easter, or sometimes not at all.

Several factors may contribute to this slipping away—family, business, and recreation interests are possibilities. A growing unwillingness to make the effort to live up to the high standards of Christianity is also a danger. When we see this pattern developing in a person, the church and its leadership need to make efforts to restore that person. [See question #2, page 352.]

B. Punishment for Disobedience (vv. 2, 3)

2, 3. For if the word spoken by angels was steadfast, and every transgression and disobedience received a just recompense of reward; how shall we escape, if we neglect so great salvation; which at the first began to be spoken by the Lord, and was confirmed unto us by them that heard him?

The word spoken by angels most likely refers to the law given at Mount Sinai. No mention of angels is made in the Exodus account of Moses receiving the law at that time. But the writer apparently has access to information not mentioned there. In Galatians 3:19 Paul speaks of the law being "ordained by angels in the hand of a mediator." See also Stephen's final words in Acts 7:53.

The writer of Hebrews uses the involvement of angels in law-giving to make a vital point. Those who disobeyed the law were justly punished—that is, they lost their hope of *salvation.* Since this was true of those who violated the old covenant, how much more certain will it be the punishment of those who violate the terms of the new covenant, which has been established by the death of God's own Son! Notice, too, that this stern warning is not directed at those who arrogantly and blatantly reject the Son. Instead, this warning is directed at those who could become guilty of *neglect* of the offer of salvation that they already have accepted. This is the "let them slip" that the writer has just mentioned in verse 1. [See question #3, page 352.]

This warning is so important that we should not move on too quickly. God had revealed His law to Moses, and the old covenant remained in force for centuries. Now the new covenant has been revealed through the *Lord.* Step by step throughout His three-year ministry, Christ had begun to set forth the terms of this new covenant. In Matthew 13:3-9, 18-23, Jesus mentioned various types of responses to His message. The writer of Hebrews is issuing a warning to those who have heard and accepted that message, but now may be drifting away. How can they possibly escape punishment if they drift away after having heard the truth?

There are times when the best way to deal with persons who are in danger of slipping away is with soft words and gentle persuasion. But there are also times when they must be confronted bluntly. The writer of Hebrews hits us squarely with the facts! [See question #4, page 352.]

Home Daily Bible Readings

Monday, May 31—Christ Is the Cornerstone (Acts 4:5-12)
Tuesday, June 1—Christ Is the Image of God (Colossians 1:15-20)
Wednesday, June 2—Christ in You, the Hope of Glory (Colossians 1:21-27)
Thursday, June 3—In Christ Are Treasures of Wisdom (Colossians 2:1-6)
Friday, June 4—Christ, the Reflection of God's Glory (Hebrews 1:1-5)
Saturday, June 5—You Established the Universe (Hebrews 1:6-13)
Sunday, June 6—Salvation Declared Through Christ (Hebrews 1:14—2:4)

C. Evidence to Believe (v. 4)

4. God also bearing them witness, both with signs and wonders, and with divers miracles, and gifts of the Holy Ghost, according to his own will.

As God has revealed His word across the centuries, He has confirmed it through *signs and wonders, and with divers miracles.* The ten plagues visited upon Egypt and the opening of the Red Sea are early examples. Throughout His earthly ministry, Jesus performed miracles that confirmed His message (John 20:30, 31).

As a further and continuing support for that message, our Lord sent *the Holy Ghost* after He had departed (John 14:26). Peter refers to this support when he notes that the message he preached was by the power of "the Holy Ghost sent down from heaven" (1 Peter 1:12). How can we ignore a salvation that comes through miraculous signs—signs that can be only from God Almighty? [See question #5, page 352.]

Conclusion

A. Facing Our Problems

If we are to stem the tide that is sweeping Christianity out of Western culture, we must first acknowledge that a problem really does exist. Once we acknowledge that there is a problem, we must then turn to ways to face it resolutely.

Realizing the importance of teaching the exclusive truth of the Christian faith is crucial. Ideally this ought to begin in our homes, the most important educational institution in the world. Unfortunately, many parents, even Christian parents, do not feel that they are capable of doing a good job of passing on their faith to their children. Even though most of us are not professional educators, we need to understand that there are many important things each of us can do—praying at mealtimes, having a Bible study with our children, and emphasizing Christian values in our conversations are examples.

Let us all make a firm commitment that we will not allow Christianity to slip away because of our neglect.

B. Prayer

Almighty God, we thank You for allowing us to share in all the joys and blessings that come to us through our Christian faith. Give us the wisdom and determination to pass this faith on to our children and to all others who have not known these joys and blessings. Through Christ we pray, amen.

C. Thought to Remember

God has spoken, and we must listen.

Learning by Doing

This page contains an alternative lesson plan emphasizing learning activities.
Classes desiring such student involvement will find these suggestions helpful.

Learning Goals

After participating in this lesson, each student will be able to:

1. List the reasons why Jesus is superior to all others in revealing God to us.

2. Explain the honor that is due Jesus as God's Son, the author of our salvation.

3. Make a statement of faith in Jesus as the Son of God.

Into the Lesson

Begin this lesson by giving a handout with the following acrostic to individuals, teams, or small groups. By doing the acrostic, the learners will discover the "key word" for the book of Hebrews. Give the worksheet the heading "The Supremacy of Jesus." Print the following instructions on the sheet. "The book of Hebrews ascribes some wonderful superlatives to Jesus. Read some of them in 1:1-9 and fill in the blanks below. As you do so, you will discover the 'key word' for the entire book of Hebrews." (This activity is also in the student book "Learning by Doing" page.)

KEY WORD: _ _ _ _ _ _

Clues:

1. Jesus is the ___ of God's glory (1:3). *brightness*
2. Jesus is ___ of all things (1:2). *heir*
3. Jesus has an ___ name (1:4). *excellent*
4. Jesus holds a ___ of righteousness (1:8). *sceptre*
5. Jesus is the ___ of God's person (1:3). *image*
6. The angels ___ Jesus (1:6). *worship*
   (Key word: *Better.*)

Make the transition to Bible study by telling the class that our study of Hebrews will unveil a Jesus who is better than anything else that life has to offer, better than any god ever imagined.

Into the Word

Prepare a short lecture on the background of the epistle to the Hebrews. Use notes in the lesson commentary Lesson Background on page 346 and on verses 1 and 2. Use the following words on a visual or the board as an outline: *Author, Date, Specific Destination, Purpose, Better, Sundry, Last Days.*

The following two activities (included in the student book) may be provided to as many groups of four or five people as your class has. Each group will do only one and should be given a sheet of poster board and a marker. Prepare written instructions for each group as follows.

Activity #1. Read Hebrews 1:1-9. Remember that the purpose of the book is to show that Jesus is better than or superior to angels, prophets, Moses, priests, and the entire Old Testament system. On the poster board list every phrase or word that describes Jesus' superiority. From your list select three or four of these descriptions and share the significance of each with the entire class.

Activity #2. Begin your study by reading Hebrews 2:1-4. This passage and other numerous reminders in this book encourage Christians to hold on to the core of their faith. Christians are still tempted by heretical doctrines. Discuss and select what your group considers the core doctrines of Christianity that must be preserved and taught. List them and be prepared to tell the rest of the class why these are important.

Allow each group to report. If you have several groups doing each activity, have one person from each group share only one or two answers.

Into Life

Read aloud the Conclusion of the lesson commentary (page 350) to class members. Ask, "How would you define *postmodernism?*" (Be prepared with a definition that you have found on the Internet, in dictionaries, or in theological reference works.) Then ask the following questions: "How is it a threat to the core values of Christianity?" "How does this definition of postmodernism describe our nation or our way of thinking? Give examples." "Hebrews 2 reminds us not to let the core values of Christianity slip away. What are some ways that moms and dads can help their children understand and endorse these Christian principles?" (Ask a "scribe" to list answers on a marker board or poster board.) "How can churches help individuals grasp these core values of Christianity? What things should your church be doing to make this a priority in teaching?" (Ask the "scribe" to list these answers also.)

Close with a chain prayer. Ask for three "links" or persons to (1) thank God for Jesus, (2) ask help for Christian homes, and (3) ask help for churches in teaching core Christian values.

Let's Talk It Over

The questions on this page are designed to promote discussion of the lesson by the class and to encourage application of the lesson Scriptures. The answers provided are only discussion starters. Let your class talk it over from there.

1. Suppose a fellow believer came to you and said, "Say, a friend gave me this book. He says it's 'another testament of Jesus Christ.' Maybe we need to see what it says and add that to our teachings at church." How would you respond to your friend's suggestion? How does today's text help you in your answer?

Many groups and individuals claim to have further words from God. In light of our text, we should be very skeptical of such claims. We have the words of Jesus from the Gospels. We also have Jesus' prediction that He will speak more of His Word through the apostles (see John 16:12-15). The New Testament, written during the time of the apostles, and written by apostles or close associates of the apostles, can rightfully claim to be the fulfillment of that promise. But books written centuries after the death of the last apostle cannot.

And what do these additional "revelations" have to say? If they contradict the inspired Word of God, they cannot be true. Invariably, every supposed revelation will contradict the Scriptures, exposing itself as false.

2. What are some examples of those who have "drifted away" from the faith? What can help people avoid "faith drift"?

An often-mentioned Biblical example of this faith drift is Demas (2 Timothy 4:10). Perhaps class members can think also of friends or family members, once active in the faith, who just seemed to "slide away" by neglect (advise caution in using real names). Remind the class that sometimes all that is needed to revive a person's waning faith are a few kind words or a kind deed.

Without careful attention to the teaching of Scripture, it is very easy to lose the Christian faith by abandoning it a little at a time over a long period. The fact that the change is *not* dramatic makes this all the easier. Daily Bible reading is a must. Understanding and applying Scripture will help us remain anchored within the faith.

3. Why do you think people "neglect so great salvation" that can be had in Christ?

People of any era always bring a lot of mental baggage with them when they consider the gospel. Sometimes people make unconscious assumptions that exclude the Christian message. If one assumes that the material world is all that

exists, then the gospel makes no sense. If one assumes that God is an impersonal "force," then the gospel is false. If one assumes that there is no absolute truth, then the gospel is optional to each individual.

To help people become able to "see" the salvation God has offered, very often we have to help them examine their assumptions. When we help them sort out the good from the faulty, we begin helping them to see Christ.

4. How can we communicate the need for salvation to people who don't believe in the concept of punishment?

There is a trend in modern cultures to abandon the idea of moral responsibility. With that goes the related idea that anyone could ever deserve to be punished. When the media reports a hideous crime, the discussion often turns to, "I wonder what *made* him do something like that?" This seems to reflect a growing attitude that people are not morally responsible for their actions. From there it is an easy step to the idea that no one really deserves to be punished because the perpetrator is a victim, too.

The Christian faith is based on the idea of one Person, Jesus, receiving the punishment for the sins of the world. Pre-evangelism for many could require that we reacquaint people with the idea that people are responsible for their own wrong behavior, and that wrong behavior deserves punishment. The "good news" of the gospel makes little sense unless one also has the "bad news" of sin and its consequences as background. Until we realize that we have done something wrong, there can be little motivation to be right with God.

5. How would you discuss with a skeptic the evidence that exists to establish the truth of the Christian faith?

We can begin our conversation by asking the skeptic, "Well, if the evidence as it stands is not sufficient, then what kind of evidence would you accept?" How the skeptic answers may reveal hidden biases—biases that may have been unknown even to the skeptic!

We should be prepared to face the fact that some will never be convinced, no matter how much evidence there is. If Jesus Himself faced this problem, we will not be exempt.

Following the Author of Our Salvation

DEVOTIONAL READING: **Philippians 2:5-11.**

BACKGROUND SCRIPTURE: **Hebrews 2:5-18.**

PRINTED TEXT: **Hebrews 2:5-18.**

Hebrews 2:5-18

5 For unto the angels hath he not put in subjection the world to come, whereof we speak.

6 But one in a certain place testified, saying, What is man, that thou art mindful of him? or the son of man, that thou visitest him?

7 Thou madest him a little lower than the angels; thou crownedst him with glory and honor, and didst set him over the works of thy hands:

8 Thou hast put all things in subjection under his feet. For in that he put all in subjection under him, he left nothing that is not put under him. But now we see not yet all things put under him.

9 But we see Jesus, who was made a little lower than the angels for the suffering of death, crowned with glory and honor; that he by the grace of God should taste death for every man.

10 For it became him, for whom are all things, and by whom are all things, in bringing many sons unto glory, to make the captain of their salvation perfect through sufferings.

11 For both he that sanctifieth and they who are sanctified are all of one: for which cause he is not ashamed to call them brethren,

12 Saying, I will declare thy name unto my brethren, in the midst of the church will I sing praise unto thee.

13 And again, I will put my trust in him. And again, Behold I and the children which God hath given me.

14 Forasmuch then as the children are partakers of flesh and blood, he also himself likewise took part of the same; that through death he might destroy him that had the power of death, that is, the devil;

15 And deliver them, who through fear of death were all their lifetime subject to bondage.

16 For verily he took not on him the nature of angels; but he took on him the seed of Abraham.

17 Wherefore in all things it behooved him to be made like unto his brethren, that he might be a merciful and faithful high priest in things pertaining to God, to make reconciliation for the sins of the people.

18 For in that he himself hath suffered being tempted, he is able to succor them that are tempted.

GOLDEN TEXT: Wherefore in all things it behooved him to be made like unto his brethren, that he might be a merciful and faithful high priest in things pertaining to God, to make reconciliation for the sins of the people.
—Hebrews 2:17.

Lesson Aims

After participating in this lesson, each student should be able to:

1. Describe how Christ's sacrifice makes reconciliation with God and atonement for our sins.

2. Explain the significance of Jesus' incarnation.

3. Express gratitude to God for His redemptive act through Jesus.

Lesson Outline

INTRODUCTION
    A. Vitamins and God
    B. Lesson Background
  I. CHRIST'S SUPERIORITY (Hebrews 2:5-9)
    A. World's Subjection (v. 5)
    B. Psalmist's Testimony (vv. 6-8)
    C. Christ's Sacrifice (v. 9)
 II. CHRIST'S WORK AND POSITION (Hebrews 2:10-18)
    A. Work of Salvation (v. 10)
      His Suffering, and Ours
    B. Position of Brother (vv. 11-13)
    C. Work of Destruction (vv. 14-16)
    D. Position of High Priest (vv. 17, 18)
      Combat Experience?
CONCLUSION
    A. Voluntary Suffering
    B. Prayer
    C. Thought to Remember

Introduction

A. Vitamins and God

As early as 1500 B.C., observers were aware of an affliction we call *scurvy*. The health problems that this malady causes became very widespread among sailors by the A.D. 1500s. That was "the age of sail," when humanity was pushing restlessly into remote corners of the world on long sea voyages. Victims of scurvy suffered from inflammation of the gums and mouth. In severe cases the teeth would loosen and fall out. The disease brought indigestion, physical weakness, and hemorrhaging of various bodily organs. One report claims that ten thousand sailors died from this affliction between A.D. 1580 and 1600.

For a long time no one had any idea what caused this problem. But gradually observers came to realize that the affliction was due to some kind of dietary deficiency. In 1747 a ship's physician noticed that adding citrus fruit to the diets of those afflicted with scurvy cured the malady. It was only in the early twentieth century, however, that we learned that scurvy is caused by a deficiency in Vitamin C (ascorbic acid). Now we knew the true nature of the cure—and the prevention!

We face a similar situation in the spiritual realm. All about us we see those suffering from the worst of all diseases—sin. Lying, envy, strife, stealing, murder, and adultery are all symptoms of a dire spiritual affliction. Many are totally ignorant of the cause of their troubles, and so they haven't the slightest idea where to look for its cure. Some feel a sense of need and desperately turn to religious fads and frauds to fill their yearning. Often this results in treating only the symptoms and not the disease itself.

If people only realized that God, as He has revealed Himself through Christ, supplies for our every spiritual need! In order for vitamins to strengthen us physically, they must be taken into the body in one form or another. In order for God to meet our eternal needs, we must allow Him to come into our lives through Christ.

B. Lesson Background

Today's lesson text picks up where last week's left off. In that lesson we were reminded of how God had revealed Himself to humanity in various ways across the centuries. As the high point of earlier revelations, God finally had revealed Himself in the ultimate through His Son, the long-awaited Messiah. The writer of Hebrews established the fact that the Son was superior to the angels and thus properly commanded mankind's full attention. We continue that theme today.

I. Christ's Superiority (Hebrews 2:5-9)

A. World's Subjection (v. 5)

5. For unto the angels hath he not put in subjection the world to come, whereof we speak.

The Son was involved in the creation of the physical world (John 1:3; Colossians 1:16; Hebrews 1:2). He also has power over *the world to come*. The writer of Hebrews is firmly convinced that when Christ came in the flesh, He inaugurated a new era. The new era will reach its fulfillment when Jesus returns in triumph to bring about the new heavens and new earth—the world to come. (See also Mark 10:30; Ephesians 1:21; Hebrews 6:5.) *Angels* are, and forever will be, involved and active in this new era, but there is no doubt that the Son is in charge.

B. Psalmist's Testimony (vv. 6-8)

6, 7. But one in a certain place testified, saying, What is man, that thou art mindful of him? or the son of man, that thou visitest him? Thou madest him a little lower than the angels; thou crownedst him with glory and honor, and didst set him over the works of thy hands.

In a certain place may strike us as a strange way to quote a passage of Scripture! But we need to remember that in those days the Scriptures were not conveniently divided into chapters and verses as our Bibles are today. Further, the readers would be familiar enough with this passage (which is Psalm 8:4-6) that they did not need book, chapter, and verse to recognize that it came from the Scriptures.

Many Bible students believe that this part of Psalm 8 has two "layers" of interpretation. First, the psalmist (David) speaks of *man* in the strictly human sense. In this sense the word *man* is generic, referring to males and females. At the same time the psalmist may be speaking prophetically of a specific man: the Messiah who was to come. Note the phrase *son of man,* which Jesus used to describe Himself in the Gospels (cf. Daniel 7:13). On the other hand, this phrase is also used extensively in the book of Ezekiel to refer to that prophet's frailty and mortality.

The writer of Hebrews quotes from this section of Psalm 8 in a context that many believe maintains these same two "layers" of interpretation. First, it applies to Jesus (cf. v. 9). At the same time the phrase "son of man" as used in Psalm 8:4 (and as reapplied here in Hebrews 2:6) can refer to mortals.

The psalmist's question *What is man?* is just as relevant today as it was when it was originally written. Many today consider humans to be no more than the product of a long evolutionary process. If true, this means that we are unique only because we have superior mental capacities that allow us to exploit the rest of nature.

But neither the psalmist nor the writer of Hebrews sees it that way. Humans have unique worth in God's sight. We are *a little lower than the angels* in that we are subject to some restrictions that angels do not face while we are on the earth. As humans, our physical bodies are limited to existence in a physical world. In our physical bodies we must face physical death. Jesus took on these same limitations when He came as a man, making Him also *a little lower than the angels* for a while.

But there's more to the story. Being "lower than the angels" is a temporary condition both for Christ (in the first century) and for us. We are made in the image of God (Genesis 1:26), but the Bible says nothing of the sort for angels. After

Christ's return, we shall judge angels (1 Corinthians 6:3).

After Christ's resurrection and ascension into Heaven, His earthly limitations disappeared when He was crowned *with glory and honor* and set over all the works of God's hands. This status, of course, exceeds the "dominion" we were given over creation (again, Genesis 1:26). The theme of Christ's humiliation followed by His glorification and reception of absolute sovereignty occurs several times in the book of Hebrews (7:27, 28; 8:1; 9:12, 24; 10:12, 13; and 12:2).

8. Thou hast put all things in subjection under his feet. For in that he put all in subjection under him, he left nothing that is not put under him. But now we see not yet all things put under him.

On God's great, final day, the world will be *in subjection* to the redeemed of humanity (1 Corinthians 6:2, 3). Even so, all things ultimately will be subjected to Christ, or put *under his feet.* Those final victories are not immediately obvious to us. Limited as we are by human frailties, it may appear to us that Satan is triumphant. On every hand we see much evidence that he is in charge and is winning. Even in our own lives we sometimes feel this way.

Yet when we seem almost completely overwhelmed by evil, this is the verse that can give us the hope we need. In the end, "our side wins" for all eternity!

C. Christ's Sacrifice (v. 9)

9. But we see Jesus, who was made a little lower than the angels for the suffering of death, crowned with glory and honor; that he by the grace of God should taste death for every man.

Much of the language here is a repeat of verse 7. By coming in the flesh, Jesus was somehow made to be *a little lower than the angels.* His humiliation became even greater when He suffered and died. As a result of all this, He was *crowned with glory and honor.* Paul expresses this same idea in Philippians 2:8, 9: "He humbled himself, and became obedient unto death, even the death

---

How to Say It

BELARUS. Beh-lah-*roos.*
COLOSSIANS. Kuh-*losh*-unz.
EISENHOWER. *Eye*-zen-how-er.
EZEKIEL. Ee-*zeek*-ee-ul or Ee-*zeek*-yul.
ISAIAH. Eye-*zay*-uh.
MESSIAH. Meh-*sigh*-uh.
NATASHA. Nuh-*tash*-ah.
SOVEREIGNTY. *sov*-er-in-tee or *sov*-ran-tee.
SUCCOR. *suh*-kur.

of the cross." On more than one occasion, Jesus mentioned to His disciples that He must experience *death* (Matthew 17:22, 23; Mark 10:45).

As a result of His suffering, He was exalted and given a name "above every name" (again, Philippians 2:9). His sacrificial death was not to benefit just one race or one nation, but was intended *for every man*. As a result, we have a responsibility to share this good news with the entire world.

II. Christ's Work and Position (Hebrews 2:10-18)

A. Work of Salvation (v. 10)

10. For it became him, for whom are all things, and by whom are all things, in bringing many sons unto glory, to make the captain of their salvation perfect through sufferings.

Him in this verse refers to God the Father, not Christ. All things are for Him and by Him. This reflects a statement made in Romans 11:36: "For of him, and through him, and to him, are all things." As part of the Father's work, *it became Him* (or "was fitting") for God to bring *many sons unto glory*. Everything that God does is fitting and appropriate. At times we may have doubts about certain actions of God, but our doubts reflect on us and on our finite weaknesses rather than on God's wisdom.

Right here is where the Jewish leaders of Jesus' day got into trouble. Their concept of what the Messiah would be like and what He would do led them to reject Jesus because He did not fit their preconceived pattern. But we ourselves are sometimes guilty of defining what we think God is like or what we think He "ought" do in given situations. We may assert, for example, that a loving God would not send sinners to Hell, but that assertion flies in the face of clear Biblical teachings to the contrary. Rather than projecting our own opinions on God, we would be wise to allow the Scriptures to speak for God's attributes and attitudes.

The captain of their salvation refers to Christ. The word for *captain* here can also be translated "author" (Hebrews 12:2) or "pioneer." All of these capture the idea that Jesus is the creator or producer of salvation for those who come after Him in seeking it. In this capacity Christ is more than just an example for others to follow. He is also the One who created the trail.

A vital part of our captain's task was to be made *perfect through sufferings*. This does not mean that Christ was ever less than morally perfect. Rather, the idea of "perfect" here is to "make complete." Under the law, God required the sacrifice of animals for sin. But that was only a temporary solution (Hebrews 10:4). Now under the new covenant God requires the suffering of His Son to deliver us from our sins. This is the sense in which the Son was "made complete" *(perfect)*. We may find this concept difficult to understand, but this is another example where we should accept the wisdom of God rather than depending on our own wisdom.

HIS SUFFERING, AND OURS

John K. Huk tells us of events concerning the time when Communists controlled the area just east of Poland known as Belarus. At first, the Communists intentionally sought out Christians to operate their stores and farms because they knew they could be trusted. By the 1930s, however, this had changed. Many believers were imprisoned; others lived under the cloud of persecution.

Take the case of Natasha, a young girl whose father worked as a laborer. The father was never jailed, but he knew that he would never be promoted. He also knew that no member of the family would be permitted to go to college. The family attended church openly near Minsk. The congregation repeatedly petitioned the government for registration that was never given.

On Natasha's first day in high school, her mother sent her off with a prayer, knowing what was likely to happen. Natasha came home nearly in tears late in the afternoon. "They assembled the students together," Natasha said. "Before the whole school the principal called me to the platform. As I stood there he kept yelling at me, 'Look at you. Our country has given you your schooling. Our country has educated you and assisted your development as a citizen. And what have you become? A believer. You have turned away from your country's principles and have become a believer. You should be ashamed.'"

Mother wrapped her arms around the girl and tried to comfort her. "I am not harmed," Natasha said. "It was difficult, but I knew my time had come."

The suffering of Christ completed His work to deliver us from the penalty of sin. Reflecting on His suffering makes our own suffering seem more endurable. We know it is temporary. Our own suffering for His Name can complete our walk with Him.   —R. H.

B. Position of Brother (vv. 11-13)

11. For both he that sanctifieth and they who are sanctified are all of one: for which cause he is not ashamed to call them brethren.

What a glorious thing to know that Christ considers us to be *brethren*! (See also Mark 3:33-35 and Romans 8:29.) [See question #1, page 360.] He is able to do this because we have been *sanctified* by His blood. *Sanctified* is one of those words we don't hear used much outside of our church buildings. It carries the idea of being "made holy" as we are set apart for God's purposes.

Through His sufferings Jesus Christ has paid the penalty necessary to bring God and humanity back together. As a result, you and I as Christians are a part of His family—we *are all of one*. This places a heavy responsibility upon us to live up to the high standards that He has set for us as members of the body of Christ. We are His heirs, an idea Paul introduces in Romans 8:17.

12, 13. Saying, I will declare thy name unto my brethren, in the midst of the church will I sing praise unto thee. And again, I will put my trust in him. And again, Behold I and the children which God hath given me.

The writer now uses three quotations from the Old Testament to show that our inclusion in Christ's family is not a new idea. The first comes from Psalm 22:22. [See question #2, page 360.]

Notice that the family relationship *(brethren)* that the writer introduces takes place in the context of the *church*. How important it is that we develop our congregations into solid "families"! To do that, we first have to learn to have the proper relationship with Christ.

The second and third references come from Isaiah 8:17 and 8:18. Together these verses express the idea of trusting God just as Isaiah realized how his own family had been used by God to reveal His will to Israel. Again, the importance of Christ's family as *brethren* must not be missed as we become more and more sanctified for His work.

C. Work of Destruction (vv. 14-16)

14. Forasmuch then as the children are partakers of flesh and blood, he also himself likewise took part of the same; that through death he might destroy him that had the power of death, that is, the devil.

Our struggle with Satan is a spiritual struggle (Ephesians 6:12). But because we are *partakers of flesh and blood,* Satan directs many of his attacks upon us through the flesh. Thus if Christ was to be tempted "in all points . . . like as we are" (Hebrews 4:15), it was necessary that He join us in the flesh.

Through His physical death and resurrection, Christ destroyed the power of death wielded by the devil. For this reason Paul can hail Christ's resurrection with these triumphant words: "O death, where is thy sting? O grave, where is thy victory?" (1 Corinthians 15:55).

15. And deliver them, who through fear of death were all their lifetime subject to bondage.

People dread the idea of being in slavery or *bondage*. For many, death is the most feared slave master—feared because its bondage seems so final. But because of our Lord's victory over the devil, we can view death as a defeated enemy. Christ is now the One who holds the "keys of hell and of death" (Revelation 1:18). [See question #3, page 360.]

16. For verily he took not on him the nature of angels; but he took on him the seed of Abraham.

Christ's birth was heralded by *angels*, but He did not come as an angel. When Jesus was born, He came as a human—specifically as a Jew in *the seed of Abraham*. This is true in the sense that Abraham was His physical ancestor (Matthew 1:2). Yet all Christians are descendants of Abraham in the more important spiritual sense (see Romans 4:9-16; 9:6-8). Jesus came as "one of us"!

D. Position of High Priest (vv. 17, 18)

17. Wherefore in all things it behooved him to be made like unto his brethren, that he might be a merciful and faithful high priest in things pertaining to God, to make reconciliation for the sins of the people.

The writer's thoughts now move to the high priesthood of Christ (cf. Hebrews 4:14–5:10; 8:1-6). In the Old Testament the *high priest* was selected from among the people—he was one of them (Hebrews 5:1). In similar fashion Christ was *in all things* fully human.

When the high priest stood before the altar in Old Testament times to offer up the sacrifices, he was bridging the chasm between God and humanity—the separation that had been created by sin. Under the terms of the new covenant, Christ serves in a similar but infinitely more effective capacity. This *reconciliation* between God and humanity was not cheap, however. The cost to

A Merciful and Faithful High Priest	
LEVITICAL PRIESTS	**JESUS AS PRIEST**
Many	One
Of the tribe of Levi	Of the tribe of Judah
Offered animal sacrifices (over and over)	Offered Himself (once)
In the order of Aaron	In the order of Melchizedek
Sacrificed for their own sins and the sins of others	Sacrificed for the sins of others; He was sinless
Served only for a limited time	Serves eternally
Served only as priests	Serves as both Priest and King
Served in a physical, temporal tabernacle	Serves in a spiritual, eternal tabernacle
Functioned under a weak and terminal covenant	Serves in a strong and endless covenant

Visual for lesson 2

Use this tabular chart to discuss the attributes of our "merciful and faithful high priest."

Christ was His suffering and death on the cross. [See question #4, page 360.]

18. For in that he himself hath suffered being tempted, he is able to succor them that are tempted.

Christ identified with us in every important struggle of our existence. Because He was tempted, yet without sin, He knew the pain that sin can bring; thus He is able to *succor* (provide help and strength for) us when we face temptation. When we pray for forgiveness for our sins, we are not praying to some distant and aloof god who does not feel our pain. Instead, our prayers arise to One "who has been there." Our prayers are to the God who has felt the pain of sin more than we can possibly imagine. [See question #5, page 360.]

COMBAT EXPERIENCE?

Sometimes we feel that our leaders don't really know what it is like to live where we live. Dwight Eisenhower was never in combat, yet his orders meant life or death to those under his command. He asked repeatedly to be sent overseas to fight during World War I, but his requests were denied. He spent the entire war in the U.S., training troops who would be sent into combat.

After that war ended, Eisenhower served with distinction on various staff jobs, but felt he would never be given the opportunity of a command. By 1941 he was a colonel. The Army Chief of Staff liked his work and promoted him to brigadier general and then to major general. Eisenhower eventually became Supreme Commander for the D-Day invasion. On December 20, 1944, Eisenhower was a five-star general.

How did a man who never saw combat relate to the men under his command? Anyone who has seen the photographs of "Ike" talking to the GIs can see that this man from a little town in Kansas understood the hopes and fears of the average soldier.

Yet Jesus understands our hopes, fears, and needs infinitely better than any human leader can. Jesus faced personal "combat" with Satan. Jesus knew poverty, rejection, pain, even death. He is Creator, Ruler, and Redeemer. If people are willing to put their trust in an Eisenhower for an earthly cause, should they not be even more willing to trust Jesus for their eternity?   —R. H.

Conclusion

A. Voluntary Suffering

We live in a world where suffering abounds. Suffering may be physical, but often the more serious and sustained suffering we endure is emotional and spiritual in nature. None of us enjoys suffering, and we go to great measures to avoid it. Modern science has made great strides in producing medicines or developing techniques that eliminate or at least alleviate much of our physical suffering. Psychologists and counselors have also developed strategies that reduce emotional suffering. With all of these resources available to us, we are able to avoid a great deal of suffering in our daily lives.

Since we are so concerned about avoiding suffering, we are always amazed when anyone chooses to suffer. As a result, we applaud those who heroically risk pain and suffering for some great cause. Examples include soldiers serving their country or someone risking his or her life to save another from danger.

If these people are worthy of our praise, how much more we should stand in utter amazement that our Lord should leave His Heavenly throne and come into this world to suffer humiliation and the cross for us! Also amazing is the fact that after God has sent His Son into the world, many continue in rebellion against Him (John 1:11). Sometimes ignorantly, but more often knowingly and arrogantly, we have defied Him. And yet our Lord came and "died for our sins according to the Scriptures" (1 Corinthians 15:3).

B. Prayer

Most gracious Father, we lift up our voices in prayer to You, knowing that You have provided for our every need. We especially thank You that You have given us Jesus Christ as our great high priest, enabling us to become reconciled to You. In His name we pray, amen.

C. Thought to Remember

By the grace of God, Christ has tasted death for every one of us.

Home Daily Bible Readings

Monday, June 7—God Has Made Jesus Messiah (Acts 2:32-36)

Tuesday, June 8—Forgiveness of Sins Through Christ (Acts 2:37-41)

Wednesday, June 9—Raised With Christ Through Faith (Colossians 2:8-12)

Thursday, June 10—Jesus Christ Is Lord (Philippians 2:5-11)

Friday, June 11—Jesus Tasted Death for Everyone (Hebrews 2:5-9)

Saturday, June 12—Jesus Is the Pioneer of Salvation (Hebrews 2:10-18)

Sunday, June 13—Christ, the Son, Was Faithful (Hebrews 3:1-6)

Learning by Doing

This page contains an alternative lesson plan emphasizing learning activities. Classes desiring such student involvement will find these suggestions helpful.

Learning Goals

After participating in this lesson, each student will be able to:

1. Describe how Christ's sacrifice makes reconciliation with God and atonement for our sins.

2. Explain the significance of Jesus' incarnation (His taking on human flesh).

3. Express gratitude to God for His redemptive act through Jesus.

Into the Lesson

Option #1. Early in the week recruit a volunteer to give a three- or four-minute report on the disease "scurvy" and the importance of getting adequate vitamin C in one's diet. Give that person a bottle of vitamin C and an orange to use as visual aids. Also give a photocopy of the introduction to today's lesson commentary (page 354) and an article from an encyclopedia or the Internet about scurvy. After the report is completed, make the transition to Bible study by using the concluding remarks in the lesson commentary introduction.

Option #2. Ask people to name their favorite author and the type of books he/she writes. List the names on a poster board. Make the transition to the lesson by saying, "Hebrews introduces us to another author." Tell the class Jesus is called the "author" of our salvation in 2:10. (While our *King James* Bibles say "captain" here, the same word is translated "author" in Hebrews 12:2, so it is appropriate to think of Jesus as the "author of our salvation.")

Into the Word

Ask people to work in reading teams of four or five people. Give each team a written copy of one of the following assignments. Distribute to all teams (except team 1) a copy of the entire lesson commentary for today's study. Give teams 1 and 2 a Bible dictionary also.

Reading Team #1. Your key word is *incarnation*. Read Hebrews 2:5-18, and then read the article in the Bible dictionary about incarnation. Define *incarnation* and identify notes of significance for believers. Select a spokesperson to report your findings.

Reading Team #2. Your key words are *lower* and *higher*. Read Hebrews 2:5-18. Clarify and explain how Jesus is both "lower" and "higher." Also explain why we needed someone with flesh

and blood—not an angel—to die in our place. Select a spokesperson to report your findings.

Reading Team #3. Your key word is *reconciliation*. Define this word and explain what it means for our relationship with God. How does *reconciliation* connect with the picture of Jesus as the "captain [or "author" (see Hebrews 12:2)] of our salvation"? Select a spokesperson to report your findings.

Reading Team #4. Your key word is *make(s)*. Read Hebrews 2:5-18. Explain the significance of each use of the word or how each of the following happens: v. 11: *makes* us holy ("sanctified"); vv. 11, 14-18: *makes* us brothers or family; v. 17: *makes* reconciliation. Select a spokesperson to report your findings to the class.

Allow each team's spokesperson to report. If you have more than one group on the same task, ask one team to report and others to add additional information that their groups discovered beyond what the reporting team gave.

Into Life

The following activity may be done as a whole class activity or in the small groups used earlier. Display four posters, each with one of the following headings: *"Jesus' Incarnation," "Jesus, Captain of Salvation," "My Reconciliation,"* or *"Celebrate Sanctification."* Tell the class or groups, "You are worship directors selecting songs for four different worship services, focusing on the theme assigned. Music helps us celebrate and give thanks. Determine appropriate choruses or songs for your song service." Have a stack of hymnbooks and chorus books available.

Conclude this study on a devotional note. Give each person a handout titled "My Prayer of Celebration and Thanksgiving." Write these open-ended statements with room for answers:

"Dear God, I have a wonderfully fresh glimpse of what You did through Jesus for me. I am thankful for the incarnation because. . . ."

"Knowing I have been sanctified, I find a new attitude of. . . ."

"My reconciliation with You as my God has changed me by. . . ."

"Above all, I thank You for Jesus, who. . . ."

Play a devotional instrumental CD or cassette quietly while individuals are writing. Close by asking God to see and hear these prayers written from the hearts of His children.

Let's Talk It Over

*The questions on this page are designed to promote discussion of the lesson
by the class and to encourage application of the lesson Scriptures. The answers
provided are only discussion starters. Let your class talk it over from there.*

**1. Throughout history there have been swings
in attitude in regard to our relationship with
Jesus. To some He has been seen as almost
untouchably removed from His followers. Our
text indicates, however, that we are *brethren* to
Jesus. In reaction to this some think of Jesus
almost as casually as a "good ol' boy" who lives
next door. On a scale with "untouchable" at one
end and "buddy" at the other, where would you
rank the proper relationship between Jesus and
His followers? Why?**

Jesus calls His followers friends in John 15:15.
However, this should not lead us to forget Jesus'
ultimate nature. He is the Lord of the universe—
"the mighty God." Our friendship with Jesus is
perhaps best viewed as one between a very gracious King and His subjects. While appreciating
the willingness of the King to call us friend, we
should never take this as a relationship between
equals.

**2. The book of Hebrews features many Old
Testament allusions and quotations, as we see
in our text. What are some things our church
can do to make sure it does not neglect the
study of the Old Testament?**

The study and practice of New Testament
Christianity includes an appreciation of the Old
Testament, as the writer of Hebrews clearly
shows us. Children's classes at your church
probably already teach the great Old Testament
stories of Noah, Samson, David and Goliath, etc.
Adult classes that use the *Standard Lesson Com-
mentary®* will be treated to Old Testament studies on a regular basis.

Years ago, an elderly preacher was asked at
his retirement party, "If you had it to do all over
again, what would you do differently?" His answer: "I'd preach more from the Old Testament!"
It is vital for your church's leadership to promote
the importance of studying the Old Testament.

**3. Do you as a Christian fear death? Should
you? Why, or why not?**

Many Christians misunderstand and fear
death. Some try to overcome their fear by thinking of death as just a "beautiful" means of "passing from this life to the next." But that is not the
picture presented in Scripture. There, death is
never anything other than an enemy.

However, Hebrews 2:14, 15 indicates that
death is a *defeated* enemy. Although it is natural
to have questions and fears about death, Christians can rest assured that Christ has taken care
of this problem for us. Our trust in Him is what
allows us to conquer our fear of this defeated foe.

**4. In the early history of the church, some
emphasized the deity of Jesus to the exclusion of
His humanity. What kind of problems could
this viewpoint cause if it began to spread in our
church today?**

Hebrews 2:14-17 emphasizes that it is Jesus'
sharing in our humanity that makes possible His
work for our salvation. The "package" that is
Jesus the Christ is not complete without both His
divinity and His humanity. He is Immanuel
(Matthew 1:23): He is *God*, and He is *with us*.

Jesus' physical body was essential for Him to
be able to do the one thing necessary for our salvation: die on the cross for sin. If Jesus did not
come in the flesh to die for sins in a physical
body, which was then raised to life, then there
was no payment of sin's penalty. This would
change the reason for our church's very existence! Instead of teaching forgiveness through His
death, we might begin to teach "works salvation"
from a god who judges people in a balance scale.

**5. We often think of temptation as being
strongest where we are the weakest. Thus, some
people draw the mistaken conclusion that Jesus'
temptations were not very "tempting": He had no
weakness to exploit, so He faced no strong temptation. How would you respond to such a claim?**

Our text makes it clear that Jesus had to face
significant moral choices in which "the easy way
out" would go against the will of the Father. (See
also Matthew 4:1-11; Hebrews 4:15.)

Scripture emphasizes that Jesus did not succumb to these powerful temptations. He experienced the temptation to disobey the Father just as
strongly and completely as we do—even much
more so because He never yielded. When we
yield to temptation, Satan does not have to turn
up the pressure any more—he has won. But since
Jesus never yielded, He faced every temptation to
the maximum amount Satan could muster. Thus
He is the perfect sacrifice for sin and the perfect
example for us in resisting temptation.

Faithful Through Obedience

DEVOTIONAL READING: 2 Corinthians 5:16–6:2.

BACKGROUND SCRIPTURE: Hebrews 3:12–4:13.

PRINTED TEXT: Hebrews 3:12–4:2, 9-13.

Hebrews 3:12-19

12 Take heed, brethren, lest there be in any of you an evil heart of unbelief, in departing from the living God.

13 But exhort one another daily, while it is called Today; lest any of you be hardened through the deceitfulness of sin.

14 For we are made partakers of Christ, if we hold the beginning of our confidence steadfast unto the end;

15 While it is said, Today if ye will hear his voice, harden not your hearts, as in the provocation.

16 For some, when they had heard, did provoke: howbeit not all that came out of Egypt by Moses.

17 But with whom was he grieved forty years? was it not with them that had sinned, whose carcasses fell in the wilderness?

18 And to whom sware he that they should not enter into his rest, but to them that believed not?

19 So we see that they could not enter in because of unbelief.

Hebrews 4:1, 2, 9-13

1 Let us therefore fear, lest, a promise being left us of entering into his rest, any of you should seem to come short of it.

2 For unto us was the gospel preached, as well as unto them: but the word preached did not profit them, not being mixed with faith in them that heard it.

. . . .

9 There remaineth therefore a rest to the people of God.

10 For he that is entered into his rest, he also hath ceased from his own works, as God did from his.

11 Let us labor therefore to enter into that rest, lest any man fall after the same example of unbelief.

12 For the word of God is quick, and powerful, and sharper than any two-edged sword, piercing even to the dividing asunder of soul and spirit, and of the joints and marrow, and is a discerner of the thoughts and intents of the heart.

13 Neither is there any creature that is not manifest in his sight: but all things are naked and opened unto the eyes of him with whom we have to do.

GOLDEN TEXT: For we are made partakers of Christ, if we hold the beginning of our confidence steadfast unto the end.—Hebrews 3:14.

Hold Fast to the Faith
Unit 1: Encouraged to Be Faithful
(Lessons 1-4)

Lesson Aims

After participating in this lesson, each student should be able to:

1. Cite the dangers of falling away from the faith and the rewards for remaining faithful.

2. Explain why God expects faithful obedience from His people.

3. Memorize one passage of Scripture to encourage faithful living.

Lesson Outline

INTRODUCTION
 A. Faithful Unto Death
 B. Lesson Background
 I. EXHORTATION TO FAITHFULNESS (Hebrews 3: 12-19; 4:1, 2)
 A. Don't Harden Hearts (3:12-19)
 The Triumph of the Ten Thousand
 B. Don't Fall Short (4:1, 2)
 II. PROMISE OF REST (Hebrews 4:9-11)
 A. Future Sabbath (vv. 9, 10)
 B. Present Effort (v. 11)
 III. POWER OF GOD (4:12, 13)
 A. Sword That Penetrates (v. 12)
 B. Sight That Penetrates (v. 13)
 People Watching
CONCLUSION
 A. Quitters
 B. History as Bunk?
 C. Prayer
 D. Thought to Remember

Introduction

A. Faithful Unto Death

In the early morning hours of February 26, 1852, the British troopship *H.M.S. Birkenhead* was sailing off the coast of Africa. Over six hundred were on board—soldiers, sailors, women, and children. Suddenly the ship struck a hidden reef and began to take on water. It was soon obvious that the ship could not be saved, and the soldiers gave a ready hand to the sailors who were beginning to lower the lifeboats. By order of the commanding officer, women and children had priority in the limited number of boats.

As the survivors pulled away from the ship, the last view they had of the sinking vessel was that of the soldiers still standing at attention until the commanding officer ordered them to save themselves by any means possible. All of the women and children survived, but many of those still on board who could not swim continued to stand in military formation as the ship went down.

Over four hundred fifty soldiers and sailors died that day, including the commanding officer and the ship's captain. Their sacrifice and self-discipline were memorialized as "the Birkenhead drill" by Rudyard Kipling (1865–1936) in his poem "Soldier an' Sailor Too":

> To take your chance in the thick of a rush,
>   with firing all about,
> Is nothing so bad when you've cover to 'and,
>   an' leave an' likin' to shout;
> But to stand an' be still to the Birken'ead drill
>   is a [very] tough bullet to chew,
> An' they done it, the Jollies—'Er Majesty's Jollies—
>   soldier an' sailor too!

Those who lost their lives that day could not be called martyrs for the cause of Christ. Yet their resoluteness is similar to what Christians have demonstrated down through the centuries. In the struggle between God and the forces of evil, a few of us may be called upon to perform dangerous duties for our Lord. In most situations God seems to ask us to perform the routine and outwardly humdrum tasks that appear to be anything but heroic. In all cases, however, God requires us to remain steadfast under every pressure—faithful unto death itself!

B. Lesson Background

The previous two lessons presented some facts that are fundamental to the Christian faith. God has spoken to humanity—first to "the fathers" through the prophets, and now "in these last days" through His Son. The Son is one with the Father, "being the brightness of his glory, and the express image of his person" (Hebrews 1:1-3). That makes the message that He brings unique.

Another vital point is that the Son is superior to the angels. Yet He humbled Himself, taking on flesh, that He might through His suffering and death destroy the devil (2:14). Finally, He stands in the presence of God as our great high priest to make reconciliation for our sins (2:17).

Now comes the "so what?" point. If all these things are true—and they are—so what? Today's lesson gives us an answer to that question. Hebrews 2:3, from two lessons ago, began to provide us with some of the answer by pointing out that there is no escape for us if we neglect the great salvation He offers. Today's lesson enlarges on this answer by urging the people to defend themselves against the sin of unbelief. That message is just as demanding on us today as it was when it was first written because both blatant, overt unbelief and the casual, noncommitted kind of "practical unbelief" are rampant.

I. Exhortation to Faithfulness (Hebrews 3:12-19; 4:1, 2)

A. Don't Harden Hearts (3:12-19)

12. Take heed, brethren, lest there be in any of you an evil heart of unbelief, in departing from the living God.

Satan is always seeking to undermine our faith, weaken it, and ultimately destroy it. Sometimes he uses forceful frontal attacks, challenging people's faith through threats and physical torture. More often, however, he uses various clever tricks to erode faith slowly, wearing it away so gently that we are scarcely aware of it until we face a real crisis and find ourselves helpless.

In the four verses previous to this one, the readers are reminded of their forefathers in the wilderness. They had witnessed God's hand upon the Egyptians, and yet they rebelled against Him. We may wonder how in the face of God's mighty works they could still fall into unbelief, but we have only to look into our own lives to find the answer. Their punishment was that "they shall not enter into my rest" (Hebrews 3:11; cf. Psalm 95:11) That "rest" refers to the promised land, which almost an entire generation did not live to see.

The writer uses this history to warn his readers that they will also lose their rest (i.e., Heaven) if they harden their hearts. Going back into Judaism is also *departing from the living God,* since that would mean rejecting God's most profound revelation: His Son. [See question #1, page 368.]

13. But exhort one another daily, while it is called Today; lest any of you be hardened through the deceitfulness of sin.

In the previous verse the readers were addressed as "brethren," indicating that they were members of a family. As such, they had a special responsibility to *exhort* or encourage one another to remain faithful. This exhortation was to be *daily,* and for good reason. Satan is relentless in his efforts to tempt, and so we need help and encouragement regularly and frequently to resist him. Through its *deceitfulness* sin promises so much but delivers only disaster. Christian fellowship is vital in helping avoid this snare (see Hebrews 10:25). [See question #2, page 368.]

THE TRIUMPH OF THE TEN THOUSAND

In 401 B.C. ten thousand Greek soldiers found themselves deep in enemy territory, leaderless, and with no food, scant weapons, and no source of supplies. They had enlisted in the army of Cyrus, named after Cyrus the Great, the conqueror of Babylon of some one hundred eighty years previous. The latter Cyrus had amassed an army of more than one hundred thousand. Many were Asiatics (barbarians), with ten thousand Greeks forming the fighting core. Cyrus was fighting his brother for their dead forefather's Persian throne.

Cyrus fought the Persians at Cunaxa and won, but he was killed in the battle. With his death the barbarian allies melted away, leaving the ten thousand Greeks to fend for themselves. Their leaders went to a conference with the Persians under guarantee of safe passage, but only one came back, stabbed and beaten. As he died, he gasped out the truth that the Persians had murdered all their officers.

Xenophon, one of the ten thousand, called a council of the lesser officers who had not been invited to that conference. "Do not despair," he told them. "We are Greeks. We are free men who can think for ourselves."

Hungry and isolated, the ten thousand marched homeward. They skillfully defeated the Persians whenever they attacked. With each crisis Xenophon would call an assembly, explain the situation, and ask for suggestions. "Whoever has a better plan, let him give it."

One day they heard a roaring sound. An ambush? Ten thousand weary soldiers came to the ready. No, it was not the enemy, it was the welcome sound of the sea. From here they could easily make it home.

How many examples from history do we need to tell us what we already know: that we need to stick together, to help each other, to "encourage one another daily"?
—R. H.

14. For we are made partakers of Christ, if we hold the beginning of our confidence steadfast unto the end.

We have the precious privilege of being, in a sense, partners with Christ. We share in His kingdom. But there is a condition that must be met to keep our position: we must be *steadfast*

How to Say It

BABYLON. *Bab*-uh-lun.
CALEB. *Kay*-leb.
CUNAXA. Koo-*nak*-suh.
CYRUS. *Sigh*-russ.
DEUTERONOMY. Due-ter-*ahn*-uh-me.
JOSHUA. *Josh*-yew-uh.
PERSIAN. *Per*-zhun.
SANTAYANA. San-tuh-*yah*-nuh.
XENOPHON. *Zee*-nuh-fun.

Visual for
lessons 3 and 4

*Leave this image posted this week and next to remind your learners to **hold on!***

unto the end. How we begin the race is important, of course. But how we finish it is vital. All of us know of those who started well in Christ's kingdom, but for one reason or another fell out of the race (cf. 2 Timothy 4:7). Some became weary and did not have the spiritual stamina to finish. Others were distracted by the worthless toys that Satan dangled before them.

15, 16. While it is said, Today if ye will hear his voice, harden not your hearts, as in the provocation. For some, when they had heard, did provoke: howbeit not all that came out of Egypt by Moses.

Verse 15 is a quotation from Psalm 95:7, 8. It reminds those of Jewish background of their long history. At the time Hebrews was written, this history, stretching back to Abraham, covered about two thousand years. History can be a powerful teaching instrument, provided that people learn from it. Unfortunately, the Jewish people did not learn the lessons from history they should have learned. But are we any different?

Harden not your hearts is an encouragement for the readers to avoid the mistakes of their forefathers in the wilderness. The readers undoubtedly have heard the account of the exodus many times, but the writer calls their attention to it in order to make an application to their current situation. God had blessed the Israelites in many ways when He used *Moses* to lead them out of *Egypt.* Yet in spite of these blessings, they had provoked God by hardening their hearts. However, *not all that came out of Egypt* fell into this trap. Caleb and Joshua were exceptions (Deuteronomy 1:36, 38). May we have their faithfulness!

17. But with whom was he grieved forty years? was it not with them that had sinned, whose carcasses fell in the wilderness?

This verse reflects Numbers 14:29, 32. That passage was written *before* the punishment took place. And it indeed came true. The sin of those *whose carcasses fell in the wilderness* was a failure to listen and to heed (Numbers 14:22). This led to unbelief, as our next verses show.

18, 19. And to whom sware he that they should not enter into his rest, but to them that believed not? So we see that they could not enter in because of unbelief.

Those who perished in the wilderness and were not able to enter into the promised land were punished *because of unbelief.* Yet God did not expect the ancient Israelites to have a blind faith—quite the opposite! *They* had seen God's glory and miracles (again, Numbers 14:22). Their failure to believe was thus inexcusable. Now that we have the Son, is our own unbelief any less inexcusable? [See question #3, page 368.]

B. Don't Fall Short (4:1, 2)

1, 2. Let us therefore fear, lest, a promise being left us of entering into his rest, any of you should seem to come short of it. For unto us was the gospel preached, as well as unto them: but the word preached did not profit them, not being mixed with faith in them that heard it.

Chapter 4 begins with a dire warning based on the history the writer has just reviewed. Most Israelites did not survive to reach the (earthly) promised land because of unbelief. But an even worse fate would befall the readers of Hebrews if they should turn away from God: eternal exclusion from Heaven.

The Hebrew Christians have heard the good news of Christ's atoning death and have accepted it. In a similar way, the Israelites who were led out of Egypt had heard (and seen) the good news that a better life awaited them once they escaped the bonds of slavery. Unfortunately, this good news *did not profit them* because their actions were not *mixed with faith.* This is the writer's first of more than thirty uses of the word *faith.* What an important concept this is, then and now!

II. Promise of Rest
(Hebrews 4:9-11)

A. Future Sabbath (vv. 9, 10)

9, 10. There remaineth therefore a rest to the people of God. For he that is entered into his rest, he also hath ceased from his own works, as God did from his.

In Hebrews 4:3-8 (not in our text for today) the author continues with Old Testament quotations and examples. Verse 9 begins the logical conclusion to all this, as we again see that important word *therefore.*

The *rest* mentioned here is, of course, Heaven. Interestingly, the Greek word translated *rest* actually means "Sabbath rest." This idea looks back to creation, when God, after six days of creative activity, rested on the seventh day (Genesis 2:1-3). It looks forward to the time when we rest from our earthly *works* (Revelation 14:13). [See question #4, page 368.]

This does not mean, however, that we are to look forward to our Heavenly rest as a place where we will do nothing. The Scriptures give us only a few hints of what Heaven will be like, but we certainly have reason to believe that we will be active there.

B. Present Effort (v. 11)

11. Let us labor therefore to enter into that rest, lest any man fall after the same example of unbelief.

As the author exhorts the readers to *labor therefore to enter into that rest,* the suggestion is not that they are to work to "earn" their salvation. That idea is foreign to New Testament teaching. Salvation comes through God's grace (Ephesians 2:8, 9). God's Son has done all the work necessary for us to enter Heaven. Yet faith without works is dead faith (James 2:26). So we work to the glory of God to show where our allegiance lies.

The readers' Jewish forefathers had fallen in the wilderness because they weren't willing to step out on faith to do the work of entering the promised land as God required. That work of faith would have realized that it was actually God working behind the scenes to defeat the enemies. Their failure is an *example of unbelief.*

III. Power of God
(Hebrews 4:12, 13)

A. Sword That Penetrates (v. 12)

12. For the word of God is quick, and powerful, and sharper than any two-edged sword, piercing even to the dividing asunder of soul and spirit, and of the joints and marrow, and is a discerner of the thoughts and intents of the heart.

The concept of God's *word* sometimes refers to Christ Himself, as in John 1:1 or Revelation 19:13. Here, however, it refers to God's revelation, written down as Scripture. *The word of God* is not just a book, which may do little more than gather dust on a shelf. It is involved in the work of judging and guiding those who carry it in their hearts and heed it.

The illustration of this power is a comparison with a sword (cf. Ephesians 6:17), specifically a *two-edged sword.* Such a sword "cuts both ways" and is powerful in all kinds of situations (cf.

Proverbs 5:3, 4; Revelation 1:16; 2:12). Just as a sharp sword in the hands of a skilled fighter can shatter bones and marrow, so the word may penetrate the inner workings of our spirits.

We may be able to hide our thoughts and intentions from those about us, but we cannot hide them from the Word. The Word not only guides our actions, it also judges whether or not we pay heed to that guidance. [See question #5, page 368.]

B. Sight That Penetrates (v. 13)

13. Neither is there any creature that is not manifest in his sight: but all things are naked and opened unto the eyes of him with whom we have to do.

Whether on the highest mountain, beneath the deepest sea, or behind the thickest wall, we cannot escape God's penetrating vision. This constant surveillance prepares us for the time when we stand before the Heavenly judgment throne. When the Lord returns, He "will bring to light the hidden things of darkness, and will make manifest the counsels of the hearts" (1 Corinthians 4:5). Wise is the person who lives life as if God were watching every move—which He is.

PEOPLE WATCHING

Do you enjoy watching people? Perhaps you have noticed how people react to one another in restaurants. At one table is a particular couple; you may see her glancing around the room, her eyes never quite meeting his. That is just as well, because he is intent on his meal. They've not exchanged a word for ten minutes. Over in a corner sits another couple. Both people lean across the table. Each responds to what the other says. Both laugh. Which pair is likely to be the couple married twenty-five years? Which pair is likely to be dating or newly married?

Researchers tell us that gestures and "body language" can reveal much. But body language can also be misleading. A youth minister was concerned about one member of the Youth Committee. Every time the youth minister spoke during a committee meeting, this man would frown and tilt his head. "He doesn't like me," thought the youth minister. Months later the youth minister realized that the man had difficulty hearing; the furrowed brow and tilted head were simply the result of his attempt to hear.

Outward gestures can be revealing, but also can be superficial and misleading. God, however, is not fooled by any body language. No secrets can be kept from Him. We cannot "schmooze" our way into favor with the God who knows our innermost secrets. Do you live your life with this truth in mind?

—R. H.

Conclusion

A. Quitters

One of the most grueling and demanding events in sports is the marathon. In an Olympic game several years ago, the winner of the women's marathon and others had already crossed the finish line, and the television cameras were ready to move on to another event. Suddenly one more runner staggered into the stadium and onto the track. It was obvious that she was totally exhausted. All she could do was stumble around the track, unable even to run in a straight line. It looked as if she would collapse at any moment, but she did manage to cross the finish line.

Later, a reporter asked her why she didn't quit when it was obvious that she could not win a medal. She replied, "I didn't spend all those months training only to come here to quit." Although she won no medals for her efforts, she won the respect of all who heard her willingness to carry on when totally exhausted with no hope of winning.

The Christian life is not a hundred yard dash. It is not something to be finished very quickly with all speed and no stamina. Rather, it is a marathon, lasting a lifetime. Unlike an Olympic marathon, however, there are no silver or bronze medals for those who finish second or third in the race of life. The eternal reward goes instead to *all* those who finish the race—but they must finish! That was what the writer of Hebrews was trying to tell the readers.

One who competes in a race must spend countless hours practicing and conditioning. Some who become Christians and later drop out of the race are those who never quite understood all that was involved in the commitment they made. They take their commitment rather lightly and thus are not seriously involved in Bible study, church attendance, and Christian service. Thus they simply lack the spiritual stamina to run such a demanding race.

Others simply may grow weary in well-doing. At the start of their Christian race they were involved and active, growing spiritually as a result. But at some point they begin to tire and drop out. Paul was well aware of this problem when he warned, "Let us not be weary in well doing: for in due season we shall reap, if we faint not" (Galatians 6:9).

Still another factor is Satan. Nothing upsets him more that seeing someone running the race well. As a result, he attempts to turn us aside by all kinds of things—material possessions, fame, physical comfort. Sometimes he is even able to use friends and family to hinder us. In Hebrews 12:1 the writer of Hebrews points to such distractions: "Let us lay aside every weight, and the sin which doth so easily beset us, and let us run with patience the race that is set before us."

B. History as Bunk?

"History is more or less bunk," Henry Ford remarked in 1916. Unfortunately, many share this view, refusing to learn from history or even bothering to study it. The writer of Hebrews, however, was an avid student of Jewish history. The Hebrew Christians certainly were not ignorant of their history. Their problem was that they did not understand how the past applied to their present situation.

The prophets of ancient Judah and Israel often referred to their past as a basis for their messages of warning and of hope. More often than not, the people closed their hearts to the prophets' words. The writer of Hebrews was doing all that he could to prevent that from happening again.

George Santayana (1863–1952) observed that those who do not remember the past are doomed to repeat it. That is the warning of the writer of Hebrews to the first-century readers—and to us.

C. Prayer

Help us, Father, to learn how to please You through obeying You. Guide us as we seek to find Your will for us, and then give us the strength, knowledge, will, and stamina to serve You in ways that will be pleasing to You. Help us avoid distractions that can keep us from the obedience that You require. Because of Jesus and in His name, amen.

D. Thought to Remember

"Ask for the old paths, . . . and walk therein" (Jeremiah 6:16).

Home Daily Bible Readings

Monday, June 14—Do Not Harden Your Hearts (Psalm 95:6-11)

Tuesday, June 15—The Israelites Rebelled in the Wilderness (Deuteronomy 1:22-33)

Wednesday, June 16—Obedience to God Brings Blessing (Deuteronomy 11:22-32)

Thursday, June 17—We Are Ambassadors for Christ (2 Corinthians 5:16–6:2)

Friday, June 18—Hold Your Confidence Firm (Hebrews 3:12-19)

Saturday, June 19—We Who Believe Enter God's Rest (Hebrews 4:1-5)

Sunday, June 20—Make Efforts to Enter That Rest (Hebrews 4:6-13)

Learning by Doing

This page contains an alternative lesson plan emphasizing learning activities.
Classes desiring such student involvement will find these suggestions helpful.

Learning Goals

After this lesson each student will be able to:

1. Cite the dangers of falling away from the faith and the rewards for remaining faithful.

2. Explain why God expects faithful obedience from His people.

3. Select and memorize one passage of Scripture to encourage faithful living.

Into the Lesson

Through the entire session display a poster that will not be used until the lesson application. The poster should read, "Let us not be weary in well doing: for in due season we shall reap, if we faint not" (Galatians 6:9). Prepare and display a second poster titled "Faithful Unto Death," with the often-used wedding vows: "Will you love, comfort, honor, and keep him (her), in sickness and in health, and forsaking all others be faithful to him (or her) so long as you both shall live?"

Divide the class into groups of two or three. Have each student tell his or her group of a couple whose marriage demonstrates these wedding vows. After a few minutes, ask two of the groups to tell of one of their models of marriage faithfulness to the entire group. Make the transition to Bible study by explaining that God often uses the model of faithfulness in marriage as an illustration of how He wants to enjoy a rich relationship with Christians, who are His bride.

Into the Word

Give a brief lecture introducing today's study, based on the Lesson Background from pages 362, 363. Emphasize the "So What?" portion of the Introduction in your comments.

Answer the following discussion questions (divided into the three major subjects of today's text) in groups of four or five people or as a whole class. Use a printed handout with space for answers (or use the appropriate page in the student book, *Adult Bible Class*). If you do this as a whole class, explain that space is included for notes to encourage retention and understanding. Also, if you do this as a whole class, read the text for each discussion before asking the questions.

God's Demand for Faithfulness (3:12-19; 4:2)

1. God expected faithfulness from the Israelites. The writer of this passage reminds us of one time when they failed. As a group, recall or retell the story of the exodus, their wanderings, and the promised land. (Ask a "scribe" to outline these events on a poster or marker board.)

2. Who did not get to enter the promised land? Why not?

3. What does Hebrews 4:2 teach about the practical side of faith?

4. What message is God giving today's believers in this passage?

Snapshots of the Reward for the Faithful (4:9-11)

1. Why would God use the word picture of "rest" as His snapshot of our Heavenly reward?

2. Look up Hebrews 11:10 and 11:16 for two other word pictures of Heaven that God chose to use. Why did He choose these "snapshots"?

3. What other word pictures of Heaven can you recall that God has used in His Word? What is your favorite "snapshot"? Why?

God's Word as a Sword (4:12, 13)

1. As the writer speaks of God's Word, what may be the significance of mentioning a sword with two sharp edges?

2. Look at the last half of verse 12. What is God's lesson to us about His Word in this verse?

3. Why is God's omniscience (v. 13) mentioned in conjunction with His Word?

Into Life

Say, "The Christian has temptations or issues, just as a husband or wife does, that may lead to unfaithfulness." Ask the class to brainstorm temptations, issues, or life events that face people the age of your class and that may lead toward unfaithfulness to God. Ask a class member to write these in view. Then ask each class member to note mentally any of the situations that are a particular danger to him or her. Explain that the next activity is designed to help the students resist Satan's attack by providing a Scriptural encouragement that can ring in their hearts or ears every day.

Point to the poster of Galatians 6:9. Note that these words were written to encourage believers who were facing tough temptations to be unfaithful to God. Give each person a three-by-five card to write the words of Galatians 6:9. As all write, repeat the words several times together as a class. Ask the learners to memorize the words by repeating them several times each day all week, as an encouragement to faithful living.

Let's Talk It Over

The questions on this page are designed to promote discussion of the lesson by the class and to encourage application of the lesson Scriptures. The answers provided are only discussion starters. Let your class talk it over from there.

1. Some people view salvation as holding a ticket to Heaven—once they have it, they can do as they please because no one can take away their "ticket." What is the danger of such a view?

The writer of Hebrews calls the failure of the Israelites in the wilderness a failing of "unbelief." While we are justified by faith, and not by works, such a callous disregard for our behavior reflects a failing of faith. Much of the book of Hebrews seems to be concerned with the possibility and danger of moving back from belief to unbelief. If "falling away" were not possible, there would be little reason for the writers of Scripture to offer such warnings.

Rather than having a ticket to Heaven, we should view salvation as a relationship with Jesus Christ. No one in a loving relationship would believe that what he or she did was not important.

2. What does it mean for a person to become "hardened" and how does it happen? What has caused you to become a little hardened at times? How did you overcome it?

The expression here seems to be equivalent to having one's heart hardened. In Scripture a heart is "hard" when it is unresponsive to God. God's Word bounces off a hard heart without affecting it. The hardness or softness of our hearts is ultimately our own responsibility.

Some people unrealistically expect God to shield them and their families from all physical harm. When serious illness or accidents occur, they become hard. We can help those who become hardened by showing love, gently pointing to the Scriptures, and helping them to see what God really has—and has not—promised.

3. Since we live among people who believe all sorts of things, how can we communicate that it is only certain beliefs that allow us to "enter into his rest"? How do you make sure that you don't fall into false beliefs or unbelief in this regard?

Assuming that a person believes that God exists, we can start by suggesting that not all beliefs and viewpoints are pleasing to God. For example, virtually all would agree that God disapproves of child abuse. The reason that most would agree with this is because of what God has "written in their hearts" (Romans 2:15).

If a belief that child abuse is pleasing to God is wrong, then this opens the door to the possibility that other beliefs are wrong and displeasing to God as well. When someone's viewpoint of "what God is like" is not consistent with another person's viewpoint, then someone must be wrong. Pointing out these logical problems can plant seeds for future conversations. Daily Bible reading and study will help us resist false beliefs.

4. How can we as Christians use the Old Testament concept of "Sabbath rest" for our lives today—if at all?

The Old Testament Sabbath—the seventh day of the week—was a day to do no regular work. This follows the example that God set in Genesis 2:2, 3 and His command in Exodus 20:8-11. For our own mental, physical, and spiritual well-being, we should seriously consider setting aside one day each week to rest as well.

We should not, however, accept the mistaken notion that Sunday is the "Christian Sabbath." Sunday—the first day of the week—is indeed a special day on the Christian calendar (Luke 24:1; Acts 20:7). It seems to be styled "the Lord's day" in Revelation 1:10. While there are good reasons not to let the normal pursuits of life crowd out our privilege and duty to meet with one another and the Lord on the first day of the week, this is not because it is some kind of Sabbath. The cross of Christ has done away with Sabbath-keeping (Colossians 2:16). However, our need for periodic rest from the normal labors of life remains.

5. Have you ever felt yourself being "cut" by God's "two-edged sword"? What was it like for you, and how did you react?

The Word of God, as we see in the text, "cuts" us in the sense that it judges us. The Word shows us what we ought to be. When we examine ourselves carefully, we see what we are. A judgment event occurs when God evaluates our actions and motives through His Word.

While this is usually painful, we need to allow the Word of God to continue to judge us. It is important to keep in mind that we are dealing with the Word of the all-knowing Creator of the universe. There is no hiding from Him. There is only room for honest self-evaluation and a reckoning with and in the truth.

Jesus: The Great High Priest

DEVOTIONAL READING: Hebrews 7:21-28.

BACKGROUND SCRIPTURE: Hebrews 4:14–5:10; 7.

PRINTED TEXT: Hebrews 4:14–5:10.

Hebrews 4:14-16

14 Seeing then that we have a great high priest, that is passed into the heavens, Jesus the Son of God, let us hold fast our profession.

15 For we have not a high priest which cannot be touched with the feeling of our infirmities; but was in all points tempted like as we are, yet without sin.

16 Let us therefore come boldly unto the throne of grace, that we may obtain mercy, and find grace to help in time of need.

Hebrews 5:1-10

1 For every high priest taken from among men is ordained for men in things pertaining to God, that he may offer both gifts and sacrifices for sins:

2 Who can have compassion on the ignorant, and on them that are out of the way; for that he himself also is compassed with infirmity.

3 And by reason hereof he ought, as for the people, so also for himself, to offer for sins.

4 And no man taketh this honor unto himself, but he that is called of God, as was Aaron.

5 So also Christ glorified not himself to be made a high priest; but he that said unto him, Thou art my Son, today have I begotten thee.

6 As he saith also in another place, Thou art a priest for ever after the order of Melchizedek.

7 Who in the days of his flesh, when he had offered up prayers and supplications with strong crying and tears unto him that was able to save him from death, and was heard in that he feared;

8 Though he were a Son, yet learned he obedience by the things which he suffered;

9 And being made perfect, he became the author of eternal salvation unto all them that obey him;

10 Called of God a high priest after the order of Melchizedek.

GOLDEN TEXT: Seeing then that we have a great high priest, that is passed into the heavens, Jesus the Son of God, let us hold fast our profession.
—Hebrews 4:14.

Lesson Aims

After participating in this lesson, each student should be able to:

1. Describe the work of Jesus on our behalf as our great high priest.

2. Tell some of the ways that we are blessed by having Jesus as our high priest.

3. Acknowledge an area of temptation and seek Jesus' help in overcoming it.

Lesson Outline

INTRODUCTION
 A. That Others Might Live
 B. Lesson Background
 I. HEAVENLY HIGH PRIEST (Hebrews 4:14-16)
  A. Immortal (v. 14)
  B. Sympathetic (v. 15)
  C. Approachable (v. 16)
 II. ISRAEL'S HIGH PRIEST (Hebrews 5:1-4)
  A. Human (v. 1)
  B. Guilty (vv. 2, 3)
  C. Called (v. 4)
 III. PERFECT HIGH PRIEST (Hebrews 5:5-10)
  A. Son of God (v. 5)
   Greedy for Glory
  B. Order of Melchizedek (v. 6)
  C. Giver of Submission (vv. 7, 8)
   The Purpose of Pain
  D. Author of Salvation (vv. 9, 10)
CONCLUSION
 A. Perfection
 B. Prayer
 C. Thought to Remember

Introduction

A. That Others Might Live

On the afternoon of January 13, 1982, Air Florida's flight 90 began its take-off roll down the runway of Washington's National Airport. But shortly after becoming airborne, the plane stalled because of ice on its wings and plunged earthward. It hit a bridge jammed with commuters and then sank into the icy Potomac River.

Rescue personnel were soon on the scene, and a helicopter hovering low overhead dropped a line to tow people to shore. Yet one of the few survivors visible in the water consistently refused to take the lifeline. Instead, he passed it on to someone else each time the helicopter returned.

That man was later identified as Arland D. Williams, Jr. He was trapped by a jammed seat belt and refused to have the helicopter spend time trying to pull him free when others needed help just as much. Mr. Williams eventually lost own battle to survive and *Time* magazine said, "If the man in the water gave a lifeline to the people gasping for survival, he was likewise giving a lifeline to those who observed him."

In a much more profound way, Christ did so as well. The "eternal lifeline" He passes to us comes at the price of His own life. Unlike the *Time* magazine conclusion, however, there is no distinction between "the people gasping for survival" and "those who observed him." All people are drowning in sin and need this great high priest to intervene on their behalf.

B. Lesson Background

The priesthood was an important part of the covenant that God revealed to Moses. Priests were "go-betweens"—representing people to God and God to the people. The law required that members of the priesthood be drawn from the descendants of Aaron (Numbers 3:10), who was from the tribe of Levi (Exodus 4:14). The concept of one man's being the "high" priest begins to be seen in Leviticus 16:32 and 21:10. The high priests were sometimes looked to as leaders or advisors to the political leaders.

In the tabernacle and later in the temple, the high priest normally presided over the offering of sacrifices. The high priest came before God not only as the chief mediator between God and those whom the priest represented, but also as a sinner himself. Some sacrifices were so sacred that they could be offered only by the high priest (Leviticus 16; Hebrews 9:7). What a responsibility!

The high priests unfortunately became overly involved in the political processes in the period between the Old and New Testaments. In about 174 B.C., ungodly rulers began to select at their whim the men to fill that office. As a result, high priests were sometimes implicated in corrupt activities. The high priest in Jesus' day is a good example. Clearly, something better was needed. The old covenant, designed to be temporary, needed to be replaced.

I. Heavenly High Priest
(Hebrews 4:14-16)
A. Immortal (v. 14)

14. Seeing then that we have a great high priest, that is passed into the heavens, Jesus the Son of God, let us hold fast our profession.

This verse begins with the important phrase *seeing then*. This phrase shows us that what comes next is the logical conclusion to the previous verses, which were part of last week's lesson. The writer already has established in Hebrews 3:1 that Jesus is a high priest. Now we have the further description *great high priest*.

This description sets Jesus in contrast to Aaron and those who followed him as priests. Those priests were all fallible human beings. Since they all died, their services as priests were limited to their own brief life spans.

Our great high priest, by contrast, can no longer die. He is able to serve as our high priest in Heaven for eternity. The phrase *passed into the heavens* speaks to the majesty and glory of Jesus Christ in this regard. Some suggest that this idea refers to Christ's ascension (Acts 1:9) during which He passed through the "immediate" heaven and on into the "ultimate" Heaven (cf. 2 Corinthians 12:2).

Since our great high priest indeed has *passed into the heavens*, it would be foolish not to *hold fast our profession*. That profession is, of course, the Christian faith rather than the Judaism that some of the first-century readers may be tempted to return to. This underscores the writer's earlier exhortations for Christians to remain true to their commitment. [See question #1, page 376.]

B. Sympathetic (v. 15)

15. For we have not a high priest which cannot be touched with the feeling of our infirmities; but was in all points tempted like as we are, yet without sin.

The idea that our *high priest* was fully human was discussed in lesson 2 (Hebrews 2:17). Here the same concept is expressed as a double negative: we do *not* have a high priest who *cannot be touched with the feeling of our infirmities*.

On many occasions we may have sympathized with others caught in painful situations. We can extend to them our encouragement, but unless we've "been there and done that," then it's difficult to know the depth of their pain. Because Christ has come in the flesh, He indeed has "been there and done that."

To be *in all points tempted like as we are* does not suggest that Christ faced every single temptation that we will ever face. But He has indeed experienced temptations that come through the flesh and those that come through pride (e.g., Matthew 4:1-11). Jesus' earthly life was by no means easy. He was besieged by Satan himself. But Christ resisted all temptations successfully. So even though He was unscarred by sin, He can empathize with us and strengthen us when we are tempted. [See question #2, page 376.]

Visual for lessons 3 and 4

*Use this visual to remind your learners that our great high priest expects us to **hold on!***

C. Approachable (v. 16)

16. Let us therefore come boldly unto the throne of grace, that we may obtain mercy, and find grace to help in time of need.

Under the Mosaic covenant only the high priest could enter the Holy of Holies to offer the yearly sacrifice of blood (Leviticus 16:29-33). All others were forbidden to enter the Holy of Holies on pain of death. But Christ's sacrifice on the cross changed all of that. At the time of His death the heavy curtain that separated the Holy of Holies from the Holy Place was torn from top to bottom, symbolically opening it for all believers to enter in (Mark 15:38).

We enter when we *come boldly* (or "with confidence") *unto the throne of grace*. One normally might approach the throne of a king with an overwhelming sense of fear, not knowing how the king will react. But when we come before Him, we can do so with confidence because He extends grace to us. When we come *in time of need*, we have every reason to believe that He will hear us and respond to that need. [See question #3, page 376.]

II. Israel's High Priest (Hebrews 5:1-4)

A. Human (v. 1)

1. For every high priest taken from among men is ordained for men in things pertaining to God, that he may offer both gifts and sacrifices for sins.

Under the Mosaic covenant the *high priest* was chosen from among the descendants of Aaron to oversee the priestly mission before God. God did not send an angel or some other Heavenly being to carry out this mission. It was most appropriate for the high priest to be one of the people whom he would represent. For this reason it was necessary for Christ to come in the flesh that He might represent the entire human race before God.

The main task of these high priests was to offer *both gifts and sacrifices for sins*. This idea covers a wide range of things presented to God, both plant and animal. How this same idea applies to Jesus is an important topic in the book of Hebrews.

B. Guilty (vv. 2, 3)

2. Who can have compassion on the ignorant, and on them that are out of the way; for that he himself also is compassed with infirmity.

A high priest ideally had to become "all things to all people" if he were to fulfill his ministry. Any priest had to meet very exacting standards for the specialized priestly ministry (see Leviticus 21:1–22:16). However, the priests' concentration on holiness tended to isolate them from those who were *ignorant* or were *out of the way,* meaning the wayward and worldly. So how could the high priest—or any priest—maintain the high standard of holiness that God demanded, yet still be able to *have compassion* on ordinary people?

The earthly high priest was best able to do this because *he himself also* was *compassed with infirmity.* Although always searching for greater holiness, the most godly high priests were still able to "connect with" those under his spiritual care because he shared their weaknesses and knew the power of temptation.

The arrogant religious leaders of Jesus' day, however, wanted nothing to do with "sinners." We see their attitude come out as they react to Jesus' association with the outcasts and the misfits of society. Those leaders criticized Him when He ate with "publicans and sinners" (Matthew 9:11). They accused Him of being "gluttonous, and a winebibber, a friend of publicans and sinners" (Matthew 11:19). Jesus' compassion stands in stark contrast with their arrogance and corruption; Jesus promised that they would be punished severely (Mark 12:38-40).

3. And by reason hereof he ought, as for the people, so also for himself, to offer for sins.

Under the Mosaic covenant, the high priest offered sacrifices not only for the people but also *for himself* (Leviticus 9:7; 16:6). However, we are told that "it is not possible that the blood of bulls and of goats should take away sins" (Hebrews 10:4). Eventually a perfect sacrifice would be required. Only Christ could provide that, by sacrificing Himself. Here is where we see a sharp difference between the old covenant priesthood and the priesthood of Christ. Christ did not offer sacrifice *for himself* because He committed no sin.

C. Called (v. 4)

4. And no man taketh this honor unto himself, but he that is called of God, as was Aaron.

The high priesthood in ancient Israel was a most honored and respected office, second only to that of the king. Yet even kings were not allowed to perform the tasks of priests (e.g., 2 Chronicles 26:16-21). Under God's plan, one did not come to the position of high priest as the result of a popular election, a military coup, or political conniving. A person who occupied this office was *called of God.*

History does not give us much specific information about how high priests were chosen, but in some way God's hand was involved in the selection process. Of course we know from history that the hand of God was sometimes circumvented, and on occasion rascals and scoundrels occupied the office. This was certainly true during Jesus' ministry when Annas and Caiaphas were high priests (Luke 3:2).

III. Perfect High Priest (Hebrews 5:5-10)

A. Son of God (v. 5)

5. So also Christ glorified not himself to be made a high priest; but he that said unto him, Thou art my Son, today have I begotten thee.

Christ did not come to earth to glorify *himself.* Instead, "being found in fashion as a man, he humbled himself, and became obedient unto death, even the death of the cross" (Philippians 2:8). It was God who glorified Him (2:9-11).

On at least two different occasions, God publicly declared Jesus to be His Son: at His baptism (Luke 3:22) and at His transfiguration (Matthew 17:5). The latter part of the verse before us is a quotation from Psalm 2:7, which prophetically looked forward to the glorification of God's Son when He came as a man. Psalm 2:7 is also used in Acts 13:33 and Hebrews 1:5.

GREEDY FOR GLORY

"Ambition," said Napoleon, "is so natural to me, so innate . . . that it is like the blood that flows in my veins." Born in 1769, young Napoleon lived in the shadow of his older brother Joseph, the favorite of their parents. Napoleon chafed under this neglect and learned to obtain by charm what he could not otherwise have.

Through his brother's influence, Napoleon was appointed lieutenant colonel in the Corsican National Guard, then became captain in the French army. He was made brigadier general at age twenty-four after helping put down a revolt. The government promoted him to major general after he provided leadership during another period of intense unrest.

Using his intelligence, his ability to judge people and situations, and his capacity for prolonged hard work, Napoleon schemed his way into more power. This led to military campaigns throughout Europe and the foundation of an empire. Napoleon crowned himself Emperor of France on December 2, 1804.

Contrast Napoleon's self-aggrandizement with Jesus, who "glorified not himself." Perhaps Napoleon recognized this as well when he observed, "Alexander, Caesar, Charlemagne, and I founded empires. But on what did we rest the creations of our genius? Upon force. Jesus Christ founded His empire upon love; and at this hour millions of people would die for Him." May we follow in the footsteps of Christ, not the Napoleons of the world. —R. H.

B. Order of Melchizedek (v. 6)

6. As he saith also in another place, Thou art a priest for ever after the order of Melchizedek.

The previous verses have been comparing and contrasting the high priesthood of Christ with the high priesthood of the old covenant. Now the writer introduces a new element: *Melchizedek.* This man is a mysterious figure, living in the time of Abraham. Melchizedek preceded Aaron and Moses by several hundred years. Not only was Melchizedek a priest of some kind, he was also "king of Salem" (Genesis 14:18). When Abraham returned from a successful campaign against the kings who had plundered Sodom and Gomorrah, he was greeted by this Melchizedek, who pronounced God's blessings upon Abraham. Abraham, in turn, paid tithes to Melchizedek (Genesis 14:19, 20).

The Aaronic priesthood originated in the tribe of Levi. Since Christ was of the tribe of Judah, He could not be a priest of the Aaronic order in the biological sense. But this restriction was set aside because Christ was a priest *after the order of Melchizedek.* This does not mean that Christ was a descendant of Melchizedek. Rather, it means that Christ was a priest of a similar kind. See Psalm 110:4; Hebrews 6:20; 7:17.

C. Giver of Submission (vv. 7, 8)

7. Who in the days of his flesh, when he had offered up prayers and supplications with strong crying and tears unto him that was able to save him from death, and was heard in that he feared.

Christ did not become a priest after He entered Heaven. His intercessory work of a priest began

How to Say It

AARONIC. Air-*ahn*-ik.
ABRAHAM. *Ay*-bruh-ham.
ANNAS. *An*-nus.
CAESAR. *See*-zur.
CAIAPHAS. *Kay*-uh-fus or *Kye*-uh-fus.
CHARLEMAGNE. *Shar*-luh-main.
CORINTHIANS. Kor-*in*-thee-unz (*th* as in *thin*).
CORSICAN. *Kor*-suh-ken.
GALATIANS. Guh-*lay*-shunz.
GETHSEMANE. Geth-*sem*-uh-nee (*G* as in *get*).
GOMORRAH. Guh-*more*-uh.
HEBREWS. *Hee*-brews.
ISAIAH. Eye-*zay*-uh.
LEVITICUS. Leh-*vit*-ih-kus.
MELCHIZEDEK. Mel-*kiz*-eh-dek.
MOSAIC. Mo-*zay*-ik.
NAPOLEON. Nuh-*poh*-lee-un (*o* as in *owe*).
PHILIPPIANS. Fih-*lip*-ee-unz.
POTOMAC. Puh-*toe*-mick.
SODOM. *Sod*-um.

while He was still on earth as He *offered up prayers and supplications with strong crying and tears.* This refers to Christ's prayers in the Garden of Gethsemane. While the Gospel accounts do not mention "strong crying and tears," they do make it clear that His prayers in the Garden were deeply emotional (Matthew 26:36-46; Mark 14:32-42; Luke 22:39-46). [See question #4, page 376.]

8. Though he were a Son, yet learned he obedience by the things which he suffered.

This verse poses something of a problem. If Christ was perfect (and He was) and if He was always obedient (and He was), then why did He have to learn *obedience* by suffering?

We begin to arrive at an answer by remembering Jesus' humanity. When Jesus came into the world as a baby, He, somehow, was able to set aside temporarily some of His divine knowledge and characteristics. Thus it could be said that He "increased in wisdom and stature" as He grew (Luke 2:52).

Leon Morris adds that Jesus "learned obedience by actually obeying." Jesus came not only ready to act, He *did* act. In so doing, He obeyed the will of the Father. That obedience purchased our salvation! [See question #5, page 376.]

THE PURPOSE OF PAIN

What if there were no pain? Dr. Paul Brand, who has worked with lepers in India, tells how tragic it is when that disease destroys nerves so that the victims no longer feel pain. Think about how the various parts of the foot absorb the weight and pressure of each step as we walk. Sometimes the toes take the brunt, then the side of the foot, then the heel. Without even thinking about it, we adjust our walk accordingly. But a leper can walk five miles and cause bleeding ulcers on his feet simply because the foot feels no pain and allows repeated pounding upon the same areas of the foot.

Hospital patients who are paralyzed or comatose need to be turned frequently for the same reason: no spot on the body can endure repeated pressure and remain undamaged. The pain of a sprained ankle alerts the brain that, "Hey, I need some recovery time! Give me a break." Why pain? Pain indicates that something is wrong and prods us to take corrective action.

Jesus felt pain, too. But it was our pain that He felt. "Feeling our pain" is more than a cliché, and is more than His mere identification with us. Pain for Jesus meant that something was wrong. That "something" was *sin*.

The ultimate pain Jesus felt was the penalty for sin He endured as He hung upon the cross. "With his stripes we are healed" (Isaiah 53:5). Will we embrace Him today, or will we be like those "having their conscience seared with a hot iron" (1 Timothy 4:2)—unable to feel the pain of sin and its welcome relief through Jesus? —R. H.

D. Author of Salvation (vv. 9, 10)

9, 10. And being made perfect, he became the author of eternal salvation unto all them that obey him; called of God a high priest after the order of Melchizedek.

Being made perfect doesn't mean that Jesus was ever "imperfect." As Leon Morris explains, "There is a perfection that results from having actually suffered; it is different from the perfec-

tion that is ready to suffer." As a result of suffering, Jesus *became the author of eternal salvation.* What a breathtaking promise: salvation that stretches into the far reaches of eternity!

But this promise is not universal; it does not extend to everyone. It is extended only to *them that obey him.* Here we are brought back to a central theme of the Hebrews epistle: faithful obedience to God through Jesus Christ. No other religion offers eternal life. Returning to Judaism would be a tragedy of the greatest proportion (Galatians 3:1–4:7; 5:1-6).

Conclusion

A. Perfection

In two thousand years of church history, from time to time there have arisen teachers and leaders who have taught that it is possible for a Christian to reach a level of maturity in which he or she is able (eventually) to live a sinless life. Practical experience, however, tells us something quite different.

Struggle as we may against temptations, we find that often we fail and fall into sin. The apostle Paul had experiences like ours. In Romans 7:19 he wrote: "For the good that I would, I do not: but the evil which I would not, that I do." In despair he cried out, "O wretched man that I am! who shall deliver me from the body of this death?" (Romans 7:24).

Paul found the answer in Jesus Christ. And so may we. Coming in the flesh, the Son of God met the same kinds of temptations that we meet—"in all points tempted like as we are" (Hebrews 4:15). Yet He was without sin, and, as our great high priest, offered Himself as a sacrifice to pay sin's penalty.

At times in our struggle against sin we feel almost overwhelmed by the power of the devil. But we have good reason to take courage because we have a Savior who has not only paid sin's price, He has also experienced our struggles against temptation. Even if we are unable to achieve moral perfection in this life, we know that we are able to enter eternity through His grace.

B. Prayer

Our Father, we come before You as believers. Yet we must pray that You will help our unbelief. Strengthen our faith and our zeal so that we can trust more fully in Him who is our mediator before You. In the name of our great high priest we pray, amen.

C. Thought to Remember

"Ye are . . . a royal priesthood" (1 Peter 2:9).

Home Daily Bible Readings

Monday, June 21—Melchizedek Blessed Abraham (Genesis 14:11-20)

Tuesday, June 22—The Lord Is a Priest Forever (Psalm 110:1-7)

Wednesday, June 23—Our High Priest Knows Our Weaknesses (Hebrews 4: 14–5:4)

Thursday, June 24—Jesus Learned Obedience Through Suffering (Hebrews 5:5-10)

Friday, June 25—A Priest Not Through Physical Descent (Hebrews 7:11-17)

Saturday, June 26—The Guarantee of a Better Covenant (Hebrews 7:18-22)

Sunday, June 27—Jesus Holds a Permanent Priesthood (Hebrews 7:23-28)

Learning by Doing

This page contains an alternative lesson plan emphasizing learning activities.
Classes desiring such student involvement will find these suggestions helpful.

Learning Goals

After participating in this lesson, each student will be able to:

1. Describe the work of Jesus on our behalf as our great high priest.

2. Tell some of the ways that we are blessed by having Jesus as our high priest.

3. Acknowledge an area of temptation and seek Jesus' help in overcoming it.

Into the Lesson

Ask a man or woman in your class who enjoys drama to come to the class dressed in a Bible-times costume. This person will give a brief lecture on the tradition and role the high priest played in Jewish life. He or she should tell of background and requirements for the role, their leadership responsibilities, their function in worship and sacrifices, and their role as mediators between people and God. The Lesson Background in the lesson commentary will be an excellent brief summary. However, a Bible dictionary will be very helpful in preparing for this introduction.

Make the transition by reminding the class that a key word in Hebrews is *better* or *superior.* Today we will discover that Jesus not only is superior to that old system, but that He becomes a very personal high priest acting on our behalf.

Into the Word

Have a volunteer read Hebrews 4:14–5:10 aloud. Tell the group we will do three brief exercises to help us grasp the grand truths of this revelation of Jesus. Provide paper and pens to each person or to study teams of two persons. After each exercise, ask people to share their findings as you write their answers on a marker board or poster.

First exercise: Read the text and find every descriptive word or phrase depicting Jesus as our high priest. We are especially interested in words that help us understand His stature or His role. *Example: "Great" (4:14). Other answers may include these: without sin (4:15), touched by our infirmities (4:15), offers sacrifices on our behalf (5:1, 3), compassionate (5:2), called by God (5:4), made perfect (5:9), etc.*

Second exercise: Scan the printed text and list the many blessings that come to us because of Jesus' work as high priest. *Example: He sympathizes with our weaknesses (4:15). Other blessings*

include that we can confidently approach God's throne (4:16), mercy and grace (4:16), eternal salvation (5:9).

Third exercise: This is the "So what?" exercise. Look at the text searching for responses expected from us as subjects to the high priest. What are we expected to do? *Answers include that we are to hold fast or hold firm to our faith (4:14) and to obey our high priest (5:9).*

Prepare and give a brief lecture for Hebrews 4:14. Remind the class that the key word for Hebrews is *better.* Three points for this mini-lecture are that Jesus is better than the Jewish priesthood because He is immortal; He makes intervention for us in Heaven, rather than in the temple Holy of Holies; and He is the divine Son of God.

Into Life

Say, "We will use two activities to apply this lesson to life. The first focuses on our responsibilities as Christ's priesthood. The second celebrates and honors Jesus Christ as our great high priest."

First, show a poster with the words "Royal Priesthood (1 Peter 2:9)" on it. Leave room on the poster for you to write class responses. Tell the class that, while we celebrate Jesus as our high priest, we also need to remember that Christians have been called to be a "royal priesthood." Ask the group, "How do Christians fulfill the duties of a royal priesthood? What is God expecting of us as we fill this role?" List the class responses on the poster. After completing this exercise, remind the class that our text told us we are to hold fast to our faith and to be obedient to our high priest. One way to do that is to fulfill our role as a royal priesthood.

Then tell the group we should celebrate Christ's position as high priest. We will do that by making an acrostic around the words *high priest.* Give teams of two people sheets of poster board and marking pens. Ask them to write the letters of the words *high priest* vertically. They are to build the acrostic with words that describe Jesus' role and the blessings He offers as our high priest. (This activity is offered on the "Learning by Doing" page of the student book, *Adult Bible Class.*)

Conclude this study by asking two people to pray. One is to thank God for His wisdom in appointing Jesus as our high priest. The second is to express commitment to being obedient to our high priest as members of the royal priesthood.

Let's Talk It Over

The questions on this page are designed to promote discussion of the lesson by the class and to encourage application of the lesson Scriptures. The answers provided are only discussion starters. Let your class talk it over from there.

1. What are some things that you have had to do personally to "hold fast" to your "profession"?

Many of us live in cultural settings where "religion" is very popular, but a profession of faith in Christ is often very *un*popular. Public prayers "in the name of Jesus" are looked down on. The claims of Christ fall not only on just uninterested ears, but often on hostile ears.

Such a situation is probably very much like that of the original recipients of the book of Hebrews. What we are being called to is unwavering confession of Christ—in word and deed—in the face of such hostility. Evangelistic outreach, obedience to traffic laws, and working to correct social injustice in the name of Christ are all part of our confession and witness. We cannot expect to make everyone happy with our profession of faith in Christ. Yet we are called upon to make the profession faithfully.

2. How does Jesus comfort you in your weaknesses? How have you comforted fellow Christians in their weaknesses?

Some think of Jesus as a strict ruler, ready to bring His "iron fist" down on us. Others tend to think of Jesus as a very mellow fellow who will overlook anything we do, no matter what. Each of these approaches misses the truth. In becoming one of us, being tempted as we are, and suffering even more than we do, Jesus understands *from experience* what life is like for us. What a comfort!

Although Jesus did not experience every single temptation and pain that we might suffer, it seems safe to say that Jesus *has* experienced every category of suffering that is found among people. When we attempt to comfort others who suffer great pain, they sometimes reply, "You can't know what it's like until you experience it." This response cannot be made to Jesus.

3. How much confidence do you have in approaching "the throne of grace"? On what do you base your confidence?

Our confidence in God and His grace can and should be very great. Our confidence should show in every aspect of our lives—especially our prayer habits. This confidence is not based on anything we have done or can do. Rather, it is based on the person and work of the Son, who has become our high priest. He has offered for us the only sacrifice for sin that we will ever need.

When we approach God's throne, we must not be tempted to try and offer Him something so that He will look favorably on us. Such an attitude would be a denial of grace. There are no people in the sight of a holy God who are worthy by their own merit. There are only those who live by His grace—and approach His throne on that basis—and those who do not.

4. What was a time that you prayed with strong emotions? Do you think your emotions made a difference in how God answered your prayers? Why, or why not?

Ultimately, we can't really know what difference our emotional state makes to God in terms of how He answers prayer. Our requests may be heard amidst our tears and still not receive the response that we desire. Jesus, the beloved Son of God, cried out to His Father over the matter of His pending death, yet He did not escape that experience. While God listened to the request of Jesus to have that hour pass from Him, this was not within God's purposes.

We can infer from this that when God does not grant our immediate desires, it is because He has some greater purpose in mind. We will not always know what these purposes are, at least not immediately. In various situations we will be called on to learn obedience to God's plans even when (or especially when) those plans go far beyond the quantity of information that God has chosen for us to have.

5. Our text says that Jesus "learned . . . obedience by the things which he suffered." Although it's often inappropriate to compare ourselves with Jesus, in what ways have you learned obedience by suffering?

In the experience of being human, Jesus learned what it was like to be subservient to others. Jesus knew exactly what it was like to be someone who reports to another, from earliest life right up to the end when He died for our sins.

We, too, must be obedient to various authorities at different points in our lives. Unlike Jesus, however, we often learn obedience when we suffer punishment due to disobedience. Examples of this kind of learning are almost endless!

Faithful to Teaching

DEVOTIONAL READING: Psalm 119:97-106.

**BACKGROUND SCRIPTURE: Hebrews
5:11–6:20.**

PRINTED TEXT: Hebrews 5:11–6:12.

Hebrews 5:11-14

11 Of whom we have many things to say,
and hard to be uttered, seeing ye are dull of
hearing.

12 For when for the time ye ought to be
teachers, ye have need that one teach you
again which be the first principles of the oracles of God; and are become such as have
need of milk, and not of strong meat.

13 For every one that useth milk is unskilful
in the word of righteousness: for he is a babe.

14 But strong meat belongeth to them that
are of full age, even those who by reason of
use have their senses exercised to discern
both good and evil.

Hebrews 6:1-12

1 Therefore leaving the principles of the
doctrine of Christ, let us go on unto perfection; not laying again the foundation of
repentance from dead works, and of faith
toward God,

2 Of the doctrine of baptisms, and of laying on of hands, and of resurrection of the
dead, and of eternal judgment.

3 And this will we do, if God permit.

4 For it is impossible for those who were
once enlightened, and have tasted of the
heavenly gift, and were made partakers of
the Holy Ghost,

5 And have tasted the good word of God,
and the powers of the world to come,

6 If they shall fall away, to renew them
again unto repentance; seeing they crucify to
themselves the Son of God afresh, and put
him to an open shame.

7 For the earth which drinketh in the rain
that cometh oft upon it, and bringeth forth
herbs meet for them by whom it is dressed,
receiveth blessing from God:

8 But that which beareth thorns and briers
is rejected, and is nigh unto cursing; whose
end is to be burned.

9 But, beloved, we are persuaded better
things of you, and things that accompany salvation, though we thus speak.

10 For God is not unrighteous to forget
your work and labor of love, which ye have
showed toward his name, in that ye have
ministered to the saints, and do minister.

11 And we desire that every one of you do
show the same diligence to the full assurance
of hope unto the end:

12 That ye be not slothful, but followers of
them who through faith and patience inherit
the promises.

GOLDEN TEXT: Therefore leaving the principles of the doctrine of Christ,
let us go on unto perfection.—Hebrews 6:1.

Hold Fast to the Faith
Unit 2: Strengthened to be Faithful
(Lessons 5-8)

Lesson Aims

After participating in this lesson, each student should be able to:

1. Cite characteristics of spiritual immaturity and spiritual maturity.

2. Describe some of the risks of prolonged spiritual immaturity.

3. Identify one step or action he or she will take toward greater spiritual maturity.

Lesson Outline

INTRODUCTION
    A. Stunted Growth
    B. Lesson Background
 I. PROBLEM STATED (Hebrews 5:11-14)
    A. Their Lethargy (v. 11)
    B. Their Stagnation (vv. 12, 13)
    C. Their Need (v. 14)
     The Need to Keep Growing
 II. SOLUTION OFFERED (Hebrews 6:1-6)
    A. Growth in Maturity (vv. 1-3)
    B. Danger of Apostasy (vv. 4-6)
     Change Is Possible
III. ILLUSTRATIONS AND CONFIDENCE (Hebrews 6: 7-12)
    A. Reap What Is Sown (vv. 7, 8)
    B. Expect Better Things (vv. 9, 10)
    D. Avoid Laziness (vv. 11, 12)
CONCLUSION
    A. Enduring—and Growing—to the End
    B. Prayer
    C. Thought to Remember

Introduction

A. Stunted Growth

In an era before the most modern surgical techniques, a beautiful baby was born to a certain couple. The baby seemed quite normal and healthy in every respect. For the first few months he grew and learned to do the things that growing babies do. But after a few more months his parents noticed that his head was not growing in proportion to his body. Before long his cooing and laughter ceased and a blank look came over his face.

A medical examination revealed that there were no fissures in the bone structure of the baby's head. The cranial bones were fused together at birth and thus could not expand to accommodate a growing brain. With the brain so compressed, it could not develop, and the boy became severely retarded. Modern medicine might have been able to correct this problem, but in those days that was not a possibility.

The spiritual problems that the first readers of the book of Hebrews faced were rather like this. When they had first become Christians, there was every reason to believe that they would continue to grow and become mature Christians. But something had stunted their spiritual growth.

B. Lesson Background

The previous lesson dealt with the fact that Christ is our great high priest. It was reassuring to learn that we have a high priest who was touched with all the infirmities of the flesh, tempted just as we are, and yet without sin. As the sinless Son of God, He can make intercession for us to the Father.

We assume that the Hebrew Christians had some understanding of this very important doctrinal truth. But the problem was that they were not always living as if they understood the responsibilities that accepting these truths brought. It was reasonable to expect them to experience growth from spiritual infancy to spiritual maturity. It is obvious that this had not happened to many of them. They were still surviving on "milk" (the rudiments of the gospel truth) when they should have been thriving on "meat" (the deeper things of the gospel).

Fortunately, however, there was a straightforward cure for the problem: move on to the "meat"! Do we really even need to point out that this problem that plagued the first-century Christians is just as much an issue today?

I. Problem Stated
(Hebrews 5:11-14)

A. Their Lethargy (v. 11)

11. Of whom we have many things to say, and hard to be uttered, seeing ye are dull of hearing.

In verses previous to this (which were in last week's lesson), the writer set forth certain aspects of Christ's priesthood, comparing and contrasting it with the old Aaronic priesthood. Then the writer injected the idea that Christ's priesthood is of the order of Melchizedek, that mysterious priest-king who ministered to Abraham (Genesis 14:18-20). We know little about Melchizedek except that his "priesthood" was distinct from the Aaronic priesthood, which was established by the law.

The writer of Hebrews apparently wants to explore this idea in greater detail, but the readers aren't ready for it. A good teacher usually senses when his or her students are not ready to pursue a subject further. Although addressing the readers through the written word rather than in a classroom presentation, the writer somehow realizes that they are not ready for the next step in the lesson. Quite frankly and bluntly, they are *dull of hearing!* [See question #1, page 384.]

B. Their Stagnation (vv. 12, 13)

12. For when for the time ye ought to be teachers, ye have need that one teach you again which be the first principles of the oracles of God; and are become such as have need of milk, and not of strong meat.

We don't know how long the recipients of this letter have been Christians. But evidently it was long enough that they *ought to be teachers* by this time. Some suggest that these were second-generation Christians. If so, that could explain their laxness, since second-generation converts can lack the zeal that motivated their parents.

But no matter what generation of Christians we are in, the Great Commission makes every Christian a teacher (Matthew 28:19, 20). There are, of course, different kinds of teachers. Some stand before a class and teach in a formal situation. Not all are gifted to teach in this way, but everyone can teach informally on a one-to-one basis.

But even at this informal level, the teacher must have information and insight to share with others (1 Peter 3:15). Perhaps as important as being able to share information is the teaching one does in his or her lifestyle. A bad example can cancel out dozens of good lessons.

It works the other way around, too: good examples aren't much use if there is not a thoughtful reason to back them up. It seems that these Hebrew Christians lack an understanding of the fundamentals of the faith and thus need to take a refresher course. What happened the first time they were taught these things? Did they not pay attention?

Or did they fail to understand some of the principles that were being taught and thus are not able to relate them effectively to other aspects of their lives? Do other things in their lives now distract them, consuming the time that should be spent in Christian spiritual growth? In short, why are they still stuck drinking *milk* when they should have moved on to solid food by now? These questions are still appropriate when we try to analyze why Christians continue to repeat this problem today!

13. For every one that useth milk is unskilful in the word of righteousness: for he is a babe.

The references to *milk* and meat in verses 12 and 13 describe two different levels of learning (cf. 1 Corinthians 3:2). Babies thrive on milk for the first several weeks of their lives; for them to try to eat solid food would be impossible and even dangerous.

Adults, on the other hand, might drink milk, but they are able to eat a much more varied diet that includes meat. Indeed, good physical health requires that we move away from a milk-only diet as we grow.

C. Their Need (v. 14)

14. But strong meat belongeth to them that are of full age, even those who by reason of use have their senses exercised to discern both good and evil.

The distinction between spiritual maturity and immaturity is not just one of learning information about Christianity. That is the simple part of achieving spiritual growth. Far more important is how information is applied in real-life situations. A mature Christian has learned *to discern both good and evil.* Some evil is easy to recognize. Examples are behaviors that the Bible clearly teaches are sinful, such as adultery. But distinguishing between good and evil is not always so clear-cut. The issue of eating meat that had been sacrificed to idols in 1 Corinthians 8 is an example of a "gray area" situation. As we work our way through that passage, we are impressed by how much discernment Paul shows. We need to have this kind of discernment as well.

THE NEED TO KEEP GROWING

Henry Ford is both famous and infamous. He started out as a machinist's apprentice in Detroit while still in his teens, repairing clocks as a sideline. An avid reader, he studied engineering in what little spare time he had. When his apprenticeship was over, he worked repairing steam engines for Westinghouse. He became chief engineer of the Edison Illuminating Company at the age of thirty.

Determined to apply the potential of the internal combustion engine to the horse-drawn wagon, he experimented with a one-cylinder engine he had made himself. Then he put a two-cylinder engine on a light carriage in June 1896. One thing led to another, and on June 16, 1903, he organized the Ford Motor Company. Henry Ford's idea was to make cars that more people could afford. By 1915, his company had sold fifteen million Model Ts.

But all was not well. Henry Ford, the creative innovator, stopped growing in wisdom. He failed to understand the changing automobile market. Competitors' cars were faster, more comfortable, and available in some color other than black. Sales of Fords declined. Finally, in 1928, Ford introduced the Model A. Despite its innovations, Ford's share of the auto market continued to decline. By 1940 it was less than 20 percent.

Henry Ford did not trust his leaders. He went so far as to form an internal department to check up on his employees and their private lives. He became increasingly eccentric, almost tyrannical, until his death in 1947. Henry Ford shows the tragedy of stagnation. The consequences were serious for him personally, for his family, and his company. Far more serious are the consequences if we as Christians neglect to keep growing spiritually.   —R. H.

II. Solution Offered
(Hebrews 6:1-6)

A. Growth in Maturity (vv. 1-3)

1. Therefore leaving the principles of the doctrine of Christ, let us go on unto perfection; not laying again the foundation of repentance from dead works, and of faith toward God.

The writer of Hebrews now moves us toward a solution. *Leaving the principles of the doctrine of Christ* is not to suggest that the Hebrew Christians abandon these principles. This *foundation* is rather like the ABCs. A child who learns these in kindergarten does not abandon this knowledge when he or she enters the first grade and begins to read. The alphabet provides the foundation upon which reading skills are built. The principles mentioned here provide the foundation upon which a Christian grows toward spiritual maturity *(perfection)*.

Peter, in his sermon on the day of Pentecost, proclaimed some of these basic *principles*. That

Let us leave the elementary teachings about Christ and go on to maturity.
Hebrews 6:1, NIV

Visual for lesson 5. *This photograph can remind your class that learning "elementary" things is only a foundation for greater maturity.*

sermon set forth Jesus as the Christ, the promised Messiah, who had been slain on the cross but had been raised from the dead. Peter made it clear that his listeners shared in the guilt for that death. When they cried out and asked what they must do, Peter responded with instructions for repentance and baptism (Acts 2:38). Their *repentance from dead works* meant that they had to turn away from Judaism that sought God's favor through observing the law. Instead, they had found God's grace through faith in Jesus Christ.

2. Of the doctrine of baptisms, and of laying on of hands, and of resurrection of the dead, and of eternal judgment.

Take a close look at the four topics listed in this verse. If asked to explain them, could you do it? These are some of the "milk" issues of spiritual growth. Those who are still stuck on understanding these will have a hard time moving on to Christian maturity!

Baptisms here is plural, suggesting that a part of knowing basic doctrine is being able to distinguish between Christian baptism and the various ceremonial washings performed by Jews of that day. *Laying on of hands* may refer to the action of the apostles by which the Holy Spirit was imparted to some first-century believers (Acts 8:14-18). The laying-on of hands was also used to recognize those who had been selected for offices in the church (1 Timothy 4:14; 2 Timothy 1:6).

The *resurrection of the dead* and *eternal judgment* are foundational doctrines that naturally go together. The resurrection mentioned here is the general resurrection of all the dead, who then must face the judgment. For Christians this will be a wonderful experience that brings joy. But to the unsaved it will bring only fear, despair, and condemnation (John 5:28, 29). This is basic!

3. And this will we do, if God permit.

This verse sums up the previous two verses, in which the writer has urged the readers to move beyond the basic principles. It also serves as a transition for the verses that follow.

B. Danger of Apostasy (vv. 4-6)

4. For it is impossible for those who were once enlightened, and have tasted of the heavenly gift, and were made partakers of the Holy Ghost.

Those who were once enlightened refers to those who had heard the gospel and responded to it as Peter instructed on the day of Pentecost (Acts 2). While three thousand who heard that sermon repented and were baptized, not everyone there that day responded positively.

Yet those who submitted to Peter's instructions received such rich blessings! Those blessings included tasting *the heavenly gift* of eternal life as they received the gift *of the Holy Ghost.*

There were other gifts as well: the joy of associating with other Christians in worship and the joy that comes from Christian service are just two. But with these blessings came some serious responsibilities, as we shall see later.

5. And have tasted the good word of God, and the powers of the world to come.

This continues the list of blessings the readers had received since becoming Christians. The *word of God* includes the Old Testament, especially those portions that predict the coming of the Messiah.

This *word* also includes the preaching of the inspired apostles. It would not necessarily have included much of what we know as the New Testament yet, because much of it had not yet been written, and what had been written had not been widely circulated.

6. If they shall fall away, to renew them again unto repentance; seeing they crucify to themselves the Son of God afresh, and put him to an open shame.

We are frightened to read the conclusion of verses 4-6: for those who *fall away,* it is impossible *to renew them again unto repentance.* Across the centuries scholars have debated the meaning of these verses.

Certainly this verse does not mean that a person cannot be restored to God's favor after committing one or even many sins. Otherwise, all of us would stand under eternal condemnation! The description here does not fit that of a careless backslider whose love for the Lord grows cold. This same issue is discussed in Hebrews 10:26-31 (see also 1 John 5:16, 17). Perhaps the most accurate interpretation is that the one who is under this severe condemnation is a former believer who has openly and maliciously rejected Christ. This would be someone who has done so in such a blatant manner that he or she has "recrucified" *the Son of God . . . , and put him to an open shame.* In effect such people are joining with those who crucified Jesus in the first place. [See question #2, page 384.]

CHANGE IS POSSIBLE

Stephen Arterburn tells the stories of Marisa, Mark, and Ben. Marisa's brother told her she was "ugly, dumb, and fat" when she was only six. Dad was gone much of the time and offered her no encouragement. To relieve her pain she buried herself in her mother's spicy novels, creating an image of herself as the sexy heroine. Marisa had her first sexual experience at age thirteen, progressed to a series of illicit relationships, to bulimia, three abortions, and genital herpes.

Mark began collecting skin magazines as a teenager and soon was deeply into pornography.

One day he skipped school, took a bus downtown, and visited a theater that showed triple-X films. After he married, he traveled for his business; adult bookstores, adult movies in his hotel room, and "men's clubs" became regular fare while on the road.

Ben, though married to Donna, progressed from adult bookstores to soliciting prostitutes. For months he hid his behavior, but one night the police arrested him. "Donna," he began when he called home, "I'm in trouble." She dreaded to hear the rest.

Three people; the same problem in different dimensions. Can those who have fallen so low recover? They can if they want to. Ben did. He and Donna are together and have a strong marriage; his addiction is under control. Marisa contemplated suicide, but has become a strong person in her own right and no longer engages in the former behaviors. Mark is still where he was, only worse. Two of the three wanted to change; one did not.

Wanting to change made the difference. If we turn away from Christ's power to change us permanently, what hope is there? —R. H.

III. Illustrations and Confidence (Hebrews 6:7-12)

A. Reap What Is Sown (vv. 7, 8)

7 For the earth which drinketh in the rain that cometh oft upon it, and bringeth forth herbs meet for them by whom it is dressed, receiveth blessing from God.

People in the first century lived closer to nature than those in industrialized societies do today, and so writers frequently based their illustrations on agriculture. Some of our Lord's most notable parables were based on agricultural practices. The

Home Daily Bible Readings

Monday, June 28—There Is No Other Gospel (Galatians 1:6-12)
Tuesday, June 29—Stand Firm in Christ's Freedom (Galatians 5:1-10)
Wednesday, June 30—Don't Abandon Your Confidence (Hebrews 10:32-39)
Thursday, July 1—Your Decrees Are My Meditation (Psalm 119:97-101)
Friday, July 2—Your Word Is a Light (Psalm 119:102-106)
Saturday, July 3—Move On to Solid Food (Hebrews 5:11—6:3)
Sunday, July 4—Do Not Become Sluggish (Hebrews 6:4-12)

[handwritten in left margin: After The thunder & lightning comes sunshine]

point that the author is making here is quite obvious: the land that is properly tilled and bears a good harvest makes the farmer happy. In the same way, a Christian whose life bears good fruit has God's approval and *blessing.*

8. But that which beareth thorns and briers is rejected, and is nigh unto cursing; whose end is to be burned.

The crop from the second soil is quite different—*thorns and briers*—even though both soils received the rain. How they were treated determined their crop yield.

The first soil is carefully tilled to eliminate weeds. The other is neglected, with disastrous results. One who lives a life dedicated to the service of the Lord will be blessed. One who misuses his or her potential, on the other hand, faces a terrible fate: *to be burned.* [See question #3, page 384.]

B. Expect Better Things (vv. 9, 10)

9. But, beloved, we are persuaded better things of you, and things that accompany salvation, though we thus speak.

After the thunder and lightning comes the sunshine. Clearly, the author does not believe that the readers have fallen into the apostasy being warned against. The writer believes *better things* of them. On occasion, God's messengers must bring words of dire warning, but these warnings are but the backdrop for God's rich blessings. [See question #4, page 384.]

10. For God is not unrighteous to forget your work and labor of love, which ye have showed toward his name, in that ye have ministered to the saints, and do minister.

Two points are worth noting here. First, God is just and will remember their *work and labor of love* (cf. Mark 9:41). Second, they have *ministered* and continue to minister *to the saints.* Hebrews 10:32-34 gives us an idea of what some of those good works were.

In Matthew 25:31-46 Jesus clearly indicates that how we treat others will be a factor in our

final judgment. When we minister to the needs of others, we minister to the Lord.

C. Avoid Laziness (vv. 11, 12)

11, 12. And we desire that every one of you do show the same diligence to the full assurance of hope unto the end: that ye be not slothful, but followers of them who through faith and patience inherit the promises.

The writer's *desire* is not just a vague, general feeling; it is aimed at *every one* of the readers personally. They were doing well up to a point, and so the writer encourages them to continue their efforts *unto the end.* We sometimes fail to encourage the faithful as much as we ought. We need to realize that even the most faithful sometimes become "weary in well doing" (Galatians 6:9).

But with the note of encouragement comes a warning to *be not slothful.* After that the section shifts back to a positive emphasis, ending with the practical suggestion to look to others who *through faith and patience inherit the promises.* Perhaps the writer is thinking of Abraham, as in Hebrews 11:8. Such pillars of faith are examples even today. [See question #5, page 384.]

Conclusion

A. Enduring—and Growing—to the End

Yogi Berra once observed that a game is "not over until it's over." What is true of a game of baseball is certainly just as true of a Christian life. Just as it is possible for a baseball team to lose the game in the last half of the last inning, the writer of Hebrews warns the readers that it is possible to fall away even if one has made a good start in the Christian life. As expressed in a previous lesson, life is much more like a marathon than a hundred-yard dash. We must persist to the end! The writer repeats this theme in Hebrews 12:1, 2. Spiritual growth helps us endure.

The apostle Paul, imprisoned and facing execution, gives us an example of steadfast faith: "I have fought a good fight, I have finished my course, I have kept the faith: henceforth there is laid up for me a crown of righteousness, which the Lord, the righteous judge, shall give me at that day" (2 Timothy 4:7, 8).

B. Prayer

Most Holy God, we thank You for the wondrous promise of eternal life. May we grow in the knowledge that we need to achieve the spiritual maturity necessary for lifelong faithfulness. In Jesus' name, amen.

C. Thought to Remember

A crown of life follows a faithful life.

How to Say It

AARONIC. Air-*ahn*-ik.
ABRAHAM. *Ay*-bruh-ham.
BULIMIA. buh-*lee*-me-uh.
CORINTHIANS. Kor-*in*-thee-unz (*th* as in *thin*).
HEBREWS. *Hee*-brews.
MELCHIZEDEK. Mel-*kiz*-eh-dek.
PENTECOST. *Pent*-ih-kost.
ZECHARIAH. *Zek*-uh-*rye*-uh (strong accent on *rye*).

Learning by Doing

This page contains an alternative lesson plan emphasizing learning activities. Classes desiring such student involvement will find these suggestions helpful.

Learning Goals

After this lesson the student will be able to:

1. Cite characteristics of spiritual immaturity and spiritual maturity.

2. Describe some of the risks of prolonged spiritual immaturity.

3. Identify one step or action he or she will take toward greater spiritual maturity.

Into the Lesson

Before class begins, mount a six-and-a-half-foot-long banner vertically on the wall before students arrive. This may be made from strips of poster board or by using a roll of white freezer paper. On the banner make the markings of a ruler and supposed measurements taken as a child was growing toward adulthood. At the top of the banner write "It'll Stunt Your Growth!"

Begin the class session by mentioning the banner and asking, "What did grandmother tell us would stunt our growth?" *(Coffee and cigarettes are common answers.)* Tell the class that stunted growth is always a concern as children mature.

Next, tell the class, "Of more concern for adults are immature attitudes and behavior." Ask the learners to identify characteristics of an immature adult. Help them by mentioning the following categories: emotional immaturity, immature decision-making, academic immaturity, social immaturity. List responses on a marker board. Then add the words *spiritual immaturity* as a category. Tell the class that you have great concerns about spiritual immaturity in today's church. Say, "God's Word will help us identify characteristics of spiritual maturity and give us tips on how to reach it."

Into the Word

Prepare a study guide with the following headings and questions. This activity will be accomplished better in small groups of two to five people than as a whole class. The study groups will need a fairly large block of time. The headings, assignments, and questions are as follows.

Characteristics of the Spiritually Immature

Jot down the characteristics or descriptions of spiritually immature Christians you find in the text. See Hebrews 5:11, 12, 13; Hebrews 6:11, 12.

What are the risks of continuing spiritual immaturity? Explain the illustrations (Hebrews 6:4-8).

What basic doctrines are known even by the immature?

Characteristics of the Spiritually Mature

Note descriptions of spiritually mature Christians in Hebrews 5:14; 6:1; 6:11, 12. What positive, encouraging note concludes these remarks?

The groups will not need to report their findings, since all have studied the same text and questions. Instead, ask these discussion questions:

1. Why are the doctrines listed in the text considered "basic," something even the spiritually immature should know?

2. Using this as a measure of maturity and immaturity, what needs do you see for our church?

Into Life

On the reverse of the handout, have printed six of these "growth-o-meters." Only one should have a sample arrow drawn on it.

Ask the class to brainstorm a list of characteristics they see in the lives of spiritually mature people. Those characteristics may come from today's text. Write the responses on a poster board. After you have created a long list, give each person five colored dots to place on the five characteristics they believe are most important demonstrations of spiritual maturity. This will require some movement of class members, so ask them to do this quickly. If you have a large class, you may display a second identical list on another side of the room and ask half the class to use it.

To make the lesson personal, ask each class member to write each of the top five characteristics selected by the class on top of one of the large "growth-o-meters" on the back of his or her study guide. (The one with an arrow is an example. The students should use the five without arrows.) All are to use this for a self-evaluation, drawing arrows to indicate how they judge their spiritual maturity. Then ask each class member to select one area to become a focus in improving his or her spiritual maturity in the next several weeks. Ask each student to place a check mark by the "growth-o-meter" selected and to note one activity or action that will begin his or her commitment to this area of spiritual growth.

Let's Talk It Over

The questions on this page are designed to promote discussion of the lesson by the class and to encourage application of the lesson Scriptures. The answers provided are only discussion starters. Let your class talk it over from there.

1. Why do you think that many Christians are so slow to learn the truths of the faith? What ill effects result from Christians remaining in the "elementary school" of the faith for so many years?

One reason for slow learning of Christian truths is that we sense no urgency for it. We intend to do it later. When everything else is done, then we will find time to study the faith. Of course, "everything else" is never done!

Another problem is that teaching these truths is a low priority in some churches. The study of Bible content is de-emphasized in favor of topical studies, current issues, or a program of support groups. As a result, many Christians get stuck at the elementary level. These Christians are never quite sure of what they believe. As a result, they remain "babies" in the faith.

Perhaps this is the reason that it is often difficult to distinguish non-Christians from Christians in lifestyle. Those who are not mature remain unable to discern good from evil, whether in their personal lives or in the culture that surrounds them.

2. Have you known someone who rejected his or her Christian faith, but later repented and confessed Christ anew? What was that person's renewed faith like? What did the church do to strengthen that person?

Answers to this question will be highly individual. You may want to caution the class about mentioning names or personal information if there are privacy concerns involved.

After class members offer some examples, you can point out that some segments of Christianity teach that it is impossible for a "true" believer ever to give up the faith. Use the thoughts in the lesson commentary to evaluate this teaching. Remind your learners that God wants *all* to come to repentance, even backsliders (2 Peter 3:9).

3. What kind of "earth" are you in the sight of God? What determines the kind and amount of "crop" you produce for Him?

The idea that we are the "farmlands" of God reminds us of Jesus' teaching in Matthew 13:3-9, 18-23, often called the "parable of the sower" (cf. Mark 4:1-9, 13-20; Luke 8:4-8, 11-15.) There we see different reactions of people to God's Word as

represented by different kinds of soil. The writer of Hebrews makes a similar comparison.

A point to stress is that it is *we* who determine what kind of farmland for God we will be. Jesus had important things to say about being fruitful for the kingdom of God (Matthew 7:15-23; 12:33; 21:43; John 15:1-8). We can be a profitable field for God or a worthless field—the choice is ours.

4. The author of Hebrews is "persuaded better things of you." What are some "better things" that you still need to attain in your Christian growth?

Answers to this question will be, of course, highly individual. Hebrews 6:9 mentions "things that accompany salvation." Although no list is given, there are hints of at least the kinds of things the author has in mind.

Forgiveness of sin for salvation is vital to understand, but there is more to Christianity than this. We are forgiven so that we can continue with the second aspect of salvation known as sanctification. Sanctification involves learning to think and live the way God desires.

Hebrews 6:10 mentions two categories of things that fit here. One is work and the other is ministering to the saints. While either of these categories could include a broad variety of activities, the point is that God wants us to change the way we live. Forgiveness is a wonderful and indispensable part of salvation, but there are also the "things that accompany salvation."

5. Just how sure are you about the promises of God? Why do you hold the level of assurance that you do?

Examine the evidence! In Hebrews 6:12 we see that "through faith and patience" we can receive an inheritance. In 6:17 Christians are called "heirs." We have it all on promise from God.

Can anything be surer than a promise of God? Hebrews 6:13-20 mentions God's promise to Abraham, and the results of that promise provide good examples of the lengths that God is willing to go on our behalf. In any case we want to avoid being like Zechariah, the father of John the Baptist. After receiving from an angel the promise of a son, Zechariah replied from a lack of faith: "Whereby shall I know this?" (Luke 1:18). If God says it, we can be sure!

Faithful to the New Covenant

DEVOTIONAL READING: Hebrews 10:5-18.

BACKGROUND SCRIPTURE: Hebrews 8, 9.

PRINTED TEXT: Hebrews 8:6-13.

Hebrews 8:6-13

6 But now hath he obtained a more excellent ministry, by how much also he is the mediator of a better covenant, which was established upon better promises.

7 For if that first covenant had been faultless, then should no place have been sought for the second.

8 For finding fault with them, he saith, Behold, the days come, saith the Lord, when I will make a new covenant with the house of Israel and with the house of Judah:

9 Not according to the covenant that I made with their fathers, in the day when I took them by the hand to lead them out of the land of Egypt; because they continued not in my covenant, and I regarded them not, saith the Lord.

10 For this is the covenant that I will make with the house of Israel after those days, saith the Lord; I will put my laws into their mind, and write them in their hearts: and I will be to them a God, and they shall be to me a people:

11 And they shall not teach every man his neighbor, and every man his brother, saying, Know the Lord: for all shall know me, from the least to the greatest.

12 For I will be merciful to their unrighteousness, and their sins and their iniquities will I remember no more.

13 In that he saith, A new covenant, he hath made the first old. Now that which decayeth and waxeth old is ready to vanish away.

GOLDEN TEXT: Now hath he obtained a more excellent ministry, by how much also he is the mediator of a better covenant, which was established upon better promises.—Hebrews 8:6.

Hold Fast to the Faith
Unit 2: Strengthened to Be Faithful
(Lessons 5-8)

Lesson Aims

After participating in this lesson, each student should be able to:

1. Contrast the elements of the old covenant God had with Israel with the new covenant God has with Christians.

2. Explain how the new covenant is superior to the old.

3. Identify one person to whom he or she can explain the benefits of the new covenant.

Lesson Outline

INTRODUCTION
    A. New Covenant
    B. Lesson Background
I. NEW COVENANT HAS COME (Hebrews 8:6-8a)
    A. The New Is Better (v. 6)
    B. The Old Was Inadequate (vv. 7, 8a)
II. NEW COVENANT WAS PREDICTED (Hebrews 8: 8b-13)
    A. Why We Need It (vv. 8b, 9)
      Fallen Heroes
    B. What It Does (vv. 10-12)
      Seeking Forgiveness
    C. The "Bottom Line" (v. 13)
CONCLUSION
    A. Change Is Threatening
    B. Prayer
    C. Thought to Remember

Introduction

A. New Covenant

Hong Kong, located just at the southern tip of China, existed for many years as a British colony. Under this "covenant" the people enjoyed the rights and privileges of British citizenship. As a result, Hong Kong grew to become one of the busiest and most prosperous cities in Southeast Asia. But in 1997 Great Britain's lease on the colony expired and Hong Kong reverted to Communist China.

As that date approached, many citizens became apprehensive about the future, and rightly so. They knew about some of the tragic conditions the Communists had brought to China. China offered a new contract, or covenant, that promised that the people could retain some of the rights and privileges that they had enjoyed under the British. But looking at the oppressive conditions on the mainland, no one was sure that the Communists would keep their promises. In the years since then Hong Kong has not been totally incorporated into mainland China, but the citizens are living under new restrictions that limit some of their freedoms.

How different it is with God's new covenant! It is superior to the old in every way. The old covenant was one of law. It set standards that people in their weakness could not meet. By contrast, the new covenant is one of grace. The standards are not any lower, but now we have a means of forgiveness when we fall short.

B. Lesson Background

A covenant can be thought of as an agreement or contract between two parties. Each party assumes certain obligations or responsibilities. Such an agreement may be made between two individuals, two countries, or between God and people. When people make covenants or contracts with each other, there is a certain give-and-take as they negotiate terms.

But this is not the case with covenants between God and people. In those instances God establishes all the terms; then He expects us to submit to them. For example, when God put Adam and Eve in the Garden of Eden, He made certain things very clear. They were to dress the garden and keep it. In return, they could expect to enjoy the fruit of all the trees except one. When they broke the covenant, they were expelled from the garden, never to return.

Much later, when God began to unfold His plans to send His Son into the world as the Savior, He entered into a covenant with Abraham (then called Abram). According to the terms of this covenant, Abraham was to journey toward a new land that God would give him. God promised to bless Abraham and protect him on his journey (Genesis 12).

The Mosaic covenant followed. Except for prophetic references to a "new covenant" (as in Jeremiah 31:31-34), this is, of course, the most significant covenant mentioned in the Old Testament. It is much more detailed than the earlier covenants, with laws and restrictions that covered a whole range of situations. Further, it was for a whole nation of Israel. Having led the Israelites out of bondage in Egypt, God entered this covenant with His people at Mount Sinai, with Moses acting as the mediator (Exodus 19, 20).

But in the hundreds of years that followed the Sinai experience, an unfortunate pattern developed. For a time the people would be obedient to the terms of the covenant, and then they would fall away, either through neglect or outright rebellion. Then God would send a messenger, usually a prophet but sometimes a king, to stir a revival. The people would then return to the covenant, but before long the vicious cycle would start all over again. Even after returning from the horrors of exile, God's people kept embracing sin. Clearly something better was needed.

I. New Covenant Has Come (Hebrews 8:6-8a)

A. The New Is Better (v. 6)

6. But now hath he obtained a more excellent ministry, by how much also he is the mediator of a better covenant, which was established upon better promises.

In previous lessons we have learned that Christ is our great high priest. Hebrews 8 now teaches us more about His functions in that capacity. For starters His *ministry* is *more excellent* than the ministry of the priests who served under the old covenant. The most obvious reason for this superiority, of course, is that He is the Son of Almighty God. As *the mediator of a better covenant* we can think of Jesus as a "go-between" (1 Timothy 2:5).

The new is superior to the old in the fact that the new covenant is built on *better promises.* Abraham was promised that he would have numerous descendants and receive God's physical blessings. Under the Mosaic covenant the people were promised a land of their own, which eventually they were able to possess. But these blessings, as precious as they were, were temporal, confined to this earth. The better promises that come through Christ are eternal. [See question #1, page 392.]

B. The Old Was Inadequate (vv. 7, 8a)

7, 8a. For if that first covenant had been faultless, then should no place have been sought for the second. For finding fault with them, he saith.

There was nothing really wrong with the *first covenant,* as far as what it was designed to do. The problem was in its application, and God found *fault with* the people who should have kept that covenant. [See question #2, page 392.] We are told that the law was "weak through the flesh" (Romans 8:3). People simply did not live up to the high standards required by the Mosaic law.

But didn't God know of this human weakness when He gave the law? Of course He did. But if God knew of this human weakness, then why did He give people a law that He knew they would not (or could not) keep? The law served several purposes, but the most important was to prepare us for the coming of Christ. In Galatians 3:24 Paul

notes that the "law was our schoolmaster to bring us unto Christ." Since the law brings us "the knowledge of sin" (Romans 3:20), it shows us our need for the forgiveness that is available only in Jesus.

The old covenant law prepared the Jewish people to receive Christ, who eventually would make His appearance in the world. This law provided a receptive context in which Christ would carry out His ministry. Thus it is apparent that from the beginning God planned a new covenant that would supersede the Mosaic covenant. (See Ephesians 1:4; 1 Peter 1:19-21.)

II. New Covenant Was Predicted (Hebrews 8:8b-13)

A. Why We Need It (vv. 8b, 9)

8b. Behold, the days come, saith the Lord, when I will make a new covenant with the house of Israel and with the house of Judah.

This is the beginning of a lengthy quotation from Jeremiah 31:31-34. Some students consider these verses from Jeremiah to be the single most important passage in the Old Testament! From the beginning God knew the weaknesses of the law. So God began to make provisions for this problem hundreds of years before Christ came.

Early in Jeremiah's career as a prophet, during the reign of good King Josiah, there was hope that the people might return to God (2 Kings 21:24–23:25). But before lasting changes could be made in the life of the nation, King Josiah and the country of Judah were caught up in the international struggles of that day. Assyria, which had been the dominant power in the area stretching from Babylon to Egypt, was being challenged by her enemies. Josiah was killed in one of the battles of this struggle (2 Kings 23:29), and the

---

How to Say It

ABRAM. *Ay*-brum.
ABRAHAM. *Ay*-bruh-ham.
ASSYRIA. Uh-*sear*-ee-uh.
BABYLON. *Bab*-uh-lun.
CORINTHIANS. Kor-*in*-thee-unz (*th* as in *thin*).
EPHESIANS. Ee-*fee*-zhunz.
GALATIANS. Guh-*lay*-shunz.
JEREMIAH. Jair-uh-*my*-uh.
JOSIAH. Jo-*sigh*-uh.
LEVITICAL. leh-*vit*-ih-kul.
MIDIANITE. *Mid*-ee-un-ite.
MOSAIC. Mo-*zay*-ik.
SOLOMON. *Sol*-o-mun.
UZZIAH. Uh-*zye*-uh.
WIESENTHAL. *Vee*-sehn-tall.

kings of Judah who followed him were either corrupt or weak.

Note that both the *house of Israel* and the *house of Judah* are to be included in this new covenant. In 931 B.C., following the death of King Solomon, the kingdom of Israel divided itself into Israel (the northern kingdom) and Judah (the southern kingdom).

Following that division, *the house of Israel* had been scattered among foreign lands (2 Kings 17:6). As Jeremiah wrote, *the house of Judah* had been partially taken into captivity in Babylon, with a much more extensive exile to follow in a few years. Yet the new covenant is intended for both of these broken parts, for the whole house of unbroken Israel (cf. Romans 9–11)—and for the rest of the world, too (see Isaiah 42:6; 49:6).

9. Not according to the covenant that I made with their fathers, in the day when I took them by the hand to lead them out of the land of Egypt; because they continued not in my covenant, and I regarded them not, saith the Lord.

The ancient Jews honored Abraham, looking to him as their father (John 8:33, 39). He was the beginning of the Hebrews as a distinct people. Although he was childless until he was a very old man, his descendants became a great nation just as God had promised (Genesis 12:2).

Even so, the Jews looked to the exodus as their beginning as a separate and distinct nation. This event left a lasting impression on their national psyche that the centuries could not erode. They realized that they had not escaped *Egypt* through their own efforts. This had been accomplished through the mighty acts of God. They realized that they were helpless until God reached out His *hand* and led them to freedom.

But memories of God's blessings in the past were not enough to keep the Israelites faithful. They *continued not* in *the covenant* that God had made with their forefathers. It is easy enough for us to be critical of the ancient Jews because they failed to live up to the covenant. But as Christians are we any better? Are we not at times just as unfaithful to our rich heritage of blessings that we have received from God?

FALLEN HEROES

After lengthy study, Professor Bobby Clinton of Fuller Seminary concluded that fewer than 30 percent of Bible leaders "finished well" (*Current Thoughts & Trends*, September 2002, p. 2). Examples to support Professor Clinton's conclusion are not hard to find. Gideon, whose three hundred men routed the Midianite army, made an idol (Judges 8:22-27). Solomon, the wisest person who ever lived, introduced the idolatry that ultimately destroyed his nation (1 Kings 11:1-13).

King Uzziah is another example. After ascending to the throne at age sixteen, he sought the Lord sincerely at first. He defeated the Philistines, rebuilt several towns he took from them, and repulsed his Arab enemies as well. Uzziah's fame spread as far as Egypt because he had become very powerful (2 Chronicles 26:1-15).

Then pride took over. Being so arrogant that he felt no place to be off limits to him, Uzziah entered the holy temple to burn incense before the altar in violation of the law. The results were frightening (2 Chronicles 26:16-21).

When the leaders of God's people lapse into disobedience, is there any doubt that people will follow their example? (See Jeremiah 44:17.) Praise God that He has sent to us our ultimate, sinless Leader: Jesus Christ. He is the author of the new covenant, and He is the Leader who never fails to set the proper example in helping us submit to that covenant that leads to eternal life. Follow Him!   —R. H.

B. What It Does (vv. 10-12)

10. For this is the covenant that I will make with the house of Israel after those days, saith the Lord; I will put my laws into their mind, and write them in their hearts: and I will be to them a God, and they shall be to me a people.

A *covenant* or a contract is in effect as long as both parties honor its provisions. But when either party fails to meet its obligations, the agreement is broken. This happened very early in the history of the Mosaic covenant, even while the people were still in the wilderness. Yet God gave them another chance, and then another, and then another.

Finally, the time had come for the new covenant. The writer continues to quote from Jeremiah in making the case. Certainly it would be with *the house of Israel* (meaning both Judah and Israel). But the new covenant includes many others, as noted in comments to verse 8b, above. "There is no difference between the Jew and the Greek: for the same Lord over all is rich unto all that call upon him" (Romans 10:12).

More than five hundred years before the writing of Hebrews, the prophet Jeremiah had predicted that after a certain length of time (*after those days*) the new covenant would go into effect. This prophecy is fulfilled in the birth, death, and resurrection of Christ, and in the outpouring of the Holy Spirit on the day of Pentecost. The new covenant is not a covenant written on tablets of stone (Exodus 20). Rather, it is a covenant in which God puts His *laws into their mind* and *in their hearts*.

In Old Testament times as well as today, the word "heart" could mean much more than the physical organ that pumps the blood through the body. It was used to describe the seat of human emotions and human will. To accept God's new covenant and live under its precepts, one must do much more than just understand it. While understanding the covenant is essential, this understanding must lead to an emotional commitment to it (Acts 2:37). This commitment, in turn, must lead to an act of the will to live up to the covenant's requirements. [See question #3, page 392.]

Under the old covenant God had again and again demonstrated to the people that He was the one and only God. Unfortunately, the people were enticed by false gods and as a result often turned their backs on Him. In this verse the writer assures us that under the new covenant God will restore that broken relationship. *I will be to them a God, and they shall be to me a people.*

11. And they shall not teach every man his neighbor, and every man his brother, saying, Know the Lord: for all shall know me, from the least to the greatest.

The phrases *they shall not teach every man his neighbor, and every man his brother* mean that people will have direct access to God under the new covenant. We do not need to go through the human intermediaries—the priests of the levitical system—that was a feature of the old covenant (cf. Isaiah 54:13; John 6:45; Hebrews 4:16; 10:19-22).

Of course, a teaching function still exists under the new covenant as the New Testament makes clear in 1 Corinthians 12:28, 29 and Ephesians 4:11, 12. Under the new covenant every Christian is a priest (1 Peter 2:9). In this capacity we have not only the opportunity but also the obligation to study and understand the new covenant.

12. For I will be merciful to their unrighteousness, and their sins and their iniquities will I remember no more.

Under the old covenant the day of Atonement was a high point in the year (Leviticus 16). It reminded the people that the sacrifices and offerings made throughout the year were not enough to atone for *their sins.* But even this important day was itself not enough, for the blood of bulls and goats cannot take away sin (Hebrews 10:4).

An outstanding feature of this new covenant, on the other hand, is God's permanent forgiveness. Because Christ takes the sin penalty upon Himself, God takes away the *sins* of His people. What a privilege to serve a God who no longer remembers our *iniquities!* [See question #4, page 392.] The writer quotes from this section of Jeremiah in Hebrews 10:16, 17 as well (see also Romans 11:27). When Christ returns, *all* Christians will *know* Him in the fullest sense of Jeremiah's original prophecy.

OLD COVENANT BY MOSES	NEW COVENANT IN JESUS
temporary	eternal
national	universal
priests from the tribe of Levi	priests from all in the covenant
sinful men as high priests	Jesus as only and sinless high priest
sealed by the blood of animals	sealed by the blood of the Lamb of God
repeated sacrifices necessary	a single and final Sacrifice
high priest enters into Holy of Holies for the people	High Priest enters Heaven to welcome the people
written on stones by the hand of God	written on hearts by the Spirit of God

Visual for lesson 6

Post this chart to help your learners see the stark differences between the old and new covenants.

SEEKING FORGIVENESS

Simon Wiesenthal had been an architect before the Nazis confined him in a concentration camp in Poland. One afternoon he was cleaning rubbish out of a hospital for wounded German soldiers being brought in from the Eastern Front. A nurse took him to the bedside of Karl, a dying SS trooper. The boy's head wrapped in bandages oozing pus.

Karl, knowing that Wiesenthal was Jewish, grabbed his hand and began to tell his story. Karl had been fighting in a Russian village where his group rounded up several hundred Jews. He and his companions had been ordered to set cans of gasoline in the house and then to fill the house with as many of the Jews as the house could hold. About two hundred were crammed inside and the doors locked.

Karl and the other soldiers tossed grenades in the windows, setting the house afire. They shot anyone who tried to escape. Karl told of a man who jumped from the second story with his clothes on fire, holding a child in his arms. The child's mother jumped next. All three were shot as they tried to crawl away.

Sobbing, Karl asked Wiesenthal to forgive him, saying that only if he were to obtain forgiveness from a Jew could he go to his grave in peace. Could Wiesenthal forgive him? Wiesenthal turned and left the room, with no word of forgiveness.

Our sins have mocked the holiness of God, in whose image we are created. But God has made forgiveness available to all. Through Christ, He forgives and remembers our sins no more. His Holy Spirit strengthens us for greater holiness daily. Even so, do we continue in sin?   —R. H.

C. The "Bottom Line" (v. 13)

13. In that he saith, A new covenant, he hath made the first old. Now that which decayeth and waxeth old is ready to vanish away.

The transition from the *old* to the *new covenant* was not instantaneous. The change took place over several decades. It began with the birth of Jesus. The process continued through the ministry of John the Baptist, through Jesus' own ministry, and through Jesus' death, resurrection, and ascension. The outpouring of the Holy Spirit on the day of Pentecost was another crucial point in the process.

From that point on the new covenant has been in effect; the old covenant cancelled. The book of Hebrews seems to be written from the perspective that temple sacrifices are continuing, however (see Hebrews 10:11), so this book probably was written before A.D. 70. In that year came the destruction of Jerusalem and its temple. With that destruction the old covenant will finally *vanish away*. [See question #5, page 392.]

Conclusion

A. Change Is Threatening

As we look back to the first century, when Christ came bringing the good news of salvation, we may wonder why everyone did not immediately respond to this wonderful message. Through His teaching, His miracles, and especially through His resurrection, Jesus gave ample proof of His identity.

There are several reasons why not everyone accepted the message that Jesus brought. Those most violent in their rejection were the religious leaders. They enjoyed prominent positions in their nation and the perks that went along with those positions. They were respected by most of the people, and they were able to live comfortably above the poverty-level experiences of many others. Those leaders were not always happy with the Roman rule that had been imposed upon them, but they had learned to make the necessary concessions to live with the situation. In their security they took a dim view of anyone who might threaten this delicate balance (John 11:48).

There were others who, though also not especially happy with the power arrangements as they existed, were unwilling to accept the gospel because it meant making a personal change. Most of us, especially as we grow older, find ourselves resistant to change. We have grown comfortable where we are. Change brings the threat of the unknown. For many throughout history, the unknown seemed to be more dangerous than the situation they were in—even if they are not entirely happy with the present situation. This may have been the case with many of the Hebrew Christians who may have been considering going back into Judaism.

Some who might have been interested in becoming Christians undoubtedly were deterred by the threat of persecution. They had seen what had happened to others who had been beaten, imprisoned, and even killed. Their hearts may have been touched by the blessings offered by the new covenant, but the price was too high. Some who were interested in becoming Christians were persuaded by friends or family against taking that step.

Human nature has not changed in the two thousand years since Christ walked the earth. Some refuse to surrender to the call of Christ because they do not want to risk their places of prominence or profit. Others are afraid of change of any kind. While most of us are not kept from becoming Christians because of fear of persecution, there are places in the world where that is a real threat. The parable of sower (Matthew 13:1-9) still confronts us today. What type of "soil" are you?

B. Prayer

We give you thanks, O Lord, that You have allowed us to live under the new covenant. Help us gain a better understanding of both the responsibilities of the new covenant and the blessings that we can enjoy under it. May we never yield to the temptations to abandon it and the wonderful personal relations with You it affords us. In our Savior's name we pray, amen.

C. Thought to Remember

May others see in us
the joy of the new covenant!

Home Daily Bible Readings

Monday, July 5—I Will Make a New Covenant (Jeremiah 31:31-37)

Tuesday, July 6—Jesus, Mediator of a Better Covenant (Hebrews 8:1-6)

Wednesday, July 7—God's Laws Written on Our Hearts (Hebrews 8:7-13)

Thursday, July 8—The Blood of Christ Secured Redemption (Hebrews 9:1-12)

Friday, July 9—The Blood of Christ Purifies Us (Hebrews 9:13-18)

Saturday, July 10—Christ's Sacrifice Removes Sin (Hebrews 9:23-28)

Sunday, July 11—Christ's Single Offering Perfects Us (Hebrews 10:10-18)

Learning by Doing

This page contains an alternative lesson plan emphasizing learning activities.
Classes desiring such student involvement will find these suggestions helpful.

Learning Goals

After this lesson the student will be able to:

1. Contrast the elements of the old covenant God had with Israel with the new covenant God has with Christians.

2. Explain how the new covenant is superior to the old one.

3. Identify one person to whom he or she can explain the benefits of the new covenant.

Into the Lesson

Display this statement as students arrive: "A covenant is a treaty or an agreement between two parties, each of which assumes certain obligations and responsibilities." Take these visual aids to class: a wedding license and a credit purchase agreement (a loan agreement for a house, appliance, automobile). Begin the class by telling the students, "We are a culture of covenants. While we may not often use the word *covenant*, it is still a great description of major decisions in our lives." Review the definition of *covenant* you have on display. Show the two examples you brought to class. Ask the class to cite obligations or responsibilities that come from each of the two.

Make the transition to Bible study by telling the class, "God has made several agreements with people down through the years. However, His greatest covenant is one that has an impact on every life in this classroom."

Into the Word

Introduce the lesson with a brief lecture based on the lesson commentary Lesson Background. Use the following words in a list as visuals for this mini-lecture: *Adam and Eve, Noah, Abraham, Mosaic covenant, a better covenant.*

Give the students a handout that has a very large heading reading, "ENJOYING _ _ _ _ _ _ _ _ _ _ _ _ s _ _." Include the following instructions: "Read Hebrews 8:6-13. Use the following clues to find words in this passage to fill in the blanks. Then use the underlined letters to complete our major heading and discover our blessing in Christ." (*Heading: Better Promises.*)

"_ _ _ _ _ _ _, the days come . . . when I will make a new covenant" (v. 8). *Behold*

He (Jesus) has obtained a more _ _ _ _ _ _-_ _ _ _ _ ministry (v. 6). *excellent*

If that first covenant had been _ _ _ _ _ _-_ _ _ _ (v. 7). *faultless*

I will make a new _ _ _ _ _ _ _ _ _ with the house of Israel (v. 8). *covenant*

I took them by the hand to lead them out of the land of _ _ _ _ _ (v. 9). *Egypt*

I _ _ _ _ _ _ _ _ _ _ them not (v. 9). *regarded*

I will _ _ _ my laws into their mind (v. 10). *put*

I will . . . _ _ _ _ _ them [my laws] in their hearts (v. 10). *write*

They shall be to me a _ _ _ _ _ _ _ (v. 10). *people*

All shall know _ _ _ (v. 11). *me*

I will remember their _ _ _ _ _ _ _ _ _ _ _ no more (v. 12). *wickedness*

That which _ _ _ _ _ _ _ _ _ is ready to vanish (v. 13). *decayeth*

Their _ _ _ _ _ . . . I remember no more (v. 12). *sins*

Under this exercise on the handout, write: "After filling in the blanks on the headline, write a few ways the blessing described in the heading is true."

After students have completed the exercise, review the answers. Use material from the commentary to help students understand the text.

Into Life

Make a poster with the heading "Covenant Blessings." Under those words make two columns headed "Old Covenant" and "New Covenant." First, ask the students what were the blessings of the old Mosaic covenant between God and Israel. Also ask what God expected of Israel. List the answers in the first column.

Then, ask what blessings God brings to His people with the new covenant and what God expects from His people today. Afterward, note similarities in the blessings and expectations.

Tell the class, "Suppose you were expected to tell someone why the new covenant is better than the old and why this is important." Ask the class to work in pairs and list reasons on the backs of their handouts of ways the new covenant is superior to the old and why this is important. After a few minutes, have members discuss their answers.

Close the session by reminding the class that a covenant is an agreement. Ask, "What is God's expectation of us? What are some of the things He would like from His people in 2004?"

Let's Talk It Over

The questions on this page are designed to promote discussion of the lesson by the class and to encourage application of the lesson Scriptures. The answers provided are only discussion starters. Let your class talk it over from there.

1. In what ways have you personally benefited from Christ's "more excellent ministry"?

The most obvious blessing is, of course, eternal life (John 5:24). Beyond that we have, under the new covenant, much more revelation from God than any of the Old Testament prophets had (1 Peter 1:12). What a privilege to be able to hold the entirety of God's Word in our hands! How we choose to benefit from that Word is, of course, up to each of us individually. We also have the ability—even the boldness—to approach God without the need of a human intercessor (Hebrews 4:16). Again, we must take personal advantage of this blessing.

2. God "found fault" with those who lived under the old covenant. Today, do you think that God is "finding fault" with you as you live under His new covenant? Why, or why not?

Even after receiving Christ as Savior, Christians unfortunately continue to sin. How we deal with that sin can go a long way toward determining whether or not God finds fault with us. Remorse, regret, and repentance keep us in God's love and forgiveness (1 John 1:9). A resolve to live a holy life is important, because God Himself is holy (1 Peter 1:15, 16).

The grace of God is not a license to sin (Romans 6:1-4; Jude 4). If we live under the illusion that it is, we can expect God's displeasure.

3. The lesson writer says understanding the new covenant must lead to a commitment, and commitment must lead to action. What actions are typical of one who has made that commitment? How could an observer notice by your actions that you have accepted the new covenant?

This is not an attempt to list the acts one must perform in order to "ratify the covenant." Such an attempt would suggest we become part of the new covenant by works, and that is faulty thinking. But the Bible does teach that we are known by our actions (Matthew 7:16-20). Once that covenant is written on our hearts, it should find expression in loving deeds. It should be seen by the choices we make. What specifically have your learners done because they are included in the new covenant? A farmer in Ohio, for example, sells his corn directly to dairy farmers and below market price because he does not want to support the liquor industry.

4. Even though the Bible tells us that God will "remember no more" our sins and iniquities, many Christians live and labor under a sense of continuing guilt. While they have been told they are forgiven, on some level they don't really believe it. They still have a picture of God weighing their lives in a balance, and the scale is tipping the wrong way! How would you counsel a fellow believer who just can't shake his or her sense of guilt?

God is not holding a scale against those in Christ. When God says He will remember our sins no more, this is not a case of God's contracting amnesia! God has knowledge of what we do wrong, but He does not count these against the Christian. Our trust in Christ is "credited" to us by God as righteousness, based upon the fact the Son died for our sin (Romans 4:5). Any scale that God holds has been tipped forever in the favor of Christians by the death and resurrection of Jesus.

Paul is an example. He had persecuted the church, and he remembered that fact with remorse throughout his life (1 Corinthians 15:9; Galatians 1:13). Yet he also knew of God's forgiveness. May we realize that "as far as the east is from the west, so far hath he removed our transgressions from us" (Psalm 103:12).

5. Since the old covenant is now obsolete, do you bother studying the Old Testament? Why or why not?

Some Christians get the idea that the only concern of the church should be the New Testament. Since the Old Testament is the Scripture of the old covenant, these believers think it is unimportant for the New Testament church.

This thinking, however, misses some important points. The Old Testament is not exclusively about the old covenant. Some vital parts of the Old Testament contain predictions regarding the new covenant. The lineage of Jesus Christ, the great high priest of the new covenant, is traced in the Old Testament. Many "realities" of the new covenant are foreshadowed by things in the old covenant (see Hebrews 8:5; 10:1). As Paul says in Romans 15:4, "For whatsoever things were written aforetime was written for our learning, that we through patience and comfort of the Scriptures might have hope."

Roll Call of the Faithful

DEVOTIONAL READING: Hebrews 11:17-26.

BACKGROUND SCRIPTURE: Hebrews 11.

PRINTED TEXT: Hebrews 11:1-13.

Hebrews 11:1-13

1 Now faith is the substance of things hoped for, the evidence of things not seen.

2 For by it the elders obtained a good report.

3 Through faith we understand that the worlds were framed by the word of God, so that things which are seen were not made of things which do appear.

4 By faith Abel offered unto God a more excellent sacrifice than Cain, by which he obtained witness that he was righteous, God testifying of his gifts: and by it he being dead yet speaketh.

5 By faith Enoch was translated that he should not see death; and was not found, because God had translated him: for before his translation he had this testimony, that he pleased God.

6 But without faith it is impossible to please him: for he that cometh to God must believe that he is, and that he is a rewarder of them that diligently seek him.

7 By faith Noah, being warned of God of things not seen as yet, moved with fear, prepared an ark to the saving of his house; by the which he condemned the world, and became heir of the righteousness which is by faith.

8 By faith Abraham, when he was called to go out into a place which he should after receive for an inheritance, obeyed; and he went out, not knowing whither he went.

9 By faith he sojourned in the land of promise, as in a strange country, dwelling in tabernacles with Isaac and Jacob, the heirs with him of the same promise:

10 For he looked for a city which hath foundations, whose builder and maker is God.

11 Through faith also Sarah herself received strength to conceive seed, and was delivered of a child when she was past age, because she judged him faithful who had promised.

12 Therefore sprang there even of one, and him as good as dead, so many as the stars of the sky in multitude, and as the sand which is by the seashore innumerable.

13 These all died in faith, not having received the promises, but having seen them afar off, and were persuaded of them, and embraced them, and confessed that they were strangers and pilgrims on the earth.

GOLDEN TEXT: Without faith it is impossible to please him: for he that cometh to God must believe that he is, and that he is a rewarder of them that diligently seek him.—Hebrews 11:6.

Hold Fast to the Faith
Unit 2: Strengthened to Be Faithful
(Lessons 5-8)

Lesson Aims

After participating in this lesson, each student should be able to:

1. Briefly recount the stories of the Bible heroes in today's text and tell how they demonstrated faith.

2. Tell a personal story of how a difficult time in life helped his or her faith to grow.

3. Identify someone who is experiencing difficulty and at least one specific way he or she can encourage that person's faith.

Lesson Outline

INTRODUCTION
  A. Mortgage on the Future
  B. Lesson Background
 I. NATURE OF FAITH (Hebrews 11:1-3)
  A. Description of Faith (vv. 1, 2)
  B. Faith in Creation (v. 3)
II. FAITH OF VARIOUS PEOPLE (Hebrews 11:4-13)
  A. Abel (v. 4)
  B. Enoch (vv. 5, 6)
  C. Noah (v. 7)
    A Job Well Done
  D. Abraham, Part 1 (vv. 8-10)
  E. Sarah (v. 11)
  F. Abraham, Part 2 (v. 12)
    Modern Heroes of the Faith
  G. Summary (v. 13)
CONCLUSION
  A. Faith on Every Hand
  B. Prayer
  C. Thought to Remember

Introduction

A. Mortgage on the Future

In the Second Punic War (218–202 B.C.) the famous Carthaginian leader Hannibal invaded Italy. He subsequently defeated in several decisive battles the best armies the Romans could put in the field. The citizens of Rome were alarmed, to say the least. Nothing but the walls of their city stood between them and total defeat.

The Roman leaders wavered in their counsel, some arguing for terms of peace and others for continued resistance. Legend has it that one courageous citizen stepped forth with an unusual idea: he offered to purchase the very parcel of land upon which Hannibal's tent stood. When asked the reason for his unusual offer, he is said to have replied, "Fellow Romans, I am taking a mortgage on the future." (Compare Jeremiah 32:1-15, 42-44.) The confident attitude of this citizen is said to have been instrumental in rallying the Romans and stiffening their resistance. Hannibal eventually withdrew.

Today we will see the writer of the Hebrew epistle "call the roll of the faithful." As we read it, we are struck by how they maintained faith in the face of dismal prospects. In hopeless conditions they demonstrated their faith by taking a mortgage on the future.

B. Lesson Background

The book of Hebrews is a book that *warns* (Hebrews 2:1-4; 3:7-19; etc.). We don't know all the reasons that the readers may have had for wanting to abandon Christianity, but fear of persecution or hardship is very likely.

The writer of this epistle marshals several arguments to convince the readers to remain true to their Christian faith. The new covenant is better than the old in having a better high priest, a better sacrifice, and a better hope. Now in Hebrews 11 the inspired writer turns to Jewish history to demonstrate that great heroes of the past had faced all kinds of challenges to their faith. But they had prevailed in spite of the danger.

Logical arguments are useful in any discussion of the Christian faith, even essential. But perhaps the most forceful argument for the power of faith in God is to look at the examples of those who have triumphed over all kinds of difficulties in their efforts to remain true to Him. The author of Hebrews selects a variety of past heroes of the faith to make just such an argument. In many ways Abraham is the greatest of those examples. The example of Abraham would be especially forceful to Jewish Christians, who looked to him as their father in the faith.

I. Nature of Faith
(Hebrews 11:1-3)

A. Description of Faith (vv. 1, 2)

1. Now faith is the substance of things hoped for, the evidence of things not seen.

This is certainly one of the most important verses in the entire Bible. Eternal life depends on *faith*. If we do not understand what faith is, we may well forfeit our hope for the life to come. Faith as described here conveys the idea of confidence in what one believes. Faith is not just vague wishful thinking; it is the complete confidence that God's promises will be fulfilled.

Right here is where modern believers have a great advantage: we can look at centuries past and see that God has indeed kept all His promises. This evidence of things that we can see in the pages of the Bible and in history provides us with *the substance of things* yet *hoped for.* Our faith is not a blind faith. [See question #1, page 400.]

2. For by it the elders obtained a good report.

The elders were those who had lived in the past (cf. Hebrews 1:1). Not all of these elders *obtained a good report,* however. Adam and Eve were expelled from the Garden of Eden for rebellion. Cain was the first murderer. But some were obedient and received God's blessings as a result. It was by faith that these were able to serve in such a way that they received God's approval. We will see some of these discussed beginning in verse 4, below.

B. Faith in Creation (v. 3)

3. Through faith we understand that the worlds were framed by the word of God, so that things which are seen were not made of things which do appear.

Where did the earth and the other heavenly bodies come from? How did they get here? Every generation has in one way or another searched for answers to these profound questions. From the primitive savage who looked into the starry heavens, to modern scientists who use the Hubble telescope to search the vast reaches of space, humanity has looked for explanations.

Some modern scientists scoff at Biblical answers as superstition of pre-modern thinking (cf. Genesis 1; Psalm 33:6, 9). They insist that they alone can give us scientific answers (cf. 2 Peter

---

How to Say It

ABRAHAM. *Ay*-bruh-ham.
CAMBODIA. Kam-*boh*-dee-uh.
CARTHAGINIAN. Kar-thuh-*jin*-ee-un.
CHALDEES. *Kal*-deez.
ELIJAH. Ee-*lye*-juh.
ENOCH. *E*-nock.
EUPHRATES. You-*fray*-teez.
HANNIBAL. *Han*-nuh-bull.
HARAN. *Hair*-un.
ISAAC. *Eye*-zuk.
JACOB. *Jay*-kub.
JARED. *Jair*-ed.
KHMER ROUGE. Kuh-*mer* Roozh.
METHUSELAH. Muh-*thoo*-zuh-luh (*th* as in *thin*).
PUNIC. *Pew*-nik.
UR. Er.
VIDYA SHARMA. *Vid*-yuh *Shar*-muh.

3:5). For example, some propose the "Big Bang" theory for the beginnings of the universe. Even if this theory were true, it does not tell us where the original matter and energy came from to produce the great explosion. At this point the scientist has to fall back on some kind of *faith* to tell us about the origins of matter and energy.

Since both Christians and non-Christians must rely on faith to answer these ultimate questions, we have a right to ask whose faith is more valid. Which is more reasonable: to have faith that the material used to form the universe somehow just "always existed," or to have faith in a God who is able to create things from nothing?

II. Faith of Various People (Hebrews 11:4-13)

A. Abel (v. 4)

4. By faith Abel offered unto God a more excellent sacrifice than Cain, by which he obtained witness that he was righteous, God testifying of his gifts: and by it he being dead yet speaketh.

The account of *Cain* and *Abel* is found in Genesis 4:1-15. Both brothers brought sacrifices to God. Cain brought "of the fruit of the ground," while Abel brought "of the firstlings of his flock." God accepted Abel's sacrifice, but rejected Cain's. This so angered Cain that he murdered his brother.

This verse gives us a clue regarding God's viewpoint. We are told that Abel offered *a more excellent sacrifice* because *he was righteous.* It is evident that the problem was not with the sacrifice itself, whether animal or grain. The important issue was that of attitude.

Abel offered his sacrifice *by faith* with a humble heart, while Cain offered his grudgingly or arrogantly. [See question #2, page 400.] As a result of his godly example, Abel still speaks to us even after *being dead* for thousands of years. [See question #3, page 400.]

B. Enoch (vv. 5, 6)

5. By faith Enoch was translated that he should not see death; and was not found, because God had translated him: for before his translation he had this testimony, that he pleased God.

There are two men named *Enoch* in Genesis. Genesis 5:21-24 allows us to conclude that the Enoch being discussed was the son of Jared and the father of Methuselah. The most important information we learn about him in that passage is that he "walked with God" (v. 24). This is significant because in Enoch's day most people were walking away from God, not with Him.

(handwritten margin note, left side, vertical: "Noah preaching of righteousness 2 Peter 2:5")

Enoch's faith is the reason the writer of Hebrews mentions him as an example. As a result of his faith, Enoch did not suffer *death* in the usual sense, for "God took him" (again, v. 24; compare the case of Elijah in 2 Kings 2:11).

Because of this unusual event, numerous Jewish myths had sprung up about Enoch. As interesting and fanciful as some of these are, we need not dwell on them and miss the main point the author is making: Enoch walked by faith and as a result was pleasing to God. Jude 14, 15 mentions a prophecy of Enoch.

6. But without faith it is impossible to please him: for he that cometh to God must believe that he is, and that he is a rewarder of them that diligently seek him.

This very important verse indicates the reason that the actions of Abel and Enoch are worthy of being mentioned in this context of *faith.* Abel and Enoch did not simply *believe* that God exists. Belief is important, but it does not go far enough by itself (see James 2:19). Abel and Enoch were among the few that *diligently* sought God. As a result, they did indeed *please* God.

All of us are painfully aware that there are times and situations when it is difficult to see any tangible evidence that God really does reward His followers. But with the evidence of history and the eye of faith we can look beyond our immediate situations and see the eternal blessings that He has in store for us.

C. Noah (v. 7)

7. By faith Noah, being warned of God of things not seen as yet, moved with fear, prepared an ark to the saving of his house; by the which he condemned the world, and became heir of the righteousness which is by faith.

(handwritten note: "Noah was 6 hundred years old")

Visual for
lesson 7

God rewards "them that diligently seek him."

from Hebrews 11:6

*This visual will remind your learners of the importance of **diligence** in the Christian walk.*

When *God* looked upon *the world* in Noah's day, He saw that it was terribly evil and corrupt. So He made the decision to cleanse it with a flood (Genesis 6:11-17). We don't know exactly how God spoke to Noah, but we do know that He ordered him to build an *ark.* Noah did "according to all that God commanded him" without any record of hesitation or questioning (Genesis 6:22).

Part of God's message to Noah was a warning *of things not seen as yet.* This is where faith comes in, and Noah really demonstrated it when he set out to build such a huge vessel. This was a tremendous undertaking, and most likely he had to carry it out in an atmosphere of ridicule from friends and neighbors. Nor was it a simple weekend project. By some calculations, this task took decades. During that time this "preacher of righteousness" (2 Peter 2:5) was unable to save any but his own family (Genesis 7:13; 1 Peter 3:20). It took a lot of faith to continue preaching under those discouraging circumstances.

A JOB WELL DONE

At the beginning of a project we often can see only dimly where it will lead. That was certainly true of Dokie Hampton's work. Before her death Dokie was a member of "The Quilters," a group of women who met regularly in Mabel Winkler's basement making quilts. Typically, they would begin in the morning, stop to eat lunch, then work on through the afternoon.

Their work was extraordinary, with hundreds and hundreds of stitches in each quilt and many separate patches of material carefully arranged and skillfully joined. These quilts were not only practical, they were works of art. Buyers gladly paid premium prices for such excellent work.

Stitching was something Dokie did quite well. In fact, she worked for a company in Akron, Ohio, sewing material to tailor-make men's suits to the wearer's exact specifications. Each stitch had to be absolutely secure so that the material would not tear. More importantly, every stitch had to be airtight! These suits were to be worn in a vacuum. If one of Dokie's stitches leaked air, the man wearing the suit could die. Who needed such clothing? American astronauts.

Dokie was one of a select handful of seamstresses assigned this task. She had only a vague notion of how her work would be used. But later on Dokie better understood the reason behind the request as she and millions of others watched on television.

Safely inside the ark on the day the rain started pouring down, Noah better understood the instructions God had given him. But the understanding came *after* faith. How much faith are we exercising today?   —R. H.

D. Abraham, Part 1 (vv. 8-10)

8. By faith Abraham, when he was called to go out into a place which he should after receive for an inheritance, obeyed; and he went out, not knowing whither he went.

The writer now causes us to consider the life of *Abraham* as an example of one who lived by faith. The Bible tells us more about the life of Abraham than the other heroes previously mentioned, and Jews look to Abraham as the father of their nation.

Abraham lived with his father and other members of his family in Ur of the Chaldees, located on the lower Euphrates River (modern Iraq). Abraham accompanied his father when he moved to Haran (Genesis 11:27-32).

God *called* Abraham *to go out into a place which he should after receive for an inheritance* after his father died. Since Abraham was seventy-five years old, it took no little faith for him to leave Haran (Genesis 12:4). When God called him out, God didn't give him a carefully marked road map showing the route he was to take and his final destination (Genesis 12:1). Rather, *he went out, not knowing whither he went.* Abraham didn't question God—he obeyed!

9. By faith he sojourned in the land of promise, as in a strange country, dwelling in tabernacles with Isaac and Jacob, the heirs with him of the same promise.

For the rest of his life Abraham lived as a nomad *in the land of promise.* That land remained a land of promise, not only for him, but also for his son *Isaac* and grandson *Jacob* as well (Genesis 35:27). Only centuries later were Abraham's descendants able to claim that land as God intended under *the same promise. Tabernacles* here means tents, indicating a nomadic lifestyle.

10. For he looked for a city which hath foundations, whose builder and maker is God.

When he left Haran, Abraham may have envisioned building *a city* in the promised land, where he could have a permanent dwelling place. But by faith he had a nobler vision: a city with *foundations* built by God. Abraham saw beyond the nomadic life that was to be his lot on earth. He saw instead the promise of a Heavenly home. The writer of Hebrews will expand on this "city" in 11:16; 12:22; and 13:14.

E. Sarah (v. 11)

11. Through faith also Sarah herself received strength to conceive seed, and was delivered of a child when she was past age, because she judged him faithful who had promised.

It may surprise us that *Sarah* is mentioned as a model of a faithful person. In fact, she doubted God's promise that Abraham would have heirs through her. At one point she encouraged her husband to take her handmaid as a secondary wife that Sarah could "obtain children by her" (Genesis 16:1-3). Later, when God sent three messengers to Abraham, Sarah overheard them tell him that she would have a son. On hearing it, she "laughed within herself" (Genesis 18:12).

Yet at some point her faith began to grow. Perhaps her attitude began to change as she watched Abraham faithfully try to carry out the Lord's mandate. We need to realize that our faith can be contagious. When others see our faithful lives, they can catch some of that faith.

F. Abraham, Part 2 (v. 12)

12. Therefore sprang there even of one, and him as good as dead, so many as the stars of the sky in multitude, and as the sand which is by the seashore innumerable.

As a result of God's power and Abraham's faith, his descendants became as numerous as the *stars of the sky* and *as the sand which is by the seashore.* The fulfillment of this promise is so important that this imagery is used in several Bible passages (Genesis 15:5; 22:17; 32:12; Exodus 32:13; Deuteronomy 1:10; 10:22). Paul discusses Abraham's profound faith in this regard in Romans 4:18, 19.

MODERN HEROES OF THE FAITH

"My first thought was that I should kill those rebels," says Vidya Sharma. Vidya lives in Katmandu, Nepal. Vidya had just learned that Maoist rebels had murdered his younger brother.

The trek to his brother's village took Vidya three days. Maoists had repeatedly threatened him, but Vidya had never considered that they would harm his family members. Rebels had come to his brother's house in the village of Toli about 11:00 P.M. and had thrown a small bomb through a window of the family home, wounding several.

The Communists broke into the house, kicking and beating indiscriminately. Yelling at Vidya's aged parents, they demanded, "Why did you permit your son to become a Christian?" Their son was the only Christian in this Hindu village. The Maoists ordered everyone out of the house and set off a much larger bomb, destroying everything. Then they shot Mahesh, Vidya's twenty-two-year-old brother.

Like the earlier Khmer Rouge in Cambodia, Maoist rebels in Nepal ranged through the countryside with their "purification" campaign, annihilating anyone they felt was against them. Because Christians generally favor democracy and believe in certain God-given rights, the Maoists saw them as enemies.

Through prayer Vidya's anger has gone, but his determination to continue his Christian work is stronger than ever. His family has suffered, his brother is dead, and his life is still threatened. But Vidya Sharma continues his important witness for Christ in this far-off spot in Southeast Asia, convinced that God knows his situation and that God's reward will far outweigh any present difficulties. May our own lives be just as faithful.

—R. H.

G. Summary (v. 13)

13. These all died in faith, not having received the promises, but having seen them afar off, and were persuaded of them, and embraced them, and confessed that they were strangers and pilgrims on the earth.

Foresight is a vital part of faith. That's what it means for these heroes to be able to see *the promises . . . afar off*. For example, Jesus said that "Abraham rejoiced to see my day" (John 8:56). [See question #4, page 400.] The way these heroes lived their lives acknowledges the fact that they were *strangers and pilgrims on the earth* (cf. Genesis 23:4; 47:9; Psalm 39:12). As Christians we also are to acknowledge that we are but strangers and sojourners on this earth (cf. 1 Peter 2:11). [See question #5, page 400.]

Conclusion

A. Faith on Every Hand

Occasionally we hear people say, "I don't take anything on faith." This is an absurd statement, for every day in countless ways we live by faith. For example, when we receive our direct deposit pay stub, we have faith that the money actually went to the bank. When we approach a bridge while driving, do we stop, pull off the road, and check the safety of the bridge? Of course not. Without even a thought we drive across the bridge. We have faith in the engineers who planned the bridge and the crews who built it.

In most situations faith does not come instantaneously, but must develop over time. Faith grows out of evidence from the past. Over the years we have lived in several different places and have had many different neighbors, some good and some otherwise. Several months ago a new neighbor moved in next door. He was a total stranger, and I had no basis for forming an opinion about him. Before long we learned that he was a Christian and that we shared many common interests. As we learned more about him, our faith in one another grew. Now we work together on all kinds of projects on his property and on mine, and I value him as a trusted friend. I have faith that He will not break our trust.

Much the same can be said about how we develop a relationship with God and acquire faith in Him. As small children we learn about God in the home and at church. This learning usually comes slowly, a little bit at a time. The rate of our learning depends on many factors, both internal and external.

We may accept Christ and become Christians at some point along the way. But that does not mean that the growth of our faith stops. Conversion is but one step—an important step to be sure—in the process of becoming mature Christians. Our faith grows through our own experiences and by observing the lives of others. That growth is not always a smooth, upward curve. Often it proceeds by jerks and starts—frequently upward, but sometimes downward as well.

If, like Abraham, we continue to look for the "city which hath foundations, whose builder and maker is God," we will not be disappointed in the end. Among those aging saints who are more mature in their faith, we see a calm, assured trust in God that grows out of a lifetime of following Him. Theirs is a faith that looks ever forward. This is the message the writer of Hebrews was trying to get across to the first-century Jewish Christians. It is a message for every generation.

B. Prayer

Gracious God, we thank You for the lives of the faithful whom You have portrayed in Scripture to serve as examples. May we be encouraged by these faithful examples to grow in our faith toward Christian maturity. May we serve in turn as faithful examples to others. In Jesus' name, amen.

C. Thought to Remember

Faith is the victory!

Home Daily Bible Readings

Monday, July 12—Abraham Did Not Weaken in Faith (Romans 4:13-22)

Tuesday, July 13—Abel and Enoch Had Faith (Hebrews 11:1-6)

Wednesday, July 14—By Faith Noah Built an Ark (Hebrews 11:7-12)

Thursday, July 15—They Desired a Heavenly Country (Hebrews 11:13-19)

Friday, July 16—Isaac, Jacob, Joseph Had Faith (Hebrews 11:20-26)

Saturday, July 17—By Faith Moses Led the Israelites (Hebrews 11:27-31)

Sunday, July 18—Others Commended for Their Faith (Hebrews 11:32-40)

Learning by Doing

This page contains an alternative lesson plan emphasizing learning activities. Classes desiring such student involvement will find these suggestions helpful.

Learning Goals

After this lesson each student will be able to:

1. Briefly recount the stories of the Bible heroes in today's text and tell how they demonstrated faith.

2. Tell a personal story of how a difficult time in life helped his or her faith to grow.

3. Identify someone who is experiencing difficulty and at least one specific way he or she can encourage that person's faith.

Into The Lesson

Write the words *FAITH MODELS* at the top of a marker board or poster board. Ask the class to name friends or acquaintances they would say are models of faith. As you add each suggested name to the list, ask others why they think that one has been chosen as a model of faith. (An exercise similar to this is in the student book, *Adult Bible Class*.)

God knows that models of faith are inspirational and motivational. Make the transition to Bible study by saying, "Many of our models and the models God chose are people who demonstrate great faith in adverse circumstances. This study should help arm us for times when Satan is attacking our personal lives."

Into the Word

This Bible study lends itself to two topics: the nature of faith and the necessity of faith. Study groups will use handouts to focus on one of these. Use the front and back of the handout to write the assignments for both groups. Divide the class into groups of no more than five people each, identifying each group as a "1" or a "2." (If you choose, use the handouts as discussion guides in a whole-class activity.)

Group #1. Distribute handouts with the heading "The Nature of Faith." The instructions under the heading should be, "Read Hebrews 11:1-13 and answer the following questions.

"A. Verse one is a classic description of faith. One writer says this is one of the most important verses in the Bible. Why or how is this true?

"B. Faith is often modeled when life circumstances are most challenging. How was the faith of the persons mentioned in our text (listed below) demonstrated, and in what circumstances? Abel (v. 4), Enoch (v. 5 and Genesis 5:17-24), Noah (v. 7), Abraham (vv. 8-13), Sarah (vv. 11, 12).

"C. As time allows, discuss how hope and faith differ."

Group #2. This group's heading should read "The Necessity of Faith." Write the following assignment: "Read today's text, Hebrews 11:1-13. Focus on the teaching in verse 6, and answer the following questions.

"A. Without faith it is impossible for us to please God. Why is faith so important for a healthy relationship with God?

"B. Faith usually grows out of experience. Illustrate this principle for the class with any example you wish. *(A simple one is to have someone turn on/off the lights; experience teaches us that the lights will go on/off using the switch. What does this principle teach us about faith in God?)*

"C. Explain or illustrate how faith continues to grow after a person becomes a Christian. What are the dangers for believers if faith does not continue to develop throughout life's walk?"

After the groups report, give a brief summary based on the lesson commentary on verse 13.

Into Life

Make three signs on letter-sized paper, each with one of the following headings: "Difficult Circumstances," "Faith's Challenge," and "Possible Testimony." Make four more signs using the following examples or some of your own choice: "Major Surgery," "Financial Setback," "Child Announces Homosexuality," and "Couple Discovers They Cannot Have Children."

Fasten the three headings side by side on the wall. Say, "We have seen Biblical models who have demonstrated faith as they faced difficult circumstances in life. Like them, we learn from our experiences and can become encouragers to other people who are facing life's challenges."

Now post the four examples under the first column, asking the class to explain why or how the faith of a person in each circumstance may be challenged (reference to second column). Ask how Christians with similar challenges who have remained faithful could encourage such a person. Ask people to volunteer personal experiences from which they have learned faith that could be encouraging to others. End this testimonial moment by asking each to identify one difficult personal event that could be used to help others. Allow prayer groups to pray for each other's faithful witness in matters both easy and difficult.

Let's Talk It Over

The questions on this page are designed to promote discussion of the lesson by the class and to encourage application of the lesson Scriptures. The answers provided are only discussion starters. Let your class talk it over from there.

1. How would you respond to the claim that faith is "accepting something that you have no good reason to think is true"?

Unfortunately, the very term *faith* has come to have this meaning in modern English. At least one dictionary definition contends that faith is "firm belief in something for which there is no proof."

When talking to people about faith, we must keep this in mind and explain carefully how the term *faith* is used in Scripture. While faith points toward "things not seen" (Hebrews 11:1), this does not mean that we have no good reason to be sure of what we hope for. Unlike modern usage of the word *faith*, the trust exhibited by those heroes mentioned in Hebrews 11 was not divorced from evidence. It was based upon a God who demonstrated His existence and power in unmistakable ways.

2. With Abel as an example, what do you think God is looking for in a sacrifice from you that would be pleasing to Him?

Apparently what made Abel's sacrifice acceptable was not directly related to *what* it was, but *how* it was offered. Abel's sacrifice was the result of faith and righteousness. This is the reason it pleased God. Cain's sacrifice somehow lacked this.

Perhaps another hint is found in Genesis 4:4, which tells us that Abel "brought of the firstlings of his flock and of the fat thereof." Was Abel's sacrifice from "his best" while Cain's was not? We cannot be certain. It *is* certain, however, that an attitude of faith will bring forth our best offering—whether of "talent, time, or treasure"—to God.

3. Thinking about how Abel continues to "speak" to us today, in what ways would you want your Christian example to "speak" to others long after God has called you home?

A life lived in faith should leave evidence of itself. While this is not necessarily dramatic, such effects should exist. Christian parents and grandparents can leave a mark on their children and grandchildren (see 2 Timothy 1:5). People of faith can have a lasting effect on the congregations where they worship and serve. Perhaps your learners can think of those, now dead, whose influence lives on at the church where you serve.

We should also remember that a life of faith can also have lasting positive effects even outside the church. The power of a Christian life to silence its critics (1 Peter 2:12) can live on long after the individual who lived it has passed away.

4. In what ways are you like (or unlike) those mentioned in Hebrews 11:13, who had not "received the promises" but "having seen them afar off, . . . were persuaded of them, and embraced them"?

We are unlike those godly people in the fact that many of the things to which they looked forward are now past reality for us. The Christ has come, has died for our sins, and is raised from the dead. The Holy Spirit has come to live within those of us who are in Christ. As Ephesians 1:13, 14 makes clear, the Holy Spirit is Himself "the earnest" or down payment from the Father on all His promises for our future.

But there are things yet to come from God for those who believe. We are going to receive new bodies fit for eternity, when the new heavens and the new earth make their appearance (1 Corinthians 15:42-44; 2 Peter 3:13; Revelation 21:1). We must look forward in faith to things and events such as these. While we have much more of the "reality" than those who lived before the time of Christ, we still have much to look forward to by faith in the power of God.

5. In what ways do you (or do you not) consider yourself to be a "stranger" and "pilgrim" on earth?

We are not strangers or aliens to God's creation as He originally fashioned it. Things changed for the worse, however, with the entrance of sin into the creation. The Bible makes a contrast between those who have been justified by faith and are being fitted for eternity in the presence of God, and those who are not. Those of us in the first condition can never be "at home" in a world that has been distorted by sin.

First Peter 2:11, 12 makes this same point: our alienation is not from God's creation as such, but rather from those "fleshly lusts, which war against" our souls. We should enjoy God's creation in nature and in our fellow human beings as He intends. We can never, however, be truly at home in a sin-corrupted world.

Faithful and Disciplined

DEVOTIONAL READING: **1 Peter 4:12-19.**

BACKGROUND SCRIPTURE: **Hebrews 12.**

PRINTED TEXT: **Hebrews 12:1-13.**

Hebrews 12:1-13

1 Wherefore, seeing we also are compassed about with so great a cloud of witnesses, let us lay aside every weight, and the sin which doth so easily beset us, and let us run with patience the race that is set before us,

2 Looking unto Jesus the author and finisher of our faith; who for the joy that was set before him endured the cross, despising the shame, and is set down at the right hand of the throne of God.

3 For consider him that endured such contradiction of sinners against himself, lest ye be wearied and faint in your minds.

4 Ye have not yet resisted unto blood, striving against sin.

5 And ye have forgotten the exhortation which speaketh unto you as unto children, My son, despise not thou the chastening of the Lord, nor faint when thou art rebuked of him:

6 For whom the Lord loveth he chasteneth, and scourgeth every son whom he receiveth.

7 If ye endure chastening, God dealeth with you as with sons; for what son is he whom the father chasteneth not?

8 But if ye be without chastisement, whereof all are partakers, then are ye bastards, and not sons.

9 Furthermore, we have had fathers of our flesh which corrected us, and we gave them reverence: shall we not much rather be in subjection unto the Father of spirits, and live?

10 For they verily for a few days chastened us after their own pleasure; but he for our profit, that we might be partakers of his holiness.

11 Now no chastening for the present seemeth to be joyous, but grievous: nevertheless, afterward it yieldeth the peaceable fruit of righteousness unto them which are exercised thereby.

12 Wherefore lift up the hands which hang down, and the feeble knees;

13 And make straight paths for your feet, lest that which is lame be turned out of the way; but let it rather be healed.

GOLDEN TEXT: If ye endure chastening, God dealeth with you as with sons.
—Hebrews 12:7.

Hold Fast to the Faith
Unit 2: Strengthened to Be Faithful
(Lessons 5-8)

Lesson Aims

After participating in this lesson, each student should be able to:

1. Identify the basic elements necessary to run a good spiritual race.

2. Express the importance of being patient and persistent when facing hardship.

3. Identify an impediment to a good spiritual race that he or she would like to lay aside.

Lesson Outline

INTRODUCTION
    A. From Junk to Jewelry
    B. Lesson Background
  I. THE RACE OF LIFE (Hebrews 12:1-3)
    A. The Task Before Us (v. 1)
      Thinking Ahead
    B. The Example Before Us (vv. 2, 3)
 II. THE DISCIPLINE OF THE FATHER (Hebrews 12:4-11)
    A. Struggle and Encouragement (vv. 4-10)
    B. Hardship and Harvest (v. 11)
III. THE NEED TO GET MOVING (Hebrews 12:12, 13)
    A. Strength, Not Feebleness (v. 12)
    B. Healing, Not Lameness (v. 13)
      Teaching by Example
CONCLUSION
    A. The Trailblazer
    B. "Hitting the Wall"
    C. Prayer
    D. Thought to Remember

Introduction

A. From Junk to Jewelry

An uncut diamond is scarcely a thing of beauty. Its odd shape and dull appearance completely conceal its true value from the untrained observer.

Then the apparently worthless bit of rock is placed in the hands of a skilled diamond cutter. He or she may spend hours cleaving the stone (cutting it in two) with special tools and then many more hours cutting, grinding, and polishing the stone before it can be mounted in a piece of jewelry. Were the stone a living thing and sensitive to pain, it might well complain of this cruel treatment. Yet when this treatment has been completed, the diamond is no longer a dull and worthless piece of stone, but a brilliant and precious jewel.

Sometimes God handles us as "diamonds in the rough." He allows suffering to come into our lives—suffering that we often cannot understand nor appreciate. Yet, when it is all over—perhaps many years later—we can see that God, the master diamond cutter, was working all along to fashion us into precious jewels. The cutting and grinding have shaped us into masterpieces.

B. Lesson Background

In last week's lesson the writer of Hebrews offered us a list of some heroes of the faith. Our study ended with Abraham, but the list is actually much longer, continuing through Isaac, Jacob, and Moses (Hebrews 11:20-29). Then the writer mentions some of the judges down to the time of Samuel and David. Other heroes are not named, but some of their sufferings are listed: violence of fire, edge of the sword, mockings, scourgings, imprisonment, being sawn asunder, and other violent mistreatment (11:34-37).

Obviously, all these heroes were humans with human shortcomings. Yet each in a personal way exemplifies a trust in God that serves as an example for those who follow.

I. The Race of Life
(Hebrews 12:1-3)

A. The Task Before Us (v. 1)

1. Wherefore, seeing we also are compassed about with so great a cloud of witnesses, let us lay aside every weight, and the sin which doth so easily beset us, and let us run with patience the race that is set before us.

As we think about *so great a cloud of witnesses* that surrounds us, we must ask, "Which way is the witnessing going?" In Hebrews 11 the author has just given us example after example of heroes of the faith. As we read that list, we could say that their accomplishments and hardships serve as witnesses to spur us on.

But the writer more likely is intending to say that those heroes themselves are now witnessing us as we work for Christ. In this case the picture is that of an athletic stadium where the runners and other athletes perform before a vast, cheering crowd. Such a crowd can be a great encouragement to the participants in an athletic contest. As Christians we see this crowd with the eye of faith.

We can also acknowledge at this point that we are always surrounded by earthly witnesses. Some of them are on our side, and some are antagonistic. Although the writer is not referring to present-day witnesses, we should nevertheless remember to conduct ourselves in such a way that we will not bring reproach to His name. [See question #1, page 408.]

Proper conduct requires that we *lay aside every weight, and the sin which doth so easily beset us.* These are really two separate ideas. Athletes, then as now, carry nothing in a race that will slow them down. Many things in life may serve as distractions from fully devoted service to Christ, although such things might not be classified as *sin* in and of themselves. An example could be spending too much time surfing the Internet (even if visiting only wholesome web sites). We must learn to shed such baggage as we "travel light" in our Christian service.

Rejecting sin is even more important. Sin saps our physical, emotional, and spiritual strength. Sin compromises our witness to non-Christians. Although we all fall back into sin at times, we cannot run a victorious race if we remain there. [See question #2, page 408.]

We also do well to remember that the Christian life is a marathon, not a sprint. Athletes train differently for a short dash than for a long-distance run. A good start out of the blocks and a sustained burst of speed are crucial for very short races. The training required to develop those skills do little to help the long-distance runner, however. *Patience* and *endurance* are much more important for the marathoner.

THINKING AHEAD

Akio Morita, cofounder of the Sony Corporation, once turned down a deal that would have made a lot of money for his company. Soon after Sony was formed, the Bulova company offered to buy one hundred thousand of Sony's transistor radios. The deal was worth more than ten times the value of Morita's company, but he declined.

Why? Even though accepting the offer would have put cash in Morita's pocket, he knew it would have done nothing for Sony because Bulova wanted to put their own name on the radios. Morita wanted to sell Sony products, not products with someone else's name on them.

In his letter of refusal Morita told the Bulova company that in fifty years the name *Sony* would be as well known as the name *Bulova,* and that the radio that he had helped create would be one step toward that goal. Had he been thinking only of the short-term, Morita might have taken the offer. But because he was thinking long-term, he did not. History shows the wisdom of Morita's decision.

The writer of Hebrews encourages us to remain faithful to the long-term goal, no matter how appealing short-term distractions may be.

Many business leaders in the secular world grasp this concept. Do we in the church understand it as well as they?   —R. H.

B. The Example Before Us (vv. 2, 3)

2. Looking unto Jesus the author and finisher of our faith; who for the joy that was set before him endured the cross, despising the shame, and is set down at the right hand of the throne of God.

If our goal is to become Christlike, we must look to *Jesus* as both our model and our inspiration. The word *author* can be understood as "pioneer" or "trailblazer." Those terms appropriately suggest that He has gone ahead to mark the path for those who will follow.

As the *finisher* of our faith Jesus has completed that which is necessary for a victorious life. He did this by enduring *the cross.* He was willing to undergo that shame because He knew the joy of doing God's will.

That joy is complete now that He sits *at the right hand of the throne of God* (Hebrews 1:3, 13; 8:1; 10:12). This indicates that He has been restored to the glory that He knew before He came into the world.

3. For consider him that endured such contradiction of sinners against himself, lest ye be wearied and faint in your minds.

The Hebrew Christians are facing ridicule and persecution. The solution is to look to Christ. Under persecution, He was unwavering in His commitment to serve God. Looking to Him is the prevention to becoming *wearied and faint.* [See question #3, page 408.]

II. The Discipline of the Father (Hebrews 12:4-11)

A. Strength and Encouragement (vv. 4-10)

4. Ye have not yet resisted unto blood, striving against sin.

Christians are under constant "inward" attack by Satan; these attacks, of course, must be met and rejected. But many will have to face physical persecution for their faith as well. At the point in

---

How to Say It

ABRAHAM. *Ay*-bruh-ham.
DEUTERONOMY. Due-ter-*ahn*-uh-me.
HEBREWS. *Hee*-brews.
ISAAC. *Eye*-zuk.
ISAIAH. Eye-*zay*-uh.
JACOB. *Jay*-kub.
JEREMIAH. Jair-uh-*my*-uh.
MOSES. *Mo*-zes or *Mo*-zez.

time that the author writes, the Hebrew Christians apparently have not yet experienced such persecution. They undoubtedly know about the deaths of Stephen (Acts 7:54-60) and James (Acts 12:2), but they themselves *have not yet resisted unto blood.* But "not yet" can mean that martyrdom looms as a real possibility, and the readers have to be ready for it. [See question #4, page 408.]

5, 6. And ye have forgotten the exhortation which speaketh unto you as unto children, My son, despise not thou the chastening of the Lord, nor faint when thou art rebuked of him: for whom the Lord loveth he chasteneth, and scourgeth every son whom he receiveth.

Every parent must deal with the problem of disobedience when rearing children. Parents make a serious mistake if they allow disobedience to go uncorrected. To do so only encourages more disobedience, to the ultimate harm of the child. Today we see all too many cases where parents have abdicated their obligation to correct and chastise their children. The results are tragic for both the parents and the children.

We certainly are not suggesting that child abuse is ever appropriate, but many of us who are older can remember when a paddling at the hands of parents or teachers had tremendous value in correcting our behavior. We need to remember that even our Lord learned "obedience by the things which he suffered" (Hebrews 5:8). We may not be able to understand the full theological implications of that verse, but we can understand the practical application of it to our own lives. If our Lord had to learn obedience by suffering, how much more does that concept apply to us?

The Old Testament shows us that the children of God confronted Him with their disobedience time and again. God did not let their disobedience go unpunished. With that fact undoubtedly in mind, the writer now injects a quotation from Proverbs 3:11, 12 to make sure that the readers remember the connection between suffering and being a child of God.

Proverbs 3:11, 12 is a passage that the readers undoubtedly have heard before. It expresses a theme designed to help the readers recall that the many things their ancestors had suffered from other nations came because of disobedience (e.g., Deuteronomy 8; Jeremiah 31:18). The suffering of the Israelites came about many times when God deliberately raised up enemies as a means of punishment.

The writer wants the readers to understand that regardless of what the future might hold, God still loves them. The sufferings that they are to undergo may be the result of evil persecution or chastisement from God for sinful disobedience. If it is to be the latter, the readers should realize that God's chastisement grows out of love; it is neither vindictive nor based on a desire for revenge.

In those dark times when God punishes His wayward children, we must not forget that His actions grow out of love, out of concern to keep us on the narrow path (Matthew 7:14). If we forget this, we are likely to become bitter and resentful, crying out in self-pity, "Why me, God, why me?" When we were being punished for our misdeeds as children, it was not always obvious to us at the time that our parents loved us. In fact, we often resented both the punishment and them. Only as the years passed and we achieved a certain level of maturity did we come to realize that they punished us because they loved us.

7. If ye endure chastening, God dealeth with you as with sons; for what son is he whom the father chasteneth not?

This thought reinforces verse 6. When we accept chastening and realize its ultimate purpose, we rejoice in knowing that this is the process He is using to help us maintain a special relationship with Him. He is dealing with us *as sons.* (See Proverbs 13:24.)

8. But if ye be without chastisement, whereof all are partakers, then are ye bastards, and not sons. *Not eligible for eternal life*

The writer makes this next point quite sharply. All first-century Jews know that illegitimate sons do not have the same legal rights and privileges that the legitimate sons have regarding the parents' estate. Those who have been disciplined and have accepted it are the ones who are the legitimate *sons* of God. But those who have not been so chastened are illegitimate children.

If ye endure chastening, God dealeth with you as with sons.
Hebrews 12:7

Visual for lesson 8

Use this visual to remind your learners of the benefits and significance of discipline.

Parents naturally will discipline their own children as appropriate. But parents are not obligated to discipline children who are not under their legal care. When certain people receive no corrective discipline from God, that is proof of their status as "outsiders." They are not members of God's family and are not eligible to receive His eternal inheritance. Rejoice that you are not one of them!

9. Furthermore, we have had fathers of our flesh which corrected us, and we gave them reverence: shall we not much rather be in subjection unto the Father of spirits, and live?

Not all children grow to respect their parents who *corrected* them. Sometimes their parents had punished them harshly or unfairly, or without showing any love in the process.

Usually, however, children do grow up to respect their parents. That respect is likely to grow as the children themselves become parents and have to deal with their own offspring. If we as children have grown to respect our parents for the love they showed us and the sacrifices they made for us, how much more should we respect our Heavenly *Father* for all that He has done for us? [See question #5, page 408.]

10. For they verily for a few days chastened us after their own pleasure; but he for our profit, that we might be partakers of his holiness.

The chastening we received from our parents lasted for only *a few days*—that is, just a few years at most. The point is not that they enjoyed punishing us, which is how we normally think of the word *pleasure*. Rather, they did it according to the best knowledge that they had.

Unfortunately, they sometimes made mistakes in disciplining us. But not so with God. He deals with us wisely, seeing beyond the present to the future that He has in store for us. He does it so that we can become *partakers of his holiness*. Because He is holy, He wants us to be holy as well (1 Peter 1:16).

B. Hardship and Harvest (v. 11)

11. Now no chastening for the present seemeth to be joyous, but grievous: nevertheless, afterward it yieldeth the peaceable fruit of righteousness unto them which are exercised thereby.

No right-thinking person is likely to seek punishment! But when we understand and accept punishment as a part of God's plan, then we will enjoy *the peaceable fruit of righteousness*. This frees us from the bitterness and resentment that often results from suffering. With such freedom comes greater devotion to the Master. God's discipline is for our eternal good. God disciplines His people out of love (Revelation 3:19).

III. The Need to Get Moving (Hebrews 12:12, 13)

A. Strength, Not Feebleness (v. 12)

12. Wherefore lift up the hands which hang down, and the feeble knees.

Runners in the marathon, which is a distance of more than twenty-six miles, speak of a certain point in the race where they "hit the wall." That point is usually around the twenty-mile mark. At that point they suddenly are overwhelmed by the feeling that every ounce of energy in their body has been exhausted and they can't go any farther. The winners, of course, somehow reach down and find the strength to finish.

The writer seems to be describing Christians who have "hit the wall." They believe that they have exhausted every ounce of their spiritual energy and can't make it to the finish line. Dangling *hands* and *feeble knees* in a runner are signs of exhaustion. Runners look for these signs in their competitors and, seeing them, take new courage.

We can be certain that Satan is watching for every sign that might indicate that Christians are completely exhausted and will become easy prey for him. Here the faltering Christians are encouraged to put every bit of energy into one last effort to make the finish line. (See Isaiah 35:3.)

B. Healing, Not Lameness (v. 13)

13. And make straight paths for your feet, lest that which is lame be turned out of the way; but let it rather be healed.

Our lesson text concludes with a reference to Proverbs 4:26. *That which is lame* refers to weaker Christians. The stronger Christians are to help them. They do this by making *straight paths* for *feet* to *follow;* those Christians who have greater spiritual maturity have a responsibility that the less mature Christians *be healed,* and that none of them *be turned out of the way.* Undoubtedly this includes setting a good example. Christian leaders will give an account for how well they lead God's flock (Hebrews 13:17).

TEACHING BY EXAMPLE

Whit Criswell was ready to commit suicide when preacher Wayne B. Smith came to Whit's house. Whit owed $380,000, which he had embezzled from his own bank. He had spent all the money, and more, on gambling. After a long discussion Wayne prayed. Before he left he told Whit, "If you need anything, call me; I'll always be your friend."

Criswell went to the state prison for two years. "Wayne came to see me," Whit says. "When I was released to [a halfway house], Wayne came by to take me to a revival at the church. Afterward he invited me to go eat with him and the guest speaker and the musical group."

After Whit was allowed to go home, Wayne kept dropping by. He asked Whit to go places with him: hospital calling, a trustees' meeting at Wayne's alma mater, a sermon study group, and speaking engagements. Wayne also invited Whit to do volunteer work in the church, and he accepted. Before very long Wayne invited Whit to join the church staff. Today Whit Criswell is minister of his own church, which has grown from one hundred fifty to over seven hundred under his leadership.

Showing is always better than talking in the Christian life. Jesus wasn't "all talk"; He showed us how to live. It's up to us to pass that example along.   —R. H.

Conclusion

A. The Trailblazer

Many of us have thrilled to the stories of Daniel Boone, who made his way from Virginia across the Appalachian Mountains into what later became the states of Tennessee and Kentucky. As he traveled through the wilderness, he blazed a trail so that others could follow him into the rich lands in the West. He blazed that trail by chopping chunks of bark from large trees along the path he took. All one had to do to follow his trail was to watch for the blaze marks.

Several years ago I was involved in blazing some trails through a large wooded tract that our Christian camp was developing. We were modern Daniel Boones, but with a difference. We didn't chop patches of bark off the trees to blaze our trails because this practice is not good for the trees, even mature trees. Instead, we used the brightly colored plastic tape that is preferred by surveyors. We simply tied them around trees as we made a way through the woods. The tape could be seen readily by anyone wishing to follow the trail.

Jesus Christ, our divine trailblazer, has done a far better job than either Daniel Boone or we. When He blazed the trail to Heaven, He was the One who knew the way. He also knew our weakness and the problems we would face during our journey. On the night that He was betrayed, He said to His disciples, "I am the way, the truth, and the life: no man cometh unto the Father, but by me" (John 14:6). May we have the courage and the strength to follow Him no matter what the cost. May we also renew our failing devotion to Him when God disciplines us.

B. "Hitting the Wall"

Earlier we mentioned the expression "hitting the wall" as used by marathon runners. It is that point in the race when a runner suddenly feels that he or she can't go any farther.

Situations like that may develop in one's Christian life. One reaches a point of feeling unable to go on; the temptation is to drop out. That was the danger that the writer saw developing in the lives of some of the Jewish Christians who would be first to read the book of Hebrews.

That "wall" could be caused by several things. One potential hazard was ridicule and persecution. The Jewish Christians had not yet "resisted unto blood," but that possibility was very real in their day. In some parts of the world today that is a very real threat.

Another potential cause for dropping out is weariness (Galatians 6:9). Some people spend their entire lives serving a certain congregation. Then they come to retirement and retire from everything. Still another "wall" that some Christians hit is self-centeredness. They become so wrapped up in the busyness of personal and congregational life that they never seem to have time for true ministry: visiting the sick, feeding the hungry, etc. When people are active in helping others, that wall evaporates.

C. Prayer

Dear Father, we thank You for sending Your Son to set the example of faithful service, regardless of what it cost Him in suffering and shame. Teach us to lay aside the weights that hinder us and to run with perseverance the race of life. In our Lord's name we pray, amen.

D. Thought to Remember

When you feel weary,
remember that cloud of witnesses.

Home Daily Bible Readings

Monday, July 19—Happy Are Those God Disciplines (Psalm 94:8-15)

Tuesday, July 20—The LORD Your God Disciplines (Deuteronomy 8:1-5)

Wednesday, July 21—Run With Perseverance (Hebrews 12:1-6)

Thursday, July 22—Discipline Yields the Fruit of Righteousness (Hebrews 12:7-11)

Friday, July 23—Make Straight Paths for Your Feet (Hebrews 12:12-17)

Saturday, July 24—Watch How You Treat God's Grace (Hebrews 12:18-24)

Sunday, July 25—Offer God an Acceptable Worship (Hebrews 12:25-29)

Learning by Doing

This page contains an alternative lesson plan emphasizing learning activities.
Classes desiring such student involvement will find these suggestions helpful.

Learning Goals

After participating in this lesson, each student will be able to:

1. Identify the basic elements necessary to run a good spiritual race.

2. Express the importance of being patient and persistent when facing hardship.

3. Identify an impediment to a good spiritual race that he or she would like to lay aside.

Into the Lesson

Plan an interview with a present or former runner (marathons, high school track, etc.) or coach of runners. If possible, have this person dress for a race. Questions for the interview include (1) Tell us about the clothing people often wear for running. Why is this important? (2) What kind of preparation and training goes into getting ready for running a long-distance race? How is this different from training for sprints? (3) What "enemies" of runners make races difficult?

Thank the person interviewed. Make the transition to Bible study by telling the class we are going to talk about running a race, but not a race that competes against other persons. It is a race that is a test of spiritual endurance.

Into the Word

Prepare and display three posters. Each poster should have one of the three following headings: "In the Grandstands," "Preparations for the Race," and "Race Strategy." Read the Scripture text together, asking all to watch for words and phrases important to each heading on the posters.

After reading the text, allow the learners time to review the Scripture and look for this information. Write their answers on the posters. Each poster should include at least the following answers:

IN THE GRANDSTANDS
A cloud of witnesses (v. 1)
PREPARATIONS FOR THE RACE
Lay aside weights and sins (v. 1)
Expect suffering (vv. 4, 5)
Strengthen arms and legs (vv. 12, 13)
RACE STRATEGY
Be patient (v. 1)
Keep looking at Jesus (v. 2)
Endure chastening (vv. 7, 8)

After these have been listed, use the following "key word" activity to interpret the Scripture.

Write one of the following "key words" on each of ten slips of paper. Then roll them up, tying them with yarn or colored string. Ask teams of two people to select one of these "scrolls." Each team is to open and explain the concept or significance this key word has in today's study.

The "key words" that are to be written on the scrolls (one per scroll) follow:

Cloud of witnesses (v. 1. Remember, some witnesses may be friendly; some are not!)
Weight (v. 1)
Patience (v. 1)
Author and Finisher (v. 2)
Contradiction (v. 3)
Blood (v. 4)
Chastening (v. 7)
Sons (vv. 7-10)
Joyous and Grievous (v. 11)
Paths (vv. 12, 13)

Into Life

Prepare the following full-page handout for each person. Answer most of these questions and assignments as a whole class. However, also give a few moments for individuals to respond to the personal questions or tasks.

HEARING CHEERING!

We all love to have people cheering us on—even in our spiritual race of life. Who are some of the people typically cheering Christians on in their spiritual race? List them here.

Now, name one or two special people who are in your cheering section.

RATS IN THE RACE!

Our Scripture tells us there are hindrances or impediments a Christian must lose in order to run a successful race. What are some of the common weights believers may find strapped to their ankles that may impede this most important race of life?

Circle one or two impediments that may keep you from running this race well.

FINISHING FINE!

How would you define or picture a person who has finished life's race well? What habits, patterns, or values do you see in this top-notch spiritual athlete?

Circle one of these qualities that you would like to practice better in this week's race. Look for ways to let this habit or quality blossom in your life as you run the race.

Let's Talk It Over

The questions on this page are designed to promote discussion of the lesson by the class and to encourage application of the lesson Scriptures. The answers provided are only discussion starters. Let your class talk it over from there.

1. Who is watching you "run the race" of the Christian life? How does knowing that they are watching affect your behavior?

Unfortunately, many unbelievers are watching and just waiting for Christians to slip up so they can gleefully point it out. Knowing that, we should be extra careful not to give them cause to celebrate our failures. On the other hand, one Christian woman admitted that she would not put a Christian bumper sticker on her car because she didn't want other drivers to associate her driving habits with Christianity. How much better if she worked harder at driving in a way that would bring honor to the Lord!

But there are others who are not looking to criticize. Young people need good role models. Adults who wrestle with the same temptations we struggle with are helped when we model the strength to overcome. May all those who witness our behavior be helped by it.

2. What sorts of things hinder you as you run the race of faith?

We all encounter things that "drag down" our faith, although those drags will vary from person to person. Our text relates these drags to sin.

Perhaps it is difficult to think honestly and objectively about the sins that beset each of us. However, a periodic inventory is a useful exercise in order to know what sins we need to guard against. Even though we have the power of the Holy Spirit, it is possible to become "entangled" in some sins. These are the kinds of sins that, if indulged, can slow us down, even to the point of pulling us out of the race of faith. The best antidote for this is to stay focused on Jesus Christ.

3. How has attention to Jesus helped you endure the hardships that can come as a result of Christian faith?

Not everything we must do in the Christian life is pleasant right now, but we must look beyond our struggles as Jesus did. As Hebrews 12:2 tells us, Jesus looked *beyond* the cross to the joy that would follow.

So when a co-worker maligns us, we remember Jesus, who endured far worse! When a supposed friend fails us, we remember Jesus was betrayed by Judas and denied by Peter—but still He persevered. When we do not get credit for all the hard work that we do, we remember that we are serving Jesus, not serving for earthly attention. Your learners can add specific details to each of these examples and many more.

4. Although almost no one in modern North America is threatened with death for Christian faith, what are some examples from around the world of Christians currently facing the prospect of martyrdom? What should you do about this sobering reality?

Although Christians often have faced persecution, some observers predict that the twenty-first century will become "the age of martyrs." Communist China has seen much persecution in recent years. The same can be said of certain Middle Eastern and African countries that are influenced by Islam.

Others countries, while they do not threaten Christians with death, require at least outward submission to the state religion in order for people to enjoy the full benefits of citizenship. Many Western countries have had such a long tradition of religious tolerance that their citizens can forget that Christians often face deadly opposition in places that do not hold the same values. There are many ways to respond, but all responses begin with prayer.

5. What are some ways that you are grateful for how your parents disciplined you as a child? How would you have been different if they hadn't? What parallels do you see to their discipline and God's?

Be cautious with this question, as it may present an opportunity for some to express bitterness toward parents who were harsh in their discipline. You can note that the writer of Hebrews makes a parallel between God's discipline and a father's discipline. A father is supposed to discipline us to make us better. God disciplines us to make us more holy.

What is assumed in Hebrews 12:7-9 is that discipline, both earthly and Heavenly, is necessary. Many parents fail to enforce obedience with their children, sometimes with very obvious results! When that attitude comes full bloom, we find people approaching God without realizing that becoming what He wants us to be will often cause discomfort.

Select Good Leaders

August 1
Lesson 9

DEVOTIONAL READING: Acts 20:17-32.

BACKGROUND SCRIPTURE: 1 Timothy 3:1-13; 5:17-19.

PRINTED TEXT: 1 Timothy 3:1-13; 5:17-19.

1 Timothy 3:1-13

1 This is a true saying, If a man desire the office of a bishop, he desireth a good work.

2 A bishop then must be blameless, the husband of one wife, vigilant, sober, of good behavior, given to hospitality, apt to teach;

3 Not given to wine, no striker, not greedy of filthy lucre; but patient, not a brawler, not covetous;

4 One that ruleth well his own house, having his children in subjection with all gravity;

5 (For if a man know not how to rule his own house, how shall he take care of the church of God?)

6 Not a novice, lest being lifted up with pride he fall into the condemnation of the devil.

7 Moreover he must have a good report of them which are without; lest he fall into reproach and the snare of the devil.

8 Likewise must the deacons be grave, not double-tongued, not given to much wine, not greedy of filthy lucre;

9 Holding the mystery of the faith in a pure conscience.

10 And let these also first be proved; then let them use the office of a deacon, being found blameless.

11 Even so must their wives be grave, not slanderers, sober, faithful in all things.

12 Let the deacons be the husbands of one wife, ruling their children and their own houses well.

13 For they that have used the office of a deacon well purchase to themselves a good degree, and great boldness in the faith which is in Christ Jesus.

1 Timothy 5:17-19

17 Let the elders that rule well be counted worthy of double honor, especially they who labor in the word and doctrine.

18 For the Scripture saith, Thou shalt not muzzle the ox that treadeth out the corn. And, The laborer is worthy of his reward.

19 Against an elder receive not an accusation, but before two or three witnesses.

GOLDEN TEXT: Holding the mystery of the faith in a pure conscience.—1 Timothy 3:9.

---

*Guidelines for
the Church's Ministry*
(Lessons 9-13)

Lesson Aims

After participating in this lesson, each student should be able to:

1. Describe the two basic offices in the early church.

2. List some of the essential qualities that church officers are expected to possess.

3. Write a letter of appreciation to a church leader who is faithfully fulfilling the required duties of the office.

Lesson Outline

INTRODUCTION
   A. The Need
   B. Lesson Background
I. QUALITIES OF ELDERS (1 Timothy 3:1-7)
   A. Desire (v. 1)
   B. Blameless and Faithful (vv. 2a, 2b)
   C. Disciplined and Hospitable (vv. 2c, 2d)
   D. Communicator (v. 2e)
   E. Not Addicted (v. 3a)
   F. Temperament (v. 3b)
   G. Orderly Family (vv. 4, 5)
   H. Spiritual Maturity (v. 6)
   I. Good Reputation (v. 7)
     The High Road to Leadership
II. QUALITIES OF DEACONS (1 Timothy 3:8-13)
   A. Respectable and Sincere (vv. 8a, 8b)
   B. Not Addicted (v. 8c)
   C. Having a Pure Conscience (v. 9)
   D. Tested (v. 10)
   E. Family Conduct (vv. 11-13)
III. CHURCH'S RESPONSIBILITIES (1 Timothy 5:17-19)
   A. Show Appreciation to Leaders (vv. 17, 18)
     Honor to Whom Honor Is Due
   B. Show Fairness to Leaders (v. 19)
CONCLUSION
   A. Church Leaders Are Different!
   B. Prayer
   C. Thought to Remember

Introduction

A. The Need

Leadership is one of the hot-button issues of our time. You cannot peruse the business section of a bookstore without seeing many books on the subject. It is of crucial importance in the church as well. There are nearly as many books on leadership in the average Christian bookstore as there are in a secular bookstore.

No one in the business world would dispute the significance a leader has on an organization. Certainly no one on a sports team would dispute it either. Enter the world of the military and you will find agreement there as well. This lesson is about Paul's advice to Timothy on how to choose good leaders for the church.

B. Lesson Background

A first-century man named Timothy received two important letters that bear his name. Timothy was Paul's son in the faith (1 Timothy 1:2). Evidently Paul had no children of his own, but Timothy was like a son to him.

Paul met Timothy, who was already a disciple, while on a missionary journey (Acts 16:1-5). Timothy became one of Paul's most trusted associates. Paul typically gave Timothy challenging assignments (1 Corinthians 4:17; 16:10; Philippians 2:19, 22; 1 Thessalonians 3:2). This may explain the need for the letters of 1 Timothy and 2 Timothy.

These two letters plus Titus are grouped together in the Scriptures and are commonly referred to as the Pastoral Epistles. They live up to their designation! Paul not only gives advice on how a church is to be pastored (shepherded), he also does some pastoring himself with Timothy and Titus.

One important area where these two disciples required the apostle's counsel concerned the issue of church leaders. As the first-century church expanded, it began to require more structured leadership in local congregations.

One distinct office that the New Testament mentions is that of "elder." This office is also known as an "overseer" or "bishop." (The Greek words *presbyteros* and *episkopos* that lie behind our English translations mean the same thing in Acts 20:17, 28 and Titus 1:5, 7). Over the centuries the word *bishop* has come to mean someone in authority over several churches, but that concept is not found in the New Testament.

Elders were also known as pastors or shepherds (Ephesians 4:11). Today, the term *pastor* is often used to designate a preaching minister, but in the New Testament it was a term used for the office of elder.

Another office was that of *deacon*. This is a Greek word that means "servant" in a general sense, but in certain contexts it refers to a specific office of the church. At some point in the expansion of first-century Christianity, local churches came to have both elders (or bishops or overseers) and deacons (see Philippians 1:1).

I. Qualities of Elders
(1 Timothy 3:1-7)

Paul gives a long list of qualities that provide a profile of a great Christian leader. [See question #1, page 416.] Some are very similar to one another and therefore related. There is also a great deal of overlap with Titus 1:6-9.

A. Desire (v. 1)

1. This is a true saying, If a man desire the office of a bishop, he desireth a good work.

When Paul relates this *true saying,* is he quoting an old adage, quoting a previous teaching of his own that Timothy is familiar with, or creating a new saying as he writes? We can't be sure. What's most important is the truthfulness of the saying itself: it is indeed an honorable thing to *desire* to be a Christian leader. There is such a thing as selfish ambition (Luke 22:24-27), but that is not the same as the humble desire and willingness to lead.

B. Blameless and Faithful (vv. 2a, 2b)

2a. A bishop then must be blameless.

The general idea of being *blameless* cannot, of course, be taken as an absolute—otherwise we would expect leaders to be perfect! It is more the idea that no one should look at a prospective elder and think, "Oh, no! Not him!" Some students think that what Paul specifically means by *blameless* can be found in the list that follows.

2b. The husband of one wife.

This phrase has sparked much debate. Most students agree that it means that an elder must be, or must have been, married. Is Paul making that an absolute requirement? If so, neither he nor Jesus could have been an elder. (And, of course, neither of them was an elder!) There is no doubt that some qualities of pastoral care are learned best in family life.

What of those who were once married but are no longer? Very few Bible students believe Paul means to exclude widowers. Literally, *husband of one wife* is a "one-wife man" or even a "one-

woman [kind of] man." (The word for *wife* in the Greek is simply the word for *woman.*) We can be certain that a bigamist, or man with a mistress, could not be considered. The issue the church struggles with today is whether or not a divorced man may be an elder. If we take this to mean "a one-woman [kind of] man," then the issue is the man's own personal faithfulness. Even if a man's wife has been unfaithful, he may still very well be a one-woman man.

Many churches look at this issue on a case-by-case basis. What is indisputable is that the quality of a person's marriage affects his ability to lead. [See question #2, page 416.]

C. Disciplined and Hospitable (vv. 2c, 2d)

2c. Vigilant, sober, of good behavior.

This verse continues with virtues that almost speak for themselves. Being *vigilant* and *sober* both point to the ability to control one's desires. (See also Titus 1:8.) *Good behavior* includes the idea of living an honorable life.

2d. Given to hospitality.

Given to hospitality is literally to be a "lover of strangers." It refers to the willingness to give food or shelter to travelers or visitors. Traveling prophets and evangelists were in particular need of such *hospitality.* Paul himself was a recipient of this type of kindness. (See Romans 12:13; Titus 1:8; Hebrews 13:2; 1 Peter 4:9; contrast 2 John 10.)

D. Communicator (v. 2e)

2e. Apt to teach.

Being *apt to teach* does not require an elder to be a distinguished orator or dynamic speaker. But he should be able to explain the gospel, at least in a private setting. Teaching is one of the spiritual gifts listed in Romans 12:7 and Ephesians 4:11.

E. Not Addicted (v. 3a)

3a. Not given to wine.

Wine was common in the ancient world, and its dangers were well known then as now. Passages such as Proverbs 21:17; 23:20, 21, 29-32 are very plain on the dangers of alcohol.

There are practical and spiritual reasons for modern Christians to practice total abstinence, but that subject is not addressed here. Paul's restriction logically may be extended to all unhealthy addictions to the various legal and illegal drugs that confront us in news reports every day.

F. Temperament (v. 3b)

3b. No striker, not greedy of filthy lucre; but patient, not a brawler, not covetous.

How to Say It

CORINTH. *Kor*-inth.

CORINTHIANS. Kor-*in*-thee-unz (*th* as in *thin*).

DEUTERONOMY. Due-ter-*ahn*-uh-me.

EPISKOPOS (Greek). ee-*pih*-skoh-pos.

NEOPHYTE. *nee*-uh-fite.

PHILIPPIANS. Fih-*lip*-ee-unz.

PRESBYTEROS (Greek). prez-*bu*-ter-os.

THESSALONIANS. *Thess*-uh-*lo*-nee-unz (strong accent on *lo*; *th* as in *thin*).

There is, of course, quite a bit of overlap between the ideas of being a *striker* and a *brawler*—they're almost the same thing. We perhaps should not see this idea as unconnected from the discussion of wine earlier in this verse when we consider that those who abuse alcohol are frequently the ones who get into fights. Those who are not convinced of this need only watch one or two episodes of the TV show *Cops* to be persuaded otherwise!

Someone who is *covetous* is in direct violation of the Tenth Commandment (Exodus 20:17). The phrase *not greedy of filthy lucre* does not appear in the oldest Greek manuscripts, although that idea is almost the same as being *covetous*. Titus 1:7 does contain this phrase with regard to elders, so the concept is certainly present in Paul's thinking.

We should be careful to remember that the acquisition of wealth is not a sin in and of itself. But both those who need money and those who already have plenty are in danger of developing a sinful attitude. See 1 Timothy 6:10.

G. Orderly Family (vv. 4, 5)

4, 5. One that ruleth well his own house, having his children in subjection with all gravity; (for if a man know not how to rule his own house, how shall he take care of the church of God?)

Once again there is a point of controversy here. Does this verse mean that the elder must have children, or is Paul simply discussing the typical or normal situation? There are men today who will not allow themselves to be considered for the office of elder because they take what Paul says quite literally.

It is certainly true that lessons learned from managing one's *own house* can affect how well a man serves as an elder. When Paul says *house,* he has in mind a household, which includes all who dwell under the same roof. If a church leader has not displayed leadership in his own home, he will find it difficult to exercise Christian leadership in *the church.* Many of the leadership and interpersonal skills learned in the home will work in the church.

H. Spiritual Maturity (v. 6)

6. Not a novice, lest being lifted up with pride he fall into the condemnation of the devil.

If we take the Greek word translated *novice* and pronounce it in English it comes out as our word *neophyte.* The danger of selecting a novice or neophyte to be elder is quite clear, and the Bible talks about the issue of *pride* in numerous places (e.g., Proverbs 11:2; 13:10; 16:18; Romans 12:16). Spiritually mature believers truly know what it means to bear the responsibility of being an elder. This knowledge will create the humility that a leader needs. [See question #3, page 416.]

I. Good Reputation (v. 7)

7. Moreover he must have a good report of them which are without; lest he fall into reproach and the snare of the devil.

Leaders should be respected. This should be true not just among Christians, but also by the community as a whole. Can the church really have a good witness if its leaders are known scoundrels?

The *snare* or trap *of the devil* is probably the sin of pride (see v. 6, above). It is assumed that the besetting sin of the devil, the sin that caused him to be cast from Heaven, was pride.

THE HIGH ROAD TO LEADERSHIP

Allen Iverson of the Philadelphia 76ers is recognized as much for his behavior off the court as his play on the court. Known as one of the "bad boys" of the NBA, he maintained this image in July, 2002, when he was charged with four felony and ten misdemeanor counts in conjunction with an alleged attack on his estranged wife.

The Reebok company, which extended an existing contract with Iverson in 2001 for fifty million dollars, did not even flinch when the charges were announced. Instead, a Reebok spokesman said, "It is Allen's celebrity status, not the facts, that continue to fuel these proceedings." Alan Brown, a sports marketing agent, said, "It might even help sales. Yes, it's the bad boy image, but the bad boy image unfortunately right now is what sells, and he's the best bad boy out there."

In a world that looks more to image than character, the church must hold true to God's Word in regard to leadership. Nowhere is this more important than in the selection of leadership for the local congregation.

What a leader does "off the court" affects the work in leading the church of the Lord Jesus. Character qualities such as being disciplined, peaceable, and above reproach are necessary in a world that too often values the opposite.

—A. E. A.

II. Qualities of Deacons (1 Timothy 3:8-13)

The Greek word *deacon* occurs nearly one hundred times in the New Testament, in various forms. Often it means simply "servant" in a general sense.

But here Paul uses this word to refer to a specific office of the church. Many students think that the very first deacons are listed in Acts 6:1-6, although the specific word *deacon* does not occur there. Many of the qualities of deacon overlap with the qualities of elder, so it will not be necessary to discuss those that are repeated.

A. Respectable and Sincere (vv. 8a, 8b)

8a. Likewise must the deacons be grave.

Grave, in the sense given here, is not a word we use much any longer. The idea is one of dignity and seriousness. Can you imagine what it would be like for a church to have deacons who took nothing seriously, who had a flippant attitude toward everything?

8b. Not double-tongued.

The negative *not double-tongued* expresses the quality of sincerity. A godly deacon is not someone who says one thing to one person and something completely different to another. A double-tongued person is probably double-minded as well (see James 1:8).

B. Not Addicted (v. 8c)

8c. Not given to much wine, not greedy of filthy lucre.

See the previous discussion in verse 3, above. Although elders have the greater authority, deacons must meet the same high standards.

C. Having a Pure Conscience (v. 9)

9. Holding the mystery of the faith in a pure conscience.

What was a great *mystery* to those who lived in Old Testament times has now been more fully revealed as the gospel of Christ (Romans 16:25, 26). What was once hidden is now revealed (Colossians 1:26). Paul desperately wants all believers to know these truths (Ephesians 3:1-6). Deacons need to understand these great truths *of the faith* and believe them with *a pure conscience.*

D. Tested (v. 10)

10. And let these also first be proved; then let them use the office of a deacon, being found blameless.

To be *proved* is to undergo testing. Some students think that this suggests that an apprenticeship for deacons is appropriate. Whatever means of testing is used, the end result must be that potential deacons be *found blameless,* as potential elders are to be (see v. 2, above). [See question #4, page 416.]

E. Family Conduct (vv. 11-13)

11. Even so must their wives be grave, not slanderers, sober, faithful in all things.

The conduct of their *wives* will reveal the quality of a potential deacon's home life. As with elders, a deacon is very unlikely to be able to

Visual for lesson 9

This visual will remind your learners of God's expectations for church leaders.

take care of the church if his home life is chaotic (see v. 4, above, and vv. 12, 13, next).

12, 13. Let the deacons be the husbands of one wife, ruling their children and their own houses well. For they that have used the office of a deacon well purchase to themselves a good degree, and great boldness in the faith which is in Christ Jesus.

Again, the ideas here mirror what Paul has already said in verse 4, above. After reminding Timothy that *deacons* are also to be good *husbands* and fathers, Paul goes on to commend deacons for their significant work. Does the mention of *a good degree* and *great boldness* speak to the deacon's excellent standing in the eyes of God, the eyes of the church, or the eyes of the community? It could be all three.

We should pause to note that there is nothing in these verses to indicate that the office of deacon is to be considered some kind of stepping-stone to the office of elder. Some might remain deacons for the rest of their lives. Each office has a purpose in the church. The two have different functions, but both are important.

III. Church's Responsibilities (1 Timothy 5:17-19)

Godly leaders are so important! Churches must not neglect their obligations to them.

A. Show Appreciation to Leaders (vv. 17, 18)

17, 18. Let the elders that rule well be counted worthy of double honor, especially they who labor in the word and doctrine. For the Scripture saith, Thou shalt not muzzle the ox that treadeth out the corn. And, The laborer is worthy of his reward.

Notice that *elders* are the ones who *rule* the church, and it appears that certain ones of those early elders were to receive some kind of *double honor.* The Scripture that Paul uses to back this up is Deuteronomy 25:4.

The way Paul uses this passage, both here and in 1 Corinthians 9:7-12, gives us the idea that the *double honor* includes some kind of pay. It seems that in many first-century churches, at least some elders may have served in full-time positions. This supports the concept of paid ministry. [See question #5, page 416.]

Although all Christians are ministers in a general sense, some are paid and have responsibility to serve full-time. But financial compensation is probably only half of this *double honor.* The other half that these elders are to receive is the honor of respect.

HONOR TO WHOM HONOR IS DUE

Selecting leaders with high integrity and good character is vital for the success of a church. But an often-overlooked ingredient in the successful church is the need for good followers.

Good followers show respect for their leaders. Sadly, however, respect for authority has eroded in modern culture. Not only is this evident with regard to leaders in government or schools, but also is apparent in the church. Resigning from church roles, withholding of offerings, missing church services, and maligning the character of the church leader is evidence of poor "followership" and lack of respect.

In all areas of life respect for those over you is vital. In the battle for Europe during World War II, Major General George S. Patton was loyal to his commanding officer, General Dwight Eisenhower, even though at times he was so disgusted with his superior that he wouldn't speak to him.

During the Korean War, however, General Douglas MacArthur failed to show proper respect to President Harry S. Truman.

MacArthur ignored the chain of command in military decision-making and began writing letters to the Veterans of Foreign Wars as well as to the Speaker of the House about what the United States should do in Korea. So President Truman fired him. As Truman explained, avoidance of World War III while containing aggression was a difficult line to walk, but that was the policy the United States had decided upon. No soldier, not even a five-star general, could challenge that policy without disturbing an essential element of democratic government.

Just as a nation is dependent upon the proper lines of respect for smooth operation, so a church needs people who respect and honor those in leadership positions. Without proper lines of respect and authority a nation is vulnerable to attacks from its enemies. And without the adherence to proper respect to appropriate authority within the church, Satan himself, the ultimate enemy, will attack and destroy. —A. E. A.

B. Show Fairness to Leaders (v. 19)

19. Against an elder receive not an accusation, but before two or three witnesses.

Leaders will always receive criticism. Sometimes they will even be the subject of slander. However, no *accusation* should be entertained unless *two or three witnesses* support it. This is consistent with Old Testament law (Deuteronomy 17:6; 19:15) and is consistent with what Paul told the church at Corinth (2 Corinthians 13:1).

Conclusion

A. Church Leaders Are Different!

Everyone agrees that leadership is complex. Some seem to exercise it intuitively. Others have to study, practice, make mistakes, and grow. While there is much the church can learn from the world on leadership techniques, the church must remember that its leaders operate by a different set of rules. There is no institution quite like the church. There is no authority quite like Christ. That is the reason we need Paul's advice. That's the reason we need the Holy Spirit's strength.

B. Prayer

Gracious Father, thank You for the privilege of service in Your church. Help us each to accept the responsibility that comes with the privilege. In Jesus' name, amen.

C. Thought to Remember

No church will grow beyond its leaders.

Home Daily Bible Readings

Monday, July 26—Select Those Full of the Spirit (Acts 6:1-7)

Tuesday, July 27—Paul Didn't Shrink From His Ministry (Acts 20:17-24)

Wednesday, July 28—Keep Watch Over the Flock (Acts 20:25-31)

Thursday, July 29—Remember Your Leaders (Hebrews 13:7-17)

Friday, July 30—A Bishop Must Be Above Reproach (1 Timothy 3:1-7)

Saturday, July 31—Deacons Must Be Serious (1 Timothy 3:8-13)

Sunday, Aug. 1—Good Leaders—Worthy of Double Honor (1 Timothy 5:17-22)

Learning by Doing

This page contains an alternative lesson plan emphasizing learning activities.
Classes desiring such student involvement will find these suggestions helpful.

Learning Goals

After this lesson each student will be able to:

1. Describe the two basic offices in the early church.

2. List some of the essential qualities that church officers are expected to possess.

3. Write a letter of appreciation to a church leader who is faithfully fulfilling the required duties of the office.

Into the Lesson

To begin the class, distribute these open-ended statements on paper and instruct your students to complete them, or direct the class to this activity in the student books, where the statements are reprinted:

1. My idea of a good elder is. . . .

2. To be a good deacon, a man must. . . .

3. The best way for a church to show appreciation for its leaders is to. . . .

When they finish, ask volunteers to share their work. Tell your class that today's lesson will deal with Paul's word to Timothy on characteristics of good leaders for the church.

Into the Word

Divide your class into an equal number of groups of four to six students. Half of your groups will do *Study A*, about elders, below. The other half will do *Study B*, about deacons. Copy the lists onto a two-column chart and give a chart to each group. Column one will list Qualifications; column two will provide space for the students to list Values. (Some examples are listed below to stimulate thought.) After they finish their work, discuss each group's findings with the whole class, comparing them with earlier comments in the "Into the Lesson" exercise.

Study A

Read 1 Timothy 3:1-7; then complete this chart, indicating the value to the church and to the elder of each qualification below.

Qualifications: desires office; blameless; one wife; vigilant; sober; good behavior; hospitable; apt to teach; not given to alcoholic beverages; not violent; not greedy; patient; not a brawler; not covetous; rules family well; submissive children; not a novice; good reputation.

Values: *If an elder "desires the office," he will not have to be recruited nor convinced; he will be* more likely to persist in service; for example, if a leader is "blameless," there will be no disagreement as to his suitability for spiritual leadership, and he will be a good model of righteousness to those within the church and those without.

Study B

Read 1 Timothy 3:8-13, then complete this chart, indicating the value to the church and to the deacon of each qualification below.

Qualifications: respectable; sincere; not given to alcoholic beverages; not greedy; good conscience; proven; respectable wife; truthful wife; sober wife; faithful wife; one wife; rules family well.

Values: *If a deacon is "respectable," people will be more likely to follow him in service projects; if he is "not an alcoholic," he is demonstrating the self-control that is a primary fruit of the Spirit.*

After reviewing the qualifications of church leaders, turn your class's attention to a discussion of the church's responsibilities to those leaders in 1 Timothy 5:17-19.

Into Life

Provide a handout with the following hypothetical situations written on it. Ask your class to suggest Scriptural answers for each situation.

1. An elder in your congregation has been accused of serious wrongdoing by another member. How should the church collectively handle the situation to be fair to the elder, the accuser, and the congregation?

2. An elder in your congregation has faithfully served in the position for over twenty-five years —much longer than anyone in the congregation's history. What would be an appropriate way to honor him and encourage him for his distinguished service?

3. A young man in your church has let it be known that he would like to be elected to the office of deacon. How should your congregation go about evaluating his qualifications? (It would be very useful to secure a copy of your congregation's bylaws or policy on selecting leaders to compare it with the class's response.)

4. A well-qualified, mature member of your congregation has been nominated to be an elder, but another member has objected to the nomination because the candidate is a widower and no longer "the husband of one wife." How should the leadership deal with such an objection?

Let's Talk It Over

*The questions on this page are designed to promote discussion of the lesson
by the class and to encourage application of the lesson Scriptures. The answers
provided are only discussion starters. Let your class talk it over from there.*

**1. The lesson writer refers to leadership
"qualities." How would that be different from
seeing Paul's list as "qualifications"? How
would this distinction help in addressing some
of the troublesome issues that arise in connection with some of the traits listed?**

Qualities are general traits that may be present
in varying degrees, while *qualifications* are absolutes. A person must meet all "qualifications,"
or he is disqualified, ineligible. A person may
possess some "qualities" to a great extent but be
deficient in others and still belong to the class of
people known by these general qualities.

Seeing these lists as *qualities* accounts for
growth in elders and deacons. Taking them as
qualifications demands a high level of maturity,
which is admirable. It may, however, disqualify
people who have made mistakes in the past without offering any way to live down those mistakes.

**2. What do you think about having divorced
men serve as elders or in paid ministry positions? What dangers are present when divorced
men are allowed to hold such positions? What
dangers are present when they are not?**

Some take the phrase "husband of one wife" to
mean that divorced men may not be elders. Certainly the need for elders and paid ministry staff
to set a good example should make us cautious
about calling a divorced man to one of these positions. But divorce is a complicated issue, and it
happens for a number of reasons. Sometimes a
person is extremely immature when he or she
marries, and the marriage fails as a result of immature behavior by one or both parties. Some
people are divorced through no fault of their own.

Prohibiting divorced people from serving in
these positions sets a high standard of fidelity for
the leadership—and thus for the church. It may,
however, prevent some capable people who have
learned some hard lessons from serving where
they are gifted. Some fear that allowing the divorced to serve opens the door for relaxed moral
standards and increases the risk that a leader
will bring scandal into the church. Others caution that outright prohibition introduces a legalism of the sort that Paul consistently opposes.

**3. Paul says an elder is not to be a "novice."
How long does someone have to be a Christian**

to be no longer a novice? What factors other
than time need to be considered?

Setting a specific number of months or years
that a man must be a Christian before he can be
an elder is probably more legalistic than Paul intended us to be. Some new Christians mature
rapidly, plunging into Bible study and other faith-
building events. Others seem to remain perpetual
"babes in Christ." Still, it would seem that a person needs time to be tested in his faith and to
weather a few storms before he is made an elder.
This takes more than a few months in most cases.

**4. How can a potential deacon be "proved"?
What kind of testing do you think is required to
be a deacon? And why do you suppose there is
not a requirement for the elder to be "proved"?**

This is similar to the requirement that an elder
not be a "novice" (v. 6). We can approach this
issue by remembering that a deacon is a "servant." He will be proved by service. Whether this
is a formal apprenticeship or merely a recognition of the candidate's servant-heart, it is service
that will distinguish a qualified deacon. Like the
elder, the deacon will need to have been a Christian—and even affiliated with the church that is
selecting him as deacon—for some period of time
for his character to become well known.

**5. If it was the "elders" who "labored in the
preaching of the word" in the New Testament
church, why do we have paid preachers today?
What advantages do you see in having a paid
preacher instead of a preaching eldership?
What advantages can you see in having preaching elders instead of a paid preacher?**

The first-century church had "evangelists"
(Acts 21:8; 2 Timothy 4:5), and that position may
resemble more closely our paid preachers today.
The New Testament pattern is rather fluid here.
In some churches one or more elders did the
preaching; others were served by evangelists.

Today we have Bible colleges and other training institutions to help people specialize in ministry. Most elders do not have that kind of
training, and their churches are better served by
those who do. But in smaller churches or in
some cultures in the world today, preaching elders may still provide the best mix of ability and
stewardship for the congregation to honor Christ.

Be Ministers of Godliness

DEVOTIONAL READING: 2 Peter 1:3-11.

BACKGROUND SCRIPTURE: 1 Timothy 4:6–5:16.

PRINTED TEXT: 1 Timothy 4:7–5:8.

1 Timothy 4:7-16

7 But refuse profane and old wives' fables, and exercise thyself rather unto godliness.

8 For bodily exercise profiteth little: but godliness is profitable unto all things, having promise of the life that now is, and of that which is to come.

9 This is a faithful saying, and worthy of all acceptation.

10 For therefore we both labor and suffer reproach, because we trust in the living God, who is the Saviour of all men, specially of those that believe.

11 These things command and teach.

12 Let no man despise thy youth; but be thou an example of the believers, in word, in conversation, in charity, in spirit, in faith, in purity.

13 Till I come, give attendance to reading, to exhortation, to doctrine.

14 Neglect not the gift that is in thee, which was given thee by prophecy, with the laying on of the hands of the presbytery.

15 Meditate upon these things; give thyself wholly to them; that thy profiting may appear to all.

16 Take heed unto thyself, and unto the doctrine; continue in them: for in doing this thou shalt both save thyself, and them that hear thee.

1 Timothy 5:1-8

1 Rebuke not an elder, but entreat him as a father; and the younger men as brethren;

2 The elder women as mothers; the younger as sisters, with all purity.

3 Honor widows that are widows indeed.

4 But if any widow have children or nephews, let them learn first to show piety at home, and to requite their parents: for that is good and acceptable before God.

5 Now she that is a widow indeed, and desolate, trusteth in God, and continueth in supplications and prayers night and day.

6 But she that liveth in pleasure is dead while she liveth.

7 And these things give in charge, that they may be blameless.

8 But if any provide not for his own, and specially for those of his own house, he hath denied the faith, and is worse than an infidel.

GOLDEN TEXT: For bodily exercise profiteth little: but godliness is profitable unto all things, having promise of the life that now is, and of that which is to come.
—1 Timothy 4:8.

Guidelines for
the Church's Ministry
(Lessons 9-13)

Lesson Aims

After participating in this lesson, each student should be able to:

1. Identify the qualities demonstrated by a faithful servant of God.

2. Express the importance of spiritual training in the life of a Christian servant.

3. Devise a spiritual training program that he or she will follow.

Lesson Outline

INTRODUCTION
    A. To the Gym, to the Church, or Both?
    B. Lesson Background
I. LIFESTYLE OF THE GODLY MINISTER (1 Timothy 4:7-10)
    A. Go Into Training (vv. 7-9)
        Training for the Long Run
    B. Trust God (v. 10)
II. DUTIES OF THE GODLY MINISTER (1 Timothy 4: 11-16)
    A. Teaching and Modeling (vv. 11, 12)
    B. Ministering and Sustaining (vv. 13, 14)
    C. Diligence and Perseverance (vv. 15, 16)
III. SKILLS OF THE GODLY MINISTER (1 Timothy 5: 1-8)
    A. Relating to Men of All Ages (v. 1)
        Reviving Respect
    B. Relating to Women of All Ages (v. 2)
    C. Relating to Widows of All Ages (vv. 3-8)
CONCLUSION
    A. It's Not Easy
    B. Prayer
    C. Thought to Remember

Introduction

A. To the Gym, to the Church, or Both?

Have you noticed how many gyms and health clubs there are around you? Have you seen the advertisements for exercise gadgets and diet programs on television, in magazines, and even on little signs posted on utility poles? No one would suggest that it is wrong to pursue good health. Good nutrition and exercise are important—even good stewardship of our lives. But Paul reminds us that whatever commitment we give to physical well-being is secondary to spiritual training.

This is just one of the issues Paul tackles in the lesson before us. He will also deal with matters of church dynamics, relationships, and doctrinal purity. A healthy church pays close attention to such issues. Our "spiritual workout" today will prepare us to witness and grow for Christ as Timothy did nearly two thousand years ago.

B. Lesson Background

Last week we studied a list of characteristics or qualities that should be present in potential leaders in the church. This week we study a passage that forced Timothy to take a long look at himself and his ministry. It is important for us to remember that these letters to Timothy are like personal notes to him—we are reading his mail.

Paul was not afraid to give Timothy the difficult assignments and the tough advice. This is what equips Timothy to deal with issues that pose challenges in the local church. As a younger minister, Timothy faced many hurdles in leading and relating to the various groups within his congregation.

Today's lesson is more than good advice from one long-dead man to another about a situation from ancient history. Those who minister to the church today have faced (or will face) many of the same challenges of the first-century church. Church leaders still need to develop the spiritual maturity and interpersonal skills that Paul urged on Timothy.

I. Lifestyle of the Godly Minister (1 Timothy 4:7-10)

A. Go Into Training (vv. 7-9)

7. But refuse profane and old wives' fables, and exercise thyself rather unto godliness.

Today we still use the expression *"old wives' tales."* It refers to the stories older women might tell their children or grandchildren at night. These are made-up stories, intended to entertain and delight the children. In this passage the phrase probably refers to old legends—made-up stories, false teachings that came from sources other than the inspired apostles—that should not be confused with the gospel. (See also 1 Timothy 1:4; 6:20; 2 Timothy 2:16; and Titus 1:14.)

Clearly Paul is ridiculing such stories. Instead of bothering with such nonsense, Timothy is to focus on something much better: *exercise . . . unto godliness.* Paul would like to see Timothy—and all Christians—replace worthless chatter with spiritual disciplines that result in drawing closer to God and His truth.

8. For bodily exercise profiteth little: but godliness is profitable unto all things, having

promise of the life that now is, and of that which is to come.

The phrase *profiteth little* should not be taken in a derogatory sense of being "totally worthless." It is simply more important to train oneself spiritually. The Greek word Paul uses here for *exercise,* or training, is the word that eventually gave us our English word *gymnasium.* The use of this word, along with certain other illustrations, suggests that Paul was a sports fan. Or at least he recognized the significance of illustrations dealing with athletics. The Greeks had originated the Olympic games, and Timothy's proximity to Greek culture while in Ephesus (1 Timothy 1:3) would make such illustrations particularly meaningful.

Paul compared the Christian life with a race in 1 Corinthians 9:24-27; Galatians 2:2; 5:7; and 2 Timothy 4:7. Although physical training has positive, earthly consequences, spiritual training has consequences for *the life that now is, and of that which is to come.* [See question #1, page 424.]

TRAINING FOR THE LONG RUN

Olympic athletes are known for the strict training regimen that they endure in preparing for the games. One such Olympian was Emil Zatopek (1922–2000), a Czech army officer who competed in the 1948, 1952, and 1956 summer Olympic games.

Zatopek did not look like the traditional distance runner. At five feet, eight inches and 145 pounds, he is spoken of as being a scrawny man with a frail frame. As he ran, he looked as if he labored for every step and would collapse from exhaustion at any moment. His style was not the classic distance runner's style either. His head bobbed from side to side, his arms flailed wildly, and his face was contorted as if he were in pain.

The training regimen Zatopek followed was not a normal pattern either. Developing his own routine, he ran at night wearing heavy boots. Preparing for the 10,000-meter race, he would run five times 200 meters, twenty times 400 meters, and five times 200 meters without sitting between runs. Instead he jogged between sets. Trainers scoffed at his efforts.

But Zatopek was rewarded when he won the 10,000-meter race in 1948. He was rewarded again in 1952 when he won an Olympic triple crown—races of 5,000 meters, 10,000 meters, and the marathon. Interestingly, Zatopek had never run the marathon before, but he won it in Olympic record time. His training made the difference between victory and defeat.

The Christian life is not a sprint. It is a distance run. All runners in this race are not the same. But the important lesson learned from

Visual for lesson 10

Use this visual to remind your learners that we must not neglect our practice of godliness.

Zatopek is to set a regimen of spiritual growth and then "run with patience the race that is set before us" (Hebrews 12:1).   —A. E. A.

9. This is a faithful saying, and worthy of all acceptation.

Paul uses the formula *this is a faithful saying* (or something very similar) in 1 Timothy 1:15; 3:1; 2 Timothy 2:11; and Titus 3:8 as well. This phrase introduces some kind of saying or proverb that is well known to Timothy, something from Paul's preaching that is familiar, or a new *saying* that Paul is creating as he writes.

In any case, we are curious about whether this *faithful saying* refers to what was taught previously in verse 8 or to what follows in verse 10. We are not sure. It would appear, however, that verse 8 best reflects the kind of proverb that would qualify as a "faithful saying."

B. Trust God (v. 10)

10. For therefore we both labor and suffer reproach, because we trust in the living God, who is the Saviour of all men, specially of those that believe.

The words used here to describe Christian travail are very strong. To *labor and suffer reproach* suggests that we give our all to the task. Paul may be referring specifically to a leader's ministry in the church, but some think that he is speaking of the more general need of all Christians to strive for a life of godliness.

Either possibility honors *the living God.* The phrase *who is the Saviour of all men* does not mean that God saves all people, but that He makes salvation available to all because of the cross. Salvation ultimately comes to *those that believe,* and not to unbelievers.

II. Duties of the Godly Minister (1 Timothy 4:11-16)

A. Teaching and Modeling (vv. 11, 12)

11. These things command and teach.

Some *things,* says Paul, need to be addressed with authority. That is the reason he can say *command* these things. Paul will later tell Timothy how to command, but here he is stressing the importance of impressing truth on the congregation. These are not just suggestions! But for Timothy to *command and teach* may pose a certain problem, as the next verse shows. [See question #2, page 424.]

12. Let no man despise thy youth; but be thou an example of the believers, in word, in conversation, in charity, in spirit, in faith, in purity.

The Greek word for *youth* can be used for a man who is of age to serve in the military. Some calculate that Timothy may be about thirty years old. Will his relative *youth* be a problem in teaching the older folks in his congregation? Perhaps!

So Paul recommends some ways to overcome this potential problem. The first concerns the way Timothy is to communicate. When the text says he is to be an *example . . . in word,* it means in speech. How often our tongue can get us into trouble! (See James 3:1-12.) On the other hand, well-chosen words can heal and encourage.

Second, Paul says Timothy should be an example *in conversation.* The meaning of this word has changed over the years. We think of *conversation* as talking to another person, but in the English of the *King James Version* it means lifestyle. Timothy's lifestyle certainly is to include everything he would do *in charity, in spirit, in faith, in purity.* These are not new concepts in Paul's writings. He stresses them numerous times, in various ways (e.g., 1 Corinthians 13; 2 Corinthians 6:3-10; 1 Thessalonians 1:3). Timothy's age will not be a problem if he demonstrates spiritual maturity. A church leader who does not give attention to the areas Paul lists is certain to fail no matter what his age; a bad example ruins credibility. [See question #3, page 424.]

B. Ministering and Sustaining (vv. 13, 14)

13. Till I come, give attendance to reading, to exhortation, to doctrine.

When Paul tells Timothy to give attention *to reading,* he most likely means the public reading of Scripture. Sadly, this is not often emphasized in many churches today. But public Scripture reading can have a powerful effect (see Nehemiah 8:1-12). What the *King James Version* translates as *exhortation* may be understood to be preaching. What is identified as *doctrine* could also be described as teaching.

This is a picture of some aspects of worship in the early church. There is a time for Scripture reading as well as a time to preach and teach what has been read. The early church often reflects the customs of the Jewish synagogue. In the synagogue it was standard practice to give words of explanation after the reading of Scripture.

With preaching or exhortation there is always a note of persuasion and decision (e.g., Acts 2:14-41). With teaching the emphasis is on the material itself—namely the facts of Scripture (e.g., Luke 24:27). We need both!

14. Neglect not the gift that is in thee, which was given thee by prophecy, with the laying on of the hands of the presbytery.

Timothy had been blessed in a certain way by *the presbytery,* or eldership. We don't know when or where this happened, but it could have been at Ephesus (1 Timothy 1:3) or even Lystra (Acts 16:1). We're not even sure about the nature of the special *gift* with which Timothy was endowed. The important thing to Paul is that Timothy actually use his spiritual gifts. Why should God give a gift to a person who has no intention of using it? Such a person may as well not have the gift at all.

The phrase *laying on of the hands* has often been seen as an ordination, although this verse does not call it as such. Still, it appears very much as if this event was a precursor to what later would be called ordination. Acts 8:18; 1 Timothy 5:22; 2 Timothy 1:6; and Hebrews 6:2 also discuss the practice of laying on of hands.

C. Diligence and Perseverance (vv. 15, 16)

15. Meditate upon these things; give thyself wholly to them; that thy profiting may appear to all.

The ministry that Timothy is involved in requires him to be totally absorbed. This complete commitment means that he will continue to grow spiritually in order that his *profiting* (progress) *may* be obvious *to all.* [See question #4, page 424.]

16. Take heed unto thyself, and unto the doctrine; continue in them: for in doing this thou shalt both save thyself, and them that hear thee.

Paul exhorts Timothy to give attention to both his life and his teaching. Many Christian leaders and servants get these out of balance. We have all met people in the church who know the Bible book, chapter, and verse but have not learned how to apply it appropriately. As a result, they bear no fruit (Luke 13:6-9).

There also are others who live out the Christian lifestyle, but show little or no interest in matters of *doctrine.* They are the ones who say, "Give us something practical! Don't bother us with tedious doctrine." Such people are spiritually shallow and may fall prey easily to false doctrine (cf. Matthew 13:5-7). A balanced Christian and a balanced leader will be concerned with both doctrine and practical application. That kind of leader will bless those who are led.

III. Skills of the Godly Minister (1 Timothy 5:1-8)

A. Relating to Men of All Ages (v. 1)

1. Rebuke not an elder, but entreat him as a father; and the younger men as brethren.

Respect for those who are older was very much a part of the fabric of the ancient world. Even so, there may be times when a younger leader needs to disagree with those who are older. When this happens, the principle of treating the older man like *a father* is helpful. (The *elder* referred to here is not necessarily someone who holds the office of elder, but can be any older man.)

To recognize someone *as a father* and others *as brethren* is the imagery of a family. When times of disagreement come, the family still has to stay together. This requires skill on the part of Timothy and all church leaders today.

REVIVING RESPECT

John Donne's classic "Meditation 17," written in 1624, reminds us that "No man is an island, entire of itself; every man is a piece of the continent, a part of the main." To emphasize this thought, Donne states that "if a clod be washed away by the sea, Europe is the less." That sounds drastic in a modern culture that puts a premium on certain people, such as celebrities and sports stars, while treating unborn infants with contempt.

Unfortunately, even in the church there is sometimes a lack of respect and regard for one another. A young person may look down upon an older person because of the heritage and traditions the older person holds. A senior saint may look down on the young because of music tastes or dress styles that are different. Fear, lack of knowledge, or outright arrogance may be the cause of these divisions within the church.

But in the end everyone really wants to be liked and respected. In his 1936 classic *How To Win Friends and Influence People,* Dale Carnegie agrees with the apostle Paul on the necessity of doing those things that make for harmony among people. Carnegie gives six principles to live by so that others will like you. These include the following:

- Be genuinely interested in other people.
- Smile.
- Remember that a person's name is to that person the sweetest and most important sound in any language.

- Be a good listener. Encourage others to talk about themselves.
- Talk in terms of the other person's interests.
- Make the other person feel important—and do it sincerely.

These simple principles will help Christians fulfill the admonition of Paul to young Timothy on how to live in community with others. This type of community living makes for a harmonious church with a glorious future. —A. E. A.

B. Relating to Women of All Ages (v. 2)

2. The elder women as mothers; the younger as sisters, with all purity.

The same basic principle from verse 1 is also applied to the *women* of the church. Paul adds the reminder that these relationships should be pursued *with all purity*. This extra caution is due to the fact that members of the opposite sex are involved. This surely needs to be heeded in our own day as well. [See question #5, page 424.]

C. Relating to Widows of All Ages (vv. 3-8)

3. Honor widows that are widows indeed.

The churches of Timothy's day evidently take seriously the responsibility of supporting financially the *widows* in the Christian community. Widows have a very difficult time supporting themselves in the ancient world. The Scripture groups "widows and fatherless" together in numerous places to describe those who are most vulnerable. (e.g., James 1:27). The church takes care of the physical needs of widows. In exchange for the financial support, these widows probably perform certain duties to help support the work of the local congregation.

The *King James Version* describes those who need support as *widows indeed*. We might rephrase that by saying the church should support those who are "really widows." Either way, what does Paul mean? It would seem that a person either is a widow or is not!

How to Say It

CZECH. Check.
CORINTHIANS. Kor-*in*-thee-unz (*th* as in *thin*).
EMIL ZATOPEK. *Ee*-mil Zuh-*toe*-peck.
EPHESUS. *Ef*-uh-sus.
LYSTRA. *Liss*-truh.
NEHEMIAH. *Nee*-huh-*my*-uh (strong accent on *my*).
PRESBYTERY. *prez*-buh-ter-ee.
SYNAGOGUE. *sin*-uh-gog.
THESSALONIANS. *Thess*-uh-*lo*-nee-unz (strong accent on *lo; th* as in *thin*).
TITUS. *Tie*-tus.

Probably what Paul has in mind is that the church should take special interest in those widows who have absolutely no one else to support them or look after them. After all, some widows may have adult children nearby. Others may be childless or have lost their children in infancy or childhood. The latter are truly desolate. A widow's own family members have the first responsibility to support the one in need.

4. But if any widow have children or nephews, let them learn first to show piety at home, and to requite their parents: for that is good and acceptable before God.

These women had supported their *children*, and it is now incumbent upon them to return the favor. In the English of the *King James Version*, the word *nephew* can be applied to grandchildren as well as to what we call a nephew today. Jesus had harsh words for those who refused to support *their parents* (Mark 7:9-13).

5. Now she that is a widow indeed, and desolate, trusteth in God, and continueth in supplications and prayers night and day.

Paul maintains that the Christian *widow* is in a unique position to trust *in God* and pray. Her tragic circumstance can bring her closer to God. It is the kind of widow who gives herself wholly to God who is a prime candidate for the church's "widow list." This kind of widow is represented by Anna in Luke 2:36, 37. This elderly woman was constantly helping and praying in the temple.

6. But she that liveth in pleasure is dead while she liveth.

Deserving widows should not be living for earthly pleasures, Paul warns. The situation he is referring to most likely concerns the behavior of some younger widows. The situation was so desperate for widows that some gave themselves over to a sinful lifestyle, either as prostitutes to

gain money, or to fornication in the attempt to find a husband or benefactor. Paul wants all widows to be true to the Christian requirements. He has more to say about the status and conduct of widows in 1 Corinthians 7.

7. And these things give in charge, that they may be blameless.

Paul's plan will keep family members from being open to the charge that they are dishonoring their mothers. It will also keep the widows from the charge that they are taking advantage of the church. When corruption is allowed to creep in, the church becomes ineffective and loses its witness.

8. But if any provide not for his own, and specially for those of his own house, he hath denied the faith, and is worse than an infidel.

This is quite an indictment! What could be worse than denying *the faith?* The kind of insensitive behavior in view here surely denies both the letter and spirit of the teaching of Jesus (again, see Mark 7:9-13).

Conditions are different today, with pensions, government social insurance, and the like. Even so, Christ expects His people to take responsibility for the care of their family members. Christian mercy should be expressed first and foremost to those closest to us. If we don't do that, then we are not likely to show mercy to anyone else. [See question #6, page 424.]

Conclusion

A. It's Not Easy

There is no doubt that service of any type is a complex matter. This is particularly true in church leadership. Those serving in that capacity not only need to understand the Scriptures, they also need to understand people. Ministry is for God and to God, but it is exercised in a setting of community.

The sheer difficulty of the task requires those who serve the church in both leadership and nonleadership positions to call forth their best. This involves not only the best in terms of personal piety, but also all the wisdom and sensitivity needed to deal with people. It is a rare person who can do it all well, but they do exist. And it's something we can all improve upon!

B. Prayer

Father, help me to evaluate myself. Help me to behave properly in my personal life as well as in the way I relate to people. May I do it all in Jesus' name and for His glory, amen.

C. Thought to Remember

Church leadership begins with holiness.

Home Daily Bible Readings

Monday, Aug. 2—Become Slaves to Righteousness (Romans 6:19-23)

Tuesday, Aug. 3—Pursue Holiness (2 Corinthians 6:14–7:1)

Wednesday, Aug. 4—Train Yourself in Godliness (1 Timothy 4:6-10)

Thursday, Aug. 5—Be an Example to Believers (1 Timothy 4:11-16)

Friday, Aug. 6—Honor Widows, Older Persons (1 Timothy 5:1-8)

Saturday, Aug. 7—Pursue Righteousness, Godliness (1 Timothy 6:11-16)

Sunday, Aug. 8—Do Good, Store Up Treasure (1 Timothy 6:17-21)

Learning by Doing

This page contains an alternative lesson plan emphasizing learning activities.
Classes desiring such student involvement will find these suggestions helpful.

Learning Goals

After participating in this lesson, each student will be able to:

1. Identify the qualities demonstrated by a faithful servant of God.

2. Express the importance of spiritual training in the life of a Christian servant.

3. Devise a spiritual training program that he or she will follow.

Into the Lesson

To begin the class, ask your students to draw a picture of their ideal evangelist or preaching minister. The picture may be realistic or abstract or even a stick figure depending on the skill of the artist. The important thing is to represent the key qualities that make God's "ideal" evangelist/preacher. You will need to provide paper and colored pencils or even crayons for the exercise. If you use the student books, space is also provided there for this activity.

Allow several minutes for your class to finish their drawings, then ask volunteers to share their work with the class and indicate which features were most important. Make a list of those important characteristics on the chalkboard, then tell your class that, as last week's lesson examined the qualities of elders and deacons, this lesson will discuss the qualities and duties of preachers.

Into the Word

Pair off your students to study today's text, 1 Timothy 4:7–5:8. Each pair will read the text and then make two lists. One will be a list of the positive traits and activities that Timothy was encouraged to have or do. The other will list the negative traits or activities that Timothy was to avoid. You will need to provide paper for this activity or point your class to their student books, where there is space for the exercise. Their lists should look something like this:

POSITIVES

1. Exercise to godliness (4:7)

2. Labor and suffer reproach (v. 10)

3. Be an example in word, in conversation, in charity, in spirit, in faith, in purity (v. 12)

4. Give attendance to reading, to exhortation, to doctrine (v. 13)

5. Meditate on/be devoted to Paul's teaching (v. 15)

6. Take heed to yourself and to doctrine (v. 16)

7. Treat older Christians as fathers and mothers, and young men and women as brothers and sisters (5:1, 2)

8. Honor widows (v. 3)

9. Teach widows and their children to be blameless (v. 7)

NEGATIVES

1. Refuse profane and old wives' fables (4:7)

2. Don't let anyone despise your youth (v. 12)

3. Don't neglect your gift (v. 14)

4. Don't rebuke an elder (5:1)

Using the lesson commentary and the following questions, discuss the importance of each positive and each negative trait or activity on the list.

1. What did Paul mean when he wrote, "exercise thyself . . . unto godliness"?

2. To what "old wives' fables" did Paul refer?

3. How does one "suffer reproach"?

4. How can a young preacher overcome presumptions about his youth?

5. Why did Paul emphasize reading, exhortation, and doctrine?

6. Why was Paul adamant about how the preacher should treat different age groups in the church?

Into Life

Ask your students to imagine that they are "personal spiritual trainers" for a young preacher just out of Bible college or seminary. Working in pairs again, they should devise a specialized weeklong training program, using today's text as a guideline. The program should include the following basic elements, plus any other duties and exercises they feel are necessary or beneficial: devotional time, Bible study time, sermon and/or lesson preparation time, professional reading time, family time, recreation/personal time, administrative duties, group worship and study time, and visitation time. After listing all the elements of the program, your teams should allocate them to a Monday through Sunday chart with hourly blocks from 6 A.M. to 10 P.M., which you will reproduce and distribute.

Ask the pairs, "How would such a chart differ for you in your own ministries? What would you delete? What do you need to add?" Ask members of the study pairs to write their own spiritual training programs and to pray for one another as each resolves to follow his or her training plan.

Let's Talk It Over

The questions on this page are designed to promote discussion of the lesson by the class and to encourage application of the lesson Scriptures. The answers provided are only discussion starters. Let your class talk it over from there.

1. Paul says that godliness is valuable not only in terms of the "life . . . which is to come" —that is, Heaven—but of "the life that now is." How have you found godliness to make your life better?

Studies have shown that people who embrace godly, holy lifestyles actually live longer. People who abuse their bodies with drugs and alcohol are afflicted with diseases that are rare among those who abstain. Those who are sexually promiscuous may contract a variety of sexually transmitted diseases.

Faith also gives people an ability to cope with the everyday stresses and anxieties of life. The fellowship of the church makes joy sweeter and pain more tolerable. Let your students give specifics about how they have found life to be better than it was before they became Christians.

2. Why is it necessary to follow a command with teaching?

Any parent in your class will know that instruction is vital to a child's development. Continually giving commands without instruction as to the reason doesn't communicate the validity of the command. Neither does it equip the youngster in making right choices when the parent is no longer around. If believers are to mature in their faith, they need to be equipped to make sound decisions and right choices on their own.

3. Are most young people in your congregation looked on as good examples? Why, or why not? How can we encourage them to be the kind of example Paul encourages Timothy to be?

Be careful not to allow this discussion to become a blame-the-bad-parents session. Children wander from the faith for a variety of reasons, and many of them return at some point.

Focus instead on the challenges that young people face—secular education that belittles Biblical authority, sensual and materialistic media, lack of challenge or motivation, etc. Then discuss ways your class can combat these issues. Note especially the value of good role models among the adults in the church.

4. Paul told Timothy to behave in such a way that his "profiting may appear to all." What is the difference between that and "showing off"?

What caution would you advise for someone who wants to take Paul's words to heart?

There is a certain balance in Scripture between letting our "light so shine before men" (Matthew 5:16) and being careful not to do things just to show off (Matthew 6:1-4). Timothy was not to conduct himself just for show. He was to get serious about his faith and ministry—to be "totally absorbed," as the lesson writer says. Paul has already told him to be an example; here Paul clarifies it. Timothy's growth in faith should be obvious. Those who follow his example will see how he is growing. If we get serious about our discipleship, others will notice.

5. Paul gives special instructions about how Timothy should treat women "with all purity." What specific safeguards should men use when working or serving with women in today's church?

Purity is all but lost in many segments of Western culture; the church ought to be one place where it can still be found! A Christian leader would be wise to be careful not be alone with a woman (unless it is his wife). This not only helps in reducing temptation, but it also avoids any appearance of evil. The careful Christian leader knows that "harmless" flirting rarely is. Your learners should be able to give several specifics about issues and situations that secular culture finds funny, but carry potential for disaster.

6. Suppose a church member tells you his wife is in a nursing home with Alzheimer's. Her health care costs are soaring. He says, "I have been advised to get a divorce so the nursing home cannot take all of my assets. I still love her, but what good will it do if I lose everything? She will never get any better. Besides, she doesn't even know me anymore. The marriage is already dead!" How would you advise your friend?

This is not a hypothetical situation. It actually happens! Our culture values only what is functional, what gives "me" a reward. Life that does not seem to be "useful" is easily written off as meaningless. Our advice to such a friend must address the sanctity of life, the sanctity of the wedding vow to be faithful "for better and for worse, in sickness and in health, for richer or for poorer," and Paul's warning.

Handle God's Word Rightly

DEVOTIONAL READING: Psalm 119:9-16.

BACKGROUND SCRIPTURE: 2 Timothy 2.

PRINTED TEXT: 2 Timothy 2:1-15.

2 Timothy 2:1-15

1 Thou therefore, my son, be strong in the grace that is in Christ Jesus.

2 And the things that thou hast heard of me among many witnesses, the same commit thou to faithful men, who shall be able to teach others also.

3 Thou therefore endure hardness, as a good soldier of Jesus Christ.

4 No man that warreth entangleth himself with the affairs of this life; that he may please him who hath chosen him to be a soldier.

5 And if a man also strive for masteries, yet is he not crowned, except he strive lawfully.

6 The husbandman that laboreth must be first partaker of the fruits.

7 Consider what I say; and the Lord give thee understanding in all things.

8 Remember that Jesus Christ of the seed of David was raised from the dead, according to my gospel:

9 Wherein I suffer trouble, as an evildoer, even unto bonds; but the word of God is not bound.

10 Therefore I endure all things for the elect's sakes, that they may also obtain the salvation which is in Christ Jesus with eternal glory.

11 It is a faithful saying: For if we be dead with him, we shall also live with him:

12 If we suffer, we shall also reign with him: if we deny him, he also will deny us:

13 If we believe not, yet he abideth faithful: he cannot deny himself.

14 Of these things put them in remembrance, charging them before the Lord that they strive not about words to no profit, but to the subverting of the hearers.

15 Study to show thyself approved unto God, a workman that needeth not to be ashamed, rightly dividing the word of truth.

Aug
15

GOLDEN TEXT: Study to show thyself approved unto God, a workman that needeth not to be ashamed, rightly dividing the word of truth.—2 Timothy 2:15.

Lesson Aims

After participating in this lesson, each student should be able to:

1. Describe the example set by a good soldier, athlete, or farmer, as explained in today's text.

2. Tell how regular Bible study can help the believer to demonstrate the qualities typified by soldiers, athletes, and farmers.

3. Identify one obstacle he or she will overcome in order to be faithful in studying God's Word.

Lesson Outline

INTRODUCTION
    A. Nothing But the Truth?
    B. Lesson Background
  I. LABORING FOR THE TRUTH (2 Timothy 2:1-7)
    A. We Are Teachers (vv. 1, 2)
    B. We Are Soldiers (vv. 3, 4)
      Enduring Hardship
    C. We Are Athletes (v. 5)
    D. We Are Farmers (vv. 6, 7)
 II. SUFFERING FOR THE TRUTH (2 Timothy 2:8-13)
    A. Christ Suffered (v. 8)
    B. Paul Suffered (vv. 9, 10)
    C. We Suffer (vv. 11-13)
      God Is There
III. CONTENDING FOR THE TRUTH (2 Timothy 2: 14, 15)
    A. Faithful in Witness (v. 14)
    B. Faithful in the Study (v. 15)
CONCLUSION
    A. It Deserves Your Best
    B. Prayer
    C. Thought to Remember

Introduction

A. Nothing But the Truth?

Today's lesson text speaks to us in two areas of life where we need reminders. First, it reminds us how blessed we are to have the Bible so accessible to us. Before the invention of the printing press, handwritten copies of the Bible were too expensive for the average person to own. Today, we can choose from a dizzying array of Bible versions and study aids in all price ranges.

Some areas of our world still do not have that kind of access. A man once spoke to a congregation with a distressing story about distributing Bibles with a Christian organization in a third-world country—and running out. People were pleading for Bibles with tears in their eyes. They begged the men to come back. Some of the children tore their Bibles so they could give parts to friends. It is easy to forget how blessed we are to have access to the Scriptures.

Second, today's text also speaks to us at a philosophical level. It assumes that there is such a thing as truth and that we can know truth. This is a somewhat foreign concept in a world that has largely rejected the concept of objective or absolute truth. Paul believed that truth existed and that God had revealed it. This lesson also reveals that Paul believed that sharing God's truth was worth the cost and sacrifice.

B. Lesson Background

The lesson presents to us Paul in his old age, facing a martyr's death (2 Timothy 4:6; Philemon 9). He is concerned that his protégé Timothy continue the same plan for spreading the gospel that Paul himself had followed.

Timothy had learned of faith from his mother and grandmother. He had learned the fullness of the Christian gospel from Paul himself. Timothy had shared Paul's hardships. Many were deserting the gospel (2 Timothy 1:15; 4:10a), but not Timothy.

The conviction of truth undoubtedly was what kept Timothy faithful. In this lesson we will see how Paul admonished Timothy to make sure that truth is passed on regardless of personal consequences. The stakes were just too high to do otherwise.

I. Laboring for the Truth (2 Timothy 2:1-7)

A. We Are Teachers (vv. 1, 2)

1. Thou therefore, my son, be strong in the grace that is in Christ Jesus.

Timothy's strength is not to be found in himself; it is a supernatural strength that comes from *Christ Jesus*. This may be something of a relief to Timothy, who some believe tends to be timid (1 Corinthians 16:10; 2 Timothy 1:7). The work of the gospel needs supernatural help. There is simply no other way to face the challenge.

2. And the things that thou hast heard of me among many witnesses, the same commit thou to faithful men, who shall be able to teach others also.

Paul wants Timothy to continue the tradition. Like a relay runner passing a baton, Timothy is to pass on to others the same faith that was passed to him. His mother, grandmother (2 Timothy 1:5), and finally Paul himself had first shared it with him; those whom Timothy instructs will then pass it on to others.

When Paul says that Timothy *heard* him share the gospel in front of *many witnesses,* we need not spend too much time wondering who those specific witnesses were. This is probably a general reference to the many times when Timothy heard Paul expound the gospel before various groups of people.

Paul continues from here to compare the Christian worker with three other kinds of workers. In certain respects, Christian workers are to be like soldiers, athletes, and farmers.

B. We Are Soldiers (vv. 3, 4)

3. Thou therefore endure hardness, as a good soldier of Jesus Christ.

No one knows *hardness* (or hardship) like a *soldier,* particularly soldiers in the ancient world. Paul has learned much about a soldier's life since he has spent considerable time in the company of soldiers while in prison. Conditions "on the road" are tough, and the soldiers are away from home for long periods of time. Add to that the threat of death, and you recognize the extraordinary commitment of the soldier.

God's men and women are to have that same kind of commitment. We are all soldiers for the cause of Christ (Philippians 2:25; Philemon 2). Paul uses military images about as frequently as sports images. (See 1 Corinthians 9:7 and Ephesians 6:10-17.)

ENDURING HARDSHIP

The difficulties and hardships faced by soldiers are many and varied. There is separation from family, the discomforts of sleeping on hard ground, exposure to the elements, and meals consisting of cold food—not to mention the constant threat of injury or death at the hands of the enemy!

Consider the paratroopers who took part in the D-day invasion in 1944. Enlisted paratroopers carried an average of seventy pounds of equipment, while officers averaged ninety pounds of gear. Adding the weight of their parachutes, each man weighed in at between ninety and one hundred twenty pounds over his body weight. These paratroopers were dropped behind enemy lines to secure needed targets. They knew that if the accompanying sea-borne assault failed, there would be no rescue.

Much planning and preparation went into that drop. However, heavy fog and enemy gunfire made it impossible to drop the paratroopers precisely as planned. Both the 82nd and the 101st Divisions suffered heavy losses. In spite of these hardships, both divisions were able to put together units and continue the invasion. Heroic efforts in the face of hardships are what led to making D-day the beginning of the end of World War II.

The Christian soldier is also faced with many hardships. For some it is leaving home and family behind for service. For others it is the extra weight of concern for the ministry of the church. For many it is witnessing the casualties of fellow Christian soldiers who fall to the assaults of the enemy. But the good soldier of the cross endures the hardships and continues the march to victory. Does that description fit you?   —A. E. A.

4. No man that warreth entangleth himself with the affairs of this life; that he may please him who hath chosen him to be a soldier.

Taking the vow or oath of enlistment means that a full-time *soldier* puts civilian priorities behind. No one can serve two masters. Just as a soldier puts aside the entanglements of the civilian world, so the Christian puts aside the entanglements of the secular world.

Paul does not mean by this that we can totally divorce ourselves from the secular world. Paul himself did secular work as a tentmaker so that he could serve the church without charge (Acts 18:3). Not every Christian can make a living from doing church work. Christians cannot avoid the responsibilities of the workaday world. Neither can we avoid the responsibilities of home life. If we were to be totally divorced from community life, we would have no one with whom to share the gospel! (See 1 Corinthians 5:9, 10.) What is forbidden is allowing oneself to be distracted by secular concerns. [See question #1, page 432.]

Another thing that soldiers know how to do is to follow lawful orders and *please* their commanders. Soldiers who do not follow orders are useless at best and a danger to their fellow soldiers at worst. Those serving in God's kingdom must have a sense of duty as soldiers for Him.

How to Say It

COLOSSIANS. Kuh-*losh*-unz.
CORINTHIANS. Kor-*in*-thee-unz (*th* as in *thin*).
EPHESIANS. Ee-*fee*-zhunz.
MESSIAH. Meh-*sigh*-uh.
NEHEMIAH. *Nee*-huh-*my*-uh (strong accent on *my*).
PHILEMON. Fih-*lee*-mun or Fye-*lee*-mun.
PHILIPPIANS. Fih-*lip*-ee-unz.
TITUS. *Tie*-tus.

C. We Are Athletes (v. 5)

5. And if a man also strive for masteries, yet is he not crowned, except he strive lawfully.

Another group that knows well what sacrifice means is that of the world-class athlete. Here Paul uses another of his sports analogies (see also last week's lesson).

This verse describes the winner of a race who receives his crown of victory. The crown or wreath awarded in the Olympic games of Paul's day corresponds with the gold medal of the modern Olympiad.

To say that the competitors must *strive lawfully* means they must compete according to the established rules. This could refer to the rules of training, but more likely it means the rules of the competition itself. The Christian must also always be aware of his or her commitment to the rules of the Lord. Just because we have been saved by grace does not mean we are free to ignore the moral laws of God. We still live under authority.

D. We Are Farmers (vv. 6, 7)

6. The husbandman that laboreth must be first partaker of the fruits.

A farmer *(husbandman)* also demonstrates the type of qualities needed in Christian leadership and service. The farmer knows how to work hard, to be patient, and to cooperate with nature and trust God.

Many of the most important things in life operate by a sowing-and-reaping rule from farming. A farmer does not reap on the same day that the seeds are sown. Crop growth takes time! In the world of spiritual development, education, and even health, we do well to operate with the patience of the farmer—trusting that in the end we will reap rewards.

The good news is that the faithful farmer is first to receive the reward of the crops. Just as a farmer eats of his or her own crops, the Christian benefits from the development of holiness of life. If we work on our spiritual maturity, we will benefit personally from the work. [See question #2, page 432.]

7. Consider what I say; and the Lord give thee understanding in all things.

Timothy is not to brush over Paul's words lightly, as if they were optional. Instead, Timothy is to *consider* those words carefully and expect to receive *understanding in all things* as a result. This involves the interaction of Timothy's own patient reasoning and the work of the Holy Spirit. This is the same interaction necessary for us to understand and apply the Bible today. The three analogies of soldier, athlete, and farmer also appear in 1 Corinthians 9:7, 24-27. If Timothy will

reflect on these things, the Lord will give him understanding.

Before moving on, let's take one more look at the figures Paul uses. There is something important that sustains all those that Paul uses in his illustrations; that something is *hope*. The good soldier sacrifices in the hope of victory, the athlete competes in the hope of a crown, and the farmer labors with the hope of a future harvest.

While there is definitely sacrifice, discipline, and hard work in the Christian life, there is also great hope. Paul himself expresses this hope as he approaches the end of his life (see 2 Timothy 4:6-8).

II. Suffering for the Truth (2 Timothy 2:8-13)

A. Christ Suffered (v. 8)

8. Remember that Jesus Christ of the seed of David was raised from the dead, according to my gospel.

For *Jesus Christ* to be *the seed of David* means that He is a descendant of David. This is an important part of identifying Jesus as the Messiah (Matthew 1:1; Romans 1:3).

Not only is Jesus described in terms of His ancestry, but also He is described in terms of His great victory over death. It is not a *dead* Christ that Timothy is to concentrate on. Neither is Timothy to think that he serves a Christ who never suffered death. Timothy is to *remember* the entire truth and therefore celebrate a risen Savior (Romans 1:4; 1 Corinthians 15:4, 20). We, too, must use these essential facts as anchor points for our faith.

B. Paul Suffered (vv. 9, 10)

9. Wherein I suffer trouble, as an evildoer, even unto bonds; but the word of God is not bound.

Paul points out that in his own situation he is being persecuted as a criminal for his faith in Jesus Christ (cf. Acts 16:23; Ephesians 3:1; Philippians 1:12-14). As in the case of Jesus, Paul is treated as a criminal even though he has committed no crime. [See question #3, page 432.]

Yet Paul can see that even though he himself is chained, the gospel goes on unchained. What a perspective! Time after time people have tried to silence truth by silencing the messenger. It does not work. God's message is far more powerful than any earthly messenger. God's truth can never be imprisoned.

10. Therefore I endure all things for the elect's sakes, that they may also obtain the salvation which is in Christ Jesus with eternal glory.

The elect are the Christians. God has foreseen their faith from eternity past, and has chosen them to spend eternity in Heaven with Him. But obtaining this *salvation* and *eternal glory* happens only through *Christ Jesus.* Paul has indeed endured all things for the sake of this group (2 Corinthians 6:3-10; 11:23-33). His upcoming martyrdom will be one more thing he will *endure . . . for the elect's sakes.*

C. We Suffer (vv. 11-13)

11. It is a faithful saying: For if we be dead with him, we shall also live with him.

We have discussed the phrase *faithful saying* in previous lessons (cf. 1 Timothy 1:15). Here the phrase serves as a lead-in to what may be a hymn or poem of the early church.

The second phrase *for if we be dead with him* leads us to wonder when it was that we died with Christ. The answer is that we died with Jesus when we became Christians. Paul told the Roman Christians that when they were baptized they "were baptized into his death" (Romans 6:3). In some way, it is in the water of baptism that we join Jesus in death, "buried with him by baptism" (Romans 6:4; cf. Colossians 2:12). Some think that these passages refer to baptism by the Holy Spirit (Matthew 3:11). These two baptisms could be thought of as two sides of a single coin —inseparable.

Following Christ's death "unto sin" (Romans 6:10), we consider ourselves "to be dead indeed unto sin" (6:11). If this interpretation is correct, then to *be dead with him* refers to dying with Christ at the time of our conversion.

However, there are some who believe that in this context Paul is talking about "daily dying" to sin rather than the initial conversion. It is interesting to note that in Romans 6:11-14 Paul indicates that our original death to sin gives rise to what may be called a daily dying to sin. So both could be in mind here as well.

For the Christian, death gives way to life, and there are two ways we live with Him. One is in the future resurrection (Romans 6:5). This will be a marvelous thing, but Paul would have us understand that we live with Jesus now also. We are already alive in Christ (Romans 6:11).

12. If we suffer, we shall also reign with him: if we deny him, he also will deny us.

It is also important to Paul that Christians commit for the long haul. They must endure. Those who *suffer* and endure (cf. Luke 9:23) are to take heart through the promise that they will *reign with* Jesus (Revelation 22:5). This should resonate with any Christian undergoing persecution. Suffering is temporary; reigning with Christ is eternal.

The second part of this verse is a solemn warning. Perhaps people had already wilted under the pressure of the persecution. But regardless of the persecution, if we reject or disown Jesus, He will disown us. In Matthew 10:33 Jesus says essentially the same thing Paul says.

GOD IS THERE

What is the source of suffering? The most basic answer is that suffering results from living life in a fallen world. Even for the follower of Christ there is pain and suffering because of this body of flesh in which we live. But a deeper issue we face as Christians is, "Where is God when we suffer? Has He abandoned us to face the pain and pressure on our own?"

Bob Russell, in a sermon delivered following the terrorist attacks in New York and Washington on September 11, 2001, helps us deal with these questions. Russell says, "Where was God last Tuesday? The same place you parents are when your sixteen-year-old gets in the car and drives off, and you say, 'Oh, I hope he listens to what I said.' [He was] the same place the father of the prodigal son was when his son was hurting in the far country—standing on the front porch, watching and hoping he would come back. [He was] the same place He was when His Son was dying on the cross and people were gloating over His death—waiting in the shadows, knowing there would be victory and resurrection."

Since God has promised never to leave us or forsake us—and this includes times of pain and suffering—it is our task as followers of the truth of God's Word to remain faithful. Paul encourages us with the reminder that, "Our light affliction, which is but for a moment, worketh for us a far more exceeding and eternal weight of glory" (2 Corinthians 4:17). —A. E. A.

Home Daily Bible Readings

Monday, Aug. 9—Keep God's Precepts Diligently (Psalm 119:1-6)

Tuesday, Aug. 10—Treasure God's Word in Your Heart (Psalm 119:9-16)

Wednesday, Aug. 11—Believers Encourage Apollos in the Word (Acts 18:24-28)

Thursday, Aug. 12—Entrust Teachings to Faithful People (2 Timothy 2:1-7)

Friday, Aug. 13—God's Word Is Not Chained (2 Timothy 2:8-13)

Saturday, Aug. 14—Rightly Explain the Word of Truth (2 Timothy 2:14-19)

Sunday, Aug. 15—The Lord's Servant, an Apt Teacher (2 Timothy 2:20-26)

13. If we believe not, yet he abideth faithful: he cannot deny himself.

The final line of this poetic section gives us a beautiful view of the faithfulness of God. Even if people are faithless and they don't believe and obey, God will still be *faithful* because it is His nature. See also Numbers 23:19; Romans 3:3, 4; and Titus 1:2.

III. Contending for the Truth
(2 Timothy 2:14, 15)

A. Faithful in Witness (v. 14)

14. Of these thing put them in remembrance, charging them before the Lord that they strive not about words to no profit, but to the subverting of the hearers.

If we tell a person something only once, it might not stick. Memory is fragile, and people need reminders (see 2 Peter 1:12; 3:1; Jude 5). In light of certain problems, Paul wants Timothy to help his congregation remember the great truths of the faith. Timothy will do this as he charges *them before the Lord*.

Perhaps some in Timothy's church have created an environment where people *strive* or go to war over *words*. It's not that words aren't important. The gospel is communicated with words! Paul is describing, rather, a situation where people are arguing over trivial matters (cf. 1 Timothy 6:4; Titus 3:9). [See question #4, page 432.]

B. Faithful in the Study (v. 15)

15. Study to show thyself approved unto God, a workman that needeth not be ashamed, rightly dividing the word of truth.

If Timothy does what Paul tells him, he will be a workman who need *not be ashamed*, since

Study to show thyself approved unto God, a workman that needeth not to be ashamed, rightly dividing the word of truth.

2 Timothy 2:15

Visual for lesson 11. *One way we show ourselves approved to God is by studying His Word. A Bible study group can help!*

he will have done what is expected. [See question #5, page 432.] What is expected is for Timothy to handle correctly *the word of truth*. The phrase *rightly dividing* may refer to "cutting up" the Word of God as the bread of life, and serving it to the congregation.

However, it is more likely that this phrase refers to cutting a straight path for people to understand the Word. So it is not so much cutting up the Word itself as it is cutting a straight path *to* the Word. This is contrasted with Paul's statement in 2 Timothy 2:17, 18 about false teachers who have swerved.

In either case it is Timothy's responsibility to do his job of teaching the Scriptures well. He must do his best to be accurate and clear as he teaches the Word of God (cf. Nehemiah 8:8).

Conclusion

A. It Deserves Your Best

When we witness to people and try to convince them to become Christians, we often stress the benefits. We often talk of the happiness and joy that comes to those who give their lives to Christ. In so doing, we sometimes make the mistake of making Christianity sound easy.

But Jesus never said it would be easy. Paul never said it would be easy. It is fulfilling, but not easy. Jesus warned people that they must take up a cross if they want to be Christians (Luke 9:23). Paul says in today's text that Timothy must sacrifice and work hard for the cause. There are some things worth sacrificing for. The Christian life is one of them.

In particular, our lesson today suggests that our great striving should be directed toward the ministry of the Word. This can mean preaching, but there are other ways to fulfill this admonition. For Timothy, who labored in the ministry of the Word as a vocation, no doubt it had special meaning. But there are many ways people can share God's Word, even if they are volunteer ministers.

Christians need the kind of all-consuming dedication that Paul speaks of in this lesson. His words to Timothy are his words to us!

B. Prayer

Dear Father, help me to appreciate the privilege of having access to Your Word and Your gospel. Remind me, too, of my obligation to study and share that Word. May I show my devotion to Jesus by laboring faithfully on His behalf. In Jesus' name, amen.

C. Thought to Remember

Be an approved worker.

Learning by Doing

This page contains an alternative lesson plan emphasizing learning activities.
Classes desiring such student involvement will find these suggestions helpful.

Learning Goals

After this lesson each student will be able to:

1. Describe the example set by a good soldier, athlete, or farmer, as explained in today's text.

2. Tell how regular Bible study can help the believer to demonstrate the qualities typified by soldiers, athletes, and farmers.

3. Identify one obstacle he or she will overcome in order to be faithful in studying God's Word.

Into the Lesson

To begin the class, distribute copies of a simple handout containing the following three headings and ask your students to complete the chart by listing several traits a person would need to be a good soldier, athlete, or farmer, respectively:

SOLDIER   ATHLETE   FARMER

For example, the soldier needs a submissive and obedient spirit; the athlete needs a competitive drive and self-discipline; the farmer needs faith and hard work. (This activity is also in the student book, *Adult Bible Class.*)

Ask students to volunteer their answers, then briefly discuss similarities of the traits of each occupation, such as dedication and perseverance. Say, "Today's lesson will compare the Christian life with each of these professions. Let's see how we can complete our spiritual responsibilities in a noble and honorable way."

Into the Word

Divide your class into pairs of students and assign to each pair one of the two exercises below. After the studies are finished, have each pair report its findings.

Exercise 1

Read 1 Corinthians 9:7, 24-27 and 2 Timothy 2:1-7 and complete the following statements:

1. Paul says a Christian is like a soldier in the following ways:

2. Paul says a Christian is like an athlete in the following ways:

3. Paul says a Christian is like a farmer in the following ways:

Exercise 2

Read 2 Timothy 2:8-13; 2 Corinthians 11:23-27; 1 Peter 2:12-24 and complete the following statements:

1. Jesus suffered for all people in the following ways:

2. Paul suffered for the church in the following ways:

3. Christians are to suffer for their faith in the following ways:

Discuss your students' answers to each exercise. Then, using the lesson commentary, explain how God expects Christians to contend faithfully for the truth of the gospel (see 2 Timothy 2:14, 15). Tie together the idea of laboring and suffering for Scriptural truth with the idea of faithfully passing on that truth to other Christians.

Into Life

For each scenario below (some also in the student book) your class should identify ways to solve the problem while upholding the absolute truths of Scripture discussed in today's lesson and general Christian principles.

1. Dave is running for Congress for the first time. He has always been a staunch pro-life advocate, but his campaign manager wants him to moderate his views (or at least to avoid the issue) so he can broaden his support in a tight race. What should he do?

2. Heather has risen to a prominent position in the accounting department of a major corporation. She has become aware that her employer is overstating the company's profits in its quarterly reports to hide the corporation's financial woes and to keep its stock price from falling. What should she do?

3. Samantha has been trying to lead her neighbor to Christ. This morning the woman called and begged Samantha, "If my husband asks, tell him we were out shopping together last night. I don't want him to know where I was." What should Samantha say?

4. Michael is fully scheduled for the coming weekend with a variety of good activities for and with his family and service projects for his local congregation. A college friend calls him with the offer of free tickets to the opening football game of their alma mater in an adjoining state. How should Michael respond?

After discussing responses to these situations, challenge class members to identify other such situations where a Christian must make a difficult choice while upholding Christian principles.

Let's Talk It Over

The questions on this page are designed to promote discussion of the lesson by the class and to encourage application of the lesson Scriptures. The answers provided are only discussion starters. Let your class talk it over from there.

1. We all know Christians who are entangled "with the affairs of this life." How is your life different because of your faith? How have you kept yourself from worldly entanglements?

Encourage your learners to be specific. Perhaps one has chosen a career path that has brought her less wealth but more time to be involved in ministry or family. Maybe another has volunteered to share his expertise in computers with others in the church when he could have used that time as a consultant and generated more income. There may be some who grew up in homes where immorality and pursuit of pleasure were prevalent and, except for finding the Lord, would likely have followed the same path.

All of us face various health, marital, and family problems. Are there some who faced such difficulties with a faith and courage they might not have had unless they had been keeping themselves pure and "unentangled"?

2. Which metaphor is most significant to you—the soldier, the athlete, or the farmer? Why? What new metaphor might Paul have used if he had been writing today?

Someone who has served in one of these positions will surely find that one to be the most significant. He or she can relate personally to the image and appreciate the level of commitment Paul is talking about.

Soldiers, athletes, and farmers were all very common in Paul's day, but many in your class may not have personal familiarity with any of these. To them Paul could have written about the patience or sacrifice of a parent, or the strict adherence to the rules practiced by an accountant. Let your learners suggest other examples.

3. Paul suffered as if he were an "evildoer" because of his ministry. How are Christians today portrayed as "evildoers"? How can we encourage one another to stand up to such misrepresentation or even outright discrimination?

Anyone today who believes in absolutes is apt to be labeled as out of touch, intolerant, narrow-minded, or even hateful. Christians are frequently accused of trying to "force" their own view of morality on others. One celebrity derided Christians as "ignorant and easily led." Your learners undoubtedly can add other examples to the list.

We can endure because we know that such difficulties are temporary and that many others down through the centuries have been through the same struggles. Paul reminds us in verse 8 that "Jesus Christ . . . was raised from the dead." In that is our hope—we, too, shall be raised. That future glory makes all our present struggles pale by comparison!

But notice that Paul had another thing that kept him going. In verse 10 it is the salvation of others that encourages him to endure. Modern Christians need to learn that perspective!

4. What "trivial matters" have caused strife in churches? Who is responsible for keeping the church focused on eternal matters when these trivial issues pop up? What can you do to help people keep the right perspective?

Trivial matters such as the color of the carpet or the walls in the sanctuary have split more than one church! Matters of personal preference, whether related to music style, kitchen equipment, the name for an adult Sunday school class, or some other issue, have also caused problems.

Of course, sensitive leaders will try to defuse such powder kegs, but isn't it the responsibility of every member to refuse to engage in such arguments? Every member can speak more about worshiping the Lord than about labels, more about winning the lost than about style of worship, more about reading the Word than about furnishings.

5. What would cause a "workman" to be "ashamed"? What specific safeguards can we put in place to be sure we are not unworthy workers?

The worker will be ashamed if the master finds him or her loafing or wasting time in fruitless efforts (cf. Matthew 25:14-30). The worker will be ashamed if the employer finds out that that employee has been working for someone else while being "on the clock."

When the King James Bible was printed in 1611, the word *study* meant to be diligent, not merely to pursue an academic interest. It is our daily diligence in faith, active service of the Lord, and immersion in the Word of God that will safeguard our fruitfulness. This fruitfulness will be a witness to others in keeping them fruitful in the Lord as well.

Remain Faithful

DEVOTIONAL READING: 1 John 5:1-5.

BACKGROUND SCRIPTURE: 2 Timothy 3:1–4:8.

PRINTED TEXT: 2 Timothy 3:1-5, 12–4:5.

2 Timothy 3:1-5, 12-17

1 This know also, that in the last days perilous times shall come.

2 For men shall be lovers of their own selves, covetous, boasters, proud, blasphemers, disobedient to parents, unthankful, unholy,

3 Without natural affection, trucebreakers, false accusers, incontinent, fierce, despisers of those that are good,

4 Traitors, heady, high-minded, lovers of pleasures more than lovers of God;

5 Having a form of godliness, but denying the power thereof: from such turn away.

· · · · · · · · · · · ·

12 Yea, and all that will live godly in Christ Jesus shall suffer persecution.

13 But evil men and seducers shall wax worse and worse, deceiving, and being deceived.

14 But continue thou in the things which thou hast learned and hast been assured of, knowing of whom thou hast learned them;

15 And that from a child thou hast known the holy Scriptures, which are able to make thee wise unto salvation through faith which is in Christ Jesus.

16 All Scripture is given by inspiration of God, and is profitable for doctrine, for reproof, for correction, for instruction in righteousness:

17 That the man of God may be perfect, thoroughly furnished unto all good works.

2 Timothy 4:1-5

1 I charge thee therefore before God, and the Lord Jesus Christ, who shall judge the quick and the dead at his appearing and his kingdom;

2 Preach the word; be instant in season, out of season; reprove, rebuke, exhort with all long-suffering and doctrine.

3 For the time will come when they will not endure sound doctrine; but after their own lusts shall they heap to themselves teachers, having itching ears;

4 And they shall turn away their ears from the truth, and shall be turned unto fables.

5 But watch thou in all things, endure afflictions, do the work of an evangelist, make full proof of thy ministry.

**Aug
22**

GOLDEN TEXT: But watch thou in all things, endure afflictions, do the work of an evangelist, make full proof of thy ministry.—2 Timothy 4:5.

Guidelines for the Church's Ministry
(Lessons 9-13)

Lesson Aims

After participating in this lesson, each student should be able to:

1. Produce a profile of the wicked people described in today's text.

2. Explain how faithfulness in teaching the Bible provides an antidote to wickedness.

3. Plan to share the Word of God with someone who needs to hear it.

Lesson Outline

INTRODUCTION
    A. Don't Count It Out
    B. Lesson Background
 I. CHARACTERISTICS OF EVIL PEOPLE (2 Timothy 3:1-5, 12, 13)
    A. Their Conduct (vv. 1-4)
    B. Their Religion (v. 5)
    C. Their Ruthlessness (vv. 12, 13)
II. ABILITY OF SCRIPTURE TO CONQUER EVIL (2 Timothy 3:14–4:5)
    A. Legacy of the Word (vv. 14, 15)
    B. Origin of the Word (v. 16a)
       The Bible Stands
    C. Purpose of the Word (vv. 16b, 17)
    D. Urgency of the Word (vv. 1, 2)
       The Priority of Preaching
    E. Alternatives to the Word (vv. 3-5)
CONCLUSION
    A. A Lifelong Learning Experience
    B. Prayer
    C. Thought to Remember

Introduction

A. Don't Count It Out

The infamous agnostic Robert G. Ingersoll (1833–1899) once declared that the Bible would soon be in the morgue. But the Bible lives on more than one hundred years after Ingersoll himself went to the morgue. Before Ingersoll, the French philosopher Voltaire (1694–1778) predicted that in a hundred years the Bible would be an outmoded and forgotten book. Fifty years after Voltaire was gone, his house was owned and used by a Bible society.

It has been popular from time to time to suggest that the Bible is obsolete and will ultimately be rejected. Nevertheless, the Bible stays on the bestseller list year after year. Those who sound its death knell eventually are the ones who end up in the grave.

Don't ever count the Bible out. There will always be some passages here and there with which we struggle (cf. 2 Peter 3:16), but the Bible has proven itself to be relevant from generation to generation.

B. Lesson Background

Last week we looked at the Bible from the perspective of the church leader, who is to teach it faithfully, accurately, and clearly. This week we will look at the incredible power of the Bible itself, the power to counter any false teaching.

Scholars are not positive about the identity of the false doctrine that threatens the church as Paul writes the Pastoral Epistles of 1 Timothy, 2 Timothy, and Titus. Some think it to be a non-Christian religious system called *gnosticism*. Others believe the problem was some kind of *Judaizing*.

Gnostic comes from a Greek word that means knowledge. The gnostics got their name from their belief that they had a secret knowledge of God and His plans. Gnostics also thought all flesh to be evil. This led some to deny themselves anything good, even legitimate pleasures. (Paul may be writing against this viewpoint in 1 Timothy 4:3.) Other gnostics proposed they could commit all kinds of sins in the flesh as long as they kept their spirits clean.

Some gnostic ideas resembled Christian ideas in a superficial way, so certain ideas could have crept into the church almost unnoticed for a time. Even though gnosticism wasn't really all that prominent during Paul's life, early forms of it may already have been developing, particularly in Ephesus, where Timothy lived (1 Timothy 1:3). John, who also ministered in Ephesus, seemed to be concerned about this doctrine in his letters.

Judaizing is the belief that Christians must follow the Jewish law in addition to believing in Christ. If this is the false doctrine that Paul has in mind, then the false teachers are urging an undue commitment to Jewish traditions (see Galatians 2:14; 1 Timothy 1:4; and Titus 1:14).

Even if neither of these two problems is around much today, Paul's warnings allow us to understand the problems that false religious ideas can cause in our twenty-first-century congregations. What is important to us isn't so much the specific false doctrine in question, but the power of the Word of God to defeat *any* false doctrine or heresy. False doctrines have come and gone as the centuries have passed, but the Bible never has lost its authority.

I. Characteristics of Evil People (2 Timothy 3:1-5, 12, 13)

A. Their Conduct (vv. 1-4)

1. This know also, that in the last days perilous times shall come.

It is important to understand what Paul meant by *the last days*. This concept was originally developed in the Old Testament, where it referred to the time when God would balance the scales of justice when He intervened to uphold His holiness. When in distress, people hoped for and prayed for "the day of the Lord" to come. It was to be a day of joy for the faithful and judgment for the wicked.

The New Testament writers applied this concept to the time after Christ's first coming. Peter, on the day of Pentecost, said that the last days had arrived (Acts 2:16, 17). The writer of Hebrews speaks of what has happened "in these last days" (Hebrews 1:2). John says "it is the last time" (1 John 2:18). See also 1 Timothy 4:1; 2 Peter 3:3.

The idea that the last days had arrived led some in the first century to maintain that Jesus would come back within just a few years. However, the concept of "the last days" does not require that. It is clear that Paul is talking to Timothy about a present problem, not a future one. It is a problem that will become even more severe as time passes.

2. For men shall be lovers of their own selves, covetous, boasters, proud, blasphemers, disobedient to parents, unthankful, unholy.

Paul commences on a list of about nineteen vices that evil people possess (cf. Romans 1:29-31). Some of these vices are what we might call "external sins," visible for all to see. Others are more "internal," being sins of thoughts and attitudes. Many of them overlap one another.

This verse begins with what may be seen as the beginning of all sin: people being *lovers of their own selves*. Is it not the foundation of sin to be so impressed with ourselves that we believe we know more than God? Christianity requires that we must put self aside and recognize that God is greater.

Covetousness, or unholy desire, is also listed. God thinks this problem to be serious enough to include a prohibition of it in the Ten Commandments (Exodus 20:17). In the verse at hand, the word used for *covetous* is technically "lovers of silver." Covetousness is essentially a selfish desire for money or material wealth. Money itself is not evil, but love of money is (1 Timothy 6:10).

Next on the list are *boasters* or braggarts. This is closely related to being *proud* (cf. Proverbs 16:18; James 4:6). Another word we could use is "conceit." One humorist tried to sum up this problem by noting that conceit is the weirdest

disease because it makes everyone sick except the one who has it! While amusing, this is not really true. The one who has this problem is suffering from a spiritual disease. Such a person is more than a mere irritation.

The term *blasphemers* is usually used for those who slander God. All slander is evil, but it is supremely dangerous to slander God.

As with covetousness, we are warned all the way back in the Ten Commandments that to be *disobedient to parents* is a sin (Exodus 20:12). Those who doubt that society has slipped in this regard need only spend a few hours "people watching" at a shopping mall to be convinced otherwise! [See question #1, page 440.]

Interestingly, ingratitude—being *unthankful*—is seen as a vice on the same plane as the rest. Many of us would be prone to not recognize ingratitude as a sin at all. To be unthankful ultimately reveals an improper attitude toward God.

This verse concludes by noting the problem of being *unholy*. The word used here stresses a lack of fellowship with God (see 1 Timothy 1:9).

3. Without natural affection, trucebreakers, false accusers, incontinent, fierce, despisers of those that are good.

Verse three continues the list of vices. *Without natural affection* refers to a lack of family love. This is a problem that Paul discusses in Romans 1:31 as well.

It follows that if people are without love, they will also be *trucebreakers*. This word means "without a treaty." It paints us a picture of relationships with irreconcilable differences.

The term *false accusers* comes from the same root as the word *devil*. It means "slanderer." The devil is the ultimate slanderer, and we help his cause when we engage in this activity.

How to Say It

AGNOSTIC. ag-*nahss*-tick.
APOLLOS. Uh-*pahl*-us.
AQUILA. *Ack*-wih-luh.
BEREANS. Buh-*ree*-unz.
GNOSTIC. *nahss*-tick.
GNOSTICISM. *nahss*-tih-*sizz*-um (strong accent on *nahss*).
HERESY. *hair*-uh-see.
JUDAIZING. *Joo*-day-ize-ing.
JUDAS ISCARIOT. *Joo*-dus Iss-*care*-e-ut.
PENTECOST. *Pent*-ih-kost.
POLYGAMOUS. puh-*lih*-guh-mus.
POLYTHEISTIC. *pah*-lee-thee-*iss*-tick (*th* as in *thin*; strong accent on *iss*).
PRISCILLA. Prih-*sil*-uh.
VOLTAIRE. Voll-*tare*.

Incontinent in the antique English of the *King James Version* means "without strength" or "lacking self-control." The lack of strength Paul is talking about is absence of moral strength.

The next quality is *fierce*, or literally "untamed." No doubt a person who does not control his or her anger and other emotions is like an untamed animal. Such people are unpredictable in their actions, and the damage they can wreak may be very great.

Those who are *despisers of those that are good* are condemned for having a corrupted view of life. We may not always be able to do good, but we ought at least to love good.

4. Traitors, heady, high-minded, lovers of pleasures more than lovers of God.

The sobering meaning of *traitors* is all too clear. There is nothing quite so painful as to be betrayed by someone whom you thought to be on your side. This word describes Judas Iscariot in Luke 6:16.

To be *heady* is the idea of being "rash" or "reckless" (see Acts 19:36). The original word gives us a picture of someone falling head forward.

The next quality, *high-minded,* is not used as a compliment even though it may sound like it. It describes someone who thinks too highly of himself or herself. This overlaps the idea of being boastful, proud, or conceited from verse 2 (see also Romans 12:3).

Those who are *lovers of pleasures more than lovers of God* are, in effect, idol worshipers. Anything that we put on the throne of our hearts instead of God is an idol.

B. Their Religion (v. 5)

5. Having a form of godliness, but denying the power thereof: from such turn away.

The evil people Paul talks about are not devoid of religion. In fact, casual observers might judge them to be very religious. But it is just *a form of godliness.* They go through the motions of religion, but they are not Christian. Even though they like the form their religion takes, they deny it has any real *power.* "They profess that they know God; but in works they deny him" (Titus 1:16). [See question #2, page 440.]

C. Their Ruthlessness (vv. 12, 13)

12. Yea, and all that will live godly in Christ Jesus shall suffer persecution.

Those who have been Christians for some time realize that God has not promised His people magical protection from *persecution.* Passages such as Matthew 16:24; John 15:20; and Acts 14:22 warn us otherwise.

13. But evil men and seducers shall wax worse and worse, deceiving, and being deceived.

The presence of Christianity will not make *evil* people better if they don't want to be made better. The presence of the Christian witness simply may make such people more determined to be *worse and worse.* Not only will these people be *deceived,* they will deceive others. The ability to lie to others and to themselves is a fundamental quality of evil people.

II. Ability of Scripture to Conquer Evil (2 Timothy 3:14–4:5)

A. Legacy of the Word (vv. 14, 15)

14. But continue thou in the things which thou hast learned and hast been assured of, knowing of whom thou hast learned them.

Timothy must not be led astray by false teachers! The gospel is not just something that Timothy "knows about"; rather, it is something that has convinced him of truth. One reason for his confidence is that he can trust those who first taught him. [See question #3, page 440.] See the next verse.

15. And that from a child thou hast known the holy Scriptures, which are able to make thee wise unto salvation through faith which is in Christ Jesus.

Timothy was taught *from a child* by his grandmother and his mother (2 Timothy 1:5). Young Jewish children were often taught Scripture verses when they were very young. The Old Testament stresses the importance of teaching God's Word to children (see Deuteronomy 4:9). The Old Testament *Scriptures* that Timothy had learned helped prepare him for later faith in Jesus (cf. John 5:39).

B. Origin of the Word (v. 16a)

16a. All Scripture is given by inspiration of God.

All Scripture ultimately comes from God. Working through human writers, God is the author and source. Second Peter 1:21 tells us a bit about how this *inspiration* took place. We can take comfort in the fact that "the Scripture cannot be broken" (John 10:35).

THE BIBLE STANDS

On one of his old history books a student once wrote, "In case of famine, eat this book; it's full of baloney! In case of flood, stand on this book; it's dry!" The world sees the Bible in much the same way: an outdated and often erroneous history book.

A nineteenth-century writer, commenting on the reliability of the Bible, states, "People for two millennia have been refuting and overthrowing this book, and yet it stands today as solid as a rock. Its circulation increases, and it is more loved and cherished and read today than ever before. People make about as much impression on this book as a man with a tack hammer would on the pyramids of Egypt.

"The hammers of infidels have been pecking away at this book for ages, but the hammers are worn out, and the anvil still endures. If this book had not been the book of God, men would have destroyed it long ago. Emperors and popes, kings and princes and rulers, scholars and intellectuals, have all tried their hand at it; they die and the book still lives."

What accounts for such durability and esteem for the Bible? Simply this: it is the Word of God. Peter reminds us that "the prophecy came not in old time by the will of man: but holy men of God spake as they were moved by the Holy Ghost" (2 Peter 1:21).

For one who believes in the inspiration of the Bible, it naturally follows that the Bible is the authority for living. To claim that the Bible is inspired by God yet reject its authority for daily living is a contradiction.   —A. E. A.

C. Purpose of the Word (vv. 16b, 17)

16b, 17. And is profitable for doctrine, for reproof, for correction, for instruction in righteousness: that the man of God may be perfect, thoroughly furnished unto all good works.

Scripture is valuable for so many things! For those who will allow it, Scripture can bring *reproof* and *correction* for all the problems listed in 2 Timothy 3:1-5. [See question #4, page 440.]

When Paul says that the purpose of Scripture is to make us *perfect*, he does not suggest we can become flawless in this life. The idea, rather, is to be "complete" or "fully equipped." This is what it means to be *thoroughly furnished* for *all good works*. It means that we will be given all we need to be mature Christians and to meet the demands of God.

The word *perfect* here is used as we might say, "He is the perfect baseball player." We don't mean that as a player he makes no mistakes; rather, we mean he has all that is necessary to be a great baseball player.

D. Urgency of the Word (vv. 1, 2)

1. I charge thee therefore before God, and the Lord Jesus Christ, who shall judge the quick and the dead at his appearing and his kingdom.

To invoke the names of *God and the Lord Jesus Christ* in this manner means that the *charge* that Paul has for Timothy is very important. We should note that the word *quick* in this context is an older word meaning "living." See Acts 10:42; Romans 14:9; and 1 Peter 4:5.

Home Daily Bible Readings

Monday, Aug. 16—Rejoice in Persecution (Luke 6:20-26)
Tuesday, Aug. 17—By Endurance You Will Gain Life (Luke 21:12-19)
Wednesday, Aug. 18—Avoid Lovers of Pleasure (2 Timothy 3:1-9)
Thursday, Aug. 19—Continue in What You Have Believed (2 Timothy 3:10-15)
Friday, Aug. 20—Be Persistent in Proclaiming the Word (2 Timothy 3:16–4:4)
Saturday, Aug. 21—I Have Kept the Faith (2 Timothy 4:5-10)
Sunday, Aug. 22—The Lord Gave Me Strength (2 Timothy 4:11-18)

2. Preach the word; be instant in season, out of season; reprove, rebuke, exhort with all long-suffering and doctrine.

The charge to *Preach the word* seems straightforward. But Paul doesn't have in mind "only when it's convenient"! To preach the Word *in season* or *out of season* means that Timothy should be prepared to preach the Word at all times, whether it is convenient or not. The same goes for us.

Notice Paul says that preaching includes reproving, rebuking, and exhorting. There are preachers who specialize in reproving and rebuking, but rarely do any exhorting or encouraging. Others *exhort* and encourage, but never *rebuke*. Biblical preaching requires that we do both. And just as God has been *long-suffering* with us (2 Peter 3:9), so our preaching is to be done with patience.

THE PRIORITY OF PREACHING

Preaching holds a prominent place in spreading the gospel message. This has been the case throughout the history of the church. It was at the preaching of Peter on the day of Pentecost that the church was born. Philip the evangelist went to Samaria proclaiming the gospel (Acts 8:5).

The apostle Paul said, "Woe is unto me, if I preach not the gospel!" (1 Corinthians 9:16). The ultimate challenge for preaching given in Scripture is Paul's rhetorical question of Romans 10:14: "How then shall they call on him in whom they have not believed? and how shall they believe in him of whom they have not heard? and how shall they hear without a preacher?"

Some would say that preaching is outdated in our world today. In *Prescription for Preaching*, Woodrow Kroll addresses this issue when he asks, "Are conditions today any different which would make the gospel message irrelevant? You might venture an answer in the affirmative. Clothes are different, styles are different, customs are different, therefore people must be different. But you are wrong. The Bible doesn't deal with clothes, styles, or customs. It deals with man's sin and God's provision for man's sin."

Kroll goes on to note that our universal sin problem remains the same, despite ever-changing clothing styles and customs. A universal problem requires a universal cure: faith in Christ. That's what makes the gospel message relevant even in the twenty-first century. —A. E. A.

E. Alternatives to the Word (vv. 3-5)

3. For the time will come when they will not endure sound doctrine; but after their own lusts shall they heap to themselves teachers, having itching ears.

This is a bit of a repeat from 1 Timothy 4:1-3. This warning to Timothy is ours as well: some people will be interested only in what they *want* to hear, not what they *need* to hear. That's what it means to have *itching ears*. [See question #5, page 440.]

4. And they shall turn away their ears from the truth, and shall be turned unto fables.

Paul also discusses the problem of *fables* in 1 Timothy 4:7 and Titus 1:14. During the time between the Old and New Testaments, Jewish writers had created a great many fanciful tales. Greek myths went back even farther than that.

But the New Testament writers always insist that their teachings rest on historical foundations, unlike those myths and legends. If Jesus did not actually live, die, and rise from the dead, then what hope do we have? (See 1 Corinthians 15:12-19.)

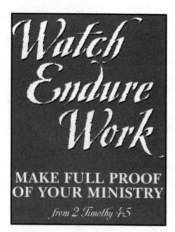

Visual for lesson 12

This visual will remind your learners of their lifelong task in preparing for church leadership.

5. But watch thou in all things, endure afflictions, do the work of an evangelist, make full proof of thy ministry.

Once again, Paul cautions Timothy to be prepared to *endure* hardship as he carries out his evangelistic ministry. The word *evangelist* is related to the word *gospel*. When Timothy does *the work of an evangelist*, he will be "telling the good news."

Acts 21:8 and Ephesians 4:11 tell us that certain people were called evangelists in the early church. Some think that an evangelist filled an office similar to that of an elder or a deacon, but this is uncertain since there are so few uses of this term in this kind of context. Someone designated as an evangelist must surely have spent most of his time sharing the gospel with unsaved people. As Timothy preaches, he is to do this as well.

Conclusion

A. A Lifelong Learning Experience

Educators extol the virtue of lifelong learning. They rightly remind us that we can never know everything, that there is always more to learn, and that we need to continue to grow. The same can be said of Bible study. Even if you began studying as a child, you can always learn more of God's will from that greatest of all books.

No less an intellect than U.S. President John Quincy Adams (1767–1848) spoke of his love for, and study of, the Bible. He made it his practice for many years to read through the Bible once a year. His plan was to read four or five chapters every morning immediately after waking up. He gave a full hour to this study and described it as "the most suitable manner of beginning the day." He went on to say that with "reference to revelation, to history, or to morality, it is an invaluable and inexhaustible mine of knowledge and virtue."

Following the example of Adams, let us commit to reading and studying the Bible every day. A good way to do this is to use a "one-year Bible" that is conveniently divided into three hundred sixty-five daily readings. Find a Bible reading plan and put it to work today!

B. Prayer

Dear Father, I desire to know Your Word, share Your Word, and order my life by Your Word. May that commitment bear fruit in my life and my church. In Jesus' name, amen.

C. Thought to Remember

"Sin will keep you from this Book, or this Book will keep you from sin."
—Dwight L. Moody (1837–1899)

Learning by Doing

This page contains an alternative lesson plan emphasizing learning activities.
Classes desiring such student involvement will find these suggestions helpful.

Learning Goals

After this lesson each student will be able to:

1. Produce a profile of the wicked people described in today's text.

2. Explain how faithfulness in teaching the Bible provides an antidote to wickedness.

3. Plan to share the Word of God with someone who needs to hear it.

Into the Lesson

Distribute copies of the agree-disagree exercise that follows and ask your students to record their opinions for each statement by circling one answer. If you use student books, refer the class to the page where this exercise is reproduced.

(1) The greatest threat to the church today is false doctrine. Agree or disagree? (2) If the Bible is not Holy Spirit inspired, we cannot depend on it for spiritual guidance. Agree or disagree? (3) The world will get better and better until the Lord returns. Agree or disagree? (4) The gospel is the only hope of salvation for the world. Agree or disagree?

Discuss students' answers briefly, noting their views. Tell your class, "Today's lesson deals with the need for Scriptural power to counter false teaching in these last days before Christ's return."

Into the Word

Use the Lesson Background section to explain the threat of gnosticism and its doctrines. Next, divide your class into several small groups to complete the two exercises that follow. Space for these exercises is provided in the student book.

Exercise 1. Ask each group to use the information from 2 Timothy 3:1-9, 12, 13 to produce a profile of the heretics depicted there by describing both their conduct (see vv. 1-4, 6-9, 12, 13) and their false religion (see v. 5).

After your groups finish their profiles, ask each to report their findings to the class. Summarize their answers on the board or on an overhead transparency, then go on to Exercise 2.

Exercise 2. Using the information from Exercise 1, plus Paul's teaching in 2 Timothy 3:14–4:5, explain the church's appropriate response to the conduct and religion of the heresy discussed earlier. Specifically, ask the groups to discuss, "How is the Bible an antidote to immoral conduct?" and, "How does the Bible help us to detect and correct false teaching?"

Into Life

Finally, ask your students to use today's lesson plus the Scriptures indicated to critique the doctrines of the imaginary cults described below.

Steve's High-flying Extraterrestrial Cult denies the existence of the Trinity, teaching that God is one being, the Chief Executive Officer (CEO), among other beings He created who exist in the "Upper Story." The CEO created this world and its inhabitants as a kind of lab experiment. Jesus was not God, but an Upper Story Being (USB) who came to earth in a UFO and took control of a human body to show others how to attain the Upper Story. To do that, a human must become a disciple of a USB, such as Jesus, while in a human body. Then, when the USB leaves earth, he takes his disciples with him, forever, to the Upper Story. *Responses: (1) There is only one true God (1 Corinthians 8:4-6). (2) Man is not a lab rat, but was made in God's image (Genesis 1, 2). (3) Jesus is not a USB, but the Son of God in the flesh (John 1:1-14; Colossians 2:9). (4) Salvation comes not by being a disciple of a USB, but by faith in the person and work of Jesus Christ (Acts 4:10-12; Romans 3:25, 26).*

Joe's Polytheistic Polygamous Cult teaches that there is an infinite number of gods, and all were once human beings before they became divine. Each worthy human today can also become a god by believing in Jesus. His nature and will are revealed in the Bible and in *The Book of Joe*, given to Joe by Jesus' Father, the God whom humans are to worship. *The Book of Joe* is the Father's final revelation to man and is superior to the Bible wherever the two disagree. *The Book of Joe* says that whoever believes in Jesus as He is revealed in that book will become a god after death. Husbands and wives will be married forever and will continue to have children in the hereafter. Faithful believers will have their own planets to colonize. *Responses: (1) There is only one true God (Isaiah 44:6-8); (2) God was never a mere mortal, and humans cannot become divine (1 Timothy 6:15, 16); (3) The Bible is God's final revelation to us before the return of Christ and the end of the world (Hebrews 1:1-3); (4) Marriage and procreation are for this life only (Luke 20:27-38).*

Suggest that the students may know someone who holds a view similar to one of these hypothetical ones. Ask each to make a commitment to talk to that one about the truth of God's Word.

Let's Talk It Over

The questions on this page are designed to promote discussion of the lesson by the class and to encourage application of the lesson Scriptures. The answers provided are only discussion starters. Let your class talk it over from there.

1. We assume that Paul is writing to adults. So we may be surprised to read "disobedient to parents" in his list of vices. To what extent should an adult Christian continue to obey his or her parents? Why?

The difference between family life in the first century and family life today may account somewhat for this command. In the first century (and in some cultures still today) it was common for more than one generation to live together in the same house. The head of the house would set the rules for everyone else, even adults, to follow.

But the principle is still valid. Adults ought to respect the wisdom and experience of their parents. They will not scorn their advice without godly reason. Paul is referring to adults who have no respect for their parents, who rebel against their heritage in general and against their own parents in particular. An adult should at least be able to sit down and have a reasonable discussion with his or her parents in order to hear their views and concerns.

2. What are some evidences that one has "a form of godliness" but lacks substance in his or her faith? How might any of us suffer from this condition to some extent? How can we avoid it?

One who has merely a form of godliness and not its substance tends to be very ritualistic. He or she will attend religious services with great regularity, but will have a lifestyle outside the church building that is very much like that of the ungodly. Such a person may also be very legalistic. This problem can show itself in instances where he or she views certain activities as sinful, while giving no attention to the heart. For example, one having a mere outward form of godliness will condemn sexual immorality, but may well harbor lust in his or her own heart.

3. What does it matter "of whom" someone has learned the truth of the gospel? What challenge is implied here for parents and teachers?

Parents and teachers need to "walk the talk," as the saying goes. Example is such a strong teacher! But the issue goes beyond that. Parents and teachers need to express a vital, personal concern for the one being taught. It needs to be clear that they have the child or student's best interest at heart. Then, when a false teacher comes along, the student will have that extra protection in evaluating the teacher's message. "I don't really know this new person, but I know what those who love me have taught—and this is different. Those who love me would not have lied to me—so this new person must be the one who is lying!"

4. If the Bible is all that verses 16 and 17 say it is, then we ought to spend considerable time in studying it! What are some ways you can realize these benefits from the Bible? What specifically do you do to know and understand its message?

This will be a good opportunity to hear how different ones among your learners conduct their quiet times and daily devotions. What devotional books can they recommend? When do they read? Is morning better, or evening? Do they read through the Bible in a year? If so, what plan do they follow?

Be sure to give attention to heart issues here as well as the form of Bible study. How do they prepare themselves to hear "reproof" and "correction" from the Bible? How do they make sure they apply what they read and learn? Does someone hold them accountable? Allow some good examples to be reported to encourage those who may not have a good daily devotional plan.

5. Suppose a preacher or teacher expresses some views that you do not like. How do you know whether it is he who is wrong, or if it is you who are guilty of what Paul describes here? What should you do if you disagree with your teacher?

We need to keep open minds and open Bibles when someone is teaching. The noble Bereans set the example for us when they compared what was taught with the Scriptures (Acts 17:11). If we disagree, we need to determine whether the issue is one of faith or one of expediency. Matters of expediency leave room for liberty of opinion.

If we disagree on issues of faith (doctrine), we need to discuss it with the teacher in private. Perhaps we misunderstood. Give the teacher an opportunity to explain and clear up the confusion. Or maybe we can explain to the teacher "the way of God more perfectly," as Aquila and Priscilla did for Apollos (Acts 18:26).

Do Good Works

DEVOTIONAL READING: James 1:19-25.

BACKGROUND SCRIPTURE: Titus 2:1–3:11.

PRINTED TEXT: Titus 2:7, 8, 11–3:10.

Titus 2:7, 8, 11-15

7 In all things showing thyself a pattern of good works: in doctrine showing uncorruptness, gravity, sincerity,

8 Sound speech, that cannot be condemned; that he that is of the contrary part may be ashamed, having no evil thing to say of you.

. . . .

11 For the grace of God that bringeth salvation hath appeared to all men,

12 Teaching us that, denying ungodliness and worldly lusts, we should live soberly, righteously, and godly, in this present world;

13 Looking for that blessed hope, and the glorious appearing of the great God and our Saviour Jesus Christ;

14 Who gave himself for us, that he might redeem us from all iniquity, and purify unto himself a peculiar people, zealous of good works.

15 These things speak, and exhort, and rebuke with all authority. Let no man despise thee.

Titus 3:1-10

1 Put them in mind to be subject to principalities and powers, to obey magistrates, to be ready to every good work,

2 To speak evil of no man, to be no brawlers, but gentle, showing all meekness unto all men.

3 For we ourselves also were sometime foolish, disobedient, deceived, serving divers lusts and pleasures, living in malice and envy, hateful, and hating one another.

4 But after that the kindness and love of God our Saviour toward man appeared,

5 Not by works of righteousness which we have done, but according to his mercy he saved us, by the washing of regeneration, and renewing of the Holy Ghost;

6 Which he shed on us abundantly through Jesus Christ our Saviour;

7 That being justified by his grace, we should be made heirs according to the hope of eternal life.

8 This is a faithful saying, and these things I will that thou affirm constantly, that they which have believed in God might be careful to maintain good works. These things are good and profitable unto men.

9 But avoid foolish questions, and genealogies, and contentions, and strivings about the law; for they are unprofitable and vain.

10 A man that is a heretic, after the first and second admonition, reject.

GOLDEN TEXT: In all things showing thyself a pattern of good works: in doctrine showing uncorruptness, gravity, sincerity, sound speech, that cannot be condemned.—Titus 2:7, 8a.

Lesson Aims

After participating in this lesson, each student should be able to:

1. Make a list of all the commands for action that Paul gave Titus in the lesson text.

2. Explain how good works demonstrate appreciation for the salvation we have through Jesus Christ.

3. Name one of Paul's commands that he or she will put into practice this week.

Lesson Outline

INTRODUCTION
    A. Do Nothings
    B. Lesson Background
I. DISCIPLINES OF A GODLY LIFE (Titus 2:7, 8, 11–3:2)
    A. Willingness to Be a Pattern (vv. 7, 8)
    B. Strength to Say "No" (vv. 11, 12)
        Just Say No
    C. Readiness for the Lord's Return (v. 13)
    D. Realization of Gospel Truth (v. 14)
    E. Reminder of Duty (v. 15)
    F. Humility of a Good Citizen (3:1, 2)
II. MOTIVATION OF THE GODLY LIFE (Titus 3:3-10)
    A. Futility of Our Past (v. 3)
    B. Completeness of Our Salvation (vv. 4-7)
        Beauty and the Beast
    C. Importance of Good Deeds (vv. 8-10)
CONCLUSION
    A. Words and Deeds
    B. Prayer
    C. Thought to Remember

Introduction

A. Do Nothings

There is an old story about a preacher who came to visit an elderly couple in their home. The wife could not hear much and therefore missed some of the conversation. After a while she asked the visiting preacher, "Now, what is it you do?" Her husband replied, "Oh, ma, he don't *do* nothing. He's a preacher."

Titus was not to be a do-nothing preacher. While Paul will remind him of the beauties of God's grace, Titus will also be told how important it is to remain committed to good deeds.

Christianity has struggled constantly about the relationship between grace and works. This lesson will help us put that issue into perspective. The church has also struggled with the relationship between doctrine and practical Christian living. This lesson will help us in that area as well.

B. Lesson Background

Many of the subjects covered in the two letters to Timothy are also covered in Titus. Some even see the letter to Titus as a kind of condensed version of 1 Timothy. It would not be surprising that Paul would say similar things to two of his key lieutenants.

An interesting comparison between Timothy and Titus may be made on the issue of circumcision. In Galatians 2:1-5 we learn that certain Jews expected Titus, a Greek, to be circumcised according to the Old Testament law. Since Titus was a Gentile, however, Paul would not require him to undergo a Jewish practice. Such a requirement would serve to bring Gentile converts "into bondage" in opposition to the "liberty which we have in Christ Jesus" (Galatians 2:4).

Timothy, on the other hand, was a Jew because his mother was Jewish. Therefore, Paul knew that it was expedient to circumcise him (Acts 16:1-3). There was no point in creating an unnecessary roadblock in Timothy's witness to his fellow Jews.

Titus must have had a strong connection to the church at Corinth, for Paul mentions him several times in 2 Corinthians. We know that Titus traveled with Paul and Barnabas on a very sensitive mission to Jerusalem (Galatians 2:1). Paul must have trusted Titus a great deal.

Paul's letters charged Timothy to correct certain problems in Ephesus. Similarly, Titus is to provide leadership on the island of Crete (Titus 1:5). The problems on Crete, however, do not seem to be as severe as those in Ephesus. The church or churches on Crete were newer, whereas Ephesus had a more established church.

I. Disciplines of a Godly Life
(Titus 2:7, 8, 11–3:2)

A. Willingness to Be a Pattern (vv. 7, 8)

7. In all things showing thyself a pattern of good works: in doctrine showing uncorruptness, gravity, sincerity.

We often profit by having an example—someone to model the behavior or practice we wish to perform. What a compliment to Titus, that Paul thought him up to the challenge of being that *pattern!* (See also 1 Timothy 4:12; 1 Peter 5:3.) [See question #1, page 448.]

Visual for lesson 13

A Pattern of Good Works
from Titus 2:7

Let this visual remind your learners that there is no such thing as being a "part-time" pattern.

Beyond his example in *good works,* Titus is to be an example in commitment to sound *doctrine.* Even though some Christians are often frustrated or bored with the study of doctrine, we must recognize its importance. Our deeds need a solid doctrinal foundation. Without such a foundation, false doctrine can take over. When that happens, our deeds can become worthless or even evil.

Titus is to show commitment to his message in certain ways. Handling doctrine with *uncorruptness* (integrity) and *gravity* (seriousness) is vital. The latter does not mean that Christians are to be grim people. Rather, it is a reminder that teaching and preaching Scripture is serious business. The word *sincerity* is not found in the oldest Greek manuscripts of this verse, but the idea is certainly not foreign to Paul (cf. 2 Corinthians 1:12; 2:17; 8:8).

8. Sound speech, that cannot be condemned; that he that is of the contrary part may be ashamed, having no evil thing to say of you.

The instruction to preach with *sound speech* probably refers to Paul's concern that Titus's preaching be above reproach. While the word *gravity* in verse 7 refers to the manner of teaching, *sound speech* probably refers to the content of what is communicated.

What is certain is that if someone teaches what is good and true, then others cannot condemn the message. At least they cannot do so with any credibility. Titus is to speak with such integrity that his opponents will be ashamed to criticize him (cf. 1 Peter 2:15).

B. Strength to Say "No" (vv. 11, 12)

11, 12. For the grace of God that bringeth salvation hath appeared to all men, teaching us that, denying ungodliness and worldly lusts, we should live soberly, righteously, and godly, in this present world.

Although God was gracious to people in Old Testament times, His *grace* comes into distinct focus in the person of Jesus Christ. It is this quality Paul has in mind when he speaks of how the grace that brings *salvation* has *appeared to* us *all.* This does not mean that all people will receive that grace. The grace has appeared to *all,* but we must accept it.

God's grace not only saves us, it also teaches us various things. Some would say that grace teaches us to sin more and more since we know we will be forgiven. Paul disagrees strenuously with that idea (Romans 6:1-4). Instead, Paul would argue that the presence of God's grace gives us the strength to say no to sin.

Ungodliness and *worldly lusts* are closely related. It is a foolish person who builds his or her life on the things of the world—things that we will surrender at death (cf. Luke 12:16-21). The way some people live, you would think they were going to live a few years in Heaven and an eternity on earth! [See question #2, page 448.]

Instead of having such a worldly attitude, we are to live *soberly* (which means self-controlled) and *righteously* (uprightly) so our lives will be *godly.* We do well to remember, "For all that is in the world, the lust of the flesh, . . . is not of the Father, but is of the world" (1 John 2:16).

JUST SAY NO

In the early 1980s Nancy Reagan, First Lady of the United States, was appalled when she learned of the prevalence of drug and alcohol abuse among children. In an effort to curb this problem she launched a campaign, aimed at elementary-aged children, called "Just Say No." The campaign began at an elementary school in Oakland, California, and it spread across the country. It was a simple message: "When someone offers you drugs, just say no." Television ad campaigns picked up on this theme. Grocery bags carried the message as well.

Yet some poked fun at the message saying that it was simplistic and therefore unrealistic. T-shirts came out saying, "I said no to drugs, but they wouldn't listen." Others called the campaign a waste of money, dismissing it as simply a "feel good" message.

In the final analysis, however, the most effec-tive way to stop a problem is never to let i⁀ It is not that *just saying no* is too simpl⁀ people think they can dabble a li⁀ culture and then can say *no* v⁀ have gone too far. But that is w⁀

The old adage is true: "If yo⁀ you're going to get burned." Wheth⁀

in drugs, alcohol, illicit sex, witchcraft, cheating on taxes, or any other sin, the best way to keep from being burned is to say no at the very outset. Simple? Yes. Simplistic? No. Effective? Most definitely!   —A. E. A.

C. Readiness for the Lord's Return (v. 13)

13. Looking for that blessed hope, and the glorious appearing of the great God and our Saviour Jesus Christ.

Having talked about the implications of Jesus' first coming, Paul now moves to the subject of the second coming. When a community in ancient times knew a king was coming, they would prepare for that visit. When we as Christians live "soberly, righteously, and godly" (v. 12, above), we will be ready for the arrival of our King. Jesus' return will be the realization of our *blessed hope.*

At first glance, it may seem that this verse is talking about two different appearings, one of our *great God* and the other of *our Saviour Jesus Christ.* It is more in line with other passages, however, to see *great God* as a description of Jesus Himself (see John 20:28; Romans 9:5; Hebrews 1:8; and 2 Peter 1:1). This is a definitive statement of the divinity of Jesus.

D. Realization of Gospel Truth (v. 14)

14. Who gave himself for us, that he might redeem us from all iniquity, and purify unto himself a peculiar people, zealous of good works.

This verse speaks to the very heart of the gospel message! When Christ *gave himself for us,* He took the penalty that the Father had decreed for our sin. The One who did this is the One who will return (v. 13, above) to claim His *people.* We show our faith in Him by our *good works* until He returns (Ephesians 2:10).

E. Reminder of Duty (v. 15)

15. These things speak, and exhort, and rebuke with all authority. Let no man despise thee.

Paul now returns to his challenge of Titus 2:1. It is similar to the challenge to Timothy in 2 Timothy 4:2. Since the message that Titus has been given to proclaim comes from an apostle, it is a message of *authority.* As long as Titus can remember this, no one will be able to intimidate him into silence or into thinking otherwise. [See question #3, page 448.]

F. Humility of a Good Citizen (3:1, 2)

1. Put them in mind to be subject to principalities and powers, to obey magistrates, to be ready to every good work.

Since we are citizens of a Heavenly kingdom, may get the idea that we are exempt from the rules of earthly governments. But both here and in Romans 13:1-7 Paul tells us otherwise. These governing authorities were not Christian rulers, but we are to obey them nonetheless. (See also 1 Peter 2:13-17.)

Christians know that without some kind of law to govern social behavior, chaos will result. So Christians obey the government. This obedience, however, is not absolute. We would not obey the government in those cases where the government tries to force us to do something against God's will (see Acts 4:19; 5:29).

Paul describes earthly governments as *principalities and powers.* Paul uses this phrase to refer to demons in Ephesians 6:12, but in the case at hand he means earthly, secular rulers.

2. To speak evil of no man, to be no brawlers, but gentle, showing all meekness unto all men.

Christians are not to slander anyone, even their enemies. Not only are Christians to *speak* no *evil,* they are also not to lash out physically. Titus is also told to show *meekness.* This does not mean weakness, but rather carries the ideas of being self-controlled and gentle (cf. Matthew 5:5).

What is it that motivates us to live a life of godliness? Paul lists several motivations in the verses that follow.

II. Motivation of the Godly Life (Titus 3:3-10)

A. Futility of Our Past (v. 3)

3. For we ourselves also were sometime foolish, disobedient, deceived, serving divers lusts and pleasures, living in malice and envy, hateful, and hating one another.

How desperate our situation was without Christ! We were *foolish,* but beyond that we were stubbornly *disobedient.* To make the situation even worse, we were *deceived.*

We know that before we accepted Christ, we were just as sinful as our neighbors (cf. Ephesians 4:18, 19). This fact should keep us from having a sense of pride. What we need instead is gratitude that God can change lives. In the state we were in previously, it was so much easier to give in to *lusts* as well as *malice and envy.* Many who give way to *hating* end up being hated by others.

B. Completeness of Our Salvation (vv. 4-7)

4. But after that the kindness and love of God our Saviour toward man appeared.

The kindness and love of God appeared in the midst of our hopelessness in the person of Jesus Christ. As the next verse shows, this was not of our doing.

5. Not by works of righteousness which we have done, but according to his mercy he saved

us, by the washing of regeneration, and renewing of the Holy Ghost.

Notice the concept of grace that is presented clearly here when we are told that *according to his mercy he saved us.* We are not saved because we are so good or so lovable (see Ephesians 2:8, 9; 2 Timothy 1:9).

The verse then speaks of *the washing of regeneration* as well as the *renewing of the Holy Ghost.* Some think that *washing of regeneration* refers to an "inner, spiritual cleansing." Others think that Paul is referring to water baptism. Indeed, it would be difficult to imagine Titus not thinking of water baptism when he reads this phrase (see also Acts 22:16; Ephesians 5:26).

Water, of course, has no power to wash away sins. It's just water. Neither does the person administering the baptism have any such power. As a result, we can conclude that Paul speaks of *washing of regeneration* in the sense that we are saved *in* the waters of baptism, but not *by* those waters (cf. Colossians 2:12).

This viewpoint upholds the importance of grace. When a person submits to baptism, it is part of an appeal for grace and a time to receive grace—it is not an attempt to earn salvation. Baptism apart from personal faith and repentance means nothing.

It is the Holy Spirit who brings about our renewal. Mere human effort cannot do this. Peter connected water baptism with receiving "the gift of the Holy Ghost", in his sermon on the day of Pentecost (Acts 2:38).

BEAUTY AND THE BEAST

Some consider the fairy tale *Beauty and the Beast* to be the most beloved love story of all time. The foundational theme of the story has been used in many movies and books throughout the years. It is the story of a spoiled prince who snubs an old beggar woman at his castle because of her unattractive appearance.

The woman warns the prince not to make judgments by appearance. Repeatedly she returns to the castle, but each time the prince turns her away. After her final dismissal, the old woman turns into a beautiful princess. She also casts a spell on the prince that turns him into a beastly looking creature. The only way to erase the ugliness of his appearance is that he learn to love another and earn her love in return. The rest of the story is a familiar one of the triumph of love over appearance.

And it is an illustration of grace as well. How ugly we were in our sin! Our sin-marred appearance was repulsive to God. But the God of grace saw beyond the ugliness of sin and He loved the unlovely. Christians often quote that most fundamental of Bible truths from John 3:16: "For God so loved the world. . . . " Unfortunately, we don't often grasp how much love that took.

There is a twist to this story of grace that we must not overlook. The beast in the fairy tale had to learn to express love to win the beauty to himself. God, on the other hand, was the beautiful one who made the first step by expressing love to ugly and sinful humanity by giving His Son for us. Paul puts it this way: "But God commendeth his love toward us, in that, while we were yet sinners, Christ died for us" (Romans 5:8).

A God who demonstrates such beautiful love deserves the best we "redeemed beasts" have to offer. And those around us having the beastliness of sin need to be pointed to the beautiful Savior.

—A. E. A.

6. Which he shed on us abundantly through Jesus Christ our Saviour.

He refers to the Holy Spirit. The outpouring of the Holy Spirit occurred on the day of Pentecost, just mentioned with verse 5, above. Since that great day each Christian has received the gift of the Holy Spirit's indwelling (Acts 2:39). Jesus promised that He would ask the Father to send the Holy Spirit (John 14:16, 17). Notice also that our God is not one who gives sparingly. God is generous and gives *abundantly*.

7. That being justified by his grace, we should be made heirs according to the hope of eternal life.

To be *justified* means to be declared righteous (Romans 3:21-26). As a result Christians also have been *made heirs* (Galatians 3:29). This is a sign of the great love that God has for us, that He would number us as His children. But there is more: to be justified and to be made heirs means having the certain *hope of eternal life.* What a God we serve!

How to Say It

ABRAHAM. *Ay*-bruh-ham.

BARNABAS. *Bar*-nuh-bus.

COLOSSIANS. Kuh-*losh*-unz.

CORINTHIANS. Kor-*in*-thee-unz (*th* as in *thin*).

CRETE. Creet.

EPHESIANS. Ee-*fee*-zhunz.

GALATIANS. Guh-*lay*-shunz.

GNOSTIC. *nahss*-tick.

GNOSTICISM. *nahss*-tih-*sizz*-um (strong accent on *nahss*).

HERESY. *hair*-uh-see.

HERETIC. *hair*-uh-tik.

LECH WALESA. Lek Wuh-*len*-suh.

TITUS. *Tie*-tus.

C. Importance of Good Deeds (vv. 8-10)

8. This is a faithful saying, and these things I will that thou affirm constantly, that they which have believed in God might be careful to maintain good works. These things are good and profitable unto men.

This verse begins with the statement *This is a faithful saying* that we have seen in previous lessons. Again, it can refer to a proverb that Titus already knows well, to some teaching that Paul has emphasized repeatedly, or to a new teaching that Paul is creating as he writes.

What Paul has to say next is so important that he wants Titus to *affirm* it *constantly:* he must be careful *to maintain good works.* "For we are his workmanship, created in Christ Jesus unto good works" (Ephesians 2:10). To recognize that Christian deeds are both *good and profitable* is to say not only that there is something inherently good about those deeds, but also that there are practical benefits. The one doing the deeds and the one receiving them both benefit. [See question #4, page 448.]

9. But avoid foolish questions, and genealogies, and contentions, and strivings about the law; for they are unprofitable and vain.

As with the previous instructions to Timothy in 2 Timothy 2:14, 16, 23, Paul warns Titus not to get involved in trivial matters. If the heresy Paul is concerned about is gnosticism, then these *genealogies* may have been gnostic genealogies. If the problem is a Jewish heresy, then the genealogies may be attempts to connect people with Old Testament characters and heroes. John the Baptist made it plain that biological descent from Abraham doesn't make a person more favored before God (Matthew 3:9). The fact Paul talks about *strivings about the law* supports the idea that the heresy was a Jewish one.

10. A man that is a heretic, after the first and second admonition, reject.

At the time Paul uses it, the word *heretic* probably means "a divisive person." Such a person may be one who ends up splitting the church over the "unprofitable and vain" issues of verse 9, above.

Titus is to warn such a person twice about the damage being done to the church. If the person keeps it up after two warnings, the result is not to be merely that Titus would give him "the cold shoulder." Something more formal, a kind of church discipline, is in mind here. This shows how dangerous Paul thought a divisive person could be and how precious is the unity of the church (see Romans 15:5, 6). [See question #5, page 448.]

Conclusion

A. Words and Deeds

The great Polish political reformer and Nobel Prize winner Lech Walesa said, "Words are plentiful; deeds are precious." Paul might well agree! But Paul may also admonish us to understand what he told Titus. Words and deeds go together. One confirms the other. Deeds without words can be interpreted in contradictory ways to those who observe them. Words without deeds may be judged insincere or hypocritical.

We Christians preach and teach God's Word. We also have Christian deeds as a natural result of the grace we have experienced. We glorify God when our words and our deeds reinforce one another. Jesus challenges us to let our light "shine before men" (Matthew 5:16). We do this in both word and deed. This is not to bring glory to us, but so that others will give glory to the Father who is in Heaven.

John Wesley (1703–1791) revealed his code of living this way: "Do all the good you can, by all the means you can, in all the ways you can, in all the places you can, at all the times you can, to all the people you can, as long as ever you can." That is a difficult challenge, but one worth adopting. In light of all God has done for us, that is the best way to live.

B. Prayer

Dear Father in Heaven, I thank You for bringing Heaven's blessings to earth. Help me to make this earth more Heavenly, even as I strive to help prepare people for Heaven. It is so easy to talk like a Christian—help me also to live like one, too. In the name of Jesus I pray, amen.

C. Thought to Remember

May we have both words and deeds, and may they not contradict one another.

Home Daily Bible Readings

Monday, Aug. 23—Generosity Glorifies God (2 Corinthians 9:10-15)

Tuesday, Aug. 24—Let Your Light Shine Before Others (Matthew 5:11-16)

Wednesday, Aug. 25—Elders Should Teach Those Younger (Titus 2:1-5)

Thursday, Aug. 26—Be a Model of Good Works (Titus 2:6-10)

Friday, Aug. 27—Be Zealous for Good Deeds (Titus 2:11-15)

Saturday, Aug. 28—Be Ready for Every Good Work (Titus 3:1-6)

Sunday, Aug. 29—Good Works Are Excellent and Profitable (Titus 3:7-11)

Learning by Doing

This page contains an alternative lesson plan emphasizing learning activities.
Classes desiring such student involvement will find these suggestions helpful.

Learning Goals

After participating in this lesson, each student will be able to:

1. Make a list of all the commands for action that Paul gave Titus in the lesson text.

2. Explain how good works demonstrate appreciation for the salvation we have through Jesus Christ.

3. Name one of Paul's commands that he or she will put into practice this week.

Into the Lesson

Ask your students to name as many activities as they can that require personal discipline to be successful. (This exercise is also found in the student book.) Suggest an answer or two, such as dieting, exercise, Bible reading, or prayer.

As your students suggest activities, list their answers on the board. When they finish, ask them to categorize the answers as activities requiring physical discipline (P), mental discipline (M), moral or ethical discipline (E), spiritual discipline (S), or some combination of the above (C). Ask volunteers to suggest which activities require the most discipline and why. After discussing their responses, tell your class that today's lesson will deal with the importance of developing Christian discipline.

Into the Word

Using material in today's Lesson Background, give a brief lecture on Titus and the situation that led Paul to write the epistle addressed to him.

For the next part of the lesson, divide your class into three groups (or multiples of three). Give the groups these assignments:

Group 1

Using a photocopy of today's printed text, mark each verse in the following way.

1. Put a plus sign (+) beside each verse that tells the reader to do something.

2. Put a minus sign (–) beside each verse that tells the reader to avoid doing something.

3. Put an exclamation point (!) beside each verse that contains a promise to the reader, or indicates something that God has done for us.

Say, "Some verses may receive more than one mark." *Their results should look like this: 2:7 (+); 8 (+, –); 11 (!); 12 (–, +); 13 (+, !); 3:1 (+); 2 (–, +); 3 (–); 4 (!); 5 (!); 6 (!); 7 (!); 8 (+); 9 (–); 10 (+).*

Group 2

Using a photocopy of today's printed text, mark each verse in the following way.

1. Put an asterisk (*) beside each verse that tells us how we should/should not behave toward others.

2. Put an ampersand (&) beside each verse that tells us how we should/should not behave toward God.

3. Put a pound sign (#) beside each verse that tells us how God behaves toward us.

Note: some verses may receive more than one type of mark. *Their results should look like this: 2:7 (*, &); 8 (*); 11 (#); 12 (&, *); 13 (&, #); 3:1 (*); 2 (*); 3 (&, *); 4 (#); 5 (#); 6 (#); 7 (#); 8 (*); 9 (&, *); 10 (*).*

Group 3

Working as a group, write a verse-by-verse paraphrase of today's text, phrasing each verse in your own words to capture the meaning of Paul's words. For example, 2:7 could be rendered, "Be a model to others by doing good deeds at every opportunity and by being sound, serious, and sincere in the way you follow Biblical doctrine."

When your groups complete their assignments, review their work in this manner: first, have someone from Group 3 read the group's paraphrase of a verse, then have Groups 1 and 2 indicate how they marked the verse. Finally, discuss the verse's meaning.

Into Life

After you have discussed today's text, ask your students to complete individually the following "Christian Discipline Inventory," which is also printed in the student book. Beneath each statement give them the choice of circling one of the following words: "Always, Usually, Never."

1. I consciously try to be a model to others by my good deeds and commitment to Biblical truth.

2. I watch the things I say and do because I don't want anyone to use my behavior as an excuse to criticize the Lord or His church.

3. I am eagerly looking for and expecting the return of Christ.

4. I try to be a good citizen so the government won't have an excuse to persecute the church.

5. I avoid wasting my time on doctrines that are not clearly taught in the New Testament.

Close with John Wesley's "code of living" (see p. 446) and challenge your students to adopt it.

Let's Talk It Over

The questions on this page are designed to promote discussion of the lesson by the class and to encourage application of the lesson Scriptures. The answers provided are only discussion starters. Let your class talk it over from there.

1. Who has been a significant example of the Christian life for you? How have you tried to follow that example? In what ways have you tried to be a good example for others?

This will be a highly personal discussion. Each learner may point to a different example—a parent, a preacher, a teacher. Perhaps there is one person in your church or your church's history whom several will identify as a good example. (If so, it would be good to let this person know how much he or she is appreciated.)

How people have followed a good example will depend on what specifically has been modeled. Perhaps a faithful saint has been regular in worship attendance in spite of physical limitations. Someone may say, "When I am tempted to skip church because I have a headache or some minor ailment, I remember Mrs. Taylor and how she is here every week even though her arthritis gives her terrible pain with every motion."

2. "Ungodliness and worldly lusts" seem to be at the heart of much of the entertainment industry. Movies, television, magazines, and other media display increasing amounts of immorality. Even the "good guys" participate. How can a Christian "deny" such ungodliness and still stay in touch with the culture?

First of all, there is more to the culture than entertainment. While that is a major part of what defines a society, there are other ways to be in touch than through those outlets. The careful disciple will pursue such avenues in addition to choosing wholesome entertainment.

Jesus is our example. He spent time with the "sinners" of His day without participating in their sin. Similarly, a modern Christian does not have to view pornography in order to "relate" to those caught in this sin. We need to build relationships with such people nonetheless in order that they might be receptive to the gospel.

3. Paul said, "Let no man despise thee." But some people will despise anything and anyone affiliated with God or morality. How do we know when to avoid confrontation in order not to be "despised," and when to stand up and let the ungodly "despise" our godly position?

Peter has a good answer for this question in 1 Peter 4:14-16. If we are reproached for being a Christian, that is to our credit. But we need to be sure we are not inviting criticism justly.

Our challenge is to speak the truth in love (Ephesians 4:15). If someone rejects the truth, that person will have to give an account for that. But if someone rejects the truth because we delivered it in a less-than-loving manner, then we will have to give an account for that!

4. Suppose someone said to you, "We are saved by grace. It doesn't matter, then, what we *do*—works are not important." How would you respond? How does verse 8 help?

Jesus "went about doing good" (Acts 10:38). If we want to be like Jesus, then, we will also do good works. We are created for good works (Ephesians 2:10). Good works are a natural byproduct of faith (James 2:17). No one who truly loves the Lord could be so callous about his or her personal behavior.

Paul agrees with this in verse 8. Any true believer will "be careful to maintain good works." Paul does not give any list of good works one must do. He does not suggest that good works must outweigh the bad. Either of these would be a matter of law-keeping and legalism. But the person who is saved by grace will be careful about his or her behavior.

5. Why do you think Paul commands such drastic measures toward a "heretic" or divisive person? What kinds of behavior qualify as punishable in this way? Why?

Splitting the church is a dangerous thing. This ties in to Paul's thought that, "If any man defile the temple of God, him shall God destroy; for the temple of God is holy, which temple ye are" (1 Corinthians 3:17). The word *defile* here means to destroy—it is the same word as the one translated *destroy* later in the verse. Each Christian is a temple. The church (the people, not the building) is the "unified whole" of those temples. Whoever destroys the church is subject to God's wrath.

Removing a person from the church was not merely punitive in the New Testament. It was intended to get a person to repent (2 Corinthians 2:5-11). It also maintained the purity of the church by removing unholy elements from it. It was used for immoral believers (1 Corinthians 5) as well as false teachers (as here).